LUKE CAGE
SECOND CHANCES VOL. 2

WRITERS
MARC MCLAURIN, D.G. CHICHESTER & GREGORY WRIGHT

PENCILERS
SCOTT BENEFIEL, PARIS CULLINS, RICHARD PACE, STEVEN BUTLER, KIRK VAN WORMER & BRIAN PELLETIER

INKERS
FRANK TURNER, JASON TEMUJIN & JIMMY PALMIOTTI WITH BUD LAROSA & STEVE GEORGE

COLORISTS
KELLY CORVESE, JIM HOSTON & JOE ROSAS WITH J.L. PAES & KEVIN SOMERS

LETTERERS
RICHARD STARKINGS, STEVE DUTRO, VICKIE WILLIAMS & JOHN GAUSHELL WITH LORETTA KROL

ASSISTANT EDITORS
KARL BOLLERS, TOM DANING & LYNAIRE BRUST

EDITORS
CHRIS COOPER, MARC MCLAURIN & CRAIG ANDERSON

FRONT COVER ARTISTS: **DWAYNE TURNER, CHRIS IVY & VERONICA GANDINI**

BACK COVER ARTISTS: **SCOTT BENEFIEL & FRANK TURNER**

COLLECTION EDITOR: **MARK D. BEAZLEY**
ASSOCIATE EDITOR: **SARAH BRUNSTAD**
ASSOCIATE MANAGER, DIGITAL ASSETS: **JOE HOCHSTEIN**
ASSOCIATE MANAGING EDITOR: **ALEX STARBUCK**
EDITOR, SPECIAL PROJECTS: **JENNIFER GRÜNWALD**
VP, PRODUCTION & SPECIAL PROJECTS: **JEFF YOUNGQUIST**

RESEARCH: **STUART VANDAL**
LAYOUT: **JEPH YORK**
PRODUCTION: **COLORTEK & JOE FRONTIRRE**
BOOK DESIGNER: **ADAM DEL RE**
SVP PRINT, SALES & MARKETING: **DAVID GABRIEL**

EDITOR IN CHIEF: **AXEL ALONSO**
CHIEF CREATIVE OFFICER: **JOE QUESADA**
PUBLISHER: **DAN BUCKLEY**
EXECUTIVE PRODUCER: **ALAN FINE**

SPECIAL THANKS TO
MIKE HANSEN

LUKE CAGE: SECOND CHANCES VOL. 2. Contains material originally published in magazine form as CAGE (1992) #13-20, TERROR INC. #11-12 and SILVER SABLE & THE WILD PACK #13-14. First printing 2016. ISBN# 978-0-7851-9507-8. Published by MARVEL WORLDWIDE, INC., a subsidiary of MARVEL ENTERTAINMENT, LLC. OFFICE OF PUBLICATION: 135 West 50th Street, New York, NY 10020. **Printed in the U.S.A.** ALAN FINE, President, Marvel Entertainment; DAN BUCKLEY, President, TV, Publishing and Brand Management; JOE QUESADA, Chief Creative Officer; TOM BREVOORT, SVP of Publishing; DAVID BOGART, SVP of Operations & Procurement, Publishing; C.B. CEBULSKI, VP of International Development & Brand Management; DAVID GABRIEL, SVP Print, Sales & Marketing; DAN CARR, Executive Director of Publishing Technology; SUSAN CRESPI, Editorial Operations Manager; ALEX MORALES, Publishing Operations Manager; STAN LEE, Chairman Emeritus. For information regarding advertising in Marvel Comics or on Marvel.com, please contact Jonathan Rheingold, VP of Custom Solutions & Ad Sales, at jrheingold@marvel.com. For Marvel subscription inquiries, please call 800-217-9158. **Manufactured between 1/22/2016 and 2/29/2016 by R.R. DONNELLEY, INC., SALEM, VA, USA.**

10 9 8 7 6 5 4 3 2 1

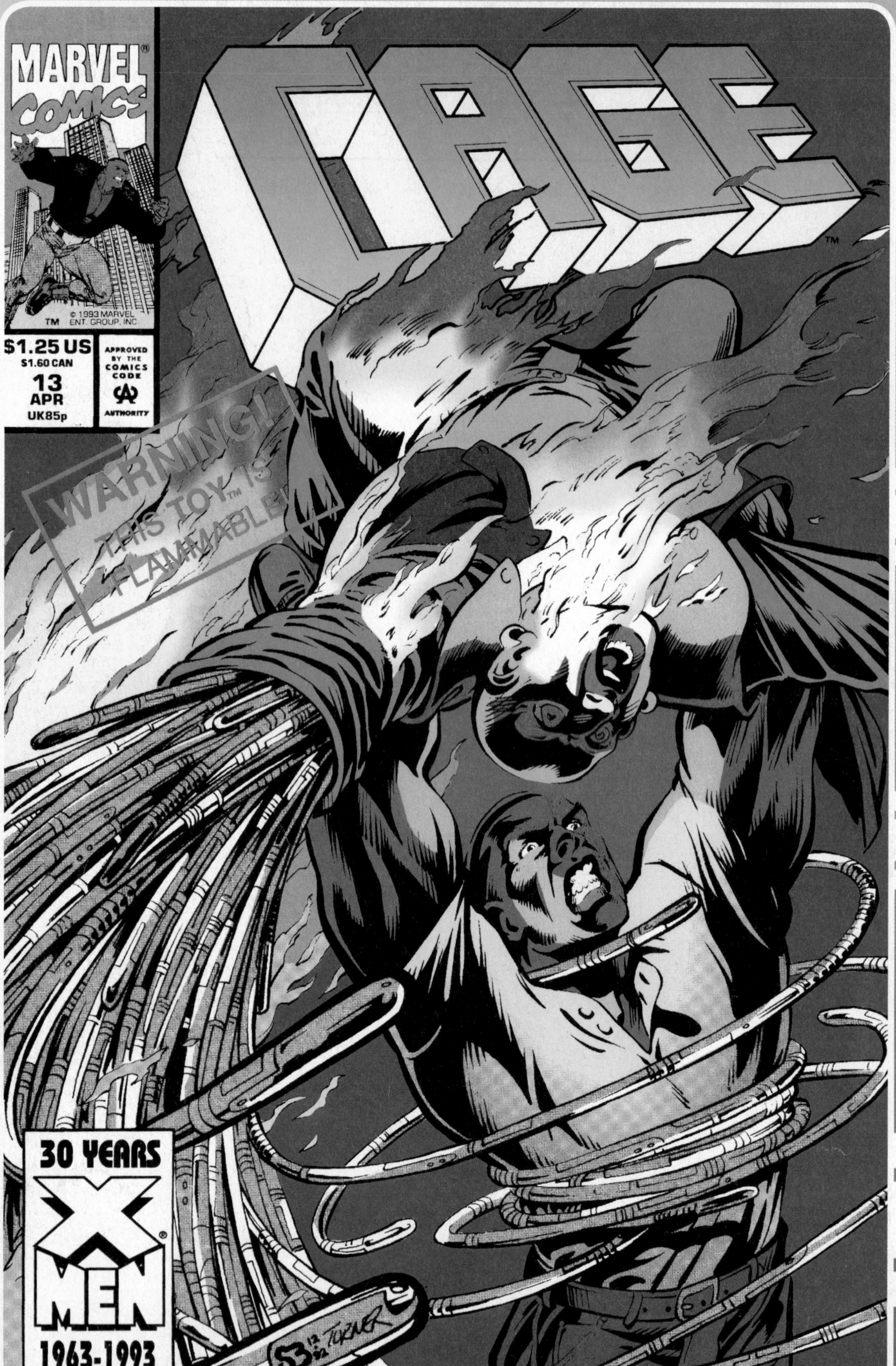

MARVEL COMICS
CAGE
© 1993 MARVEL ENT. GROUP, INC.
$1.25 US
$1.60 CAN
13
APR
UK85p
APPROVED BY THE COMICS CODE AUTHORITY
WARNING! THIS TOY IS FLAMMABLE!
30 YEARS X-MEN 1963-1993

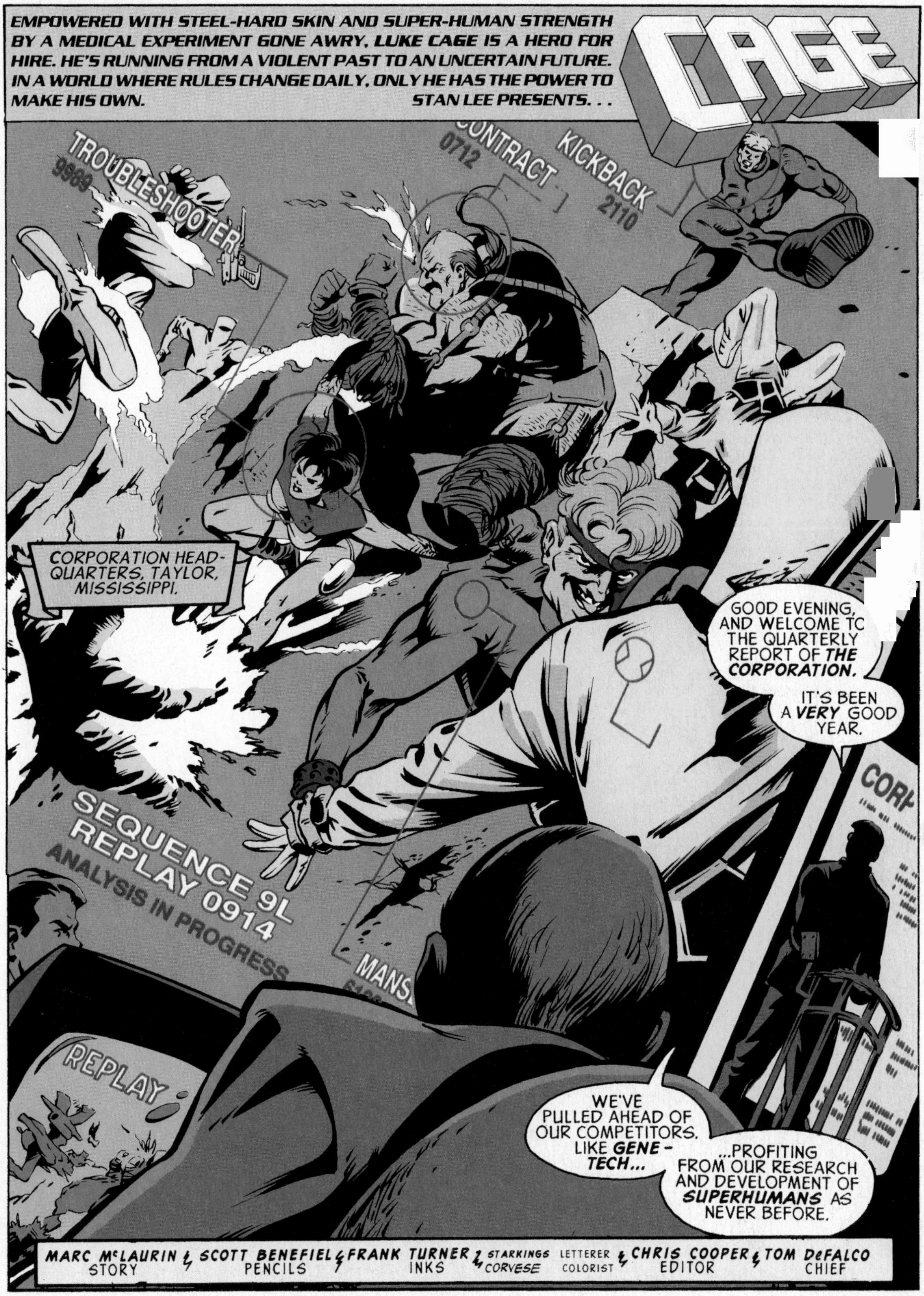
EMPOWERED WITH STEEL-HARD SKIN AND SUPER-HUMAN STRENGTH BY A MEDICAL EXPERIMENT GONE AWRY, LUKE CAGE IS A HERO FOR HIRE. HE'S RUNNING FROM A VIOLENT PAST TO AN UNCERTAIN FUTURE. IN A WORLD WHERE RULES CHANGE DAILY, ONLY HE HAS THE POWER TO MAKE HIS OWN.
STAN LEE PRESENTS. . .
CAGE
TROUBLESHOOTER 9989
CONTRACT 0712
KICKBACK 2110
CORPORATION HEAD-QUARTERS, TAYLOR, MISSISSIPPI.
GOOD EVENING, AND WELCOME TO THE QUARTERLY REPORT OF THE CORPORATION.
IT'S BEEN A VERY GOOD YEAR.
SEQUENCE 9L REPLAY 0914
ANALYSIS IN PROGRESS
REPLAY
WE'VE PULLED AHEAD OF OUR COMPETITORS. LIKE GENE-TECH...
...PROFITING FROM OUR RESEARCH AND DEVELOPMENT OF SUPERHUMANS AS NEVER BEFORE.
MARC McLAURIN STORY & SCOTT BENEFIEL PENCILS & FRANK TURNER INKS & STARKINGS LETTERER & CORVESE COLORIST & CHRIS COOPER EDITOR & TOM DeFALCO CHIEF

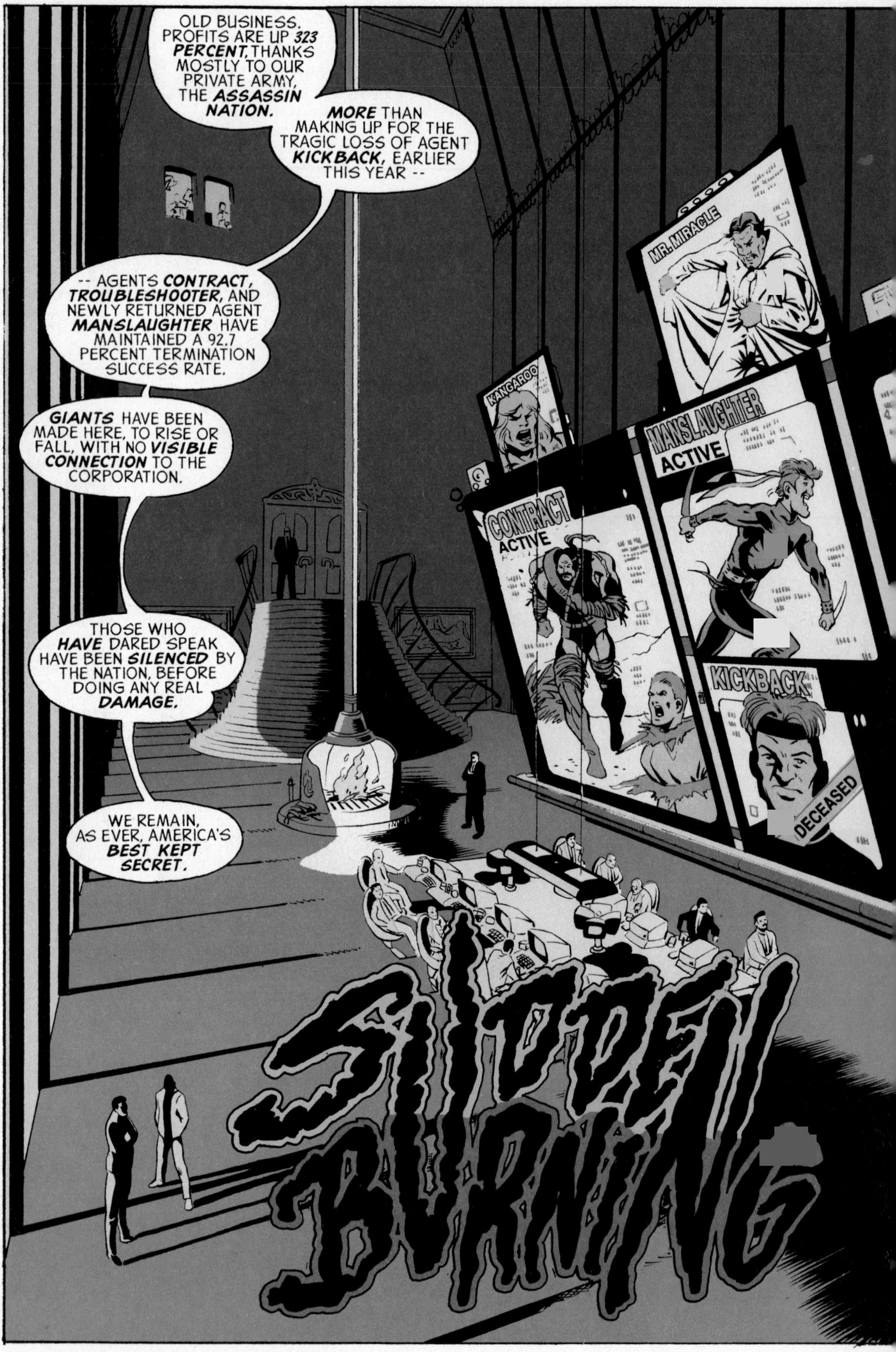

OLD BUSINESS. PROFITS ARE UP 323 PERCENT, THANKS MOSTLY TO OUR PRIVATE ARMY, THE ASSASSIN NATION.
MORE THAN MAKING UP FOR THE TRAGIC LOSS OF AGENT KICKBACK, EARLIER THIS YEAR --
-- AGENTS CONTRACT, TROUBLESHOOTER, AND NEWLY RETURNED AGENT MANSLAUGHTER HAVE MAINTAINED A 92.7 PERCENT TERMINATION SUCCESS RATE.
GIANTS HAVE BEEN MADE HERE, TO RISE OR FALL, WITH NO VISIBLE CONNECTION TO THE CORPORATION.
THOSE WHO HAVE DARED SPEAK HAVE BEEN SILENCED BY THE NATION, BEFORE DOING ANY REAL DAMAGE.
WE REMAIN, AS EVER, AMERICA'S BEST KEPT SECRET.
MR. MIRACLE
KANGAROO
MANSLAUGHTER
ACTIVE
CONTRACT
ACTIVE
KICKBACK
DECEASED
SUDDEN BURNING

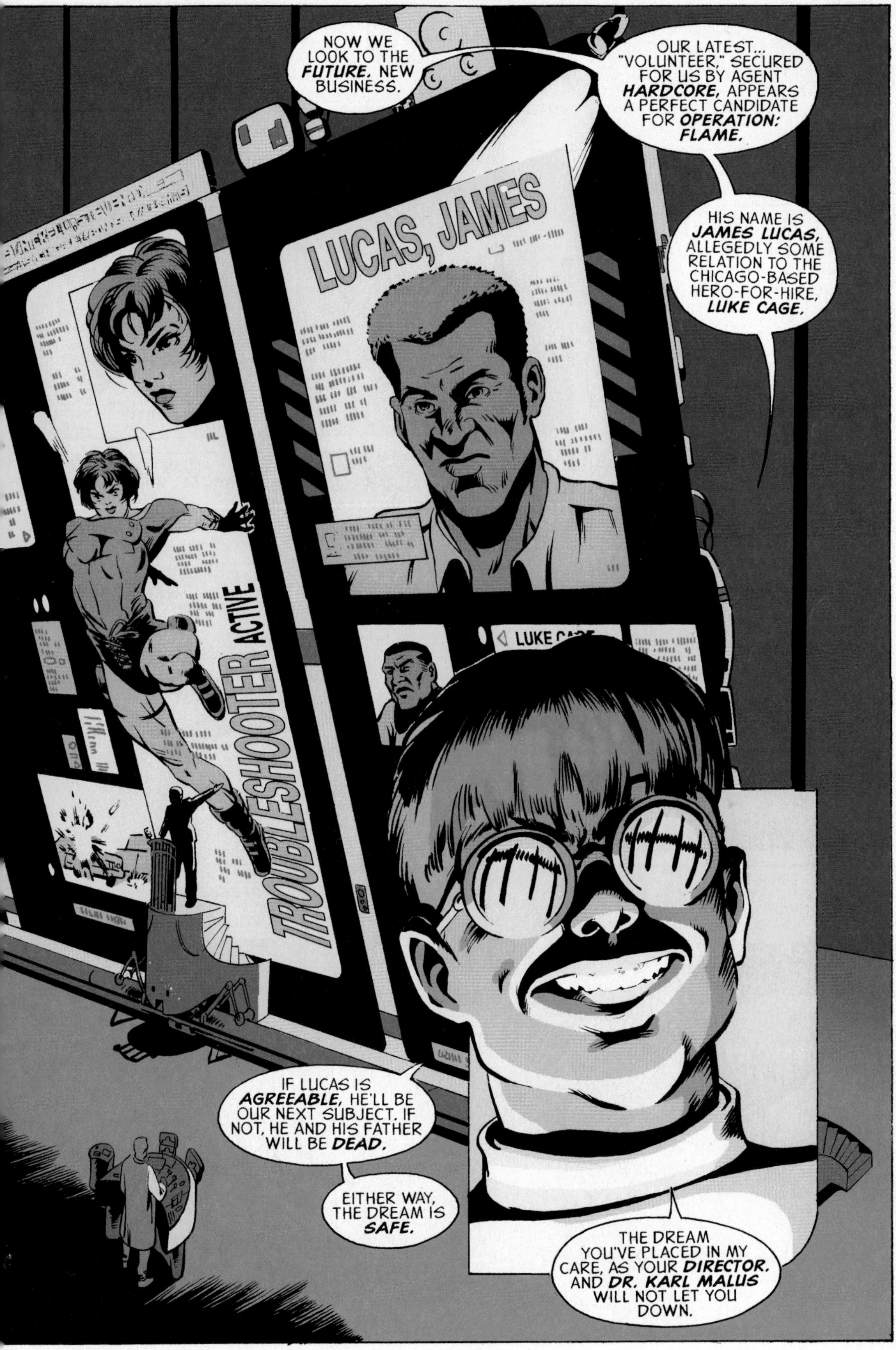
NOW WE LOOK TO THE FUTURE. NEW BUSINESS.
OUR LATEST... "VOLUNTEER," SECURED FOR US BY AGENT HARDCORE, APPEARS A PERFECT CANDIDATE FOR OPERATION: FLAME.
HIS NAME IS JAMES LUCAS, ALLEGEDLY SOME RELATION TO THE CHICAGO-BASED HERO-FOR-HIRE, LUKE CAGE.
LUCAS, JAMES
TROUBLESHOOTER ACTIVE
IF LUCAS IS AGREEABLE, HE'LL BE OUR NEXT SUBJECT. IF NOT, HE AND HIS FATHER WILL BE DEAD.
EITHER WAY, THE DREAM IS SAFE.
THE DREAM YOU'VE PLACED IN MY CARE, AS YOUR DIRECTOR. AND DR. KARL MALUS WILL NOT LET YOU DOWN.

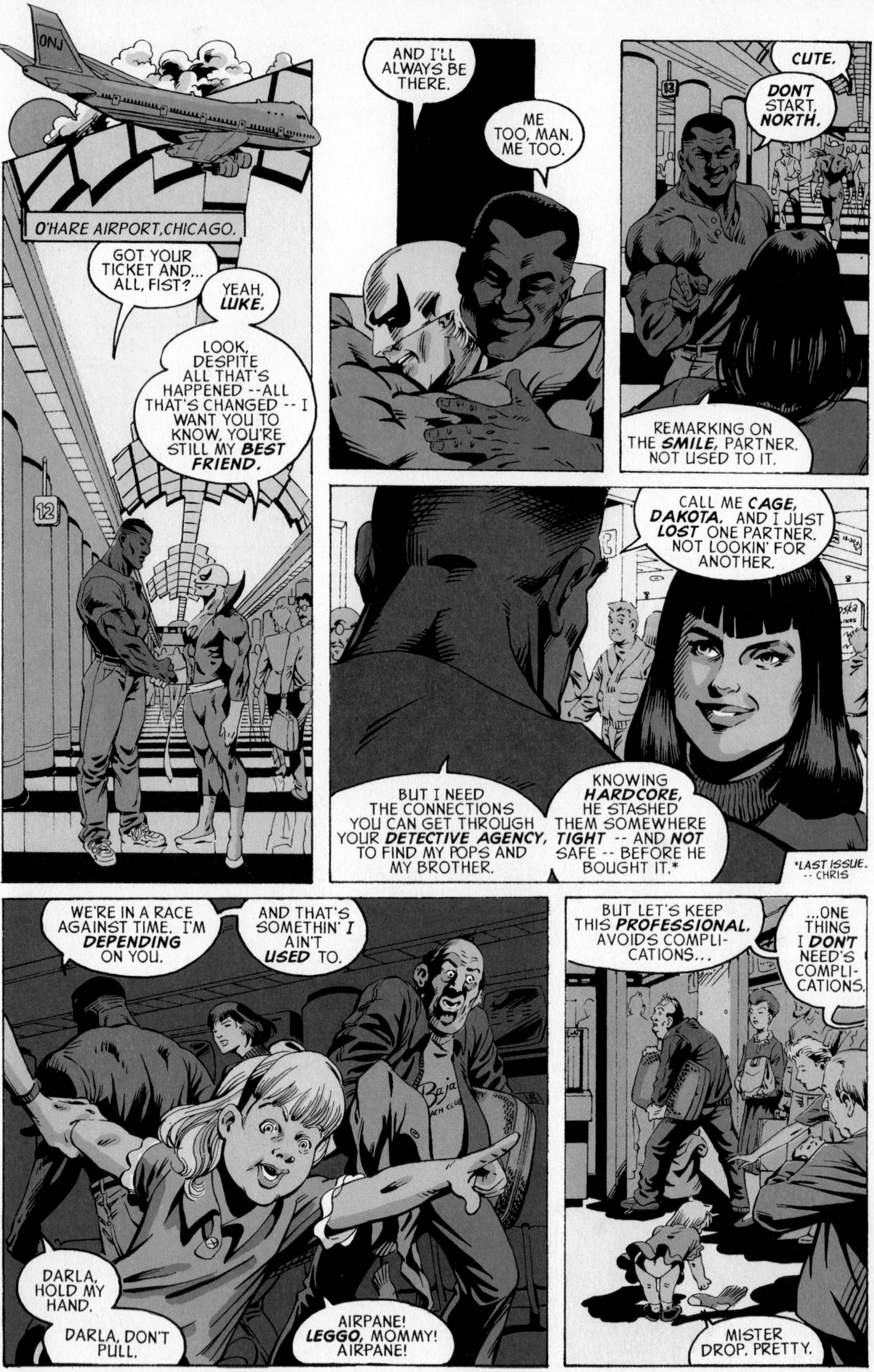
O'HARE AIRPORT, CHICAGO.
GOT YOUR TICKET AND... ALL, FIST?
YEAH, LUKE.
LOOK, DESPITE ALL THAT'S HAPPENED --ALL THAT'S CHANGED -- I WANT YOU TO KNOW, YOU'RE STILL MY BEST FRIEND.
AND I'LL ALWAYS BE THERE.
ME TOO, MAN. ME TOO.
CUTE.
DON'T START, NORTH.
REMARKING ON THE SMILE, PARTNER. NOT USED TO IT.
CALL ME CAGE, DAKOTA. AND I JUST LOST ONE PARTNER. NOT LOOKIN' FOR ANOTHER.
BUT I NEED THE CONNECTIONS YOU CAN GET THROUGH YOUR DETECTIVE AGENCY, TO FIND MY POPS AND MY BROTHER.
KNOWING HARDCORE, HE STASHED THEM SOMEWHERE TIGHT -- AND NOT SAFE -- BEFORE HE BOUGHT IT.*
*LAST ISSUE. -- CHRIS
WE'RE IN A RACE AGAINST TIME. I'M DEPENDING ON YOU.
AND THAT'S SOMETHIN' I AIN'T USED TO.
DARLA, HOLD MY HAND.
DARLA, DON'T PULL.
AIRPANE! LEGGO, MOMMY! AIRPANE!
BUT LET'S KEEP THIS PROFESSIONAL. AVOIDS COMPLI- CATIONS...
...ONE THING I DON'T NEED'S COMPLI- CATIONS.
MISTER DROP. PRETTY.

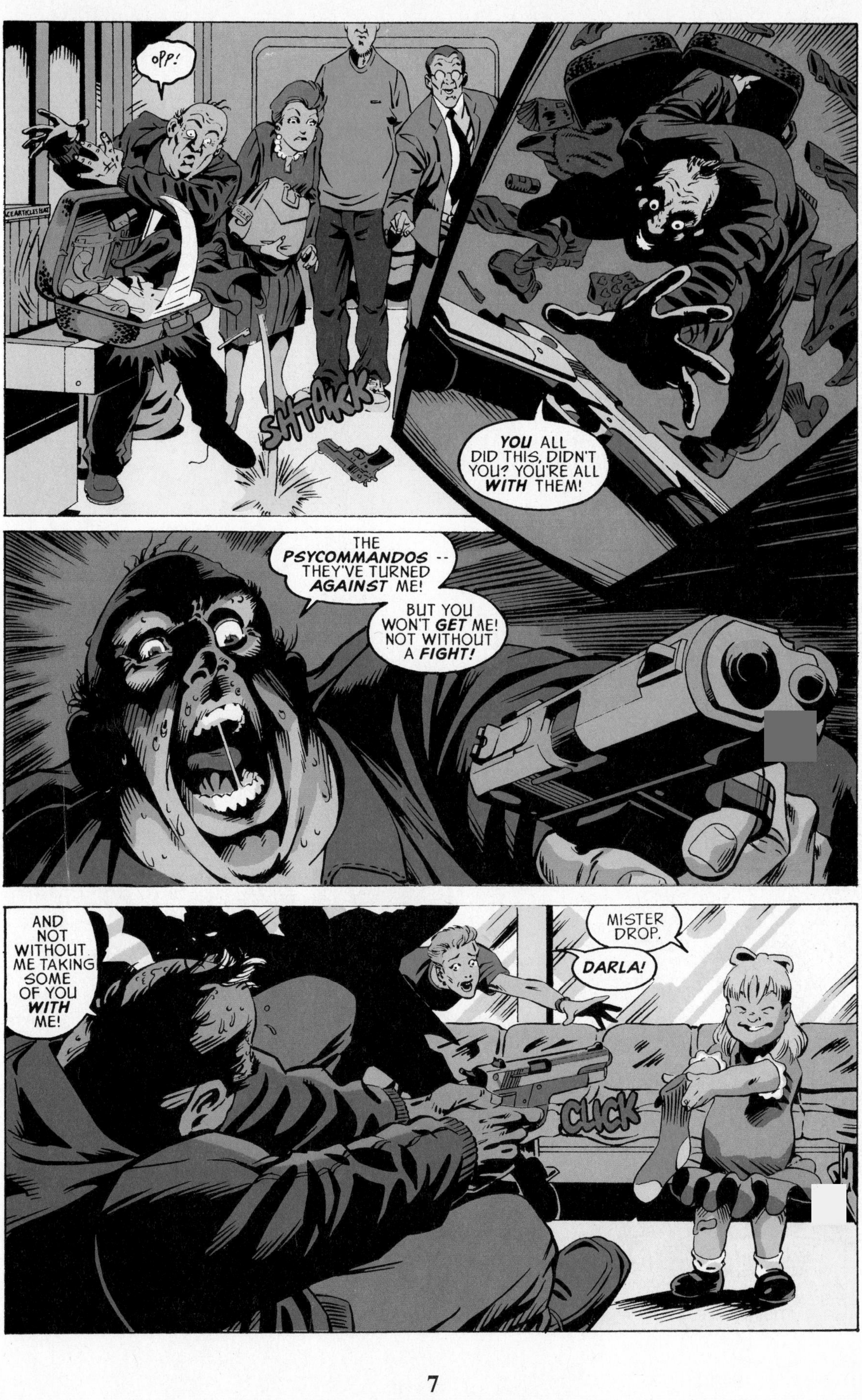
OPP!
SHTAKK
YOU ALL DID THIS, DIDN'T YOU? YOU'RE ALL WITH THEM!
THE PSYCOMMANDOS -- THEY'VE TURNED AGAINST ME!
BUT YOU WON'T GET ME! NOT WITHOUT A FIGHT!
AND NOT WITHOUT ME TAKING SOME OF YOU WITH ME!
MISTER DROP.
DARLA!
CLICK

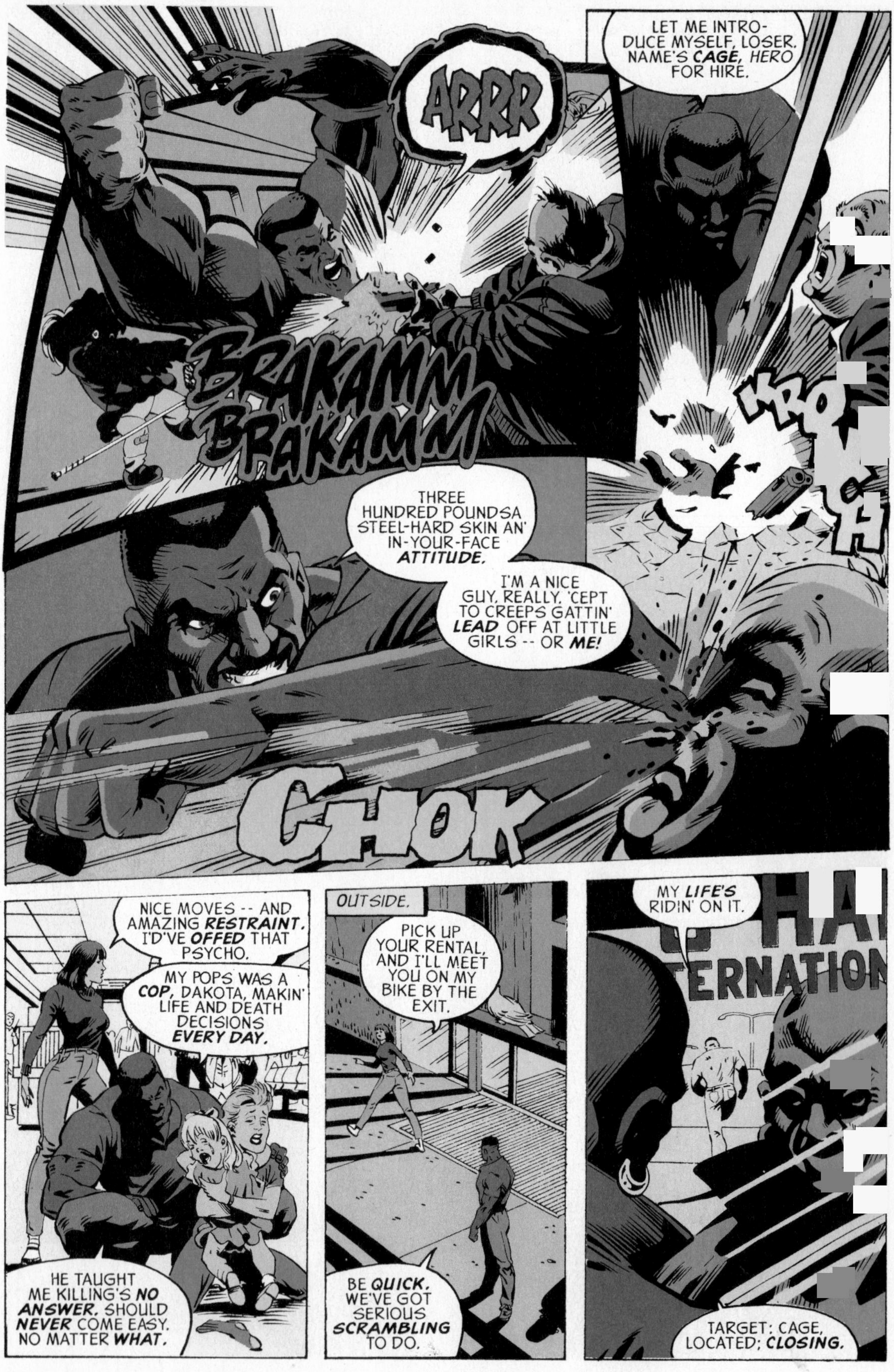
ARRR
BRAKAMM BRAKAMM
LET ME INTRODUCE MYSELF, LOSER. NAME'S CAGE, HERO FOR HIRE.
KRO
THREE HUNDRED POUNDSA STEEL-HARD SKIN AN' IN-YOUR-FACE ATTITUDE.
I'M A NICE GUY, REALLY, 'CEPT TO CREEPS GATTIN' LEAD OFF AT LITTLE GIRLS -- OR ME!
CHOK
NICE MOVES -- AND AMAZING RESTRAINT. I'D'VE OFFED THAT PSYCHO.
MY POPS WAS A COP, DAKOTA, MAKIN' LIFE AND DEATH DECISIONS EVERY DAY.
HE TAUGHT ME KILLING'S NO ANSWER. SHOULD NEVER COME EASY. NO MATTER WHAT.
OUTSIDE.
PICK UP YOUR RENTAL, AND I'LL MEET YOU ON MY BIKE BY THE EXIT.
BE QUICK. WE'VE GOT SERIOUS SCRAMBLING TO DO.
MY LIFE'S RIDIN' ON IT.
TERNATION
TARGET: CAGE, LOCATED; CLOSING.

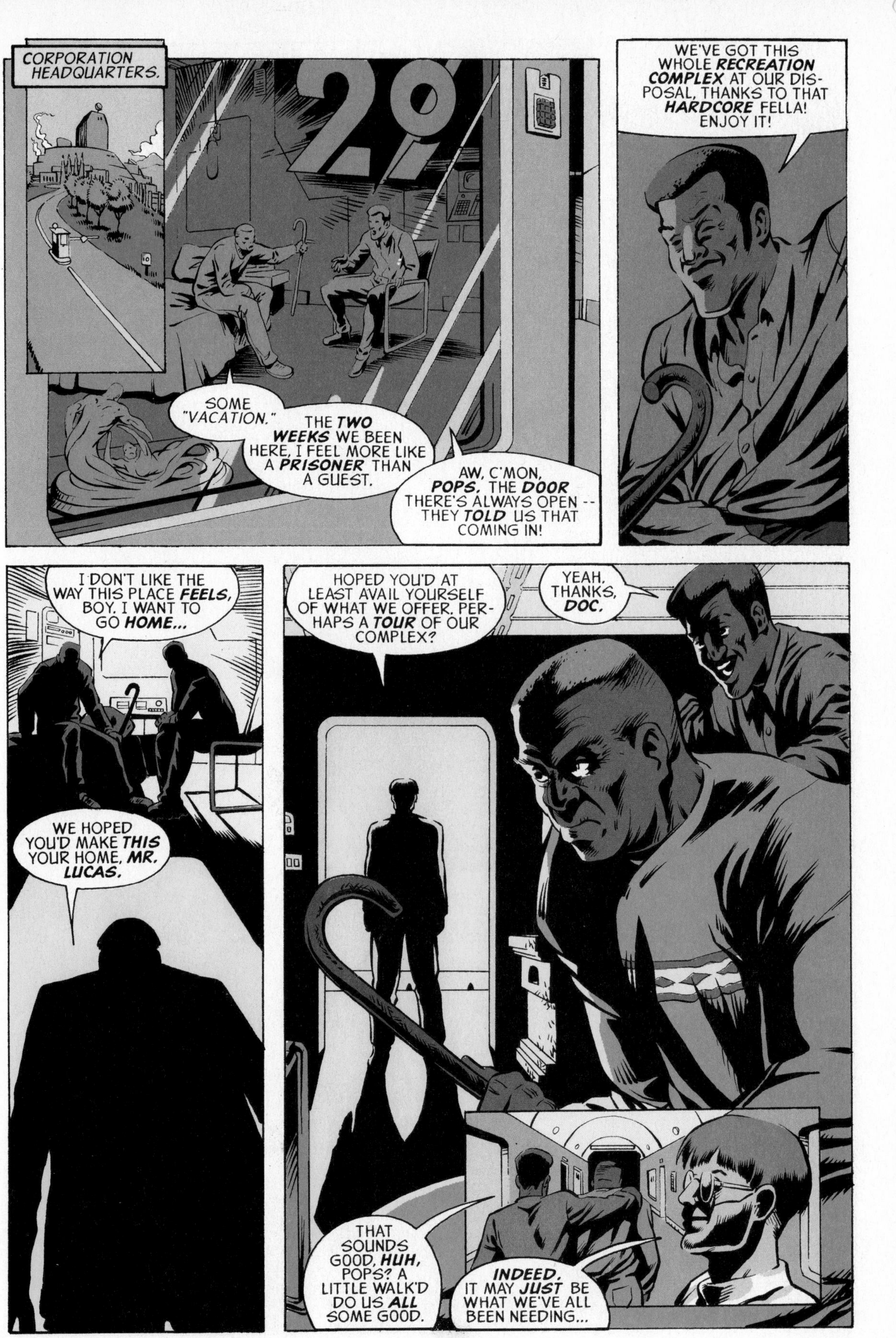
CORPORATION HEADQUARTERS.
SOME "VACATION."
THE TWO WEEKS WE BEEN HERE, I FEEL MORE LIKE A PRISONER THAN A GUEST.
AW, C'MON, POPS. THE DOOR THERE'S ALWAYS OPEN -- THEY TOLD US THAT COMING IN!
WE'VE GOT THIS WHOLE RECREATION COMPLEX AT OUR DISPOSAL, THANKS TO THAT HARDCORE FELLA! ENJOY IT!
I DON'T LIKE THE WAY THIS PLACE FEELS, BOY. I WANT TO GO HOME...
WE HOPED YOU'D MAKE THIS YOUR HOME, MR. LUCAS.
HOPED YOU'D AT LEAST AVAIL YOURSELF OF WHAT WE OFFER. PERHAPS A TOUR OF OUR COMPLEX?
YEAH, THANKS, DOC.
THAT SOUNDS GOOD, HUH, POPS? A LITTLE WALK'D DO US ALL SOME GOOD.
INDEED. IT MAY JUST BE WHAT WE'VE ALL BEEN NEEDING...

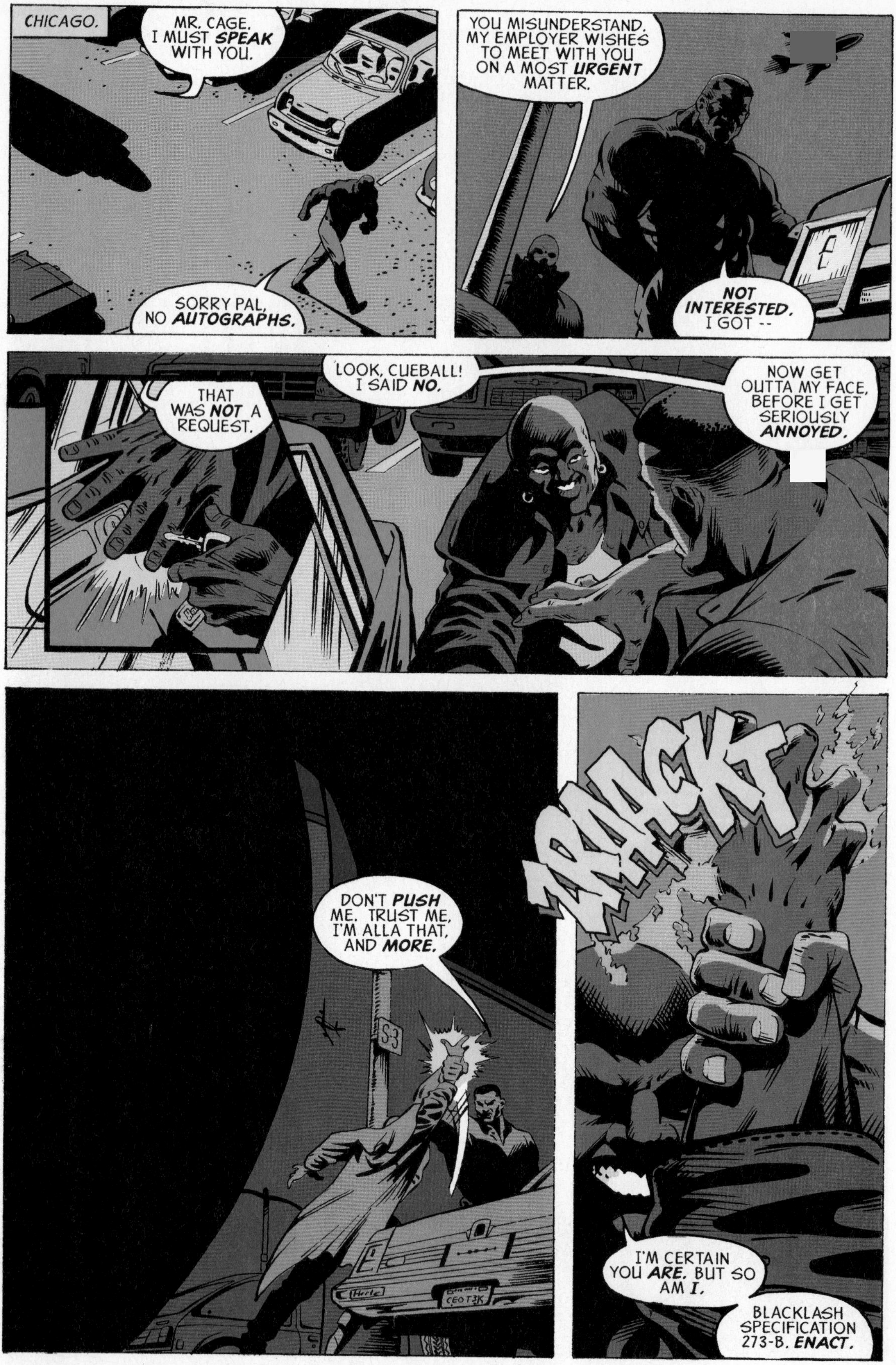
CHICAGO.
MR. CAGE. I MUST SPEAK WITH YOU.
SORRY PAL, NO AUTOGRAPHS.
YOU MISUNDERSTAND. MY EMPLOYER WISHES TO MEET WITH YOU ON A MOST URGENT MATTER.
NOT INTERESTED. I GOT --
THAT WAS NOT A REQUEST.
LOOK, CUEBALL! I SAID NO.
NOW GET OUTTA MY FACE, BEFORE I GET SERIOUSLY ANNOYED.
DON'T PUSH ME. TRUST ME, I'M ALLA THAT, AND MORE.
ZRACK!
I'M CERTAIN YOU ARE. BUT SO AM I.
BLACKLASH SPECIFICATION 273-B. ENACT.

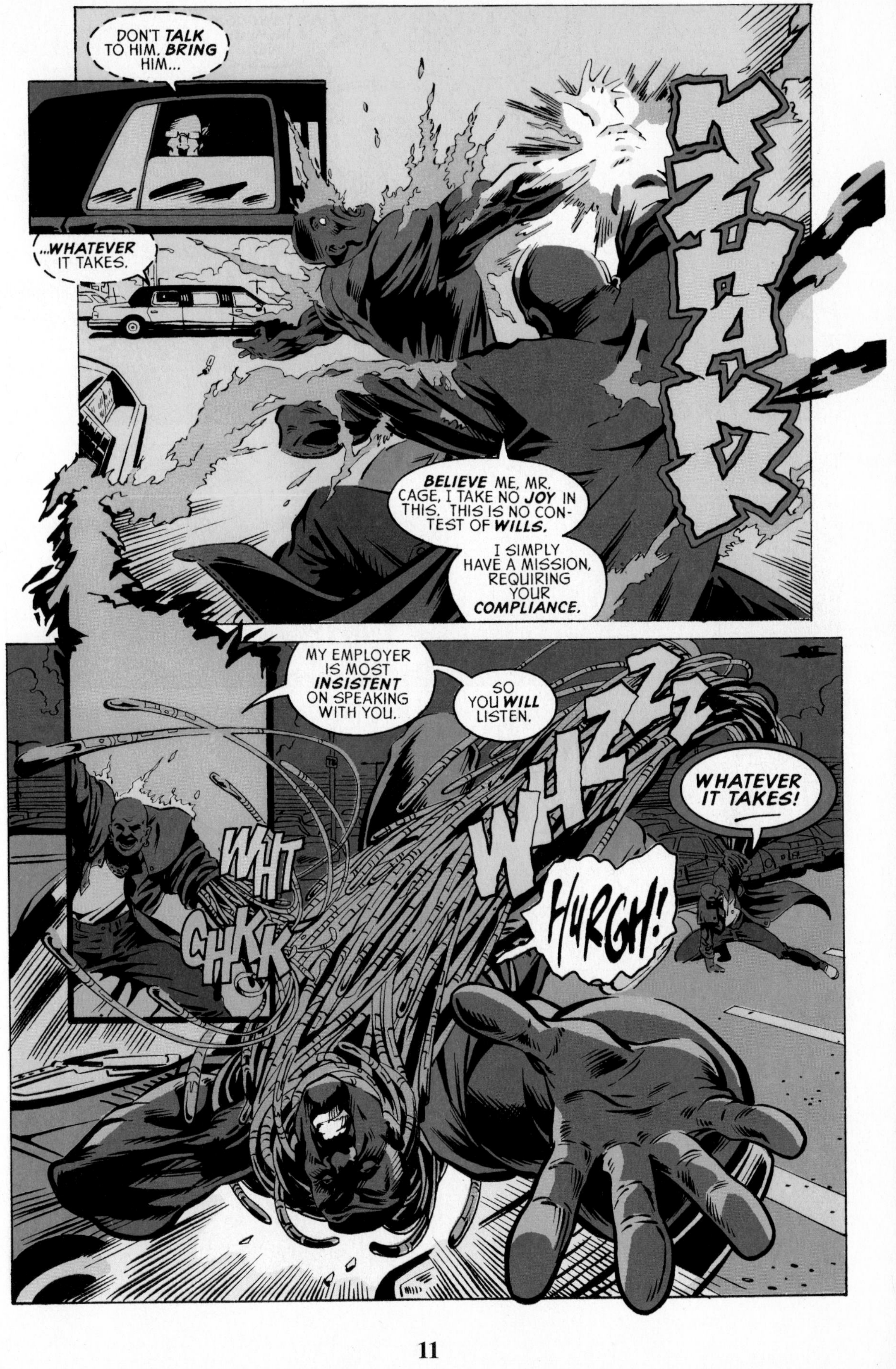

DON'T TALK TO HIM. BRING HIM...
...WHATEVER IT TAKES.
ZHAK
BELIEVE ME, MR. CAGE, I TAKE NO JOY IN THIS. THIS IS NO CONTEST OF WILLS.
I SIMPLY HAVE A MISSION, REQUIRING YOUR COMPLIANCE.
MY EMPLOYER IS MOST INSISTENT ON SPEAKING WITH YOU.
SO YOU WILL LISTEN.
WHZZZ
WHATEVER IT TAKES!
WHT
CHKK
HURGH!

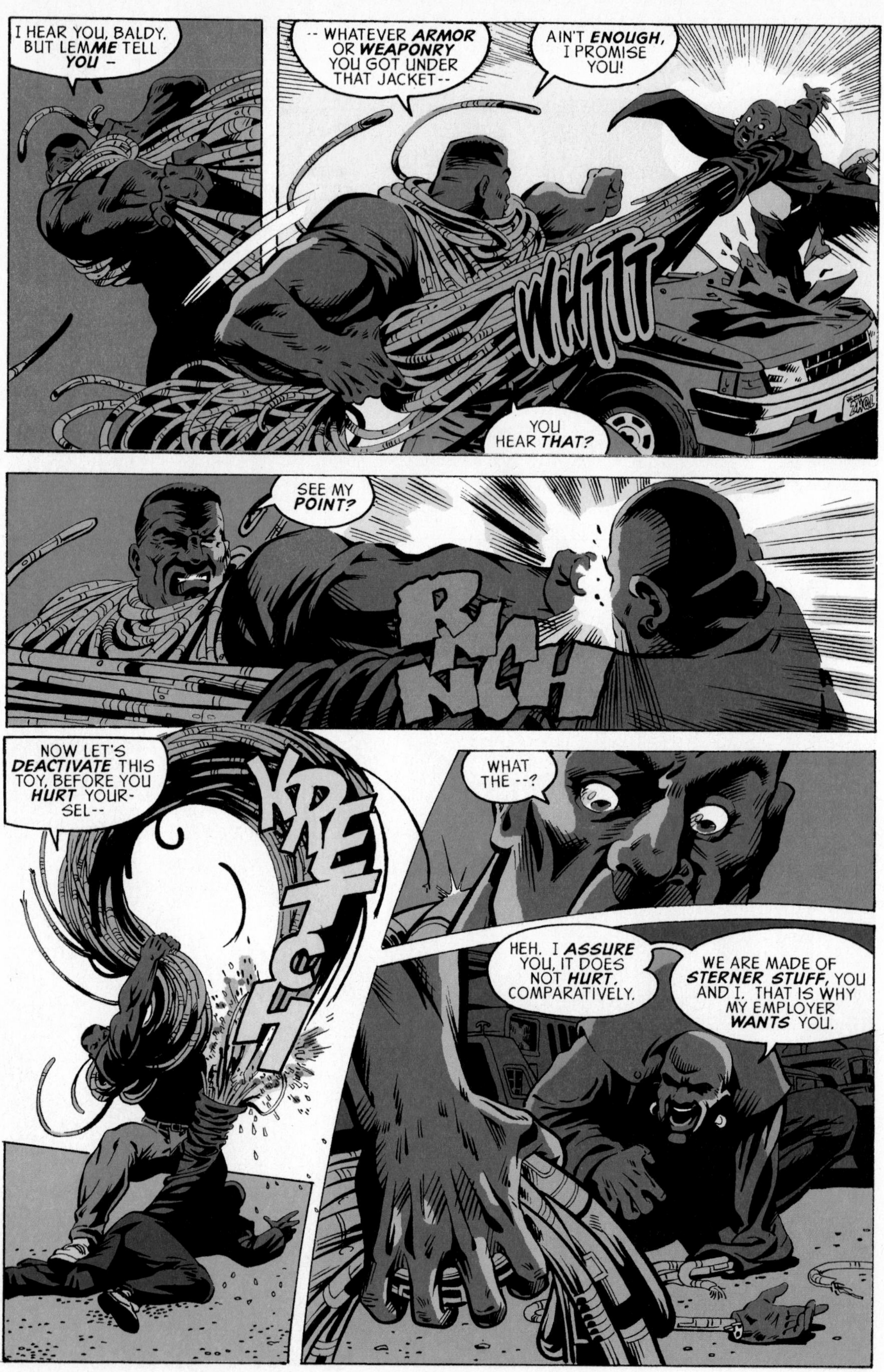
I HEAR YOU, BALDY. BUT LEMME TELL YOU –
-- WHATEVER ARMOR OR WEAPONRY YOU GOT UNDER THAT JACKET--
AIN'T ENOUGH, I PROMISE YOU!
WHTTT
YOU HEAR THAT?
SEE MY POINT?
RNCH
NOW LET'S DEACTIVATE THIS TOY, BEFORE YOU HURT YOUR-SEL--
KRETCH
WHAT THE --?
HEH. I ASSURE YOU, IT DOES NOT HURT, COMPARATIVELY.
WE ARE MADE OF STERNER STUFF, YOU AND I. THAT IS WHY MY EMPLOYER WANTS YOU.

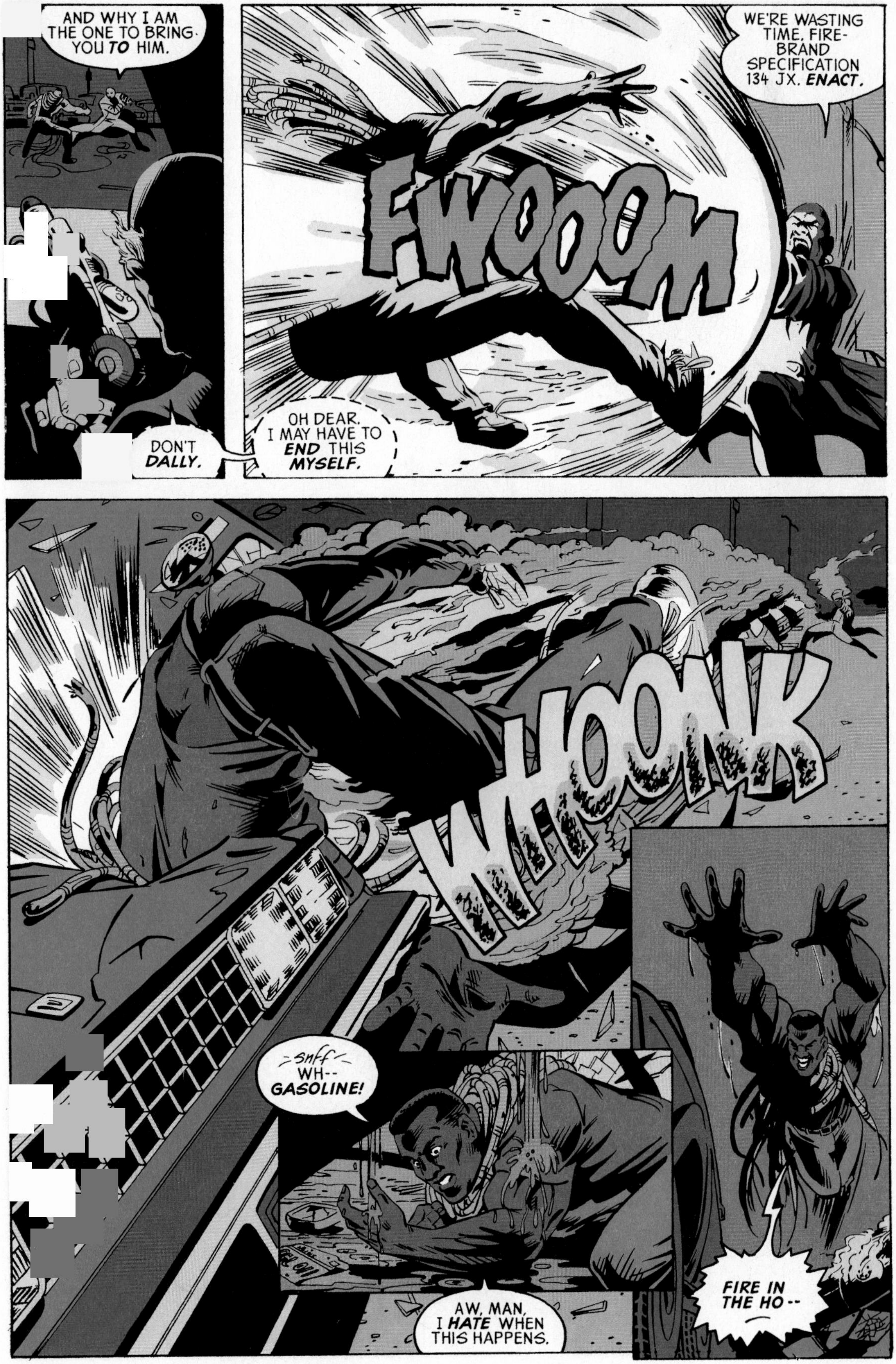
AND WHY I AM THE ONE TO BRING YOU *TO* HIM.
DON'T *DALLY.*
WE'RE WASTING TIME. FIRE-BRAND SPECIFICATION 134 JX. *ENACT.*
FWOOOM
OH DEAR. I MAY HAVE TO *END* THIS *MYSELF.*
WHOONK
-snff- WH-- *GASOLINE!*
AW, MAN, I *HATE* WHEN THIS HAPPENS.
FIRE IN THE HO--

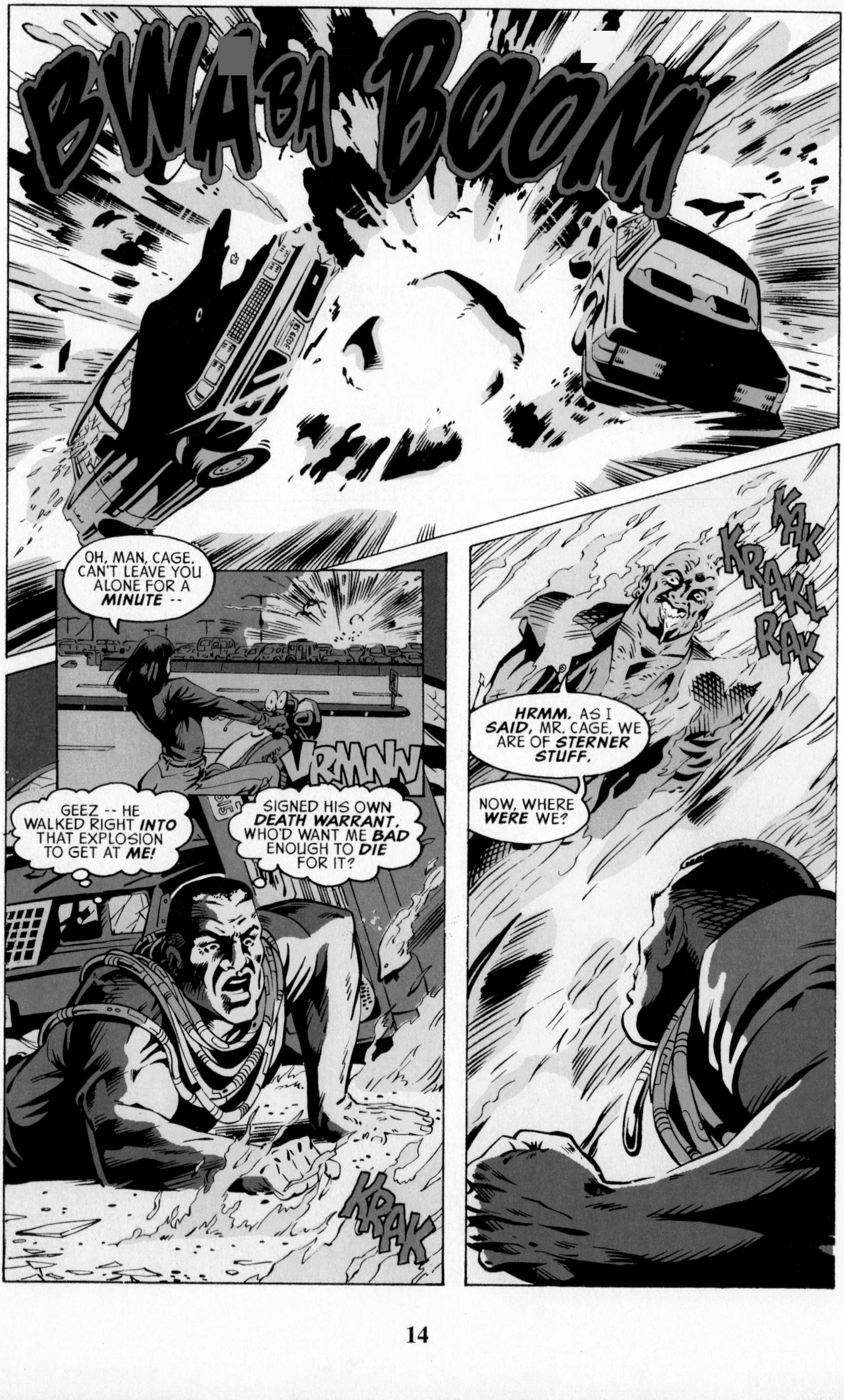
BWA BA BOOM
OH, MAN, CAGE. CAN'T LEAVE YOU ALONE FOR A *MINUTE* --
VRMNN
GEEZ -- HE WALKED RIGHT *INTO* THAT EXPLOSION TO GET AT *ME!*
SIGNED HIS OWN *DEATH WARRANT.* WHO'D WANT ME *BAD* ENOUGH TO *DIE* FOR IT?
KRAK
KAK
KRAKL
RAK
HRMM. AS I *SAID,* MR. CAGE, WE ARE OF *STERNER STUFF.*
NOW, WHERE *WERE* WE?

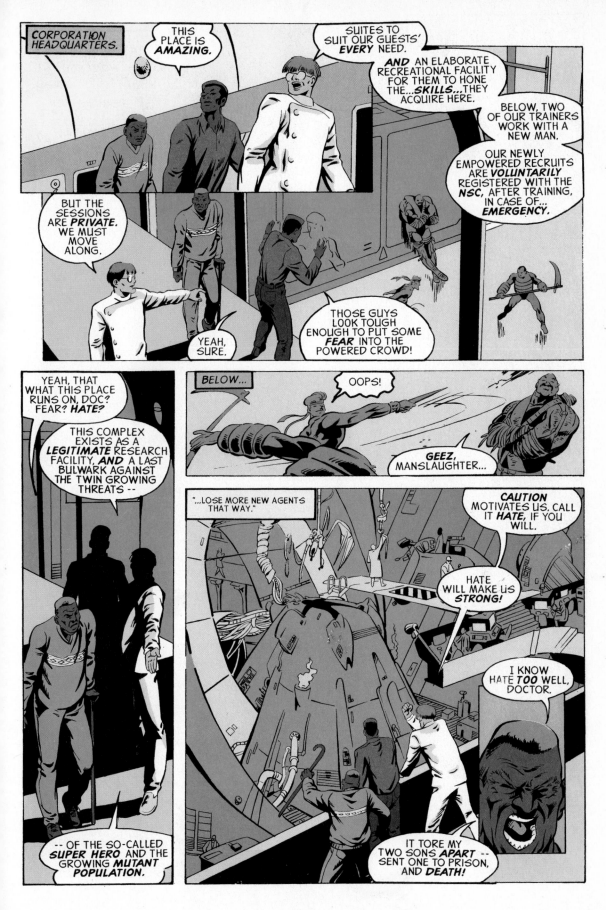

CORPORATION HEADQUARTERS.

THIS PLACE IS *AMAZING*.

SUITES TO SUIT OUR GUESTS' *EVERY* NEED.

AND AN ELABORATE RECREATIONAL FACILITY FOR THEM TO HONE THE...*SKILLS*...THEY ACQUIRE HERE.

BELOW, TWO OF OUR TRAINERS WORK WITH A NEW MAN.

OUR NEWLY EMPOWERED RECRUITS ARE *VOLUNTARILY* REGISTERED WITH THE *NSC*, AFTER TRAINING, IN CASE OF... *EMERGENCY*.

BUT THE SESSIONS ARE *PRIVATE*. WE MUST MOVE ALONG.

YEAH, SURE.

THOSE GUYS LOOK TOUGH ENOUGH TO PUT SOME *FEAR* INTO THE POWERED CROWD!

YEAH, THAT WHAT THIS PLACE RUNS ON, DOC? FEAR? *HATE*?

THIS COMPLEX EXISTS AS A *LEGITIMATE* RESEARCH FACILITY, *AND* A LAST BULWARK AGAINST THE TWIN GROWING THREATS --

BELOW...

OOPS!

GEEZ, MANSLAUGHTER...

"...LOSE MORE NEW AGENTS THAT WAY."

CAUTION MOTIVATES US. CALL IT *HATE*, IF YOU WILL.

HATE WILL MAKE US *STRONG*!

I KNOW HATE *TOO* WELL, DOCTOR.

-- OF THE SO-CALLED *SUPER HERO* AND THE GROWING *MUTANT* POPULATION.

IT TORE MY TWO SONS *APART* -- SENT ONE TO PRISON, AND *DEATH*!

15

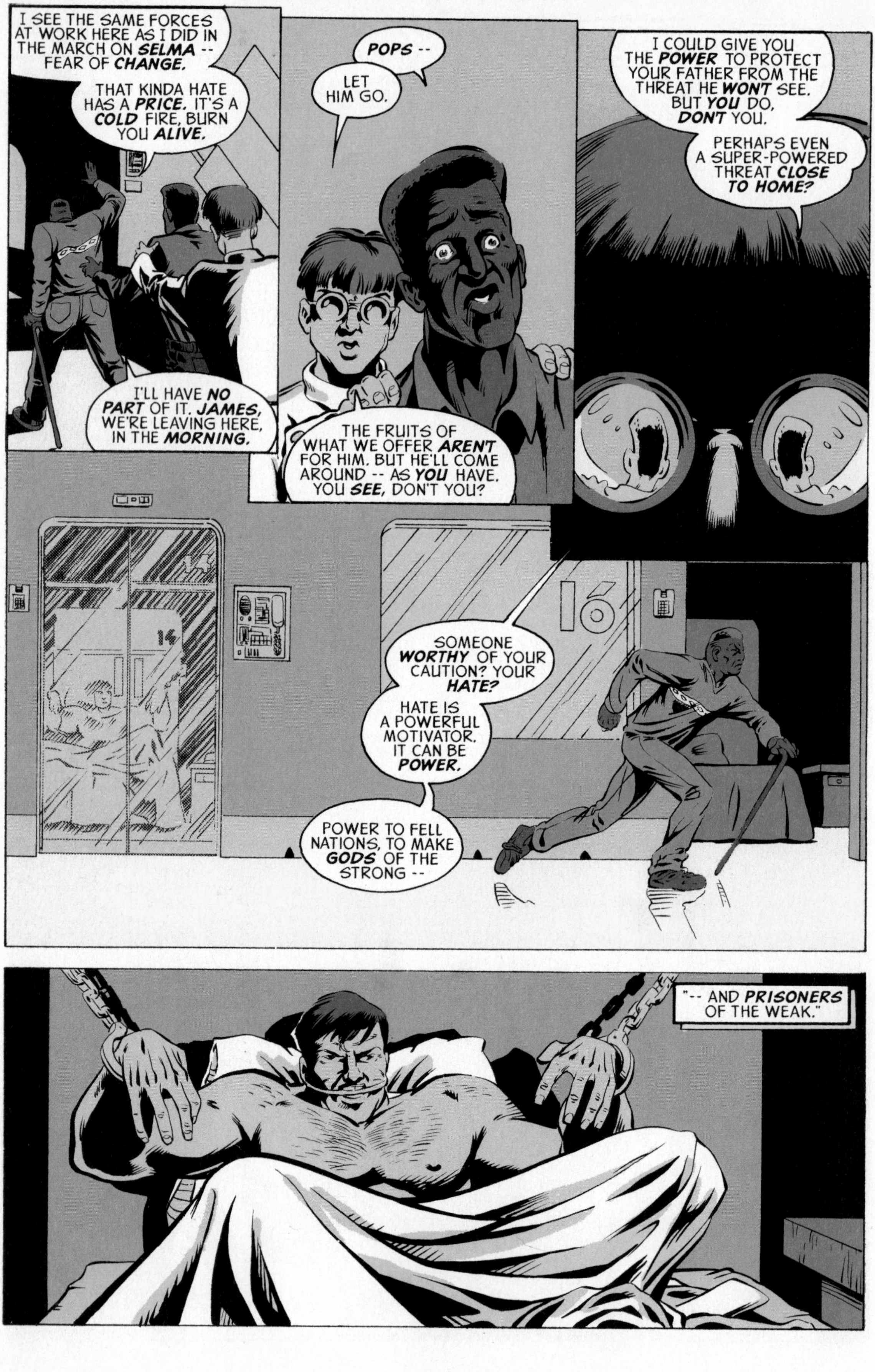
I SEE THE SAME FORCES AT WORK HERE AS I DID IN THE MARCH ON SELMA -- FEAR OF CHANGE.
THAT KINDA HATE HAS A PRICE. IT'S A COLD FIRE, BURN YOU ALIVE.
I'LL HAVE NO PART OF IT. JAMES, WE'RE LEAVING HERE, IN THE MORNING.
POPS --
LET HIM GO.
THE FRUITS OF WHAT WE OFFER AREN'T FOR HIM. BUT HE'LL COME AROUND -- AS YOU HAVE. YOU SEE, DON'T YOU?
I COULD GIVE YOU THE POWER TO PROTECT YOUR FATHER FROM THE THREAT HE WON'T SEE. BUT YOU DO, DON'T YOU.
PERHAPS EVEN A SUPER-POWERED THREAT CLOSE TO HOME?
16
SOMEONE WORTHY OF YOUR CAUTION? YOUR HATE?
HATE IS A POWERFUL MOTIVATOR. IT CAN BE POWER.
POWER TO FELL NATIONS, TO MAKE GODS OF THE STRONG --
"-- AND PRISONERS OF THE WEAK."

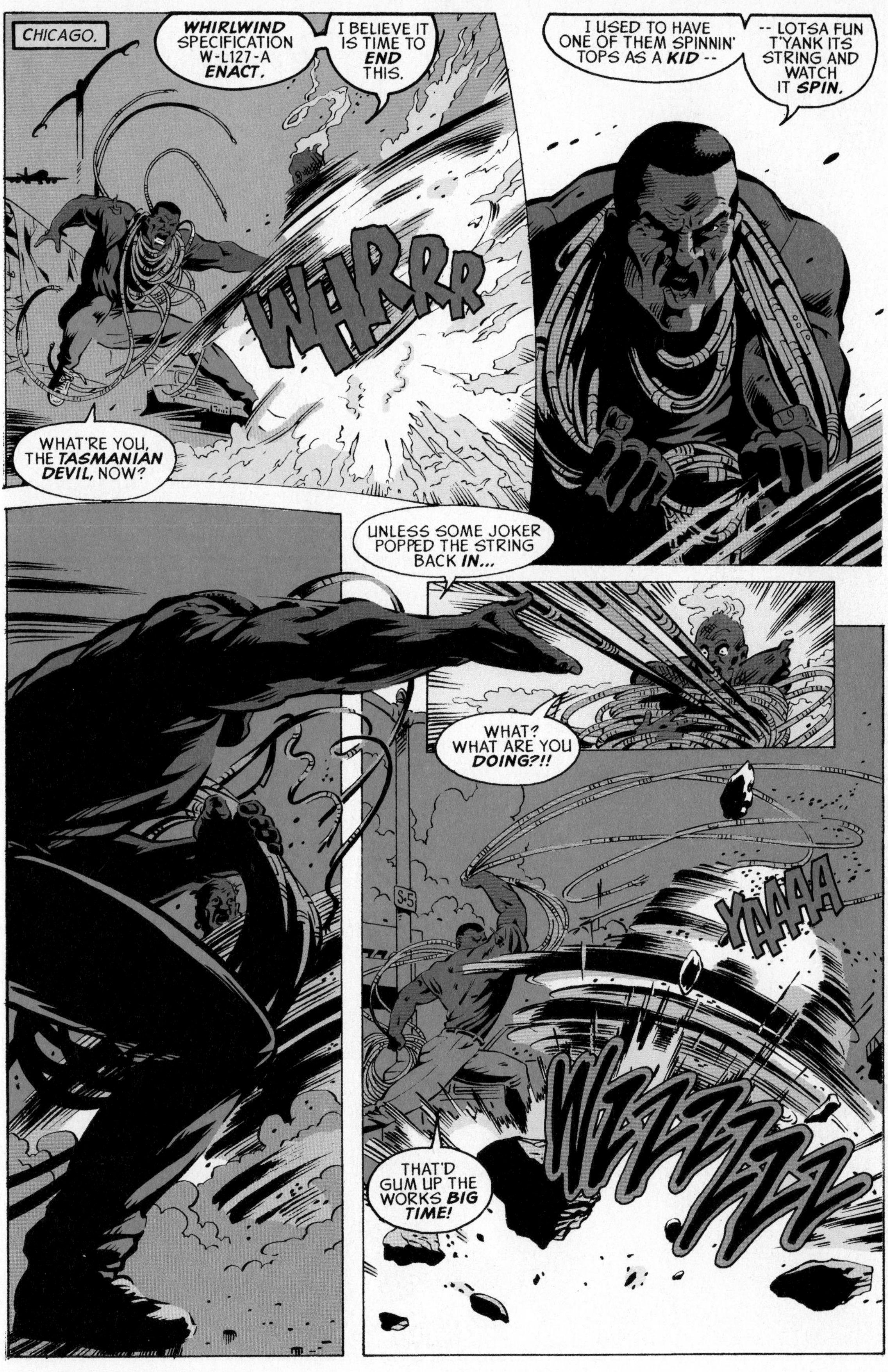
CHICAGO.
WHIRLWIND SPECIFICATION W-L127-A ENACT.
I BELIEVE IT IS TIME TO END THIS.
WHRRRR
WHAT'RE YOU, THE TASMANIAN DEVIL, NOW?
I USED TO HAVE ONE OF THEM SPINNIN' TOPS AS A KID --
-- LOTSA FUN T'YANK ITS STRING AND WATCH IT SPIN.
UNLESS SOME JOKER POPPED THE STRING BACK IN...
WHAT? WHAT ARE YOU DOING?!!
YAAAA
THAT'D GUM UP THE WORKS BIG TIME!

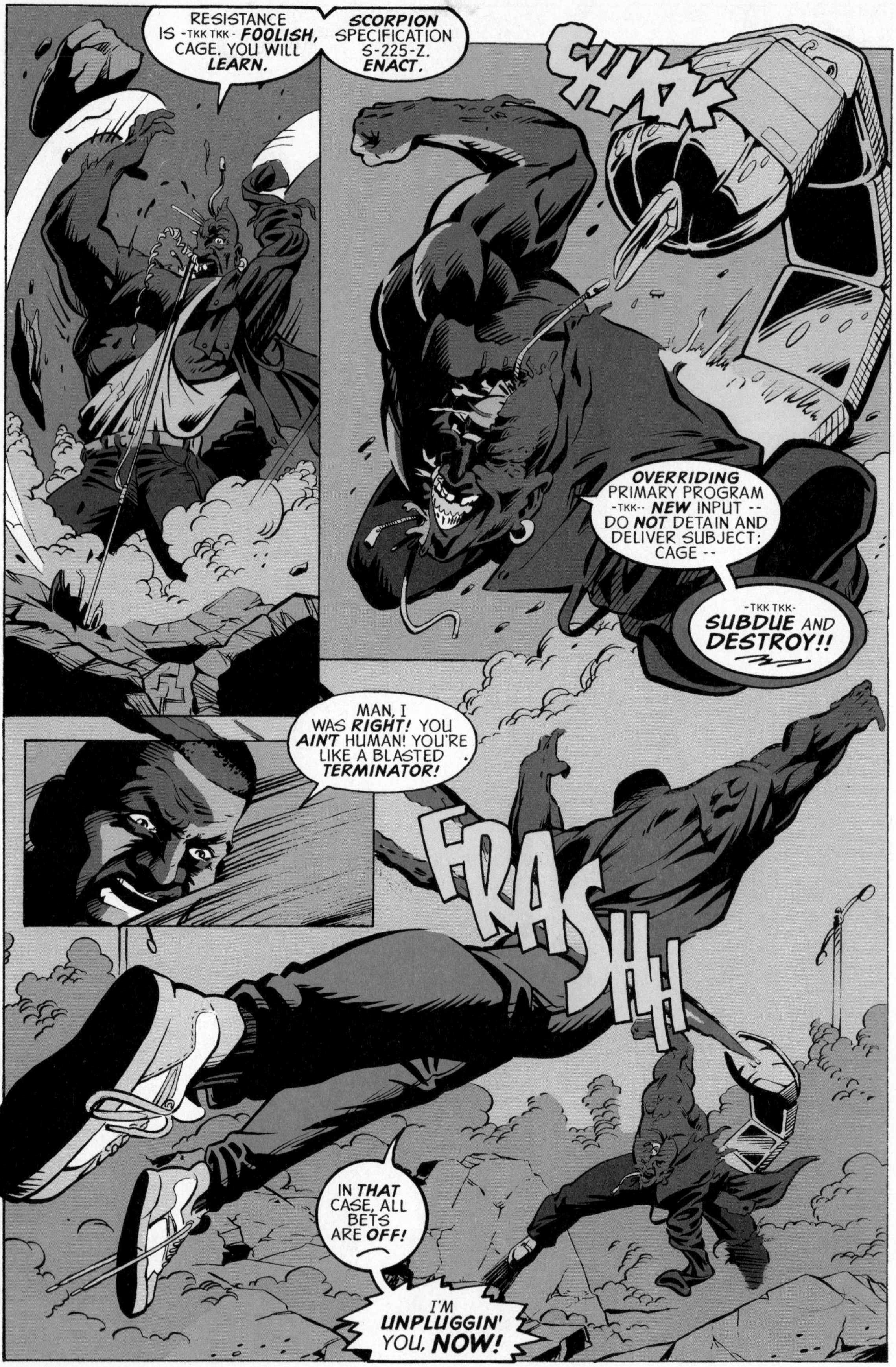

RESISTANCE IS -TKK TKK- FOOLISH, CAGE. YOU WILL LEARN.
SCORPION SPECIFICATION S-225-Z. ENACT.
CHAK
OVERRIDING PRIMARY PROGRAM -TKK-- NEW INPUT -- DO NOT DETAIN AND DELIVER SUBJECT: CAGE --
-TKK TKK- SUBDUE AND DESTROY!!
MAN, I WAS RIGHT! YOU AIN'T HUMAN! YOU'RE LIKE A BLASTED TERMINATOR!
FRASHH
IN THAT CASE, ALL BETS ARE OFF!
I'M UNPLUGGIN' YOU, NOW!

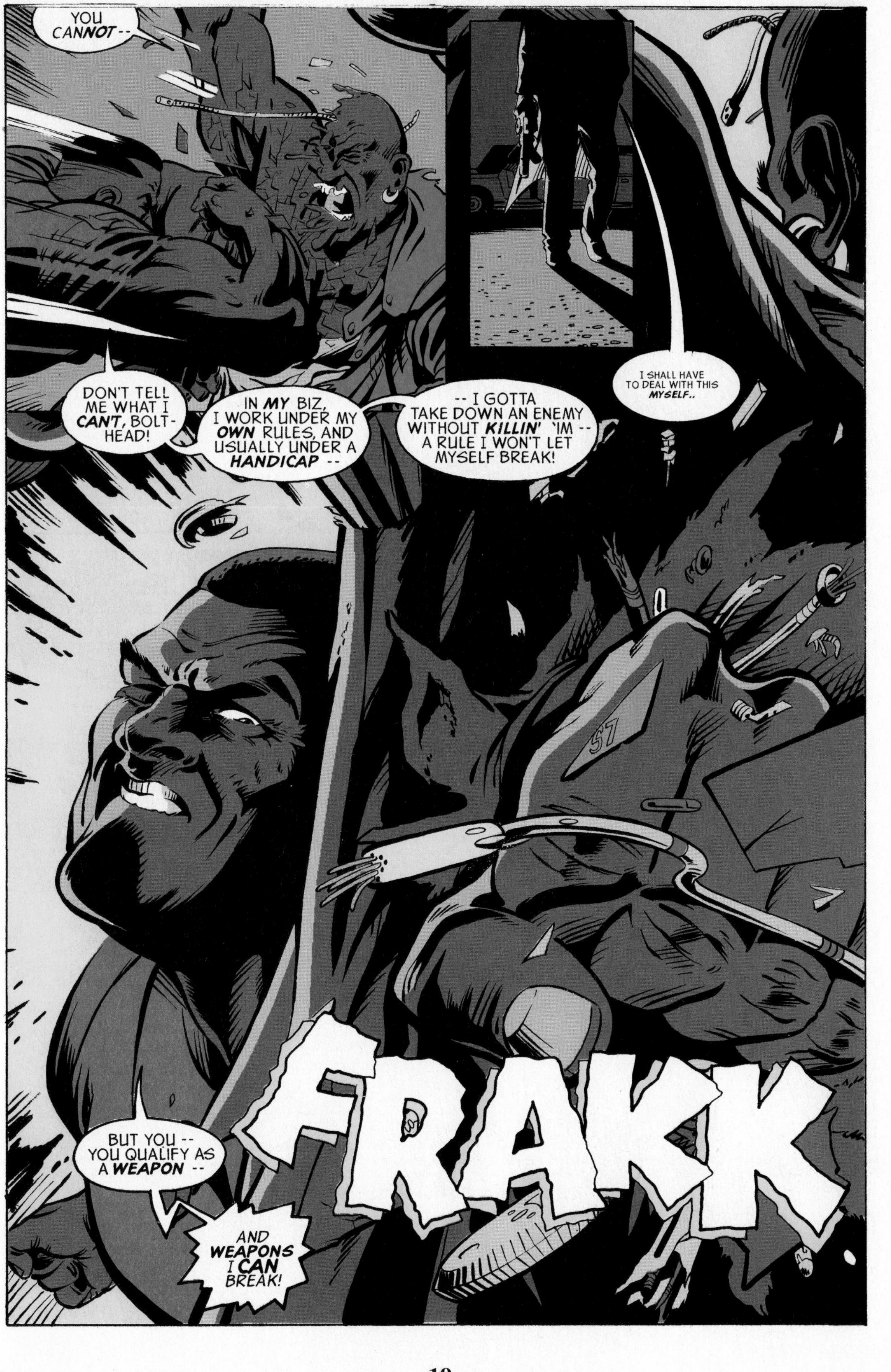
YOU CANNOT --
I SHALL HAVE TO DEAL WITH THIS MYSELF..
DON'T TELL ME WHAT I CAN'T, BOLT-HEAD!
IN MY BIZ, I WORK UNDER MY OWN RULES, AND USUALLY UNDER A HANDICAP --
-- I GOTTA TAKE DOWN AN ENEMY WITHOUT KILLIN' 'IM -- A RULE I WON'T LET MYSELF BREAK!
BUT YOU -- YOU QUALIFY AS A WEAPON --
FRAKK
AND WEAPONS I CAN BREAK!

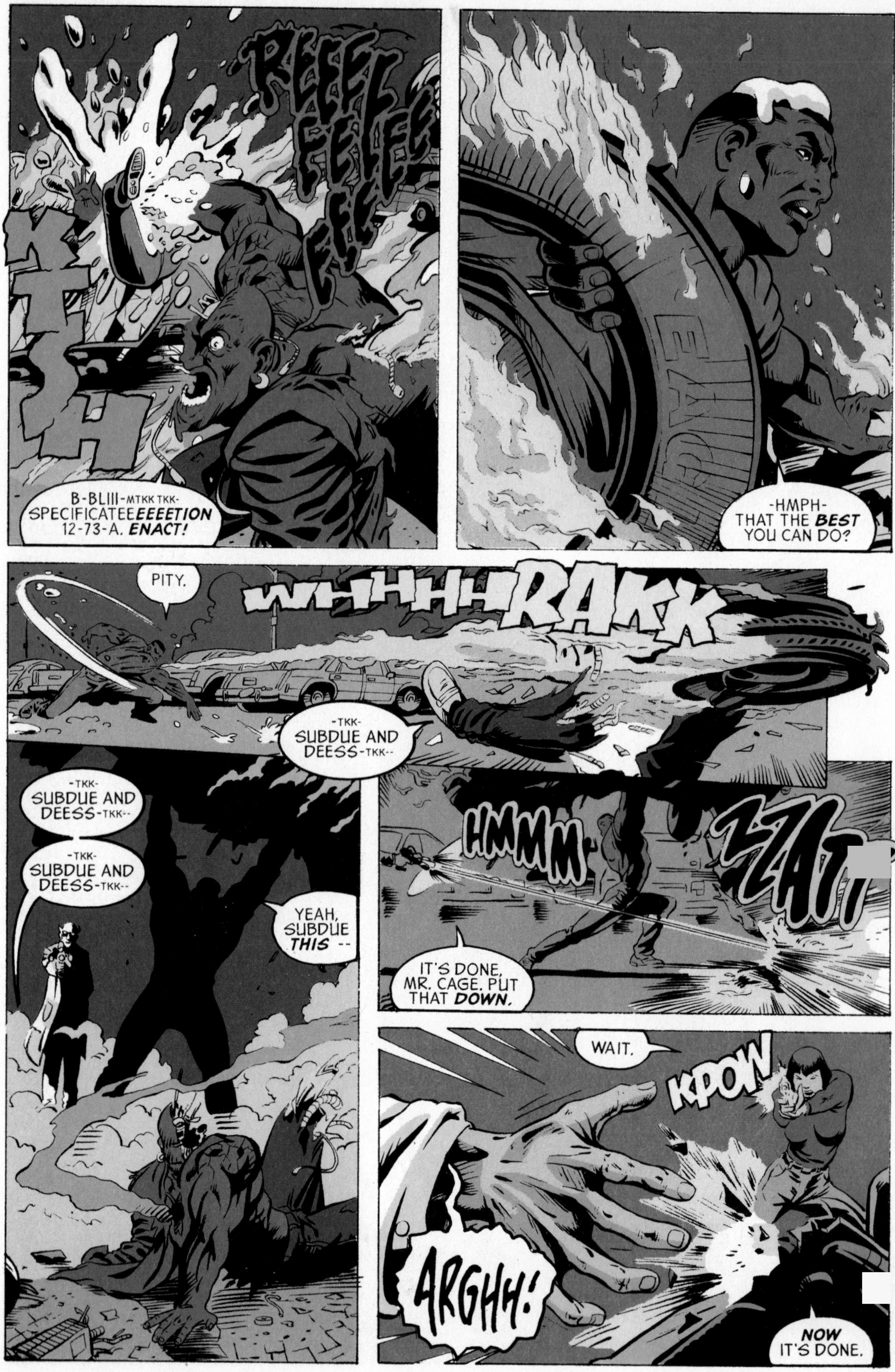
REEEEEEEEEEEE
B-BLIII-MTKK TKK-
SPECIFICATEEEEEEETION
12-73-A. ENACT!
-HMPH-
THAT THE BEST
YOU CAN DO?
PITY.
WHHHHRAKK
-TKK-
SUBDUE AND
DEESS-TKK--
-TKK-
SUBDUE AND
DEESS-TKK--
-TKK-
SUBDUE AND
DEESS-TKK--
YEAH,
SUBDUE
THIS --
HMMM
ZZAT
IT'S DONE,
MR. CAGE. PUT
THAT DOWN.
WAIT.
KPOW
ARGHH!
NOW
IT'S DONE.

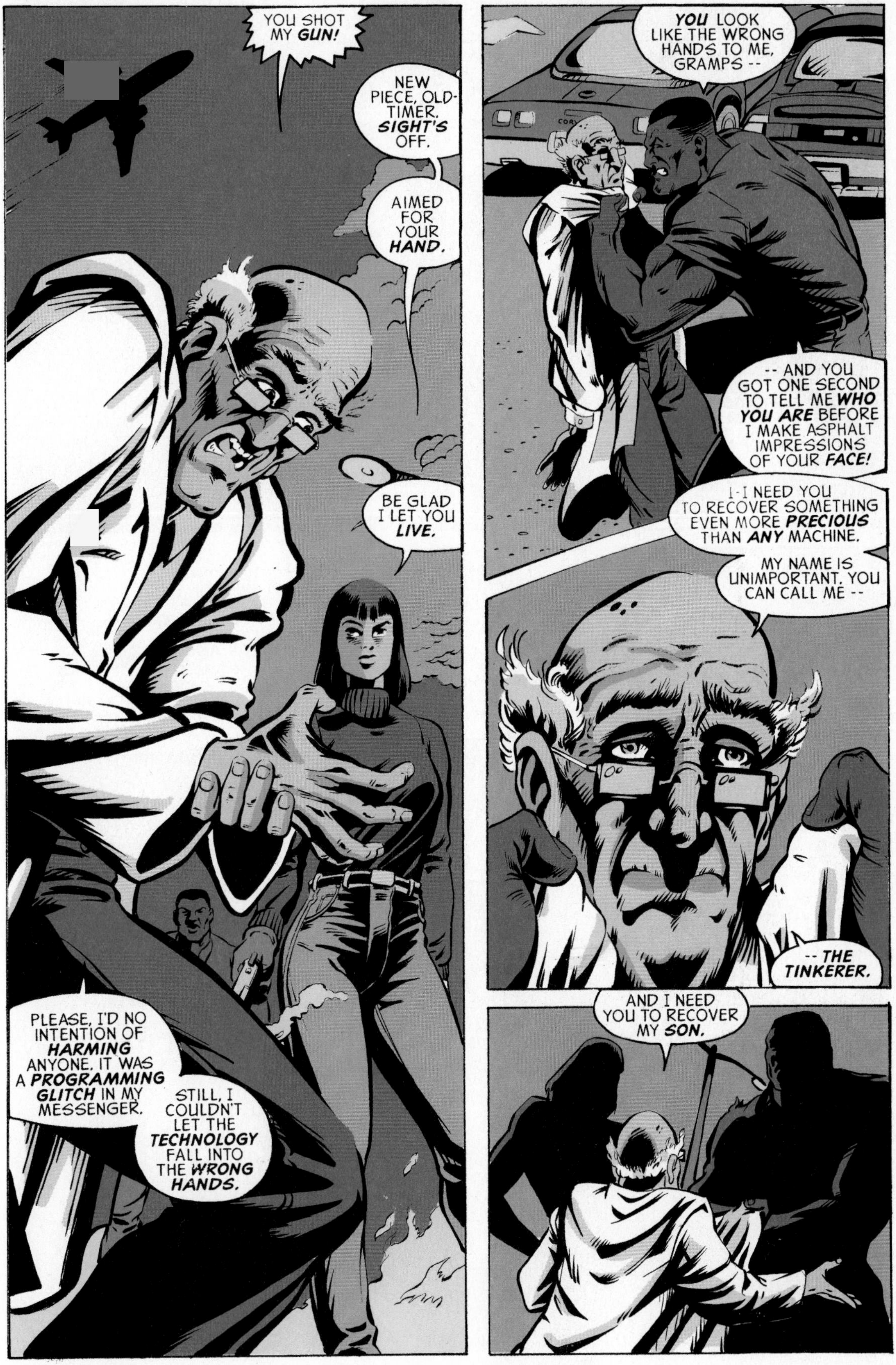

YOU SHOT MY GUN!
NEW PIECE, OLD-TIMER. SIGHT'S OFF.
AIMED FOR YOUR HAND.
BE GLAD I LET YOU LIVE.
PLEASE, I'D NO INTENTION OF HARMING ANYONE. IT WAS A PROGRAMMING GLITCH IN MY MESSENGER.
STILL, I COULDN'T LET THE TECHNOLOGY FALL INTO THE WRONG HANDS.
YOU LOOK LIKE THE WRONG HANDS TO ME, GRAMPS --
-- AND YOU GOT ONE SECOND TO TELL ME WHO YOU ARE BEFORE I MAKE ASPHALT IMPRESSIONS OF YOUR FACE!
I-I NEED YOU TO RECOVER SOMETHING EVEN MORE PRECIOUS THAN ANY MACHINE.
MY NAME IS UNIMPORTANT. YOU CAN CALL ME --
-- THE TINKERER.
AND I NEED YOU TO RECOVER MY SON.

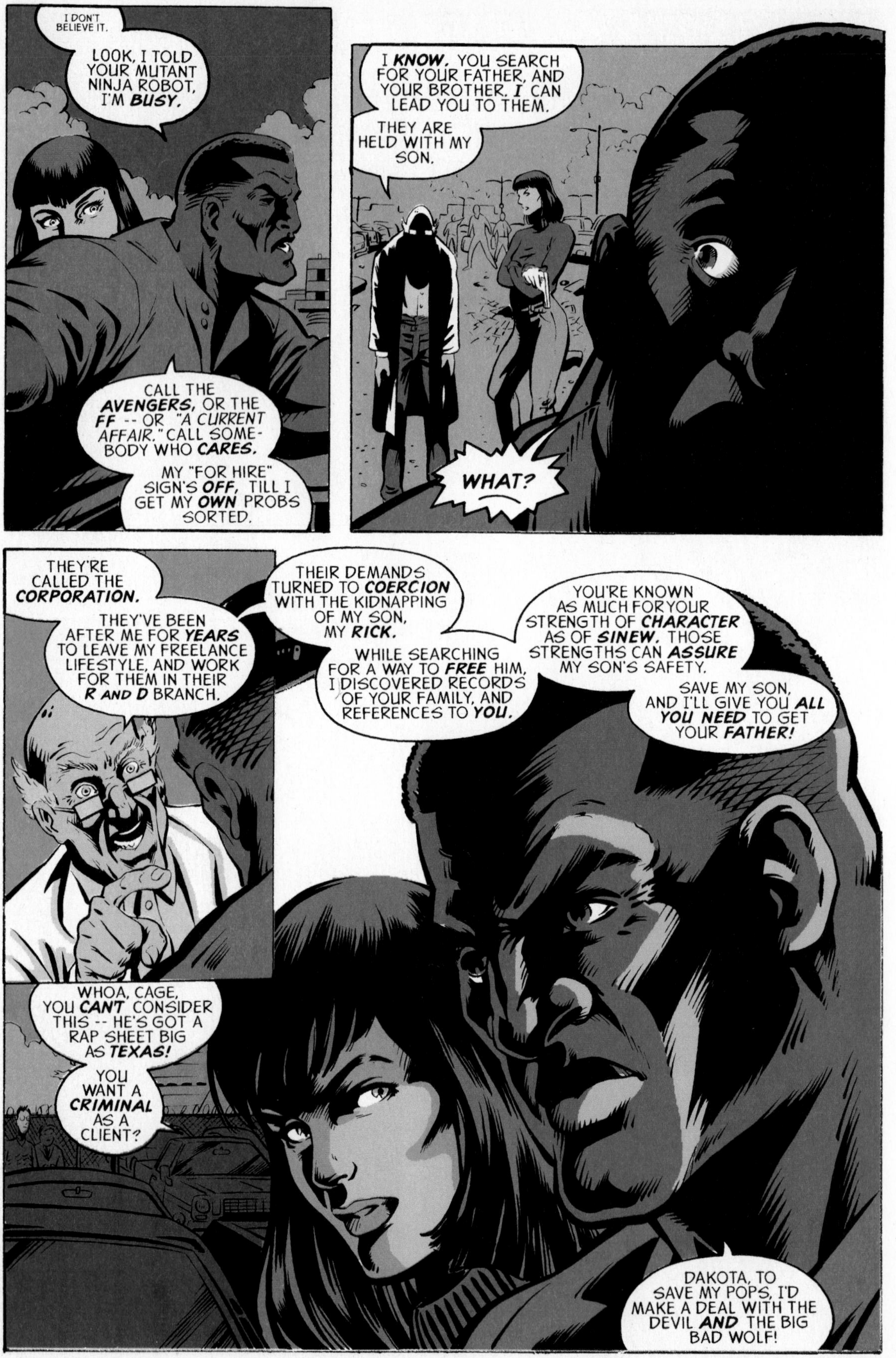
I DON'T BELIEVE IT.
LOOK, I TOLD YOUR MUTANT NINJA ROBOT, I'M BUSY.
CALL THE AVENGERS, OR THE FF -- OR "A CURRENT AFFAIR." CALL SOMEBODY WHO CARES.
MY "FOR HIRE" SIGN'S OFF, TILL I GET MY OWN PROBS SORTED.
I KNOW. YOU SEARCH FOR YOUR FATHER, AND YOUR BROTHER. I CAN LEAD YOU TO THEM.
THEY ARE HELD WITH MY SON.
WHAT?
THEY'RE CALLED THE CORPORATION.
THEY'VE BEEN AFTER ME FOR YEARS TO LEAVE MY FREELANCE LIFESTYLE, AND WORK FOR THEM IN THEIR R AND D BRANCH.
THEIR DEMANDS TURNED TO COERCION WITH THE KIDNAPPING OF MY SON, MY RICK.
WHILE SEARCHING FOR A WAY TO FREE HIM, I DISCOVERED RECORDS OF YOUR FAMILY, AND REFERENCES TO YOU.
YOU'RE KNOWN AS MUCH FOR YOUR STRENGTH OF CHARACTER AS OF SINEW. THOSE STRENGTHS CAN ASSURE MY SON'S SAFETY.
SAVE MY SON, AND I'LL GIVE YOU ALL YOU NEED TO GET YOUR FATHER!
WHOA, CAGE, YOU CAN'T CONSIDER THIS -- HE'S GOT A RAP SHEET BIG AS TEXAS!
YOU WANT A CRIMINAL AS A CLIENT?
DAKOTA, TO SAVE MY POPS, I'D MAKE A DEAL WITH THE DEVIL AND THE BIG BAD WOLF!

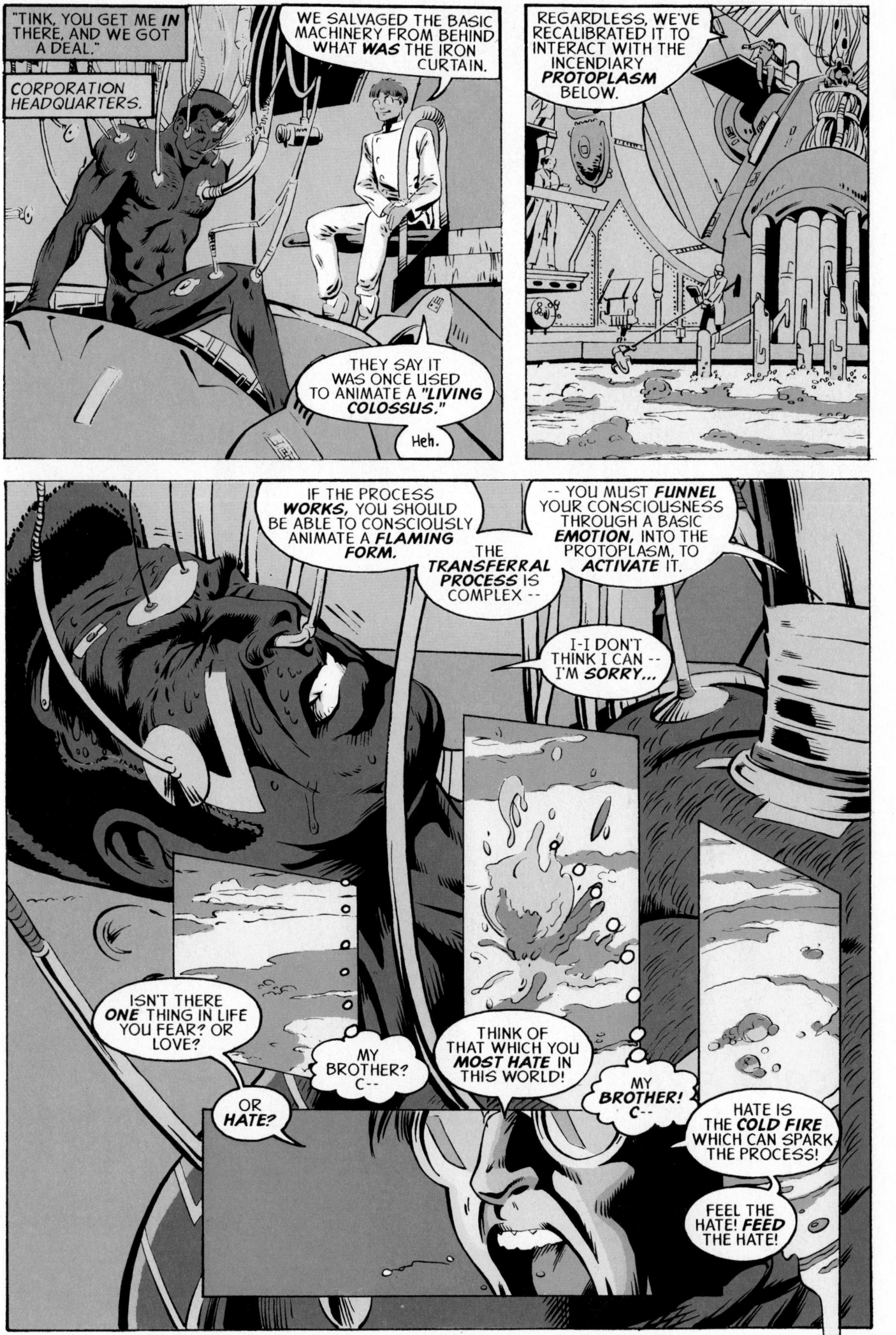
"TINK, YOU GET ME IN THERE, AND WE GOT A DEAL."
CORPORATION HEADQUARTERS.
WE SALVAGED THE BASIC MACHINERY FROM BEHIND WHAT WAS THE IRON CURTAIN.
THEY SAY IT WAS ONCE USED TO ANIMATE A "LIVING COLOSSUS."
Heh.
REGARDLESS, WE'VE RECALIBRATED IT TO INTERACT WITH THE INCENDIARY PROTOPLASM BELOW.
IF THE PROCESS WORKS, YOU SHOULD BE ABLE TO CONSCIOUSLY ANIMATE A FLAMING FORM.
THE TRANSFERRAL PROCESS IS COMPLEX --
-- YOU MUST FUNNEL YOUR CONSCIOUSNESS THROUGH A BASIC EMOTION, INTO THE PROTOPLASM, TO ACTIVATE IT.
I-I DON'T THINK I CAN -- I'M SORRY...
ISN'T THERE ONE THING IN LIFE YOU FEAR? OR LOVE?
OR HATE?
MY BROTHER? C--
THINK OF THAT WHICH YOU MOST HATE IN THIS WORLD!
MY BROTHER! C--
HATE IS THE COLD FIRE WHICH CAN SPARK THE PROCESS!
FEEL THE HATE! FEED THE HATE!

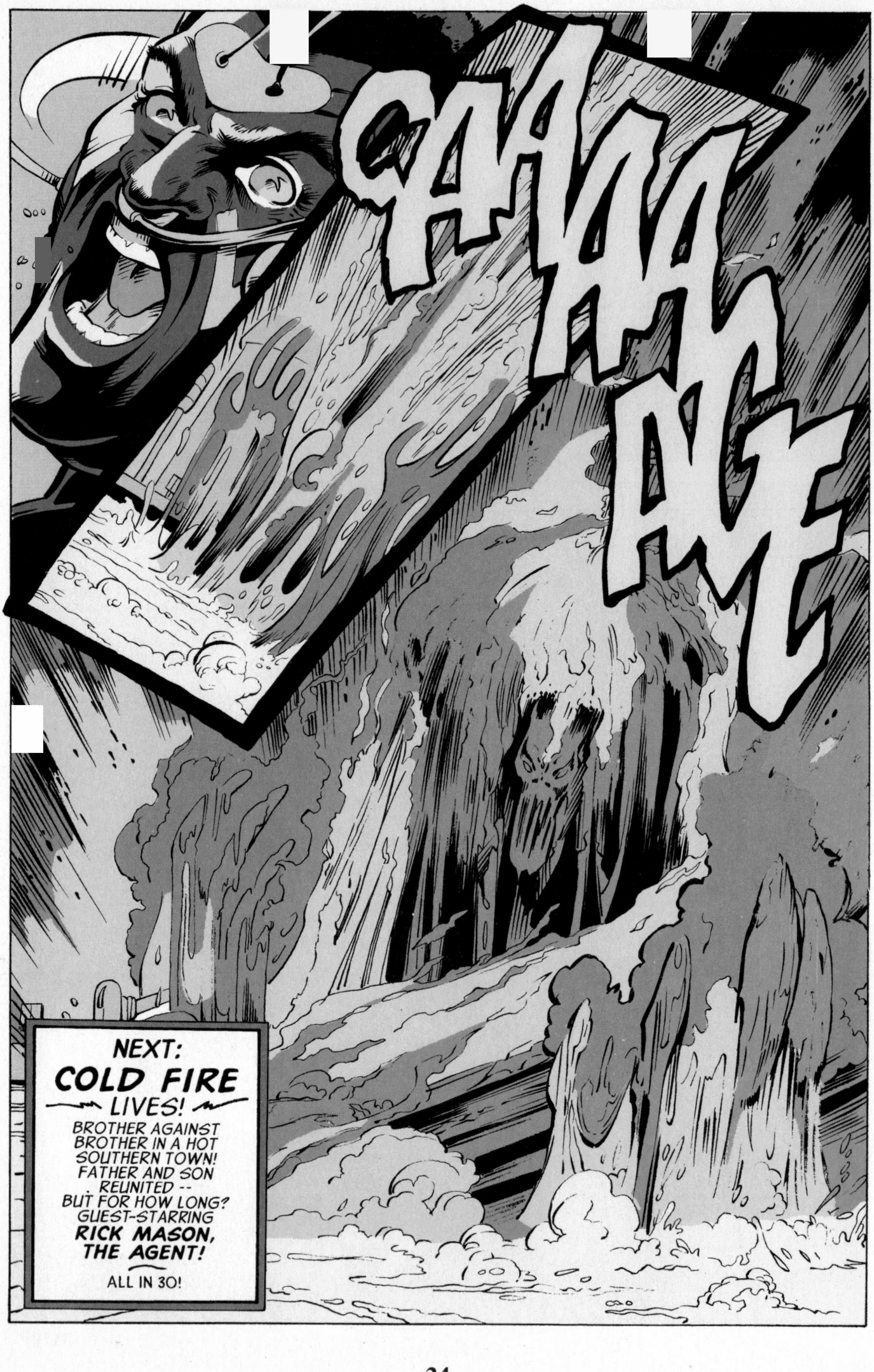
GAAAAAGE
NEXT:
COLD FIRE
LIVES!
BROTHER AGAINST BROTHER IN A HOT SOUTHERN TOWN! FATHER AND SON REUNITED -- BUT FOR HOW LONG? GUEST-STARRING
RICK MASON, THE AGENT!
ALL IN 30!

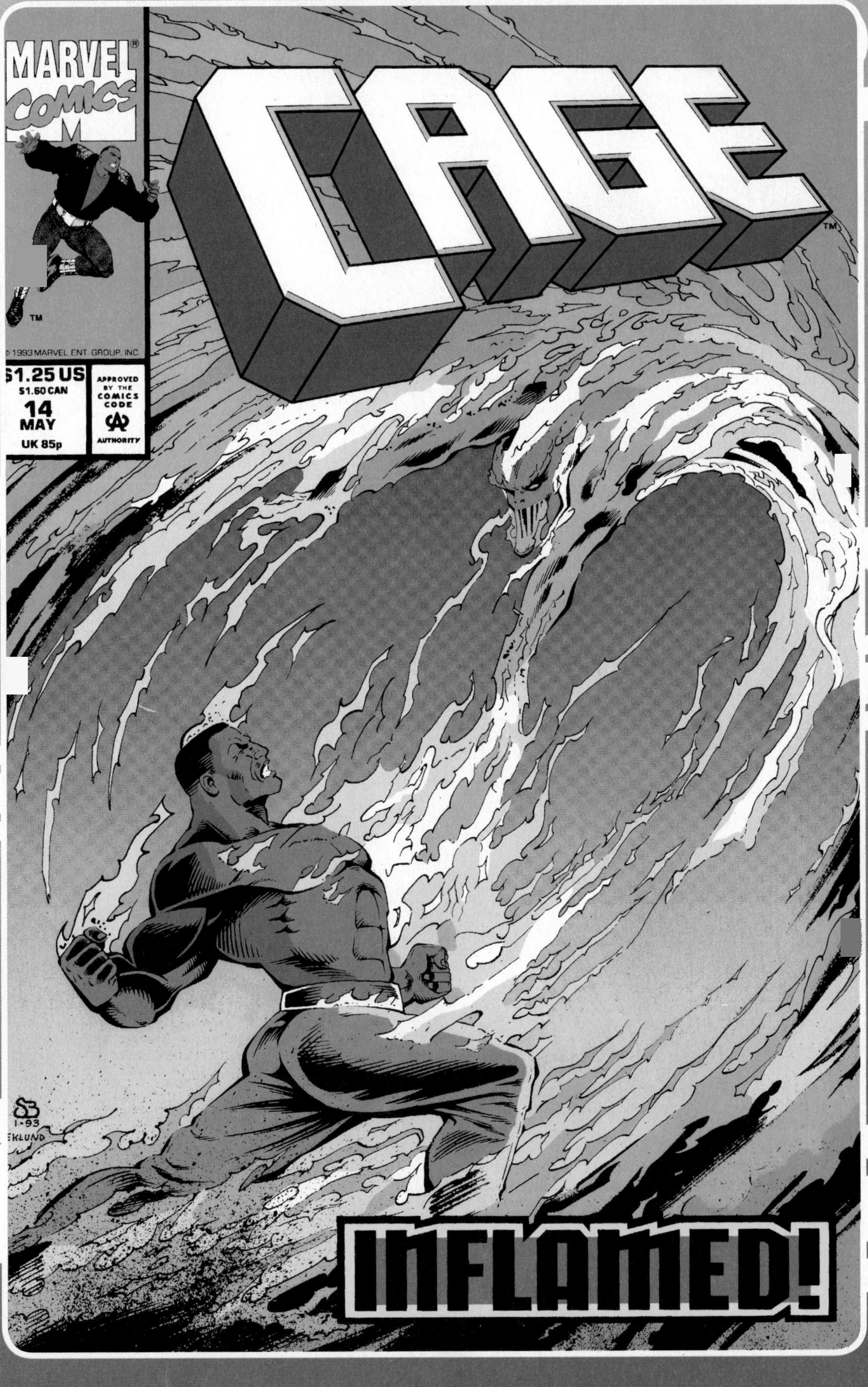
MARVEL COMICS
CAGE
© 1993 MARVEL ENT. GROUP, INC.
$1.25 US
$1.60 CAN
14
MAY
UK 85p
APPROVED BY THE COMICS CODE AUTHORITY
INFLAMED!

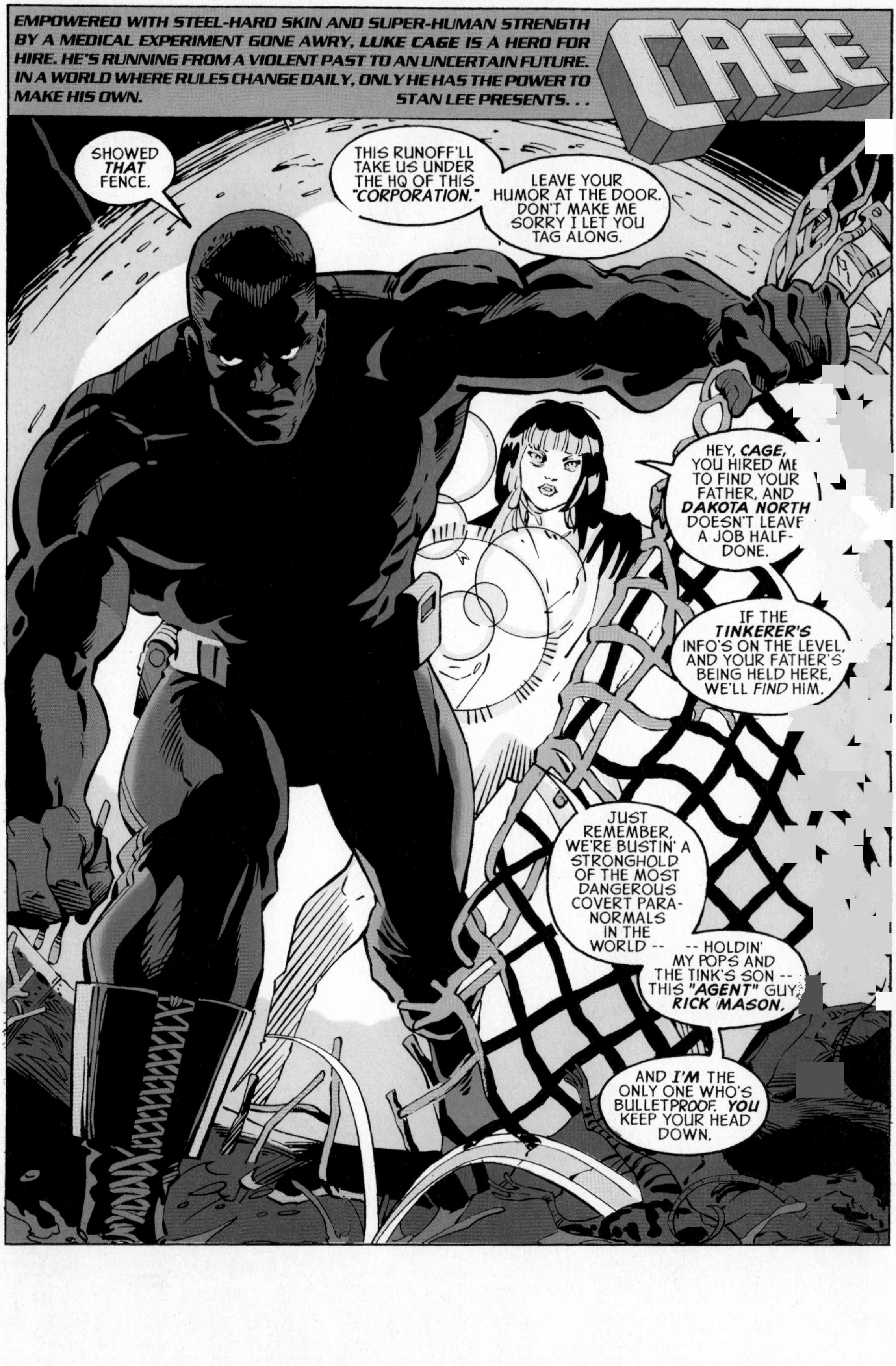
EMPOWERED WITH STEEL-HARD SKIN AND SUPER-HUMAN STRENGTH BY A MEDICAL EXPERIMENT GONE AWRY, LUKE CAGE IS A HERO FOR HIRE. HE'S RUNNING FROM A VIOLENT PAST TO AN UNCERTAIN FUTURE. IN A WORLD WHERE RULES CHANGE DAILY, ONLY HE HAS THE POWER TO MAKE HIS OWN.
STAN LEE PRESENTS. . .
CAGE
SHOWED THAT FENCE.
THIS RUNOFF'LL TAKE US UNDER THE HQ OF THIS "CORPORATION."
LEAVE YOUR HUMOR AT THE DOOR. DON'T MAKE ME SORRY I LET YOU TAG ALONG.
HEY, CAGE, YOU HIRED ME TO FIND YOUR FATHER, AND DAKOTA NORTH DOESN'T LEAVE A JOB HALF-DONE.
IF THE TINKERER'S INFO'S ON THE LEVEL, AND YOUR FATHER'S BEING HELD HERE, WE'LL FIND HIM.
JUST REMEMBER, WE'RE BUSTIN' A STRONGHOLD OF THE MOST DANGEROUS COVERT PARA-NORMALS IN THE WORLD --
-- HOLDIN' MY POPS AND THE TINK'S SON -- THIS "AGENT" GUY RICK MASON.
AND I'M THE ONLY ONE WHO'S BULLETPROOF. YOU KEEP YOUR HEAD DOWN.

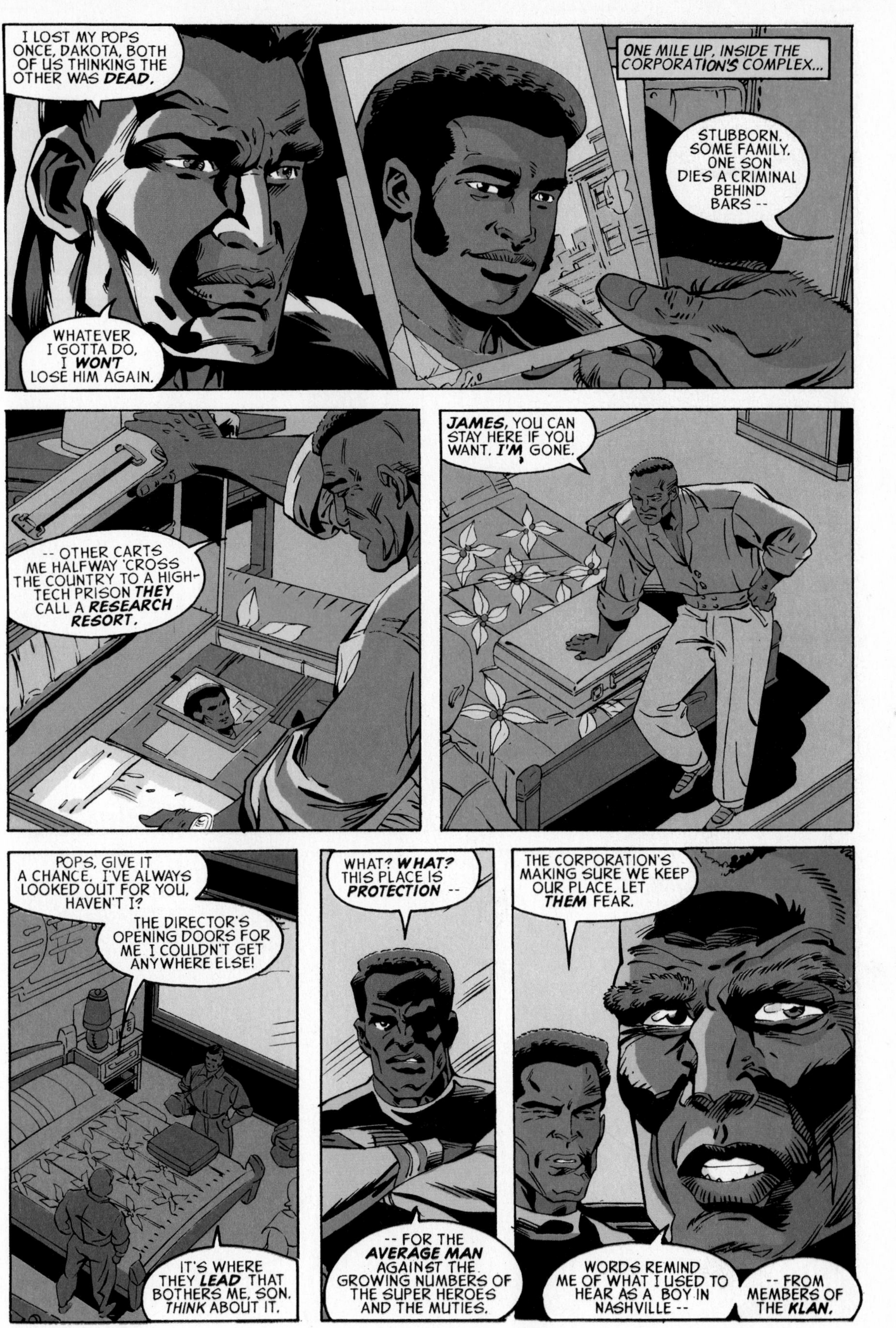
I LOST MY POPS ONCE, DAKOTA, BOTH OF US THINKING THE OTHER WAS DEAD.
ONE MILE UP, INSIDE THE CORPORATION'S COMPLEX...
STUBBORN. SOME FAMILY. ONE SON DIES A CRIMINAL BEHIND BARS --
WHATEVER I GOTTA DO, I WON'T LOSE HIM AGAIN.
-- OTHER CARTS ME HALFWAY 'CROSS THE COUNTRY TO A HIGH-TECH PRISON THEY CALL A RESEARCH RESORT.
JAMES, YOU CAN STAY HERE IF YOU WANT. I'M GONE.
POPS, GIVE IT A CHANCE. I'VE ALWAYS LOOKED OUT FOR YOU, HAVEN'T I?
THE DIRECTOR'S OPENING DOORS FOR ME I COULDN'T GET ANYWHERE ELSE!
IT'S WHERE THEY LEAD THAT BOTHERS ME, SON. THINK ABOUT IT.
WHAT? WHAT? THIS PLACE IS PROTECTION --
-- FOR THE AVERAGE MAN AGAINST THE GROWING NUMBERS OF THE SUPER HEROES AND THE MUTIES.
THE CORPORATION'S MAKING SURE WE KEEP OUR PLACE. LET THEM FEAR.
WORDS REMIND ME OF WHAT I USED TO HEAR AS A BOY IN NASHVILLE --
-- FROM MEMBERS OF THE KLAN.

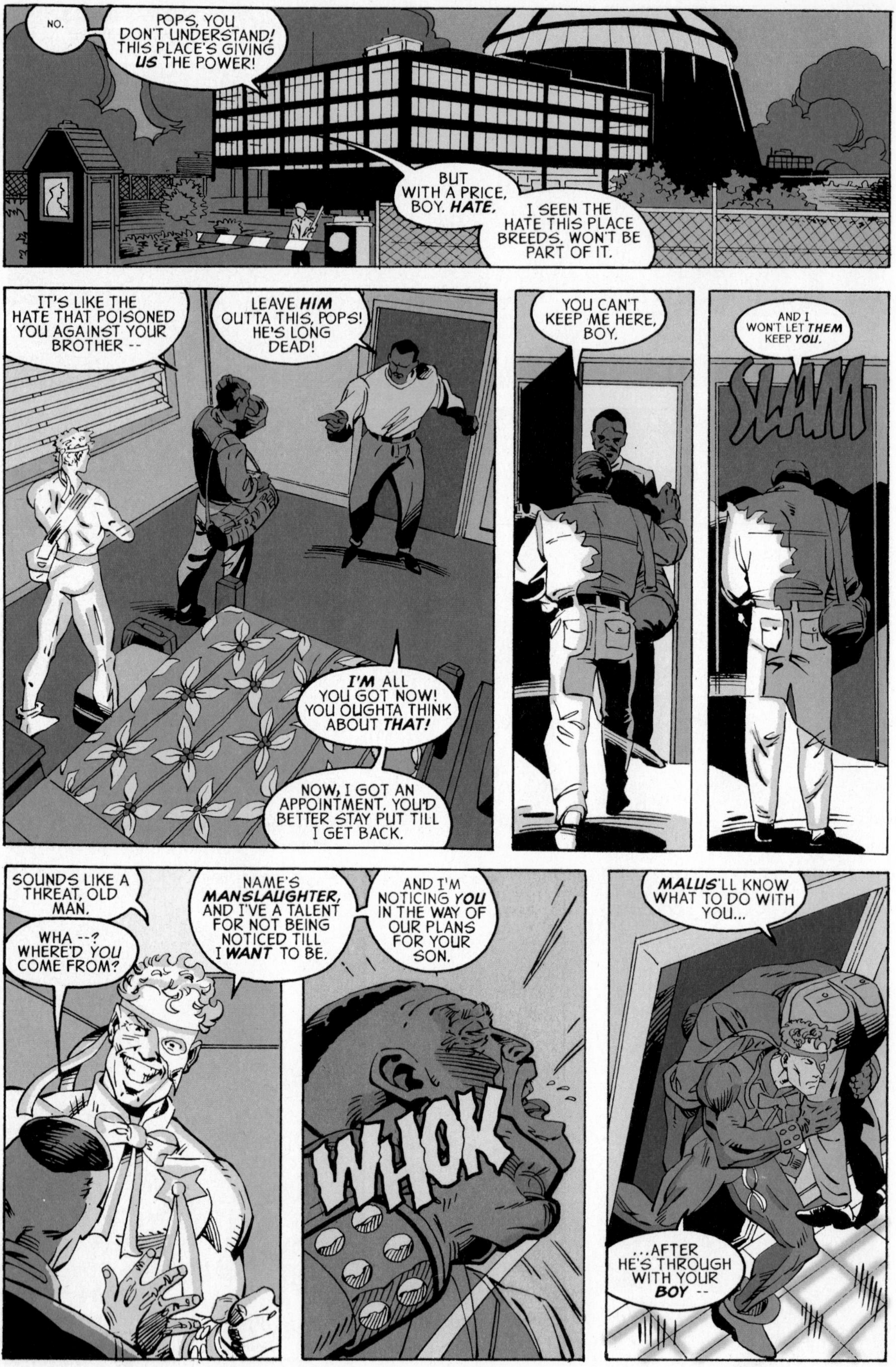
NO.
POPS, YOU DON'T UNDERSTAND! THIS PLACE'S GIVING US THE POWER!
BUT WITH A PRICE, BOY. HATE.
I SEEN THE HATE THIS PLACE BREEDS. WON'T BE PART OF IT.
IT'S LIKE THE HATE THAT POISONED YOU AGAINST YOUR BROTHER --
LEAVE HIM OUTTA THIS, POPS! HE'S LONG DEAD!
I'M ALL YOU GOT NOW! YOU OUGHTA THINK ABOUT THAT!
NOW, I GOT AN APPOINTMENT. YOU'D BETTER STAY PUT TILL I GET BACK.
YOU CAN'T KEEP ME HERE, BOY.
AND I WON'T LET THEM KEEP YOU.
SLAM
SOUNDS LIKE A THREAT, OLD MAN.
WHA --? WHERE'D YOU COME FROM?
NAME'S MANSLAUGHTER, AND I'VE A TALENT FOR NOT BEING NOTICED TILL I WANT TO BE.
AND I'M NOTICING YOU IN THE WAY OF OUR PLANS FOR YOUR SON.
WHOK
MALUS'LL KNOW WHAT TO DO WITH YOU...
...AFTER HE'S THROUGH WITH YOUR BOY --

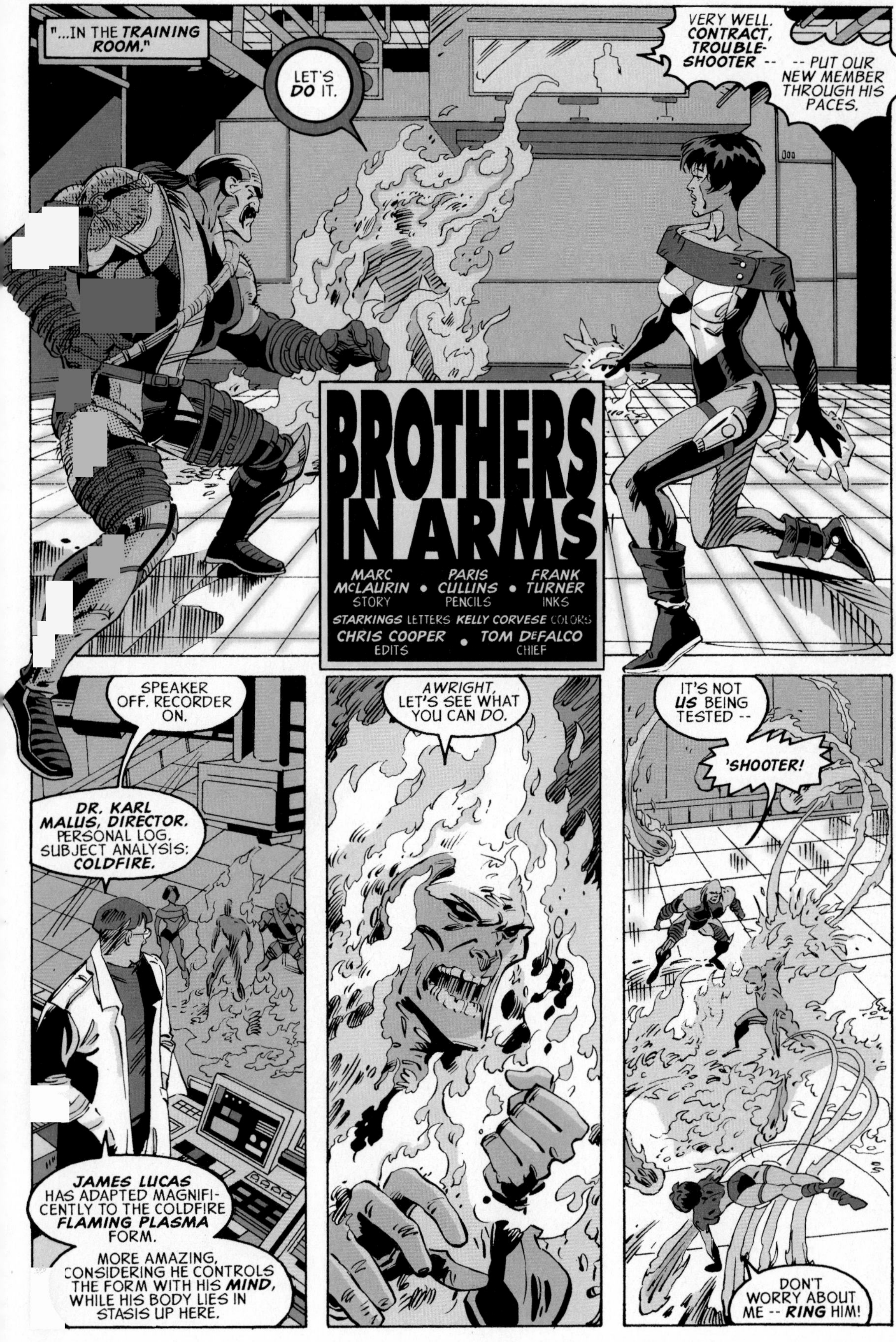
"...IN THE TRAINING ROOM."
LET'S DO IT.
VERY WELL. CONTRACT, TROUBLE-SHOOTER --
-- PUT OUR NEW MEMBER THROUGH HIS PACES.
BROTHERS IN ARMS
MARC McLAURIN STORY • PARIS CULLINS PENCILS • FRANK TURNER INKS
STARKINGS LETTERS KELLY CORVESE COLORS
CHRIS COOPER EDITS • TOM DeFALCO CHIEF
SPEAKER OFF. RECORDER ON.
DR. KARL MALUS, DIRECTOR. PERSONAL LOG. SUBJECT ANALYSIS: COLDFIRE.
JAMES LUCAS HAS ADAPTED MAGNIFI-CENTLY TO THE COLDFIRE FLAMING PLASMA FORM.
MORE AMAZING, CONSIDERING HE CONTROLS THE FORM WITH HIS MIND, WHILE HIS BODY LIES IN STASIS UP HERE.
AWRIGHT, LET'S SEE WHAT YOU CAN DO.
IT'S NOT US BEING TESTED --
'SHOOTER!
DON'T WORRY ABOUT ME -- RING HIM!

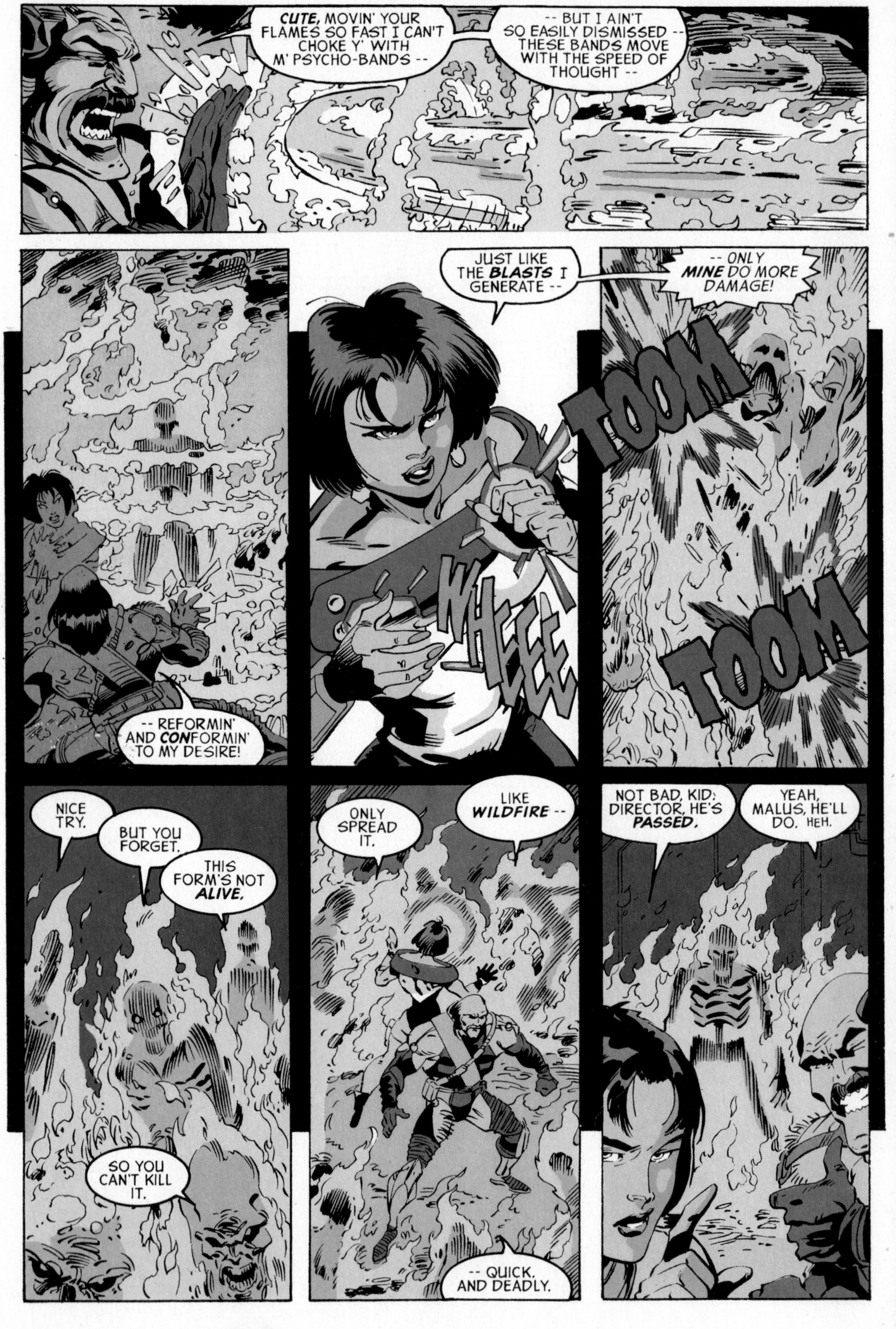

CUTE, MOVIN' YOUR FLAMES SO FAST I CAN'T CHOKE Y' WITH M' PSYCHO-BANDS --
-- BUT I AIN'T SO EASILY DISMISSED -- THESE BANDS MOVE WITH THE SPEED OF THOUGHT --
-- REFORMIN' AND CONFORMIN' TO MY DESIRE!
JUST LIKE THE BLASTS I GENERATE --
WHEEE
-- ONLY MINE DO MORE DAMAGE!
TOOM
TOOM
NICE TRY.
BUT YOU FORGET.
THIS FORM'S NOT ALIVE.
SO YOU CAN'T KILL IT.
LIKE WILDFIRE --
ONLY SPREAD IT.
-- QUICK, AND DEADLY.
NOT BAD, KID: DIRECTOR, HE'S PASSED.
YEAH, MALUS, HE'LL DO. HEH.

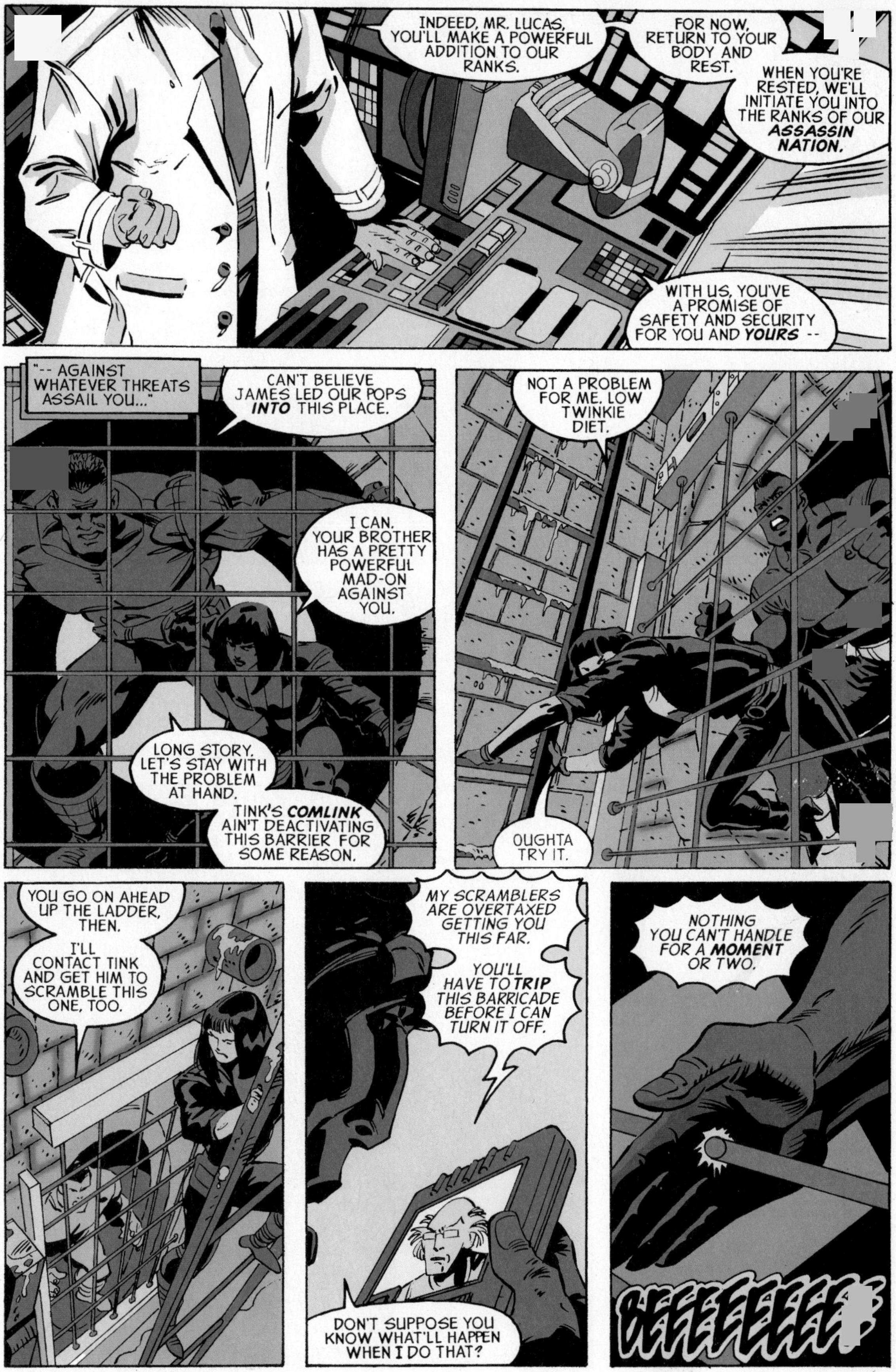
INDEED, MR. LUCAS, YOU'LL MAKE A POWERFUL ADDITION TO OUR RANKS.
FOR NOW, RETURN TO YOUR BODY AND REST.
WHEN YOU'RE RESTED, WE'LL INITIATE YOU INTO THE RANKS OF OUR **ASSASSIN NATION.**
WITH US, YOU'VE A PROMISE OF SAFETY AND SECURITY FOR YOU AND **YOURS** --
"-- AGAINST WHATEVER THREATS ASSAIL YOU..."
CAN'T BELIEVE JAMES LED OUR POPS **INTO** THIS PLACE.
I CAN. YOUR BROTHER HAS A PRETTY POWERFUL MAD-ON AGAINST YOU.
LONG STORY. LET'S STAY WITH THE PROBLEM AT HAND.
TINK'S **COMLINK** AIN'T DEACTIVATING THIS BARRIER FOR SOME REASON.
NOT A PROBLEM FOR ME. LOW TWINKIE DIET.
OUGHTA TRY IT.
YOU GO ON AHEAD UP THE LADDER, THEN.
I'LL CONTACT TINK AND GET HIM TO SCRAMBLE THIS ONE, TOO.
MY SCRAMBLERS ARE OVERTAXED GETTING YOU THIS FAR.
YOU'LL HAVE TO **TRIP** THIS BARRICADE BEFORE I CAN TURN IT OFF.
DON'T SUPPOSE YOU KNOW WHAT'LL HAPPEN WHEN **I** DO THAT?
NOTHING YOU CAN'T HANDLE FOR A **MOMENT** OR TWO.
BEEEEEEEE

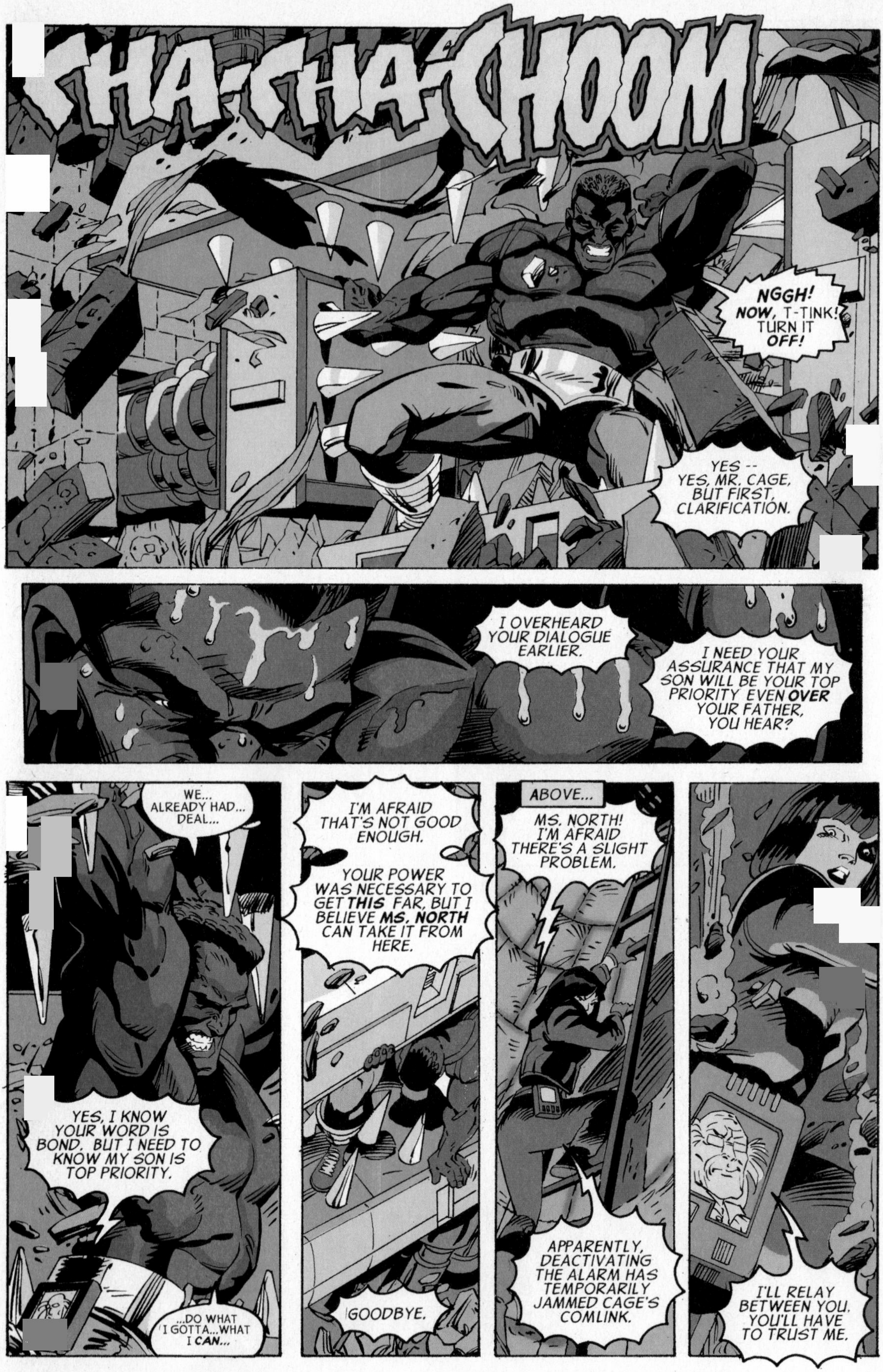
CHA-CHA-CHOOM
NGGH! NOW, T-TINK! TURN IT OFF!
YES -- YES, MR. CAGE, BUT FIRST, CLARIFICATION.
I OVERHEARD YOUR DIALOGUE EARLIER.
I NEED YOUR ASSURANCE THAT MY SON WILL BE YOUR TOP PRIORITY EVEN OVER YOUR FATHER, YOU HEAR?
WE... ALREADY HAD... DEAL...
YES, I KNOW YOUR WORD IS BOND. BUT I NEED TO KNOW MY SON IS TOP PRIORITY.
...DO WHAT I GOTTA... WHAT I CAN...
I'M AFRAID THAT'S NOT GOOD ENOUGH.
YOUR POWER WAS NECESSARY TO GET THIS FAR, BUT I BELIEVE MS. NORTH CAN TAKE IT FROM HERE.
GOODBYE.
ABOVE...
MS. NORTH! I'M AFRAID THERE'S A SLIGHT PROBLEM.
APPARENTLY, DEACTIVATING THE ALARM HAS TEMPORARILY JAMMED CAGE'S COMLINK.
I'LL RELAY BETWEEN YOU. YOU'LL HAVE TO TRUST ME.

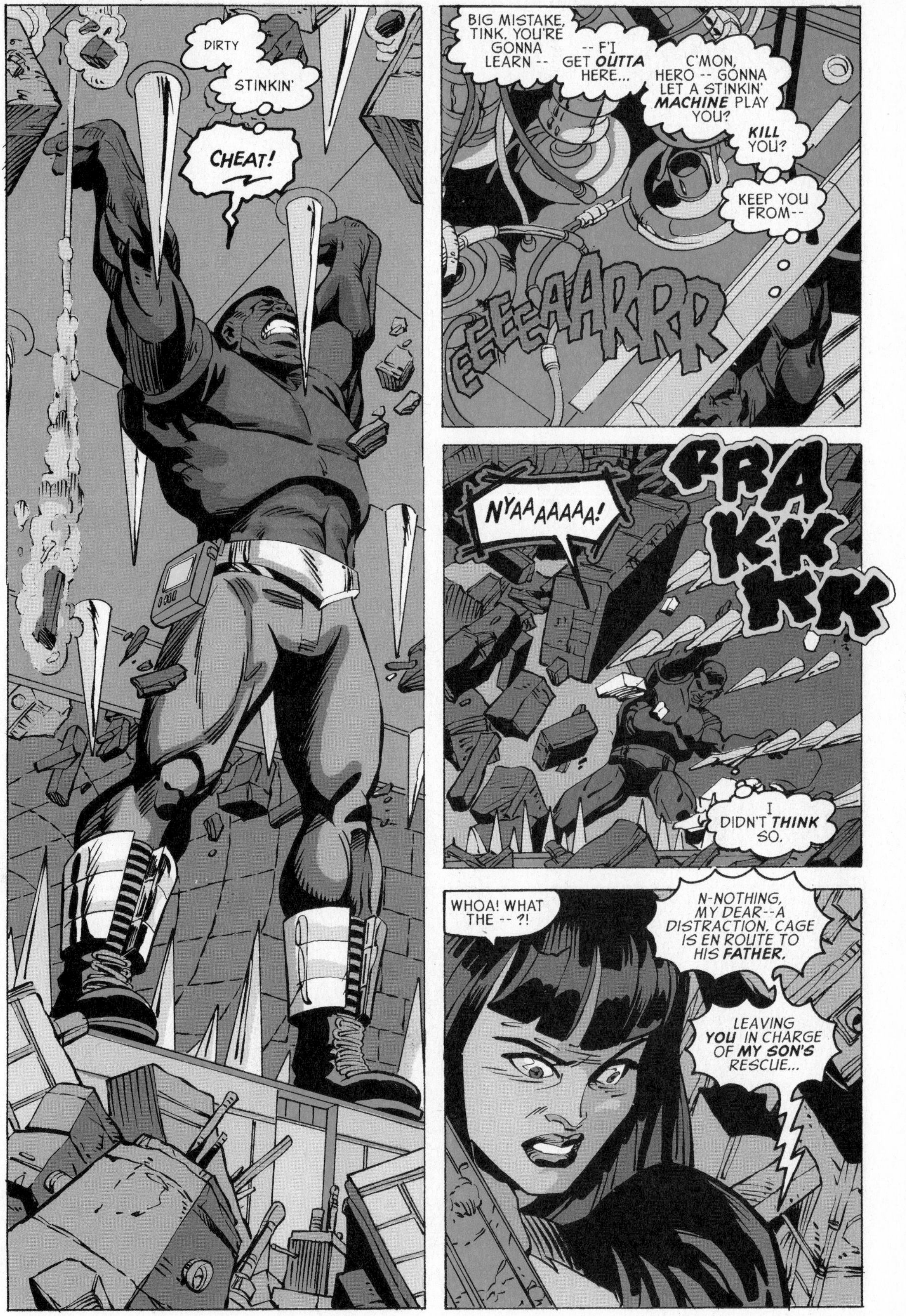
DIRTY
STINKIN'
CHEAT!
BIG MISTAKE, TINK. YOU'RE GONNA LEARN --
-- F'I GET OUTTA HERE...
C'MON, HERO -- GONNA LET A STINKIN' MACHINE PLAY YOU?
KILL YOU?
KEEP YOU FROM--
EEEEAARRRR
NYAAAAAAA!
PRAKKKK
I DIDN'T THINK SO.
WHOA! WHAT THE -- ?!
N-NOTHING, MY DEAR--A DISTRACTION. CAGE IS EN ROUTE TO HIS FATHER.
LEAVING YOU IN CHARGE OF MY SON'S RESCUE...

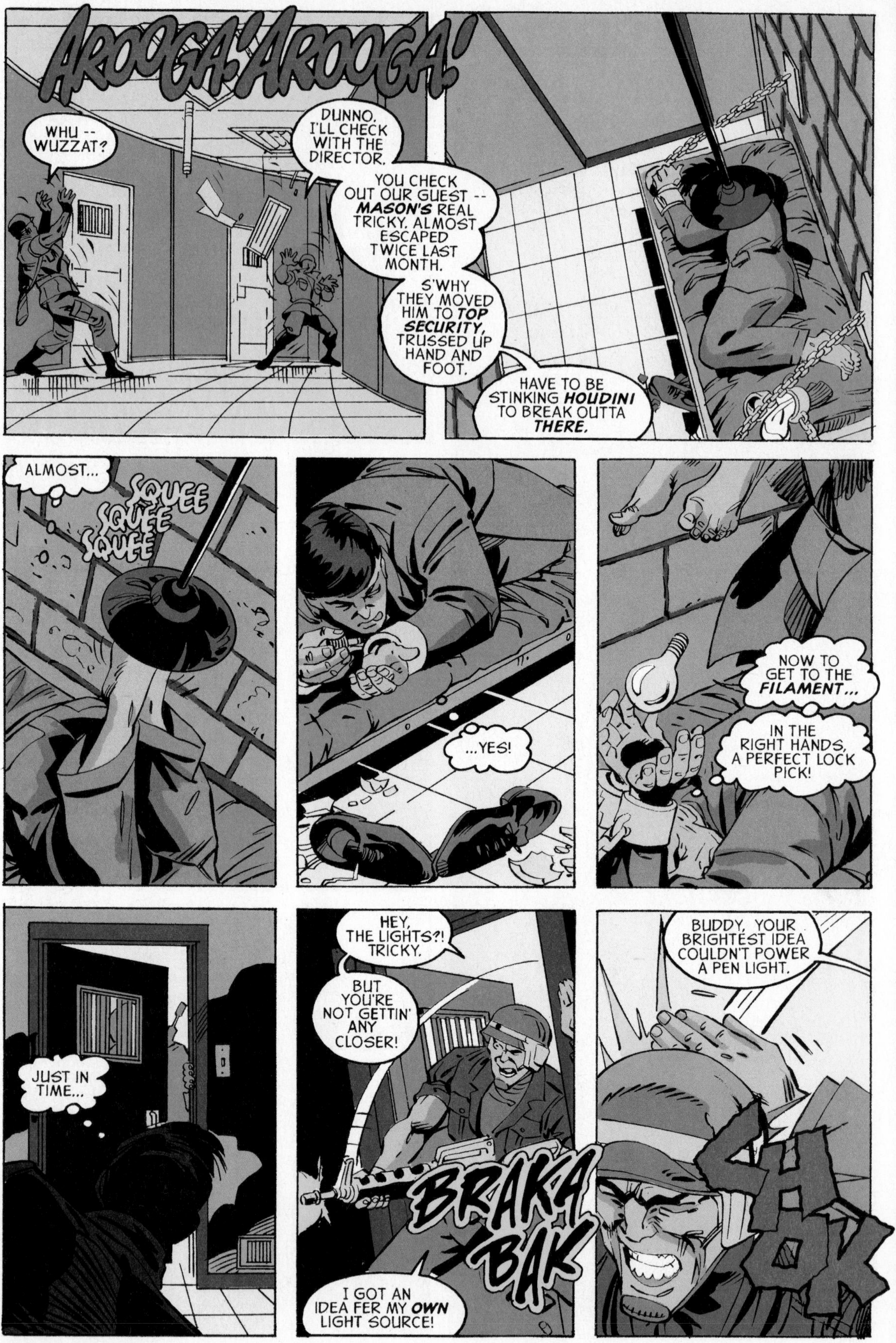
AROOGA'AROOGA!
WHU -- WUZZAT?
DUNNO. I'LL CHECK WITH THE DIRECTOR.
YOU CHECK OUT OUR GUEST -- MASON'S REAL TRICKY. ALMOST ESCAPED TWICE LAST MONTH.
S'WHY THEY MOVED HIM TO TOP SECURITY, TRUSSED UP HAND AND FOOT.
HAVE TO BE STINKING HOUDINI TO BREAK OUTTA THERE.
ALMOST...
SQUEE SQUEE SQUEE
...YES!
NOW TO GET TO THE FILAMENT...
IN THE RIGHT HANDS, A PERFECT LOCK PICK!
JUST IN TIME...
HEY, THE LIGHTS?! TRICKY.
BUT YOU'RE NOT GETTIN' ANY CLOSER!
BRAKA BAK
I GOT AN IDEA FER MY OWN LIGHT SOURCE!
BUDDY, YOUR BRIGHTEST IDEA COULDN'T POWER A PEN LIGHT.
CHOK

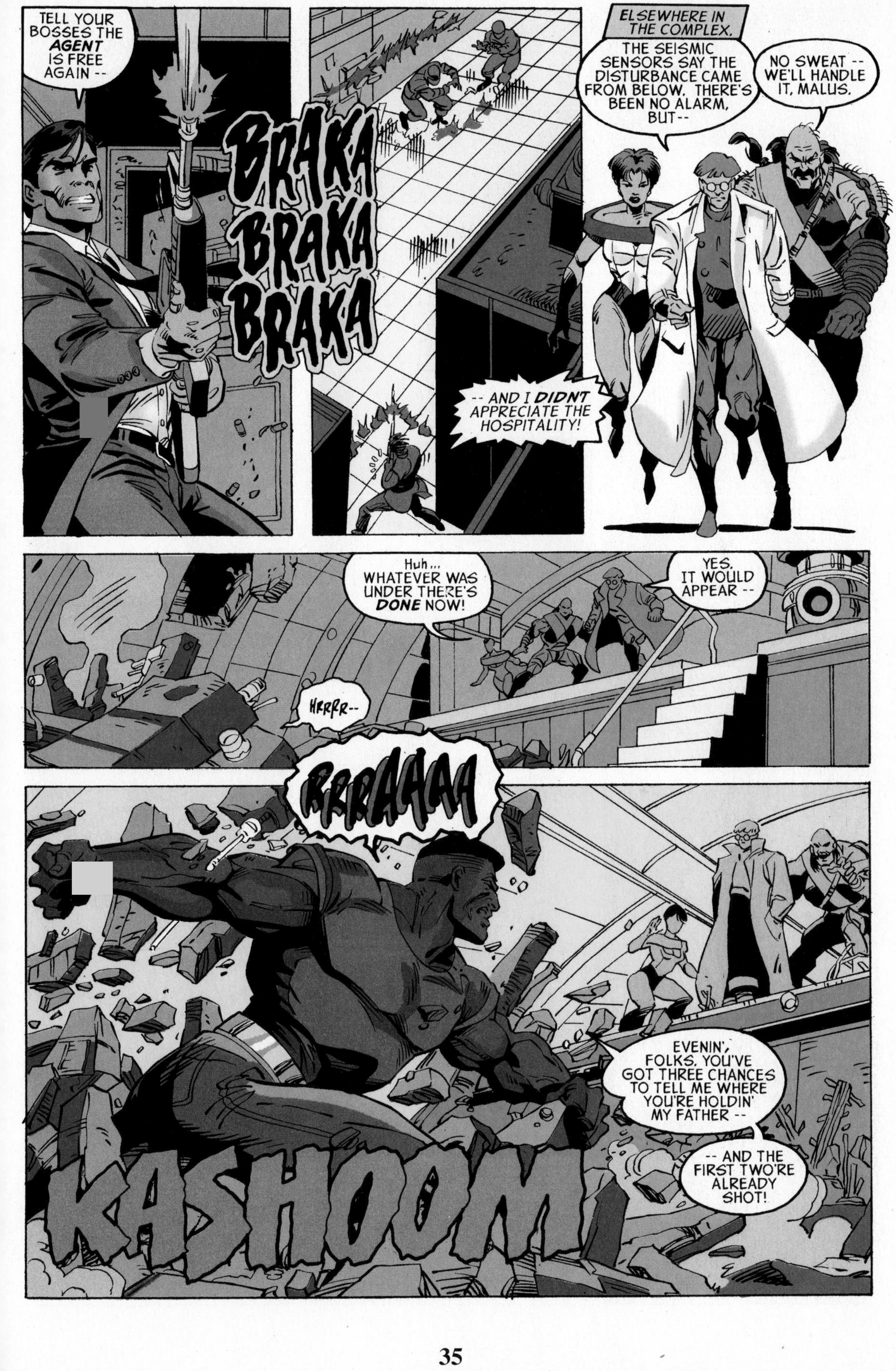

TELL YOUR BOSSES THE **AGENT** IS FREE AGAIN --
BRAKA BRAKA BRAKA
-- AND I **DIDNT** APPRECIATE THE HOSPITALITY!
ELSEWHERE IN THE COMPLEX.
THE SEISMIC SENSORS SAY THE DISTURBANCE CAME FROM BELOW. THERE'S BEEN NO ALARM, BUT--
NO SWEAT -- WE'LL HANDLE IT, MALUS.
Huh... WHATEVER WAS UNDER THERE'S **DONE** NOW!
YES. IT WOULD APPEAR --
HRRRR--
RRRAAAAA
KASHOOM
EVENIN', FOLKS. YOU'VE GOT THREE CHANCES TO TELL ME WHERE YOU'RE HOLDIN' MY FATHER --
-- AND THE FIRST TWO'RE ALREADY SHOT!

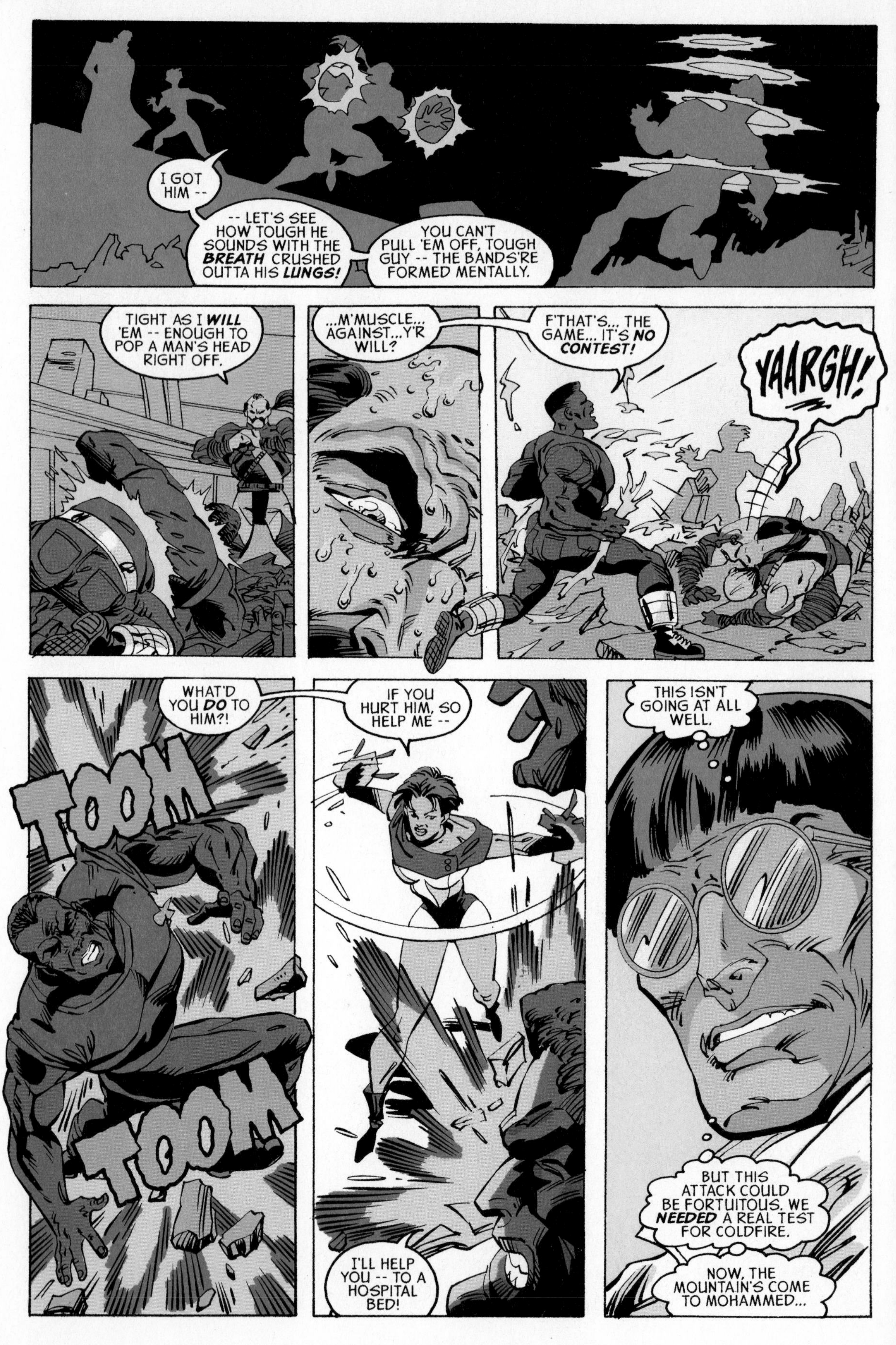
I GOT HIM --
-- LET'S SEE HOW TOUGH HE SOUNDS WITH THE **BREATH** CRUSHED OUTTA HIS **LUNGS!**
YOU CAN'T PULL 'EM OFF, TOUGH GUY -- THE BANDS'RE FORMED MENTALLY.
TIGHT AS I **WILL** 'EM -- ENOUGH TO POP A MAN'S HEAD RIGHT OFF.
...M'MUSCLE... AGAINST...Y'R WILL?
F'THAT'S... THE GAME... IT'S **NO CONTEST!**
YAARGH!
WHAT'D YOU **DO** TO HIM?!
IF YOU HURT HIM, SO HELP ME --
THIS ISN'T GOING AT ALL WELL.
TOOM
TOOM
I'LL HELP YOU -- TO A HOSPITAL BED!
BUT THIS ATTACK COULD BE FORTUITOUS. WE **NEEDED** A REAL TEST FOR COLDFIRE.
NOW, THE MOUNTAIN'S COME TO MOHAMMED...

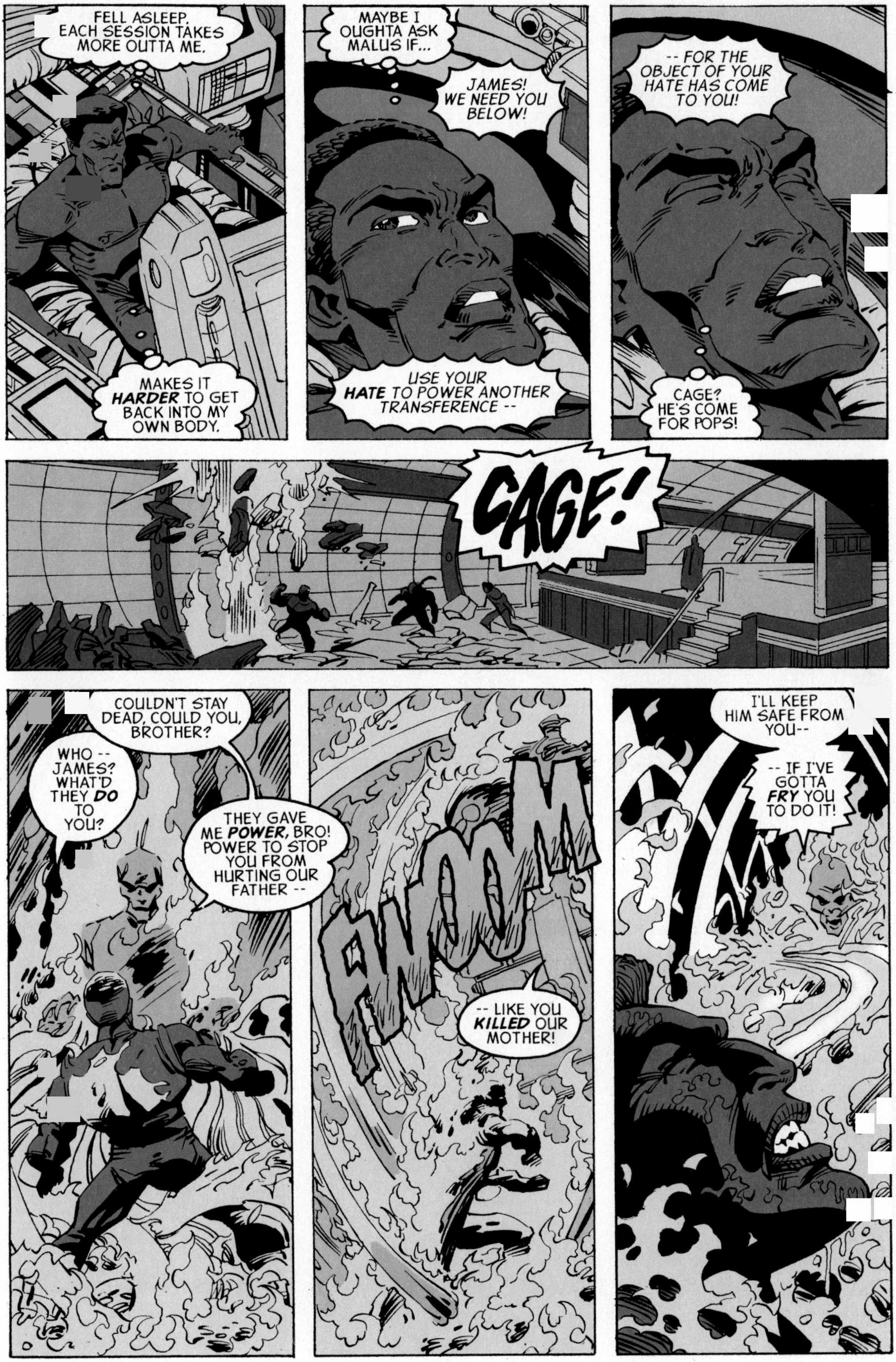
FELL ASLEEP. EACH SESSION TAKES MORE OUTTA ME.
MAKES IT HARDER TO GET BACK INTO MY OWN BODY.
MAYBE I OUGHTA ASK MALUS IF...
JAMES! WE NEED YOU BELOW!
USE YOUR HATE TO POWER ANOTHER TRANSFERENCE --
-- FOR THE OBJECT OF YOUR HATE HAS COME TO YOU!
CAGE? HE'S COME FOR POPS!
CAGE!
COULDN'T STAY DEAD, COULD YOU, BROTHER?
WHO -- JAMES? WHAT'D THEY DO TO YOU?
THEY GAVE ME POWER, BRO! POWER TO STOP YOU FROM HURTING OUR FATHER --
PHOOOM
-- LIKE YOU KILLED OUR MOTHER!
I'LL KEEP HIM SAFE FROM YOU--
-- IF I'VE GOTTA FRY YOU TO DO IT!

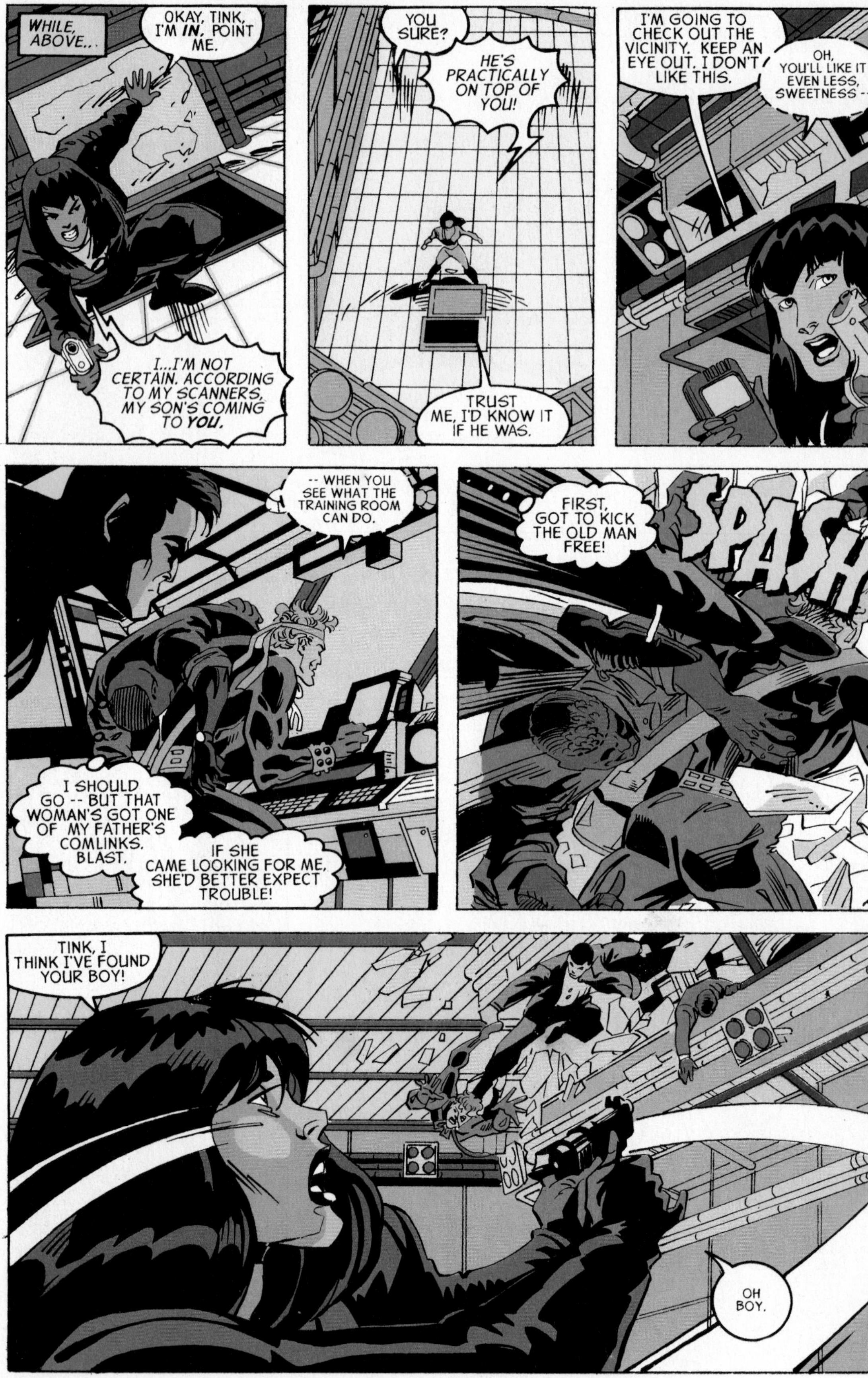
WHILE, ABOVE...
OKAY, TINK, I'M IN, POINT ME.
I...I'M NOT CERTAIN. ACCORDING TO MY SCANNERS, MY SON'S COMING TO YOU.
YOU SURE?
HE'S PRACTICALLY ON TOP OF YOU!
TRUST ME, I'D KNOW IT IF HE WAS.
I'M GOING TO CHECK OUT THE VICINITY. KEEP AN EYE OUT. I DON'T LIKE THIS.
OH, YOU'LL LIKE IT EVEN LESS, SWEETNESS --
-- WHEN YOU SEE WHAT THE TRAINING ROOM CAN DO.
I SHOULD GO -- BUT THAT WOMAN'S GOT ONE OF MY FATHER'S COMLINKS. BLAST.
IF SHE CAME LOOKING FOR ME, SHE'D BETTER EXPECT TROUBLE!
FIRST, GOT TO KICK THE OLD MAN FREE!
SPASH
TINK, I THINK I'VE FOUND YOUR BOY!
OH BOY.

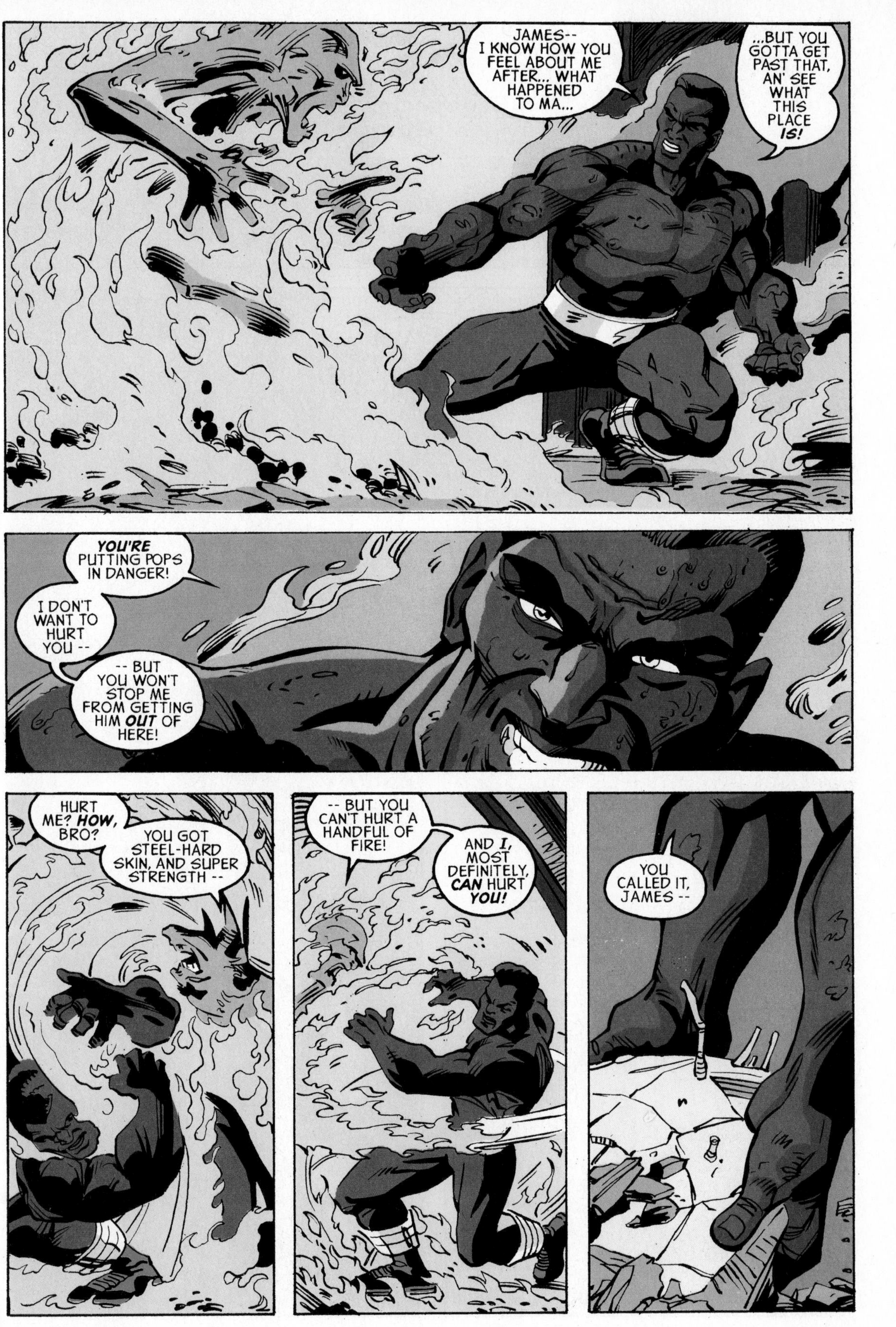
JAMES-- I KNOW HOW YOU FEEL ABOUT ME AFTER... WHAT HAPPENED TO MA...
...BUT YOU GOTTA GET PAST THAT, AN' SEE WHAT THIS PLACE IS!
YOU'RE PUTTING POPS IN DANGER!
I DON'T WANT TO HURT YOU --
-- BUT YOU WON'T STOP ME FROM GETTING HIM OUT OF HERE!
HURT ME? HOW, BRO?
YOU GOT STEEL-HARD SKIN, AND SUPER STRENGTH --
-- BUT YOU CAN'T HURT A HANDFUL OF FIRE!
AND I, MOST DEFINITELY, CAN HURT YOU!
YOU CALLED IT, JAMES --

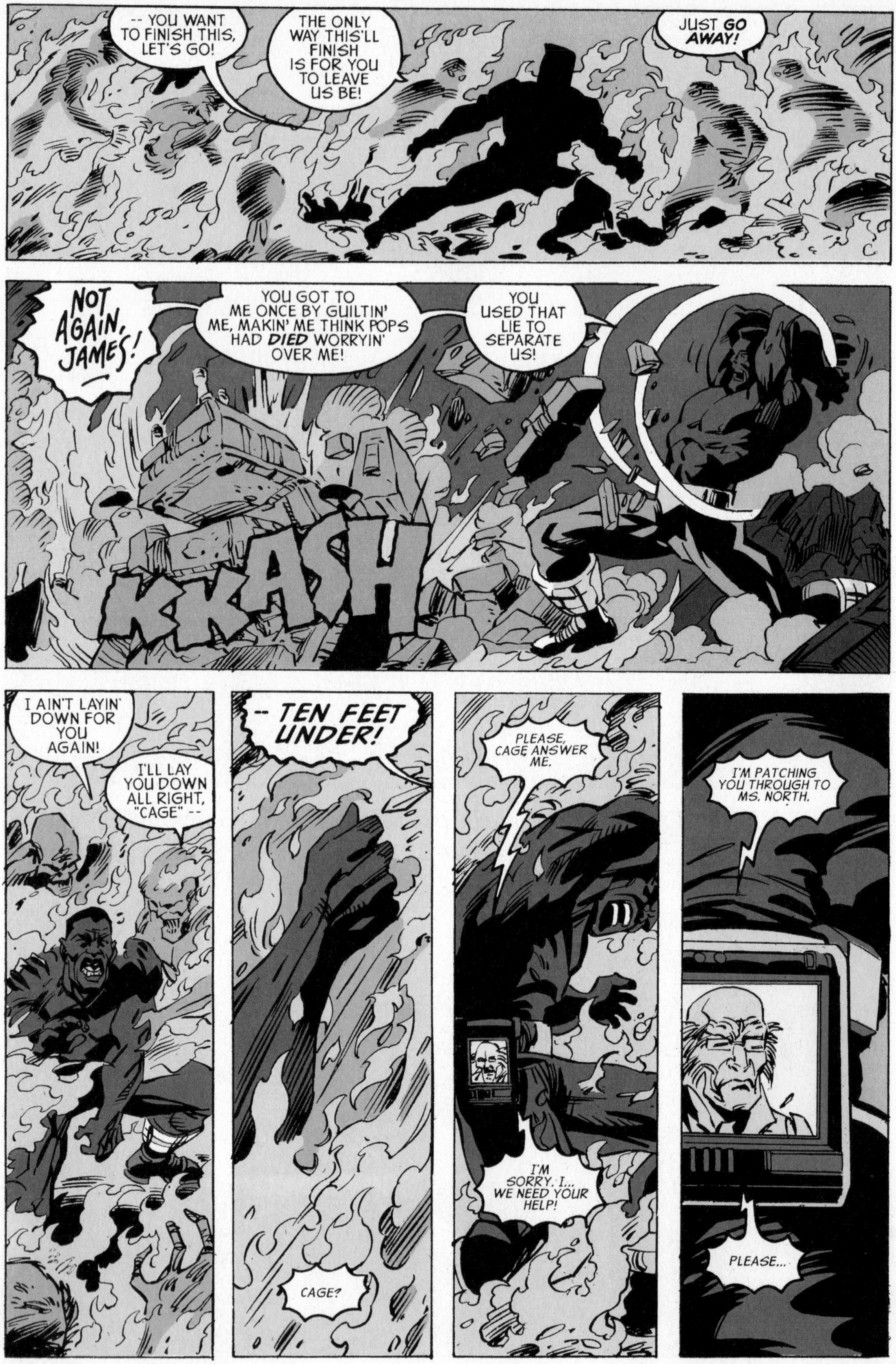
-- YOU WANT TO FINISH THIS, LET'S GO!
THE ONLY WAY THIS'LL FINISH IS FOR YOU TO LEAVE US BE!
JUST GO AWAY!
NOT AGAIN, JAMES!
YOU GOT TO ME ONCE BY GUILTIN' ME, MAKIN' ME THINK POPS HAD DIED WORRYIN' OVER ME!
YOU USED THAT LIE TO SEPARATE US!
KKASH
I AIN'T LAYIN' DOWN FOR YOU AGAIN!
I'LL LAY YOU DOWN ALL RIGHT, "CAGE" --
-- TEN FEET UNDER!
CAGE?
PLEASE, CAGE ANSWER ME.
I'M SORRY. I... WE NEED YOUR HELP!
I'M PATCHING YOU THROUGH TO MS. NORTH.
PLEASE...

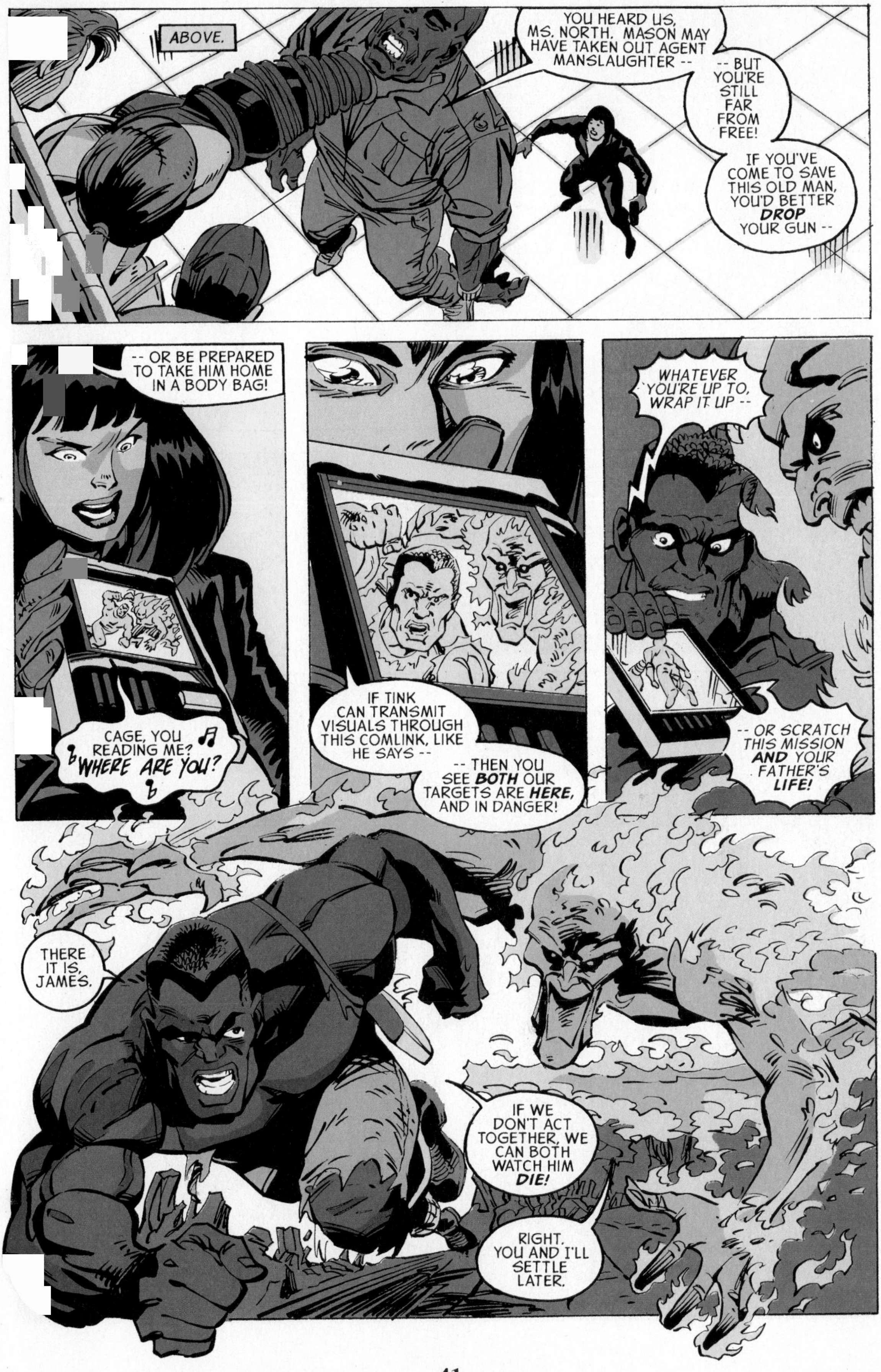
ABOVE.
YOU HEARD US, MS. NORTH. MASON MAY HAVE TAKEN OUT AGENT MANSLAUGHTER --
-- BUT YOU'RE STILL FAR FROM FREE!
IF YOU'VE COME TO SAVE THIS OLD MAN, YOU'D BETTER DROP YOUR GUN --
-- OR BE PREPARED TO TAKE HIM HOME IN A BODY BAG!
CAGE, YOU READING ME? WHERE ARE YOU?
IF TINK CAN TRANSMIT VISUALS THROUGH THIS COMLINK, LIKE HE SAYS --
-- THEN YOU SEE BOTH OUR TARGETS ARE HERE, AND IN DANGER!
WHATEVER YOU'RE UP TO, WRAP IT UP --
-- OR SCRATCH THIS MISSION AND YOUR FATHER'S LIFE!
THERE IT IS, JAMES.
IF WE DON'T ACT TOGETHER, WE CAN BOTH WATCH HIM DIE!
RIGHT. YOU AND I'LL SETTLE LATER.

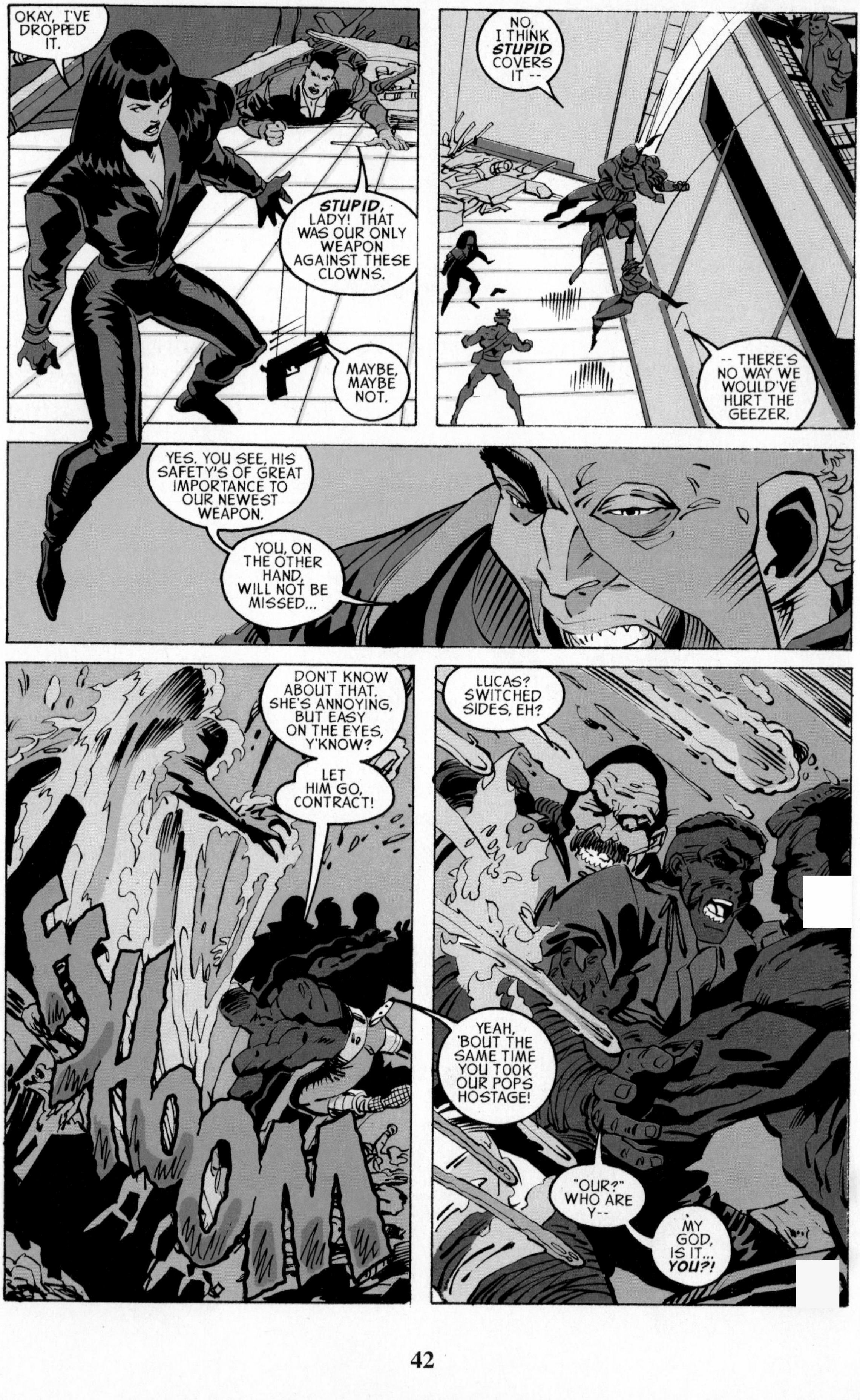
OKAY, I'VE DROPPED IT.
STUPID, LADY! THAT WAS OUR ONLY WEAPON AGAINST THESE CLOWNS.
MAYBE, MAYBE NOT.
NO, I THINK STUPID COVERS IT --
-- THERE'S NO WAY WE WOULD'VE HURT THE GEEZER.
YES, YOU SEE, HIS SAFETY'S OF GREAT IMPORTANCE TO OUR NEWEST WEAPON.
YOU, ON THE OTHER HAND, WILL NOT BE MISSED...
DON'T KNOW ABOUT THAT. SHE'S ANNOYING, BUT EASY ON THE EYES, Y'KNOW?
LET HIM GO, CONTRACT!
LUCAS? SWITCHED SIDES, EH?
YEAH, 'BOUT THE SAME TIME YOU TOOK OUR POPS HOSTAGE!
"OUR?" WHO ARE Y--
MY GOD, IS IT... YOU?!

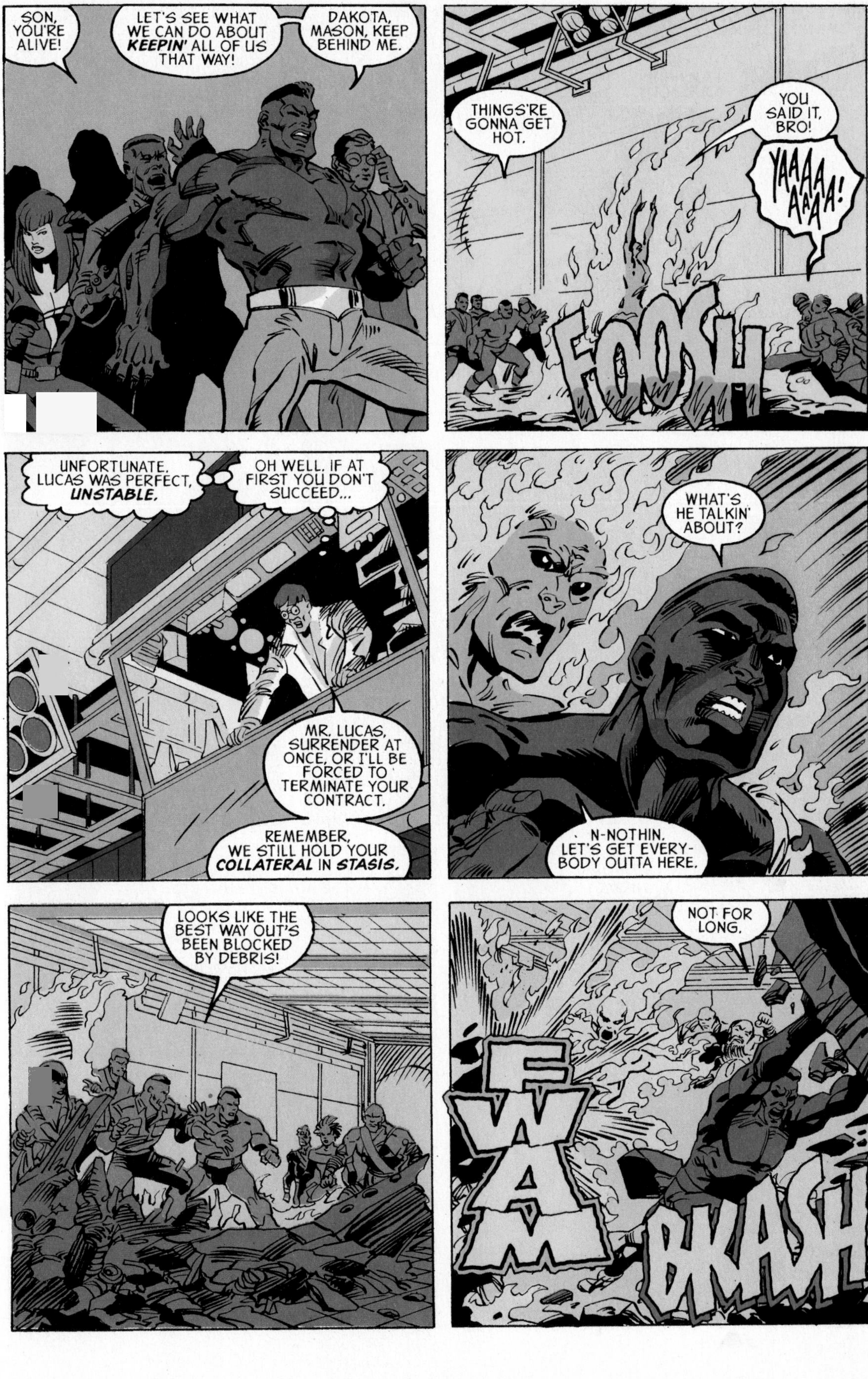
SON, YOU'RE ALIVE!
LET'S SEE WHAT WE CAN DO ABOUT KEEPIN' ALL OF US THAT WAY!
DAKOTA, MASON, KEEP BEHIND ME.
THINGS'RE GONNA GET HOT.
YOU SAID IT, BRO!
YAAAAAAAA!
FOOSH
UNFORTUNATE. LUCAS WAS PERFECT. UNSTABLE.
OH WELL. IF AT FIRST YOU DON'T SUCCEED...
MR. LUCAS, SURRENDER AT ONCE, OR I'LL BE FORCED TO TERMINATE YOUR CONTRACT.
REMEMBER, WE STILL HOLD YOUR COLLATERAL IN STASIS.
WHAT'S HE TALKIN' ABOUT?
N-NOTHIN. LET'S GET EVERY-BODY OUTTA HERE.
LOOKS LIKE THE BEST WAY OUT'S BEEN BLOCKED BY DEBRIS!
NOT FOR LONG.
FWAM
BKASH

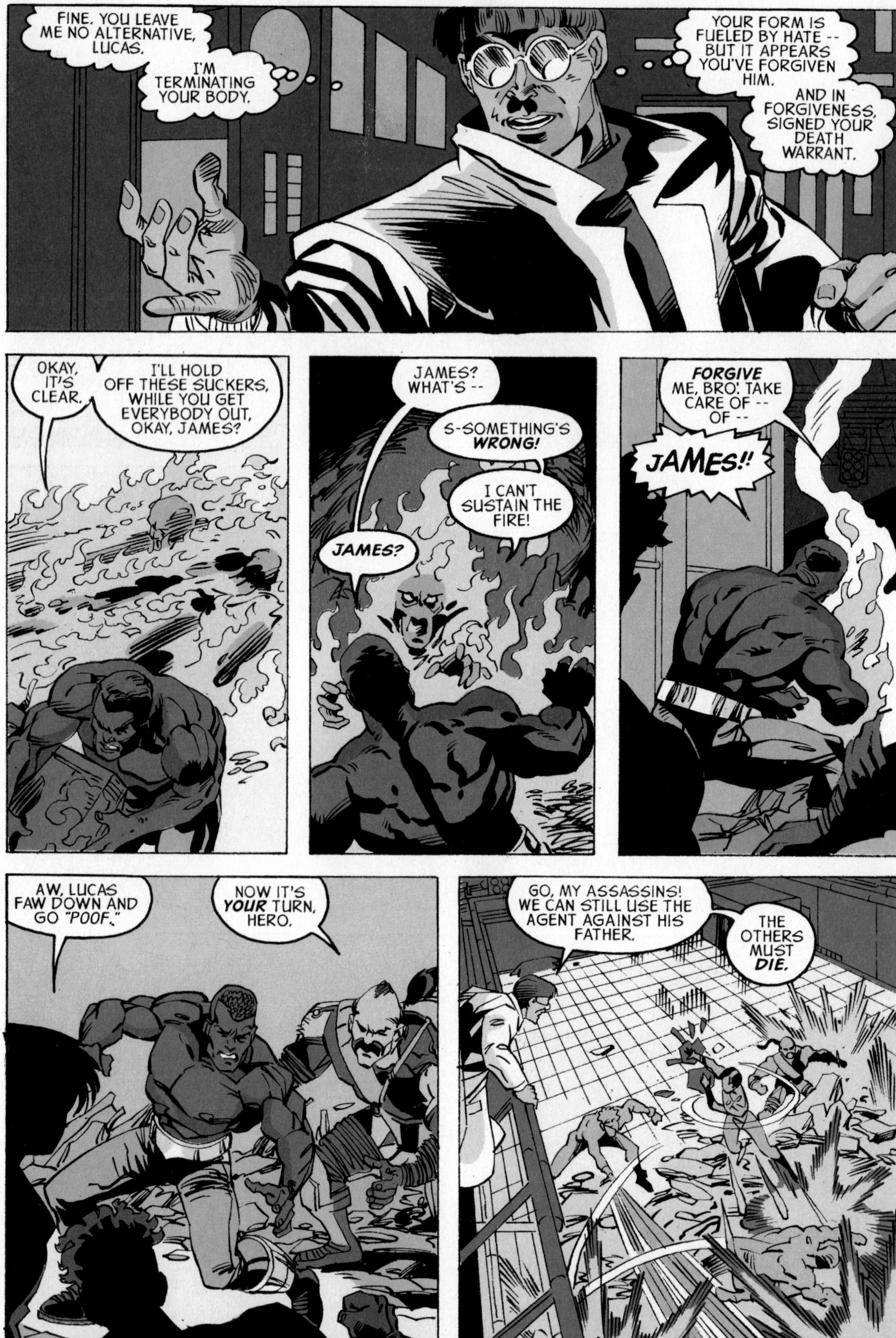
FINE. YOU LEAVE ME NO ALTERNATIVE, LUCAS.
I'M TERMINATING YOUR BODY.
YOUR FORM IS FUELED BY HATE -- BUT IT APPEARS YOU'VE FORGIVEN HIM.
AND IN FORGIVENESS, SIGNED YOUR DEATH WARRANT.
OKAY, IT'S CLEAR.
I'LL HOLD OFF THESE SUCKERS, WHILE YOU GET EVERYBODY OUT, OKAY, JAMES?
JAMES? WHAT'S --
S-SOMETHING'S *WRONG!*
I CAN'T SUSTAIN THE FIRE!
JAMES?
FORGIVE ME, BRO! TAKE CARE OF -- OF --
JAMES!!
AW, LUCAS FAW DOWN AND GO "POOF."
NOW IT'S *YOUR* TURN, HERO.
GO, MY ASSASSINS! WE CAN STILL USE THE AGENT AGAINST HIS FATHER.
THE OTHERS MUST *DIE.*

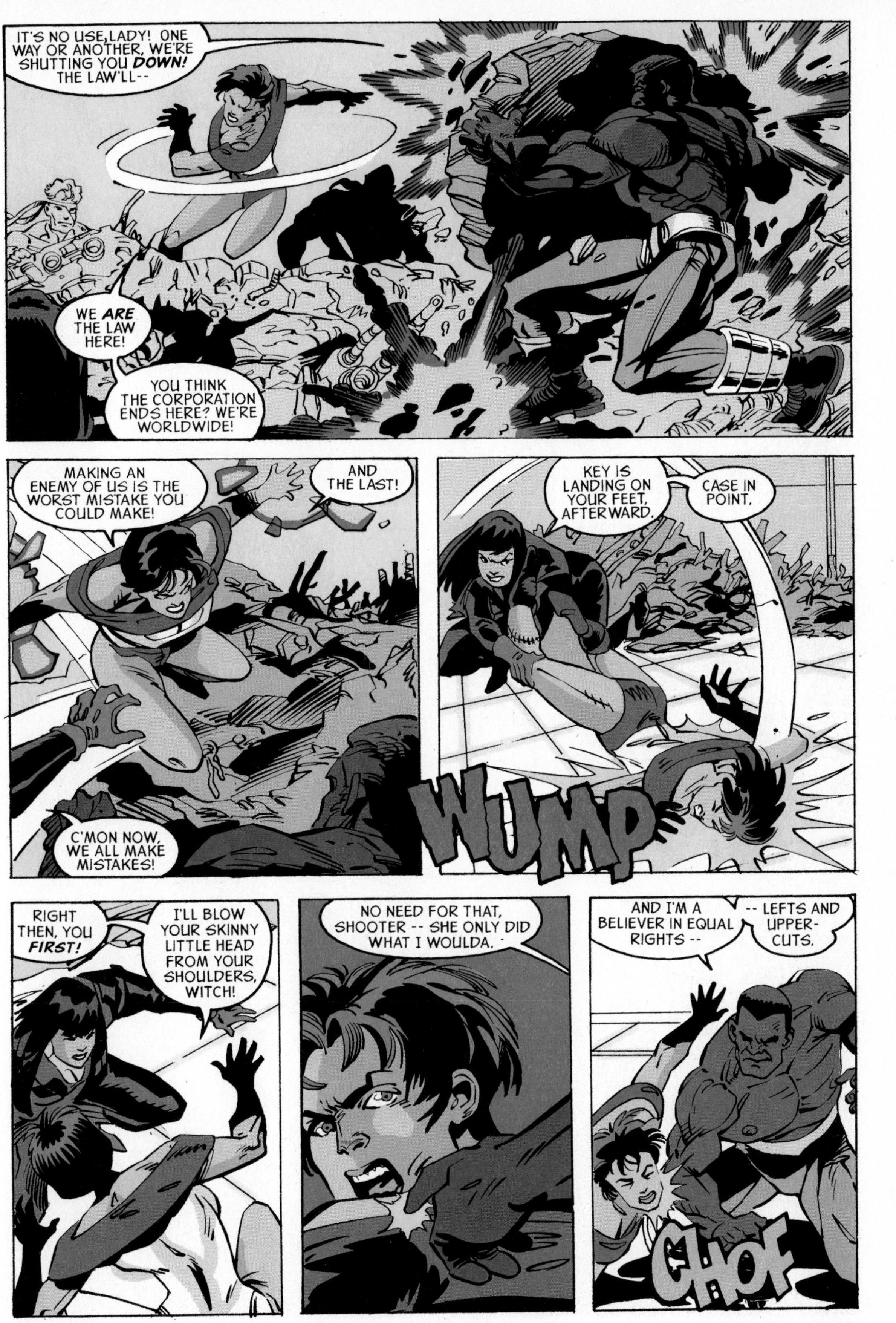
IT'S NO USE, LADY! ONE WAY OR ANOTHER, WE'RE SHUTTING YOU DOWN! THE LAW'LL--
WE ARE THE LAW HERE!
YOU THINK THE CORPORATION ENDS HERE? WE'RE WORLDWIDE!
MAKING AN ENEMY OF US IS THE WORST MISTAKE YOU COULD MAKE!
AND THE LAST!
C'MON NOW, WE ALL MAKE MISTAKES!
KEY IS LANDING ON YOUR FEET, AFTERWARD.
CASE IN POINT.
WUMP
RIGHT THEN, YOU FIRST!
I'LL BLOW YOUR SKINNY LITTLE HEAD FROM YOUR SHOULDERS, WITCH!
NO NEED FOR THAT, SHOOTER -- SHE ONLY DID WHAT I WOULDA.
AND I'M A BELIEVER IN EQUAL RIGHTS --
-- LEFTS AND UPPER-CUTS.
CHOF

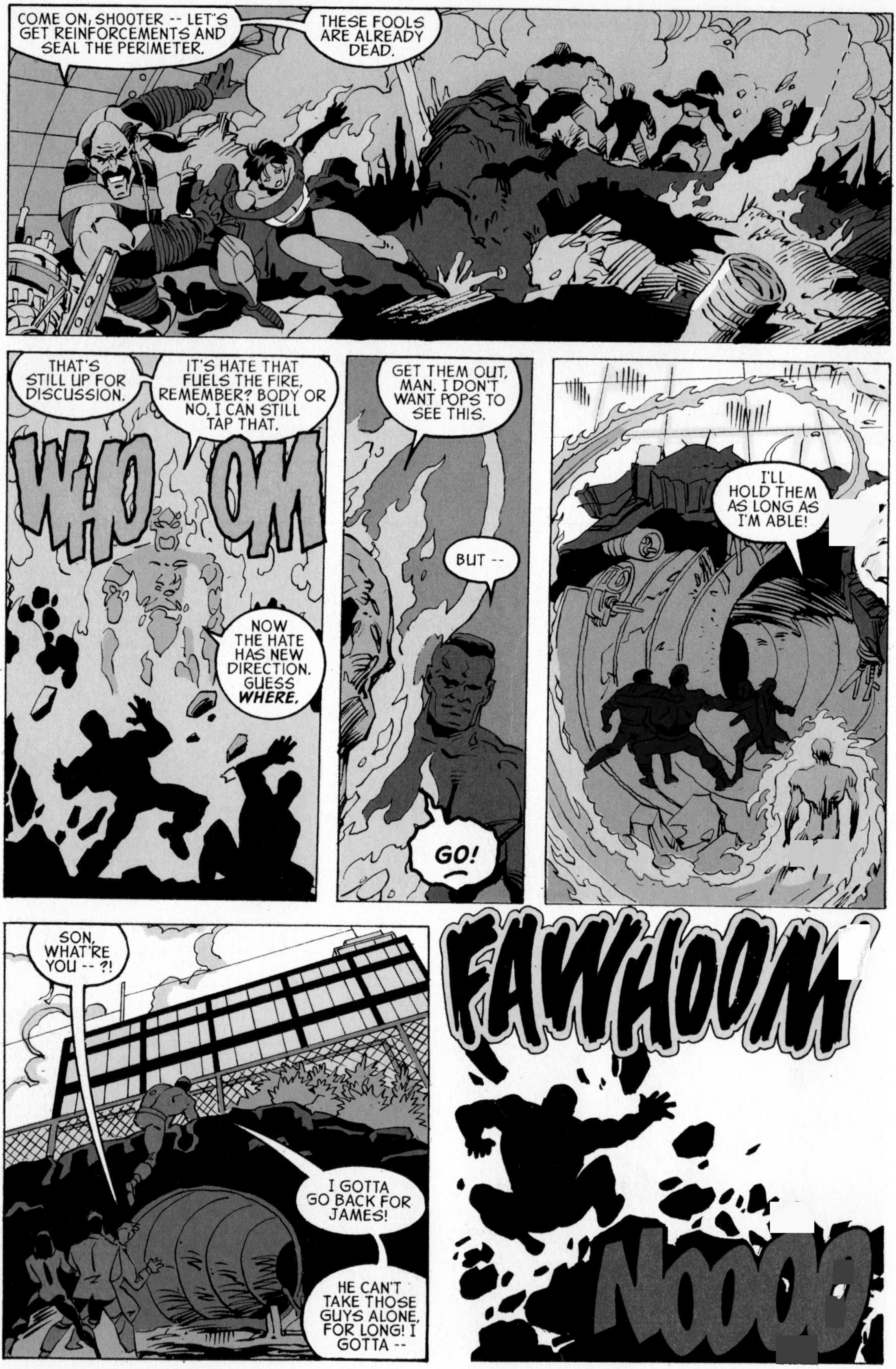
COME ON, SHOOTER -- LET'S GET REINFORCEMENTS AND SEAL THE PERIMETER.
THESE FOOLS ARE ALREADY DEAD.
THAT'S STILL UP FOR DISCUSSION.
IT'S HATE THAT FUELS THE FIRE, REMEMBER? BODY OR NO, I CAN STILL TAP THAT.
WHOOM
NOW THE HATE HAS NEW DIRECTION. GUESS WHERE.
GET THEM OUT, MAN. I DON'T WANT POPS TO SEE THIS.
BUT --
GO!
I'LL HOLD THEM AS LONG AS I'M ABLE!
SON, WHAT'RE YOU -- ?!
I GOTTA GO BACK FOR JAMES!
HE CAN'T TAKE THOSE GUYS ALONE, FOR LONG! I GOTTA --
FAWHOOM
NOOOO

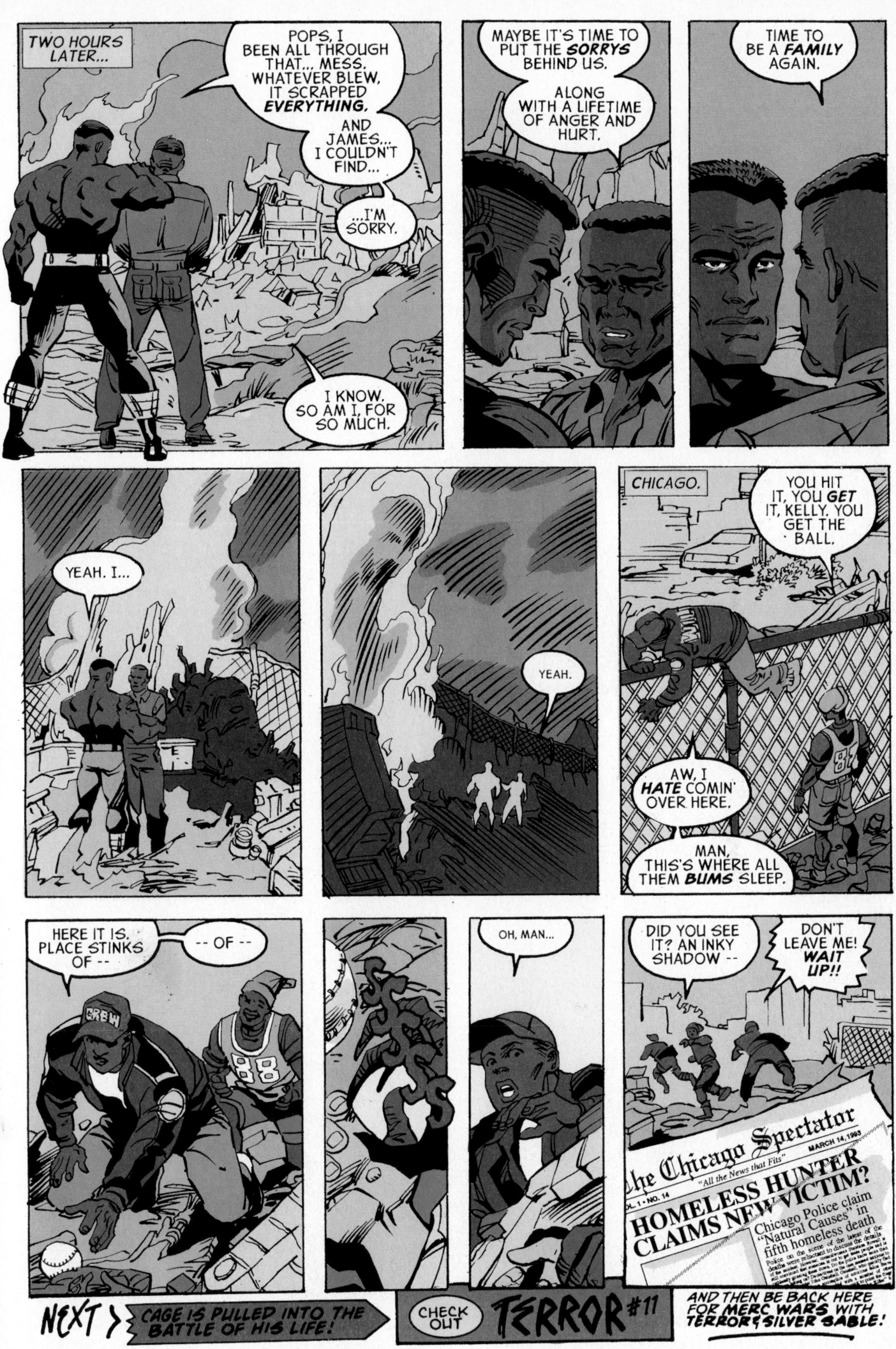
TWO HOURS LATER...
POPS, I BEEN ALL THROUGH THAT... MESS. WHATEVER BLEW, IT SCRAPPED EVERYTHING.
AND JAMES... I COULDN'T FIND...
...I'M SORRY.
I KNOW. SO AM I, FOR SO MUCH.
MAYBE IT'S TIME TO PUT THE SORRYS BEHIND US.
ALONG WITH A LIFETIME OF ANGER AND HURT.
TIME TO BE A FAMILY AGAIN.
YEAH. I...
YEAH.
CHICAGO.
YOU HIT IT, YOU GET IT, KELLY. YOU GET THE BALL.
AW, I HATE COMIN' OVER HERE.
MAN, THIS'S WHERE ALL THEM BUMS SLEEP.
HERE IT IS. PLACE STINKS OF --
-- OF --
OH, MAN...
DID YOU SEE IT? AN INKY SHADOW --
DON'T LEAVE ME! WAIT UP!!
Chicago Spectator
MARCH 14, 1993
"All the News that Fits"
HOMELESS HUNTER CLAIMS NEW VICTIM?
Chicago Police claim "Natural Causes" in fifth homeless death
NEXT > CAGE IS PULLED INTO THE BATTLE OF HIS LIFE!
CHECK OUT TERROR #11
AND THEN BE BACK HERE FOR MERC WARS WITH TERROR & SILVER SABLE!

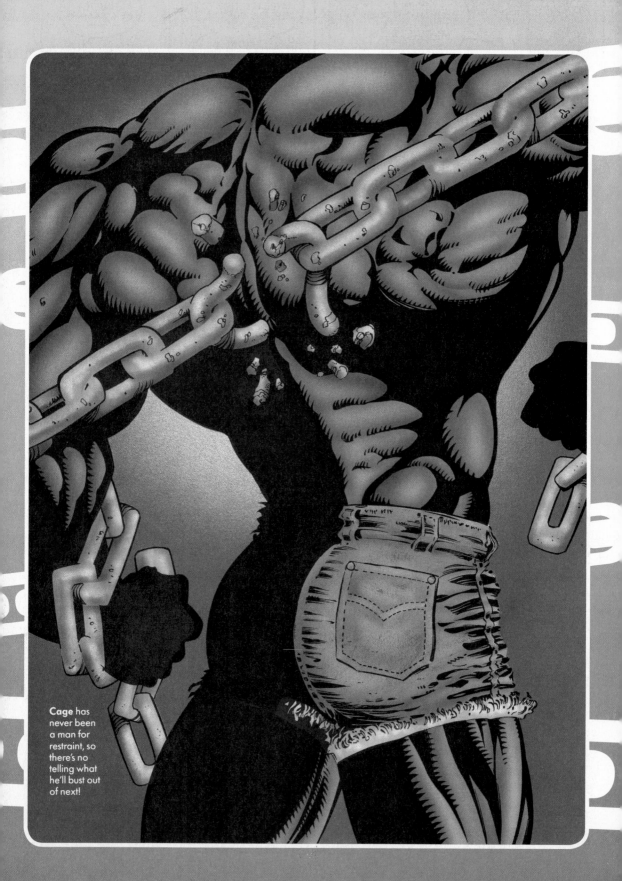

Cage has never been a man for restraint, so there's no telling what he'll bust out of next!

MARVEL SWIMSUIT SPECIAL #4 PINUP BY JAMES FRY, HARRY CANDELARIO & TOM SMITH

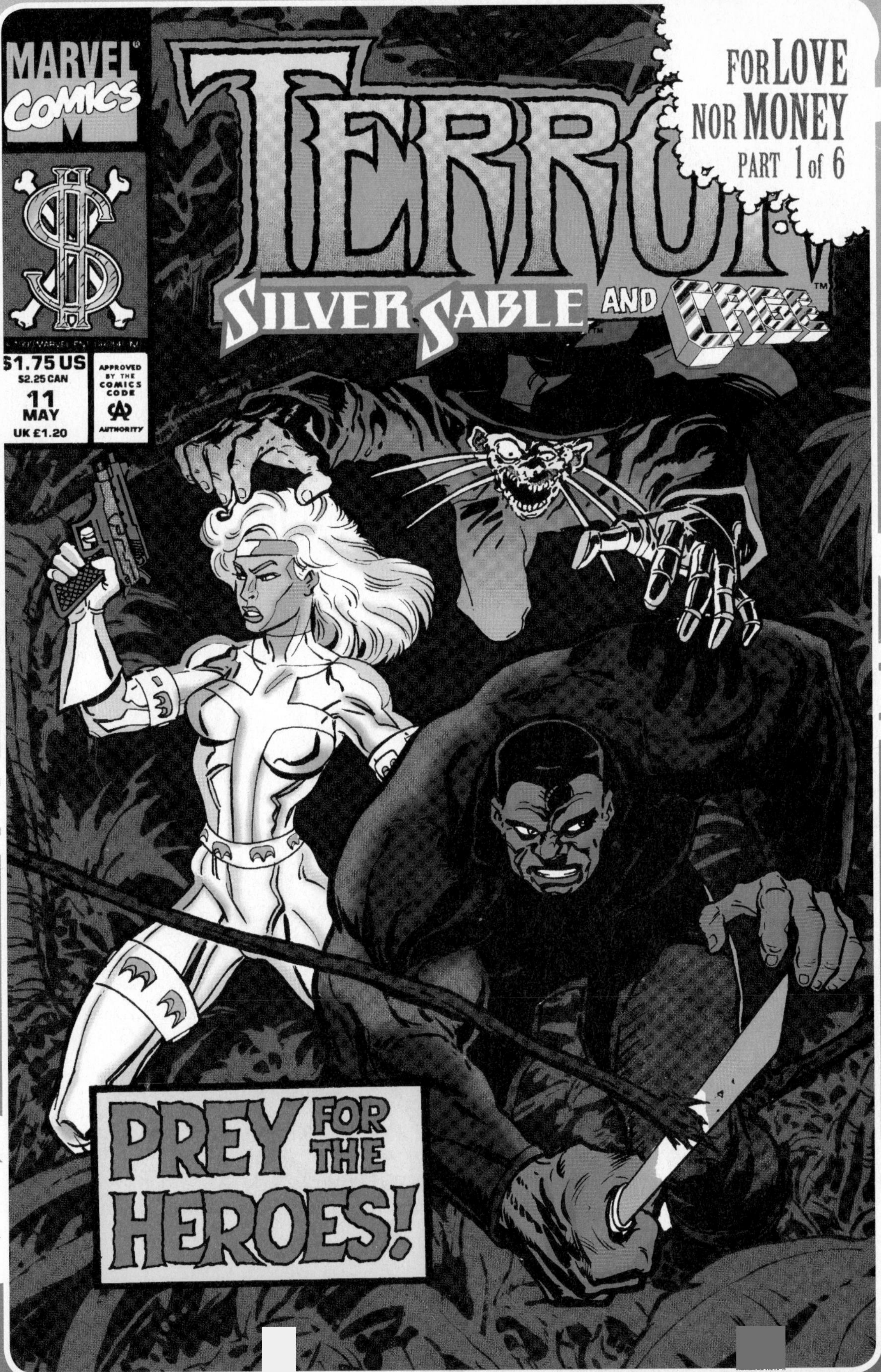
MARVEL COMICS
TERRO
SILVER SABLE AND CAGE
FOR LOVE NOR MONEY
PART 1 of 6
$1.75 US
$2.25 CAN
11
MAY
UK £1.20
APPROVED BY THE COMICS CODE AUTHORITY
PREY FOR THE HEROES!

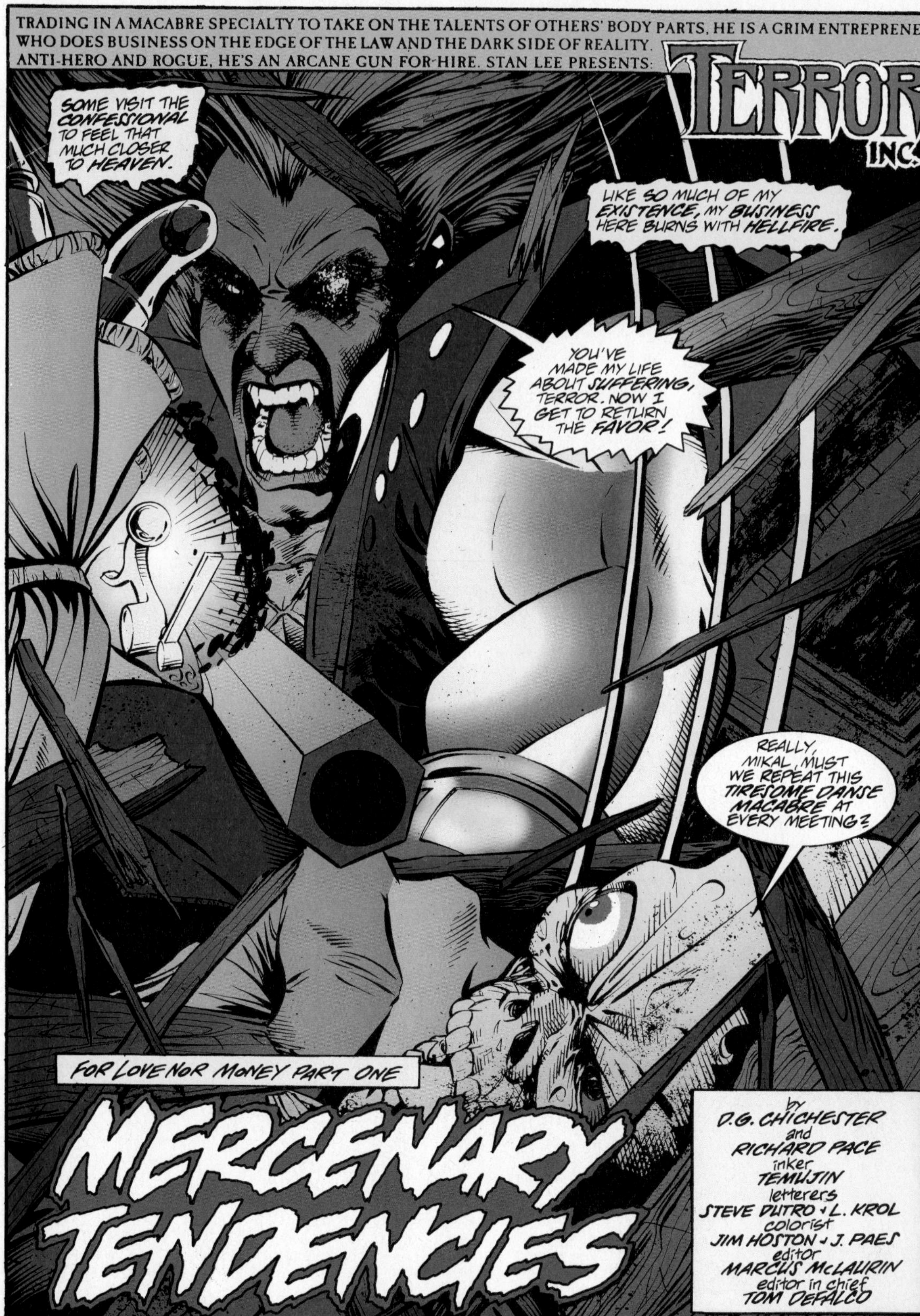
TRADING IN A MACABRE SPECIALTY TO TAKE ON THE TALENTS OF OTHERS' BODY PARTS, HE IS A GRIM ENTREPRENEUR WHO DOES BUSINESS ON THE EDGE OF THE LAW AND THE DARK SIDE OF REALITY. ANTI-HERO AND ROGUE, HE'S AN ARCANE GUN FOR-HIRE. STAN LEE PRESENTS:
TERROR INC.
SOME VISIT THE CONFESSIONAL TO FEEL THAT MUCH CLOSER TO HEAVEN.
LIKE SO MUCH OF MY EXISTENCE, MY BUSINESS HERE BURNS WITH HELLFIRE.
YOU'VE MADE MY LIFE ABOUT SUFFERING, TERROR. NOW I GET TO RETURN THE FAVOR!
REALLY, MIKAL, MUST WE REPEAT THIS TIRESOME DANSE MACABRE AT EVERY MEETING?
FOR LOVE NOR MONEY PART ONE
MERCENARY TENDENCIES
by D.G. CHICHESTER and RICHARD PACE inker TEMUJIN letterers STEVE DUTRO & L. KROL colorist JIM HOSTON & J. PAES editor MARCUS McLAURIN editor in chief TOM DEFALCO

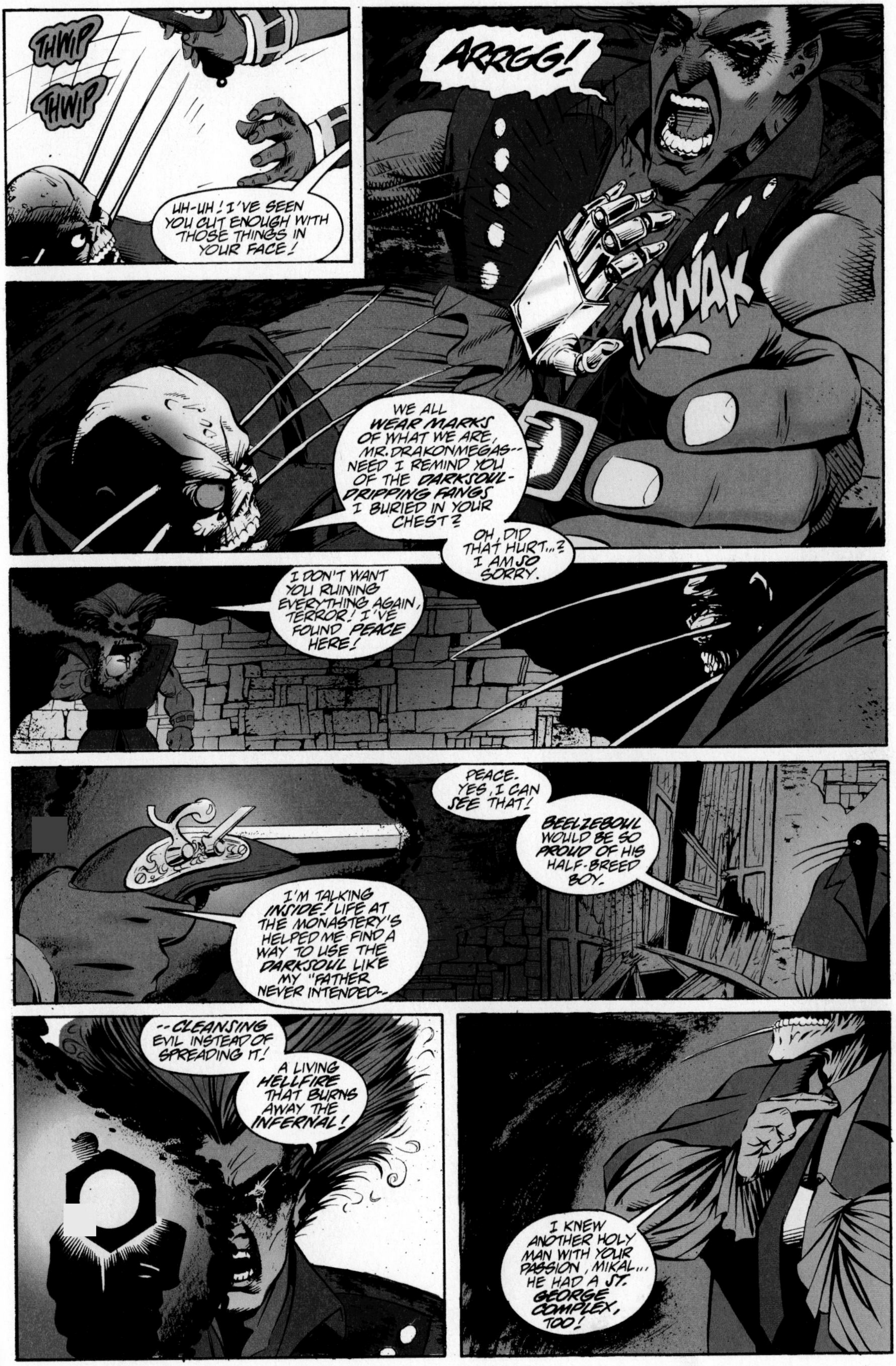
THWIP
THWIP
UH-UH! I'VE SEEN YOU CUT ENOUGH WITH THOSE THINGS IN YOUR FACE!
ARRGG!
THWAK
WE ALL WEAR MARKS OF WHAT WE ARE, MR. DRAKONMEGAS-- NEED I REMIND YOU OF THE DARKSOUL-DRIPPING FANGS I BURIED IN YOUR CHEST?
OH, DID THAT HURT...? I AM SO SORRY.
I DON'T WANT YOU RUINING EVERYTHING AGAIN, TERROR! I'VE FOUND PEACE HERE!
PEACE. YES, I CAN SEE THAT!
BEELZEBOUL WOULD BE SO PROUD OF HIS HALF-BREED BOY.
I'M TALKING INSIDE! LIFE AT THE MONASTERY'S HELPED ME FIND A WAY TO USE THE DARKSOUL LIKE MY "FATHER NEVER INTENDED--
--CLEANSING EVIL INSTEAD OF SPREADING IT!
A LIVING HELLFIRE THAT BURNS AWAY THE INFERNAL!
I KNEW ANOTHER HOLY MAN WITH YOUR PASSION, MIKAL... HE HAD A ST. GEORGE COMPLEX, TOO!

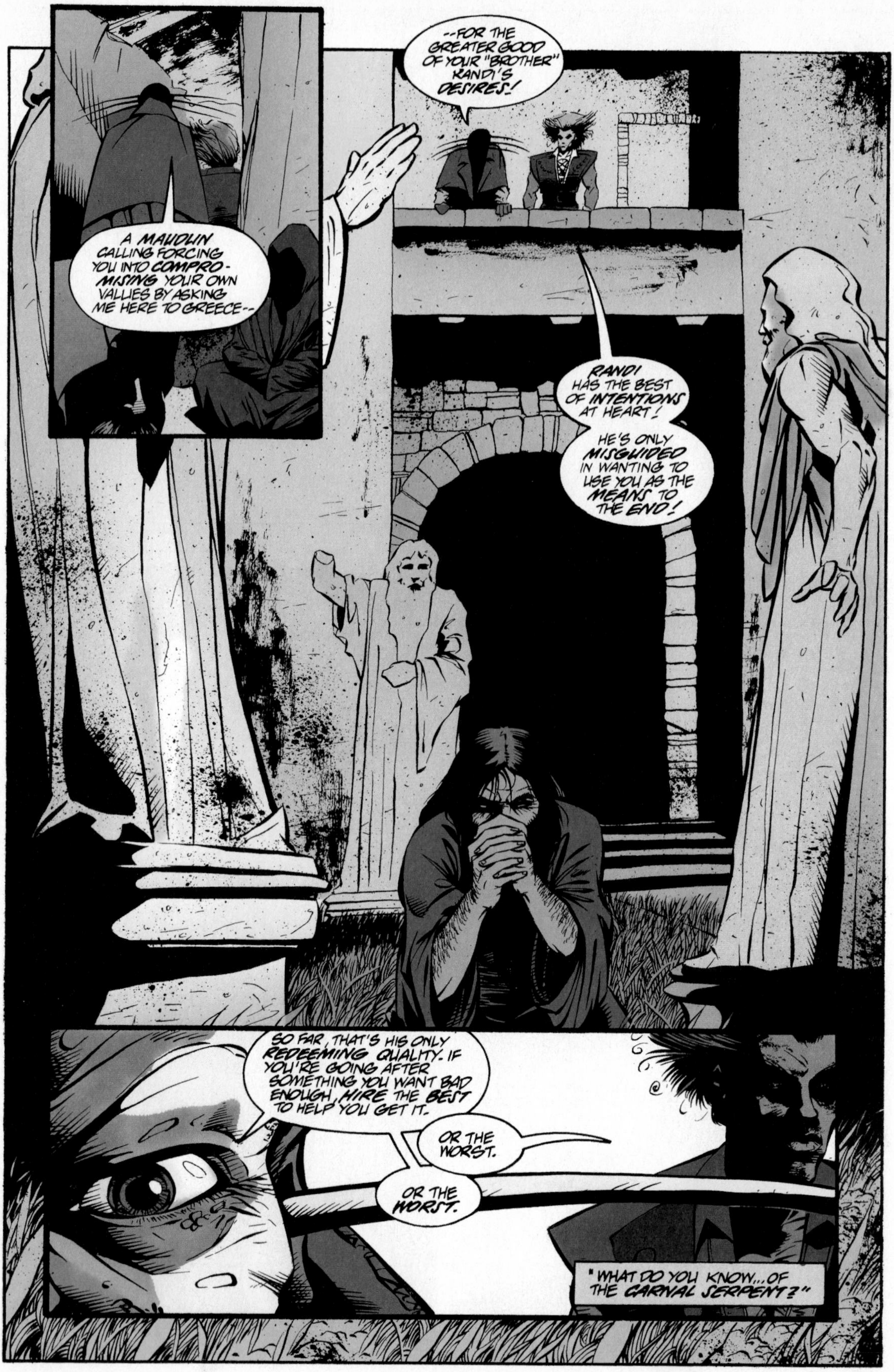
A MAUDLIN CALLING FORCING YOU INTO COMPRO-MISING YOUR OWN VALUES BY ASKING ME HERE TO GREECE--
--FOR THE GREATER GOOD OF YOUR "BROTHER" RANDI'S DESIRES!
RANDI HAS THE BEST OF INTENTIONS AT HEART!
HE'S ONLY MISGUIDED IN WANTING TO USE YOU AS THE MEANS TO THE END!
SO FAR, THAT'S HIS ONLY REDEEMING QUALITY. IF YOU'RE GOING AFTER SOMETHING YOU WANT BAD ENOUGH, HIRE THE BEST TO HELP YOU GET IT.
OR THE WORST.
OR THE WORST.
"WHAT DO YOU KNOW...OF THE CARNAL SERPENT?"

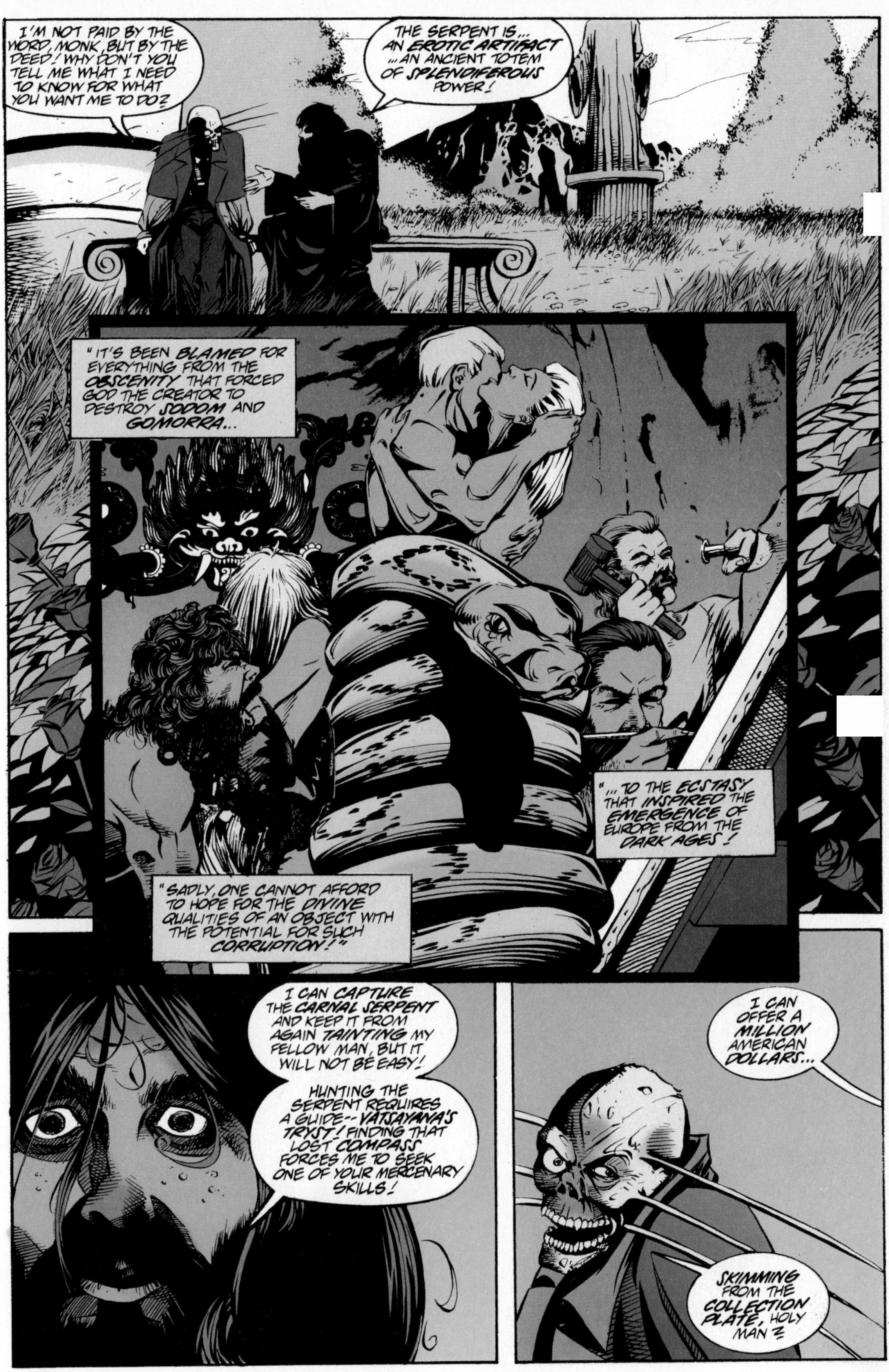
I'M NOT PAID BY THE WORD, MONK, BUT BY THE DEED! WHY DON'T YOU TELL ME WHAT I NEED TO KNOW FOR WHAT YOU WANT ME TO DO?
THE SERPENT IS... AN EROTIC ARTIFACT ...AN ANCIENT TOTEM OF SPLENDIFEROUS POWER!
"IT'S BEEN BLAMED FOR EVERYTHING FROM THE OBSCENITY THAT FORCED GOD THE CREATOR TO DESTROY SODOM AND GOMORRA...
"...TO THE ECSTASY THAT INSPIRED THE EMERGENCE OF EUROPE FROM THE DARK AGES!
"SADLY, ONE CANNOT AFFORD TO HOPE FOR THE DIVINE QUALITIES OF AN OBJECT WITH THE POTENTIAL FOR SUCH CORRUPTION!"
I CAN CAPTURE THE CARNAL SERPENT AND KEEP IT FROM AGAIN TAINTING MY FELLOW MAN, BUT IT WILL NOT BE EASY!
HUNTING THE SERPENT REQUIRES A GUIDE--VATSAYANA'S TRYST! FINDING THAT LOST COMPASS FORCES ME TO SEEK ONE OF YOUR MERCENARY SKILLS!
I CAN OFFER A MILLION AMERICAN DOLLARS...
SKIMMING FROM THE COLLECTION PLATE, HOLY MAN?

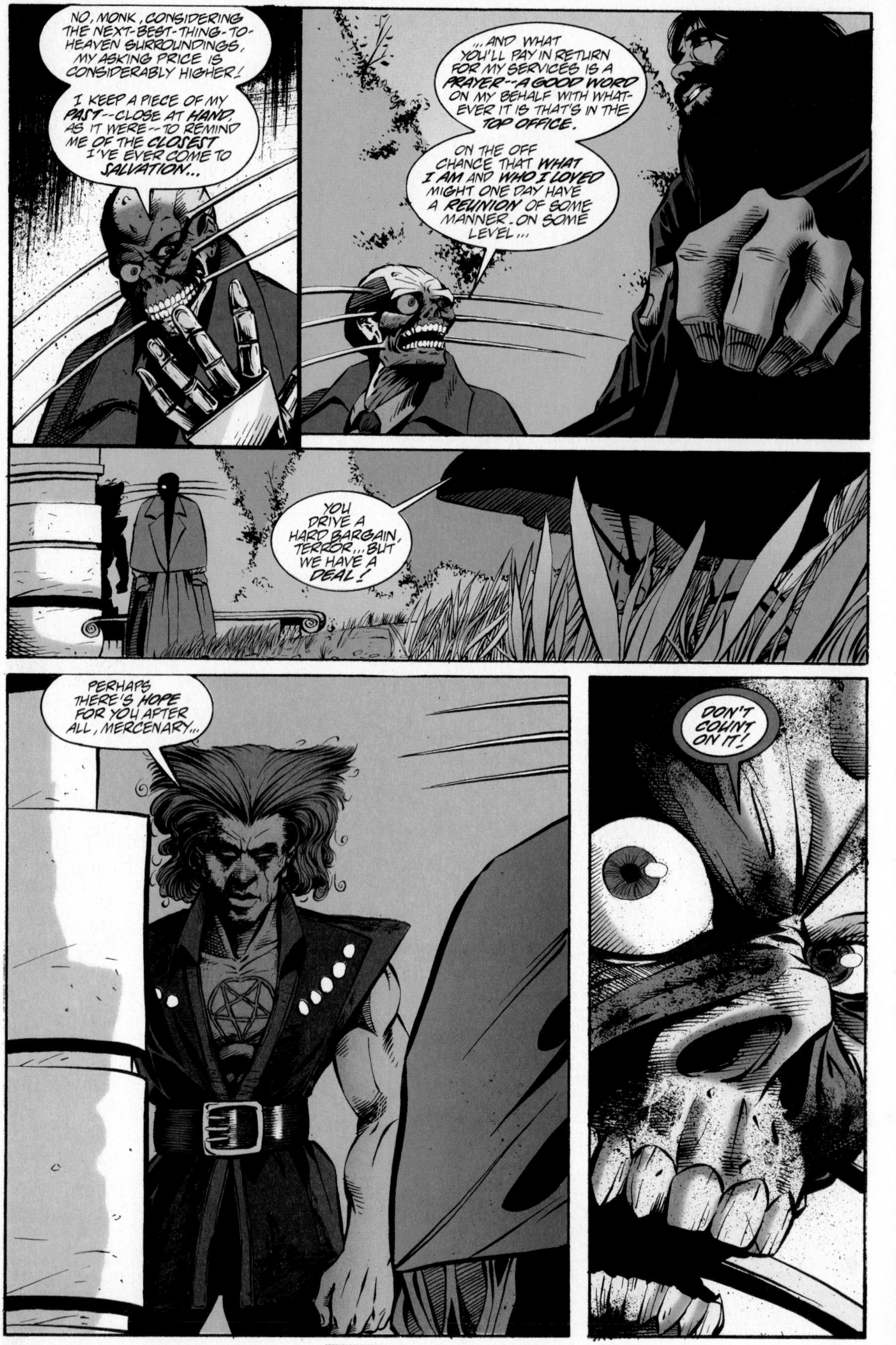
NO, MONK, CONSIDERING THE NEXT-BEST-THING-TO-HEAVEN SURROUNDINGS, MY ASKING PRICE IS CONSIDERABLY HIGHER!
I KEEP A PIECE OF MY PAST--CLOSE AT HAND, AS IT WERE--TO REMIND ME OF THE CLOSEST I'VE EVER COME TO SALVATION...
...AND WHAT YOU'LL PAY IN RETURN FOR MY SERVICES IS A PRAYER--A GOOD WORD ON MY BEHALF WITH WHATEVER IT IS THAT'S IN THE TOP OFFICE.
ON THE OFF CHANCE THAT WHAT I AM AND WHO I LOVED MIGHT ONE DAY HAVE A REUNION OF SOME MANNER. ON SOME LEVEL...
YOU DRIVE A HARD BARGAIN, TERROR... BUT WE HAVE A DEAL!
PERHAPS THERE'S HOPE FOR YOU AFTER ALL, MERCENARY...
DON'T COUNT ON IT!

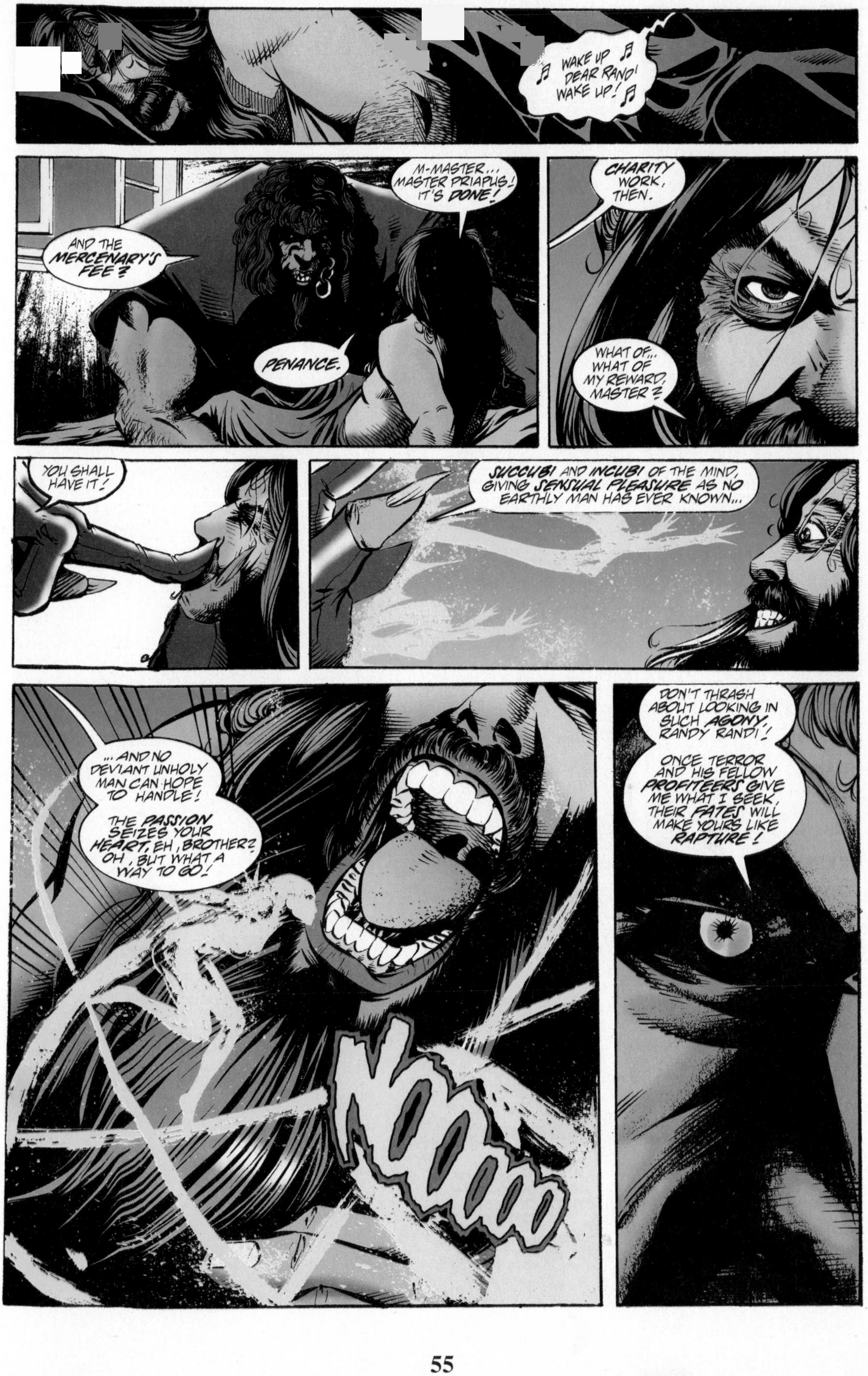
WAKE UP DEAR RAND! WAKE UP!
M-MASTER... MASTER PRIAPUS! IT'S DONE!
AND THE MERCENARY'S FEE?
PENANCE.
CHARITY WORK, THEN.
WHAT OF... WHAT OF MY REWARD, MASTER?
YOU SHALL HAVE IT!
SUCCUBI AND INCUBI OF THE MIND, GIVING SENSUAL PLEASURE AS NO EARTHLY MAN HAS EVER KNOWN...
...AND NO DEVIANT UNHOLY MAN CAN HOPE TO HANDLE!
THE PASSION SEIZES YOUR HEART, EH, BROTHER? OH, BUT WHAT A WAY TO GO!
NOOOOO
DON'T THRASH ABOUT LOOKING IN SUCH AGONY, RANDY RANDI!
ONCE TERROR AND HIS FELLOW PROFITEERS GIVE ME WHAT I SEEK, THEIR FATES WILL MAKE YOURS LIKE RAPTURE!

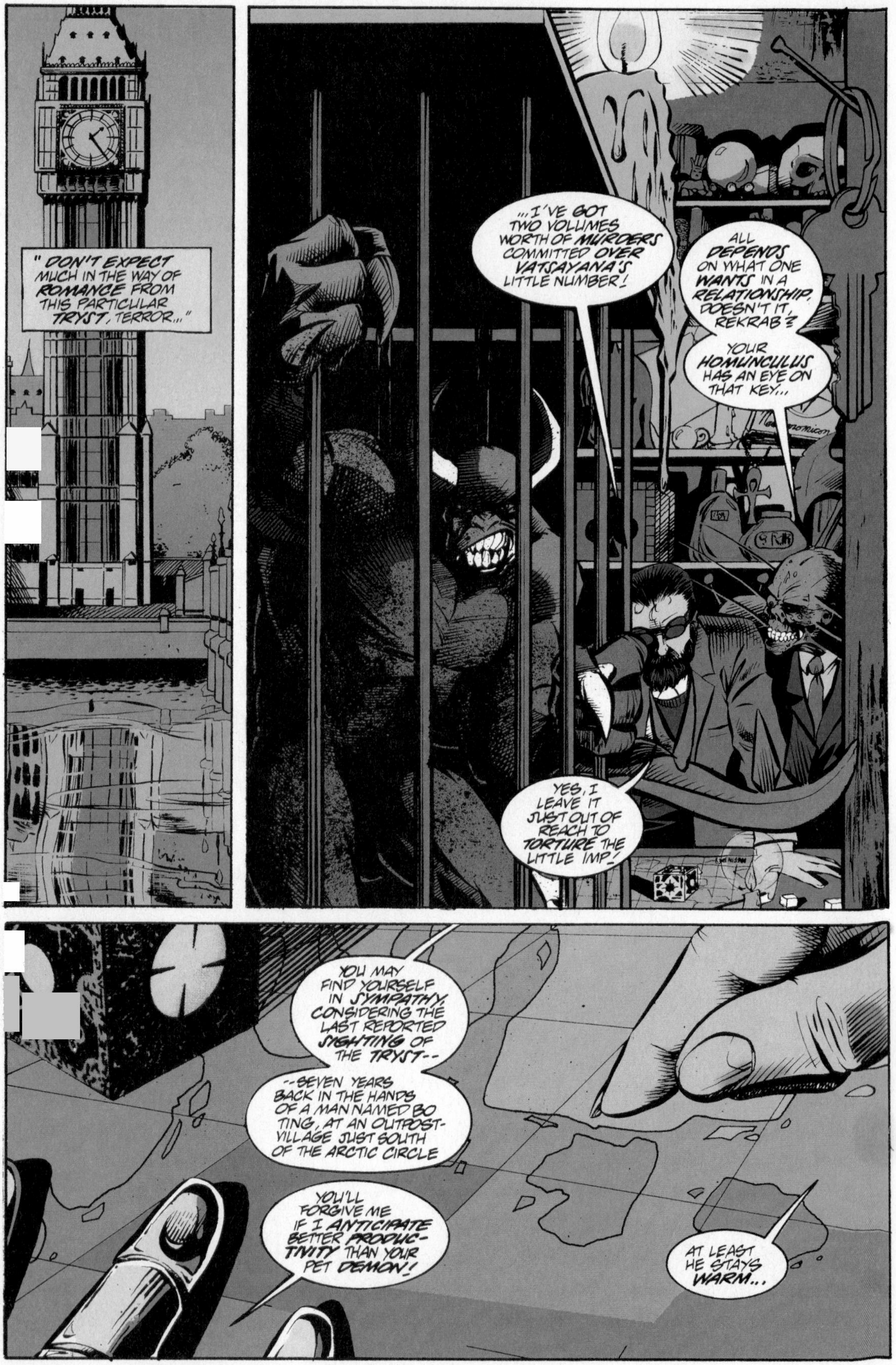
"DON'T EXPECT MUCH IN THE WAY OF ROMANCE FROM THIS PARTICULAR TRYST, TERROR..."
...I'VE GOT TWO VOLUMES WORTH OF MURDERS COMMITTED OVER VATSAYANA'S LITTLE NUMBER!
ALL DEPENDS ON WHAT ONE WANTS IN A RELATIONSHIP, DOESN'T IT, REKRAB?
YOUR HOMUNCULUS HAS AN EYE ON THAT KEY...
YES, I LEAVE IT JUST OUT OF REACH TO TORTURE THE LITTLE IMP!
YOU MAY FIND YOURSELF IN SYMPATHY, CONSIDERING THE LAST REPORTED SIGHTING OF THE TRYST--
--SEVEN YEARS BACK IN THE HANDS OF A MAN NAMED BO TING, AT AN OUTPOST-VILLAGE JUST SOUTH OF THE ARCTIC CIRCLE
YOU'LL FORGIVE ME IF I ANTICIPATE BETTER PRODUCTIVITY THAN YOUR PET DEMON!
AT LEAST HE STAYS WARM...

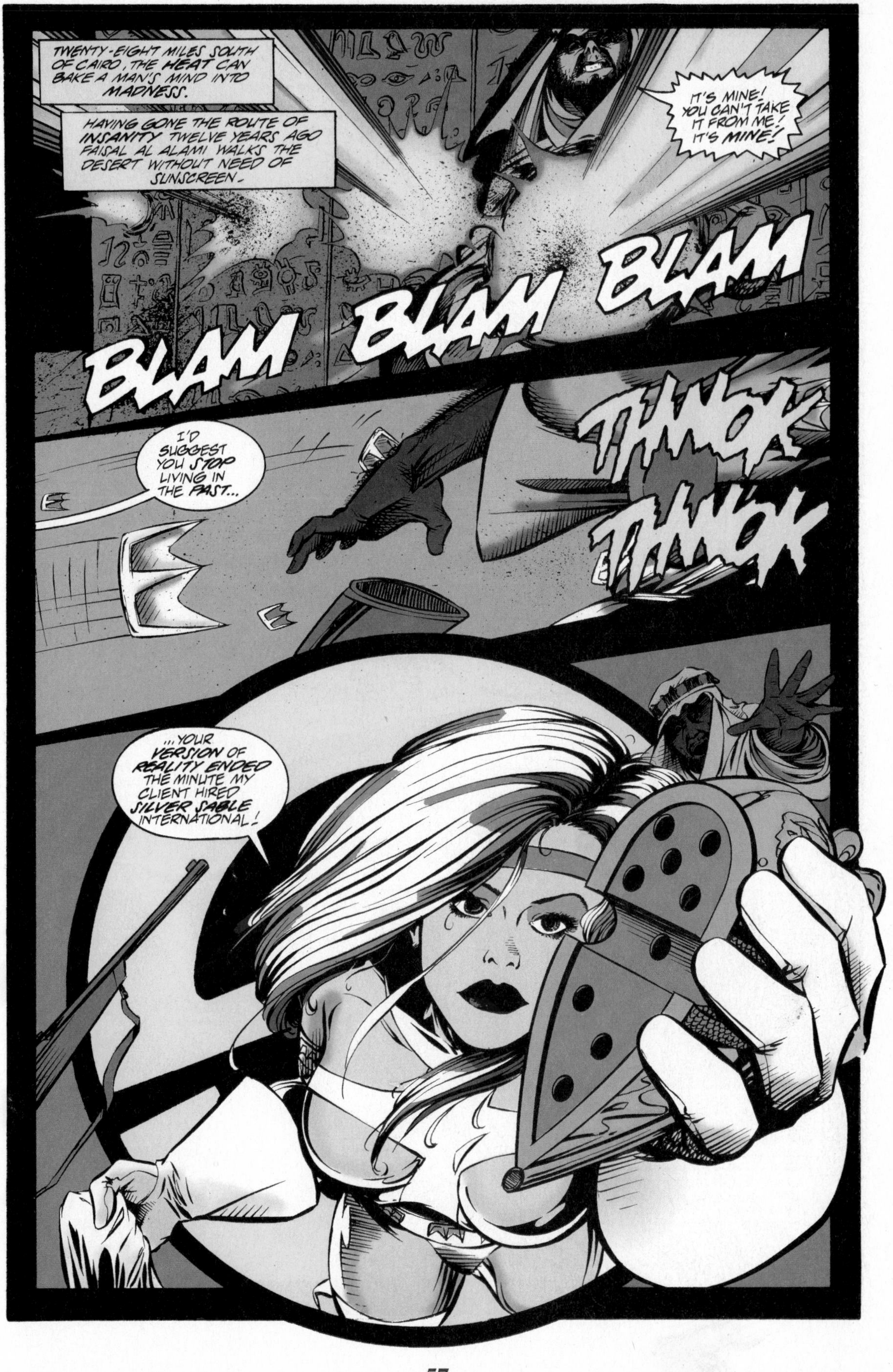
TWENTY-EIGHT MILES SOUTH OF CAIRO, THE HEAT CAN BAKE A MAN'S MIND INTO MADNESS.
HAVING GONE THE ROUTE OF INSANITY TWELVE YEARS AGO FAISAL AL ALAMI WALKS THE DESERT WITHOUT NEED OF SUNSCREEN.
IT'S MINE! YOU CAN'T TAKE IT FROM ME! IT'S MINE!
BLAM BLAM BLAM BLAM
I'D SUGGEST YOU STOP LIVING IN THE PAST...
THWOK THWOK
...YOUR VERSION OF REALITY ENDED THE MINUTE MY CLIENT HIRED SILVER SABLE INTERNATIONAL!

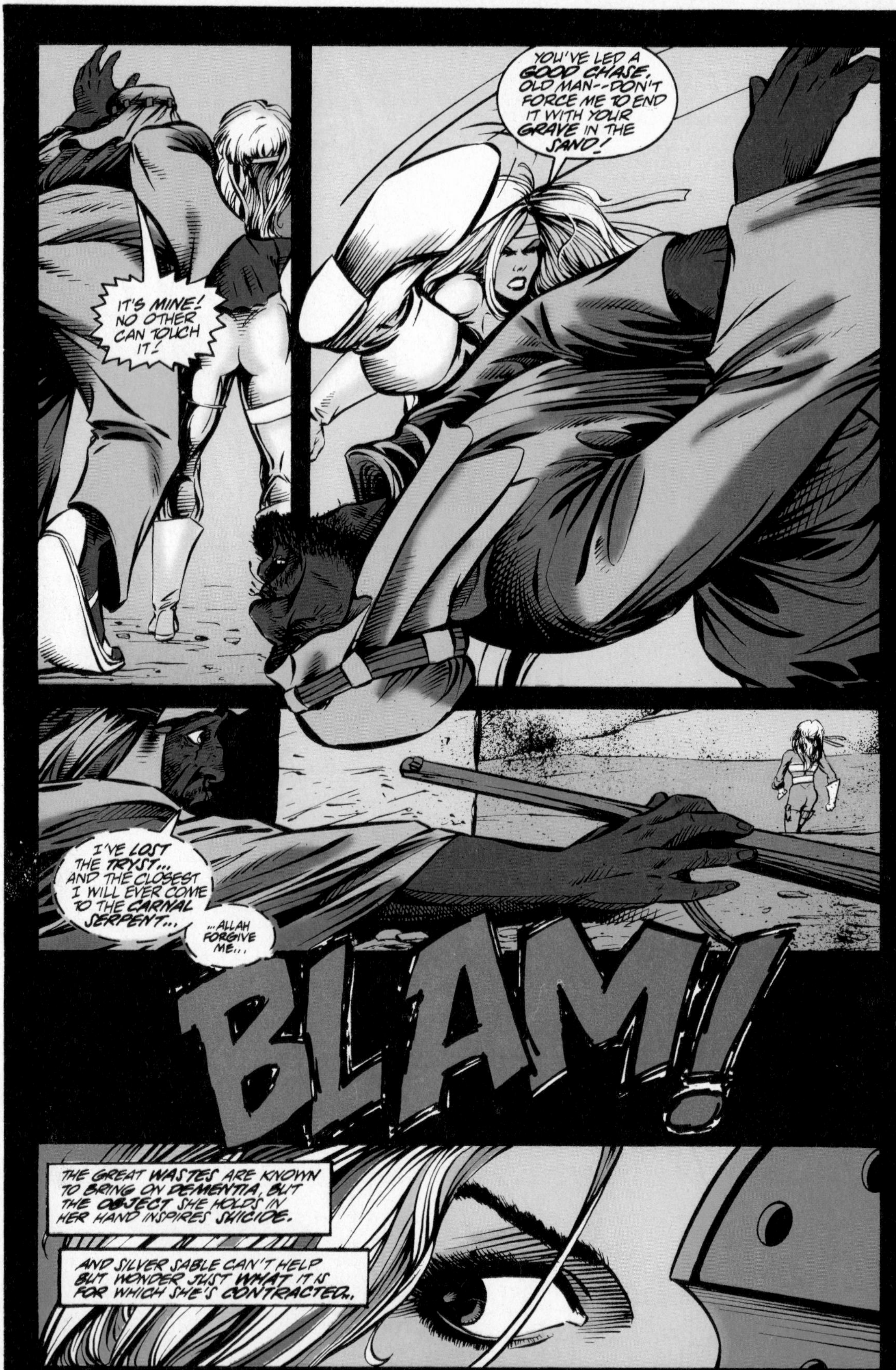
YOU'VE LED A GOOD CHASE, OLD MAN--DON'T FORCE ME TO END IT WITH YOUR GRAVE IN THE SAND!
IT'S MINE! NO OTHER CAN TOUCH IT!
I'VE LOST THE TRYST... AND THE CLOSEST I WILL EVER COME TO THE CARNAL SERPENT...
...ALLAH FORGIVE ME...
BLAM!
THE GREAT WASTES ARE KNOWN TO BRING ON DEMENTIA, BUT THE OBJECT SHE HOLDS IN HER HAND INSPIRES SUICIDE.
AND SILVER SABLE CAN'T HELP BUT WONDER JUST WHAT IT IS FOR WHICH SHE'S CONTRACTED..

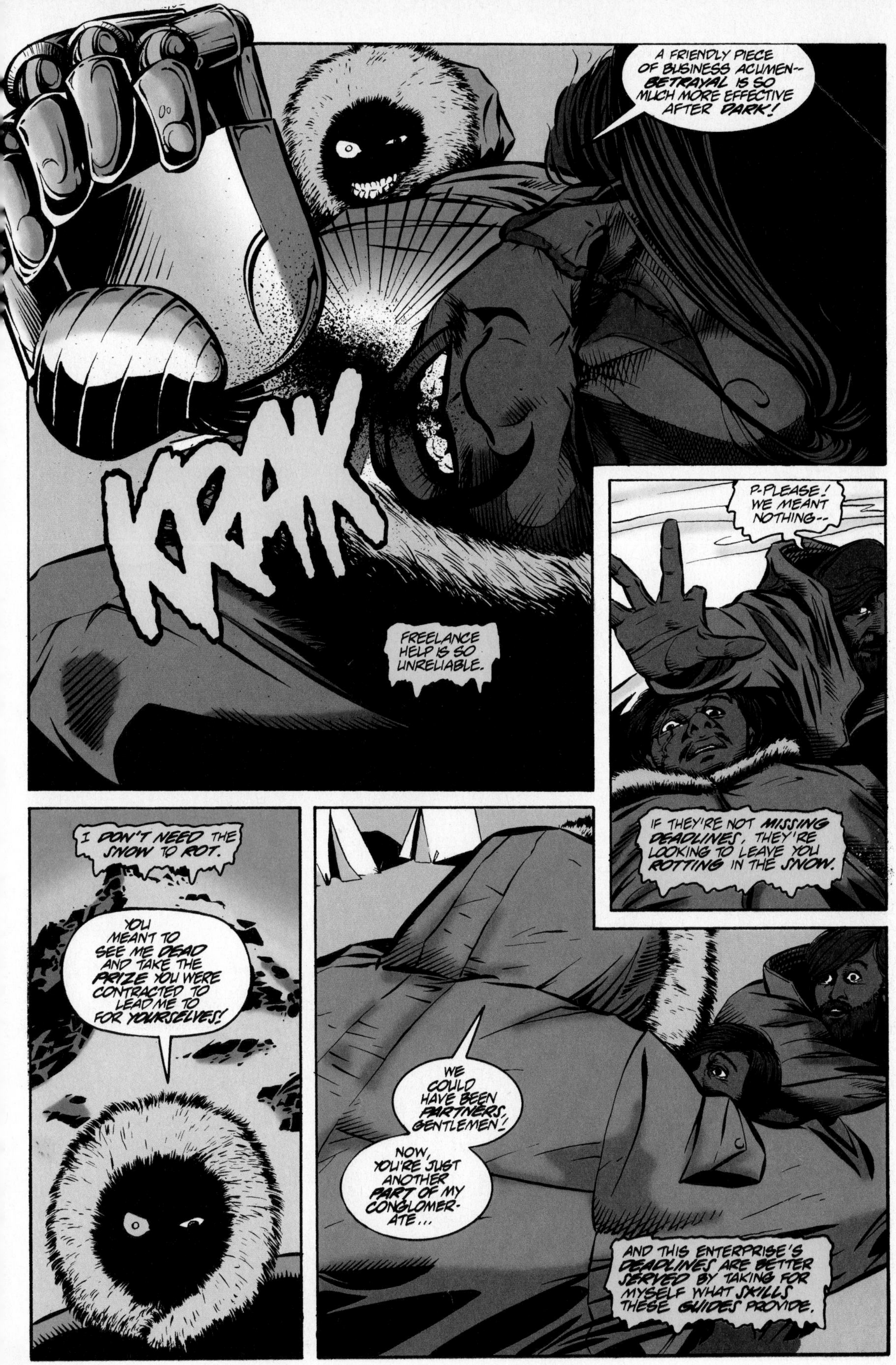
A FRIENDLY PIECE OF BUSINESS ACUMEN-- BETRAYAL IS SO MUCH MORE EFFECTIVE AFTER DARK!
KRAK
FREELANCE HELP IS SO UNRELIABLE.
P-PLEASE! WE MEANT NOTHING--
IF THEY'RE NOT MISSING DEADLINES, THEY'RE LOOKING TO LEAVE YOU ROTTING IN THE SNOW.
I DON'T NEED THE SNOW TO ROT.
YOU MEANT TO SEE ME DEAD AND TAKE THE PRIZE YOU WERE CONTRACTED TO LEAD ME TO FOR YOURSELVES!
WE COULD HAVE BEEN PARTNERS, GENTLEMEN!
NOW, YOU'RE JUST ANOTHER PART OF MY CONGLOMER-ATE...
AND THIS ENTERPRISE'S DEADLINES ARE BETTER SERVED BY TAKING FOR MYSELF WHAT SKILLS THESE GUIDES PROVIDE.

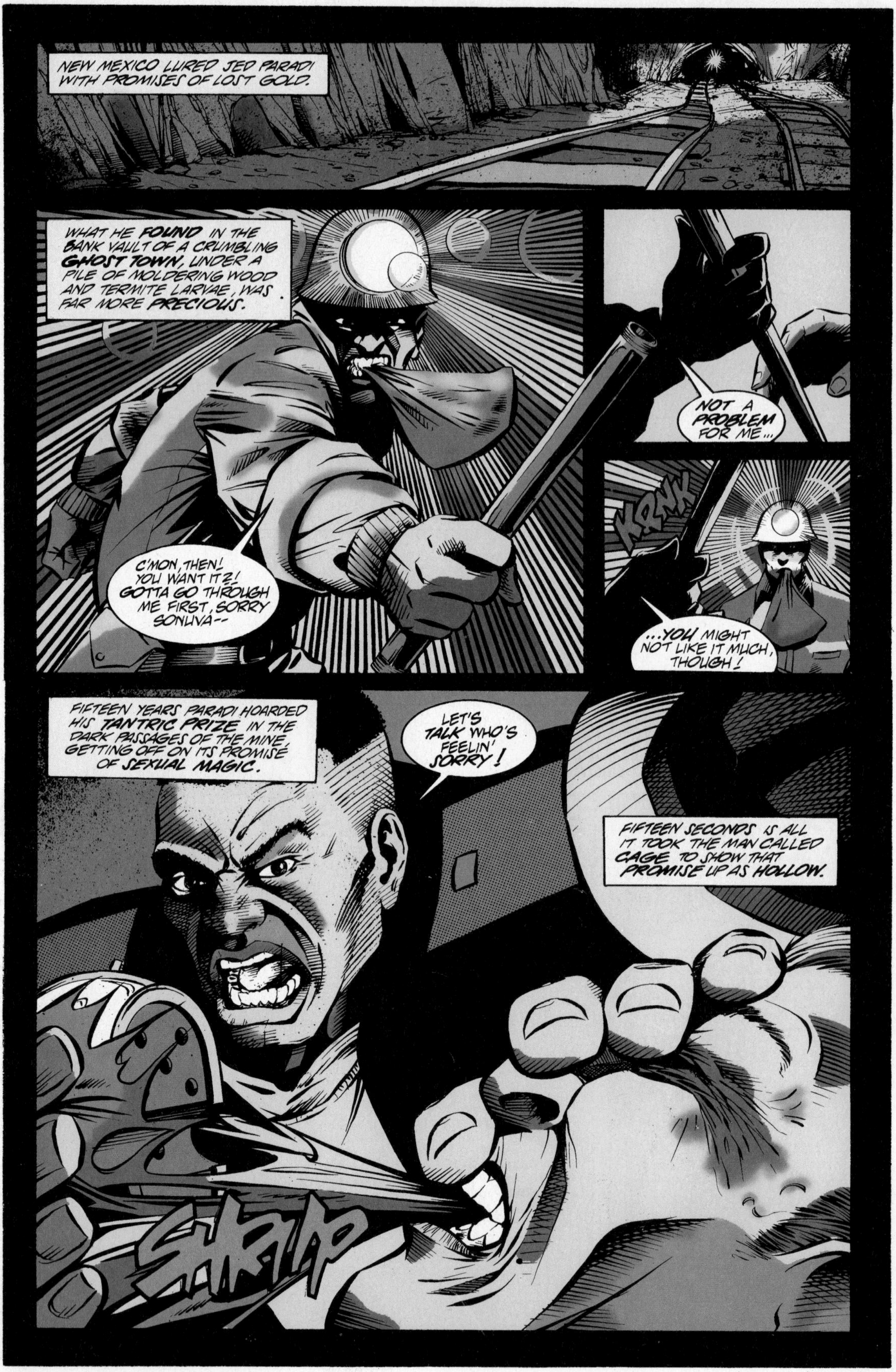
NEW MEXICO LURED JED PARADI WITH PROMISES OF LOST GOLD.
WHAT HE FOUND IN THE BANK VAULT OF A CRUMBLING GHOST TOWN, UNDER A PILE OF MOLDERING WOOD AND TERMITE LARVAE, WAS FAR MORE PRECIOUS.
C'MON, THEN! YOU WANT IT?! GOTTA GO THROUGH ME FIRST, SORRY SONUVA--
NOT A PROBLEM FOR ME...
KRNK
...YOU MIGHT NOT LIKE IT MUCH, THOUGH!
FIFTEEN YEARS PARADI HOARDED HIS TANTRIC PRIZE IN THE DARK PASSAGES OF THE MINE, GETTING OFF ON ITS PROMISE OF SEXUAL MAGIC.
LET'S TALK WHO'S FEELIN' SORRY!
FIFTEEN SECONDS IS ALL IT TOOK THE MAN CALLED CAGE TO SHOW THAT PROMISE UP AS HOLLOW.
SHRIP

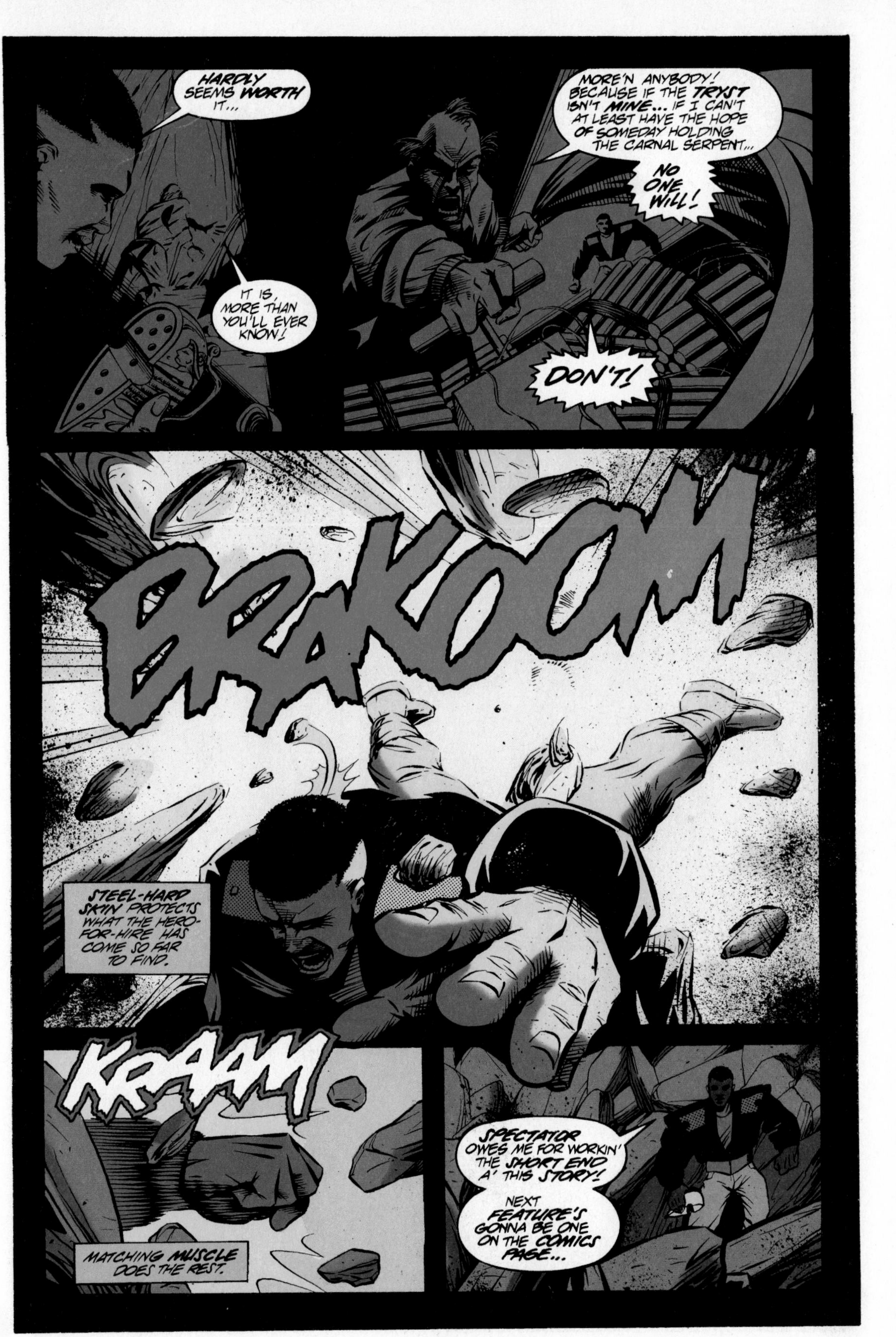
HARDLY SEEMS WORTH IT...
IT IS, MORE THAN YOU'LL EVER KNOW!
MORE'N ANYBODY! BECAUSE IF THE TRYST ISN'T MINE... IF I CAN'T AT LEAST HAVE THE HOPE OF SOMEDAY HOLDING THE CARNAL SERPENT...
NO ONE WILL!
DON'T!
BRAKOOM
STEEL-HARD SKIN PROTECTS WHAT THE HERO-FOR-HIRE HAS COME SO FAR TO FIND.
KRAAM
MATCHING MUSCLE DOES THE REST.
SPECTATOR OWES ME FOR WORKIN' THE SHORT END A' THIS STORY!
NEXT FEATURE'S GONNA BE ONE ON THE COMICS PAGE...

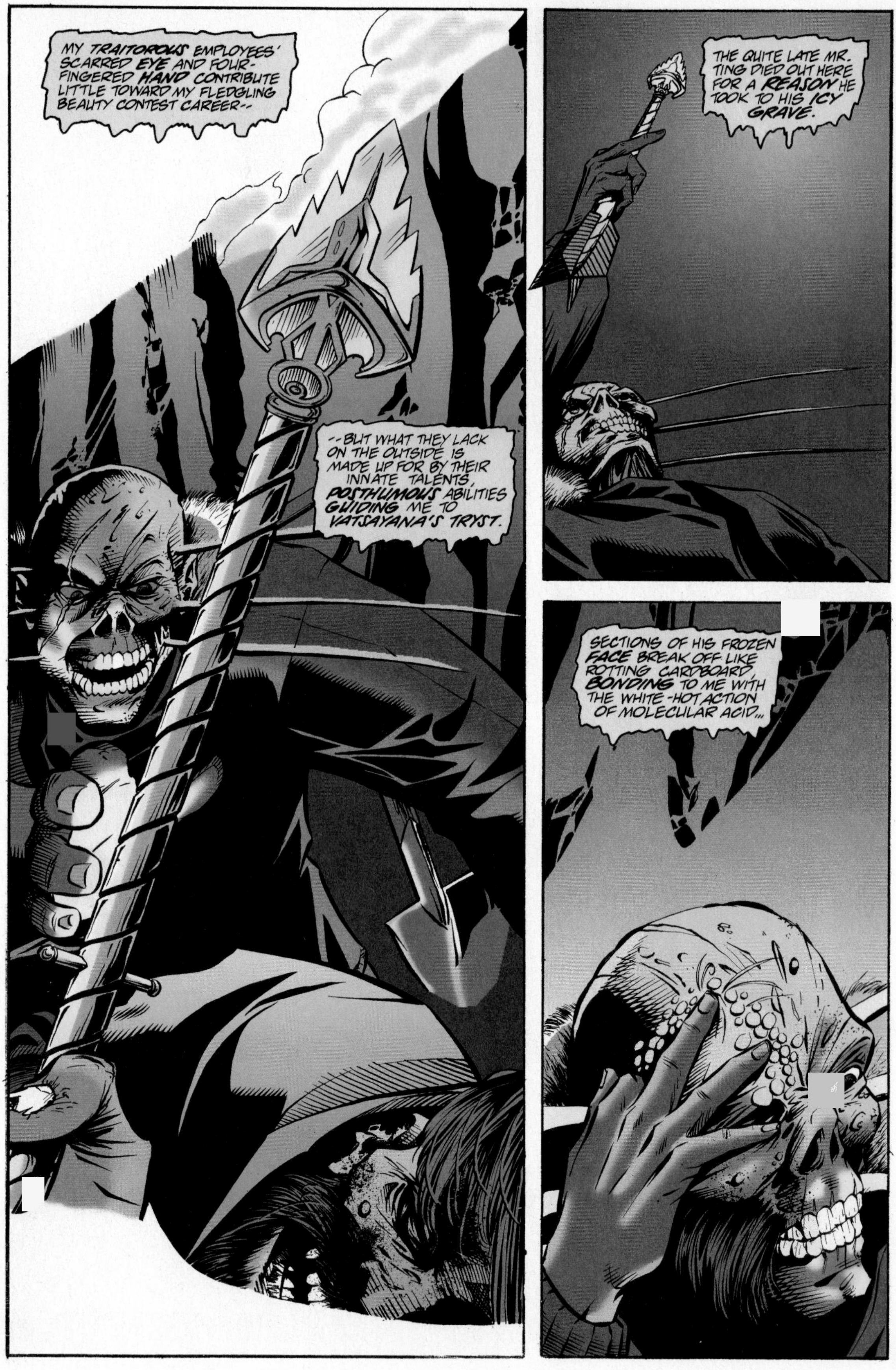
MY TRAITOROUS EMPLOYEES' SCARRED EYE AND FOUR-FINGERED HAND CONTRIBUTE LITTLE TOWARD MY FLEDGLING BEAUTY CONTEST CAREER--
--BUT WHAT THEY LACK ON THE OUTSIDE IS MADE UP FOR BY THEIR INNATE TALENTS, POSTHUMOUS ABILITIES GUIDING ME TO VATSAYANA'S TRYST.
THE QUITE LATE MR. TING DIED OUT HERE FOR A REASON HE TOOK TO HIS ICY GRAVE.
SECTIONS OF HIS FROZEN FACE BREAK OFF LIKE ROTTING CARDBOARD, BONDING TO ME WITH THE WHITE-HOT ACTION OF MOLECULAR ACID...

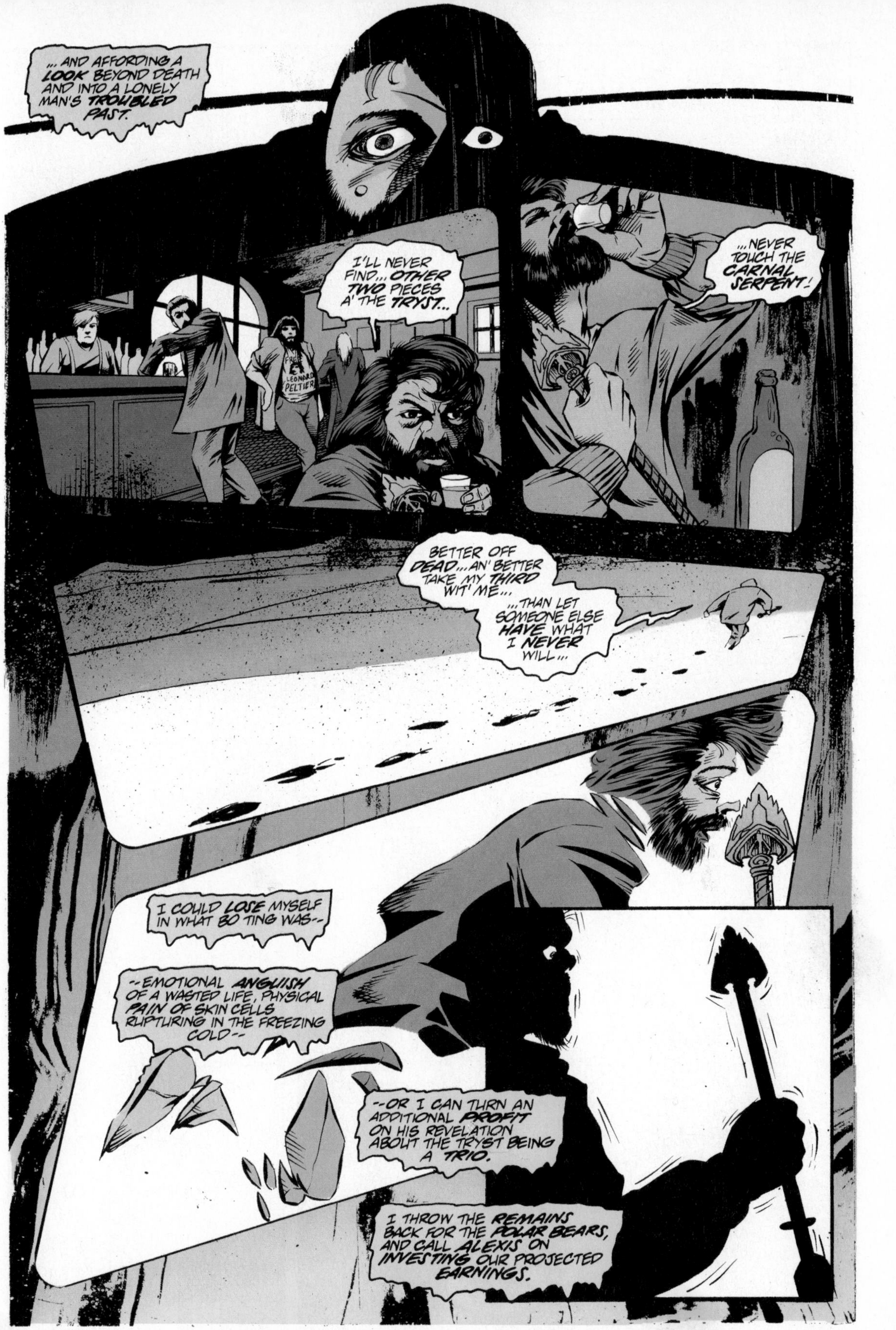
...AND AFFORDING A LOOK BEYOND DEATH AND INTO A LONELY MAN'S TROUBLED PAST.
I'LL NEVER FIND... OTHER TWO PIECES A' THE TRYST...
...NEVER TOUCH THE CARNAL SERPENT!
FREE LEONARD PELTIER
BETTER OFF DEAD... AN' BETTER TAKE MY THIRD WIT' ME...
...THAN LET SOMEONE ELSE HAVE WHAT I NEVER WILL...
I COULD LOSE MYSELF IN WHAT BO TING WAS--
--EMOTIONAL ANGUISH OF A WASTED LIFE, PHYSICAL PAIN OF SKIN CELLS RUPTURING IN THE FREEZING COLD--
--OR I CAN TURN AN ADDITIONAL PROFIT ON HIS REVELATION ABOUT THE TRYST BEING A TRIO.
I THROW THE REMAINS BACK FOR THE POLAR BEARS, AND CALL ALEXIS ON INVESTING OUR PROJECTED EARNINGS.

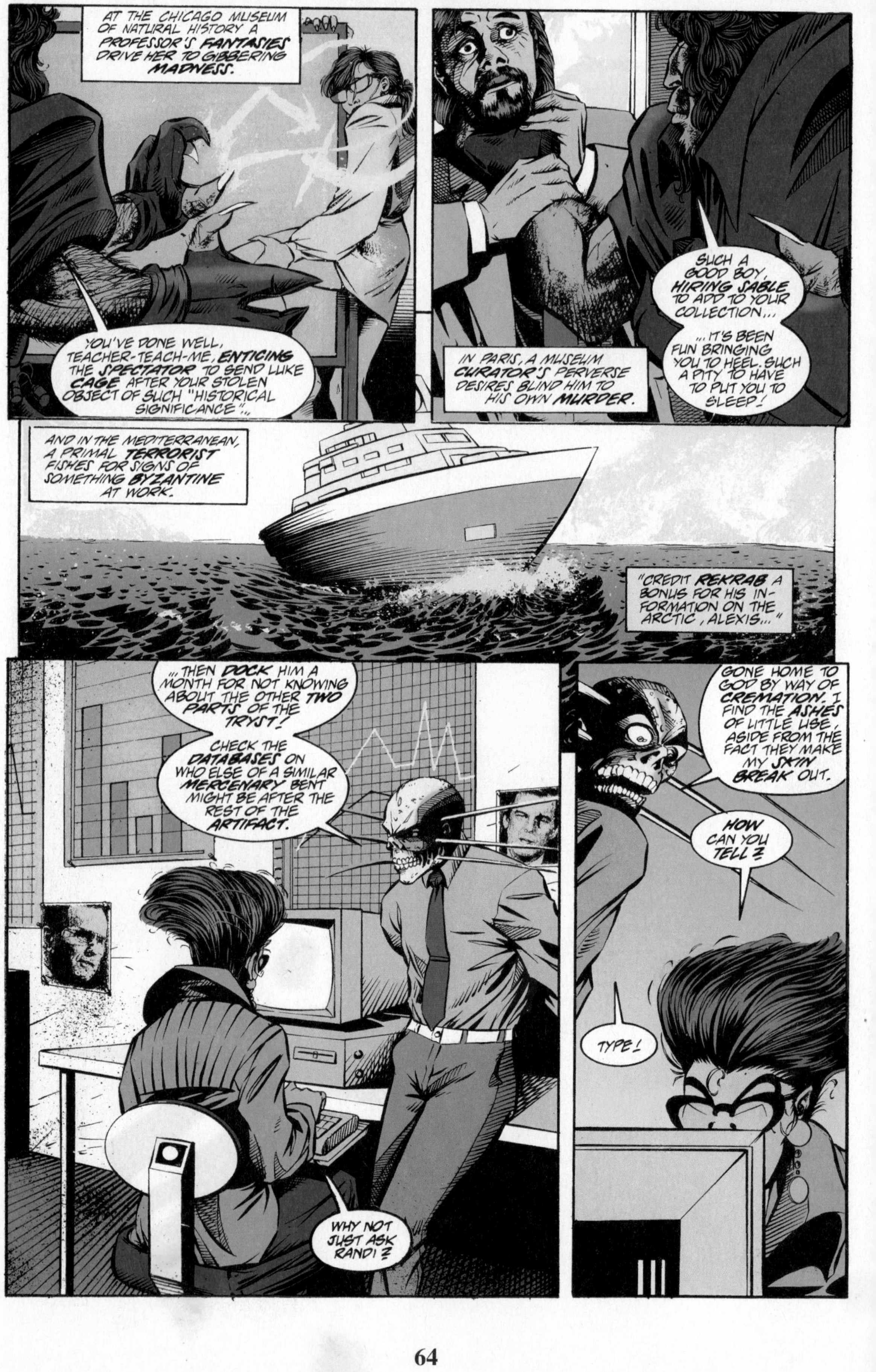
AT THE CHICAGO MUSEUM OF NATURAL HISTORY A PROFESSOR'S FANTASIES DRIVE HER TO GIBBERING MADNESS.
YOU'VE DONE WELL, TEACHER-TEACH-ME, ENTICING THE SPECTATOR TO SEND LUKE CAGE AFTER YOUR STOLEN OBJECT OF SUCH "HISTORICAL SIGNIFICANCE"...
IN PARIS, A MUSEUM CURATOR'S PERVERSE DESIRES BLIND HIM TO HIS OWN MURDER.
SUCH A GOOD BOY, HIRING SABLE TO ADD TO YOUR COLLECTION...
...IT'S BEEN FUN BRINGING YOU TO HEEL. SUCH A PITY TO HAVE TO PUT YOU TO SLEEP!
AND IN THE MEDITERRANEAN, A PRIMAL TERRORIST FISHES FOR SIGNS OF SOMETHING BYZANTINE AT WORK.
"CREDIT REKRAB A BONUS FOR HIS INFORMATION ON THE ARCTIC, ALEXIS..."
..THEN DOCK HIM A MONTH FOR NOT KNOWING ABOUT THE OTHER TWO PARTS OF THE TRYST!
CHECK THE DATABASES ON WHO ELSE OF A SIMILAR MERCENARY BENT MIGHT BE AFTER THE REST OF THE ARTIFACT.
WHY NOT JUST ASK RANDI?
GONE HOME TO GOD BY WAY OF CREMATION. I FIND THE ASHES OF LITTLE USE, ASIDE FROM THE FACT THEY MAKE MY SKIN BREAK OUT.
HOW CAN YOU TELL?
TYPE!

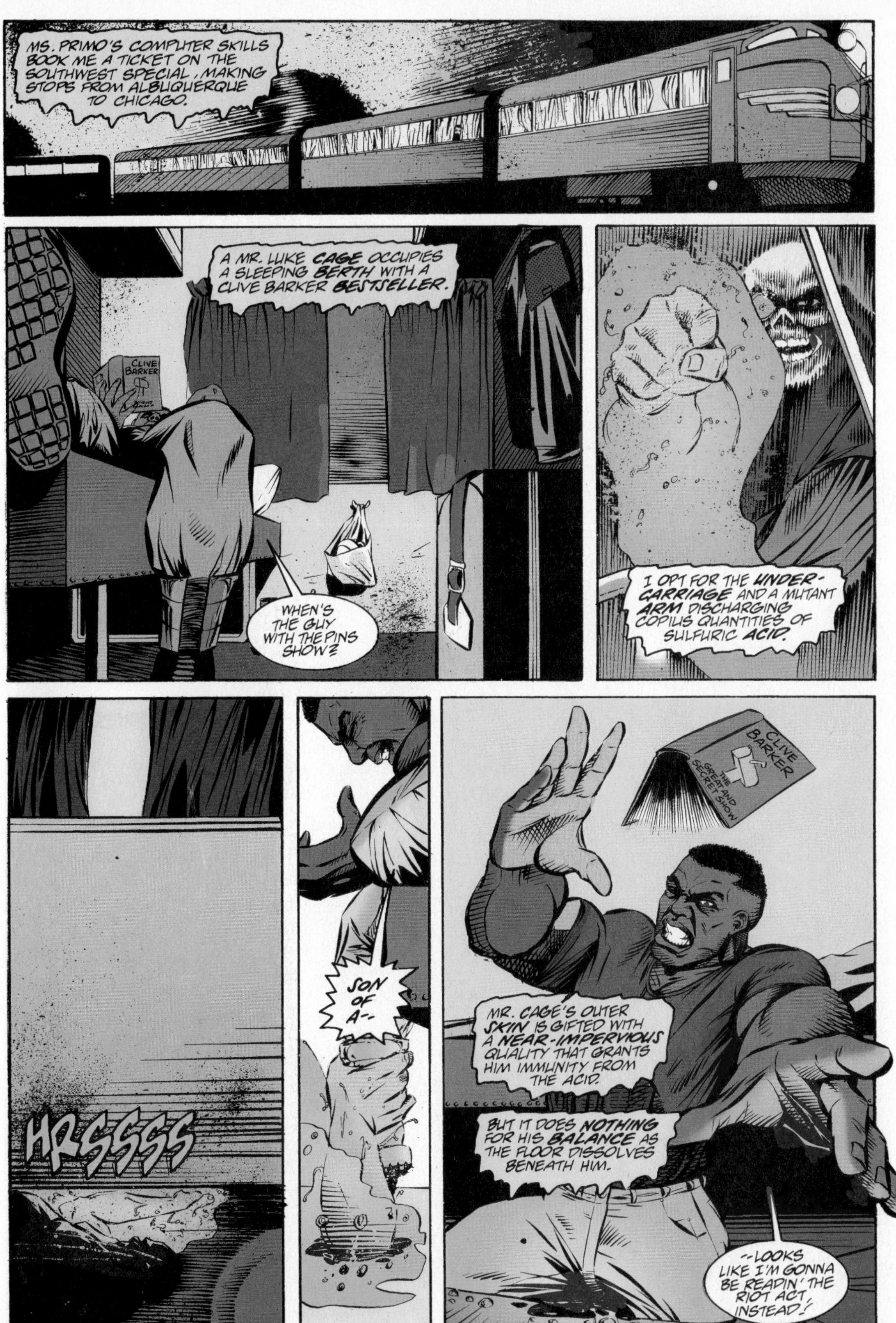
MS. PRIMO'S COMPUTER SKILLS BOOK ME A TICKET ON THE SOUTHWEST SPECIAL, MAKING STOPS FROM ALBUQUERQUE TO CHICAGO.
A MR. LUKE CAGE OCCUPIES A SLEEPING BERTH WITH A CLIVE BARKER BESTSELLER.
CLIVE BARKER
WHEN'S THE GUY WITH THE PINS SHOW?
I OPT FOR THE UNDER-CARRIAGE AND A MUTANT ARM DISCHARGING COPIUS QUANTITIES OF SULFURIC ACID.
HRSSSS
SON OF A--
CLIVE BARKER
THE GREAT AND SECRET SHOW
MR. CAGE'S OUTER SKIN IS GIFTED WITH A NEAR-IMPERVIOUS QUALITY THAT GRANTS HIM IMMUNITY FROM THE ACID.
BUT IT DOES NOTHING FOR HIS BALANCE AS THE FLOOR DISSOLVES BENEATH HIM.
--LOOKS LIKE I'M GONNA BE READIN' THE RIOT ACT, INSTEAD!

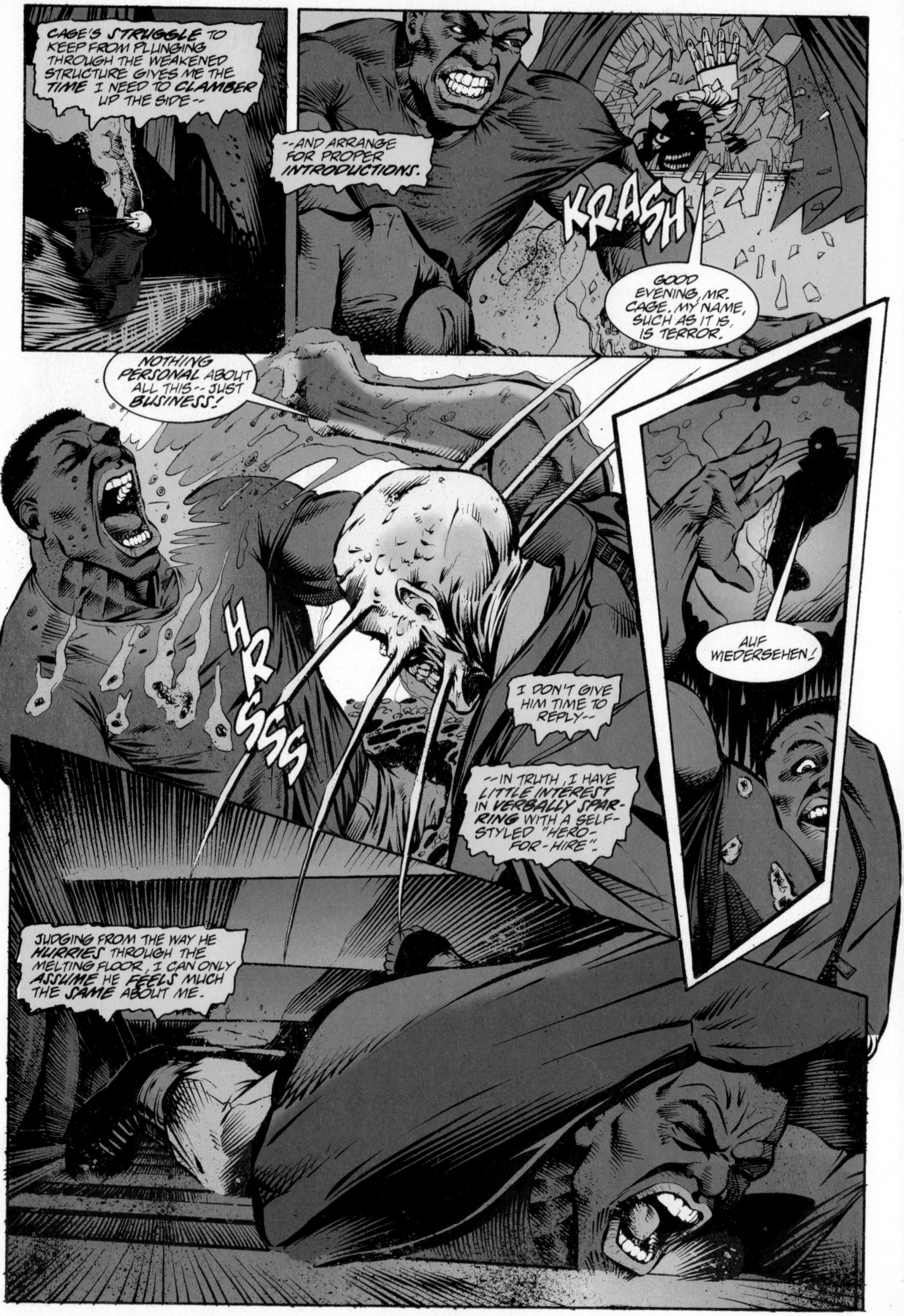
CAGE'S STRUGGLE TO KEEP FROM PLUNGING THROUGH THE WEAKENED STRUCTURE GIVES ME THE TIME I NEED TO CLAMBER UP THE SIDE--
--AND ARRANGE FOR PROPER INTRODUCTIONS.
KRASH
GOOD EVENING, MR. CAGE. MY NAME, SUCH AS IT IS, IS TERROR.
NOTHING PERSONAL ABOUT ALL THIS--JUST BUSINESS!
AUF WIEDERSEHEN!
HRSSSS
I DON'T GIVE HIM TIME TO REPLY--
--IN TRUTH, I HAVE LITTLE INTEREST IN VERBALLY SPARRING WITH A SELF-STYLED "HERO-FOR-HIRE".
JUDGING FROM THE WAY HE HURRIES THROUGH THE MELTING FLOOR, I CAN ONLY ASSUME HE FEELS MUCH THE SAME ABOUT ME.

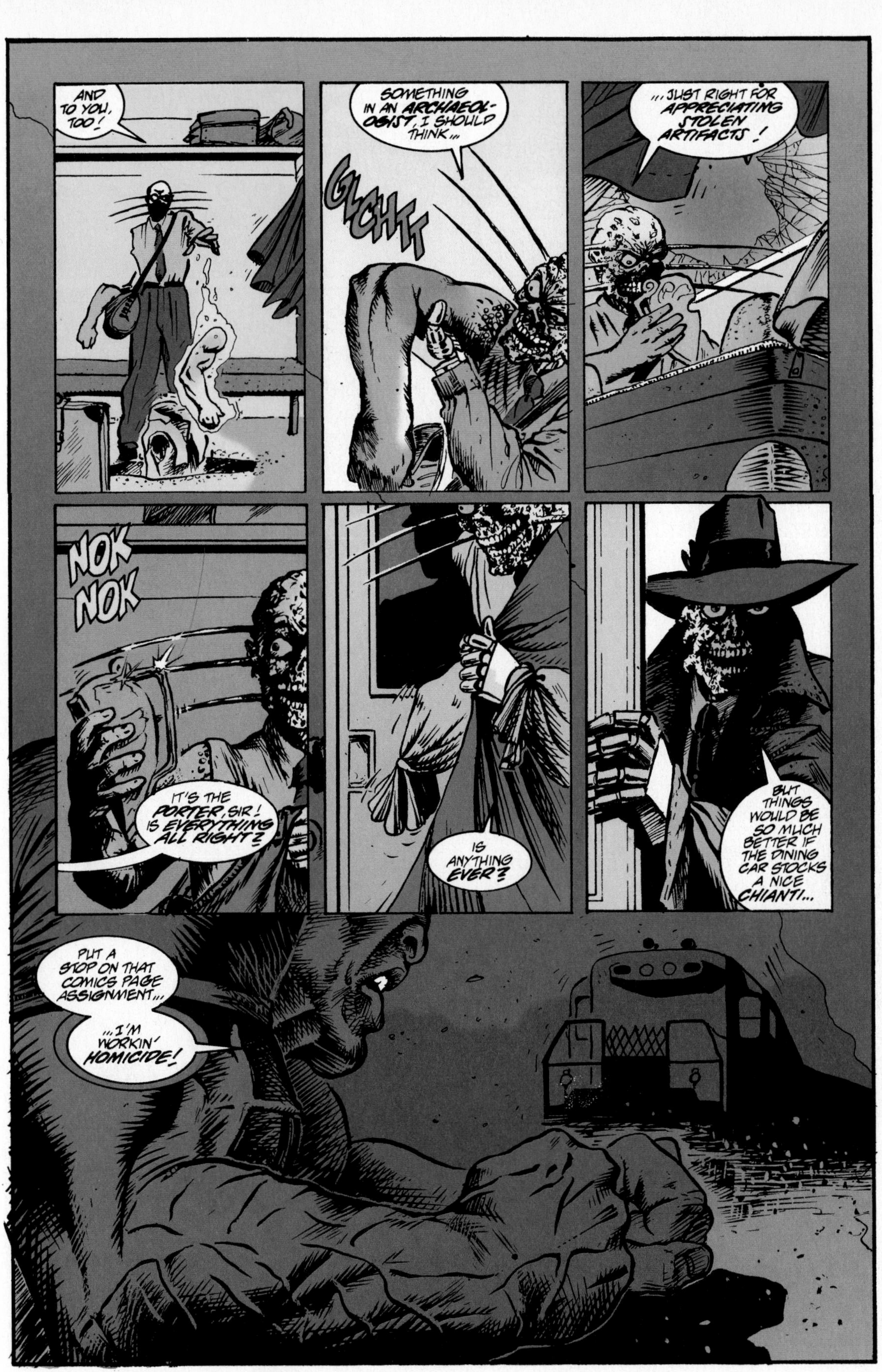
AND TO YOU, TOO!
SOMETHING IN AN ARCHAEOL-OGIST, I SHOULD THINK...
GLCHTT
...JUST RIGHT FOR APPRECIATING STOLEN ARTIFACTS!
NOK NOK
IT'S THE PORTER, SIR! IS EVERYTHING ALL RIGHT?
IS ANYTHING EVER?
BUT THINGS WOULD BE SO MUCH BETTER IF THE DINING CAR STOCKS A NICE CHIANTI...
PUT A STOP ON THAT COMICS PAGE ASSIGNMENT...
...I'M WORKIN' HOMICIDE!

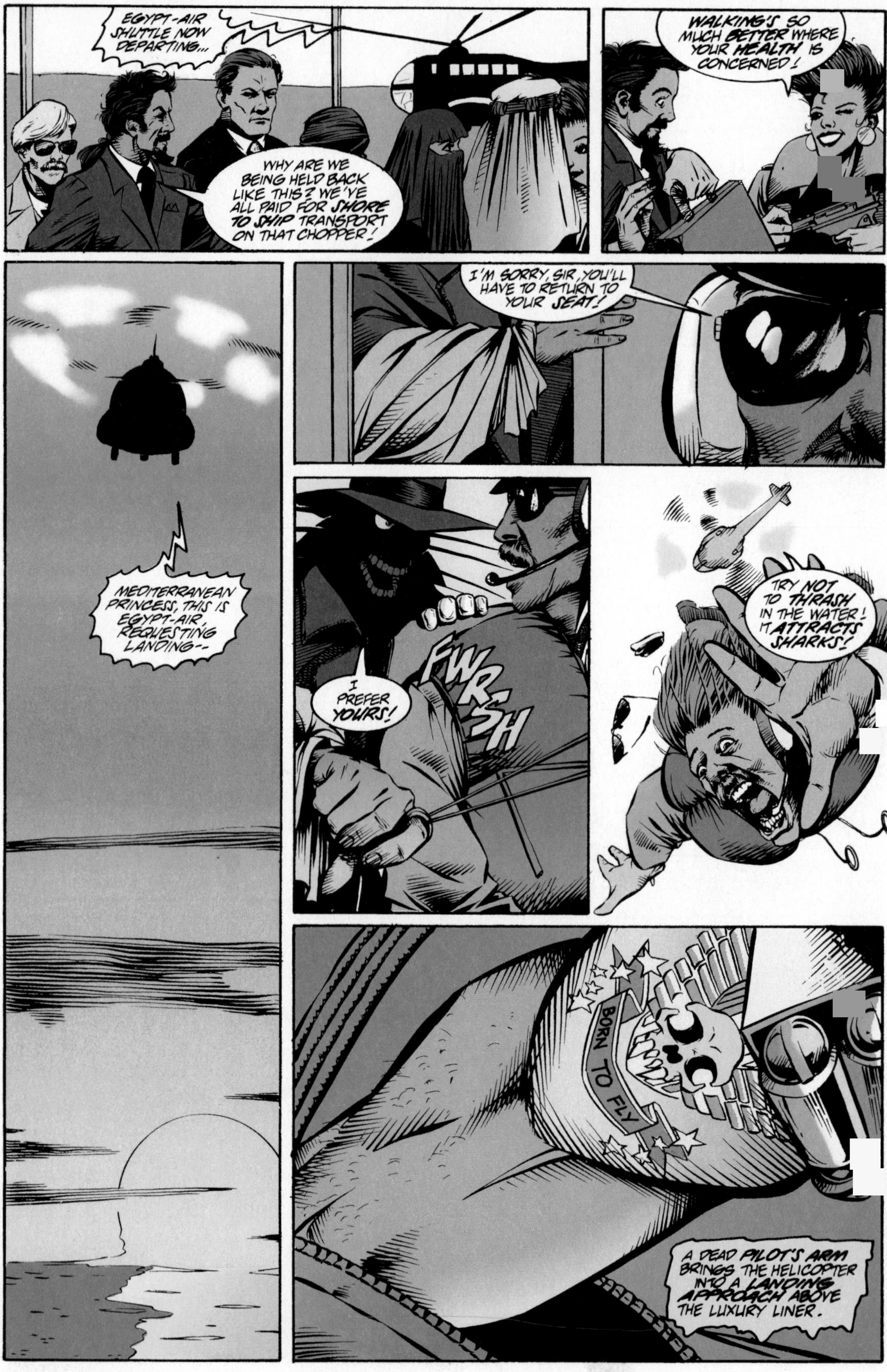

EGYPT-AIR SHUTTLE NOW DEPARTING...
WHY ARE WE BEING HELD BACK LIKE THIS? WE'VE ALL PAID FOR SHORE TO SHIP TRANSPORT ON THAT CHOPPER!
WALKING'S SO MUCH BETTER WHERE YOUR HEALTH IS CONCERNED!
MEDITERRANEAN PRINCESS, THIS IS EGYPT-AIR, REQUESTING LANDING--
I'M SORRY, SIR, YOU'LL HAVE TO RETURN TO YOUR SEAT!
I PREFER YOURS!
FWRSH
TRY NOT TO THRASH IN THE WATER! IT ATTRACTS SHARKS!
BORN TO FLY
A DEAD PILOT'S ARM BRINGS THE HELICOPTER INTO A LANDING APPROACH ABOVE THE LUXURY LINER.

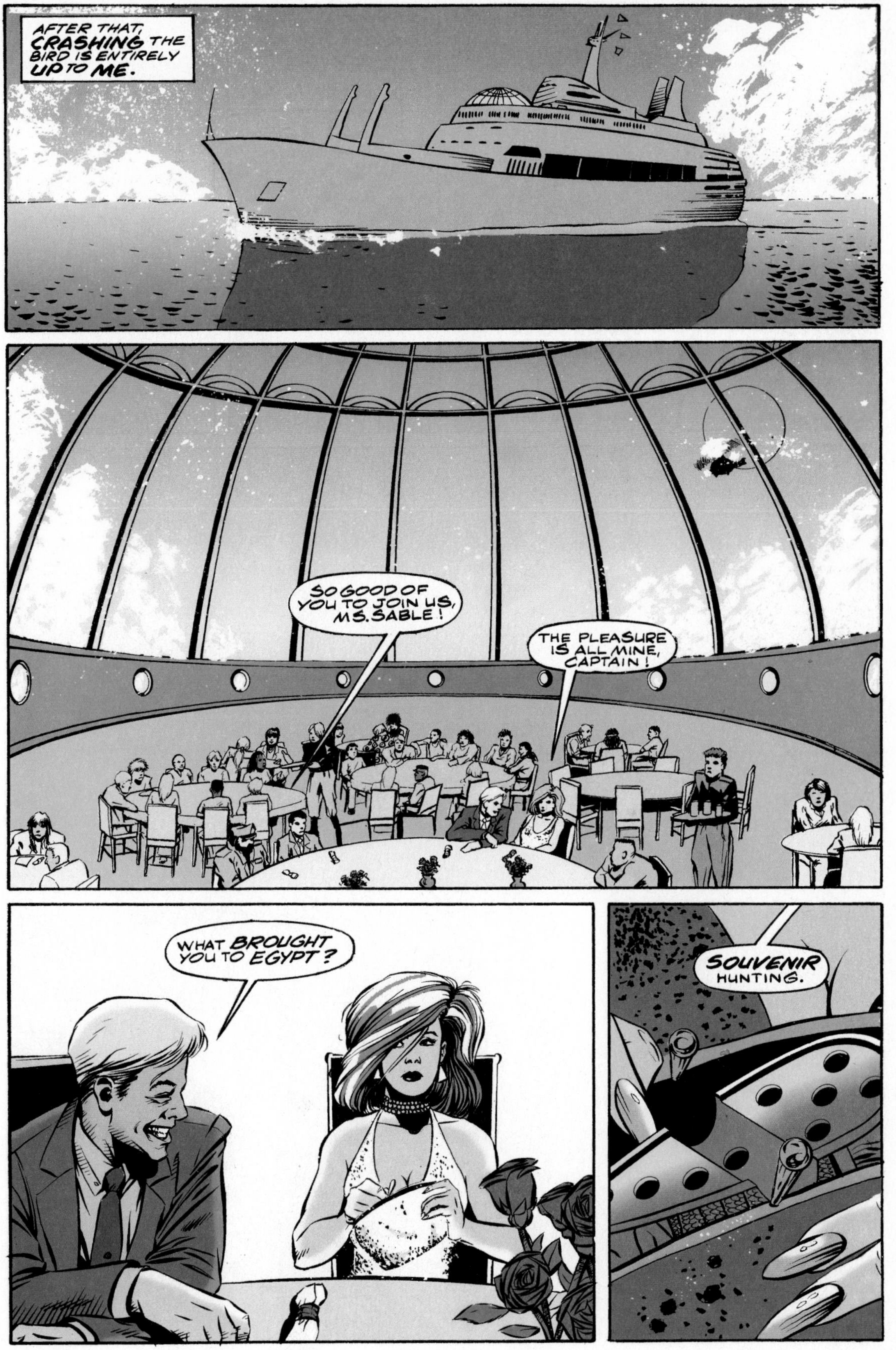
AFTER THAT, CRASHING THE BIRD IS ENTIRELY UP TO ME.
SO GOOD OF YOU TO JOIN US, MS. SABLE!
THE PLEASURE IS ALL MINE, CAPTAIN!
WHAT BROUGHT YOU TO EGYPT?
SOUVENIR HUNTING.

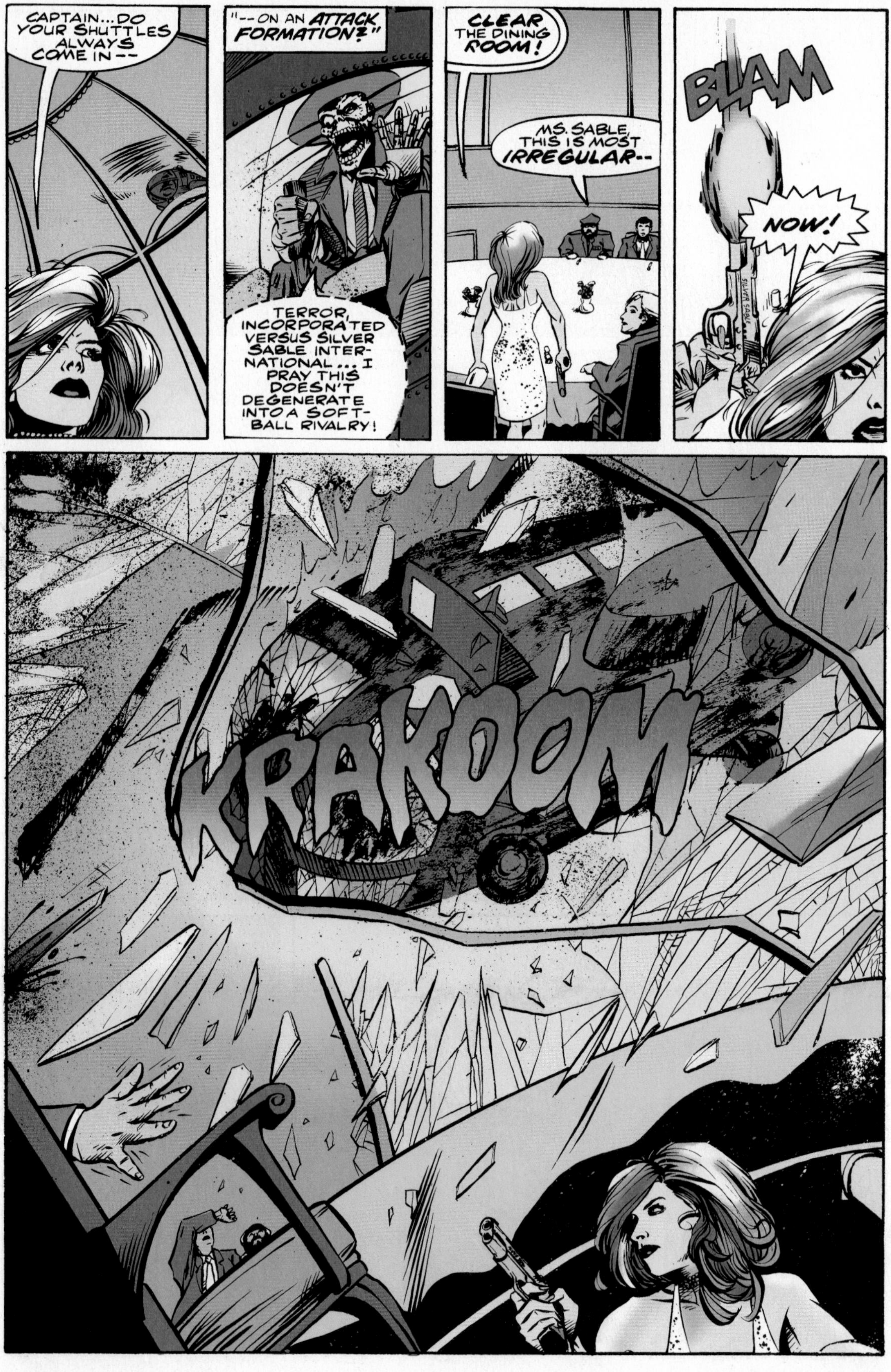
CAPTAIN...DO YOUR SHUTTLES ALWAYS COME IN--
"--ON AN ATTACK FORMATION?"
TERROR, INCORPORATED VERSUS SILVER SABLE INTERNATIONAL... I PRAY THIS DOESN'T DEGENERATE INTO A SOFTBALL RIVALRY!
CLEAR THE DINING ROOM!
MS. SABLE, THIS IS MOST IRREGULAR--
BLAM
NOW!
KRAKOOM

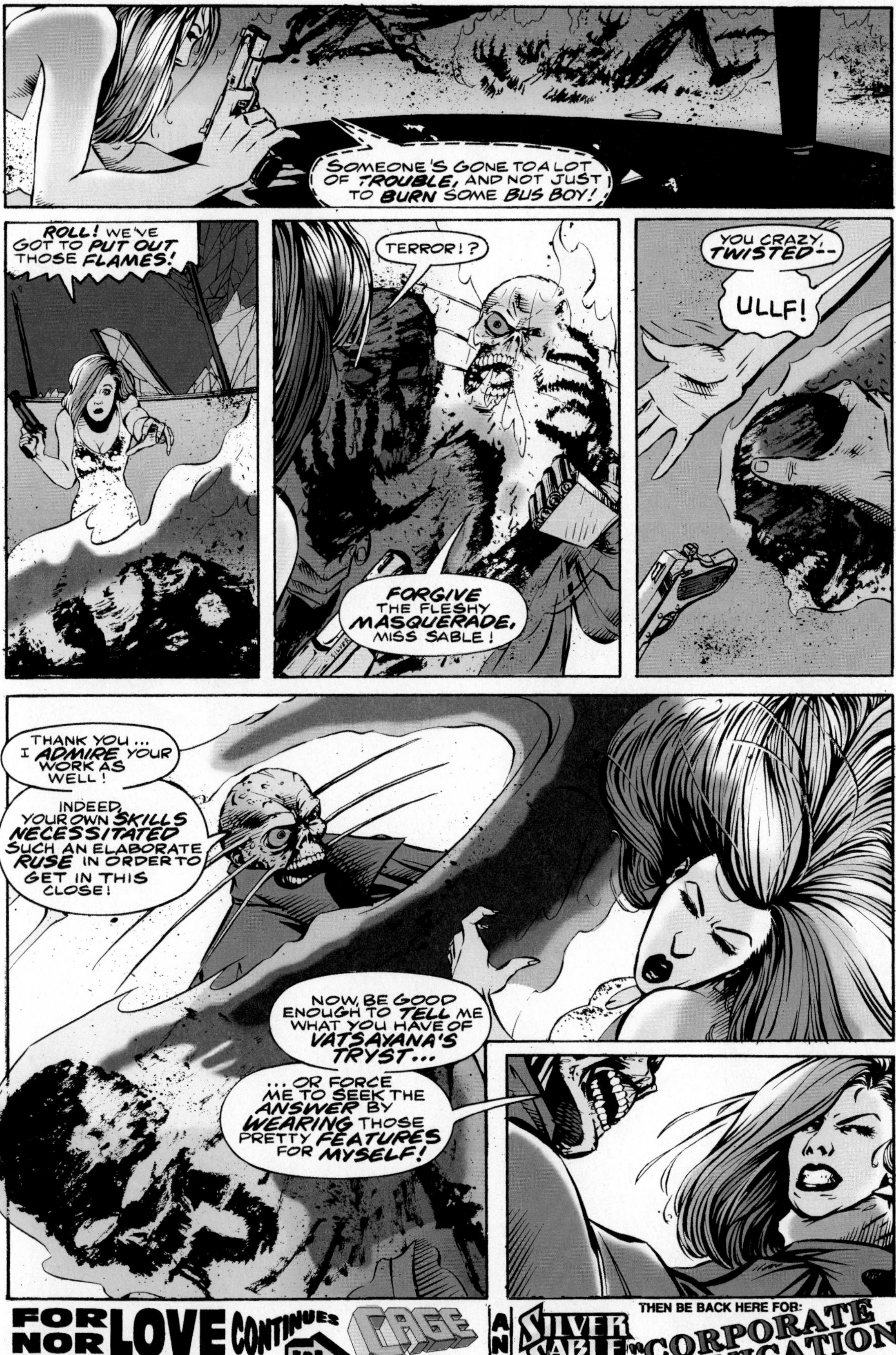

SOMEONE'S GONE TO A LOT OF TROUBLE, AND NOT JUST TO BURN SOME BUS BOY!
ROLL! WE'VE GOT TO PUT OUT THOSE FLAMES!
TERROR!?
FORGIVE THE FLESHY MASQUERADE, MISS SABLE!
YOU CRAZY, TWISTED--
ULLF!
THANK YOU... I ADMIRE YOUR WORK AS WELL!
INDEED, YOUR OWN SKILLS NECESSITATED SUCH AN ELABORATE RUSE IN ORDER TO GET IN THIS CLOSE!
NOW, BE GOOD ENOUGH TO TELL ME WHAT YOU HAVE OF VATSAYANA'S TRYST...
...OR FORCE ME TO SEEK THE ANSWER BY WEARING THOSE PRETTY FEATURES FOR MYSELF!
FOR LOVE NOR MONEY CONTINUES IN CAGE #15 AND SILVER SABLE #13
THEN BE BACK HERE FOR: "CORPORATE FORNICATION" DON'T MISS IT!

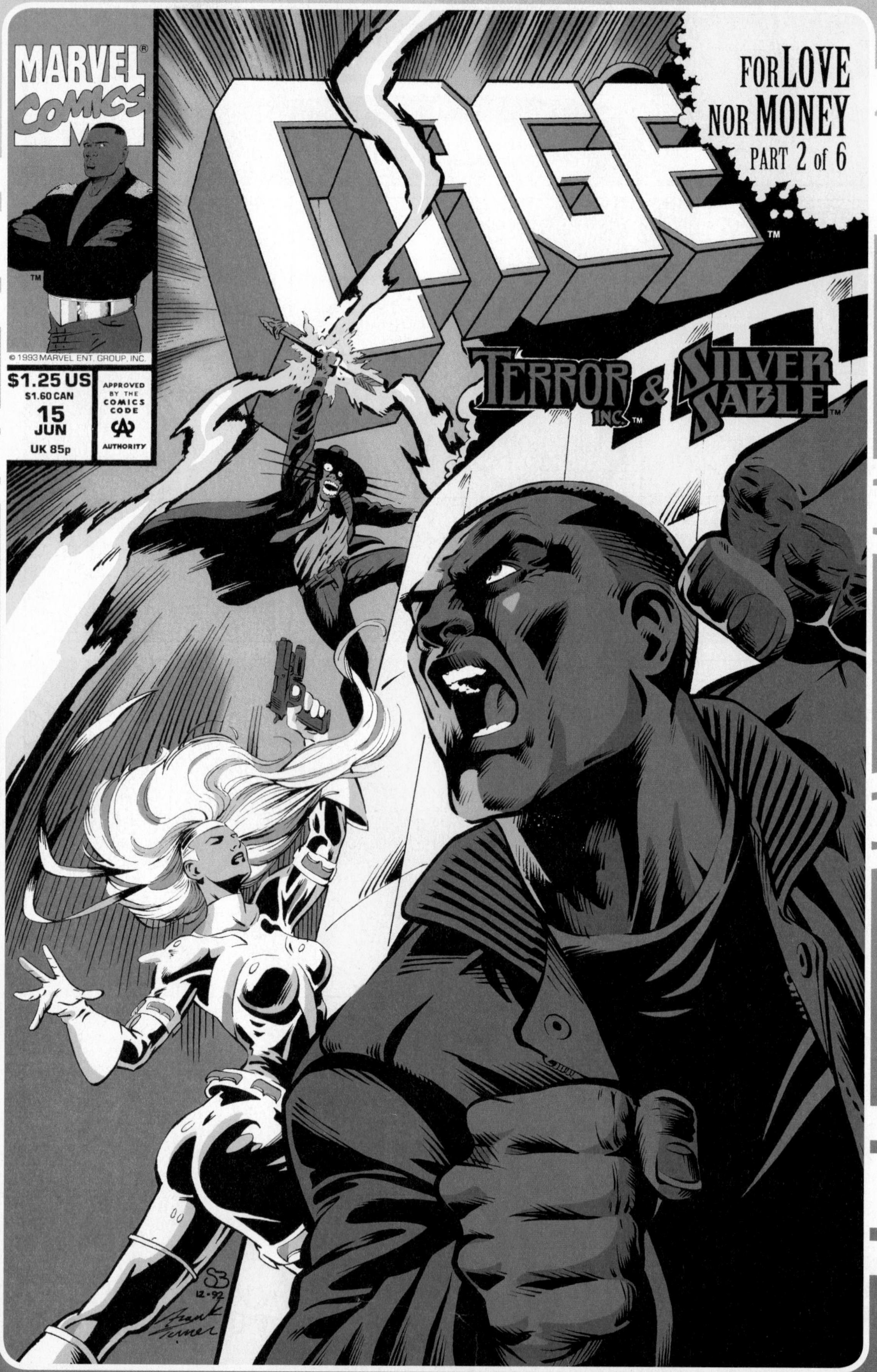
MARVEL COMICS
CAGE
FOR LOVE NOR MONEY PART 2 of 6
© 1993 MARVEL ENT. GROUP, INC.
$1.25 US
$1.60 CAN
15
JUN
UK 85p
APPROVED BY THE COMICS CODE AUTHORITY
TERROR INC. & SILVER SABLE

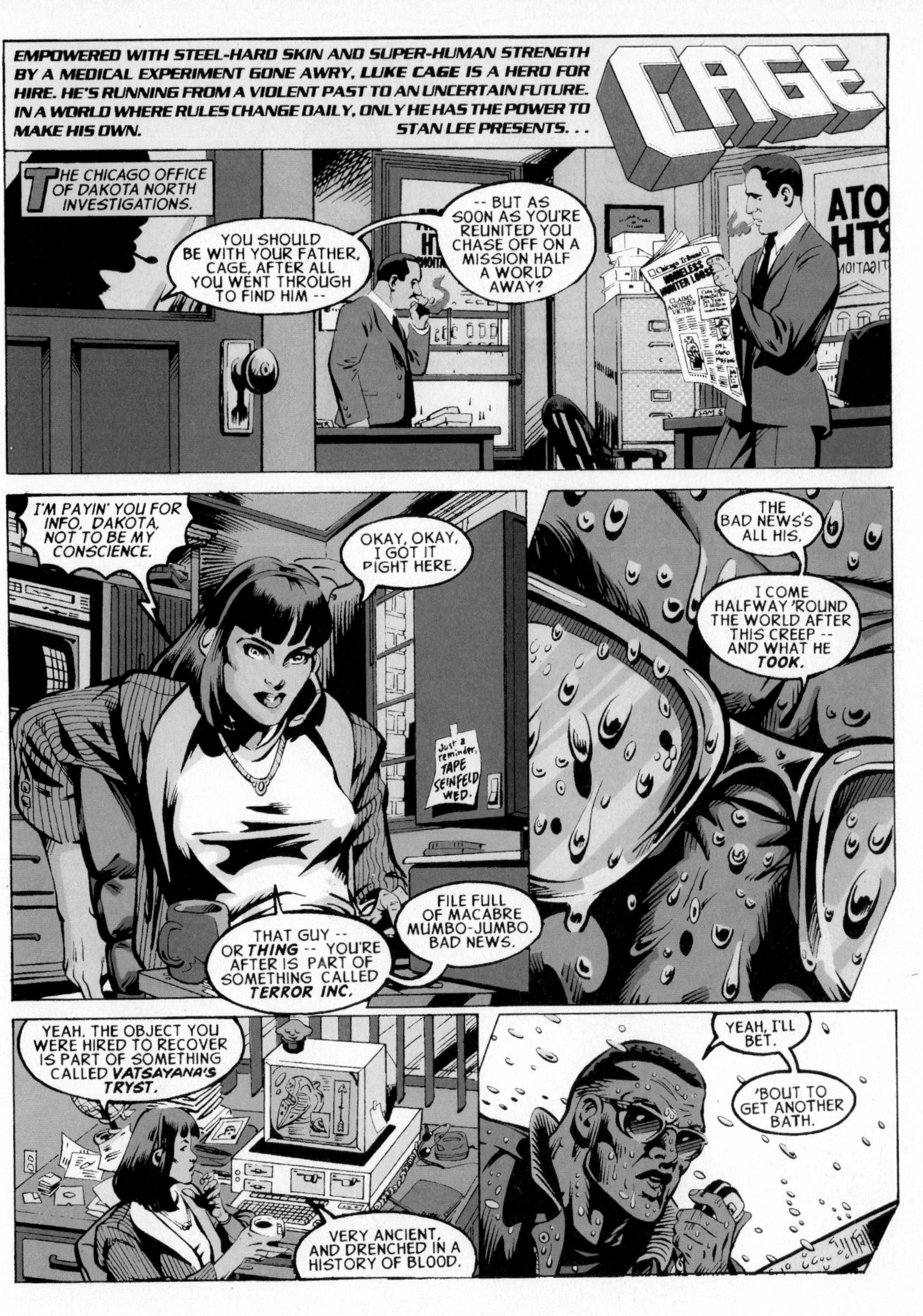
EMPOWERED WITH STEEL-HARD SKIN AND SUPER-HUMAN STRENGTH BY A MEDICAL EXPERIMENT GONE AWRY, LUKE CAGE IS A HERO FOR HIRE. HE'S RUNNING FROM A VIOLENT PAST TO AN UNCERTAIN FUTURE. IN A WORLD WHERE RULES CHANGE DAILY, ONLY HE HAS THE POWER TO MAKE HIS OWN.
STAN LEE PRESENTS. . .
CAGE
THE CHICAGO OFFICE OF DAKOTA NORTH INVESTIGATIONS.
YOU SHOULD BE WITH YOUR FATHER, CAGE, AFTER ALL YOU WENT THROUGH TO FIND HIM --
-- BUT AS SOON AS YOU'RE REUNITED YOU CHASE OFF ON A MISSION HALF A WORLD AWAY?
I'M PAYIN' YOU FOR INFO, DAKOTA, NOT TO BE MY CONSCIENCE.
OKAY, OKAY, I GOT IT RIGHT HERE.
Just a reminder, TAPE SEINFELD WED.
THAT GUY -- OR THING -- YOU'RE AFTER IS PART OF SOMETHING CALLED TERROR INC.
FILE FULL OF MACABRE MUMBO-JUMBO. BAD NEWS.
THE BAD NEWS'S ALL HIS.
I COME HALFWAY 'ROUND THE WORLD AFTER THIS CREEP -- AND WHAT HE TOOK.
YEAH. THE OBJECT YOU WERE HIRED TO RECOVER IS PART OF SOMETHING CALLED VATSAYANA'S TRYST.
VERY ANCIENT, AND DRENCHED IN A HISTORY OF BLOOD.
YEAH, I'LL BET.
'BOUT TO GET ANOTHER BATH.

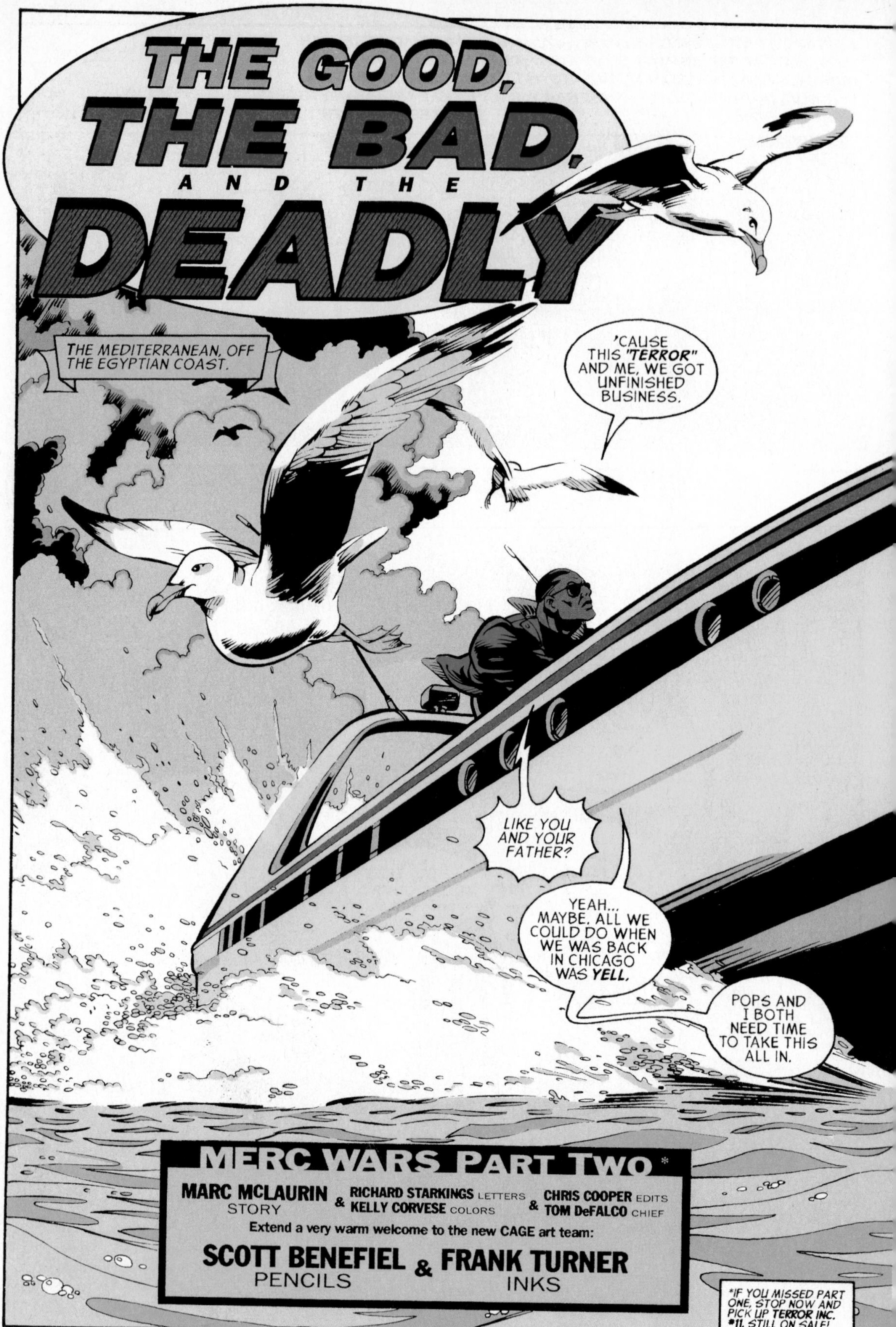
THE GOOD, THE BAD, AND THE DEADLY
THE MEDITERRANEAN, OFF THE EGYPTIAN COAST.
'CAUSE THIS "TERROR" AND ME, WE GOT UNFINISHED BUSINESS.
LIKE YOU AND YOUR FATHER?
YEAH... MAYBE. ALL WE COULD DO WHEN WE WAS BACK IN CHICAGO WAS YELL.
POPS AND I BOTH NEED TIME TO TAKE THIS ALL IN.
MERC WARS PART TWO*
MARC MCLAURIN STORY & RICHARD STARKINGS LETTERS KELLY CORVESE COLORS & CHRIS COOPER EDITS TOM DeFALCO CHIEF
Extend a very warm welcome to the new CAGE art team:
SCOTT BENEFIEL PENCILS & FRANK TURNER INKS
*IF YOU MISSED PART ONE, STOP NOW AND PICK UP TERROR INC. #11, STILL ON SALE! --CHRIS

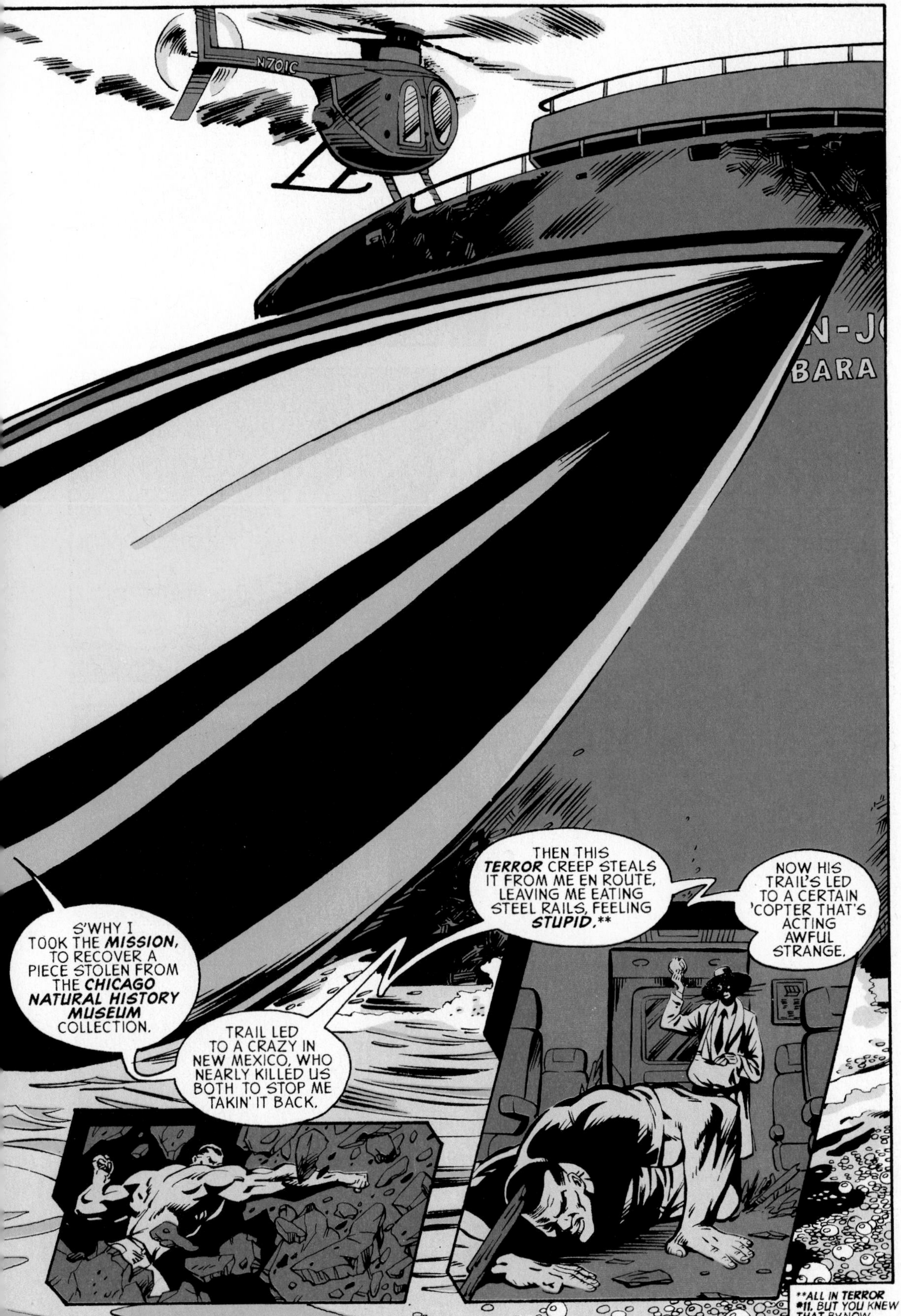
N701C
N-JO
BARA
S'WHY I TOOK THE MISSION, TO RECOVER A PIECE STOLEN FROM THE CHICAGO NATURAL HISTORY MUSEUM COLLECTION.
TRAIL LED TO A CRAZY IN NEW MEXICO, WHO NEARLY KILLED US BOTH TO STOP ME TAKIN' IT BACK.
THEN THIS TERROR CREEP STEALS IT FROM ME EN ROUTE, LEAVING ME EATING STEEL RAILS, FEELING STUPID.**
NOW HIS TRAIL'S LED TO A CERTAIN 'COPTER THAT'S ACTING AWFUL STRANGE.
**ALL IN TERROR #11. BUT YOU KNEW THAT BY NOW, HMM? --CHRIS.

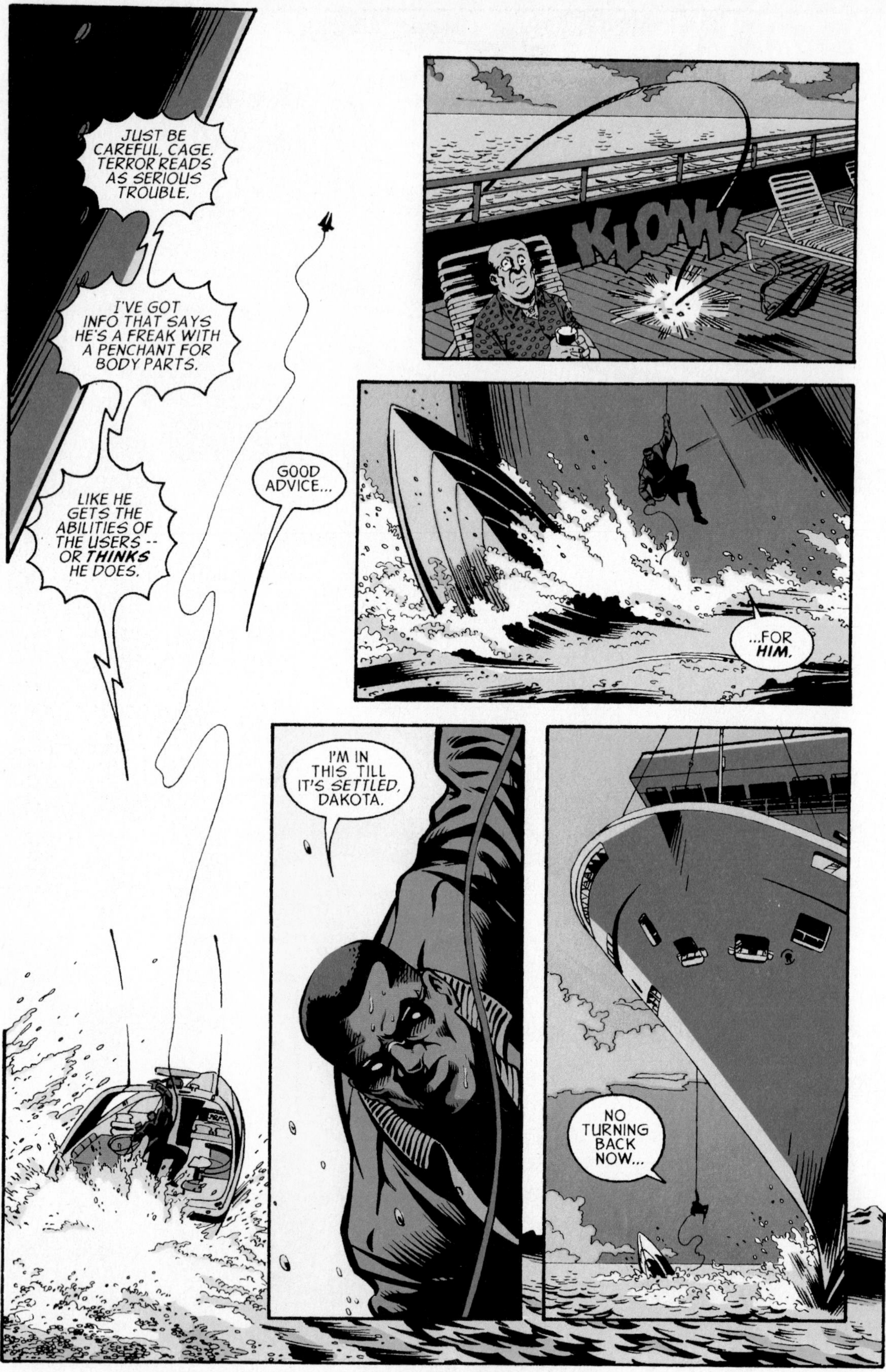
JUST BE CAREFUL, CAGE. TERROR READS AS SERIOUS TROUBLE.
I'VE GOT INFO THAT SAYS HE'S A FREAK WITH A PENCHANT FOR BODY PARTS.
LIKE HE GETS THE ABILITIES OF THE USERS -- OR THINKS HE DOES.
GOOD ADVICE...
KLONK
...FOR HIM.
I'M IN THIS TILL IT'S SETTLED, DAKOTA.
NO TURNING BACK NOW...

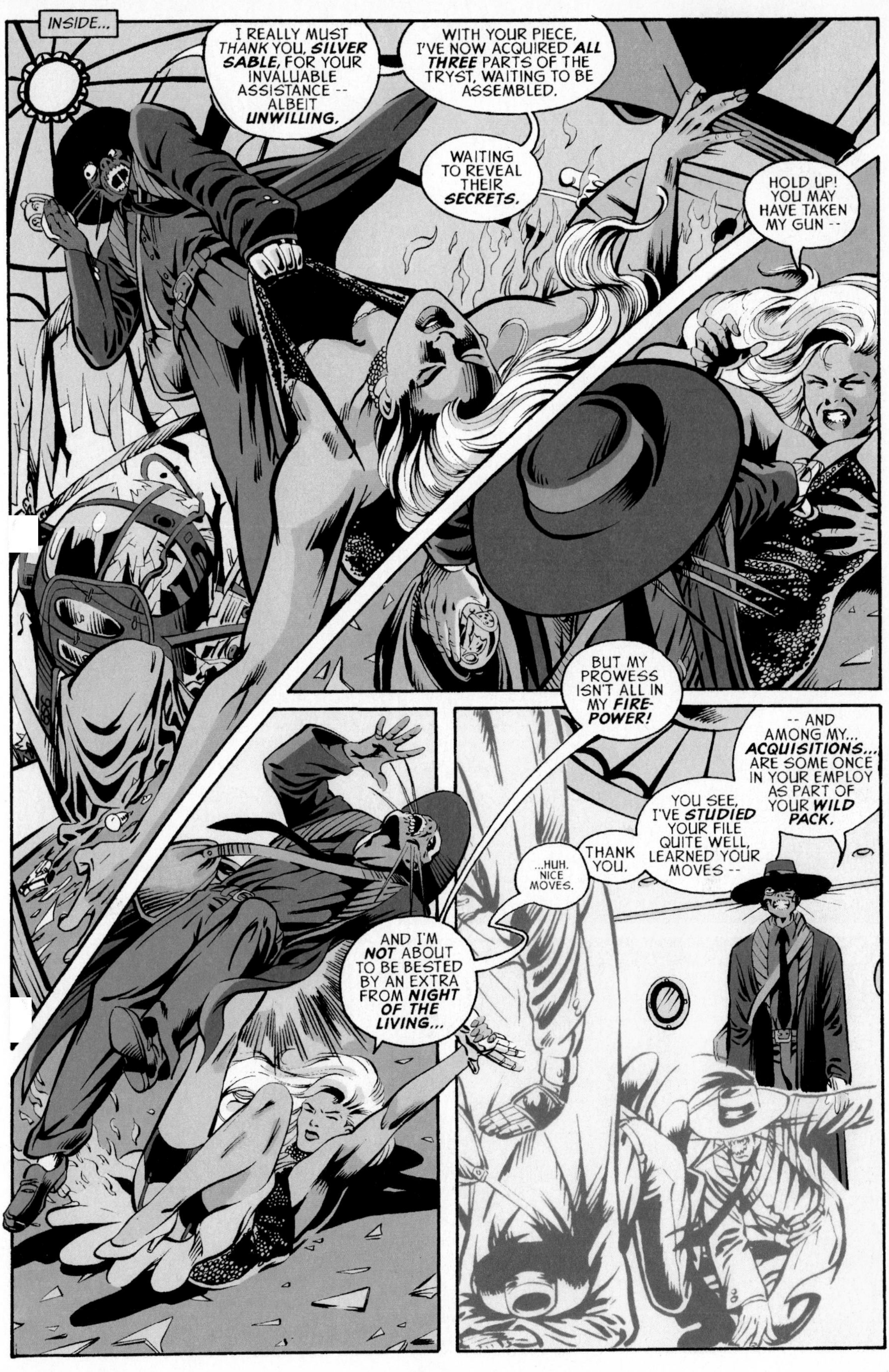

INSIDE...
I REALLY MUST THANK YOU, SILVER SABLE, FOR YOUR INVALUABLE ASSISTANCE -- ALBEIT UNWILLING.
WITH YOUR PIECE, I'VE NOW ACQUIRED ALL THREE PARTS OF THE TRYST, WAITING TO BE ASSEMBLED.
WAITING TO REVEAL THEIR SECRETS.
HOLD UP! YOU MAY HAVE TAKEN MY GUN --
BUT MY PROWESS ISN'T ALL IN MY FIRE-POWER!
AND I'M NOT ABOUT TO BE BESTED BY AN EXTRA FROM NIGHT OF THE LIVING...
...HUH. NICE MOVES.
THANK YOU.
YOU SEE, I'VE STUDIED YOUR FILE QUITE WELL, LEARNED YOUR MOVES --
-- AND AMONG MY... ACQUISITIONS... ARE SOME ONCE IN YOUR EMPLOY AS PART OF YOUR WILD PACK.

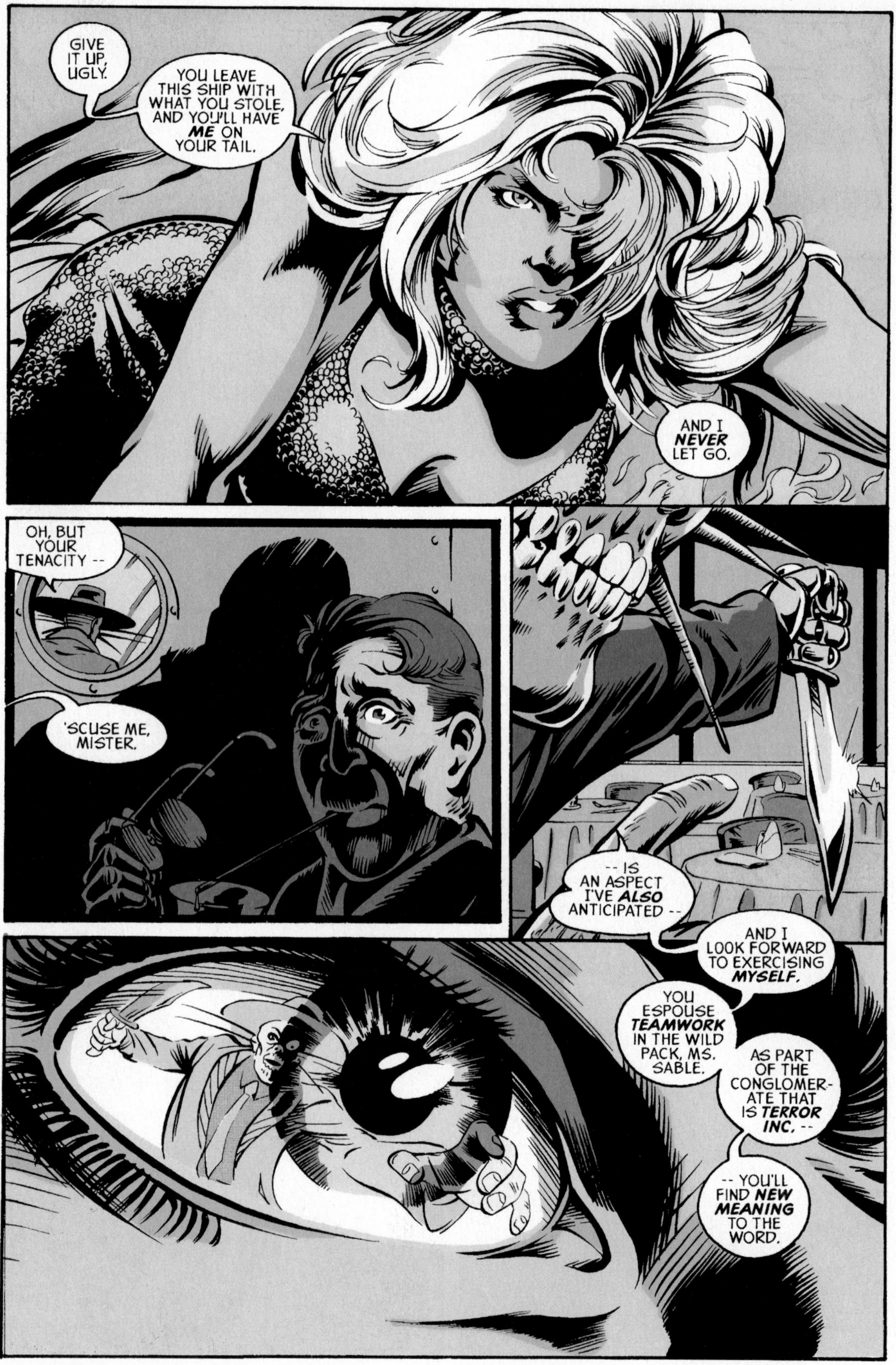
GIVE IT UP, UGLY.
YOU LEAVE THIS SHIP WITH WHAT YOU STOLE, AND YOU'LL HAVE *ME* ON YOUR TAIL.
AND I *NEVER* LET GO.
OH, BUT YOUR TENACITY --
'SCUSE ME, MISTER.
-- IS AN ASPECT I'VE *ALSO* ANTICIPATED --
AND I LOOK FORWARD TO EXERCISING *MYSELF.*
YOU ESPOUSE *TEAMWORK* IN THE WILD PACK, MS. SABLE.
AS PART OF THE CONGLOMERATE THAT IS *TERROR INC.* --
-- YOU'LL FIND *NEW MEANING* TO THE WORD.

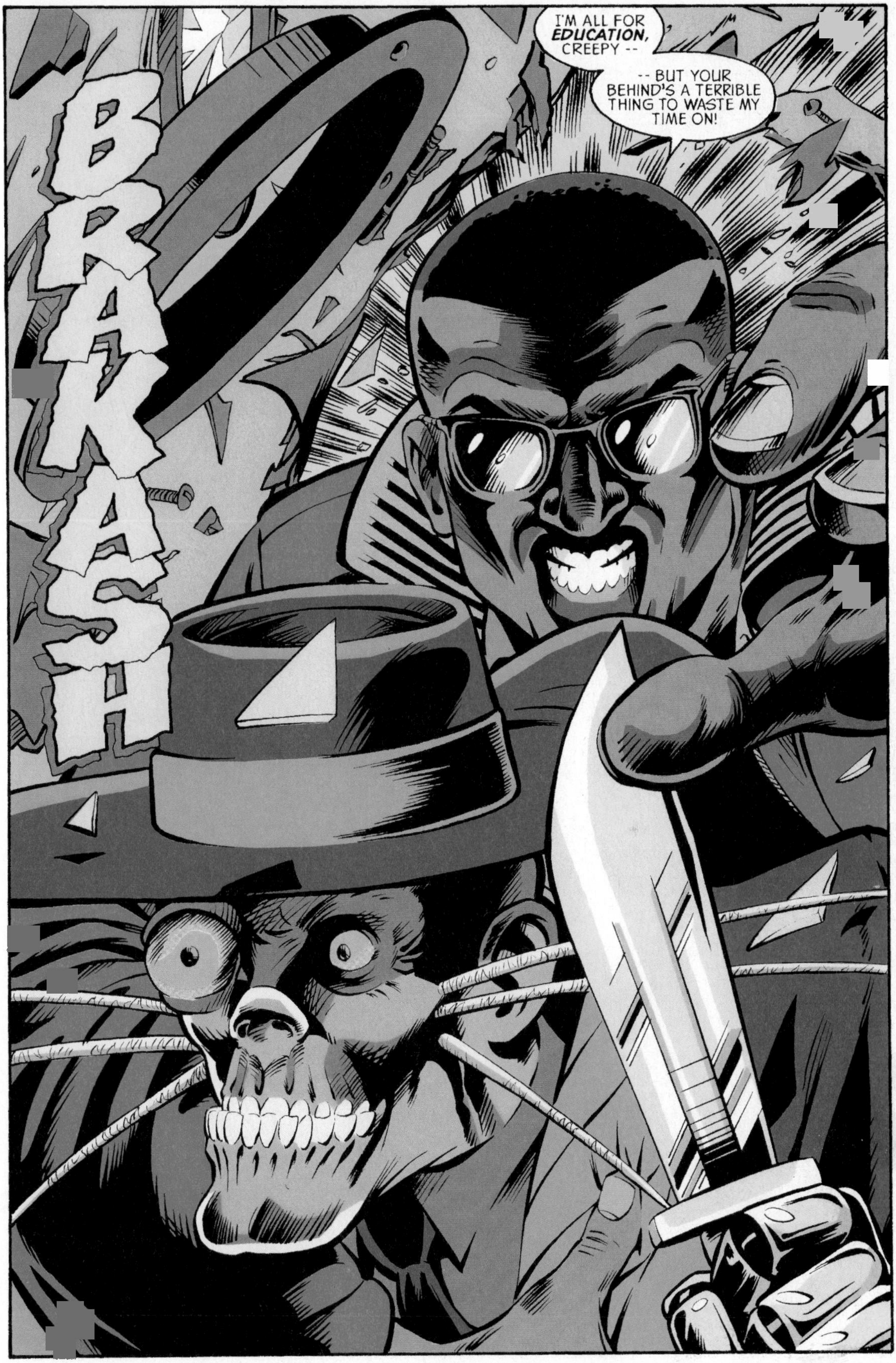
BRAKASH
I'M ALL FOR EDUCATION, CREEPY --
-- BUT YOUR BEHIND'S A TERRIBLE THING TO WASTE MY TIME ON!

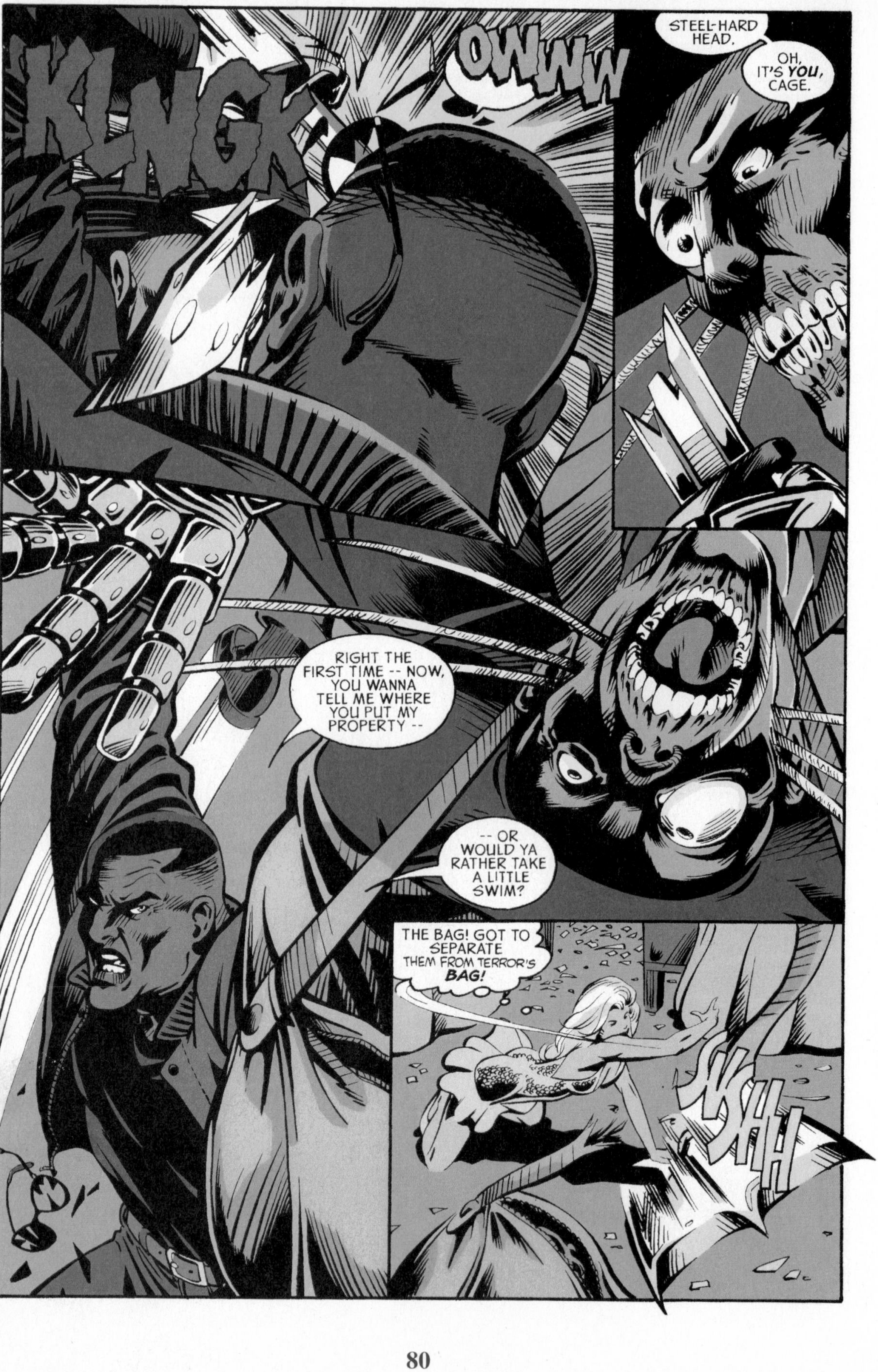
KLNGK
OWWW
STEEL-HARD HEAD.
OH, IT'S YOU, CAGE.
RIGHT THE FIRST TIME -- NOW, YOU WANNA TELL ME WHERE YOU PUT MY PROPERTY --
-- OR WOULD YA RATHER TAKE A LITTLE SWIM?
THE BAG! GOT TO SEPARATE THEM FROM TERROR'S BAG!
SSHH

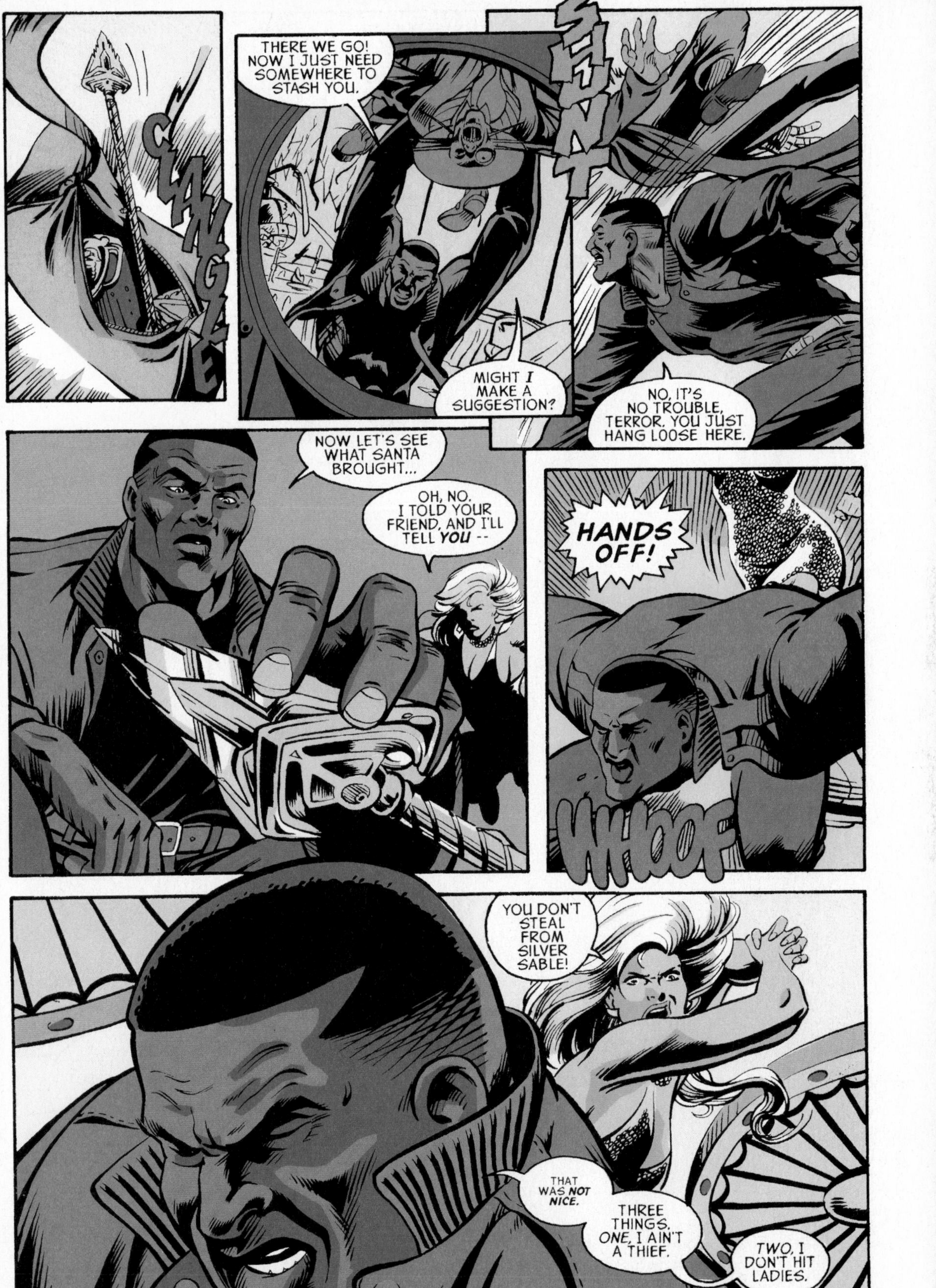
CLANGLE
THERE WE GO! NOW I JUST NEED SOMEWHERE TO STASH YOU.
MIGHT I MAKE A SUGGESTION?
SHUNT
NO, IT'S NO TROUBLE, TERROR. YOU JUST HANG LOOSE HERE.
NOW LET'S SEE WHAT SANTA BROUGHT...
OH, NO. I TOLD YOUR FRIEND, AND I'LL TELL YOU --
HANDS OFF!
WHOOF
YOU DON'T STEAL FROM SILVER SABLE!
THAT WAS NOT NICE.
THREE THINGS. ONE, I AIN'T A THIEF.
TWO, I DON'T HIT LADIES.

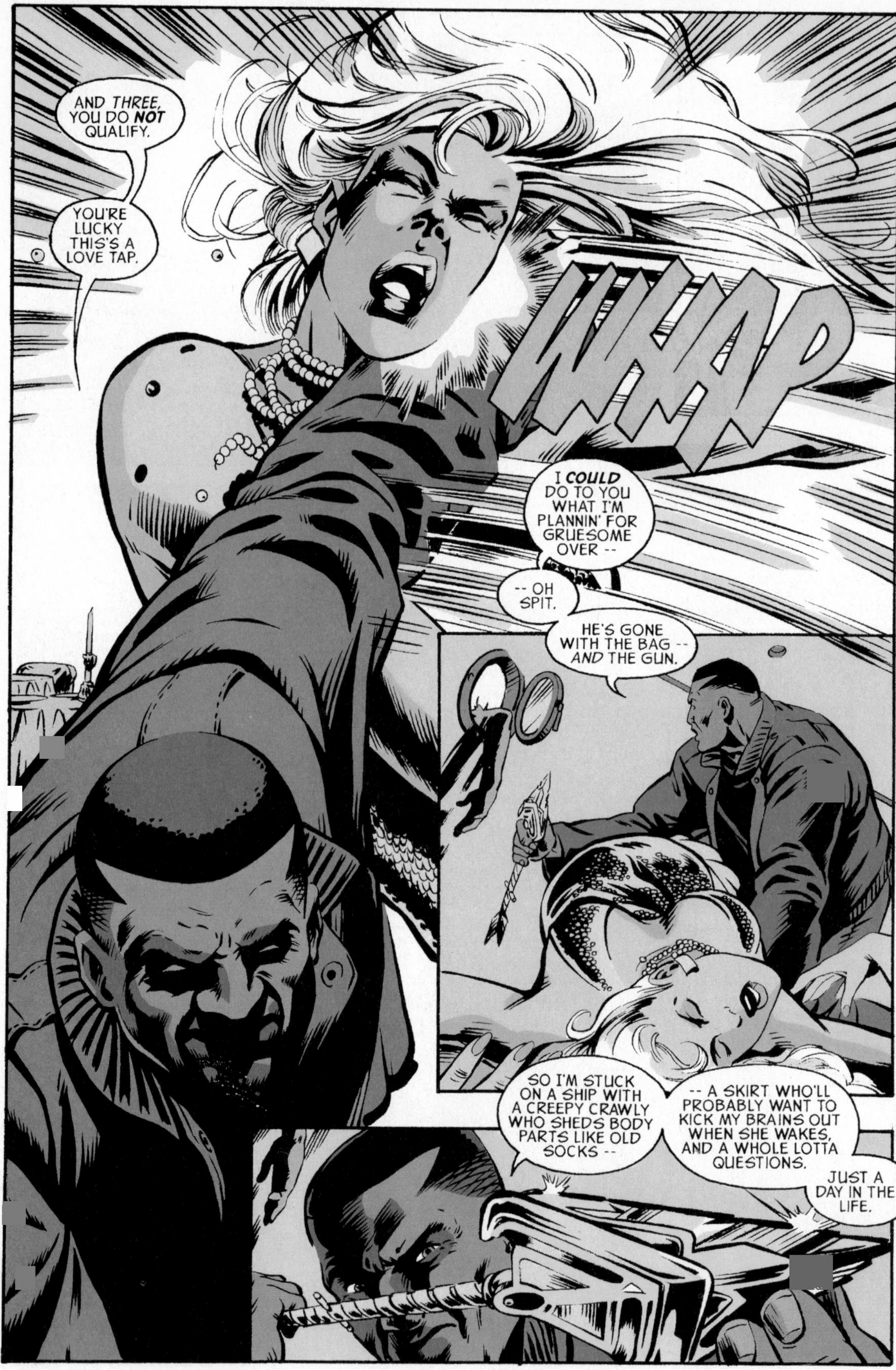
AND *THREE*, YOU DO ***NOT*** QUALIFY.
YOU'RE LUCKY THIS'S A LOVE TAP.
WHAP
I ***COULD*** DO TO YOU WHAT I'M PLANNIN' FOR GRUESOME OVER --
-- OH SPIT.
HE'S GONE WITH THE BAG -- *AND* THE GUN.
SO I'M STUCK ON A SHIP WITH A CREEPY CRAWLY WHO SHEDS BODY PARTS LIKE OLD SOCKS --
-- A SKIRT WHO'LL PROBABLY WANT TO KICK MY BRAINS OUT WHEN SHE WAKES, AND A WHOLE LOTTA QUESTIONS.
JUST A DAY IN THE LIFE.

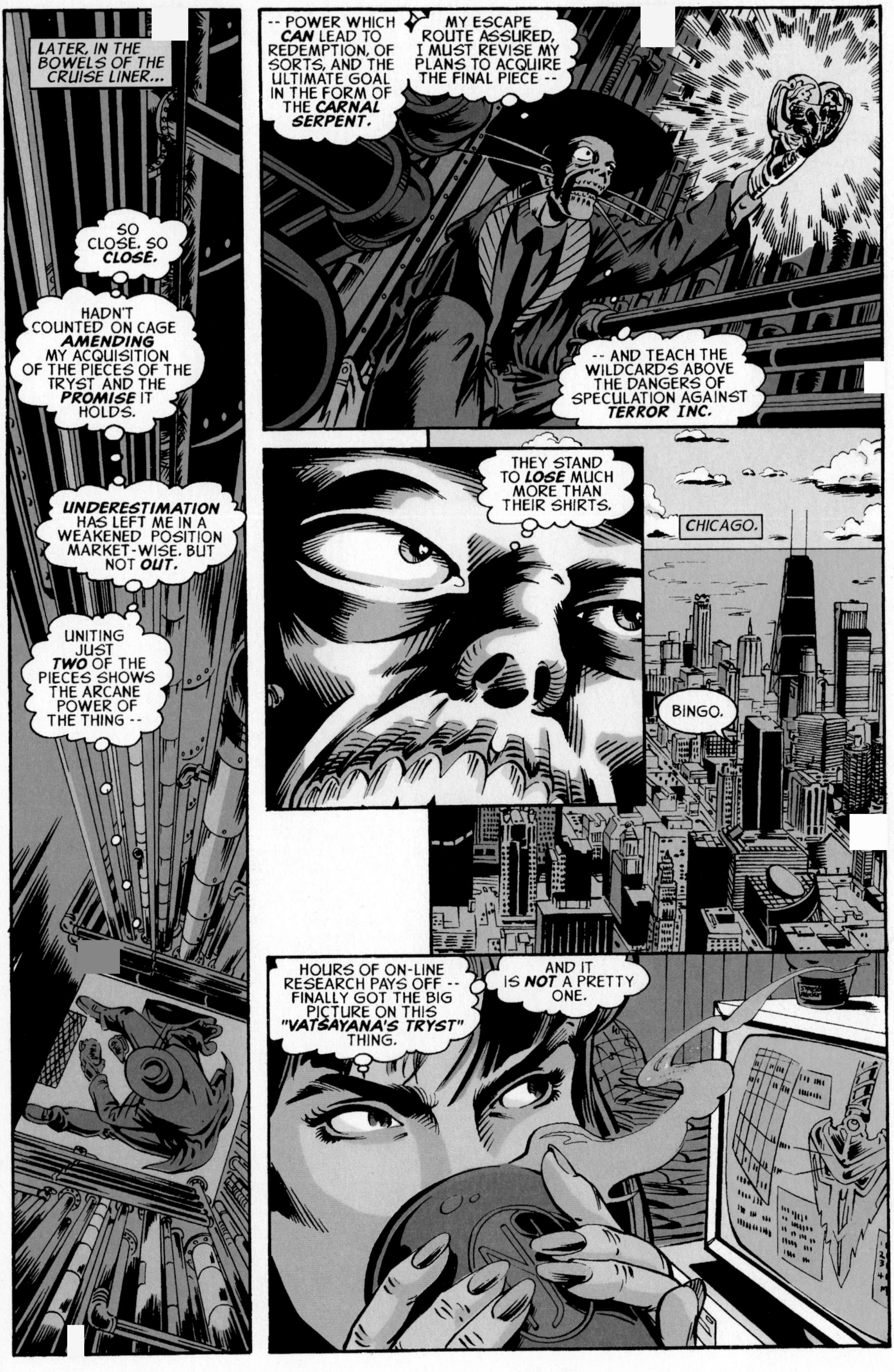
LATER, IN THE BOWELS OF THE CRUISE LINER...
SO CLOSE. SO CLOSE.
HADN'T COUNTED ON CAGE AMENDING MY ACQUISITION OF THE PIECES OF THE TRYST AND THE PROMISE IT HOLDS.
UNDERESTIMATION HAS LEFT ME IN A WEAKENED POSITION MARKET-WISE. BUT NOT OUT.
UNITING JUST TWO OF THE PIECES SHOWS THE ARCANE POWER OF THE THING --
-- POWER WHICH CAN LEAD TO REDEMPTION, OF SORTS, AND THE ULTIMATE GOAL IN THE FORM OF THE CARNAL SERPENT.
MY ESCAPE ROUTE ASSURED, I MUST REVISE MY PLANS TO ACQUIRE THE FINAL PIECE --
-- AND TEACH THE WILDCARDS ABOVE THE DANGERS OF SPECULATION AGAINST TERROR INC.
THEY STAND TO LOSE MUCH MORE THAN THEIR SHIRTS.
CHICAGO.
BINGO.
HOURS OF ON-LINE RESEARCH PAYS OFF -- FINALLY GOT THE BIG PICTURE ON THIS "VATSAYANA'S TRYST" THING.
AND IT IS NOT A PRETTY ONE.

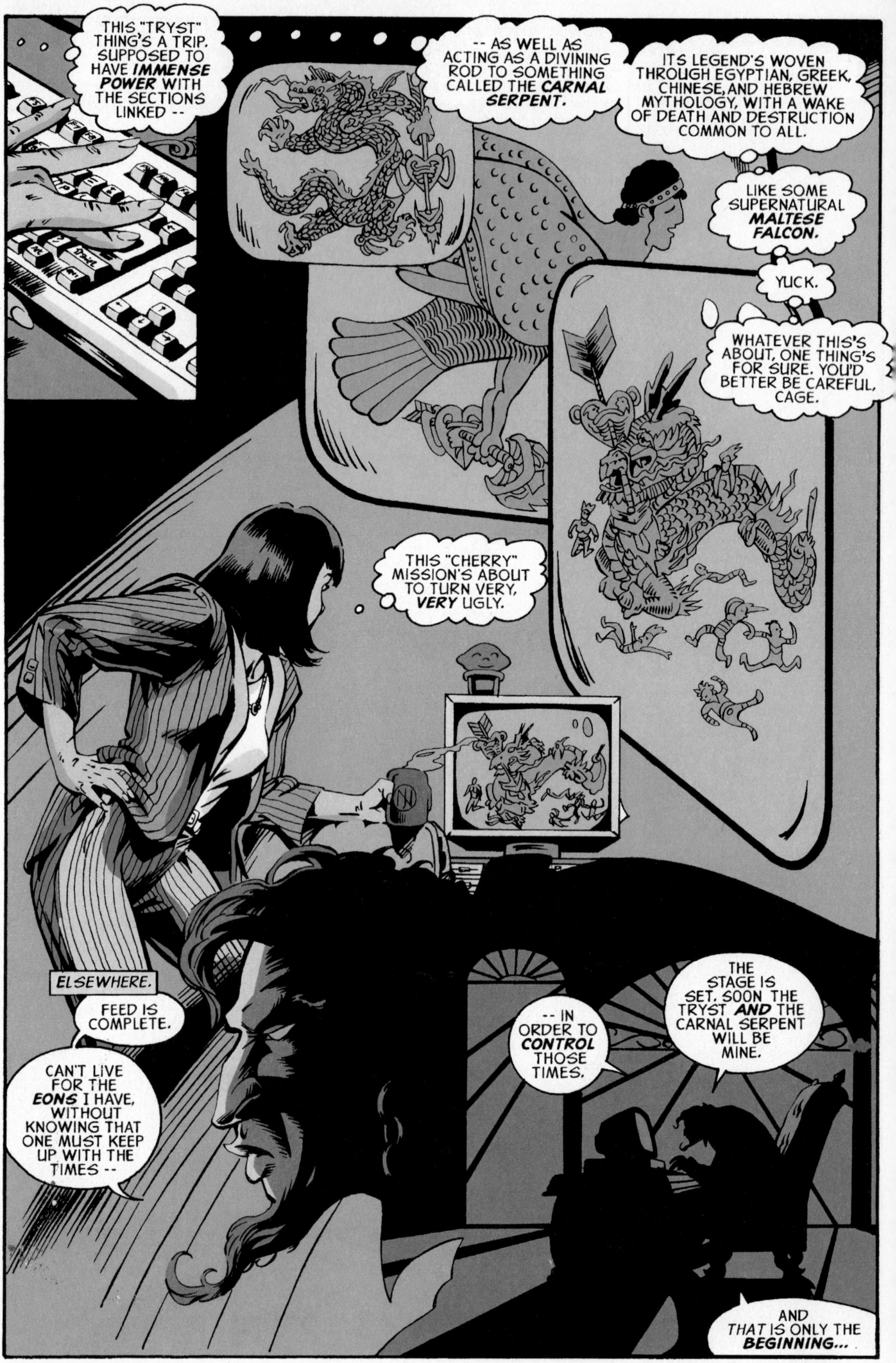

THIS "TRYST" THING'S A TRIP. SUPPOSED TO HAVE **IMMENSE POWER** WITH THE SECTIONS LINKED --
-- AS WELL AS ACTING AS A DIVINING ROD TO SOMETHING CALLED THE **CARNAL SERPENT.**
ITS LEGEND'S WOVEN THROUGH EGYPTIAN, GREEK, CHINESE, AND HEBREW MYTHOLOGY, WITH A WAKE OF DEATH AND DESTRUCTION COMMON TO ALL.
LIKE SOME SUPERNATURAL **MALTESE FALCON.**
YUCK.
WHATEVER THIS'S ABOUT, ONE THING'S FOR SURE. YOU'D BETTER BE CAREFUL, CAGE.
THIS "CHERRY" MISSION'S ABOUT TO TURN VERY, **VERY** UGLY.
ELSEWHERE.
FEED IS COMPLETE.
CAN'T LIVE FOR THE **EONS** I HAVE, WITHOUT KNOWING THAT ONE MUST KEEP UP WITH THE TIMES --
-- IN ORDER TO **CONTROL** THOSE TIMES.
THE STAGE IS SET. SOON THE TRYST **AND** THE CARNAL SERPENT WILL BE MINE.
AND *THAT* IS ONLY THE **BEGINNING...**

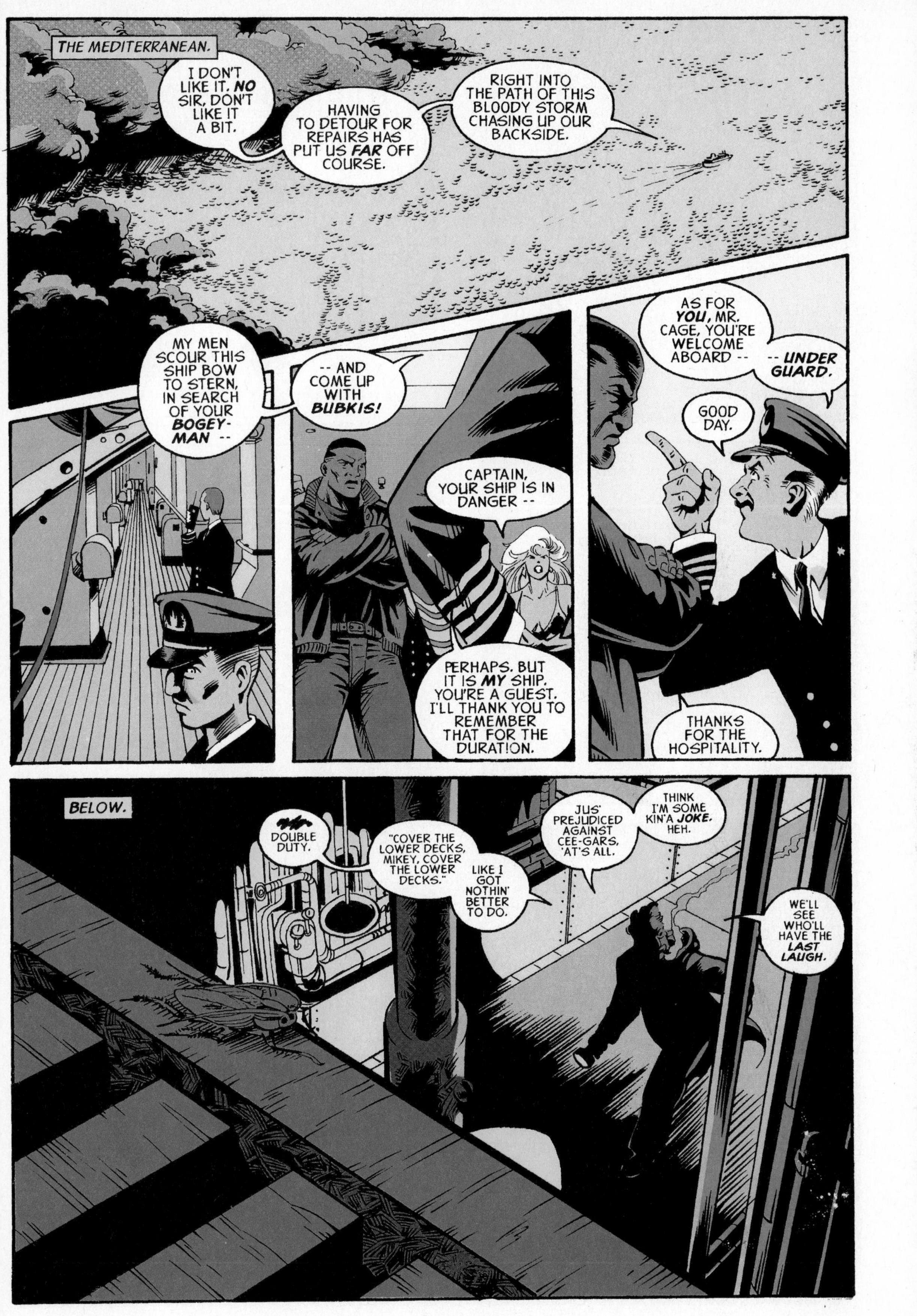
THE MEDITERRANEAN.
I DON'T LIKE IT. NO SIR, DON'T LIKE IT A BIT.
HAVING TO DETOUR FOR REPAIRS HAS PUT US FAR OFF COURSE.
RIGHT INTO THE PATH OF THIS BLOODY STORM CHASING UP OUR BACKSIDE.
MY MEN SCOUR THIS SHIP BOW TO STERN, IN SEARCH OF YOUR BOGEY-MAN --
-- AND COME UP WITH BUBKIS!
CAPTAIN, YOUR SHIP IS IN DANGER --
PERHAPS. BUT IT IS MY SHIP. YOU'RE A GUEST. I'LL THANK YOU TO REMEMBER THAT FOR THE DURATION.
AS FOR YOU, MR. CAGE, YOU'RE WELCOME ABOARD --
-- UNDER GUARD.
GOOD DAY.
THANKS FOR THE HOSPITALITY.
BELOW.
DOUBLE DUTY.
"COVER THE LOWER DECKS, MIKEY, COVER THE LOWER DECKS."
LIKE I GOT NOTHIN' BETTER TO DO.
JUS' PREJUDICED AGAINST CEE-GARS, 'AT'S ALL.
THINK I'M SOME KIN'A JOKE. HEH.
WE'LL SEE WHO'LL HAVE THE LAST LAUGH.

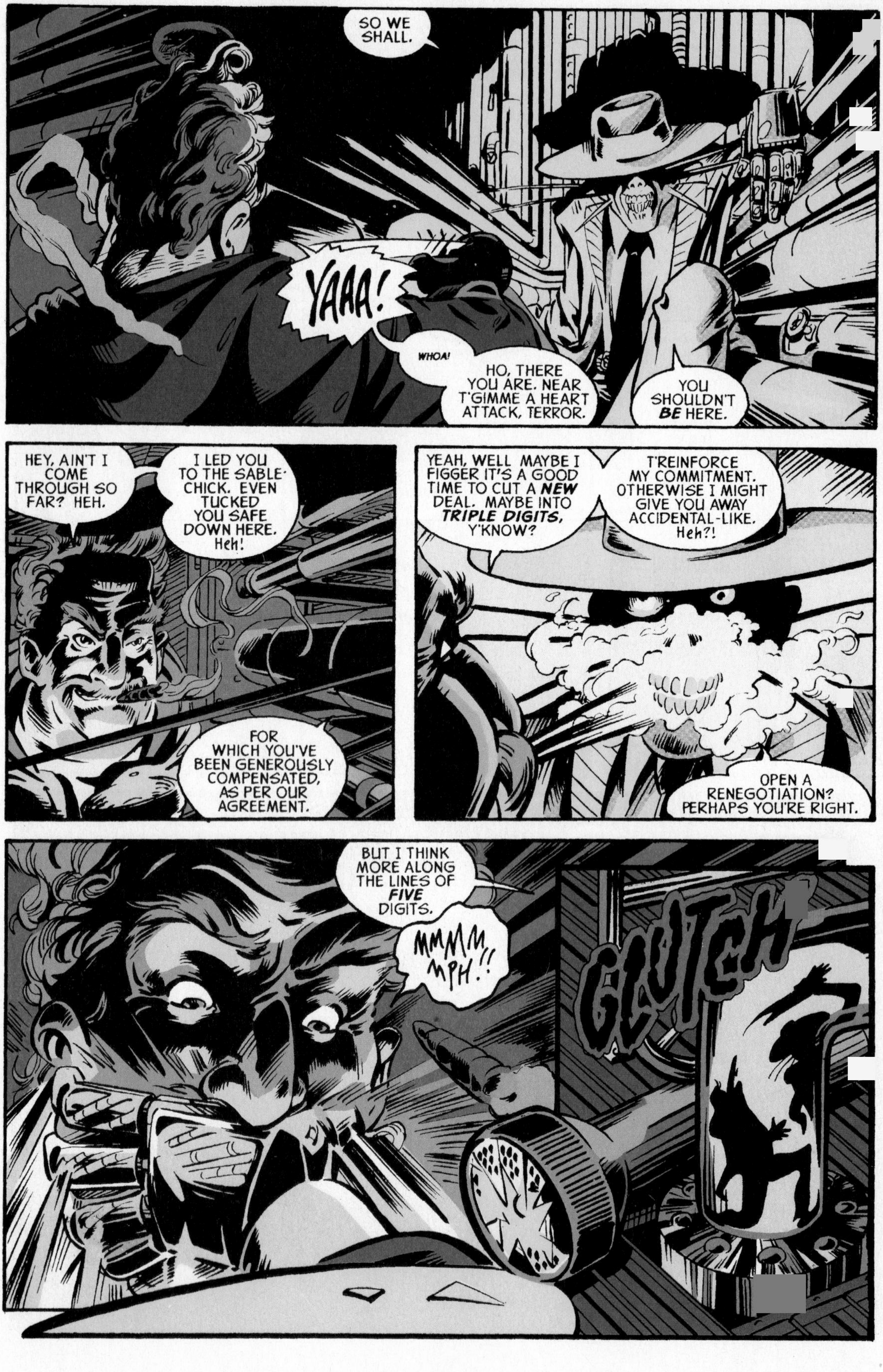
SO WE SHALL.
YAAA!
WHOA!
HO, THERE YOU ARE. NEAR T'GIMME A HEART ATTACK, TERROR.
YOU SHOULDN'T BE HERE.
HEY, AIN'T I COME THROUGH SO FAR? HEH.
I LED YOU TO THE SABLE-CHICK. EVEN TUCKED YOU SAFE DOWN HERE. Heh!
FOR WHICH YOU'VE BEEN GENEROUSLY COMPENSATED, AS PER OUR AGREEMENT.
YEAH, WELL MAYBE I FIGGER IT'S A GOOD TIME TO CUT A NEW DEAL. MAYBE INTO TRIPLE DIGITS, Y'KNOW?
T'REINFORCE MY COMMITMENT. OTHERWISE I MIGHT GIVE YOU AWAY ACCIDENTAL-LIKE. Heh?!
OPEN A RENEGOTIATION? PERHAPS YOU'RE RIGHT.
BUT I THINK MORE ALONG THE LINES OF FIVE DIGITS.
MMMM MPH!!
GLUTCH

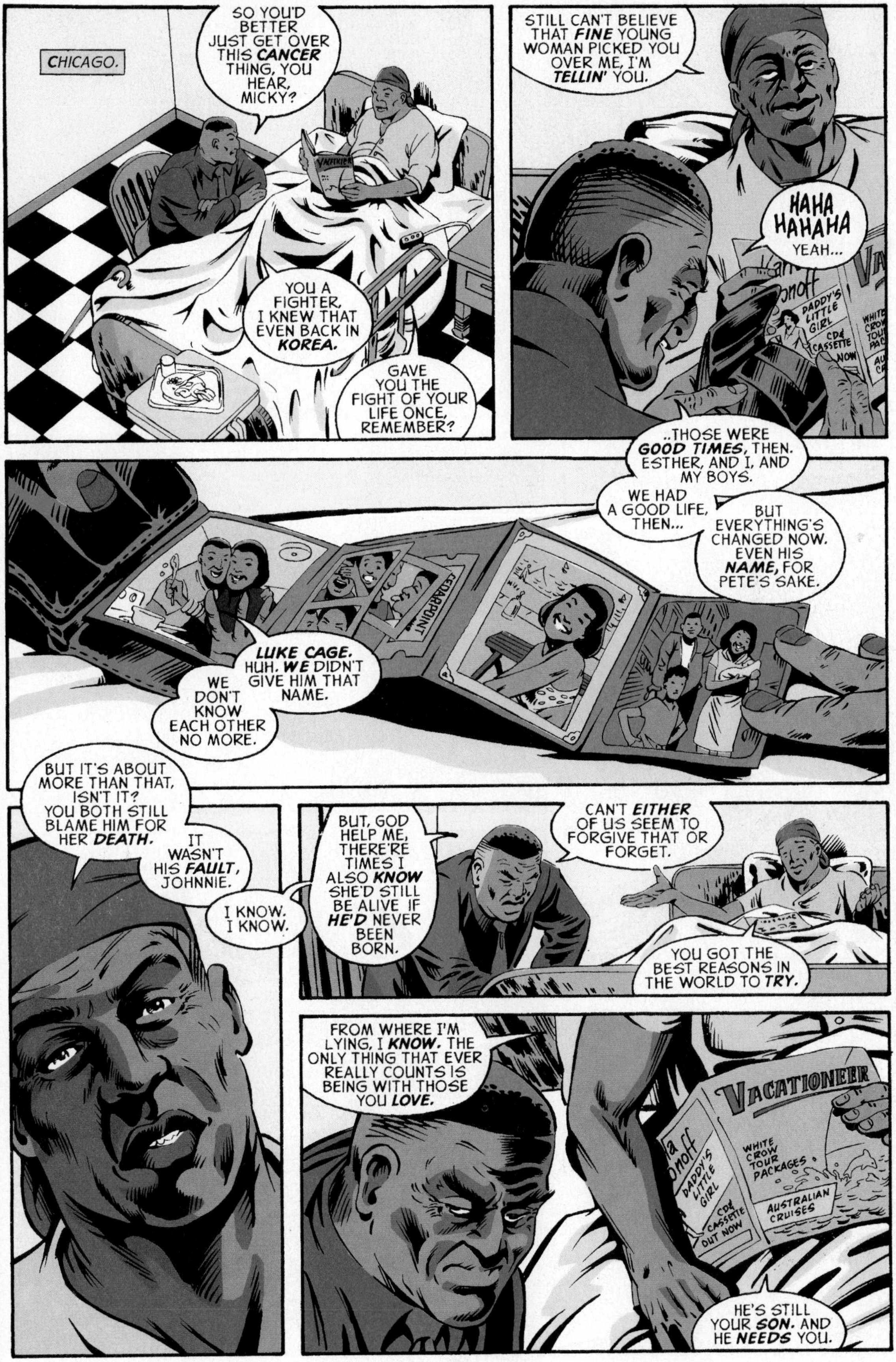
CHICAGO.
SO YOU'D BETTER JUST GET OVER THIS CANCER THING, YOU HEAR, MICKY?
YOU A FIGHTER, I KNEW THAT EVEN BACK IN KOREA.
GAVE YOU THE FIGHT OF YOUR LIFE ONCE, REMEMBER?
STILL CAN'T BELIEVE THAT FINE YOUNG WOMAN PICKED YOU OVER ME, I'M TELLIN' YOU.
HAHA HAHAHA YEAH...
DADDY'S LITTLE GIRL
CD& CASSETTE NOW
..THOSE WERE GOOD TIMES, THEN. ESTHER, AND I, AND MY BOYS.
WE HAD A GOOD LIFE, THEN...
BUT EVERYTHING'S CHANGED NOW. EVEN HIS NAME, FOR PETE'S SAKE.
CEDARPOINT
LUKE CAGE. HUH. WE DIDN'T GIVE HIM THAT NAME.
WE DON'T KNOW EACH OTHER NO MORE.
BUT IT'S ABOUT MORE THAN THAT, ISN'T IT? YOU BOTH STILL BLAME HIM FOR HER DEATH.
IT WASN'T HIS FAULT, JOHNNIE.
I KNOW. I KNOW.
BUT, GOD HELP ME, THERE'RE TIMES I ALSO KNOW SHE'D STILL BE ALIVE IF HE'D NEVER BEEN BORN.
CAN'T EITHER OF US SEEM TO FORGIVE THAT OR FORGET.
YOU GOT THE BEST REASONS IN THE WORLD TO TRY.
FROM WHERE I'M LYING, I KNOW. THE ONLY THING THAT EVER REALLY COUNTS IS BEING WITH THOSE YOU LOVE.
VACATIONEER
DADDY'S LITTLE GIRL
CD& CASSETTE OUT NOW
WHITE CROW TOUR PACKAGES
AUSTRALIAN CRUISES
HE'S STILL YOUR SON. AND HE NEEDS YOU.

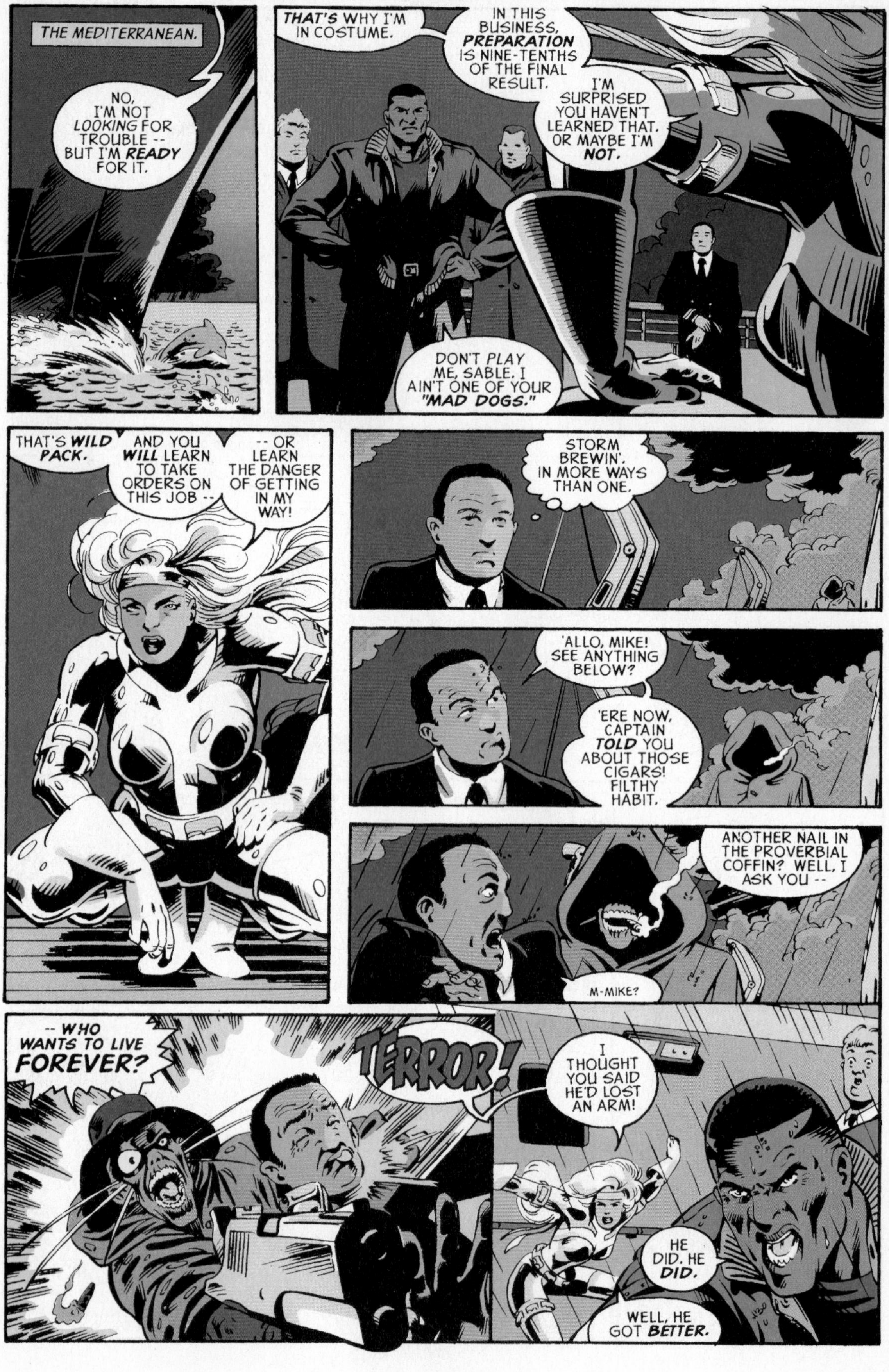
THE MEDITERRANEAN.
NO, I'M NOT LOOKING FOR TROUBLE -- BUT I'M READY FOR IT.
THAT'S WHY I'M IN COSTUME.
IN THIS BUSINESS, PREPARATION IS NINE-TENTHS OF THE FINAL RESULT.
I'M SURPRISED YOU HAVEN'T LEARNED THAT. OR MAYBE I'M NOT.
DON'T PLAY ME, SABLE. I AIN'T ONE OF YOUR "MAD DOGS."
THAT'S WILD PACK.
AND YOU WILL LEARN TO TAKE ORDERS ON THIS JOB --
-- OR LEARN THE DANGER OF GETTING IN MY WAY!
STORM BREWIN'. IN MORE WAYS THAN ONE.
'ALLO, MIKE! SEE ANYTHING BELOW?
'ERE NOW, CAPTAIN TOLD YOU ABOUT THOSE CIGARS! FILTHY HABIT.
ANOTHER NAIL IN THE PROVERBIAL COFFIN? WELL, I ASK YOU --
M-MIKE?
-- WHO WANTS TO LIVE FOREVER?
TERROR!
I THOUGHT YOU SAID HE'D LOST AN ARM!
HE DID. HE DID.
WELL, HE GOT BETTER.

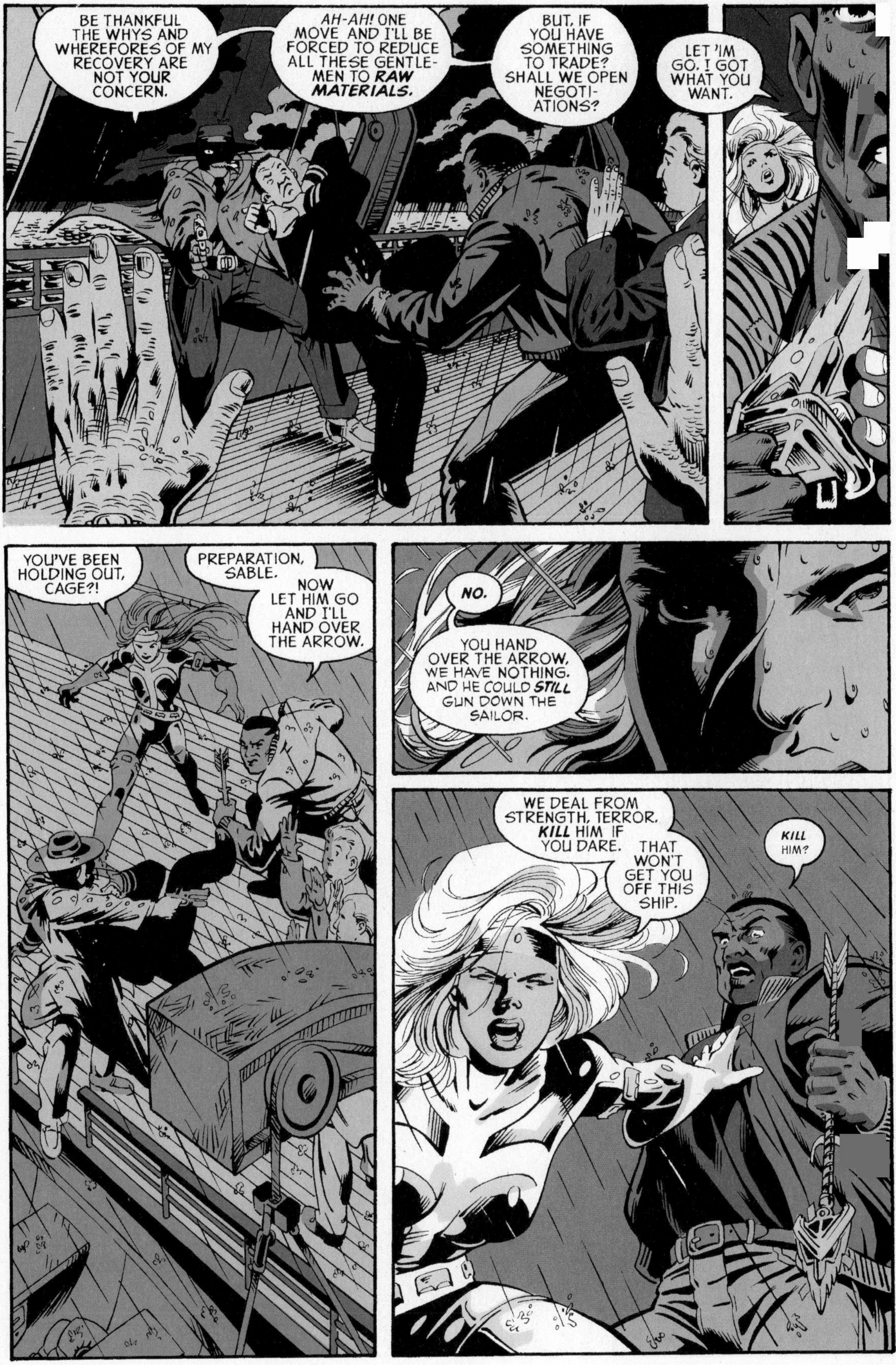
BE THANKFUL THE WHYS AND WHEREFORES OF MY RECOVERY ARE NOT YOUR CONCERN.
AH-AH! ONE MOVE AND I'LL BE FORCED TO REDUCE ALL THESE GENTLE-MEN TO RAW MATERIALS.
BUT, IF YOU HAVE SOMETHING TO TRADE? SHALL WE OPEN NEGOTI-ATIONS?
LET 'IM GO. I GOT WHAT YOU WANT.
YOU'VE BEEN HOLDING OUT, CAGE?!
PREPARATION, SABLE.
NOW LET HIM GO AND I'LL HAND OVER THE ARROW.
NO.
YOU HAND OVER THE ARROW, WE HAVE NOTHING. AND HE COULD STILL GUN DOWN THE SAILOR.
WE DEAL FROM STRENGTH, TERROR. KILL HIM IF YOU DARE.
THAT WON'T GET YOU OFF THIS SHIP.
KILL HIM?

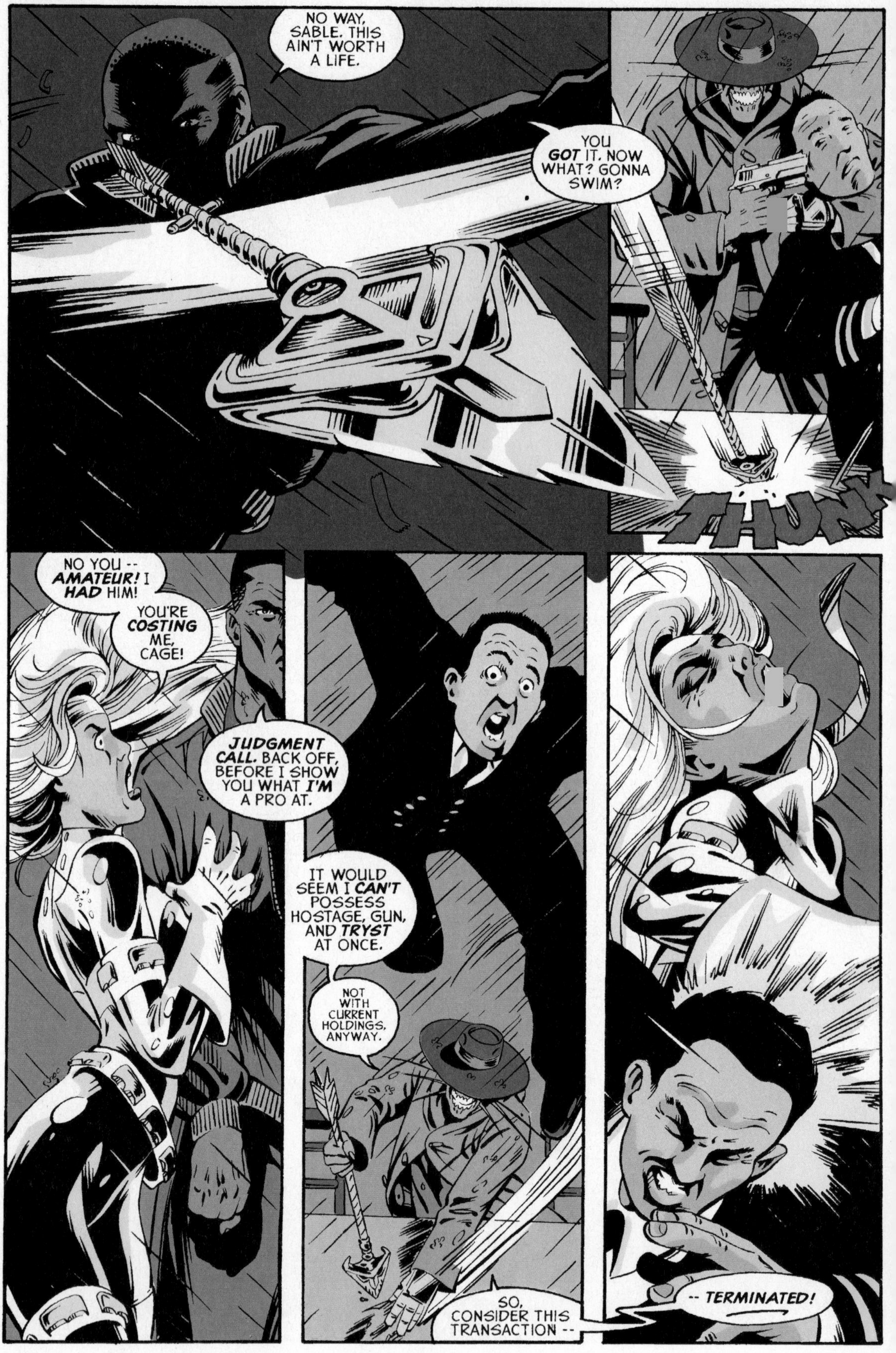
NO WAY, SABLE. THIS AIN'T WORTH A LIFE.
YOU GOT IT. NOW WHAT? GONNA SWIM?
THUNK
NO YOU -- AMATEUR! I HAD HIM!
YOU'RE COSTING ME, CAGE!
JUDGMENT CALL. BACK OFF, BEFORE I SHOW YOU WHAT I'M A PRO AT.
IT WOULD SEEM I CAN'T POSSESS HOSTAGE, GUN, AND TRYST AT ONCE.
NOT WITH CURRENT HOLDINGS, ANYWAY.
SO, CONSIDER THIS TRANSACTION --
-- TERMINATED!

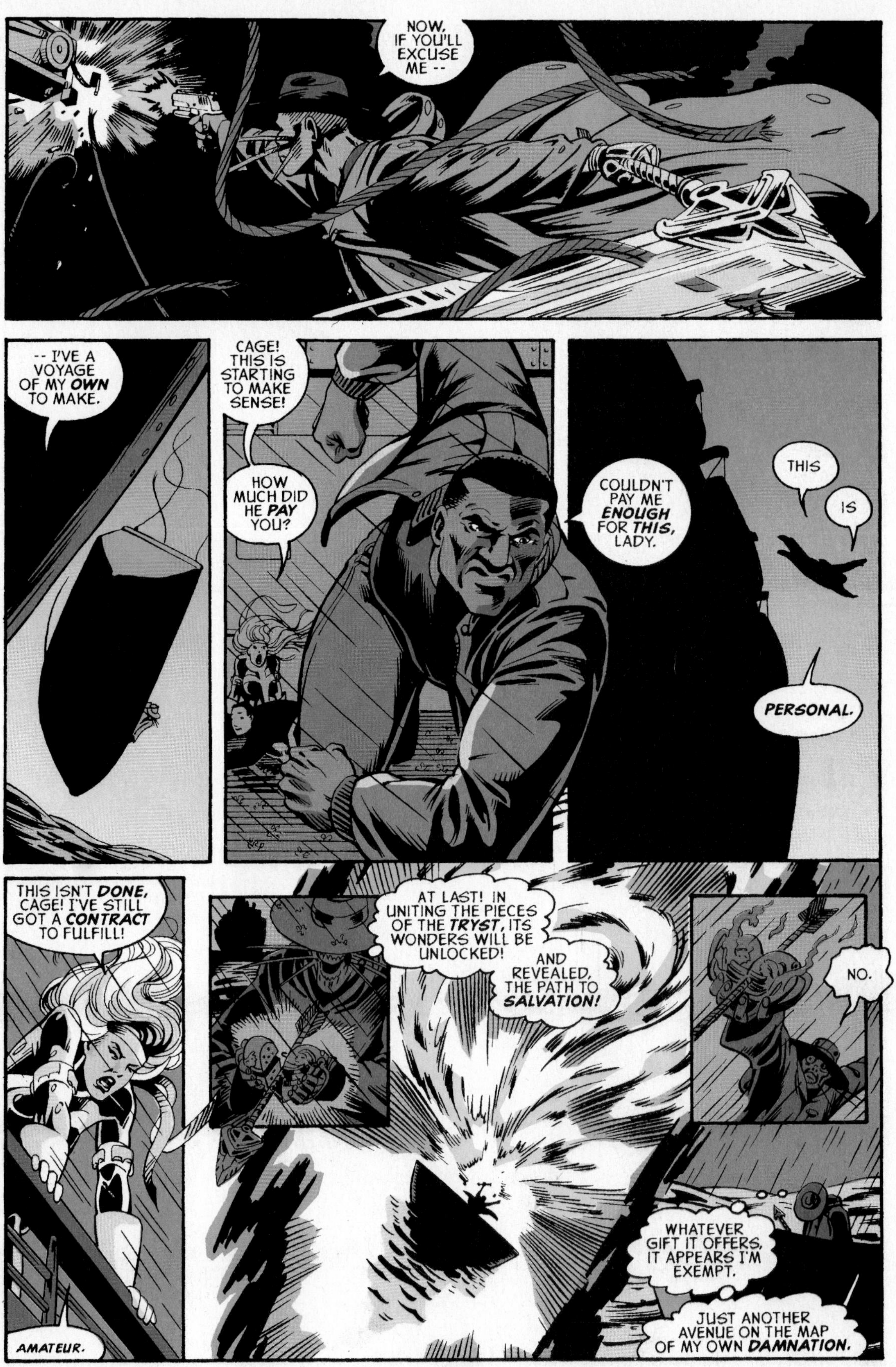
NOW, IF YOU'LL EXCUSE ME --
-- I'VE A VOYAGE OF MY OWN TO MAKE.
CAGE! THIS IS STARTING TO MAKE SENSE!
HOW MUCH DID HE PAY YOU?
COULDN'T PAY ME ENOUGH FOR THIS, LADY.
THIS
IS
PERSONAL.
THIS ISN'T DONE, CAGE! I'VE STILL GOT A CONTRACT TO FULFILL!
AMATEUR.
AT LAST! IN UNITING THE PIECES OF THE TRYST, ITS WONDERS WILL BE UNLOCKED!
AND REVEALED, THE PATH TO SALVATION!
NO.
WHATEVER GIFT IT OFFERS, IT APPEARS I'M EXEMPT.
JUST ANOTHER AVENUE ON THE MAP OF MY OWN DAMNATION.

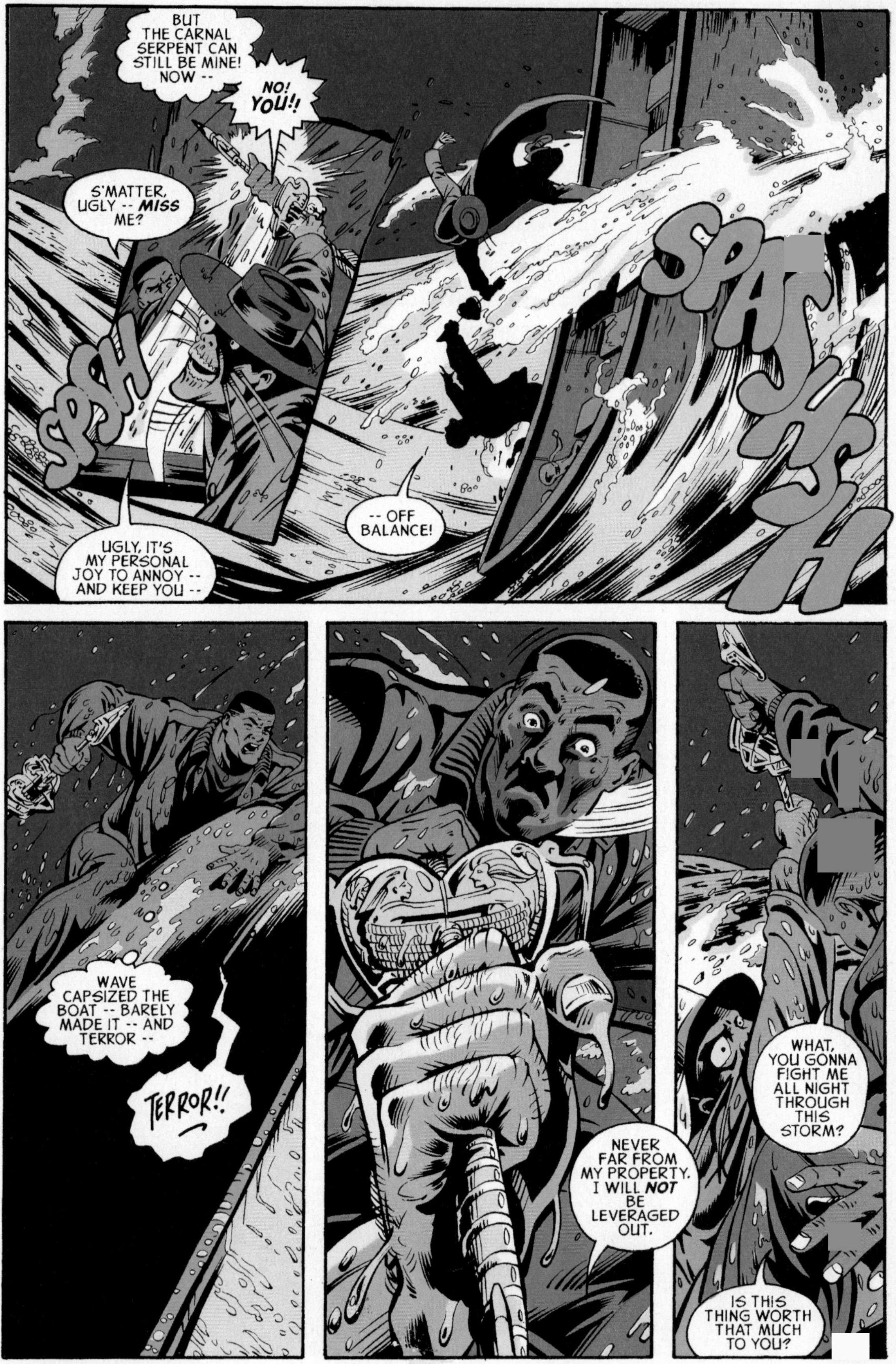

BUT THE CARNAL SERPENT CAN STILL BE MINE! NOW --
NO! YOU!!
S'MATTER, UGLY -- **MISS** ME?
SPOSH
UGLY, IT'S MY PERSONAL JOY TO ANNOY -- AND KEEP YOU --
-- OFF BALANCE!
WAVE CAPSIZED THE BOAT -- BARELY MADE IT -- AND TERROR --
TERROR!!
NEVER FAR FROM MY PROPERTY. I WILL **NOT** BE LEVERAGED OUT.
WHAT, YOU GONNA FIGHT ME ALL NIGHT THROUGH THIS STORM?
IS THIS THING WORTH THAT MUCH TO YOU?

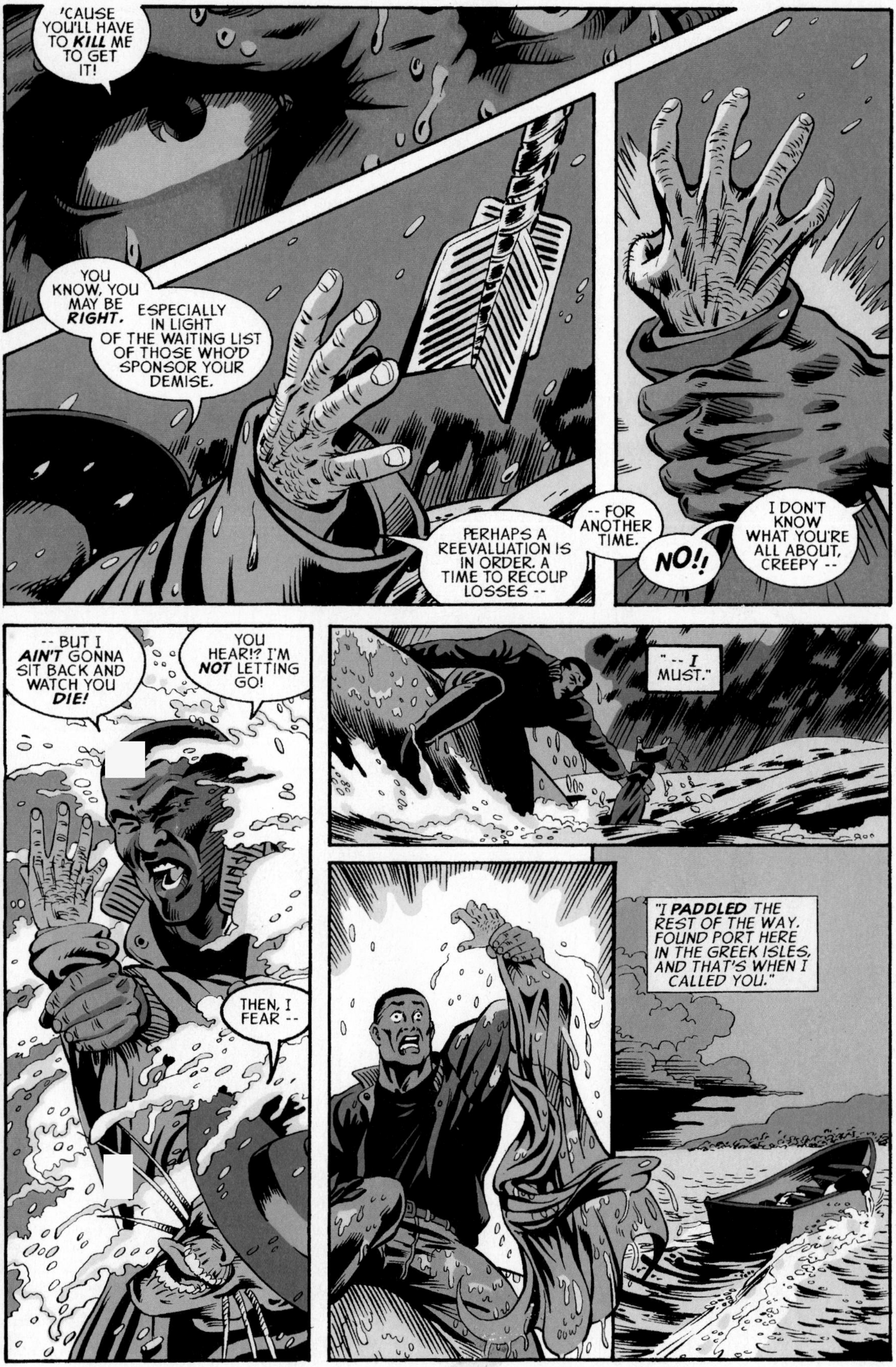
'CAUSE YOU'LL HAVE TO KILL ME TO GET IT!
YOU KNOW, YOU MAY BE RIGHT.
ESPECIALLY IN LIGHT OF THE WAITING LIST OF THOSE WHO'D SPONSOR YOUR DEMISE.
PERHAPS A REEVALUATION IS IN ORDER. A TIME TO RECOUP LOSSES --
-- FOR ANOTHER TIME.
NO!!
I DON'T KNOW WHAT YOU'RE ALL ABOUT, CREEPY --
-- BUT I AIN'T GONNA SIT BACK AND WATCH YOU DIE!
YOU HEAR!? I'M NOT LETTING GO!
THEN, I FEAR --
" -- I MUST."
"I PADDLED THE REST OF THE WAY. FOUND PORT HERE IN THE GREEK ISLES, AND THAT'S WHEN I CALLED YOU."

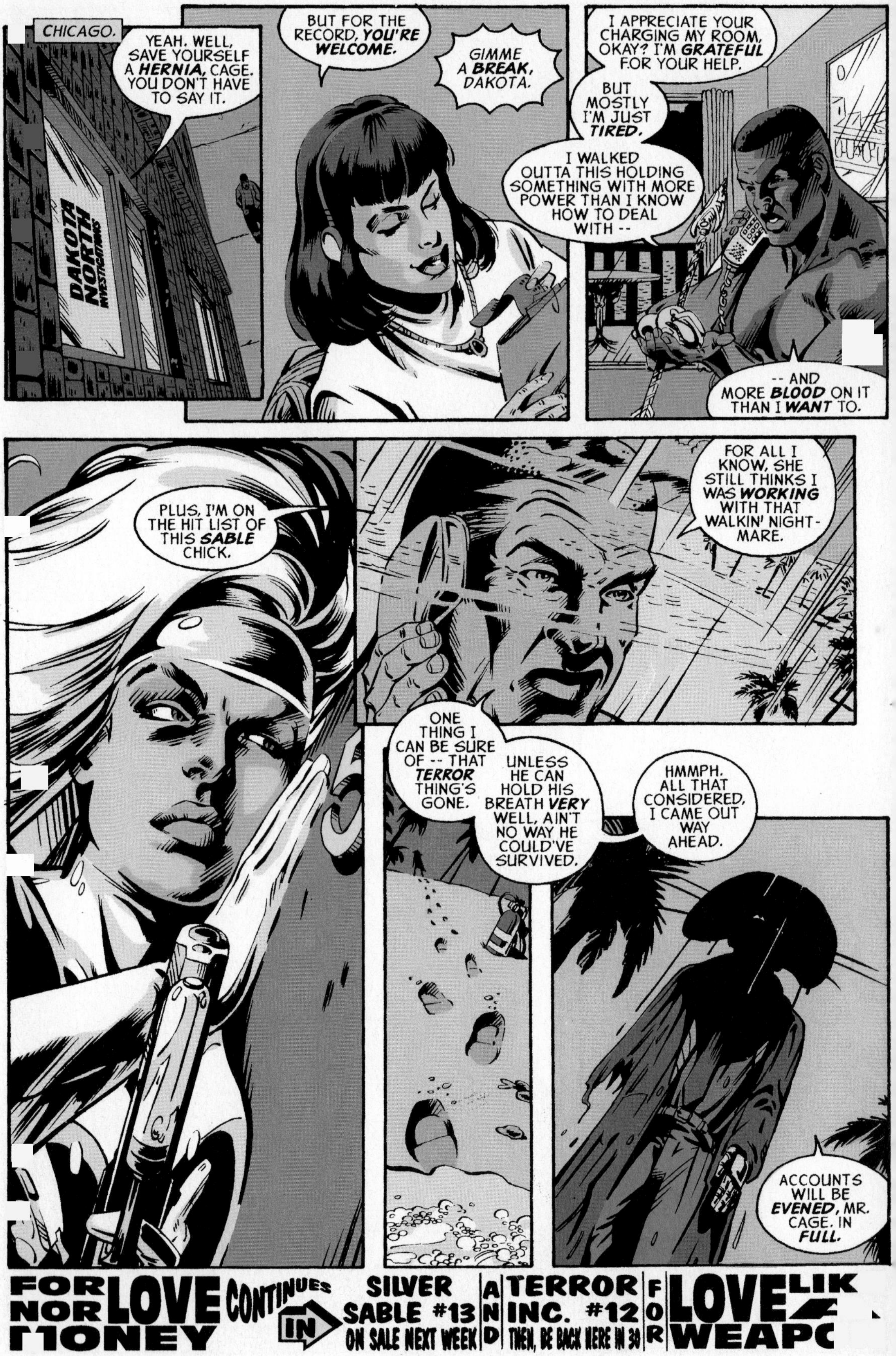

CHICAGO.
YEAH. WELL, SAVE YOURSELF A HERNIA, CAGE. YOU DON'T HAVE TO SAY IT.
DAKOTA NORTH INVESTIGATIONS
BUT FOR THE RECORD, YOU'RE WELCOME.
GIMME A BREAK, DAKOTA.
I APPRECIATE YOUR CHARGING MY ROOM, OKAY? I'M GRATEFUL FOR YOUR HELP.
BUT MOSTLY I'M JUST TIRED.
I WALKED OUTTA THIS HOLDING SOMETHING WITH MORE POWER THAN I KNOW HOW TO DEAL WITH --
-- AND MORE BLOOD ON IT THAN I WANT TO.
PLUS, I'M ON THE HIT LIST OF THIS SABLE CHICK.
FOR ALL I KNOW, SHE STILL THINKS I WAS WORKING WITH THAT WALKIN' NIGHT-MARE.
ONE THING I CAN BE SURE OF -- THAT TERROR THING'S GONE.
UNLESS HE CAN HOLD HIS BREATH VERY WELL, AIN'T NO WAY HE COULD'VE SURVIVED.
HMMPH. ALL THAT CONSIDERED, I CAME OUT WAY AHEAD.
ACCOUNTS WILL BE EVENED, MR. CAGE. IN FULL.

FOR LOVE NOR MONEY CONTINUES IN SILVER SABLE #13 ON SALE NEXT WEEK AND TERROR INC. #12 THEN, BE BACK HERE IN 30 FOR LOVE LIKE A WEAPO

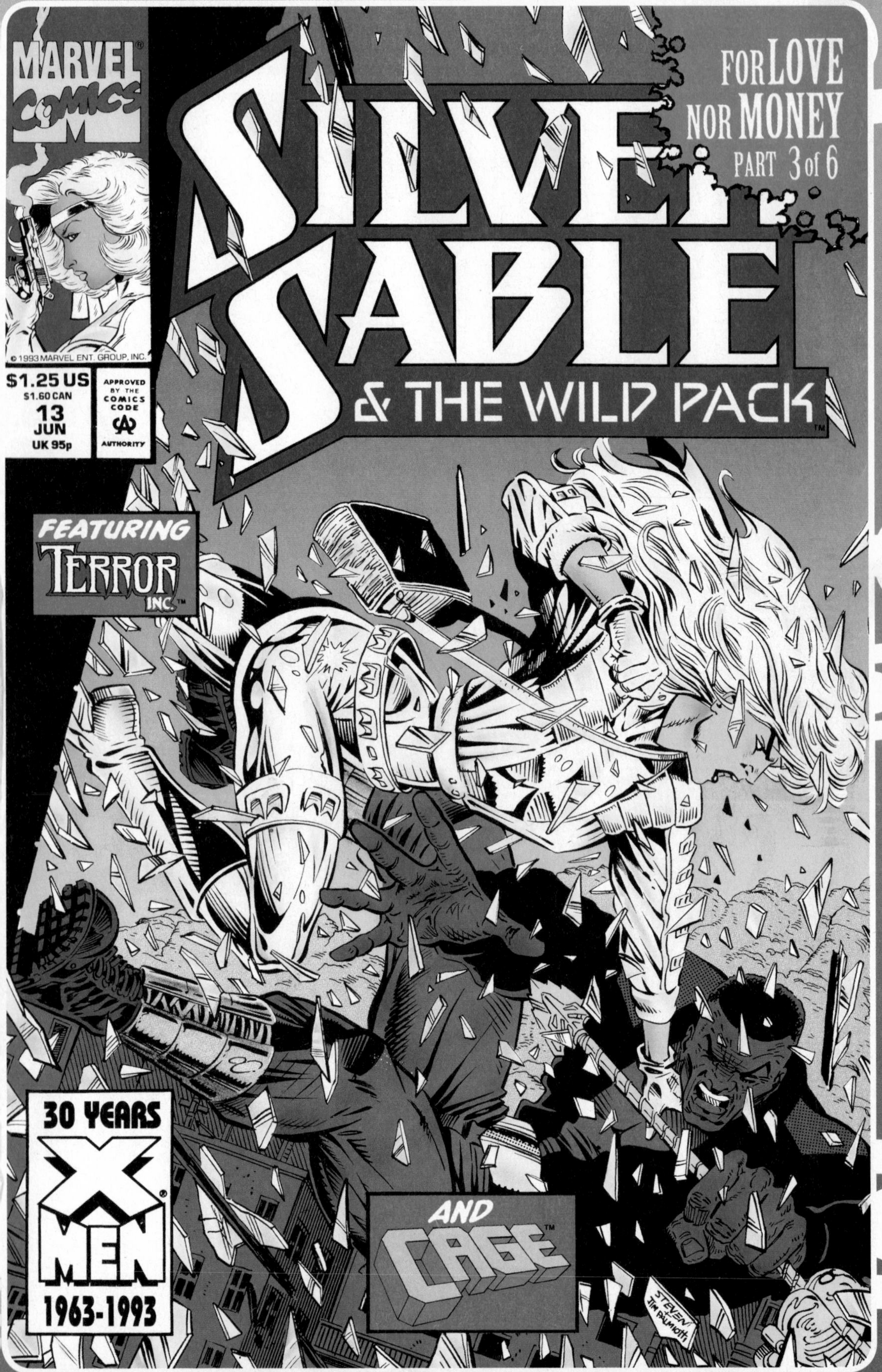
MARVEL COMICS
© 1993 MARVEL ENT. GROUP, INC.
$1.25 US
$1.60 CAN
13
JUN
UK 95p
APPROVED BY THE COMICS CODE AUTHORITY
FOR LOVE NOR MONEY
PART 3 of 6
SILVE
SABLE
& THE WILD PACK
FEATURING
TERROR INC.
30 YEARS
X-MEN
1963-1993
AND
CAGE

RELENTLESSLY TRAINED IN MULTIPLE FORMS OF HAND-TO-HAND AND ARMED COMBAT, SILVER SABL WAS DESTINED TO INHERIT THE COMMAND OF HER FATHER'S PROFESSIONAL SOLDIER UNIT, TH WILD PACK. UNDER THE AUSPICES OF SILVER SABLE INTERNATIONAL, SHE HAS SINCE TRANSFORME THEM INTO THE ULTIMATE MERCENARY COMBAT FORCE, NOW THE ECONOMIC FOUNDATION OF HER BELOVE HOMELAND, SYMKARIA.

STAN LEE PRESENTS. . .SILVER SABLE AND THE WILD PAC

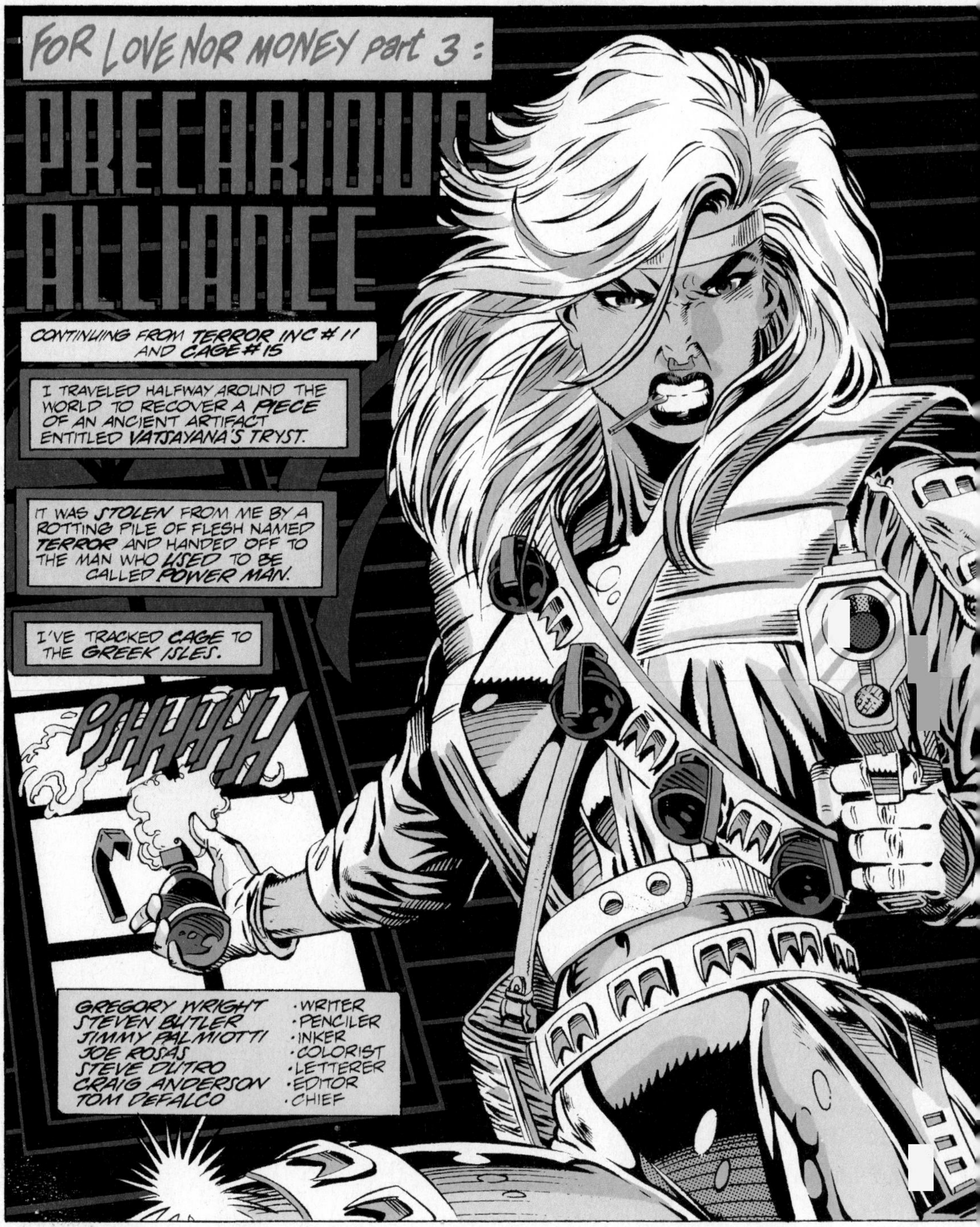
FOR LOVE NOR MONEY part 3:
PRECARIOUS ALLIANCE
CONTINUING FROM TERROR INC #11 AND CAGE #15
I TRAVELED HALFWAY AROUND THE WORLD TO RECOVER A PIECE OF AN ANCIENT ARTIFACT ENTITLED VATSAYANA'S TRYST.
IT WAS STOLEN FROM ME BY A ROTTING PILE OF FLESH NAMED TERROR AND HANDED OFF TO THE MAN WHO USED TO BE CALLED POWER MAN.
I'VE TRACKED CAGE TO THE GREEK ISLES.
PHHHH
GREGORY WRIGHT ·WRITER
STEVEN BUTLER ·PENCILER
JIMMY PALMIOTTI ·INKER
JOE ROSAS ·COLORIST
STEVE DUTRO ·LETTERER
CRAIG ANDERSON ·EDITOR
TOM DEFALCO ·CHIEF

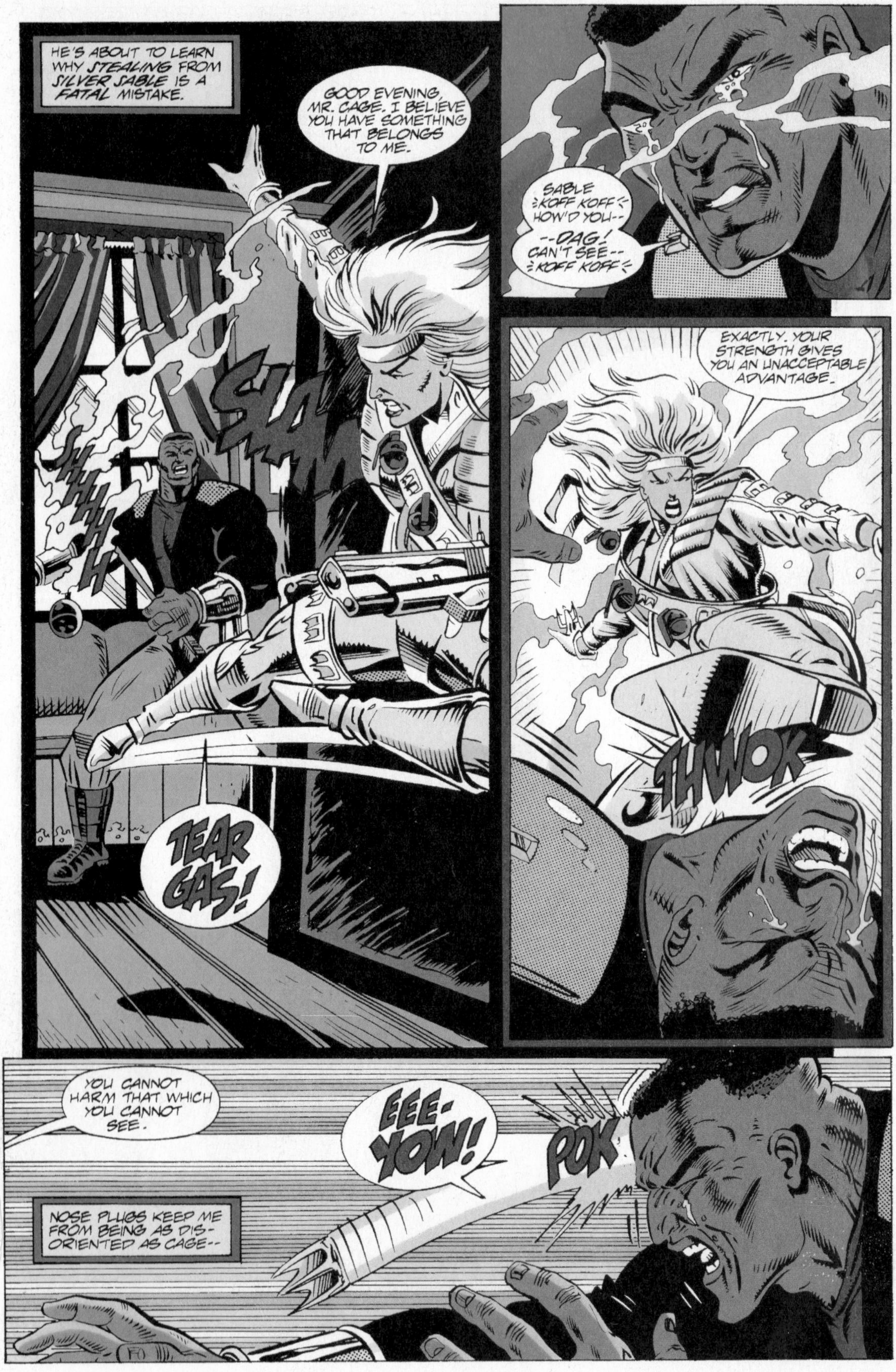
HE'S ABOUT TO LEARN WHY STEALING FROM SILVER SABLE IS A FATAL MISTAKE.
GOOD EVENING, MR. CAGE. I BELIEVE YOU HAVE SOMETHING THAT BELONGS TO ME.
SLAM
SHHHHH
TEAR GAS!
SABLE KOFF KOFF HOW'D YOU--
--DAG! CAN'T SEE-- KOFF KOFF
EXACTLY. YOUR STRENGTH GIVES YOU AN UNACCEPTABLE ADVANTAGE.
THWOK
YOU CANNOT HARM THAT WHICH YOU CANNOT SEE.
EEE-YOW!
POK
NOSE PLUGS KEEP ME FROM BEING AS DIS-ORIENTED AS CAGE--

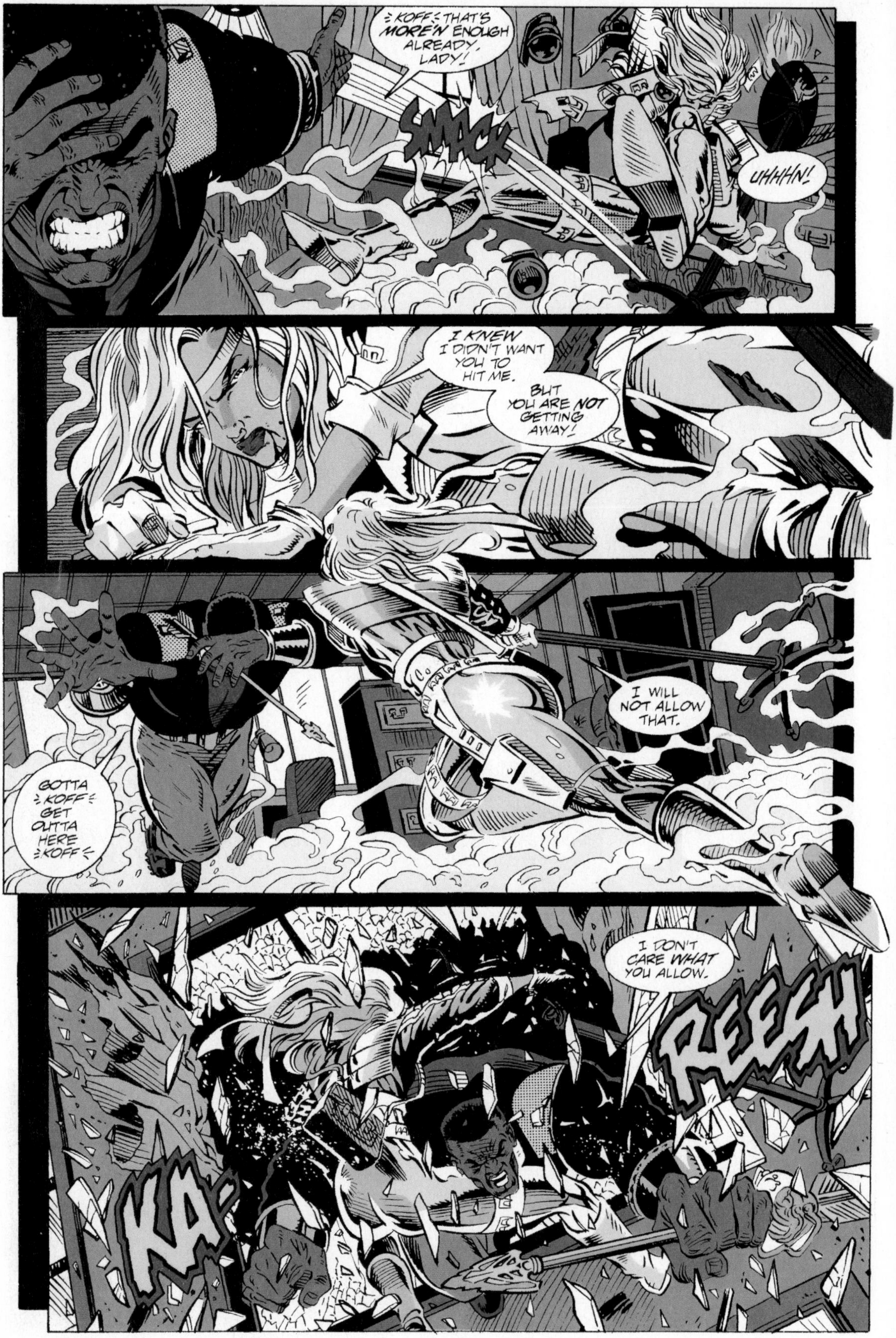

KOFF THAT'S MORE'N ENOUGH ALREADY, LADY!
SMACK
UHHHN!
I KNEW I DIDN'T WANT YOU TO HIT ME.
BUT YOU ARE NOT GETTING AWAY!
I WILL NOT ALLOW THAT.
GOTTA KOFF GET OUTTA HERE KOFF
I DON'T CARE WHAT YOU ALLOW.
REESH
KA

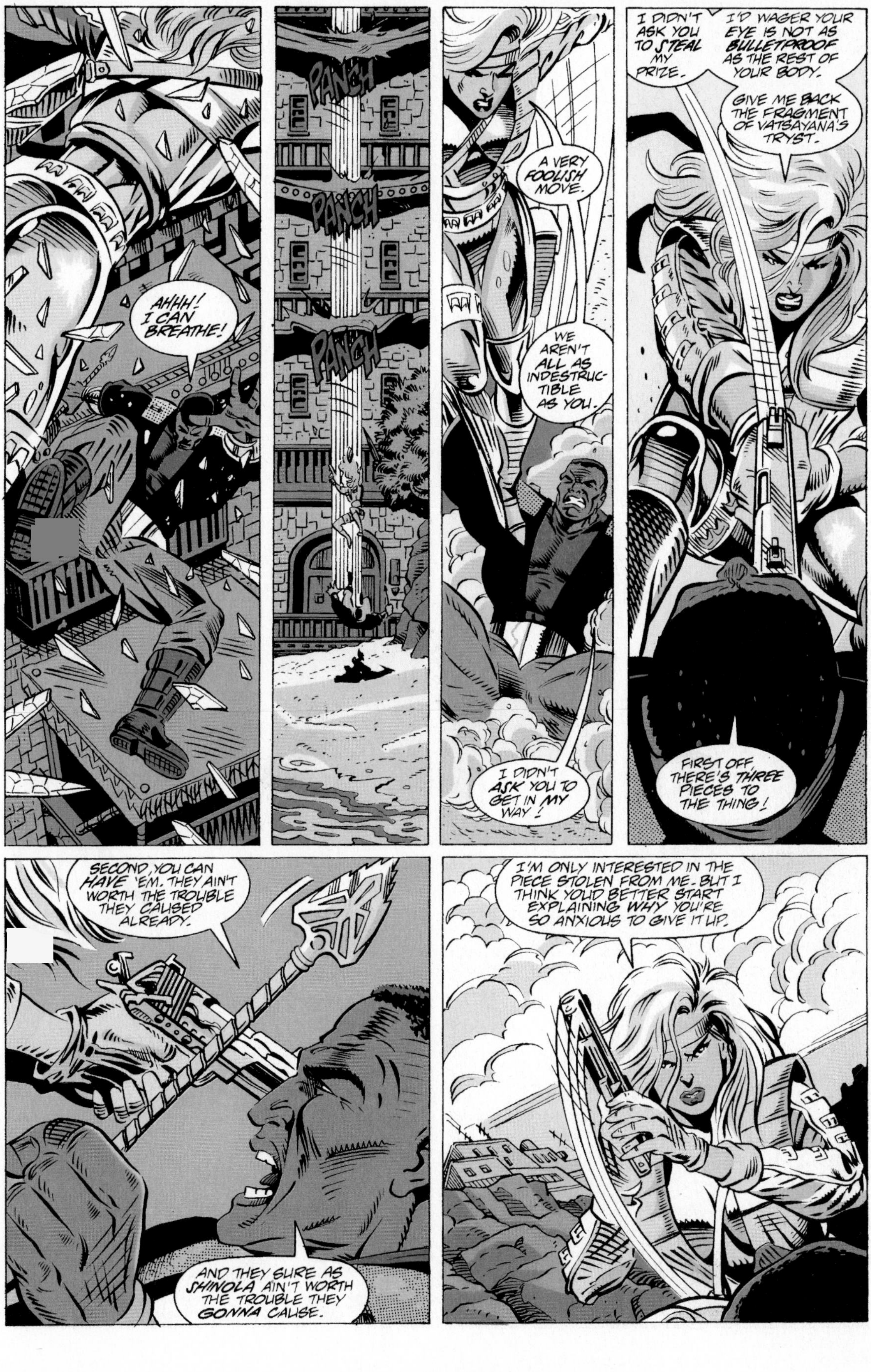
AHHH! I CAN BREATHE!
PANCH
PANCH
PANCH
A VERY FOOLISH MOVE.
WE AREN'T ALL AS INDESTRUC-TIBLE AS YOU.
I DIDN'T ASK YOU TO GET IN MY WAY!
I DIDN'T ASK YOU TO STEAL MY PRIZE.
I'D WAGER YOUR EYE IS NOT AS BULLETPROOF AS THE REST OF YOUR BODY.
GIVE ME BACK THE FRAGMENT OF VATSAYANA'S TRYST.
FIRST OFF, THERE'S THREE PIECES TO THE THING!
SECOND, YOU CAN HAVE 'EM. THEY AIN'T WORTH THE TROUBLE THEY CAUSED ALREADY.
AND THEY SURE AS SHINOLA AIN'T WORTH THE TROUBLE THEY GONNA CAUSE.
I'M ONLY INTERESTED IN THE PIECE STOLEN FROM ME. BUT I THINK YOU'D BETTER START EXPLAINING WHY YOU'RE SO ANXIOUS TO GIVE IT UP.

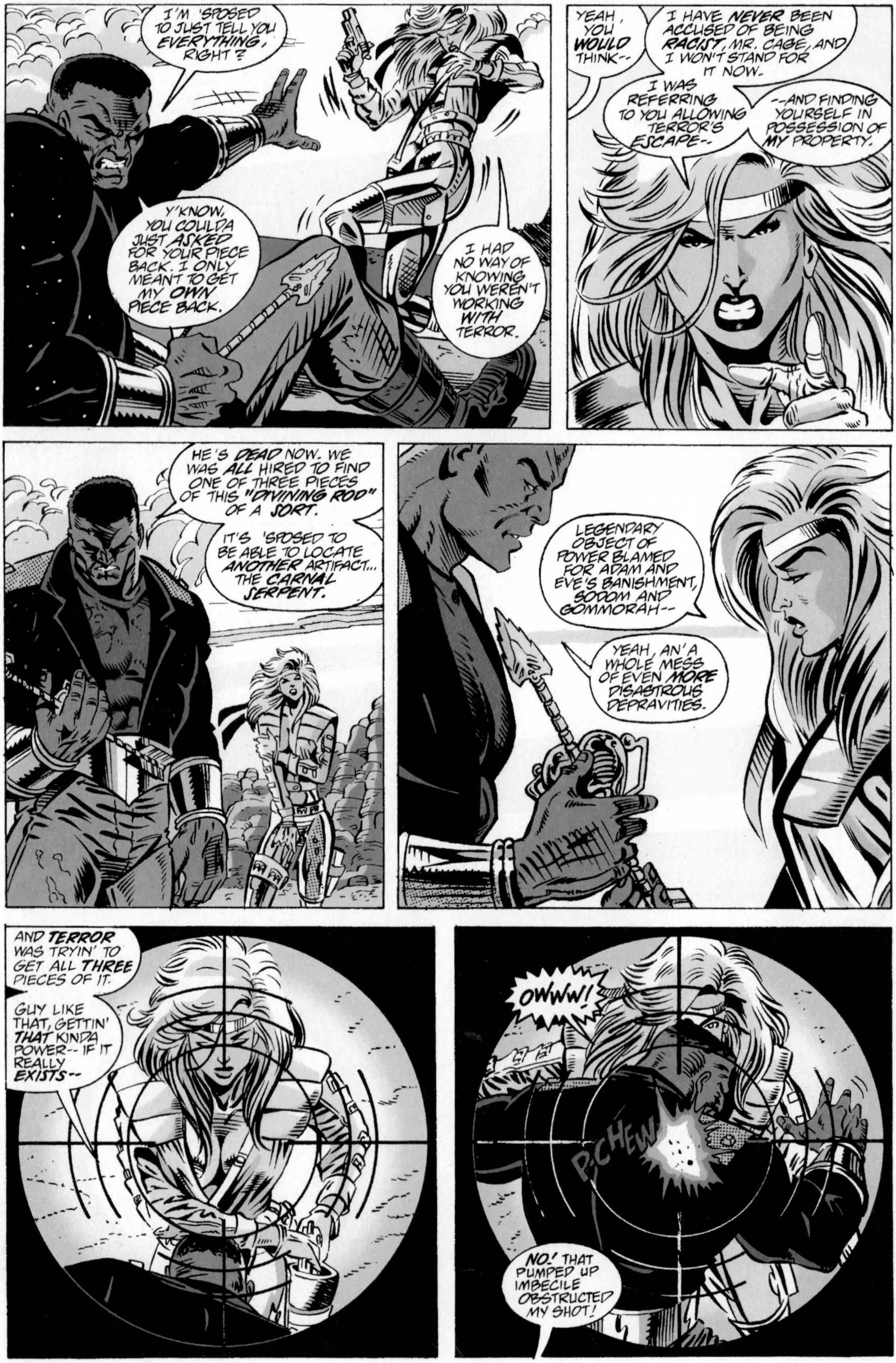
I'M 'SPOSED TO JUST TELL YOU EVERYTHING, RIGHT?
Y'KNOW, YOU COULDA JUST ASKED FOR YOUR PIECE BACK. I ONLY MEANT TO GET MY OWN PIECE BACK.
I HAD NO WAY OF KNOWING YOU WEREN'T WORKING WITH TERROR.
YEAH, YOU WOULD THINK--
I HAVE NEVER BEEN ACCUSED OF BEING RACIST, MR. CAGE, AND I WON'T STAND FOR IT NOW.
I WAS REFERRING TO YOU ALLOWING TERROR'S ESCAPE--
--AND FINDING YOURSELF IN POSSESSION OF MY PROPERTY.
HE'S DEAD NOW. WE WAS ALL HIRED TO FIND ONE OF THREE PIECES OF THIS "DIVINING ROD" OF A SORT.
IT'S 'SPOSED TO BE ABLE TO LOCATE ANOTHER ARTIFACT... THE CARNAL SERPENT.
LEGENDARY OBJECT OF POWER BLAMED FOR ADAM AND EVE'S BANISHMENT, SODOM AND GOMMORAH--
YEAH, AN'A WHOLE MESS OF EVEN MORE DISASTROUS DEPRAVITIES.
AND TERROR WAS TRYIN' TO GET ALL THREE PIECES OF IT.
GUY LIKE THAT, GETTIN' THAT KINDA POWER-- IF IT REALLY EXISTS--
OWWW!
BCHEW
NO! THAT PUMPED UP IMBECILE OBSTRUCTED MY SHOT!

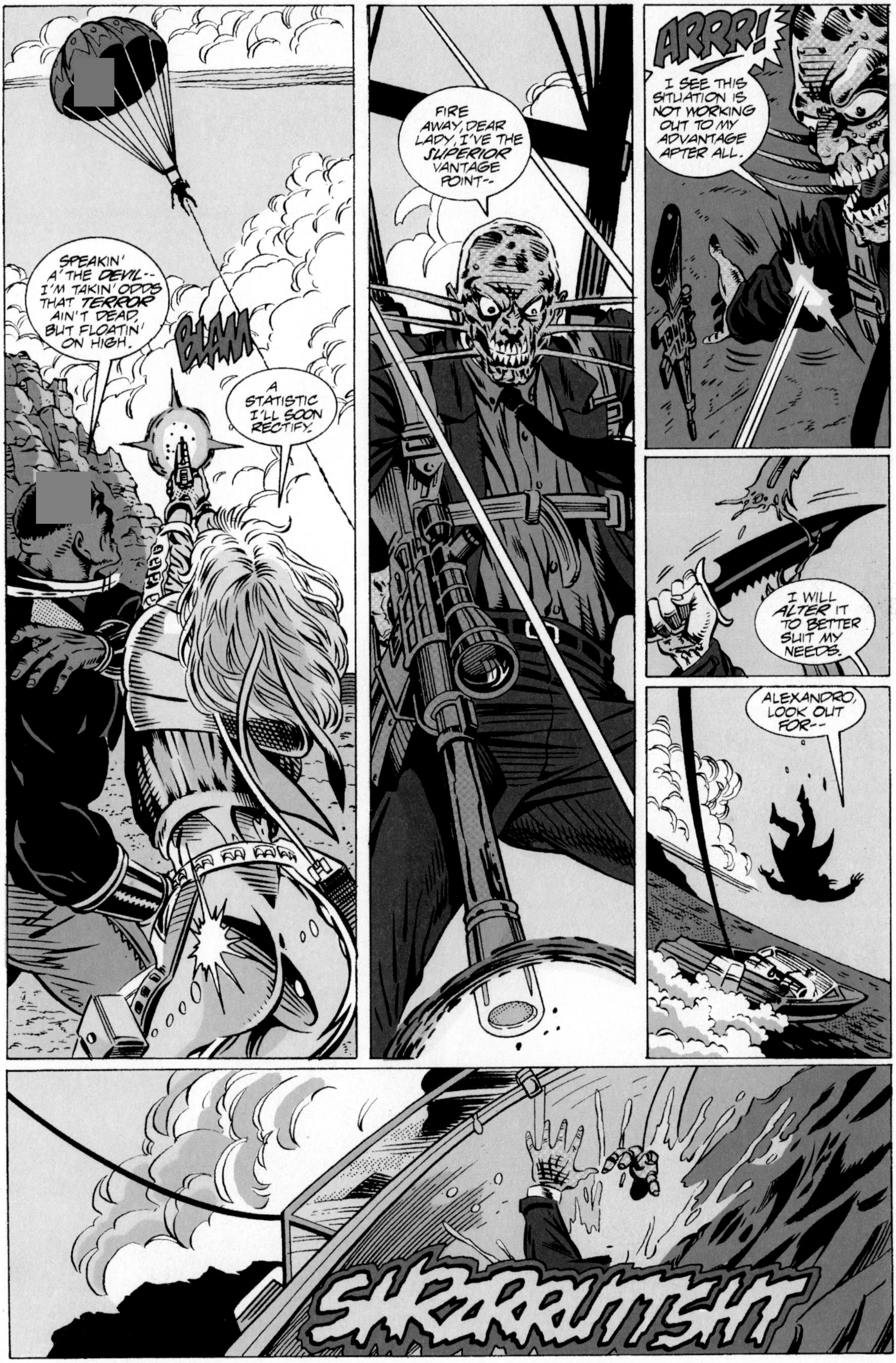
SPEAKIN' A' THE DEVIL-- I'M TAKIN' ODDS THAT TERROR AIN'T DEAD, BUT FLOATIN' ON HIGH.
BLAM
A STATISTIC I'LL SOON RECTIFY.
FIRE AWAY, DEAR LADY, I'VE THE SUPERIOR VANTAGE POINT-.
ARRR!
I SEE THIS SITUATION IS NOT WORKING OUT TO MY ADVANTAGE AFTER ALL.
I WILL ALTER IT TO BETTER SUIT MY NEEDS.
ALEXANDRO, LOOK OUT FOR--
SKRRRUTSH

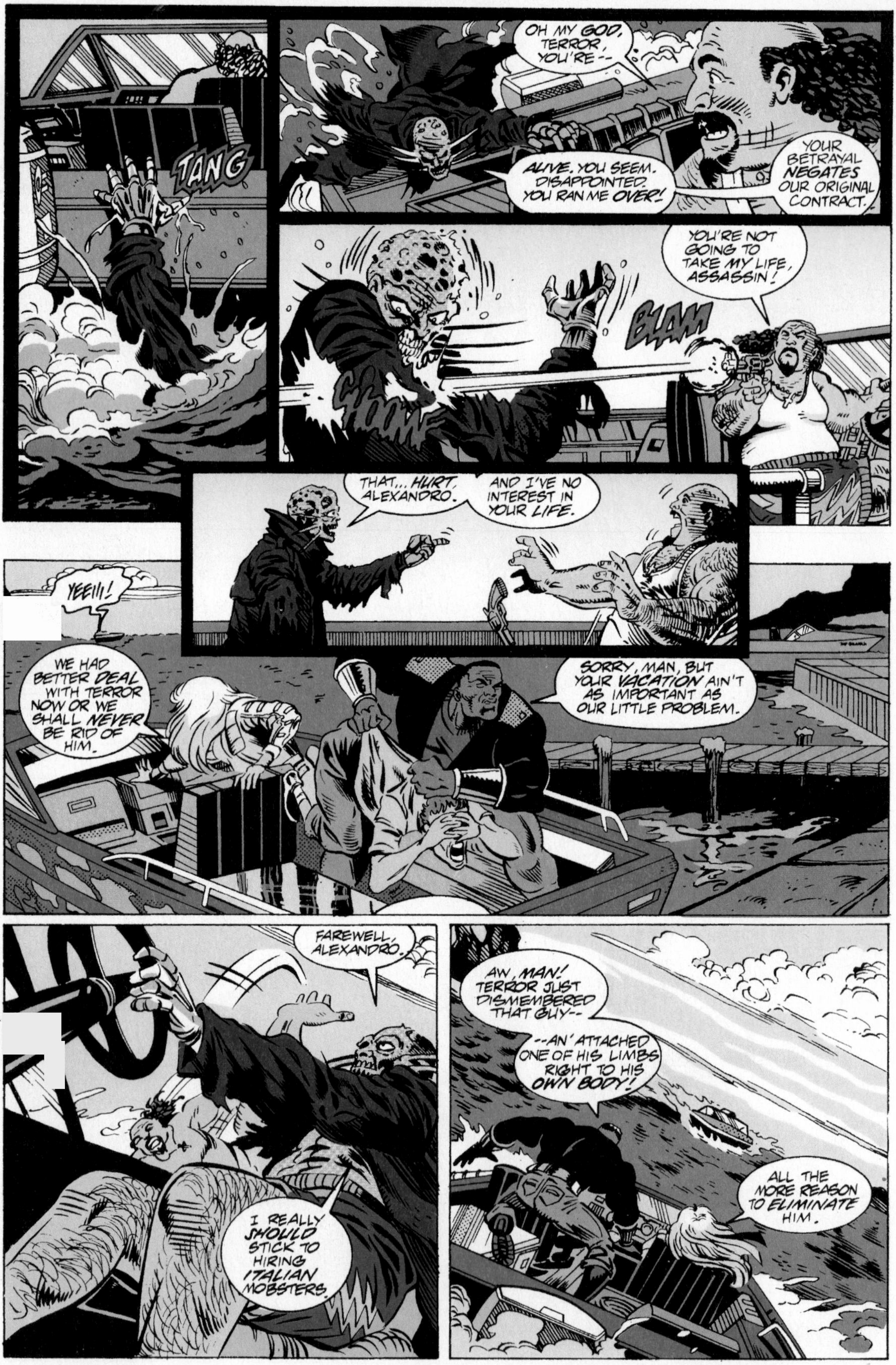
TANG
OH MY GOD, TERROR, YOU'RE--
ALIVE. YOU SEEM. DISAPPOINTED. YOU RAN ME OVER!
YOUR BETRAYAL NEGATES OUR ORIGINAL CONTRACT.
YOU'RE NOT GOING TO TAKE MY LIFE, ASSASSIN!
BLAM
THAT... HURT, ALEXANDRO.
AND I'VE NO INTEREST IN YOUR LIFE.
YEEIII!
WE HAD BETTER DEAL WITH TERROR NOW OR WE SHALL NEVER BE RID OF HIM.
SORRY, MAN, BUT YOUR VACATION AIN'T AS IMPORTANT AS OUR LITTLE PROBLEM.
FAREWELL, ALEXANDRO.
I REALLY SHOULD STICK TO HIRING ITALIAN MOBSTERS.
AW, MAN! TERROR JUST DISMEMBERED THAT GUY--
--AN' ATTACHED ONE OF HIS LIMBS RIGHT TO HIS OWN BODY!
ALL THE MORE REASON TO ELIMINATE HIM.

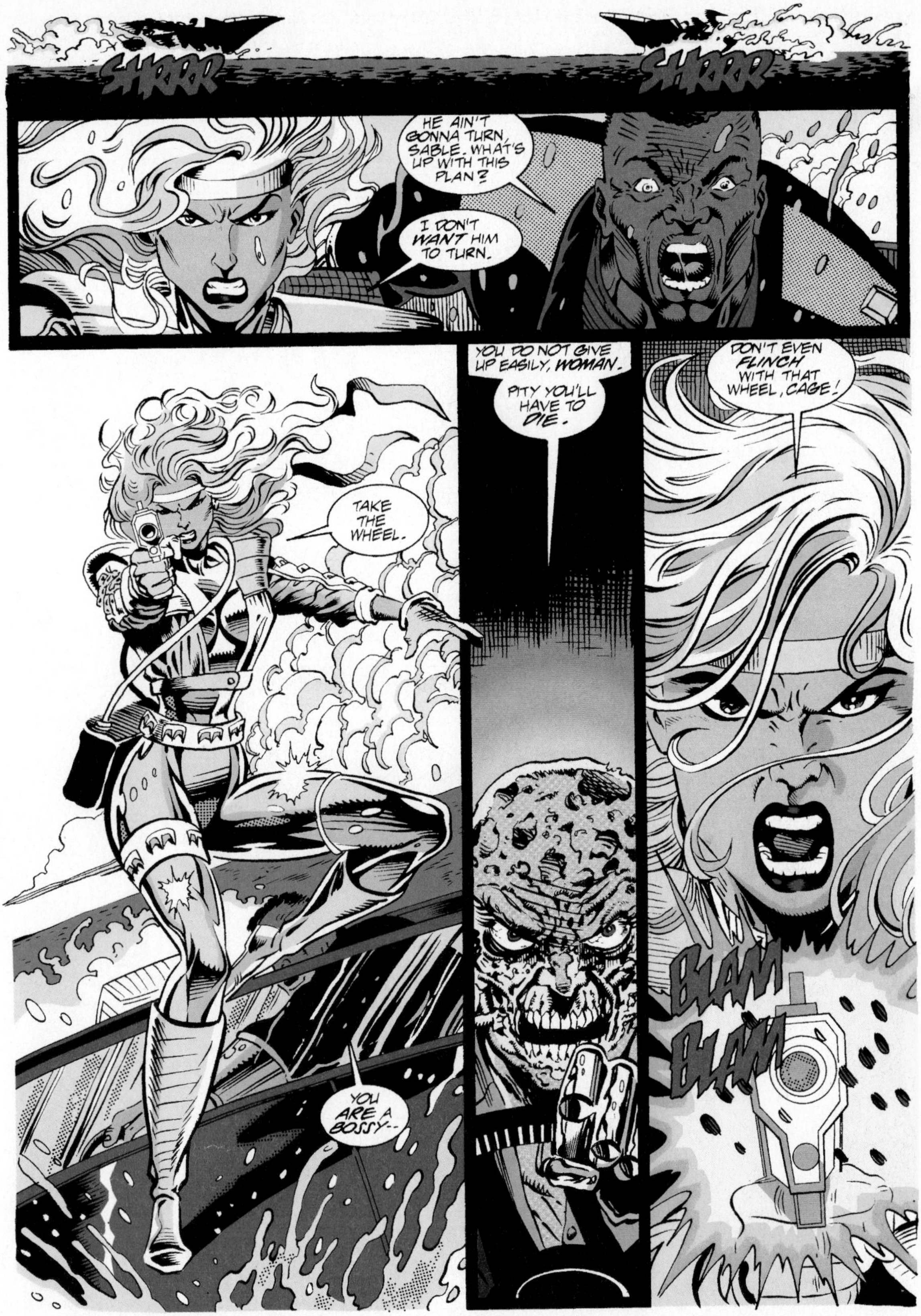
SHRRR
SHRRR
HE AIN'T GONNA TURN, SABLE. WHAT'S UP WITH THIS PLAN?
I DON'T WANT HIM TO TURN.
TAKE THE WHEEL.
YOU ARE A BOSSY--
YOU DO NOT GIVE UP EASILY, WOMAN.
PITY YOU'LL HAVE TO DIE.
DON'T EVEN FLINCH WITH THAT WHEEL, CAGE!
BLAM
BLAM

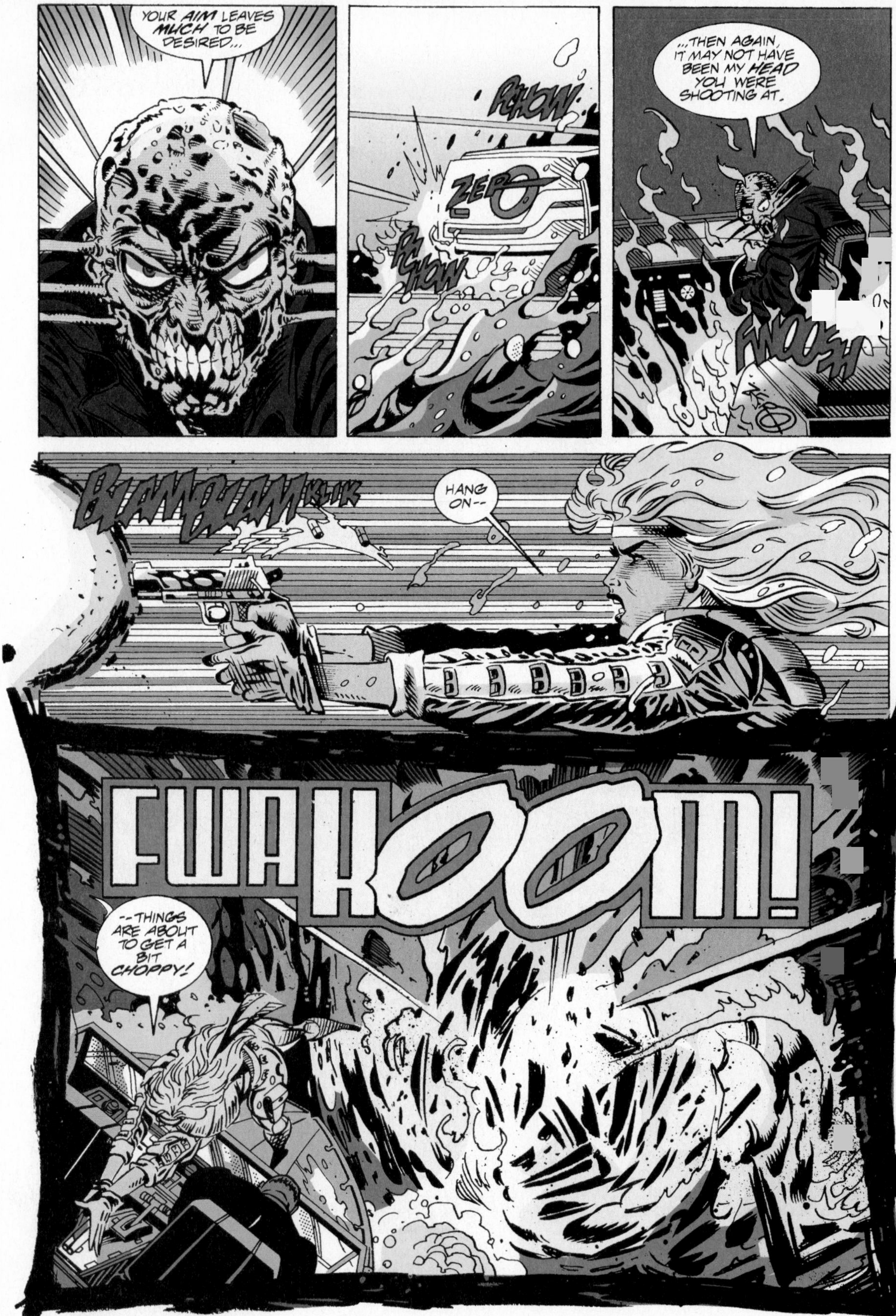

YOUR AIM LEAVES MUCH TO BE DESIRED...
PCHOW
ZERO
PCHOW
...THEN AGAIN, IT MAY NOT HAVE BEEN MY HEAD YOU WERE SHOOTING AT.
FWOOSH
BLAM BLAM KLIK
HANG ON--
FWAKOOM!
--THINGS ARE ABOUT TO GET A BIT CHOPPY!

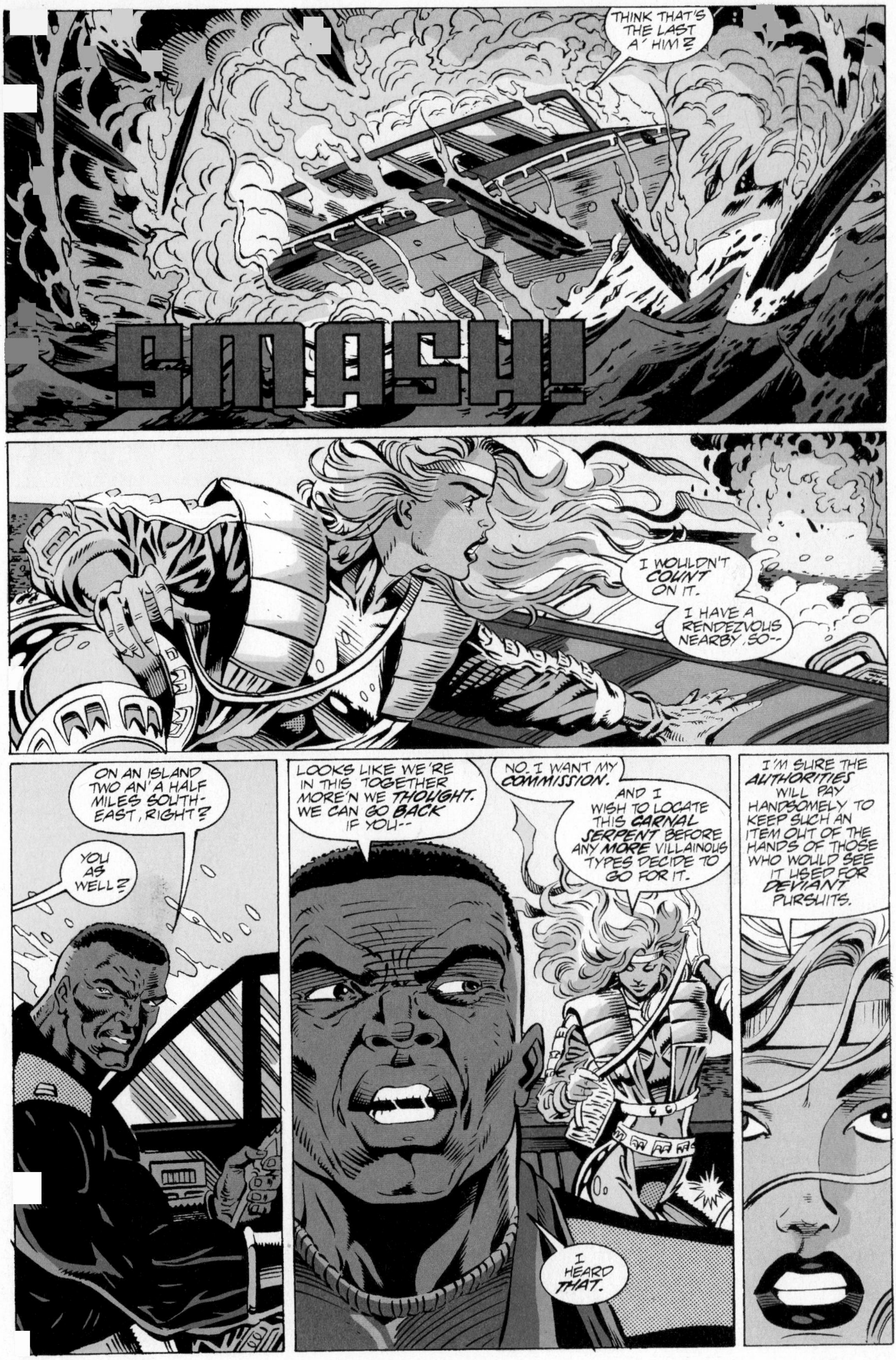
THINK THAT'S THE LAST A' HIM?
SMASH!
I WOULDN'T COUNT ON IT.
I HAVE A RENDEZVOUS NEARBY. SO--
ON AN ISLAND TWO AN' A HALF MILES SOUTH-EAST, RIGHT?
YOU AS WELL?
LOOKS LIKE WE'RE IN THIS TOGETHER MORE'N WE THOUGHT. WE CAN GO BACK IF YOU--
NO. I WANT MY COMMISSION.
AND I WISH TO LOCATE THIS CARNAL SERPENT BEFORE ANY MORE VILLAINOUS TYPES DECIDE TO GO FOR IT.
I HEARD THAT.
I'M SURE THE AUTHORITIES WILL PAY HANDSOMELY TO KEEP SUCH AN ITEM OUT OF THE HANDS OF THOSE WHO WOULD SEE IT USED FOR DEVIANT PURSUITS.

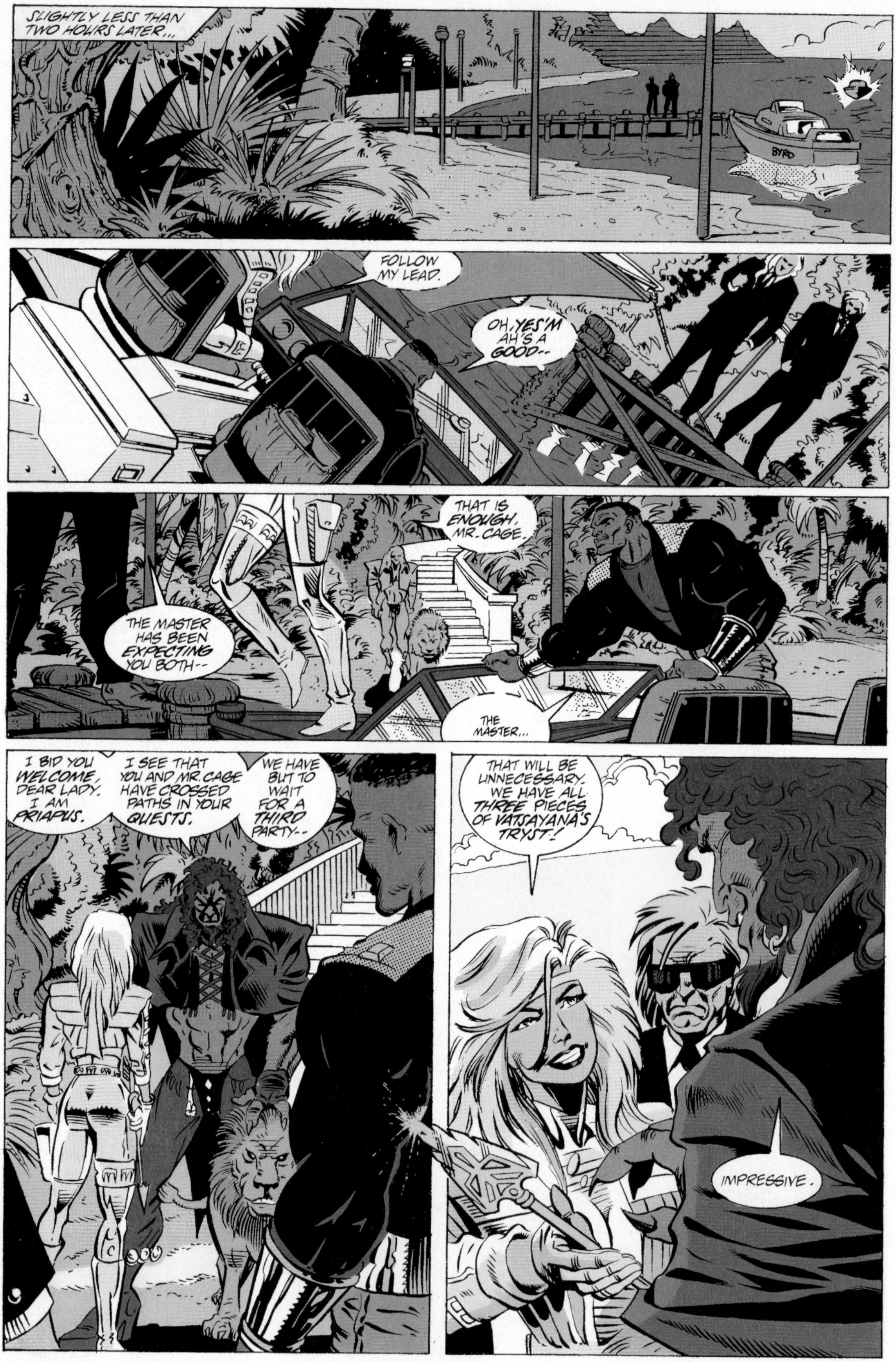
SLIGHTLY LESS THAN TWO HOURS LATER...
BYRD
FOLLOW MY LEAD.
OH, YES'M AH'S A GOOD--
THAT IS ENOUGH, MR. CAGE.
THE MASTER HAS BEEN EXPECTING YOU BOTH--
THE MASTER...
I BID YOU WELCOME, DEAR LADY. I AM PRIAPUS.
I SEE THAT YOU AND MR. CAGE HAVE CROSSED PATHS IN YOUR QUESTS.
WE HAVE BUT TO WAIT FOR A THIRD PARTY--
THAT WILL BE UNNECESSARY. WE HAVE ALL THREE PIECES OF VATSAYANA'S TRYST!
IMPRESSIVE.

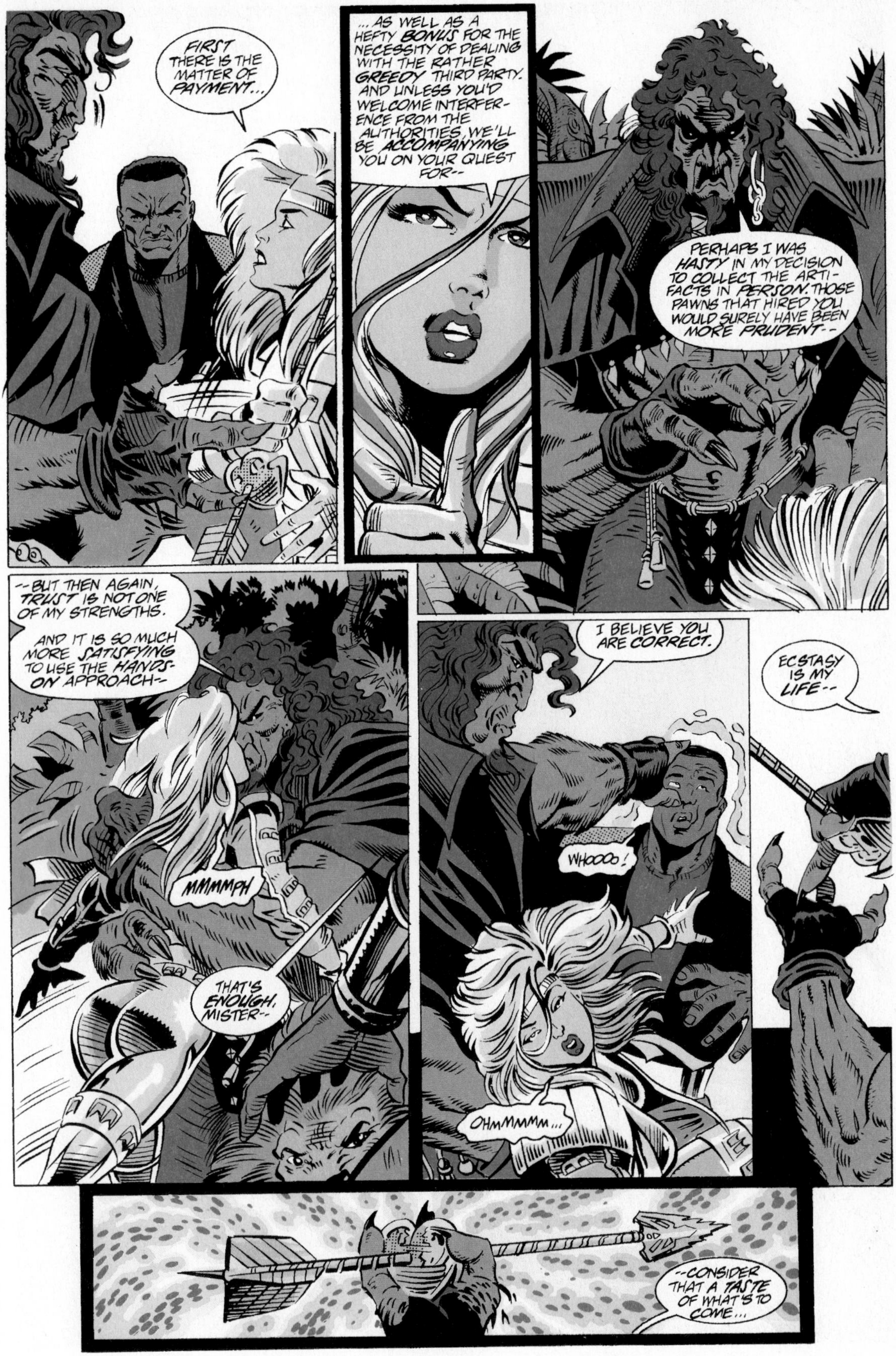
FIRST THERE IS THE MATTER OF PAYMENT...
...AS WELL AS A HEFTY BONUS FOR THE NECESSITY OF DEALING WITH THE RATHER GREEDY THIRD PARTY. AND UNLESS YOU'D WELCOME INTERFERENCE FROM THE AUTHORITIES, WE'LL BE ACCOMPANYING YOU ON YOUR QUEST FOR--
PERHAPS I WAS HASTY IN MY DECISION TO COLLECT THE ARTIFACTS IN PERSON. THOSE PAWNS THAT HIRED YOU WOULD SURELY HAVE BEEN MORE PRUDENT--
--BUT THEN AGAIN, TRUST IS NOT ONE OF MY STRENGTHS.
AND IT IS SO MUCH MORE SATISFYING TO USE THE HANDS-ON APPROACH--
MMMMPH
THAT'S ENOUGH, MISTER--
I BELIEVE YOU ARE CORRECT.
ECSTASY IS MY LIFE--
WHOOOO!
OHMMMMM...
--CONSIDER THAT A TASTE OF WHAT'S TO COME...

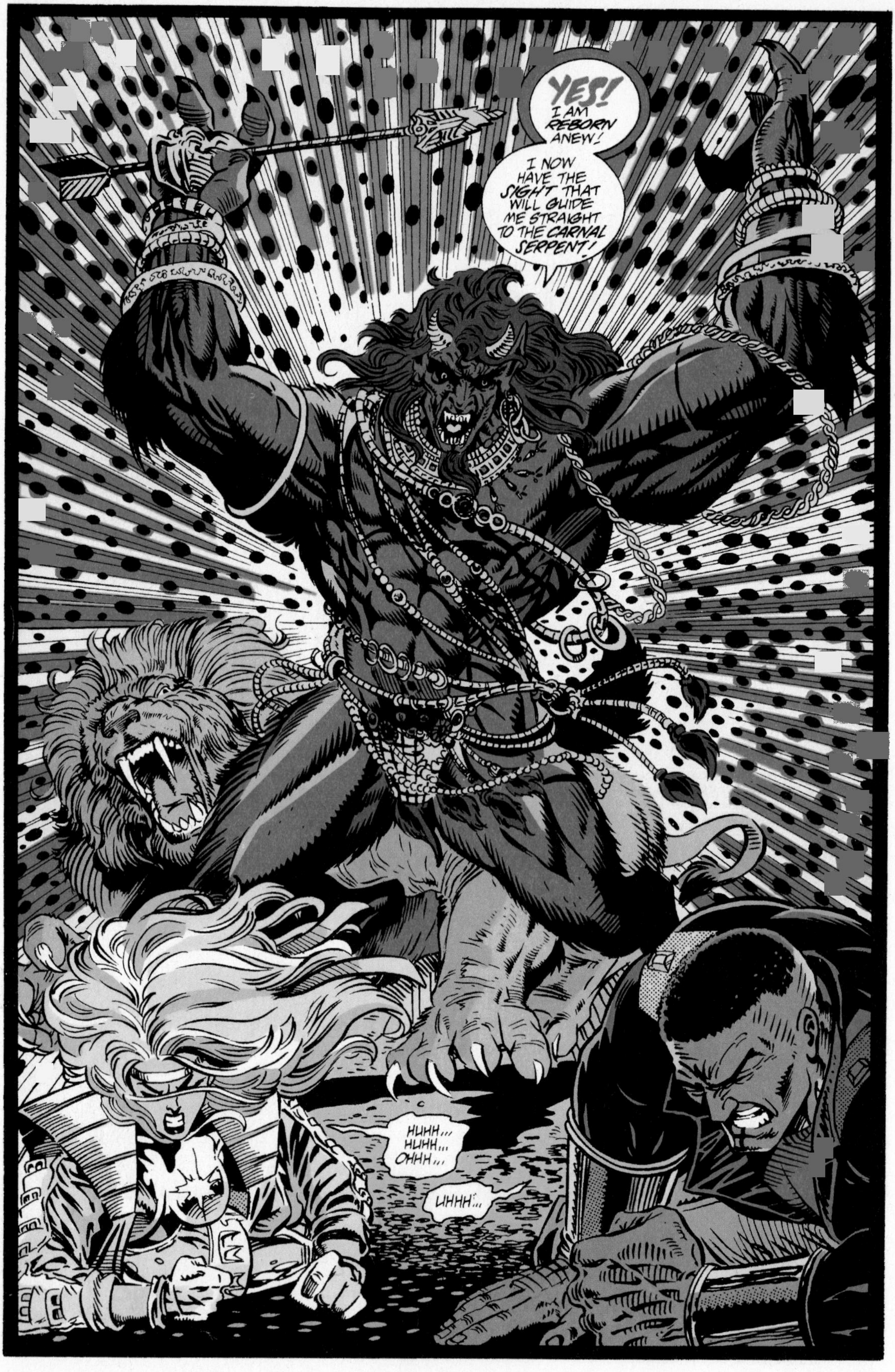
YES! I AM REBORN ANEW!
I NOW HAVE THE SIGHT THAT WILL GUIDE ME STRAIGHT TO THE CARNAL SERPENT!
HUHH... HUHH... OHHH...
UHHH...

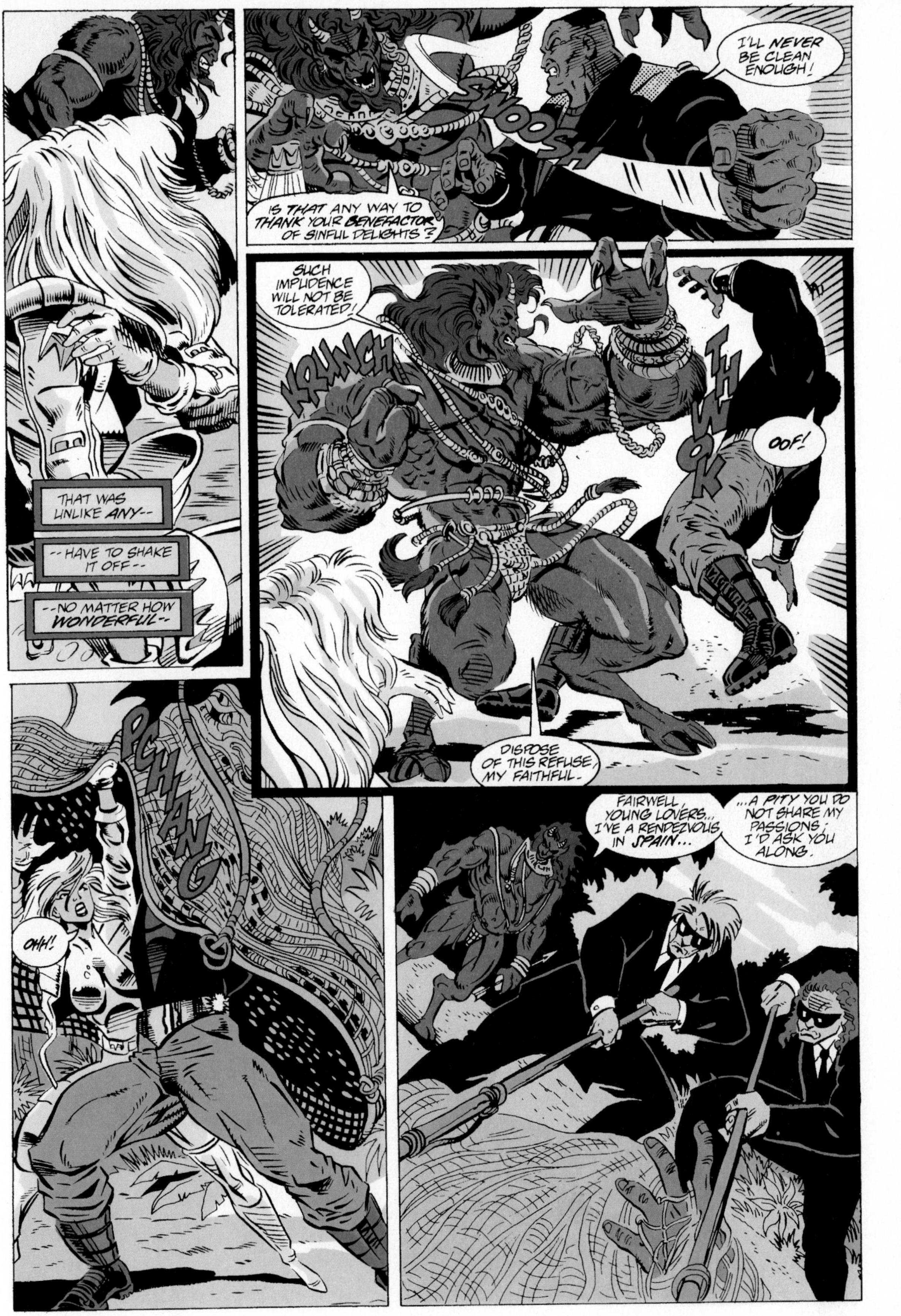
I'LL NEVER BE CLEAN ENOUGH!
SNOOSH
IS THAT ANY WAY TO THANK YOUR BENEFACTOR OF SINFUL DELIGHTS?
THAT WAS UNLIKE ANY--
--HAVE TO SHAKE IT OFF--
--NO MATTER HOW WONDERFUL--
SUCH IMPUDENCE WILL NOT BE TOLERATED!
KRUNCH
THWOK
OOF!
DISPOSE OF THIS REFUSE, MY FAITHFUL.
PCHANG
OHH!
FAIRWELL, YOUNG LOVERS... I'VE A RENDEZVOUS IN SPAIN...
...A PITY YOU DO NOT SHARE MY PASSIONS, I'D ASK YOU ALONG.

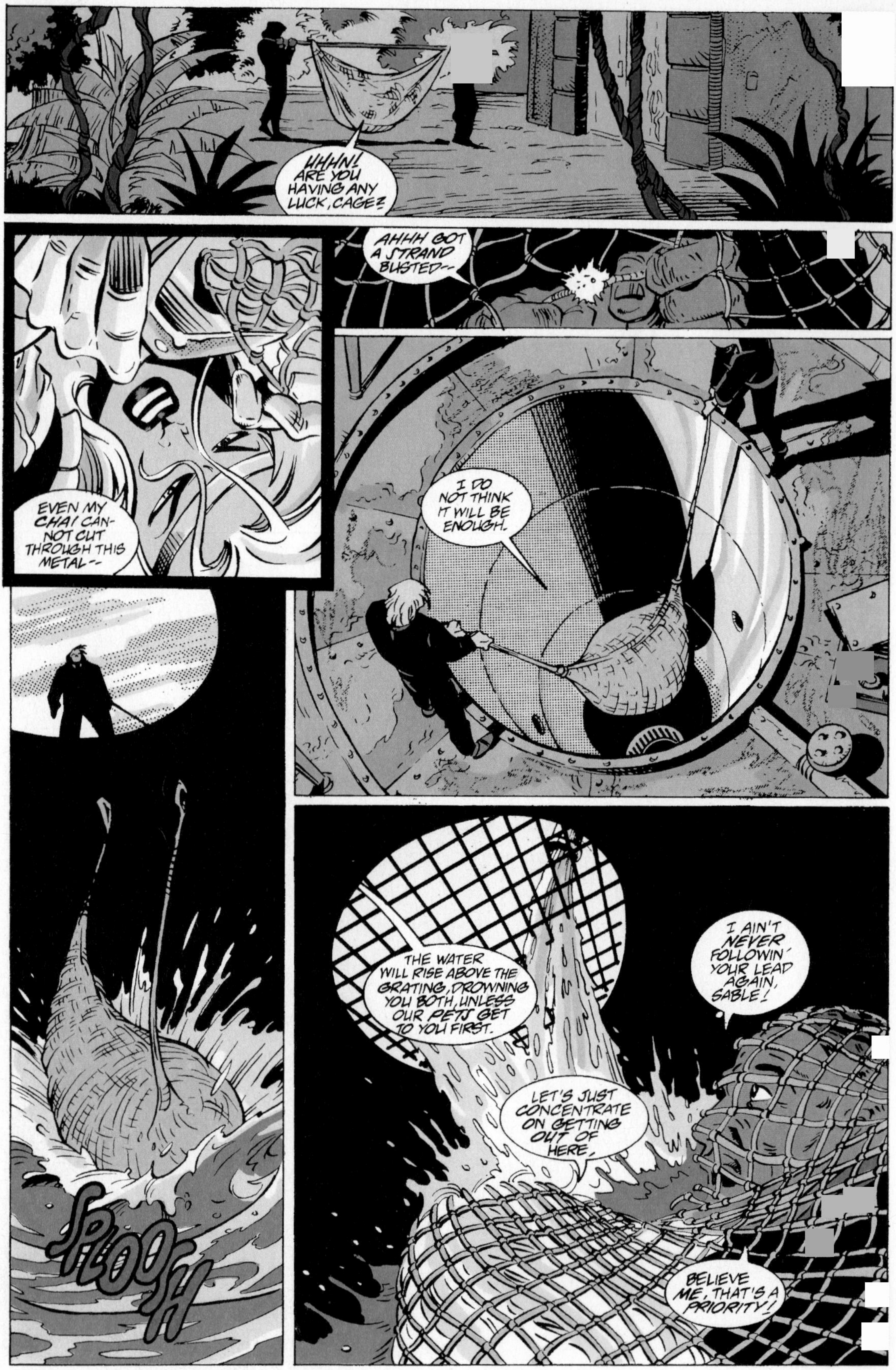

UHHN! ARE YOU HAVING ANY LUCK, CAGE?
AHHH GOT A STRAND BUSTED--
EVEN MY CHAI CAN-NOT CUT THROUGH THIS METAL--
I DO NOT THINK IT WILL BE ENOUGH.
SPLOOSH
THE WATER WILL RISE ABOVE THE GRATING, DROWNING YOU BOTH, UNLESS OUR PETS GET TO YOU FIRST.
I AIN'T NEVER FOLLOWIN' YOUR LEAD AGAIN, SABLE!
LET'S JUST CONCENTRATE ON GETTING OUT OF HERE.
BELIEVE ME, THAT'S A PRIORITY!

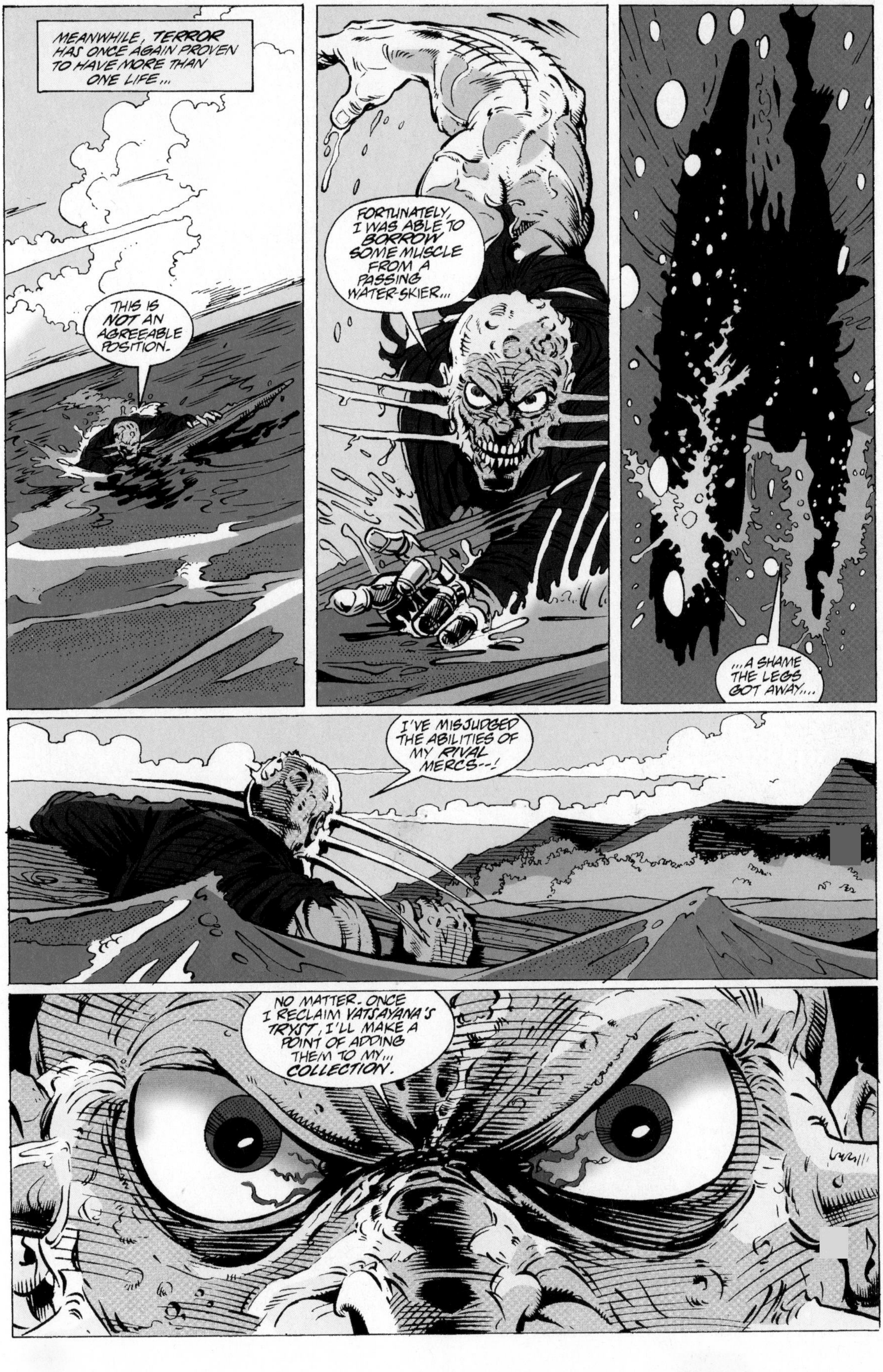
MEANWHILE, TERROR HAS ONCE AGAIN PROVEN TO HAVE MORE THAN ONE LIFE...
THIS IS NOT AN AGREEABLE POSITION.
FORTUNATELY, I WAS ABLE TO BORROW SOME MUSCLE FROM A PASSING WATER-SKIER...
...A SHAME THE LEGS GOT AWAY...
I'VE MISJUDGED THE ABILITIES OF MY RIVAL MERCS--!
NO MATTER. ONCE I RECLAIM VATSAYANA'S TRYST, I'LL MAKE A POINT OF ADDING THEM TO MY... COLLECTION.

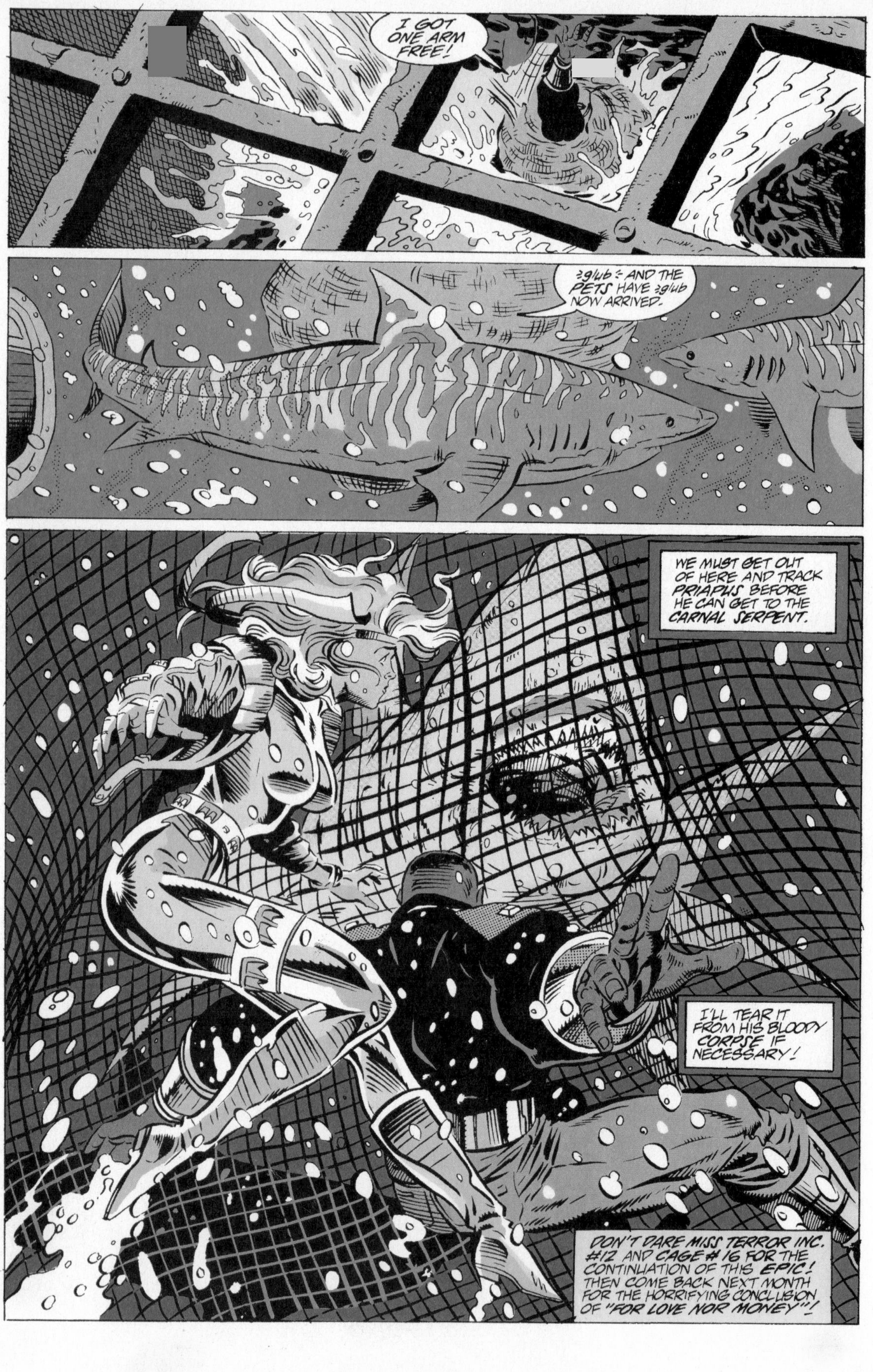
I GOT ONE ARM FREE!
=glub= AND THE PETS HAVE =glub= NOW ARRIVED.
WE MUST GET OUT OF HERE AND TRACK PRIAPUS BEFORE HE CAN GET TO THE CARNAL SERPENT.
I'LL TEAR IT FROM HIS BLOODY CORPSE IF NECESSARY!
DON'T DARE MISS TERROR INC. #12 AND CAGE #16 FOR THE CONTINUATION OF THIS EPIC! THEN COME BACK NEXT MONTH FOR THE HORRIFYING CONCLUSION OF "FOR LOVE NOR MONEY"!

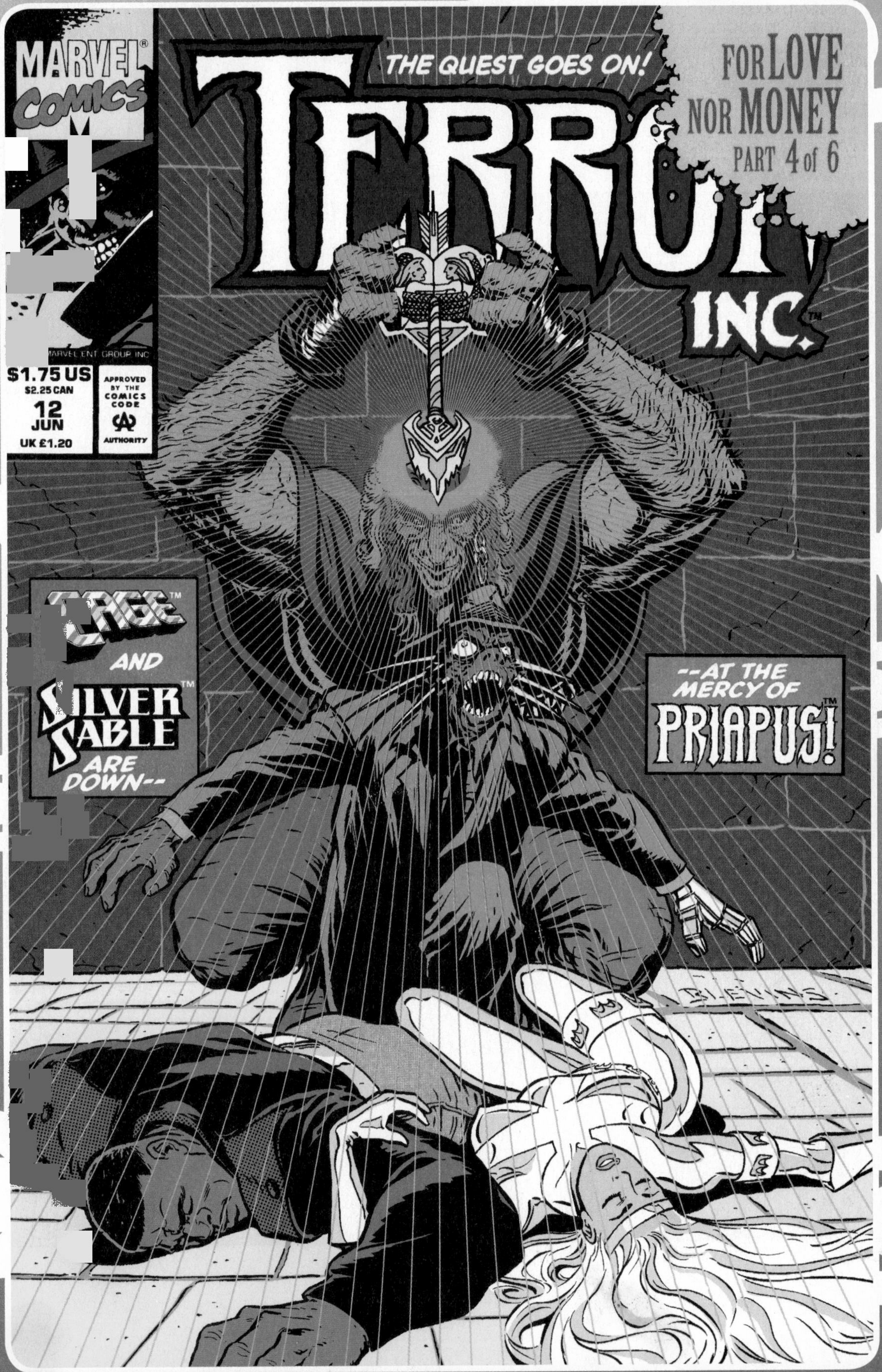
MARVEL COMICS
THE QUEST GOES ON!
TERROR INC.
FOR LOVE NOR MONEY PART 4 of 6
$1.75 US
$2.25 CAN
12
JUN
UK £1.20
APPROVED BY THE COMICS CODE AUTHORITY
CAGE AND SILVER SABLE ARE DOWN--
--AT THE MERCY OF PRIAPUS!
BLEVINS

TRADING IN A MACABRE SPECIALTY TO TAKE ON THE TALENTS OF OTHERS' BODY PARTS, HE IS A [illegible]TREPRENEUR WHO DOES BUSINESS ON THE EDGE OF THE LAW AND THE DARK SIDE OF REALITY.
ANTI-HERO AND ROGUE, HE'S AN ARCANE GUN FOR HIRE. STAN LEE PRESENTS:

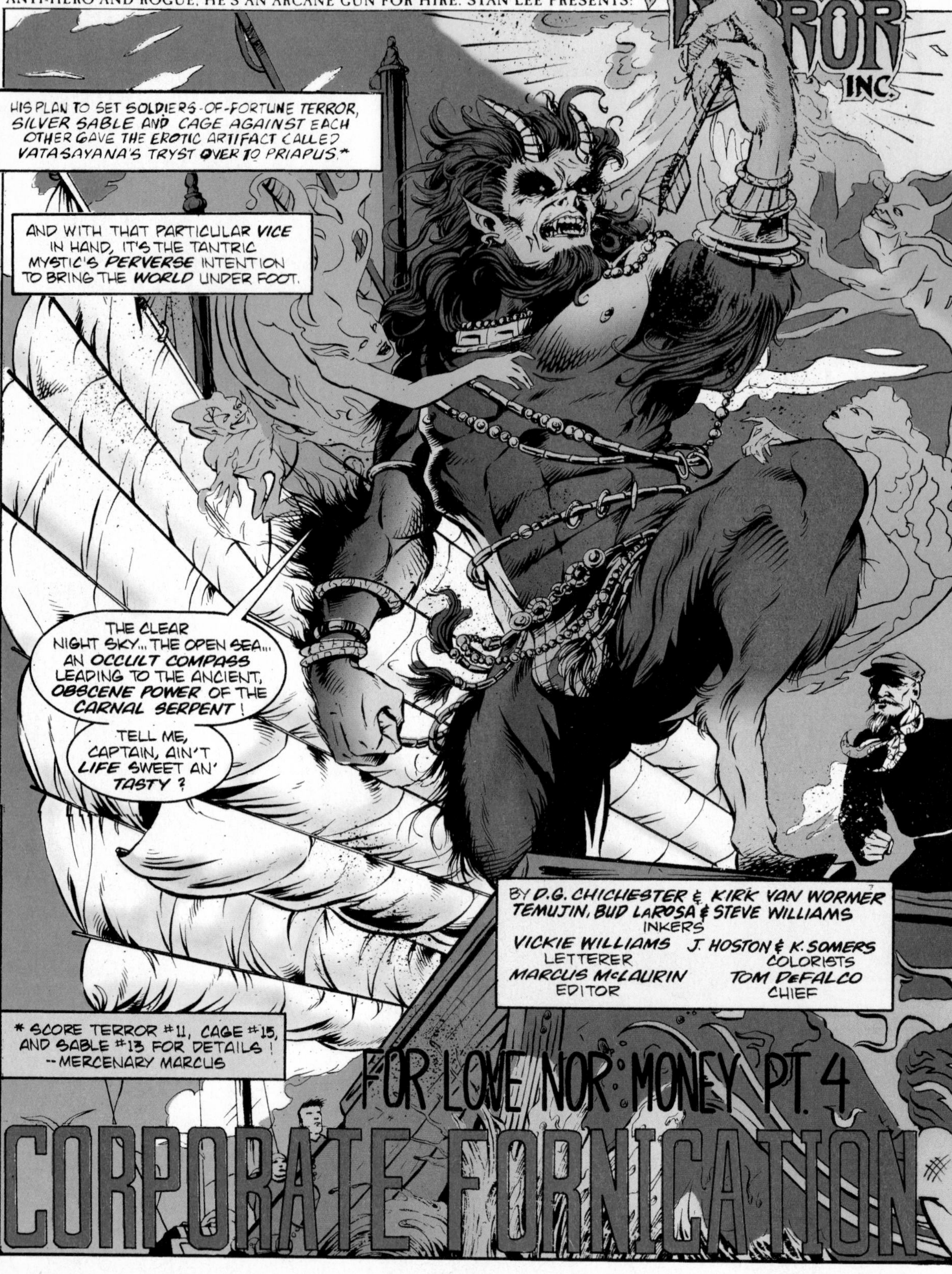
INC.
HIS PLAN TO SET SOLDIERS-OF-FORTUNE TERROR, SILVER SABLE AND CAGE AGAINST EACH OTHER GAVE THE EROTIC ARTIFACT CALLED VATASAYANA'S TRYST OVER TO PRIAPUS.*
AND WITH THAT PARTICULAR VICE IN HAND, IT'S THE TANTRIC MYSTIC'S PERVERSE INTENTION TO BRING THE WORLD UNDER FOOT.
THE CLEAR NIGHT SKY... THE OPEN SEA... AN OCCULT COMPASS LEADING TO THE ANCIENT, OBSCENE POWER OF THE CARNAL SERPENT!
TELL ME, CAPTAIN, AIN'T LIFE SWEET AN' TASTY?
BY D.G. CHICHESTER & KIRK VAN WORMER
TEMUJIN, BUD LAROSA & STEVE WILLIAMS
INKERS
VICKIE WILLIAMS
LETTERER
J. HOSTON & K. SOMERS
COLORISTS
MARCUS McLAURIN
EDITOR
TOM DEFALCO
CHIEF
* SCORE TERROR #11, CAGE #15, AND SABLE #13 FOR DETAILS! --MERCENARY MARCUS
FOR LOVE NOR MONEY PT. 4
CORPORATE FORNICATION

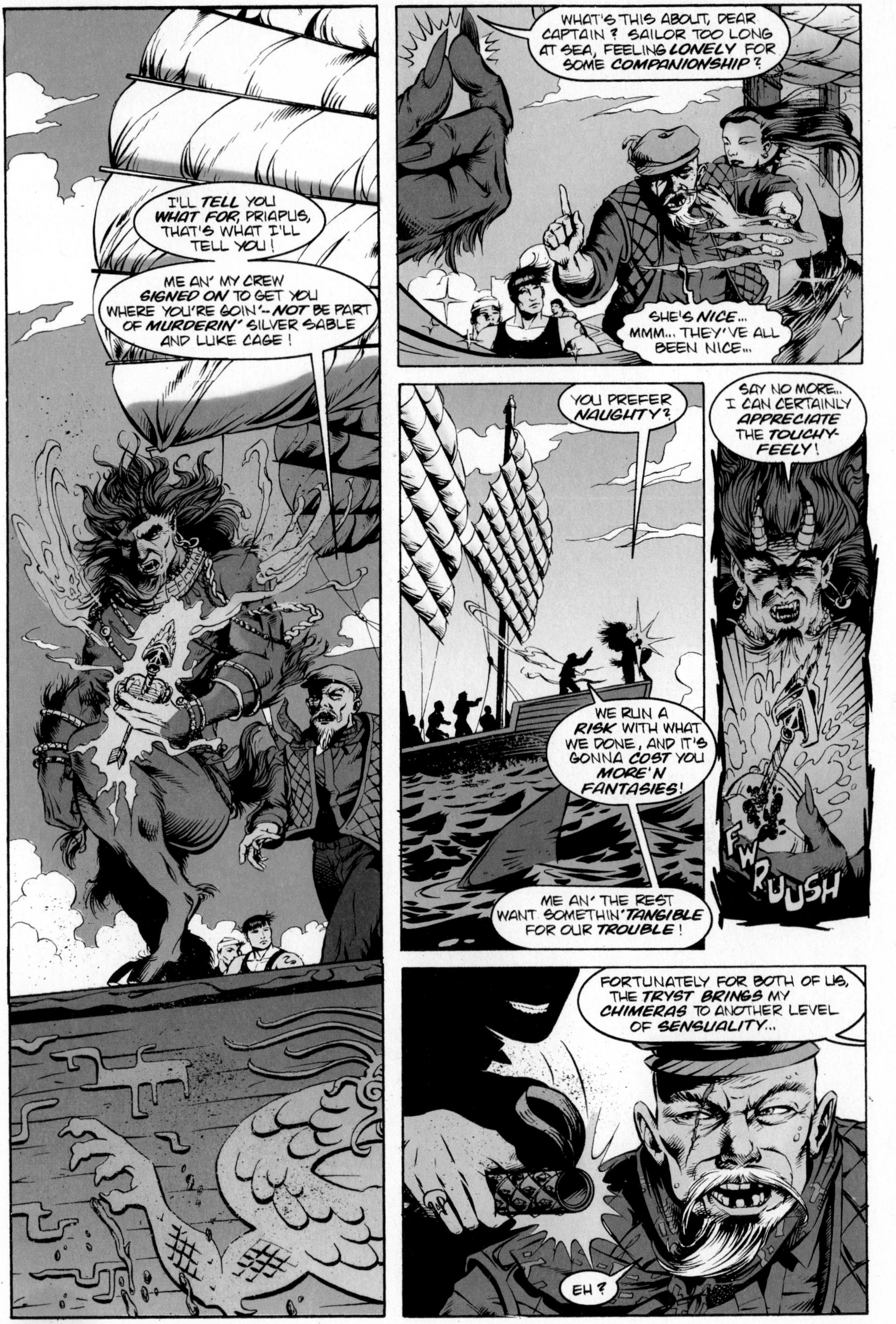
I'LL TELL YOU WHAT FOR, PRIAPUS, THAT'S WHAT I'LL TELL YOU!
ME AN' MY CREW SIGNED ON TO GET YOU WHERE YOU'RE GOIN'-- NOT BE PART OF MURDERIN' SILVER SABLE AND LUKE CAGE!
WHAT'S THIS ABOUT, DEAR CAPTAIN? SAILOR TOO LONG AT SEA, FEELING LONELY FOR SOME COMPANIONSHIP?
SHE'S NICE... MMM... THEY'VE ALL BEEN NICE...
YOU PREFER NAUGHTY?
WE RUN A RISK WITH WHAT WE DONE, AND IT'S GONNA COST YOU MORE'N FANTASIES!
ME AN' THE REST WANT SOMETHIN' TANGIBLE FOR OUR TROUBLE!
SAY NO MORE... I CAN CERTAINLY APPRECIATE THE TOUCHY-FEELY!
FWRUUSH
FORTUNATELY FOR BOTH OF US, THE TRYST BRINGS MY CHIMERAS TO ANOTHER LEVEL OF SENSUALITY...
EH?

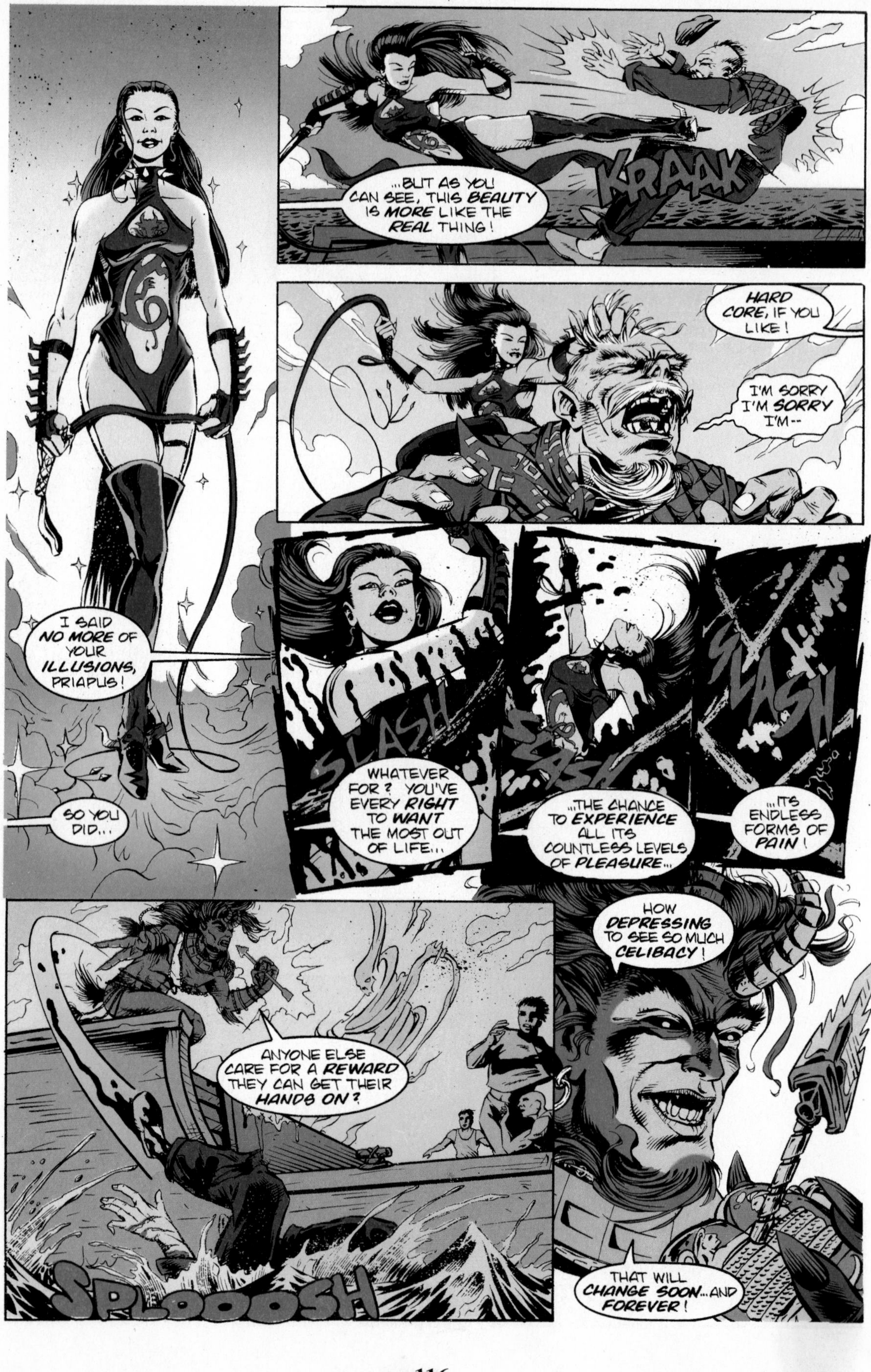
...BUT AS YOU CAN SEE, THIS BEAUTY IS MORE LIKE THE REAL THING!
KRAAAK
HARD CORE, IF YOU LIKE!
I'M SORRY I'M SORRY I'M--
I SAID NO MORE OF YOUR ILLUSIONS, PRIAPUS!
SO YOU DID...
SLASH
WHATEVER FOR? YOU'VE EVERY RIGHT TO WANT THE MOST OUT OF LIFE...
SLASH
...THE CHANCE TO EXPERIENCE ALL ITS COUNTLESS LEVELS OF PLEASURE...
SLASH
...ITS ENDLESS FORMS OF PAIN!
ANYONE ELSE CARE FOR A REWARD THEY CAN GET THEIR HANDS ON?
SPLOOOSH
HOW DEPRESSING TO SEE SO MUCH CELIBACY!
THAT WILL CHANGE SOON...AND FOREVER!

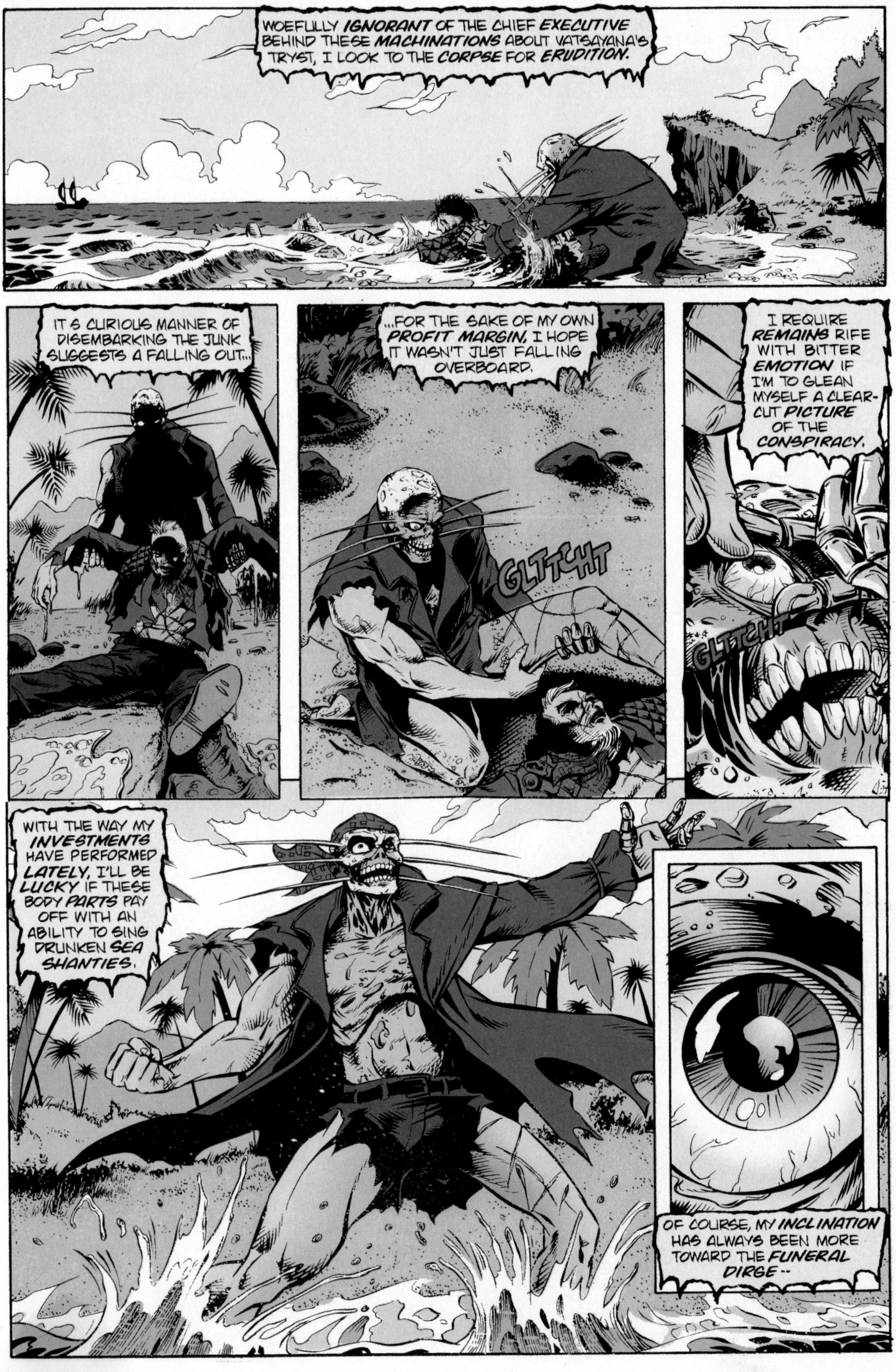
WOEFULLY IGNORANT OF THE CHIEF EXECUTIVE BEHIND THESE MACHINATIONS ABOUT VATSAYANA'S TRYST, I LOOK TO THE CORPSE FOR ERUDITION.
ITS CURIOUS MANNER OF DISEMBARKING THE JUNK SUGGESTS A FALLING OUT...
...FOR THE SAKE OF MY OWN PROFIT MARGIN, I HOPE IT WASN'T JUST FALLING OVERBOARD.
GLTTCHT
I REQUIRE REMAINS RIFE WITH BITTER EMOTION IF I'M TO GLEAN MYSELF A CLEAR-CUT PICTURE OF THE CONSPIRACY.
GLTTCHT
WITH THE WAY MY INVESTMENTS HAVE PERFORMED LATELY, I'LL BE LUCKY IF THESE BODY PARTS PAY OFF WITH AN ABILITY TO SING DRUNKEN SEA SHANTIES.
OF COURSE, MY INCLINATION HAS ALWAYS BEEN MORE TOWARD THE FUNERAL DIRGE --

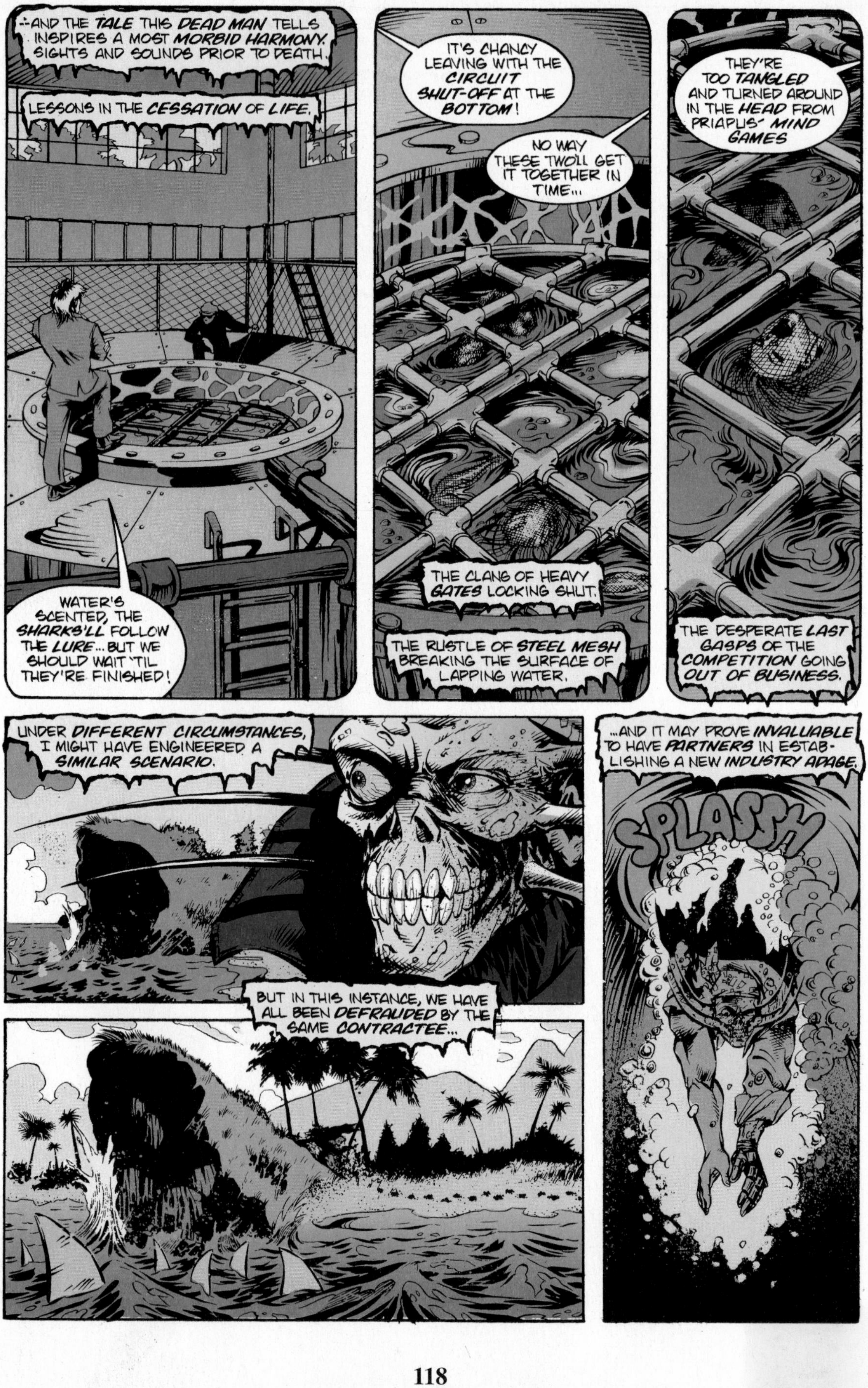

...AND THE TALE THIS DEAD MAN TELLS INSPIRES A MOST MORBID HARMONY. SIGHTS AND SOUNDS PRIOR TO DEATH.
LESSONS IN THE CESSATION OF LIFE.
WATER'S SCENTED, THE SHARKS'LL FOLLOW THE LURE... BUT WE SHOULD WAIT 'TIL THEY'RE FINISHED!
IT'S CHANCY LEAVING WITH THE CIRCUIT SHUT-OFF AT THE BOTTOM!
NO WAY THESE TWO'LL GET IT TOGETHER IN TIME...
THE CLANG OF HEAVY GATES LOCKING SHUT.
THE RUSTLE OF STEEL MESH BREAKING THE SURFACE OF LAPPING WATER.
THEY'RE TOO TANGLED AND TURNED AROUND IN THE HEAD FROM PRIAPUS' MIND GAMES
THE DESPERATE LAST GASPS OF THE COMPETITION GOING OUT OF BUSINESS.
UNDER DIFFERENT CIRCUMSTANCES, I MIGHT HAVE ENGINEERED A SIMILAR SCENARIO.
BUT IN THIS INSTANCE, WE HAVE ALL BEEN DEFRAUDED BY THE SAME CONTRACTEE...
...AND IT MAY PROVE INVALUABLE TO HAVE PARTNERS IN ESTAB-LISHING A NEW INDUSTRY ADAGE.
SPLASSH

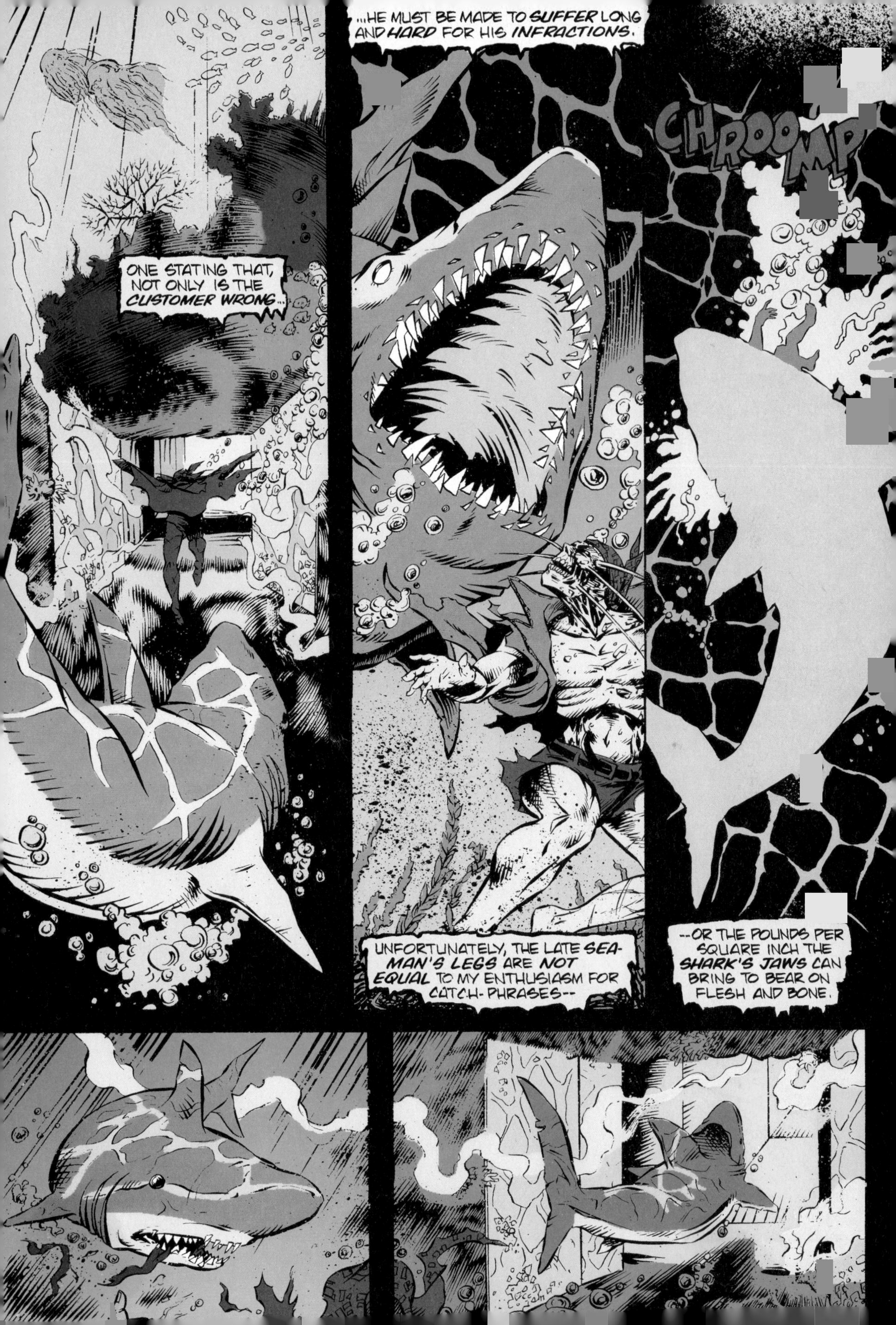
ONE STATING THAT, NOT ONLY IS THE CUSTOMER WRONG...
...HE MUST BE MADE TO SUFFER LONG AND HARD FOR HIS INFRACTIONS.
CHROOMP
UNFORTUNATELY, THE LATE SEA-MAN'S LEGS ARE NOT EQUAL TO MY ENTHUSIASM FOR CATCH-PHRASES--
--OR THE POUNDS PER SQUARE INCH THE SHARK'S JAWS CAN BRING TO BEAR ON FLESH AND BONE.

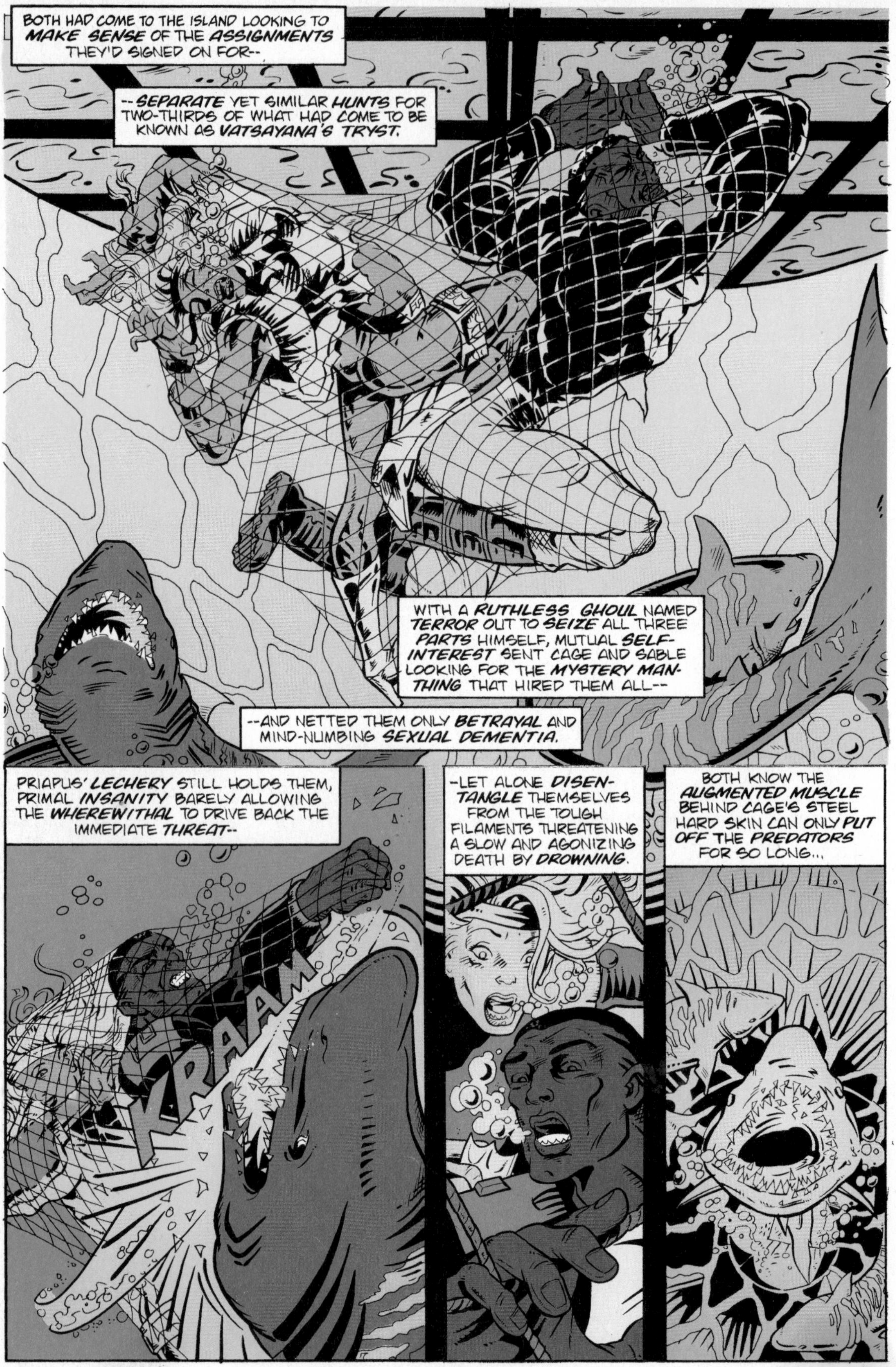
BOTH HAD COME TO THE ISLAND LOOKING TO MAKE SENSE OF THE ASSIGNMENTS THEY'D SIGNED ON FOR--
--SEPARATE YET SIMILAR HUNTS FOR TWO-THIRDS OF WHAT HAD COME TO BE KNOWN AS VATSAYANA'S TRYST.
WITH A RUTHLESS GHOUL NAMED TERROR OUT TO SEIZE ALL THREE PARTS HIMSELF, MUTUAL SELF-INTEREST SENT CAGE AND SABLE LOOKING FOR THE MYSTERY MAN-THING THAT HIRED THEM ALL--
--AND NETTED THEM ONLY BETRAYAL AND MIND-NUMBING SEXUAL DEMENTIA.
PRIAPUS' LECHERY STILL HOLDS THEM, PRIMAL INSANITY BARELY ALLOWING THE WHEREWITHAL TO DRIVE BACK THE IMMEDIATE THREAT--
KRAAM
-LET ALONE DISEN-TANGLE THEMSELVES FROM THE TOUGH FILAMENTS THREATENING A SLOW AND AGONIZING DEATH BY DROWNING.
BOTH KNOW THE AUGMENTED MUSCLE BEHIND CAGE'S STEEL HARD SKIN CAN ONLY PUT OFF THE PREDATORS FOR SO LONG...

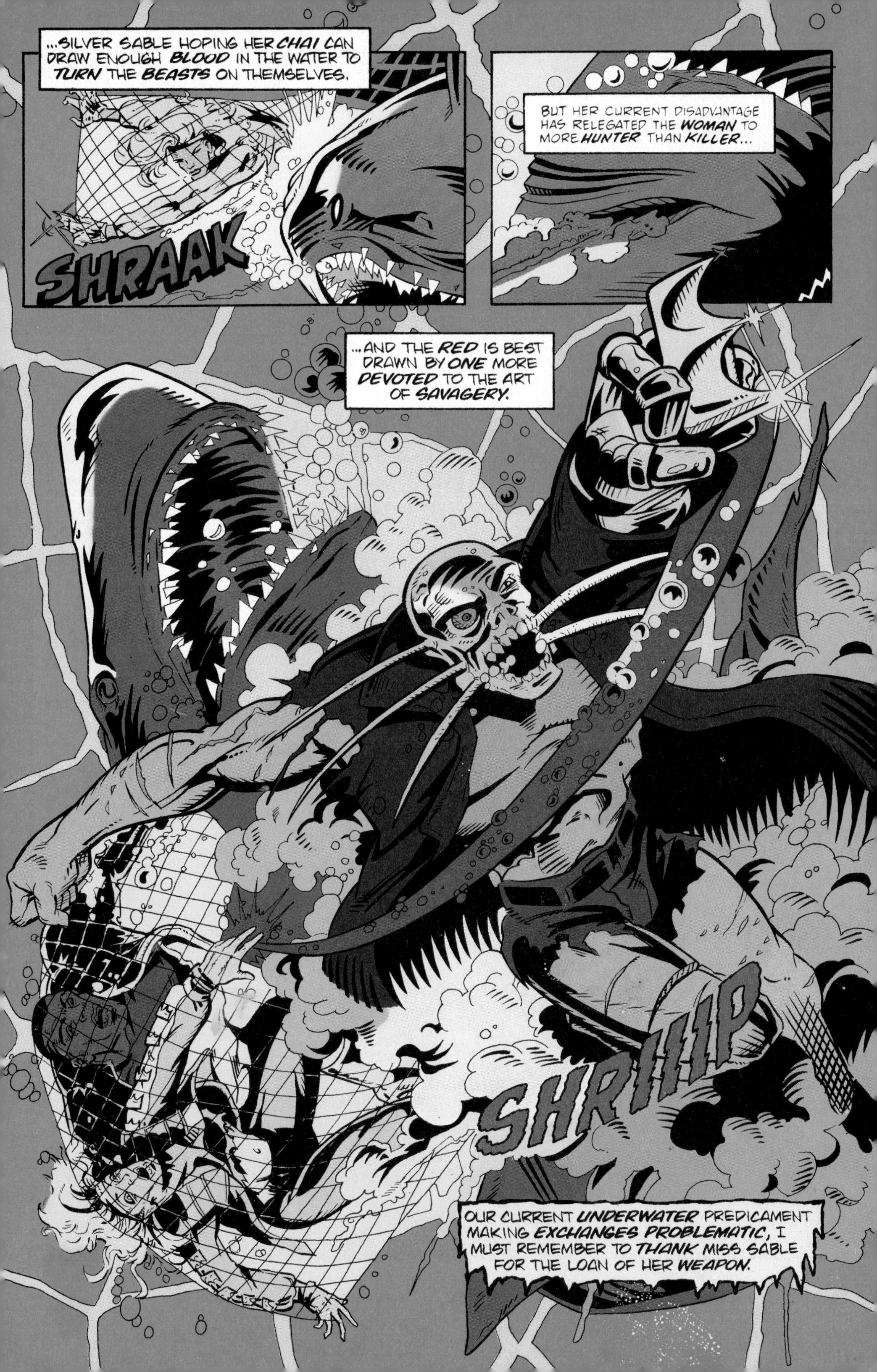
...SILVER SABLE HOPING HER CHAI CAN DRAW ENOUGH BLOOD IN THE WATER TO TURN THE BEASTS ON THEMSELVES.
SHRAAK
BUT HER CURRENT DISADVANTAGE HAS RELEGATED THE WOMAN TO MORE HUNTER THAN KILLER...
...AND THE RED IS BEST DRAWN BY ONE MORE DEVOTED TO THE ART OF SAVAGERY.
SHRIIIP
OUR CURRENT UNDERWATER PREDICAMENT MAKING EXCHANGES PROBLEMATIC, I MUST REMEMBER TO THANK MISS SABLE FOR THE LOAN OF HER WEAPON.

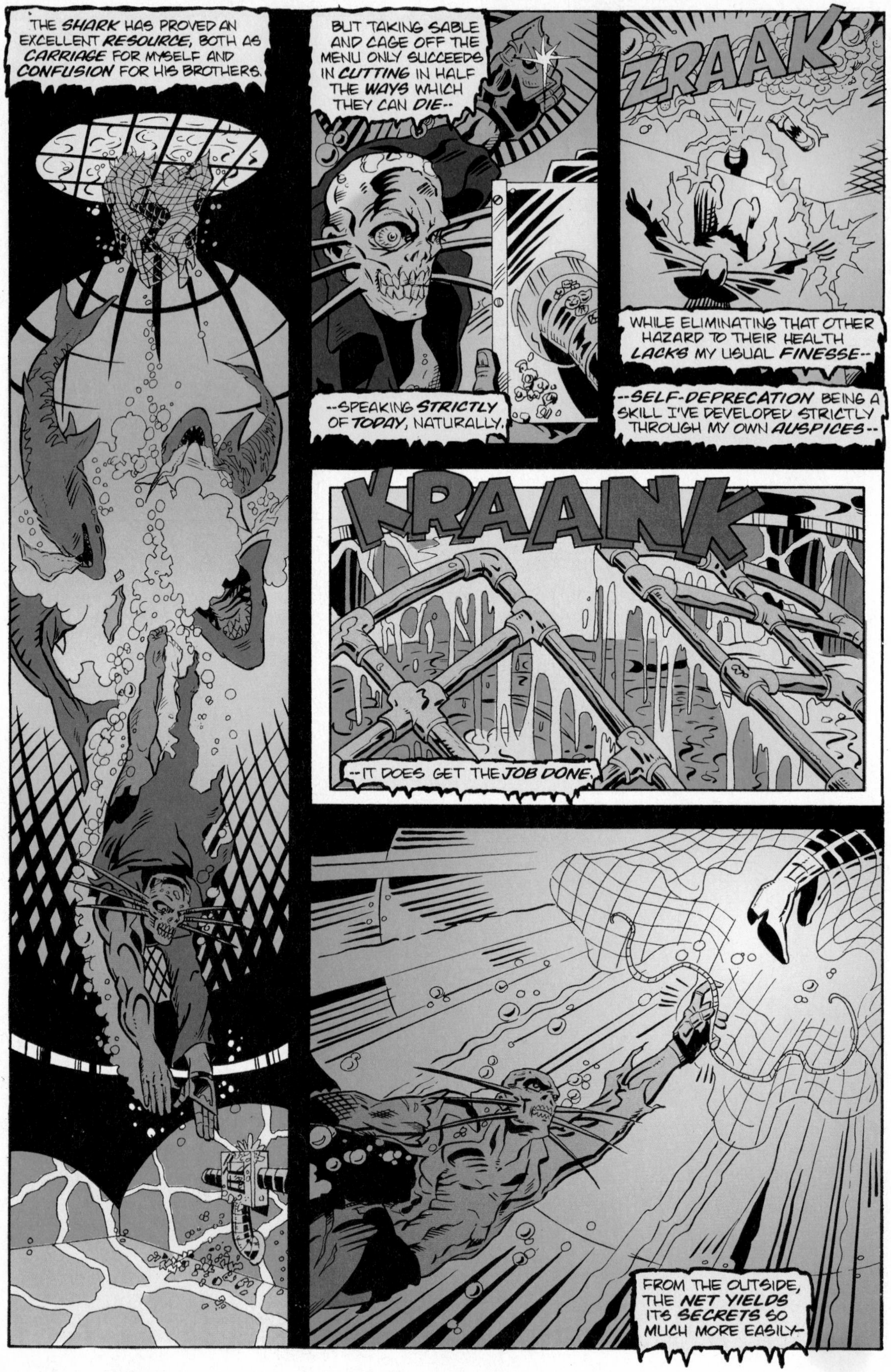
THE SHARK HAS PROVED AN EXCELLENT RESOURCE, BOTH AS CARRIAGE FOR MYSELF AND CONFUSION FOR HIS BROTHERS.
BUT TAKING SABLE AND CAGE OFF THE MENU ONLY SUCCEEDS IN CUTTING IN HALF THE WAYS WHICH THEY CAN DIE--
--SPEAKING STRICTLY OF TODAY, NATURALLY.
ZRAAK
WHILE ELIMINATING THAT OTHER HAZARD TO THEIR HEALTH LACKS MY USUAL FINESSE--
--SELF-DEPRECATION BEING A SKILL I'VE DEVELOPED STRICTLY THROUGH MY OWN AUSPICES--
KRAANK
--IT DOES GET THE JOB DONE.
FROM THE OUTSIDE, THE NET YIELDS ITS SECRETS SO MUCH MORE EASILY--

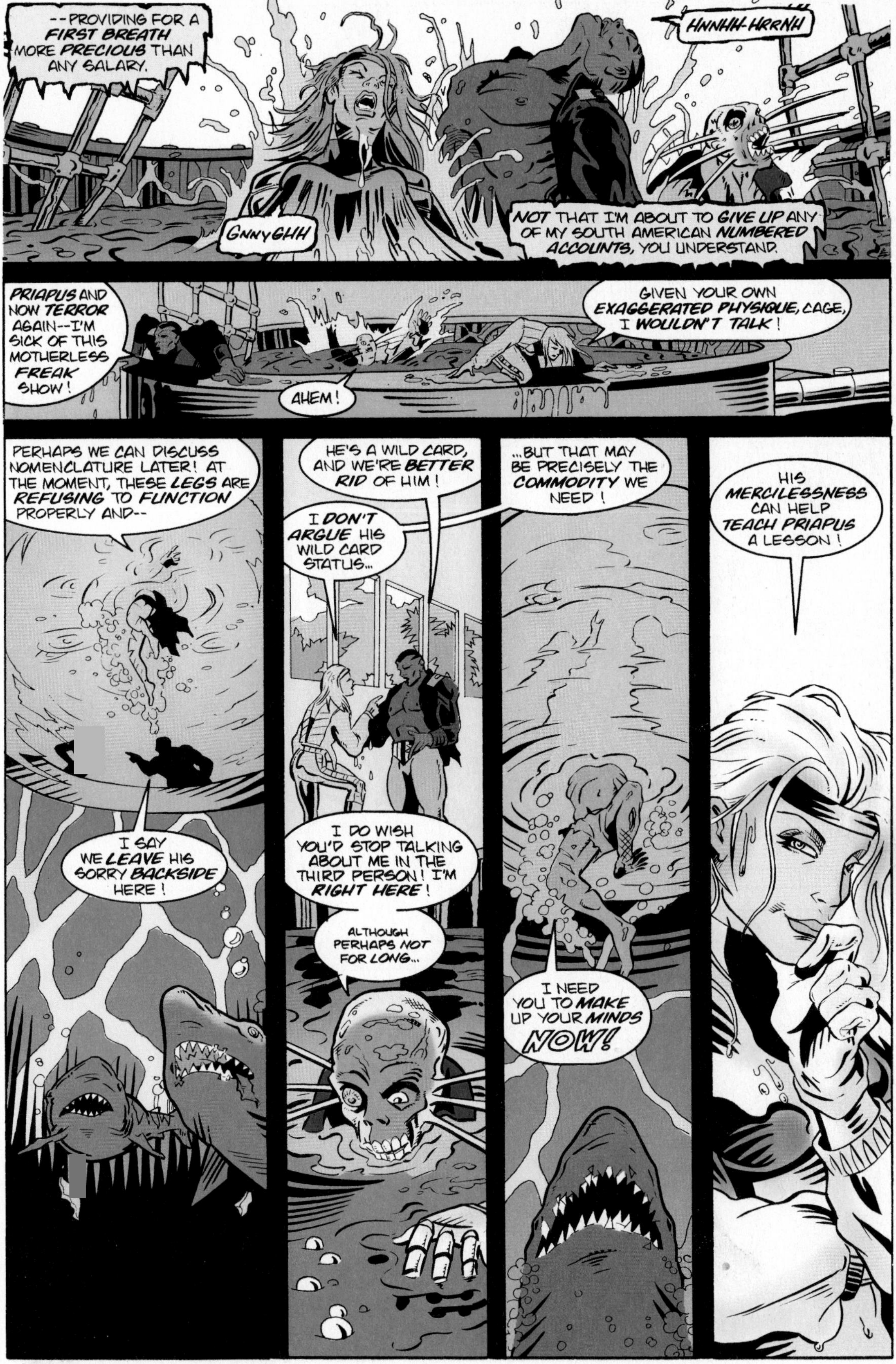
--PROVIDING FOR A FIRST BREATH MORE PRECIOUS THAN ANY SALARY.
HNNHH-HRRNH
GNNYGHH
NOT THAT I'M ABOUT TO GIVE UP ANY OF MY SOUTH AMERICAN NUMBERED ACCOUNTS, YOU UNDERSTAND.
PRIAPUS AND NOW TERROR AGAIN--I'M SICK OF THIS MOTHERLESS FREAK SHOW!
GIVEN YOUR OWN EXAGGERATED PHYSIQUE, CAGE, I WOULDN'T TALK!
AHEM!
PERHAPS WE CAN DISCUSS NOMENCLATURE LATER! AT THE MOMENT, THESE LEGS ARE REFUSING TO FUNCTION PROPERLY AND--
I SAY WE LEAVE HIS SORRY BACKSIDE HERE!
HE'S A WILD CARD, AND WE'RE BETTER RID OF HIM!
I DON'T ARGUE HIS WILD CARD STATUS...
...BUT THAT MAY BE PRECISELY THE COMMODITY WE NEED!
I DO WISH YOU'D STOP TALKING ABOUT ME IN THE THIRD PERSON! I'M RIGHT HERE!
ALTHOUGH PERHAPS NOT FOR LONG...
I NEED YOU TO MAKE UP YOUR MINDS NOW!
HIS MERCILESSNESS CAN HELP TEACH PRIAPUS A LESSON!

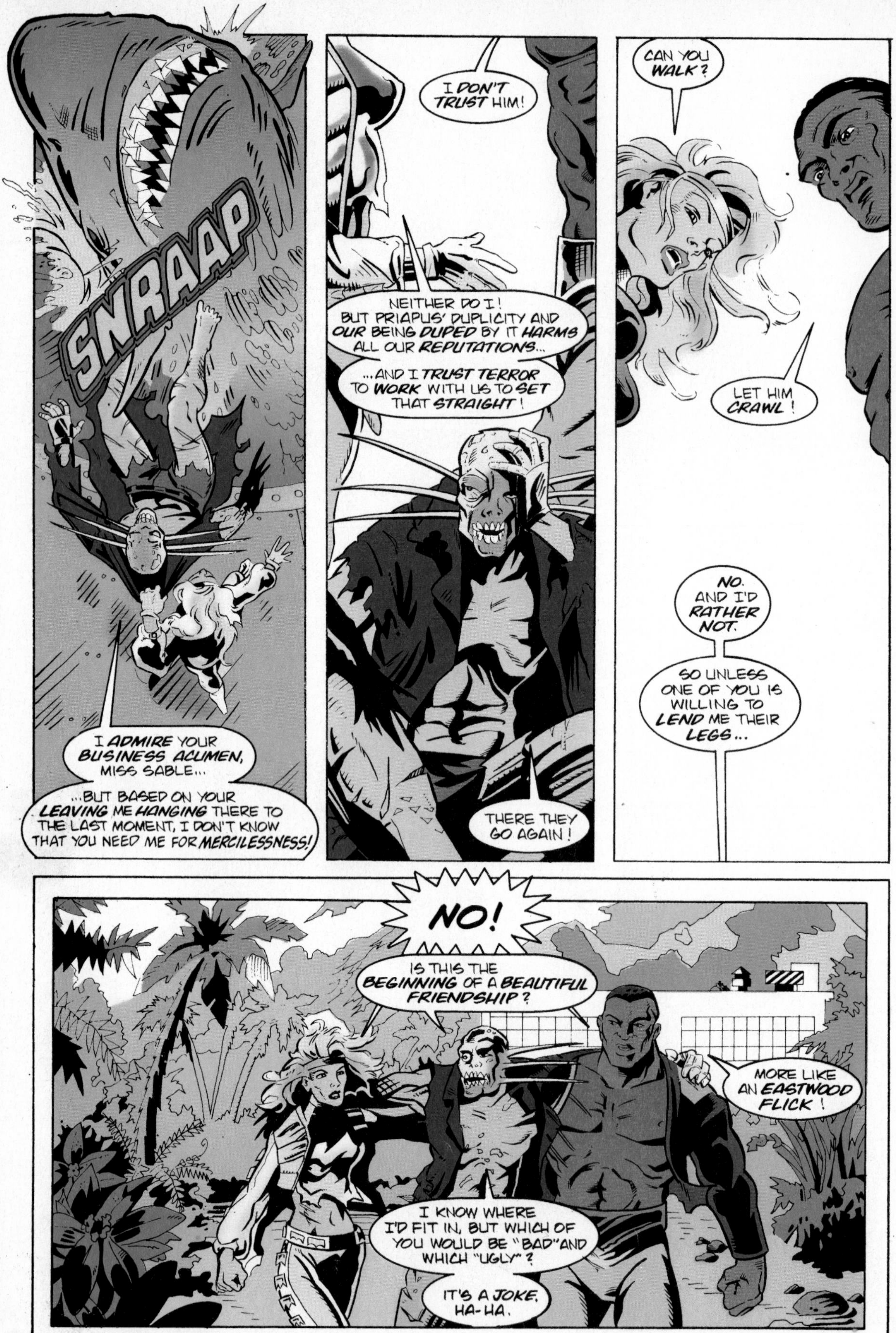
SNRAAP
I ADMIRE YOUR BUSINESS ACUMEN, MISS SABLE...
...BUT BASED ON YOUR LEAVING ME HANGING THERE TO THE LAST MOMENT, I DON'T KNOW THAT YOU NEED ME FOR MERCILESSNESS!
I DON'T TRUST HIM!
NEITHER DO I! BUT PRIAPUS' DUPLICITY AND OUR BEING DUPED BY IT HARMS ALL OUR REPUTATIONS...
...AND I TRUST TERROR TO WORK WITH US TO SET THAT STRAIGHT!
THERE THEY GO AGAIN!
CAN YOU WALK?
LET HIM CRAWL!
NO. AND I'D RATHER NOT.
SO UNLESS ONE OF YOU IS WILLING TO LEND ME THEIR LEGS...
NO!
IS THIS THE BEGINNING OF A BEAUTIFUL FRIENDSHIP?
MORE LIKE AN EASTWOOD FLICK!
I KNOW WHERE I'D FIT IN, BUT WHICH OF YOU WOULD BE "BAD" AND WHICH "UGLY"?
IT'S A JOKE. HA-HA.

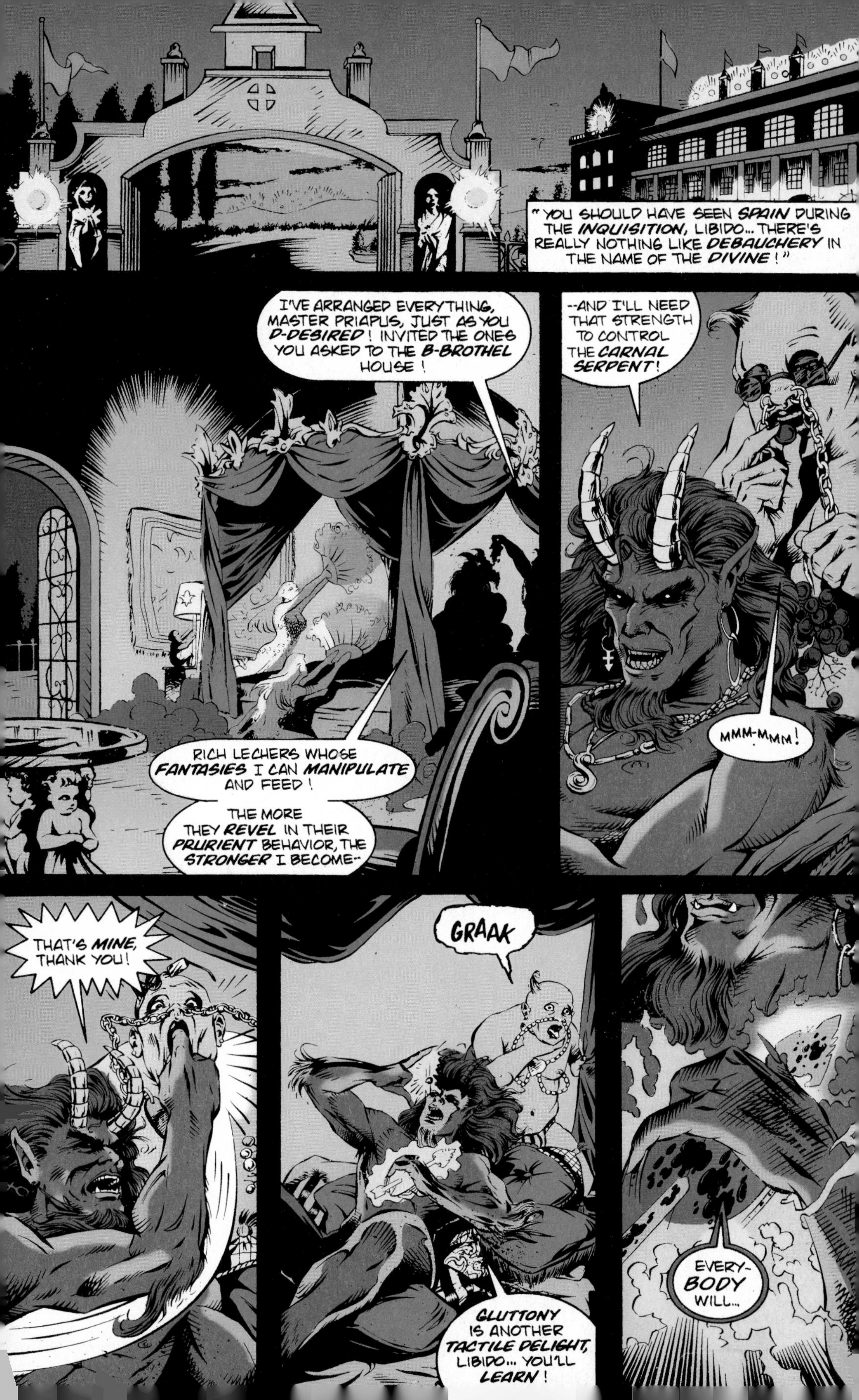
"YOU SHOULD HAVE SEEN SPAIN DURING THE INQUISITION, LIBIDO... THERE'S REALLY NOTHING LIKE DEBAUCHERY IN THE NAME OF THE DIVINE!"
I'VE ARRANGED EVERYTHING, MASTER PRIAPUS, JUST AS YOU D-DESIRED! INVITED THE ONES YOU ASKED TO THE B-BROTHEL HOUSE!
RICH LECHERS WHOSE FANTASIES I CAN MANIPULATE AND FEED!
THE MORE THEY REVEL IN THEIR PRURIENT BEHAVIOR, THE STRONGER I BECOME--
--AND I'LL NEED THAT STRENGTH TO CONTROL THE CARNAL SERPENT!
MMM-MMM!
THAT'S MINE, THANK YOU!
GRAAK
GLUTTONY IS ANOTHER TACTILE DELIGHT, LIBIDO... YOU'LL LEARN!
EVERY-BODY WILL...

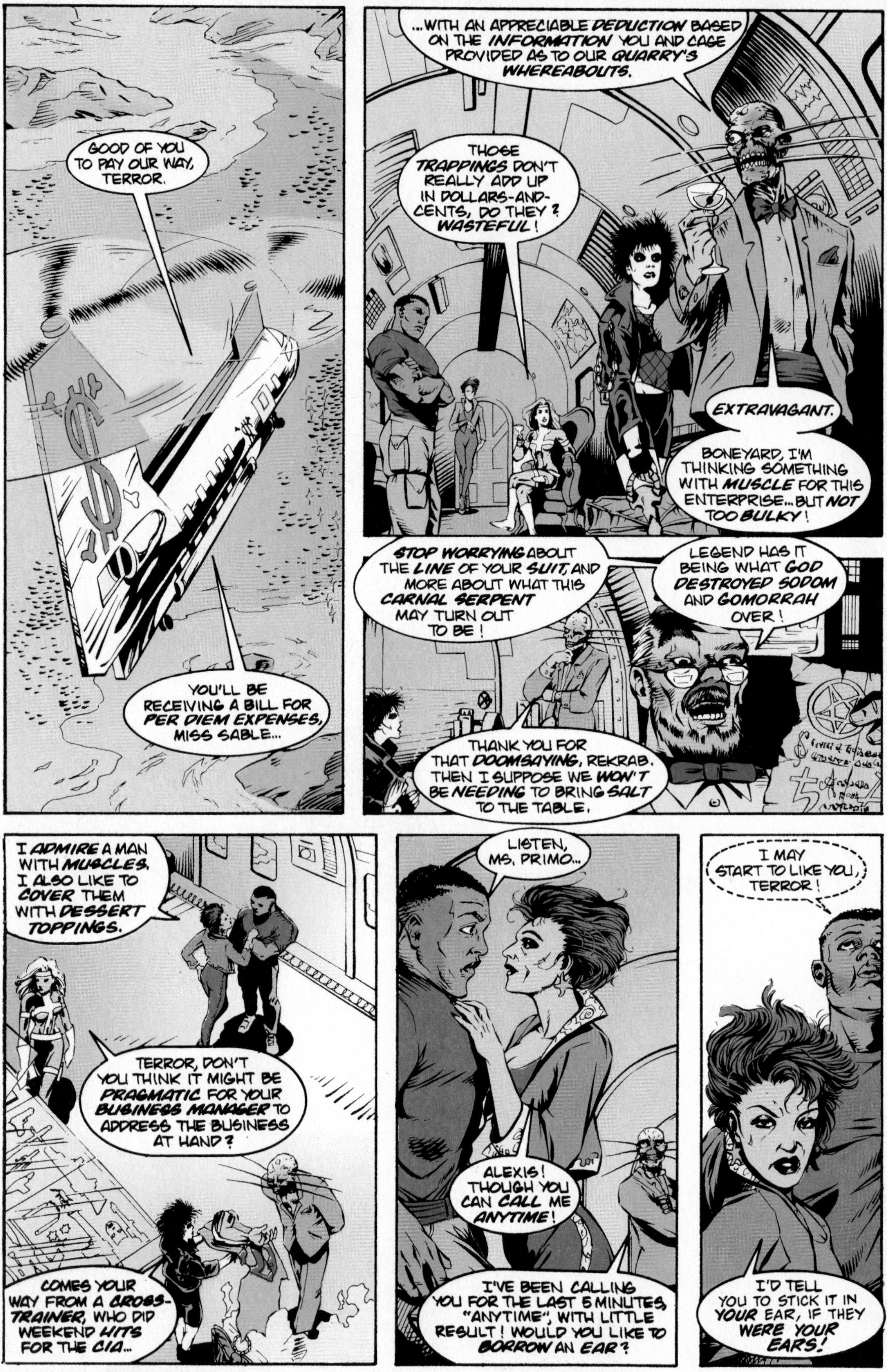
GOOD OF YOU TO PAY OUR WAY, TERROR.
YOU'LL BE RECEIVING A BILL FOR PER DIEM EXPENSES, MISS SABLE...
...WITH AN APPRECIABLE DEDUCTION BASED ON THE INFORMATION YOU AND CAGE PROVIDED AS TO OUR QUARRY'S WHEREABOUTS.
THOSE TRAPPINGS DON'T REALLY ADD UP IN DOLLARS-AND-CENTS, DO THEY? WASTEFUL!
EXTRAVAGANT.
BONEYARD, I'M THINKING SOMETHING WITH MUSCLE FOR THIS ENTERPRISE... BUT NOT TOO BULKY!
STOP WORRYING ABOUT THE LINE OF YOUR SUIT, AND MORE ABOUT WHAT THIS CARNAL SERPENT MAY TURN OUT TO BE!
LEGEND HAS IT BEING WHAT GOD DESTROYED SODOM AND GOMORRAH OVER!
THANK YOU FOR THAT DOOMSAYING, REKRAB. THEN I SUPPOSE WE WON'T BE NEEDING TO BRING SALT TO THE TABLE.
I ADMIRE A MAN WITH MUSCLES. I ALSO LIKE TO COVER THEM WITH DESSERT TOPPINGS.
TERROR, DON'T YOU THINK IT MIGHT BE PRAGMATIC FOR YOUR BUSINESS MANAGER TO ADDRESS THE BUSINESS AT HAND?
COMES YOUR WAY FROM A CROSS-TRAINER, WHO DID WEEKEND HITS FOR THE CIA...
LISTEN, MS. PRIMO...
ALEXIS! THOUGH YOU CAN CALL ME ANYTIME!
I'VE BEEN CALLING YOU FOR THE LAST 5 MINUTES, "ANYTIME", WITH LITTLE RESULT! WOULD YOU LIKE TO BORROW AN EAR?
I MAY START TO LIKE YOU, TERROR!
I'D TELL YOU TO STICK IT IN YOUR EAR, IF THEY WERE YOUR EARS!

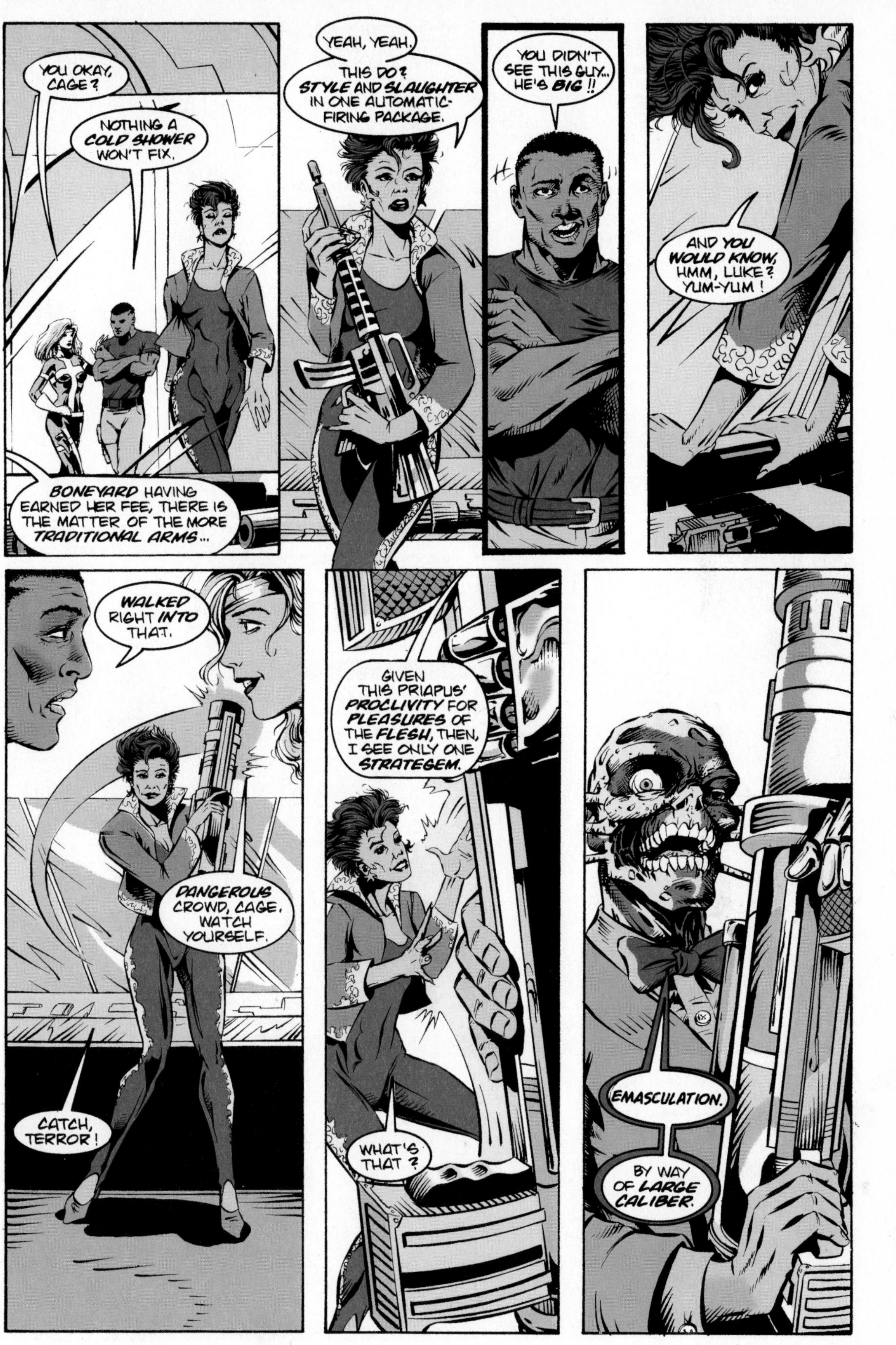
You okay, Cage?
Nothing a cold shower won't fix.
Boneyard having earned her fee, there is the matter of the more traditional arms...
Yeah, yeah.
This do? Style and slaughter in one automatic-firing package.
You didn't see this guy... he's big!!
And you would know, hmm, Luke? Yum-yum!
Walked right into that.
Dangerous crowd, Cage. Watch yourself.
Catch, Terror!
Given this Priapus' proclivity for pleasures of the flesh, then, I see only one strategem.
What's that?
Emasculation.
By way of large caliber.

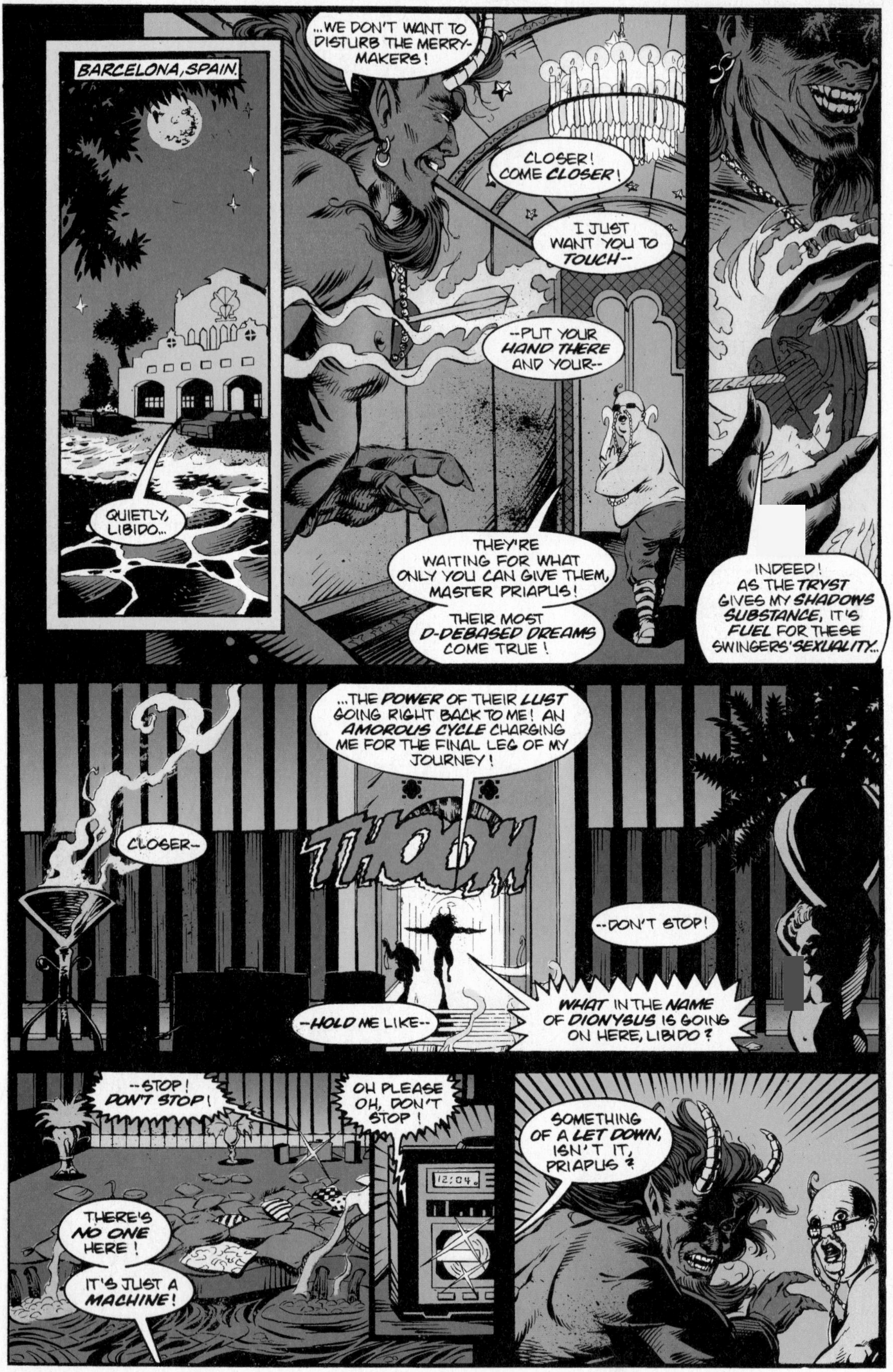
BARCELONA, SPAIN.
QUIETLY, LIBIDO...
...WE DON'T WANT TO DISTURB THE MERRY-MAKERS!
CLOSER! COME CLOSER!
I JUST WANT YOU TO TOUCH--
--PUT YOUR HAND THERE AND YOUR--
THEY'RE WAITING FOR WHAT ONLY YOU CAN GIVE THEM, MASTER PRIAPUS!
THEIR MOST D-DEBASED DREAMS COME TRUE!
INDEED! AS THE TRYST GIVES MY SHADOWS SUBSTANCE, IT'S FUEL FOR THESE SWINGERS' SEXUALITY...
...THE POWER OF THEIR LUST GOING RIGHT BACK TO ME! AN AMOROUS CYCLE CHARGING ME FOR THE FINAL LEG OF MY JOURNEY!
CLOSER-
THOOM
--DON'T STOP!
--HOLD ME LIKE--
WHAT IN THE NAME OF DIONYSUS IS GOING ON HERE, LIBIDO?
--STOP! DON'T STOP!
OH PLEASE OH, DON'T STOP!
12:04
THERE'S NO ONE HERE!
IT'S JUST A MACHINE!
SOMETHING OF A LET DOWN, ISN'T IT, PRIAPUS?

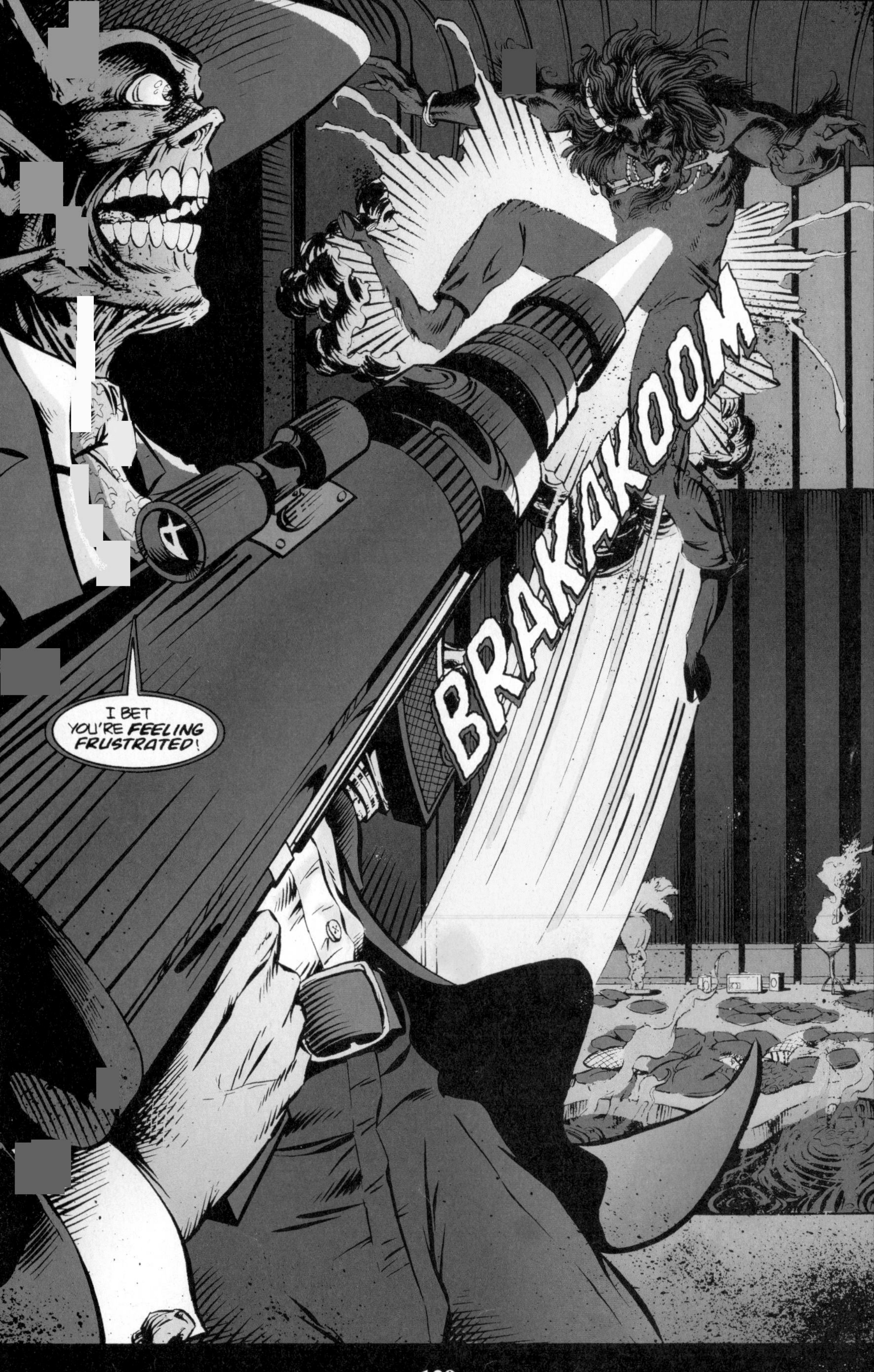
I BET YOU'RE FEELING FRUSTRATED!
BRAKAKOOM

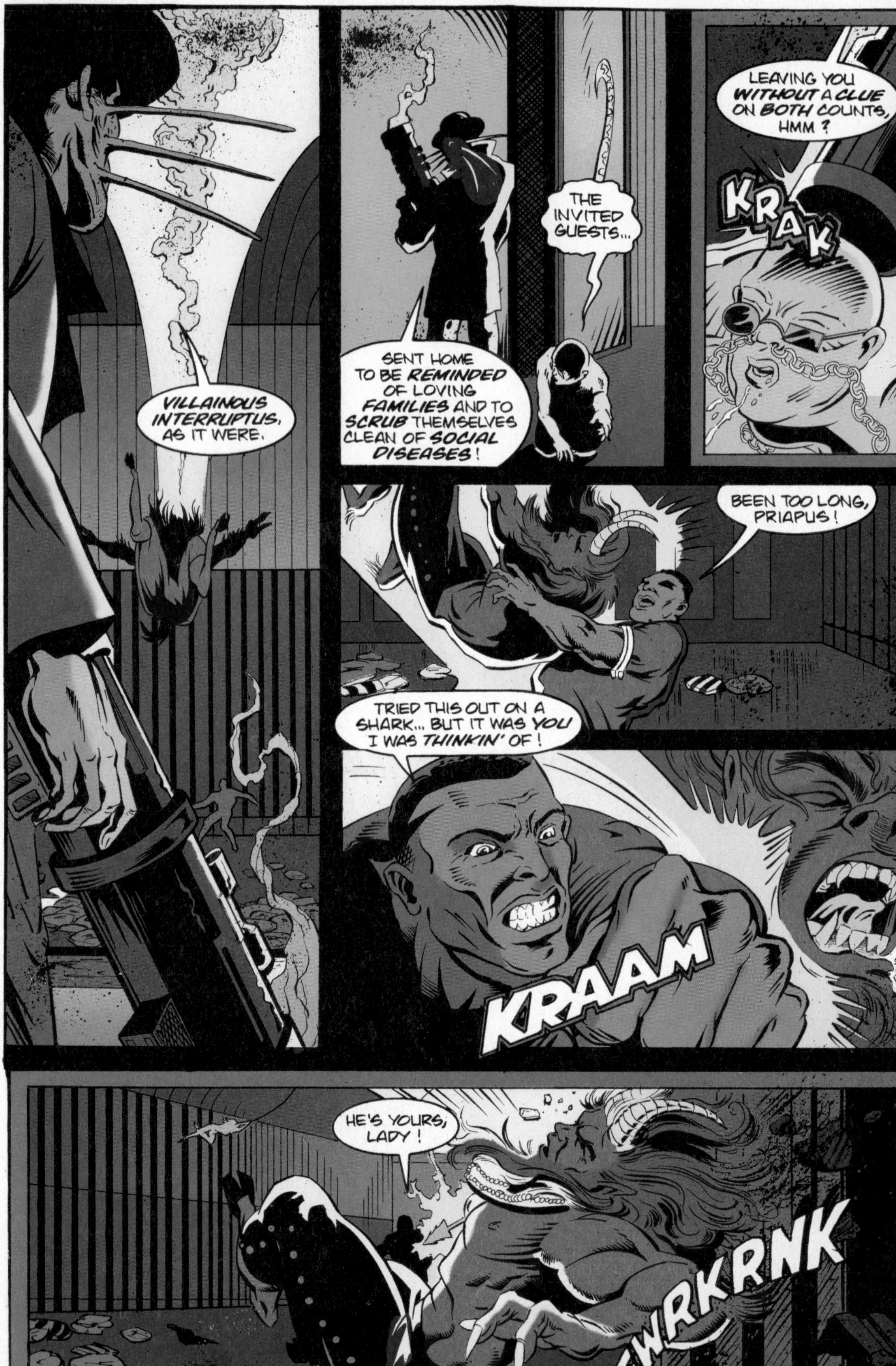
VILLAINOUS INTERRUPTUS, AS IT WERE.
SENT HOME TO BE REMINDED OF LOVING FAMILIES AND TO SCRUB THEMSELVES CLEAN OF SOCIAL DISEASES!
THE INVITED GUESTS...
LEAVING YOU WITHOUT A CLUE ON BOTH COUNTS, HMM?
KRAK
BEEN TOO LONG, PRIAPUS!
TRIED THIS OUT ON A SHARK... BUT IT WAS YOU I WAS THINKIN' OF!
KRAAM
HE'S YOURS, LADY!
FWRKRNK

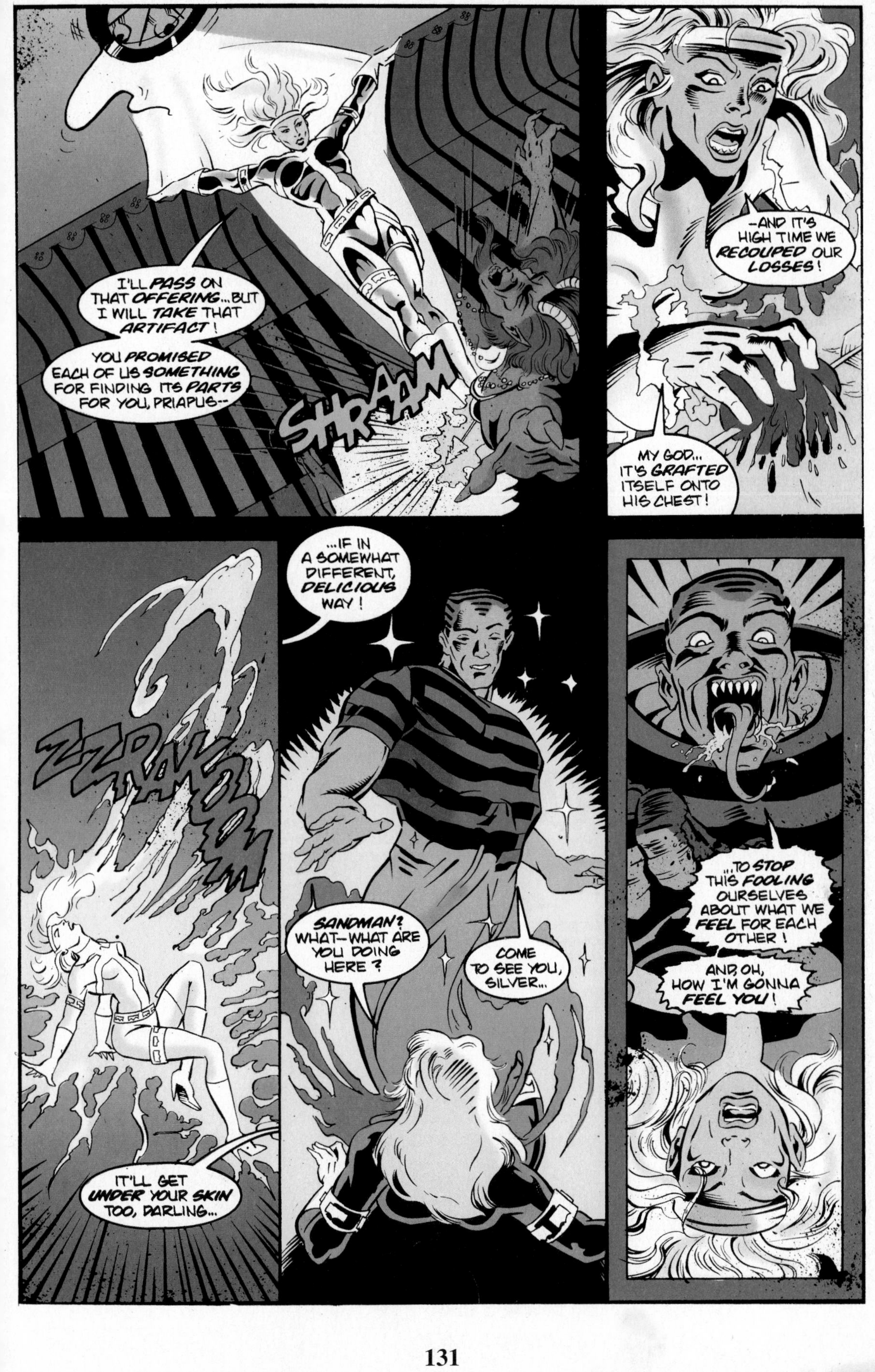
I'LL PASS ON THAT OFFERING...BUT I WILL TAKE THAT ARTIFACT!
YOU PROMISED EACH OF US SOMETHING FOR FINDING ITS PARTS FOR YOU, PRIAPUS--
SHRAAM
-AND IT'S HIGH TIME WE RECOUPED OUR LOSSES!
MY GOD... IT'S GRAFTED ITSELF ONTO HIS CHEST!
ZZRAKOOM
IT'LL GET UNDER YOUR SKIN TOO, DARLING...
...IF IN A SOMEWHAT DIFFERENT, DELICIOUS WAY!
SANDMAN? WHAT-WHAT ARE YOU DOING HERE?
COME TO SEE YOU, SILVER...
...TO STOP THIS FOOLING OURSELVES ABOUT WHAT WE FEEL FOR EACH OTHER!
AND, OH, HOW I'M GONNA FEEL YOU!

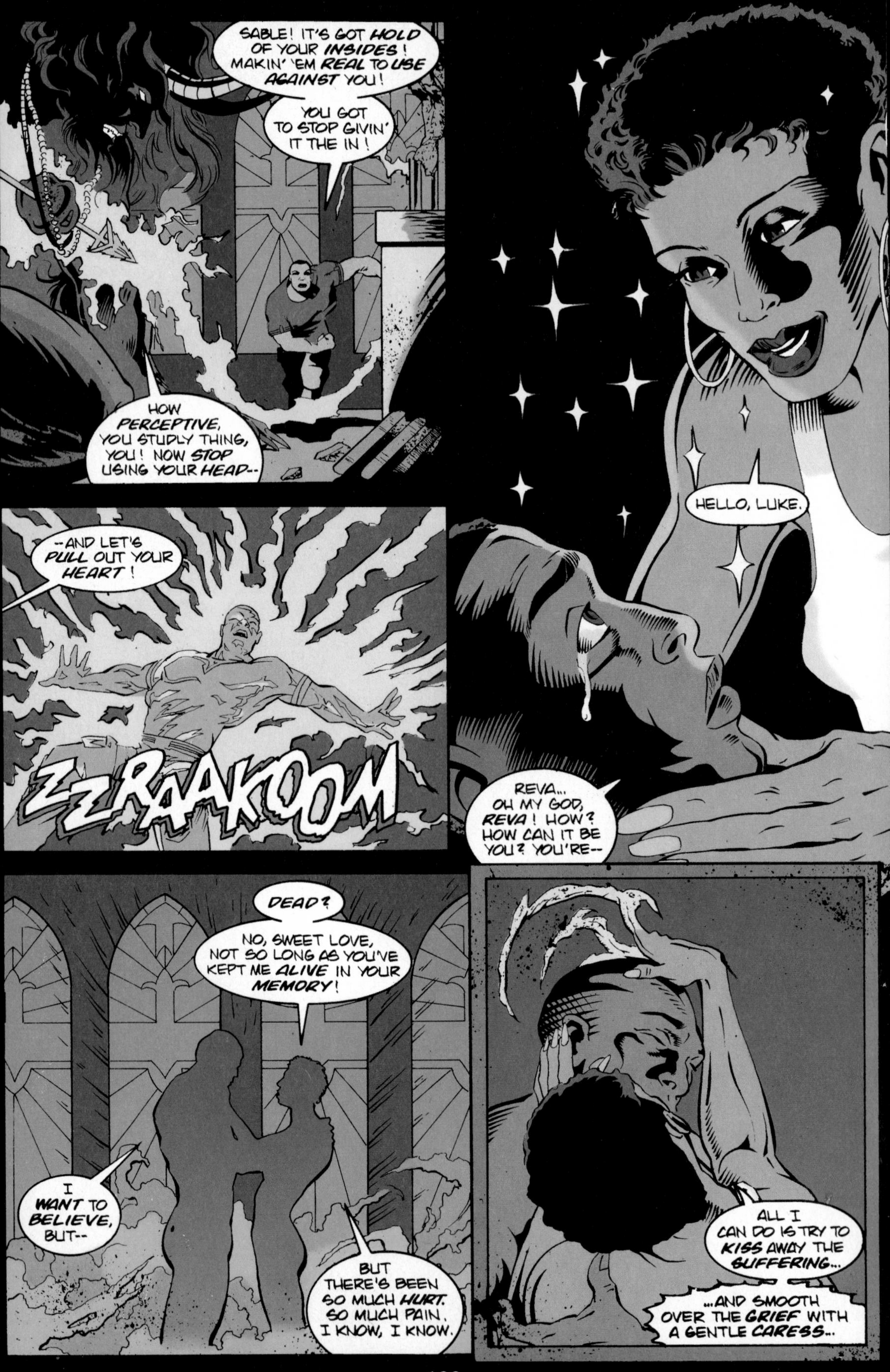
SABLE! IT'S GOT HOLD OF YOUR INSIDES! MAKIN' 'EM REAL TO USE AGAINST YOU!
YOU GOT TO STOP GIVIN' IT THE IN!
HOW PERCEPTIVE, YOU STUDLY THING, YOU! NOW STOP USING YOUR HEAD--
--AND LET'S PULL OUT YOUR HEART!
ZZRAAKOOM
HELLO, LUKE.
REVA... OH MY GOD, REVA! HOW? HOW CAN IT BE YOU? YOU'RE--
DEAD?
NO, SWEET LOVE, NOT SO LONG AS YOU'VE KEPT ME ALIVE IN YOUR MEMORY!
I WANT TO BELIEVE, BUT--
BUT THERE'S BEEN SO MUCH HURT. SO MUCH PAIN. I KNOW, I KNOW.
ALL I CAN DO IS TRY TO KISS AWAY THE SUFFERING...
...AND SMOOTH OVER THE GRIEF WITH A GENTLE CARESS...

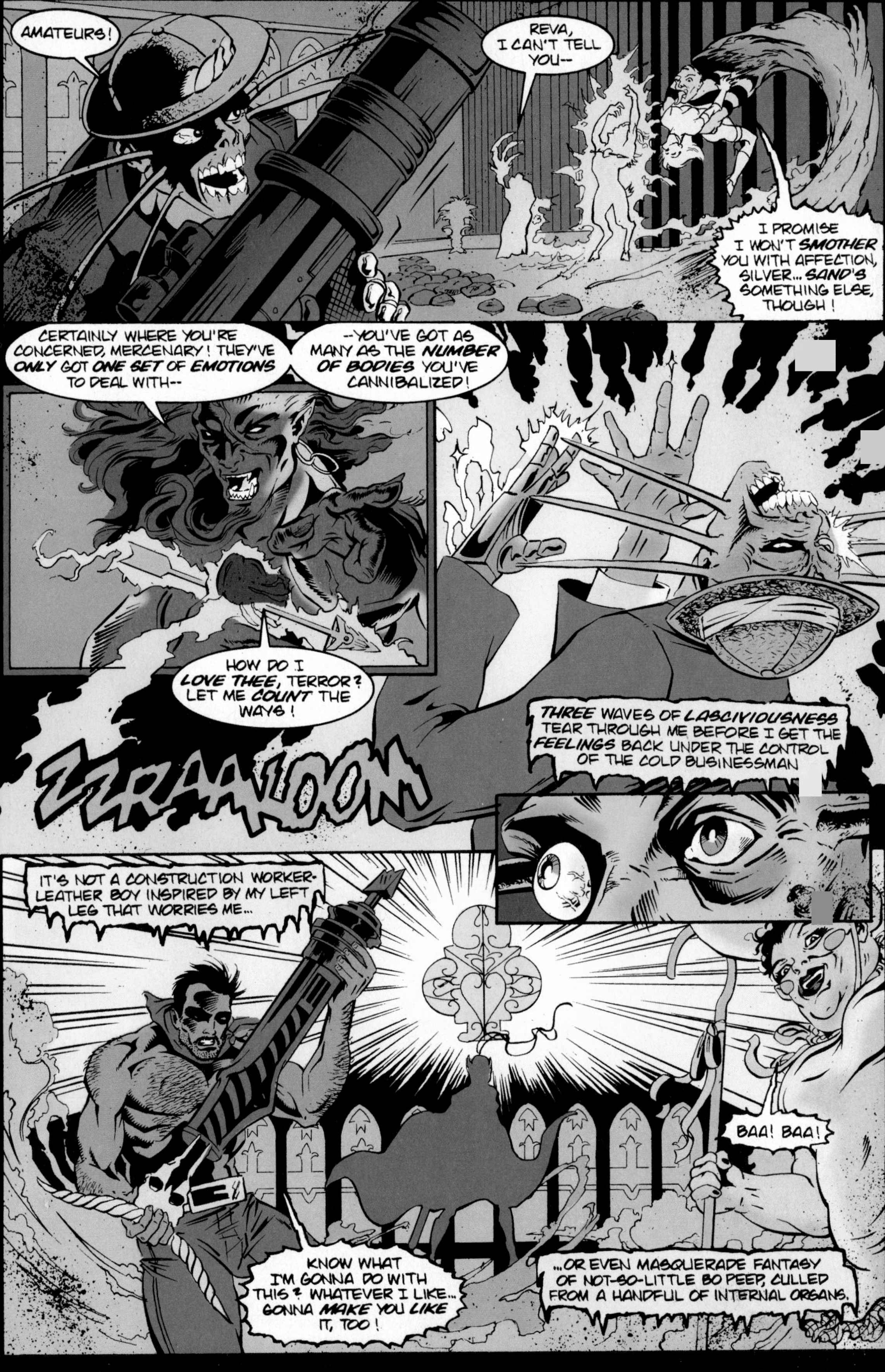

AMATEURS!
REVA, I CAN'T TELL YOU--
I PROMISE I WON'T SMOTHER YOU WITH AFFECTION, SILVER... SAND'S SOMETHING ELSE, THOUGH !
CERTAINLY WHERE YOU'RE CONCERNED, MERCENARY! THEY'VE ONLY GOT ONE SET OF EMOTIONS TO DEAL WITH--
--YOU'VE GOT AS MANY AS THE NUMBER OF BODIES YOU'VE CANNIBALIZED!
HOW DO I LOVE THEE, TERROR? LET ME COUNT THE WAYS !
ZZRAALOOM
THREE WAVES OF LASCIVIOUSNESS TEAR THROUGH ME BEFORE I GET THE FEELINGS BACK UNDER THE CONTROL OF THE COLD BUSINESSMAN
IT'S NOT A CONSTRUCTION WORKER-LEATHER BOY INSPIRED BY MY LEFT LEG THAT WORRIES ME...
BAA! BAA!
KNOW WHAT I'M GONNA DO WITH THIS? WHATEVER I LIKE... GONNA MAKE YOU LIKE IT, TOO !
...OR EVEN MASQUERADE FANTASY OF NOT-SO-LITTLE BO PEEP, CULLED FROM A HANDFUL OF INTERNAL ORGANS.

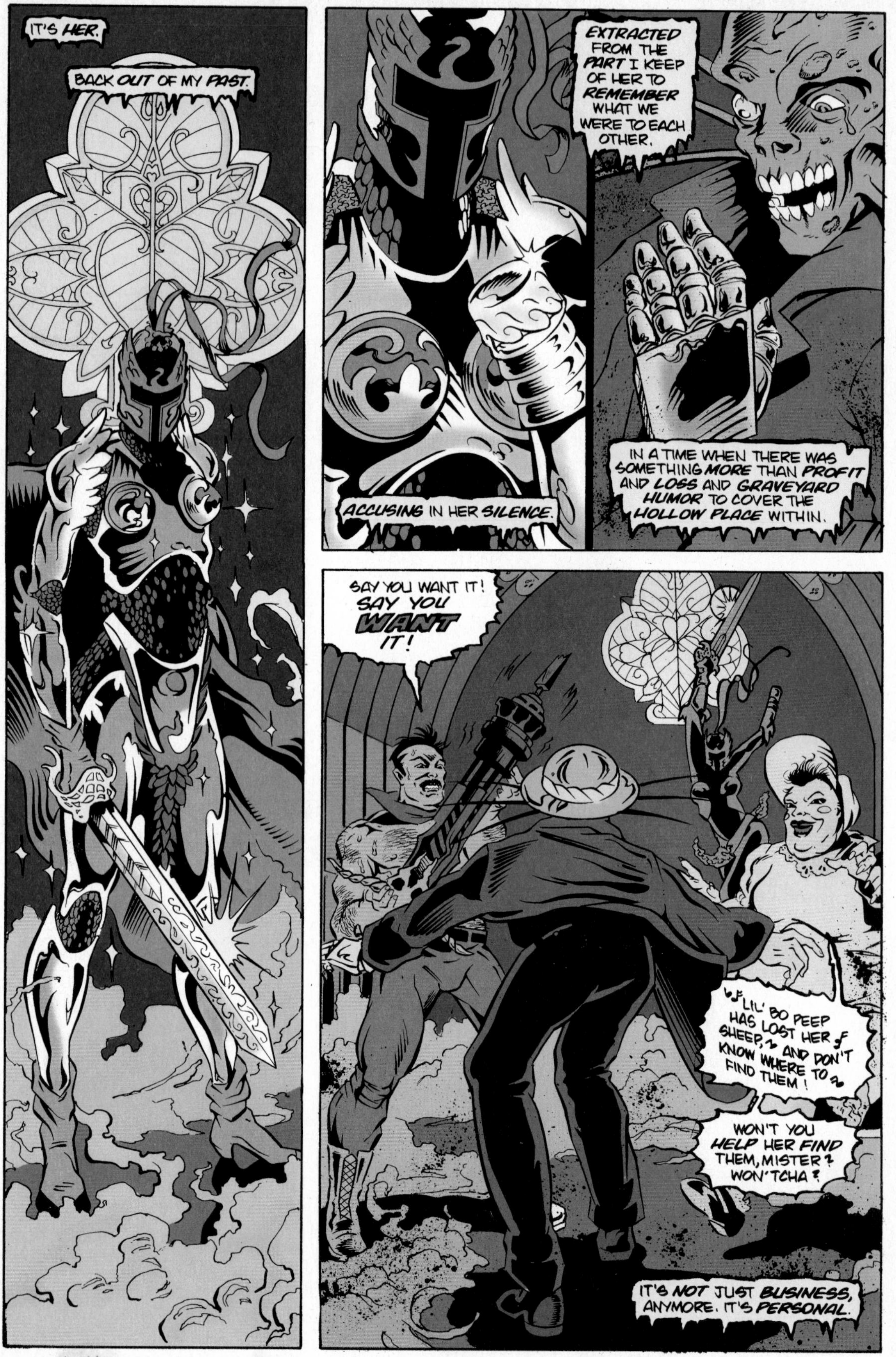
IT'S HER.
BACK OUT OF MY PAST.
EXTRACTED FROM THE PART I KEEP OF HER TO REMEMBER WHAT WE WERE TO EACH OTHER.
ACCUSING IN HER SILENCE.
IN A TIME WHEN THERE WAS SOMETHING MORE THAN PROFIT AND LOSS AND GRAVEYARD HUMOR TO COVER THE HOLLOW PLACE WITHIN.
SAY YOU WANT IT! SAY YOU WANT IT!
LIL' BO PEEP HAS LOST HER SHEEP, AND DON'T KNOW WHERE TO FIND THEM!
WON'T YOU HELP HER FIND THEM, MISTER? WON'TCHA?
IT'S NOT JUST BUSINESS, ANYMORE. IT'S PERSONAL.

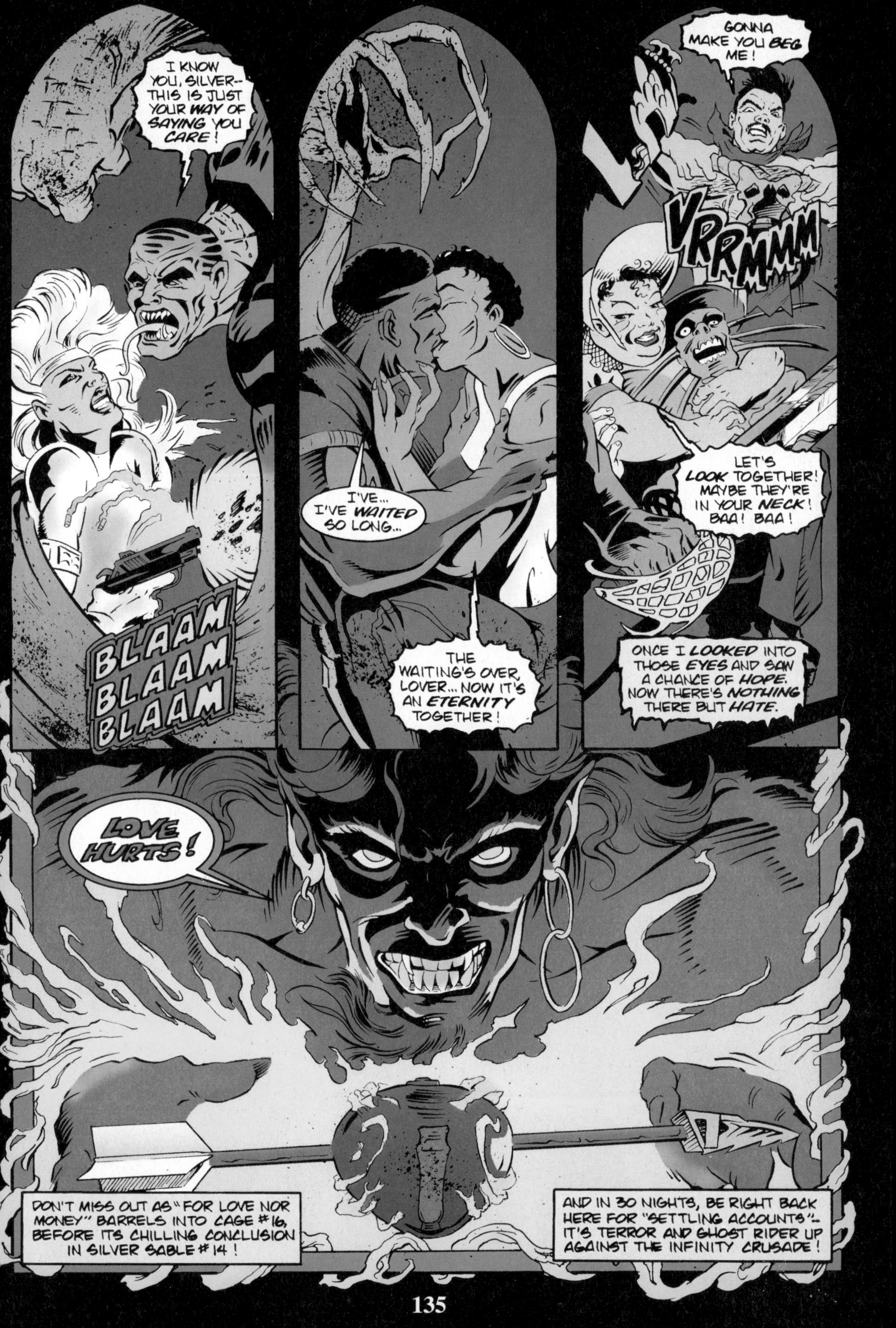
I KNOW YOU, SILVER-- THIS IS JUST YOUR WAY OF SAYING YOU CARE!
BLAAM BLAAM BLAAM
I'VE... I'VE WAITED SO LONG...
THE WAITING'S OVER, LOVER... NOW IT'S AN ETERNITY TOGETHER!
GONNA MAKE YOU BEG ME!
VRRMMM
LET'S LOOK TOGETHER! MAYBE THEY'RE IN YOUR NECK! BAA! BAA!
ONCE I LOOKED INTO THOSE EYES AND SAW A CHANCE OF HOPE. NOW THERE'S NOTHING THERE BUT HATE.
LOVE HURTS!
DON'T MISS OUT AS "FOR LOVE NOR MONEY" BARRELS INTO CAGE #16, BEFORE ITS CHILLING CONCLUSION IN SILVER SABLE #14!
AND IN 30 NIGHTS, BE RIGHT BACK HERE FOR "SETTLING ACCOUNTS"-- IT'S TERROR AND GHOST RIDER UP AGAINST THE INFINITY CRUSADE!

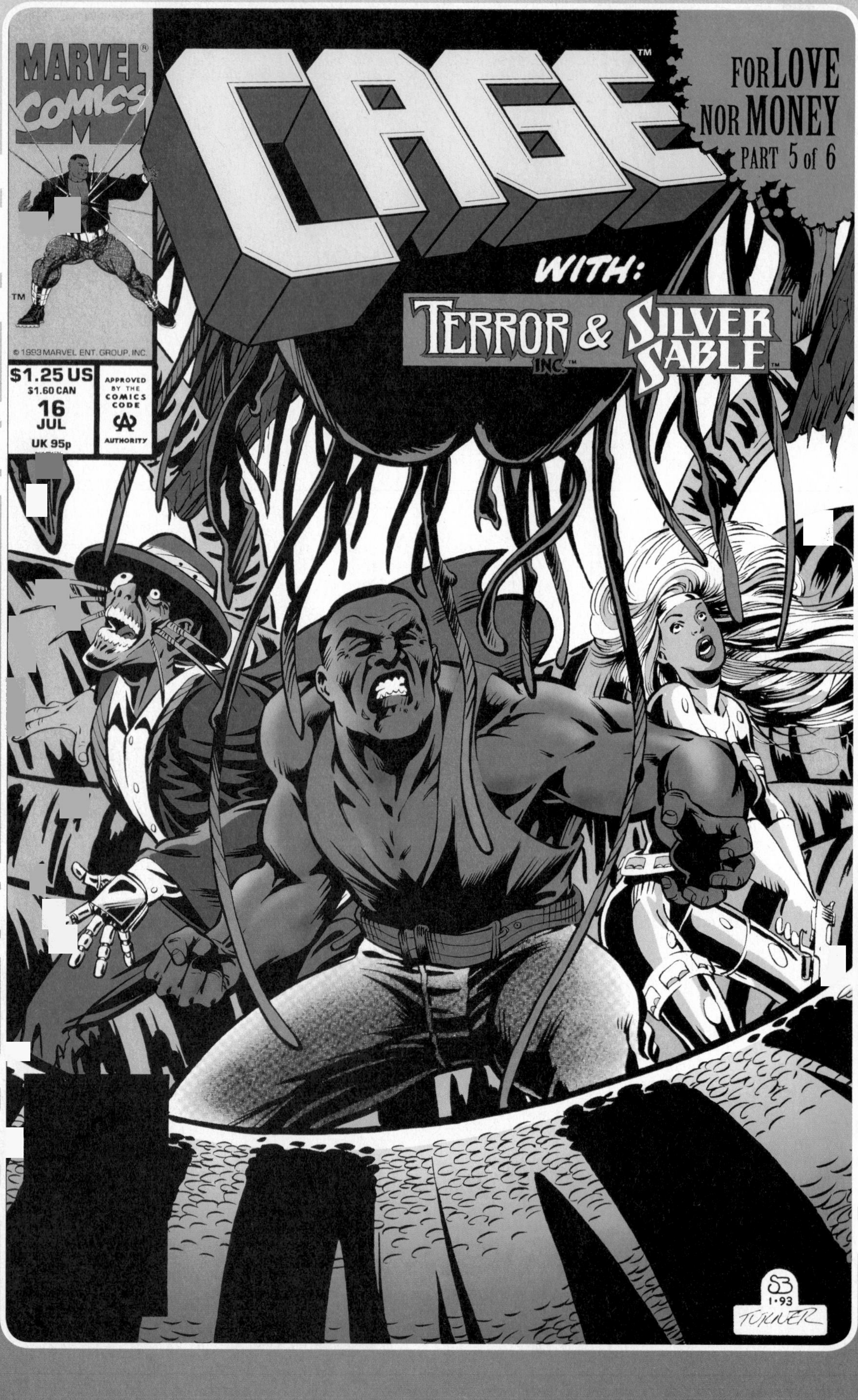
MARVEL COMICS
CAGE™
FOR LOVE NOR MONEY
PART 5 of 6
WITH:
TERROR INC.™ & SILVER SABLE™
© 1993 MARVEL ENT. GROUP, INC.
$1.25 US
$1.60 CAN
16
JUL
UK 95p
APPROVED BY THE COMICS CODE AUTHORITY
SB 1·93
TURNER

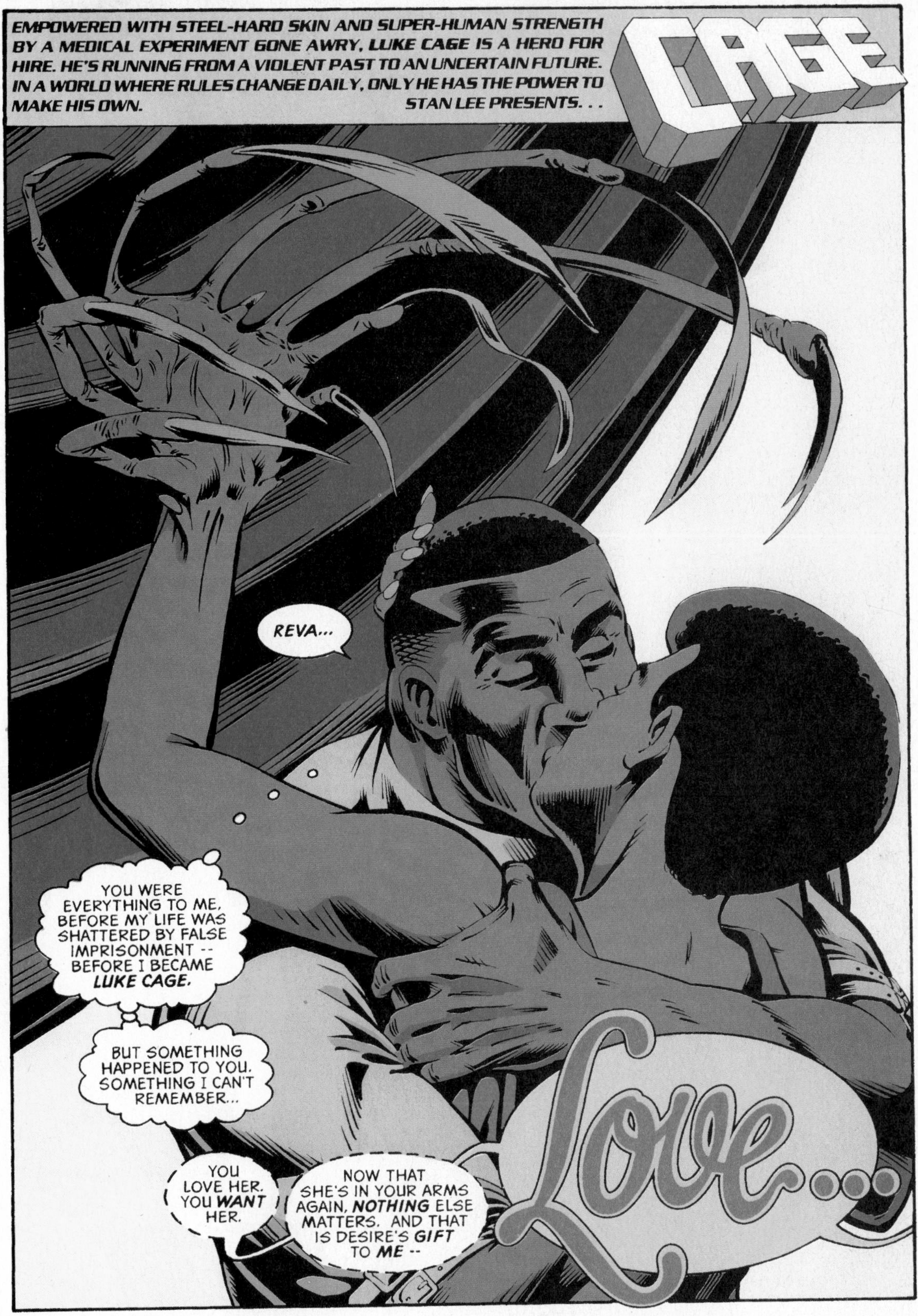

EMPOWERED WITH STEEL-HARD SKIN AND SUPER-HUMAN STRENGTH BY A MEDICAL EXPERIMENT GONE AWRY, LUKE CAGE IS A HERO FOR HIRE. HE'S RUNNING FROM A VIOLENT PAST TO AN UNCERTAIN FUTURE. IN A WORLD WHERE RULES CHANGE DAILY, ONLY HE HAS THE POWER TO MAKE HIS OWN.
STAN LEE PRESENTS. . .
CAGE
REVA...
YOU WERE EVERYTHING TO ME, BEFORE MY LIFE WAS SHATTERED BY FALSE IMPRISONMENT -- BEFORE I BECAME LUKE CAGE.
BUT SOMETHING HAPPENED TO YOU. SOMETHING I CAN'T REMEMBER...
YOU LOVE HER. YOU WANT HER.
NOW THAT SHE'S IN YOUR ARMS AGAIN, NOTHING ELSE MATTERS. AND THAT IS DESIRE'S GIFT TO ME --
Love...

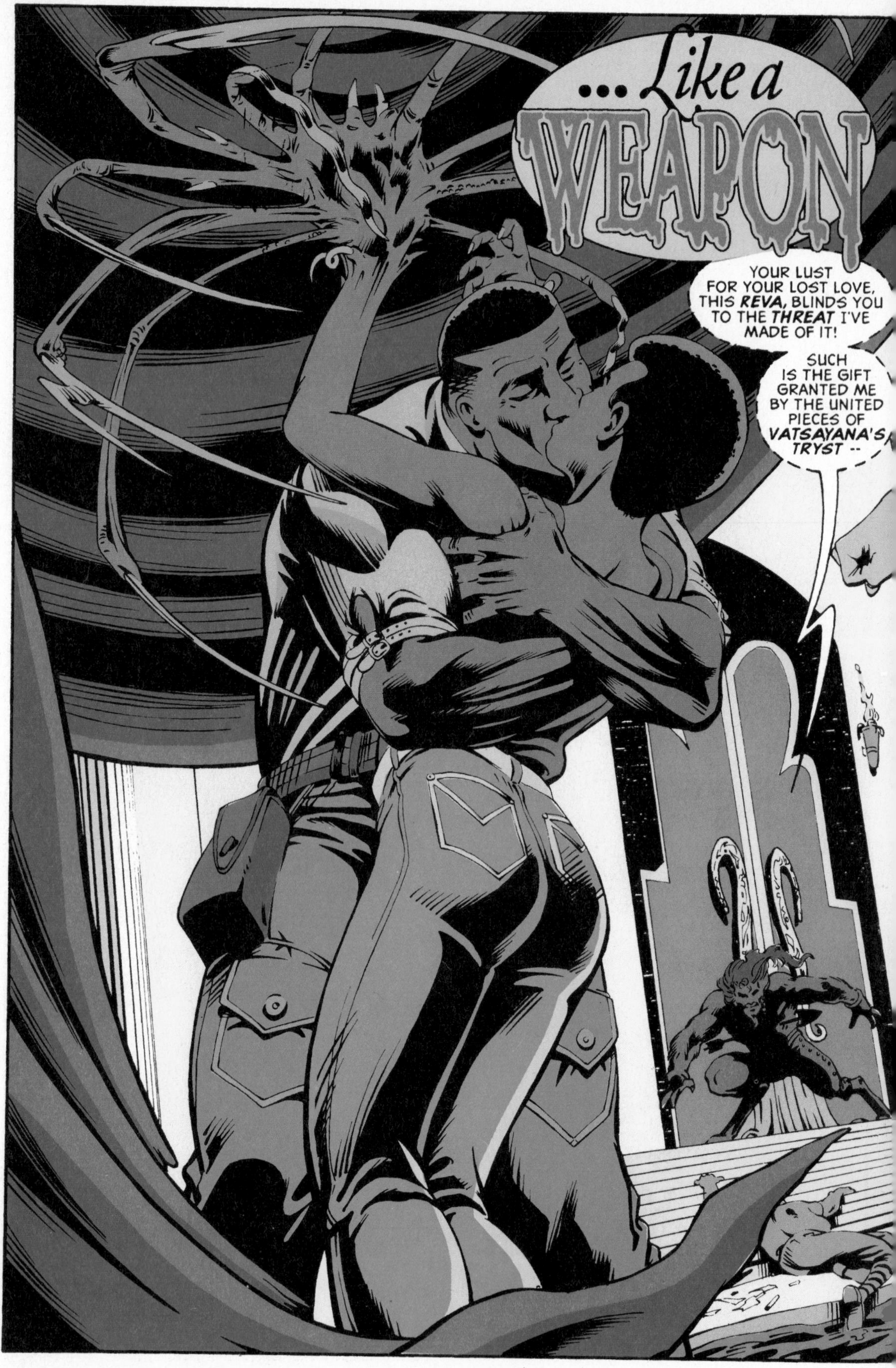
...Like a WEAPON
YOUR LUST FOR YOUR LOST LOVE, THIS REVA, BLINDS YOU TO THE THREAT I'VE MADE OF IT!
SUCH IS THE GIFT GRANTED ME BY THE UNITED PIECES OF VATSAYANA'S TRYST --

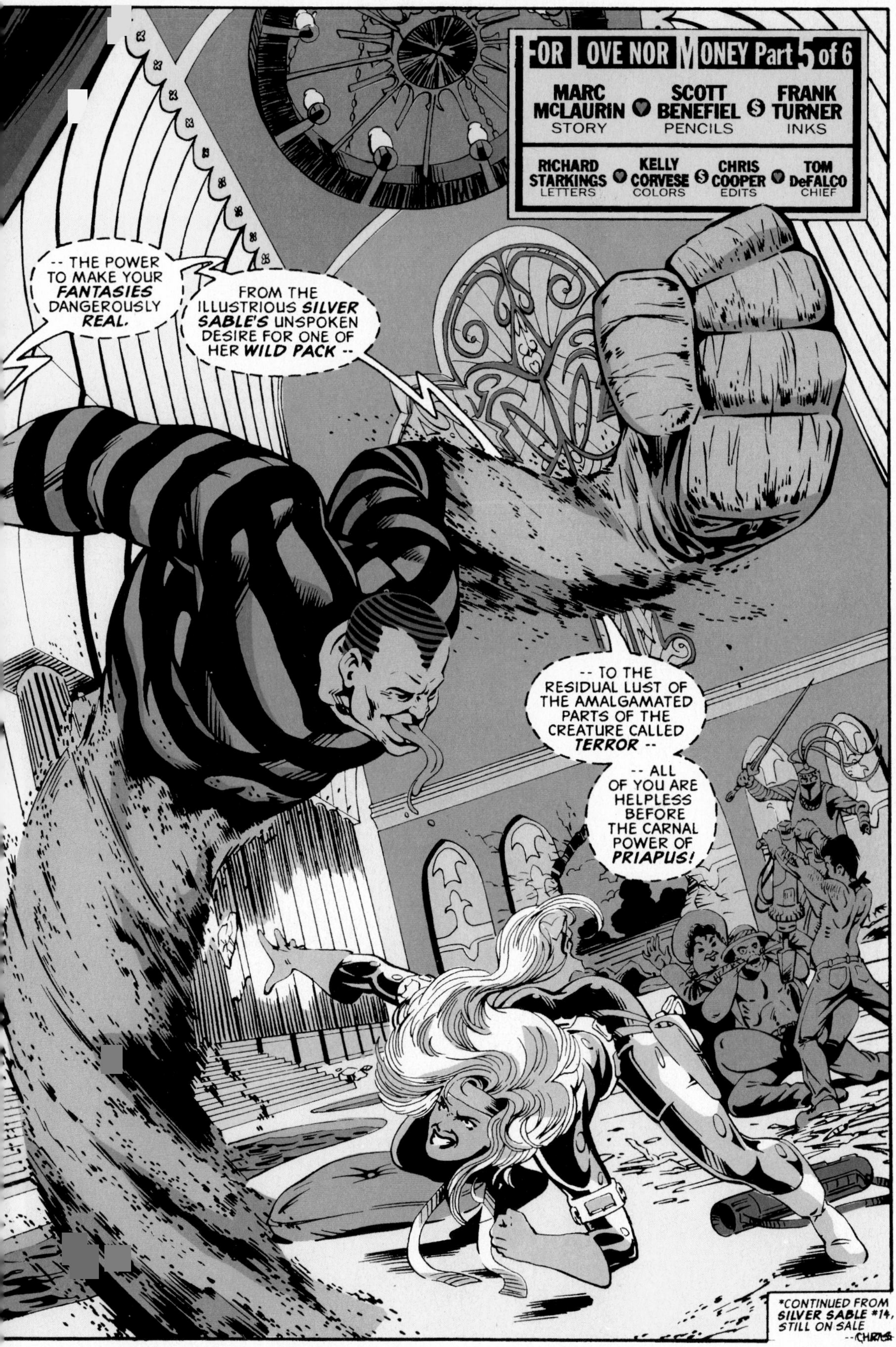
FOR LOVE NOR MONEY Part 5 of 6
MARC McLAURIN STORY
SCOTT BENEFIEL PENCILS
FRANK TURNER INKS
RICHARD STARKINGS LETTERS
KELLY CORVESE COLORS
CHRIS COOPER EDITS
TOM DeFALCO CHIEF
-- THE POWER TO MAKE YOUR FANTASIES DANGEROUSLY REAL.
FROM THE ILLUSTRIOUS SILVER SABLE'S UNSPOKEN DESIRE FOR ONE OF HER WILD PACK --
-- TO THE RESIDUAL LUST OF THE AMALGAMATED PARTS OF THE CREATURE CALLED TERROR --
-- ALL OF YOU ARE HELPLESS BEFORE THE CARNAL POWER OF PRIAPUS!
*CONTINUED FROM SILVER SABLE #14, STILL ON SALE --CHRIS

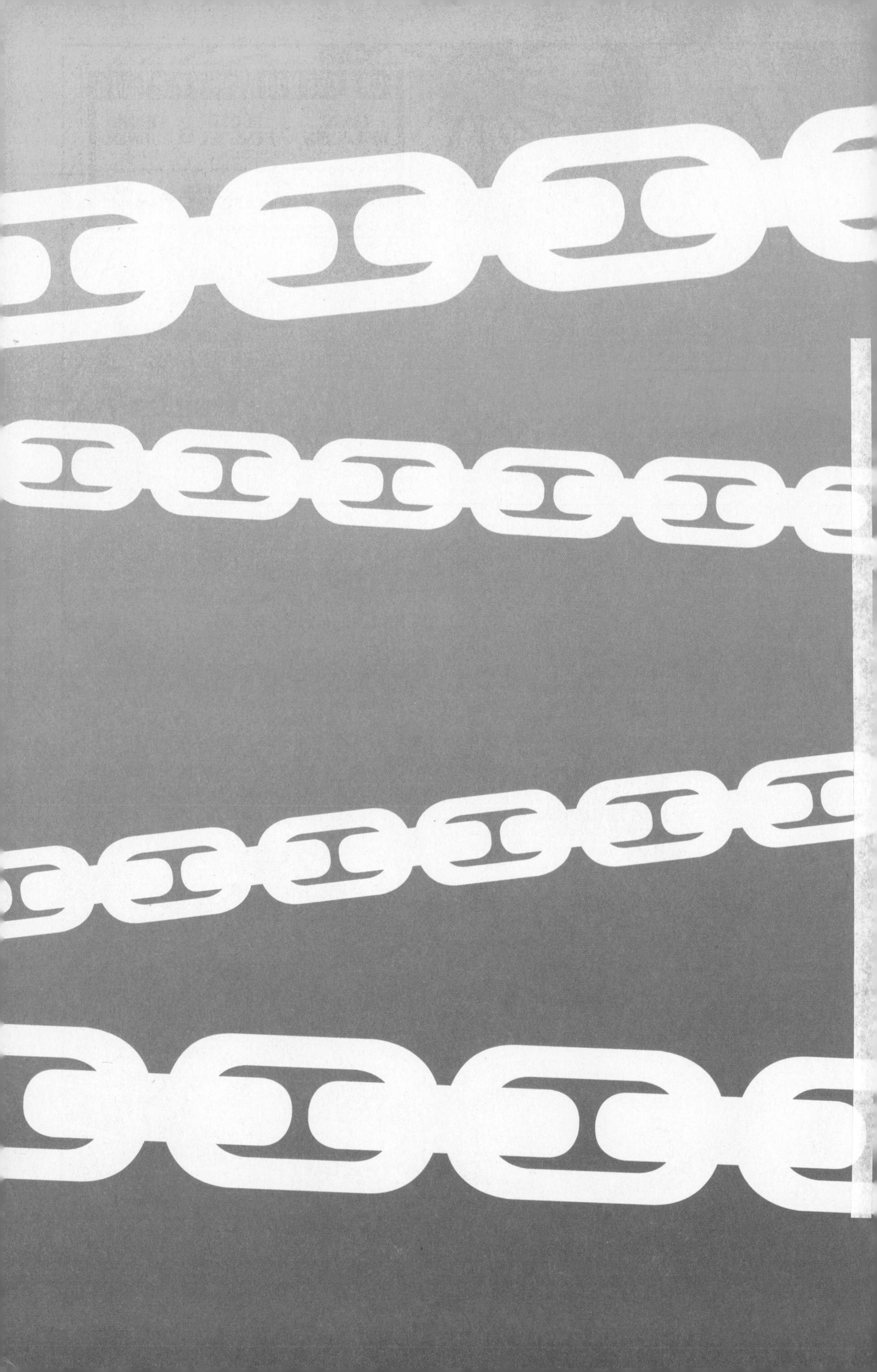

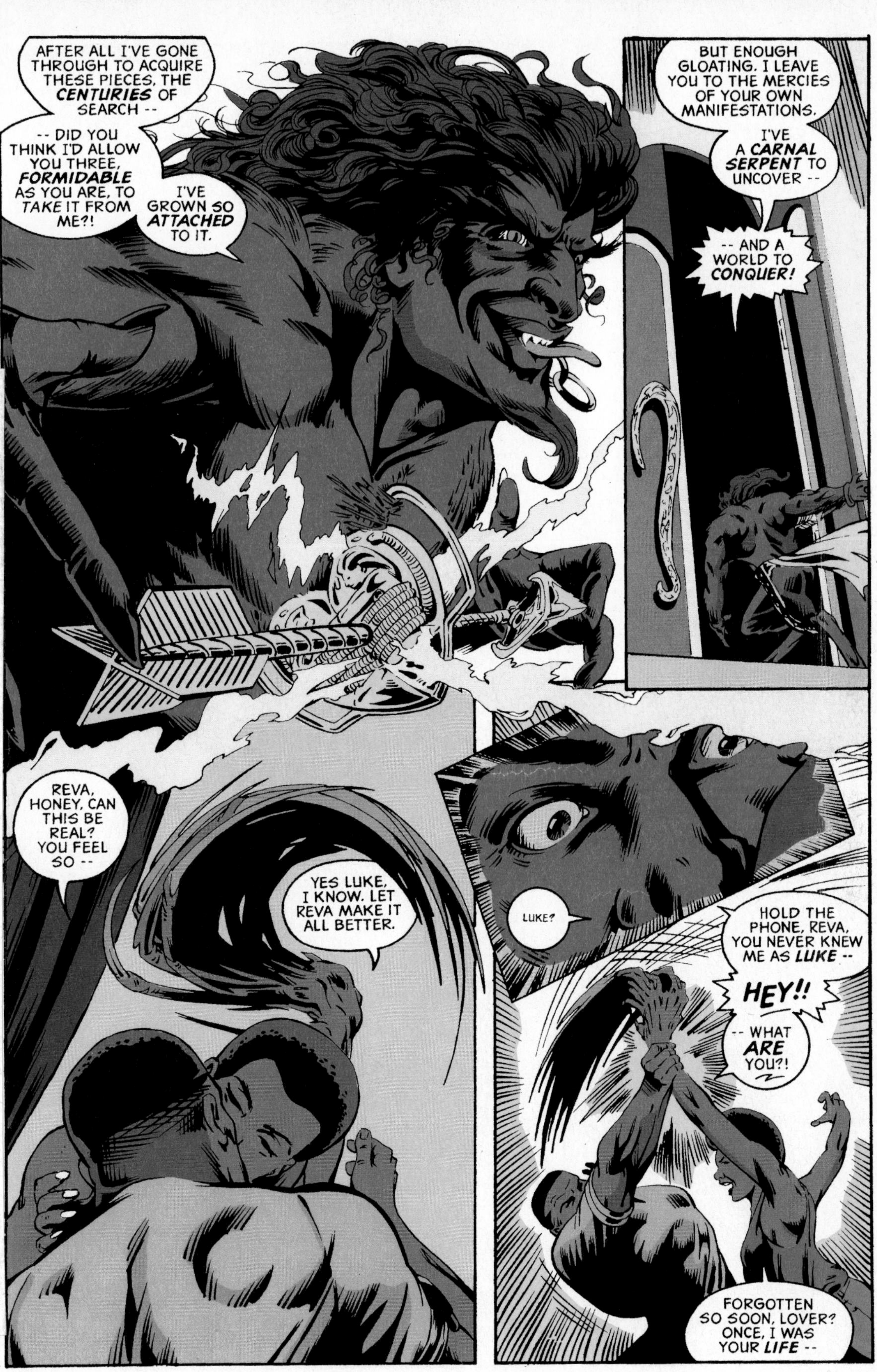
AFTER ALL I'VE GONE THROUGH TO ACQUIRE THESE PIECES, THE CENTURIES OF SEARCH --
-- DID YOU THINK I'D ALLOW YOU THREE, FORMIDABLE AS YOU ARE, TO TAKE IT FROM ME?!
I'VE GROWN SO ATTACHED TO IT.
BUT ENOUGH GLOATING. I LEAVE YOU TO THE MERCIES OF YOUR OWN MANIFESTATIONS.
I'VE A CARNAL SERPENT TO UNCOVER --
-- AND A WORLD TO CONQUER!
REVA, HONEY, CAN THIS BE REAL? YOU FEEL SO --
YES LUKE, I KNOW. LET REVA MAKE IT ALL BETTER.
LUKE?
HOLD THE PHONE, REVA, YOU NEVER KNEW ME AS LUKE --
HEY!!
-- WHAT ARE YOU?!
FORGOTTEN SO SOON, LOVER? ONCE, I WAS YOUR LIFE --

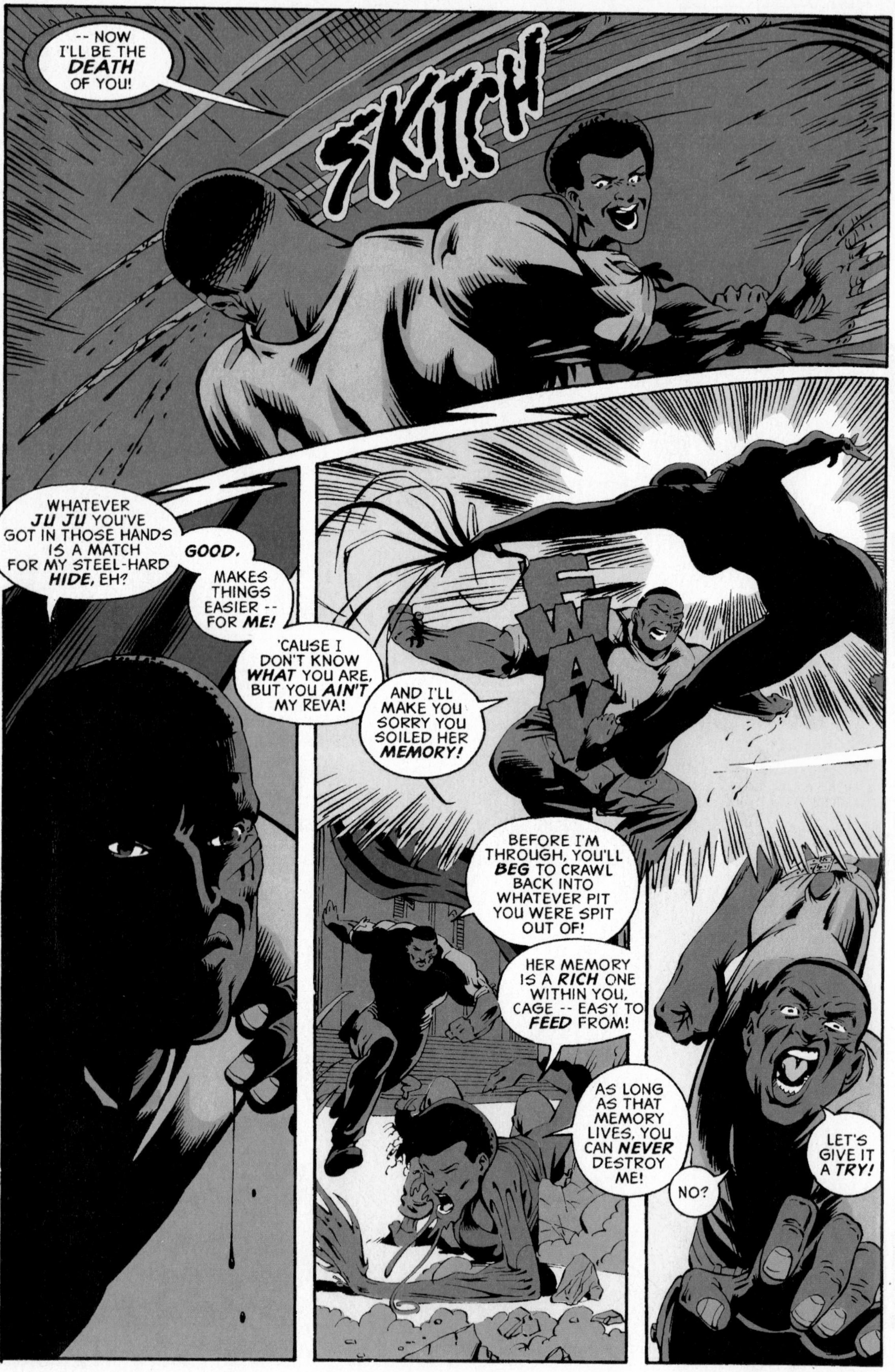
-- NOW I'LL BE THE DEATH OF YOU!
SKITCH
WHATEVER JU JU YOU'VE GOT IN THOSE HANDS IS A MATCH FOR MY STEEL-HARD HIDE, EH?
GOOD.
MAKES THINGS EASIER -- FOR ME!
'CAUSE I DON'T KNOW WHAT YOU ARE, BUT YOU AIN'T MY REVA!
AND I'LL MAKE YOU SORRY YOU SOILED HER MEMORY!
FWAK
BEFORE I'M THROUGH, YOU'LL BEG TO CRAWL BACK INTO WHATEVER PIT YOU WERE SPIT OUT OF!
HER MEMORY IS A RICH ONE WITHIN YOU, CAGE -- EASY TO FEED FROM!
AS LONG AS THAT MEMORY LIVES, YOU CAN NEVER DESTROY ME!
NO?
LET'S GIVE IT A TRY!

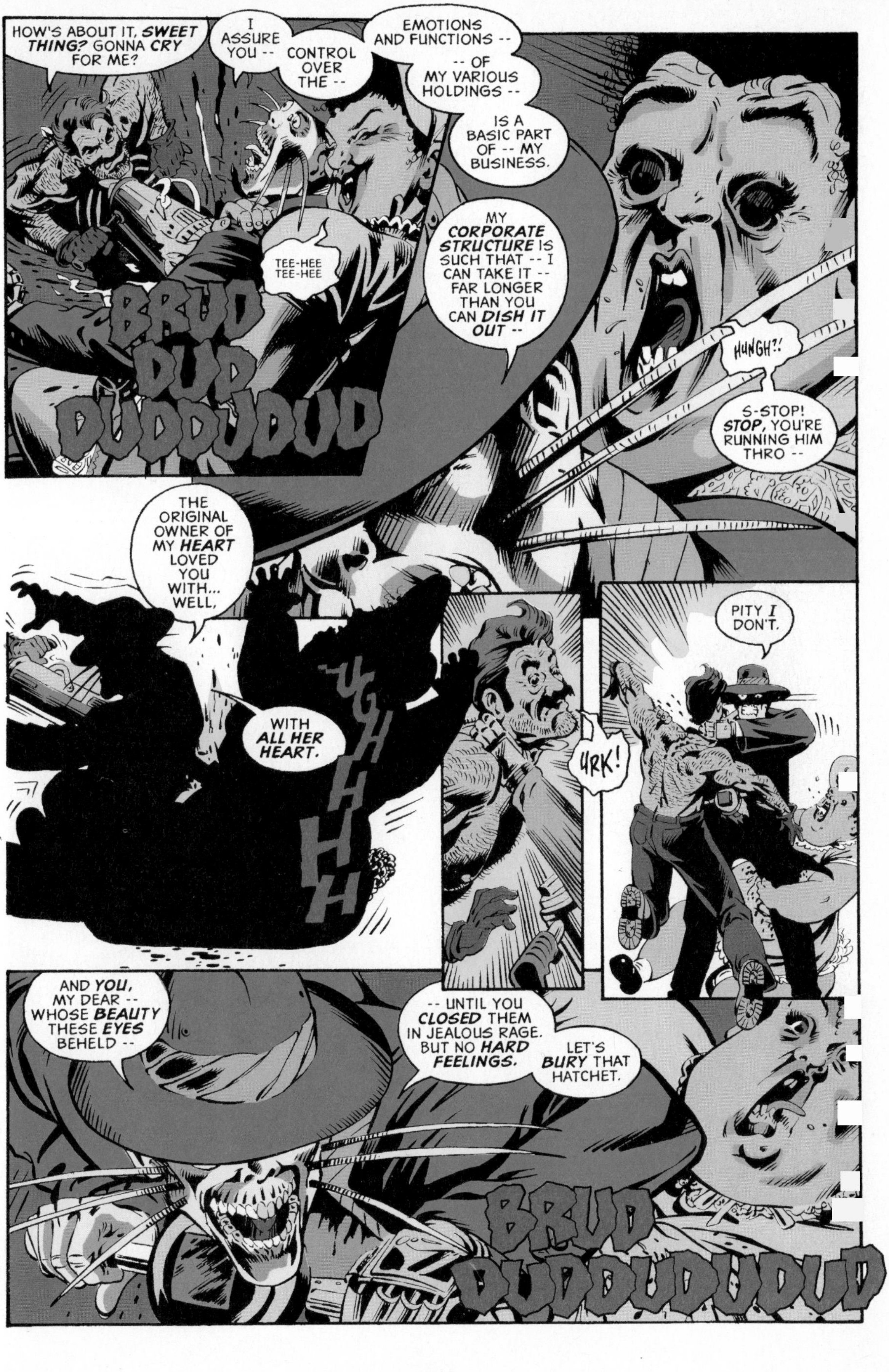
HOW'S ABOUT IT, SWEET THING? GONNA CRY FOR ME?
I ASSURE YOU --
CONTROL OVER THE --
EMOTIONS AND FUNCTIONS --
-- OF MY VARIOUS HOLDINGS --
IS A BASIC PART OF -- MY BUSINESS.
TEE-HEE TEE-HEE
MY CORPORATE STRUCTURE IS SUCH THAT -- I CAN TAKE IT -- FAR LONGER THAN YOU CAN DISH IT OUT --
BRUD DUD DUDDUDUD
HUNGH?!
S-STOP! STOP, YOU'RE RUNNING HIM THRO --
THE ORIGINAL OWNER OF MY HEART LOVED YOU WITH... WELL,
WITH ALL HER HEART.
UGHHHHHH
URK!
PITY I DON'T.
AND YOU, MY DEAR -- WHOSE BEAUTY THESE EYES BEHELD --
-- UNTIL YOU CLOSED THEM IN JEALOUS RAGE. BUT NO HARD FEELINGS.
LET'S BURY THAT HATCHET.
BRUD DUDDUDUDUD

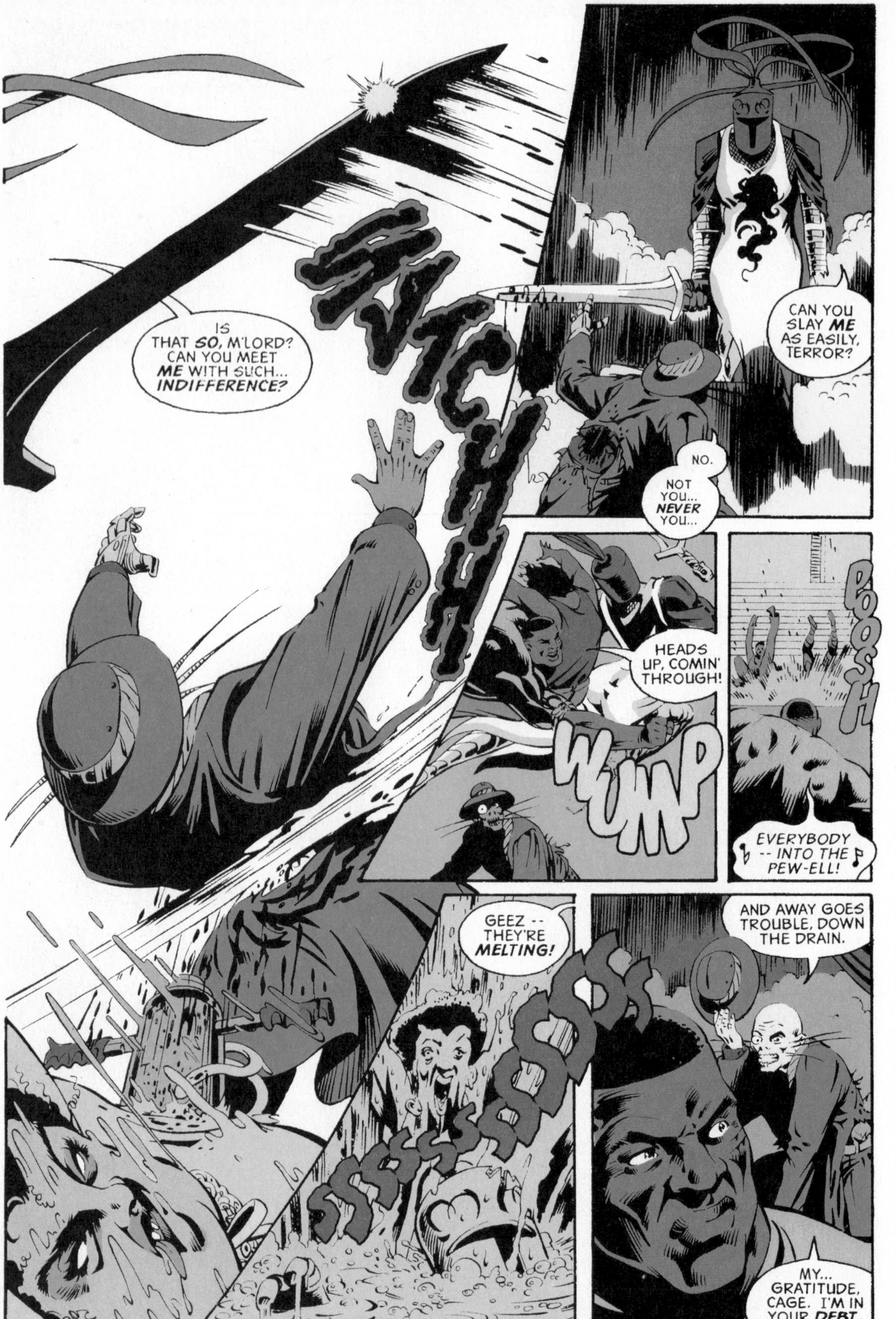

CAN YOU SLAY ME AS EASILY, TERROR?
IS THAT SO, M'LORD? CAN YOU MEET ME WITH SUCH... INDIFFERENCE?
SHTCHHHH
NO.
NOT YOU... NEVER YOU...
HEADS UP, COMIN' THROUGH!
WUMP
POOSH
EVERYBODY -- INTO THE PEW-ELL!
GEEZ -- THEY'RE MELTING!
SSSSSSSSSS
AND AWAY GOES TROUBLE, DOWN THE DRAIN.
MY... GRATITUDE, CAGE. I'M IN YOUR DEBT.

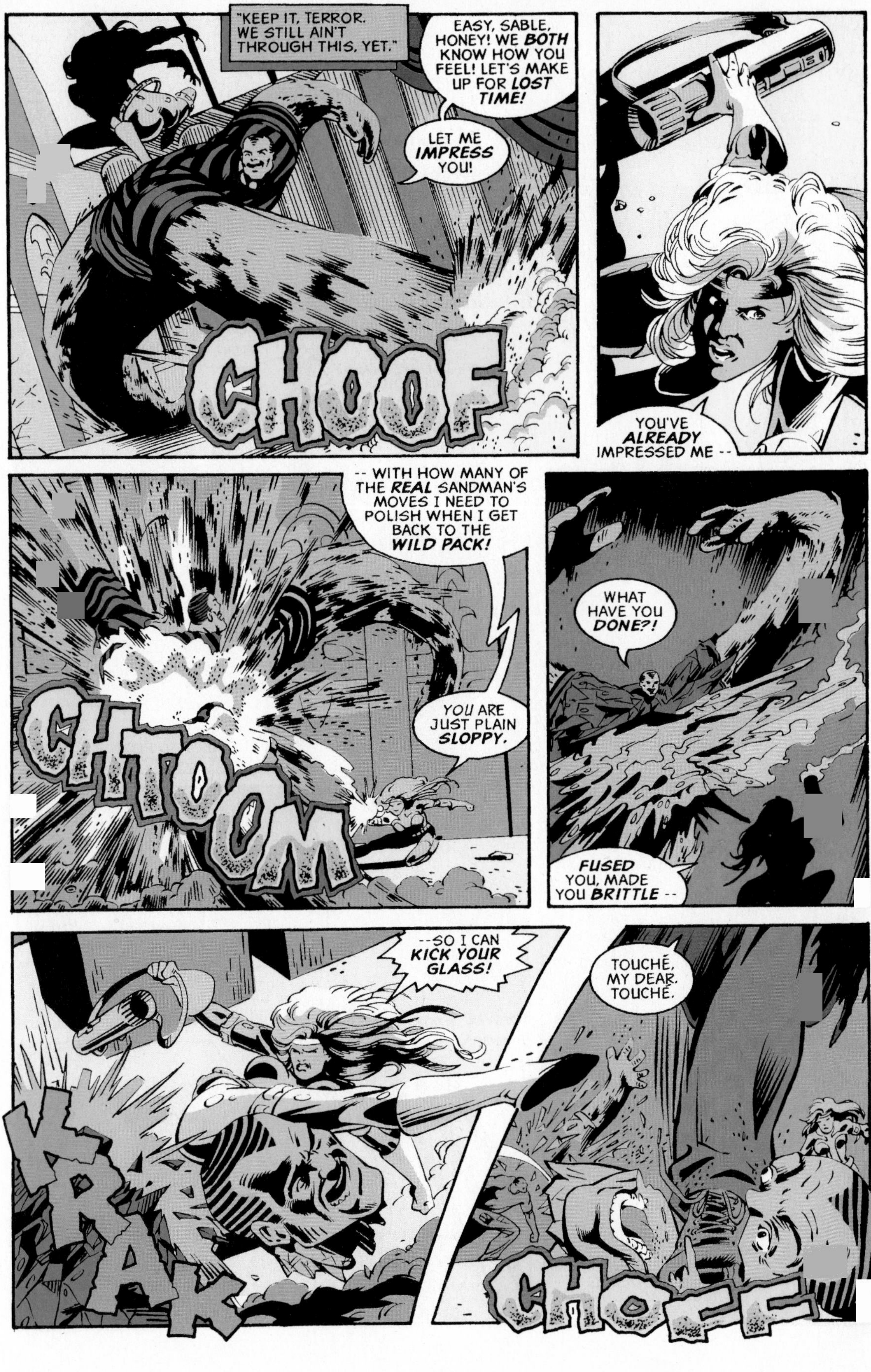
"KEEP IT, TERROR. WE STILL AIN'T THROUGH THIS, YET."
EASY, SABLE, HONEY! WE BOTH KNOW HOW YOU FEEL! LET'S MAKE UP FOR LOST TIME!
LET ME IMPRESS YOU!
CHOOF
YOU'VE ALREADY IMPRESSED ME --
-- WITH HOW MANY OF THE REAL SANDMAN'S MOVES I NEED TO POLISH WHEN I GET BACK TO THE WILD PACK!
YOU ARE JUST PLAIN SLOPPY.
CHTOOM
WHAT HAVE YOU DONE?!
FUSED YOU, MADE YOU BRITTLE --
--SO I CAN KICK YOUR GLASS!
TOUCHÉ, MY DEAR. TOUCHÉ.
KRAK
CHOOF

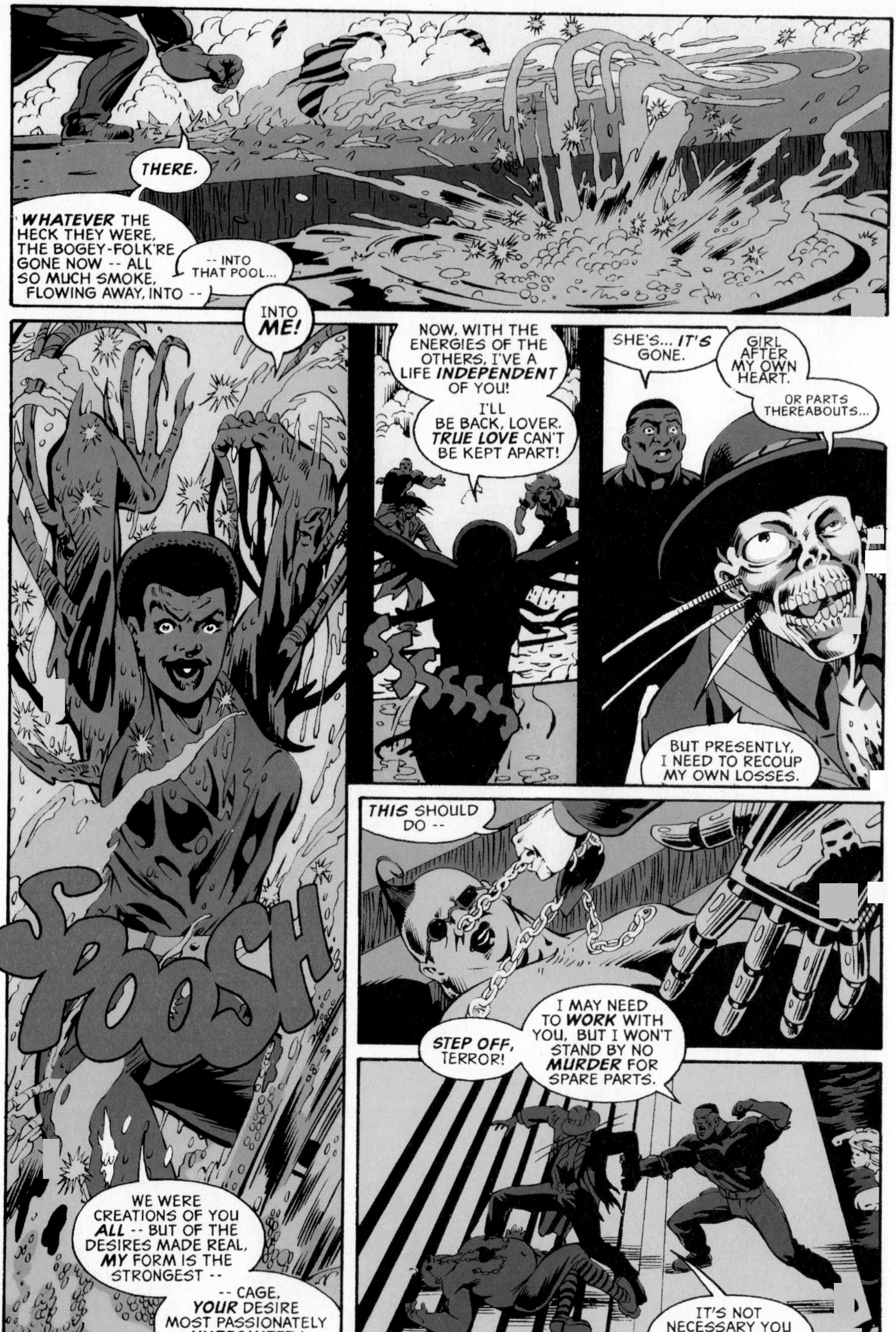
THERE.
WHATEVER THE HECK THEY WERE, THE BOGEY-FOLK'RE GONE NOW -- ALL SO MUCH SMOKE, FLOWING AWAY, INTO --
-- INTO THAT POOL...
INTO ME!
POOSH
WE WERE CREATIONS OF YOU ALL -- BUT OF THE DESIRES MADE REAL, MY FORM IS THE STRONGEST --
-- CAGE, YOUR DESIRE MOST PASSIONATELY UNREQUITED!
NOW, WITH THE ENERGIES OF THE OTHERS, I'VE A LIFE INDEPENDENT OF YOU!
I'LL BE BACK, LOVER. TRUE LOVE CAN'T BE KEPT APART!
SSSSSS
SHE'S... IT'S GONE.
GIRL AFTER MY OWN HEART.
OR PARTS THEREABOUTS...
BUT PRESENTLY, I NEED TO RECOUP MY OWN LOSSES.
THIS SHOULD DO --
STEP OFF, TERROR!
I MAY NEED TO WORK WITH YOU, BUT I WON'T STAND BY NO MURDER FOR SPARE PARTS.
IT'S NOT NECESSARY YOU STAND AT ALL...

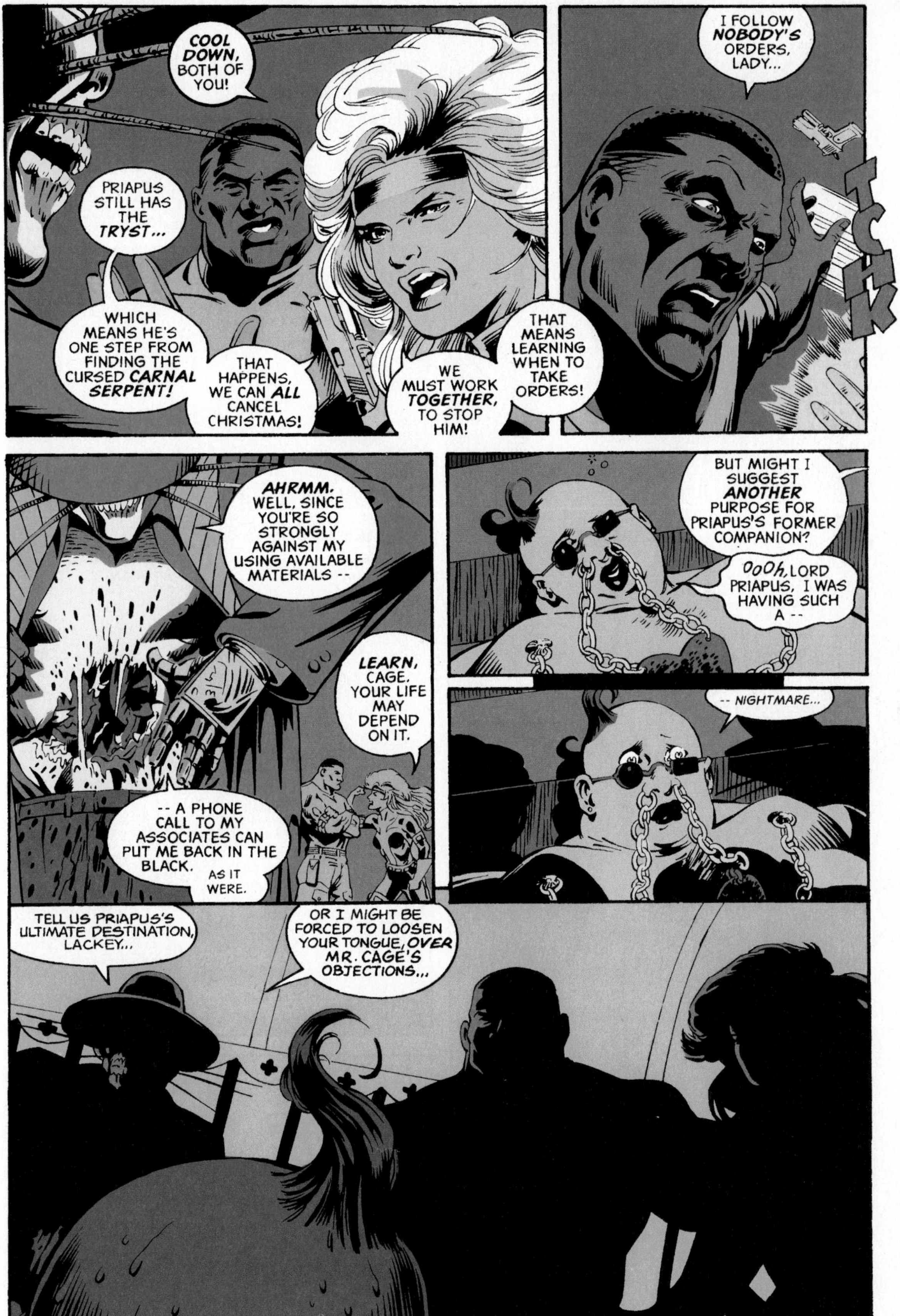

COOL DOWN, BOTH OF YOU!
PRIAPUS STILL HAS THE TRYST...
WHICH MEANS HE'S ONE STEP FROM FINDING THE CURSED CARNAL SERPENT!
THAT HAPPENS, WE CAN ALL CANCEL CHRISTMAS!
WE MUST WORK TOGETHER, TO STOP HIM!
THAT MEANS LEARNING WHEN TO TAKE ORDERS!
I FOLLOW NOBODY'S ORDERS, LADY...
TCHK
AHRMM. WELL, SINCE YOU'RE SO STRONGLY AGAINST MY USING AVAILABLE MATERIALS --
LEARN, CAGE. YOUR LIFE MAY DEPEND ON IT.
-- A PHONE CALL TO MY ASSOCIATES CAN PUT ME BACK IN THE BLACK.
AS IT WERE.
BUT MIGHT I SUGGEST ANOTHER PURPOSE FOR PRIAPUS'S FORMER COMPANION?
Oooh, LORD PRIAPUS, I WAS HAVING SUCH A --
-- NIGHTMARE...
TELL US PRIAPUS'S ULTIMATE DESTINATION, LACKEY...
OR I MIGHT BE FORCED TO LOOSEN YOUR TONGUE, OVER MR. CAGE'S OBJECTIONS...

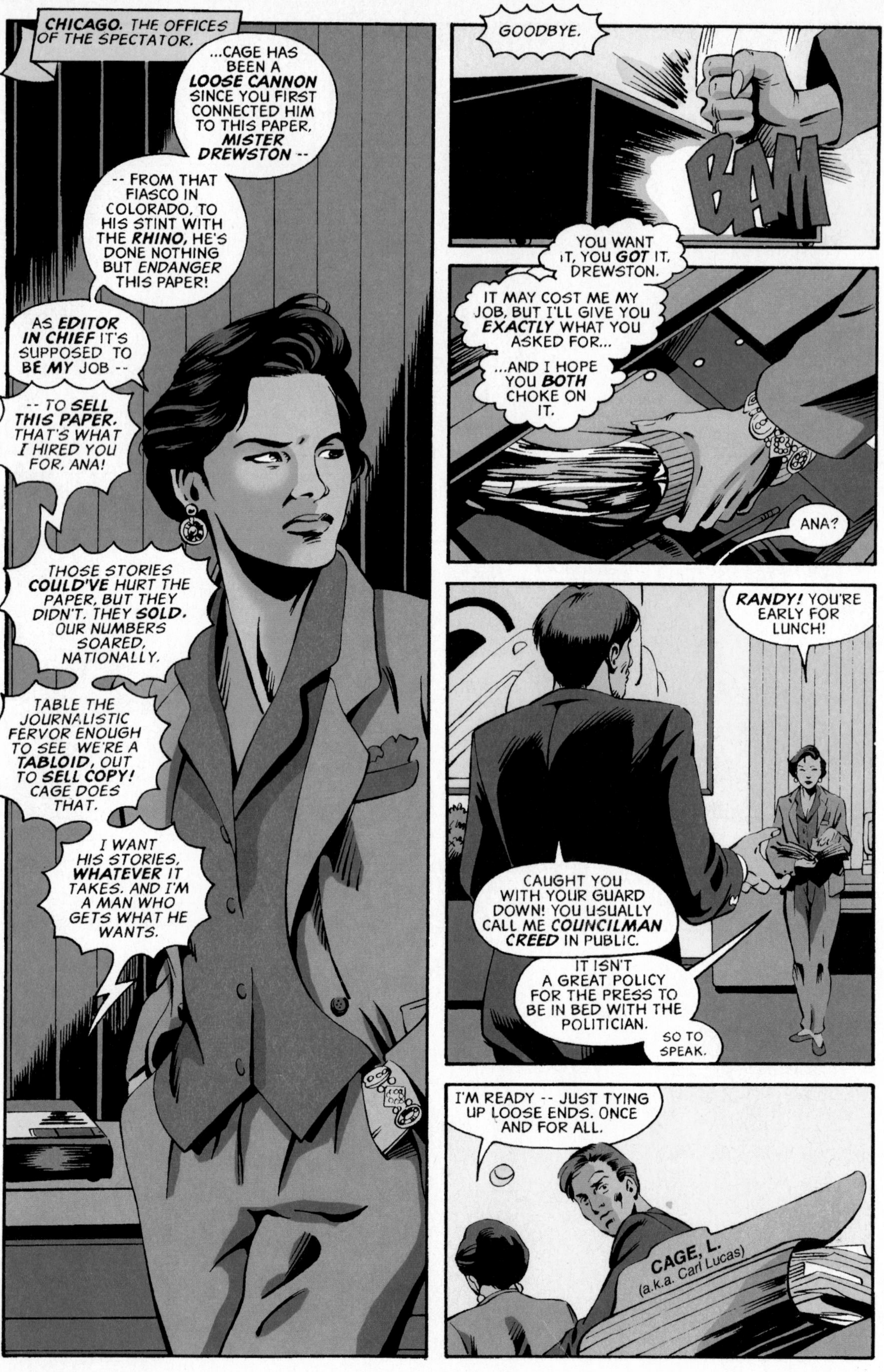

CHICAGO. THE OFFICES OF THE SPECTATOR.
...CAGE HAS BEEN A LOOSE CANNON SINCE YOU FIRST CONNECTED HIM TO THIS PAPER, MISTER DREWSTON --
-- FROM THAT FIASCO IN COLORADO, TO HIS STINT WITH THE RHINO, HE'S DONE NOTHING BUT ENDANGER THIS PAPER!
AS EDITOR IN CHIEF IT'S SUPPOSED TO BE MY JOB --
-- TO SELL THIS PAPER. THAT'S WHAT I HIRED YOU FOR, ANA!
THOSE STORIES COULD'VE HURT THE PAPER, BUT THEY DIDN'T. THEY SOLD. OUR NUMBERS SOARED, NATIONALLY.
TABLE THE JOURNALISTIC FERVOR ENOUGH TO SEE WE'RE A TABLOID, OUT TO SELL COPY! CAGE DOES THAT.
I WANT HIS STORIES, WHATEVER IT TAKES. AND I'M A MAN WHO GETS WHAT HE WANTS.
GOODBYE.
BAM
YOU WANT IT, YOU GOT IT, DREWSTON.
IT MAY COST ME MY JOB, BUT I'LL GIVE YOU EXACTLY WHAT YOU ASKED FOR...
...AND I HOPE YOU BOTH CHOKE ON IT.
ANA?
RANDY! YOU'RE EARLY FOR LUNCH!
CAUGHT YOU WITH YOUR GUARD DOWN! YOU USUALLY CALL ME COUNCILMAN CREED IN PUBLIC.
IT ISN'T A GREAT POLICY FOR THE PRESS TO BE IN BED WITH THE POLITICIAN.
SO TO SPEAK.
I'M READY -- JUST TYING UP LOOSE ENDS. ONCE AND FOR ALL.
CAGE, L.
(a.k.a. Carl Lucas)

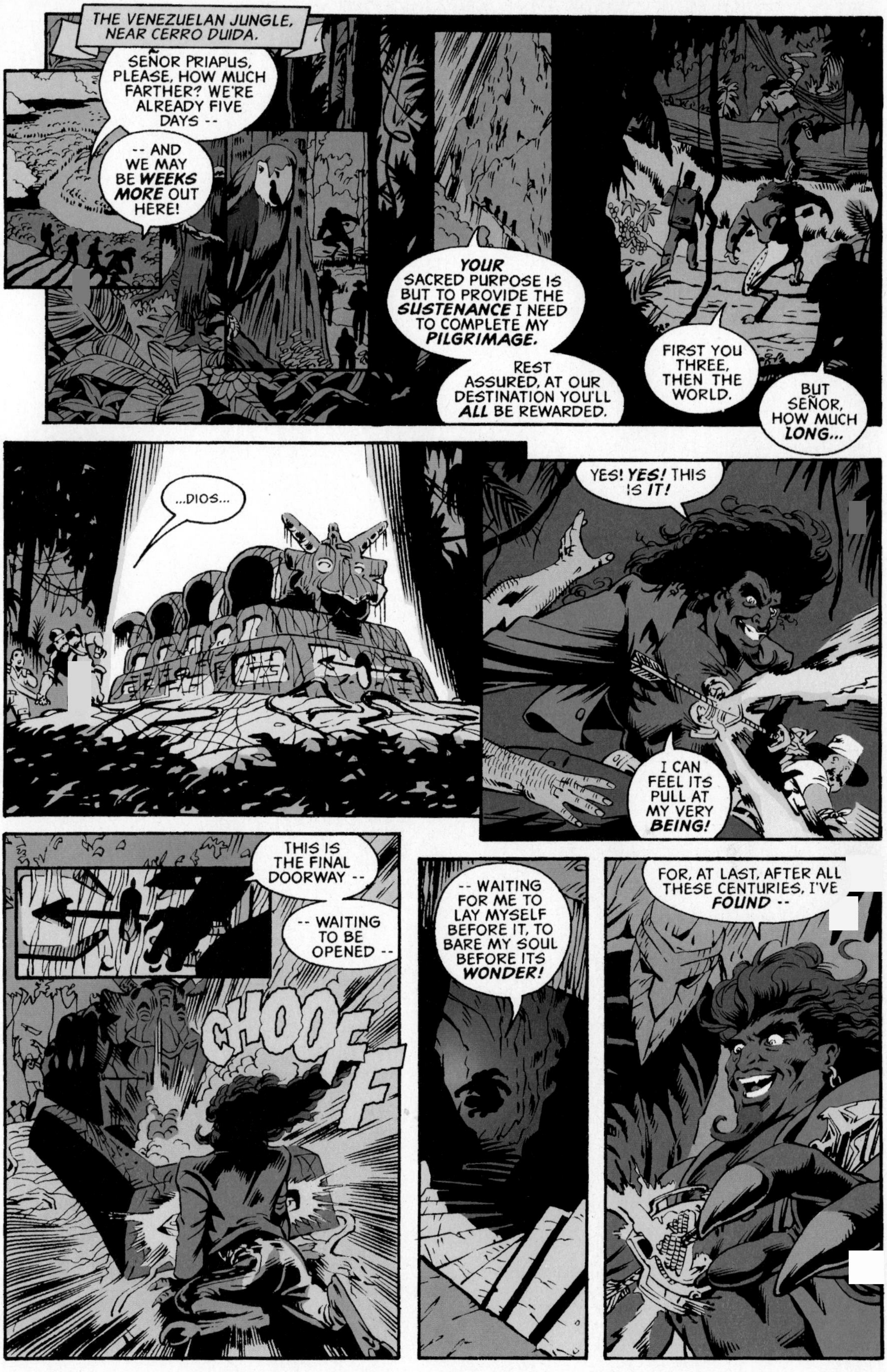
THE VENEZUELAN JUNGLE, NEAR CERRO DUIDA.
SEÑOR PRIAPUS, PLEASE, HOW MUCH FARTHER? WE'RE ALREADY FIVE DAYS --
-- AND WE MAY BE WEEKS MORE OUT HERE!
YOUR SACRED PURPOSE IS BUT TO PROVIDE THE SUSTENANCE I NEED TO COMPLETE MY PILGRIMAGE.
REST ASSURED, AT OUR DESTINATION YOU'LL ALL BE REWARDED.
FIRST YOU THREE, THEN THE WORLD.
BUT SEÑOR, HOW MUCH LONG...
...DIOS...
YES! YES! THIS IS IT!
I CAN FEEL ITS PULL AT MY VERY BEING!
THIS IS THE FINAL DOORWAY --
-- WAITING TO BE OPENED --
CHOOFF
-- WAITING FOR ME TO LAY MYSELF BEFORE IT, TO BARE MY SOUL BEFORE ITS WONDER!
FOR, AT LAST, AFTER ALL THESE CENTURIES, I'VE FOUND --

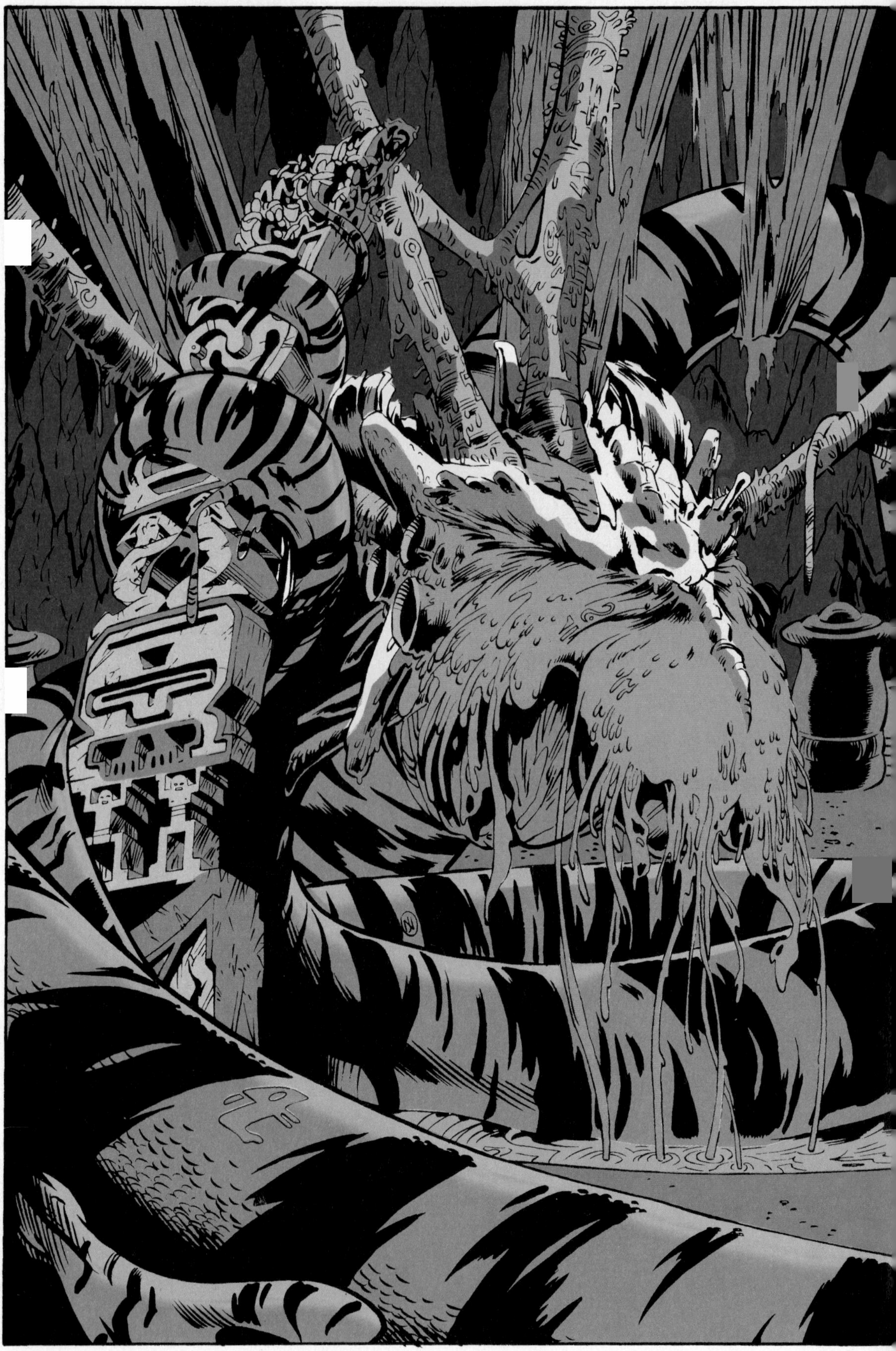

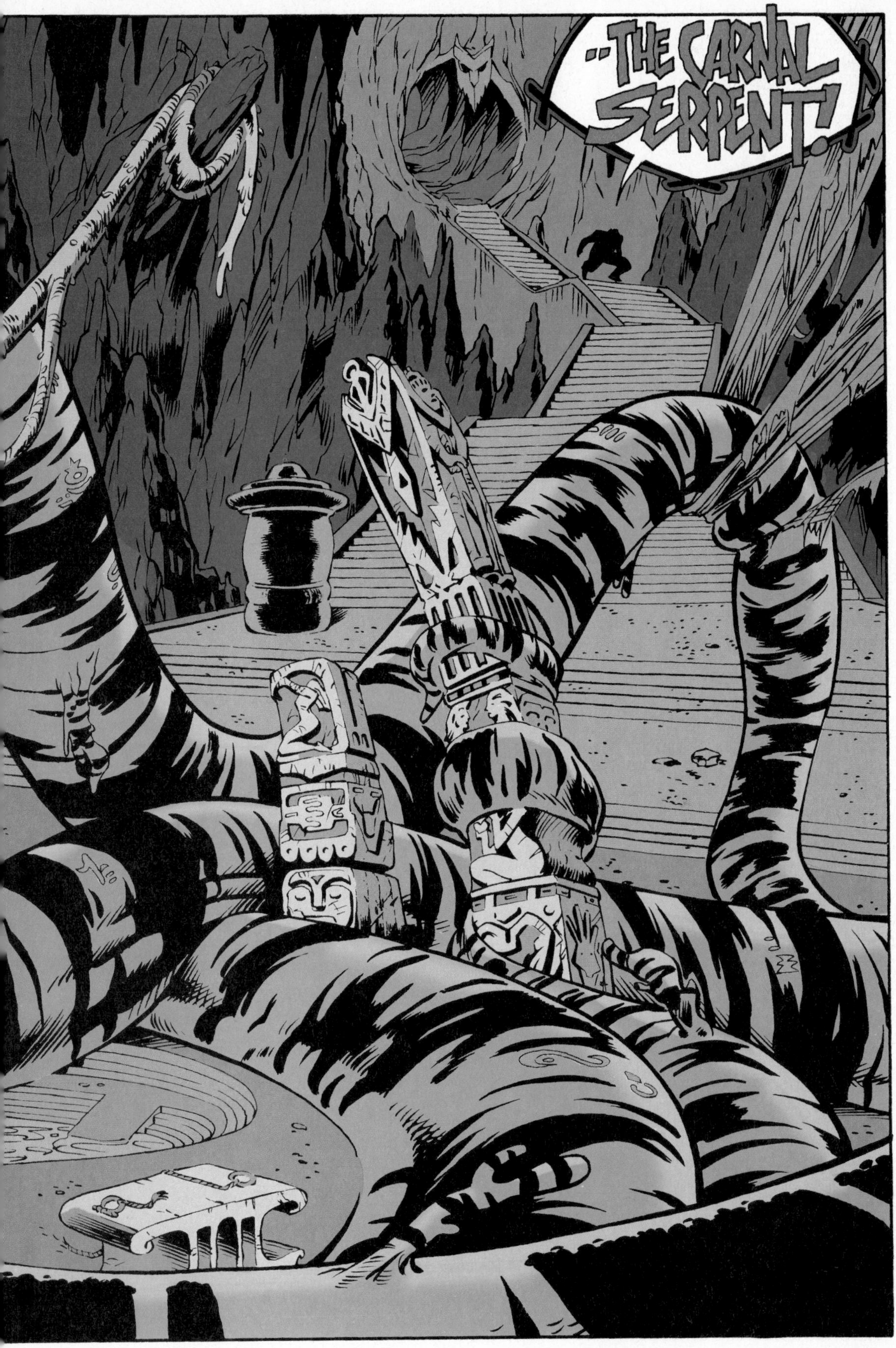
..THE CARNAL SERPENT!

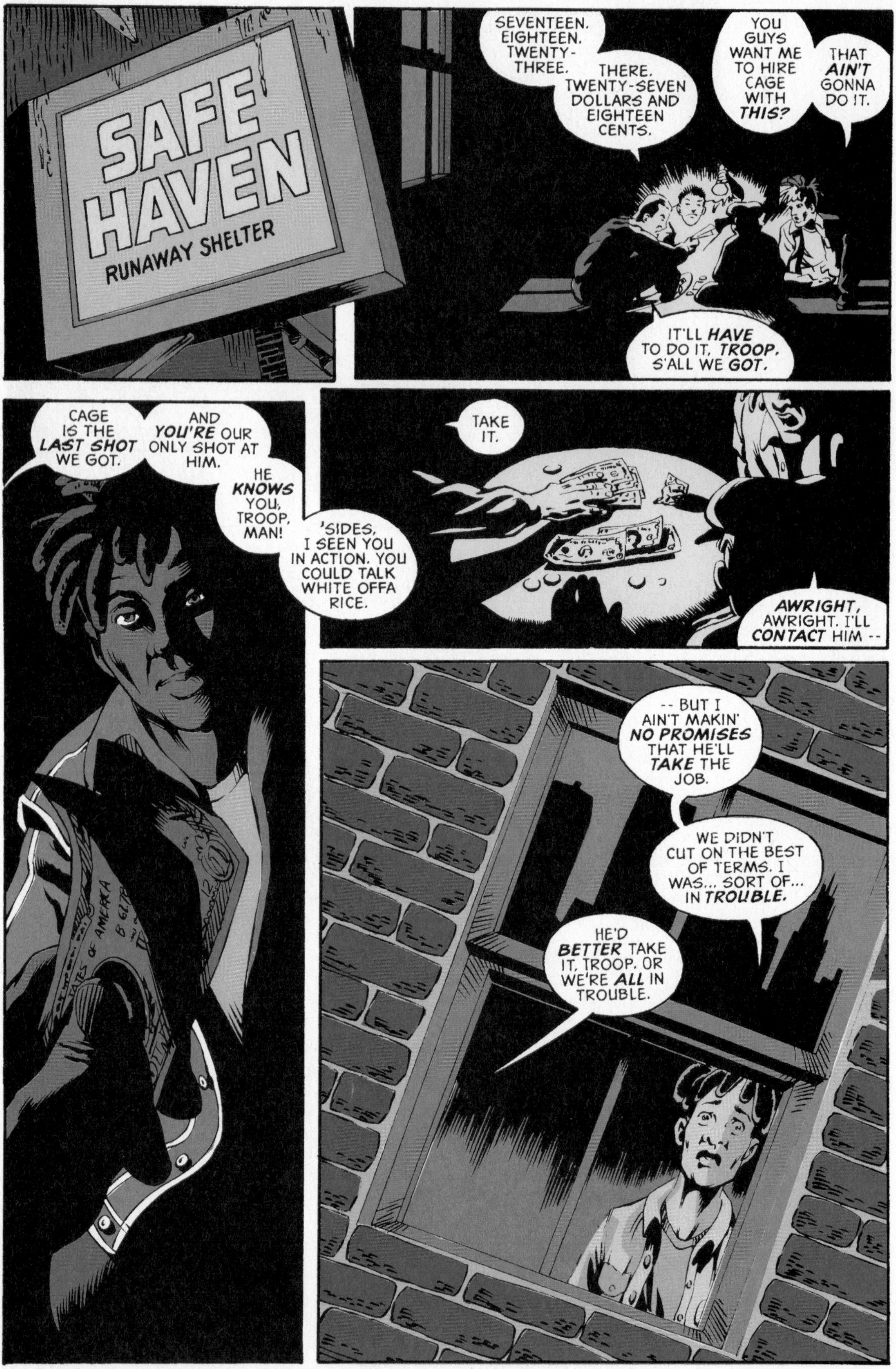
SAFE HAVEN
RUNAWAY SHELTER
SEVENTEEN. EIGHTEEN. TWENTY-THREE.
THERE. TWENTY-SEVEN DOLLARS AND EIGHTEEN CENTS.
YOU GUYS WANT ME TO HIRE CAGE WITH THIS?
THAT AIN'T GONNA DO IT.
IT'LL HAVE TO DO IT, TROOP. S'ALL WE GOT.
CAGE IS THE LAST SHOT WE GOT.
AND YOU'RE OUR ONLY SHOT AT HIM.
HE KNOWS YOU, TROOP, MAN!
'SIDES, I SEEN YOU IN ACTION. YOU COULD TALK WHITE OFFA RICE.
TAKE IT.
AWRIGHT, AWRIGHT. I'LL CONTACT HIM --
-- BUT I AIN'T MAKIN' NO PROMISES THAT HE'LL TAKE THE JOB.
WE DIDN'T CUT ON THE BEST OF TERMS. I WAS... SORT OF... IN TROUBLE.
HE'D BETTER TAKE IT, TROOP. OR WE'RE ALL IN TROUBLE.

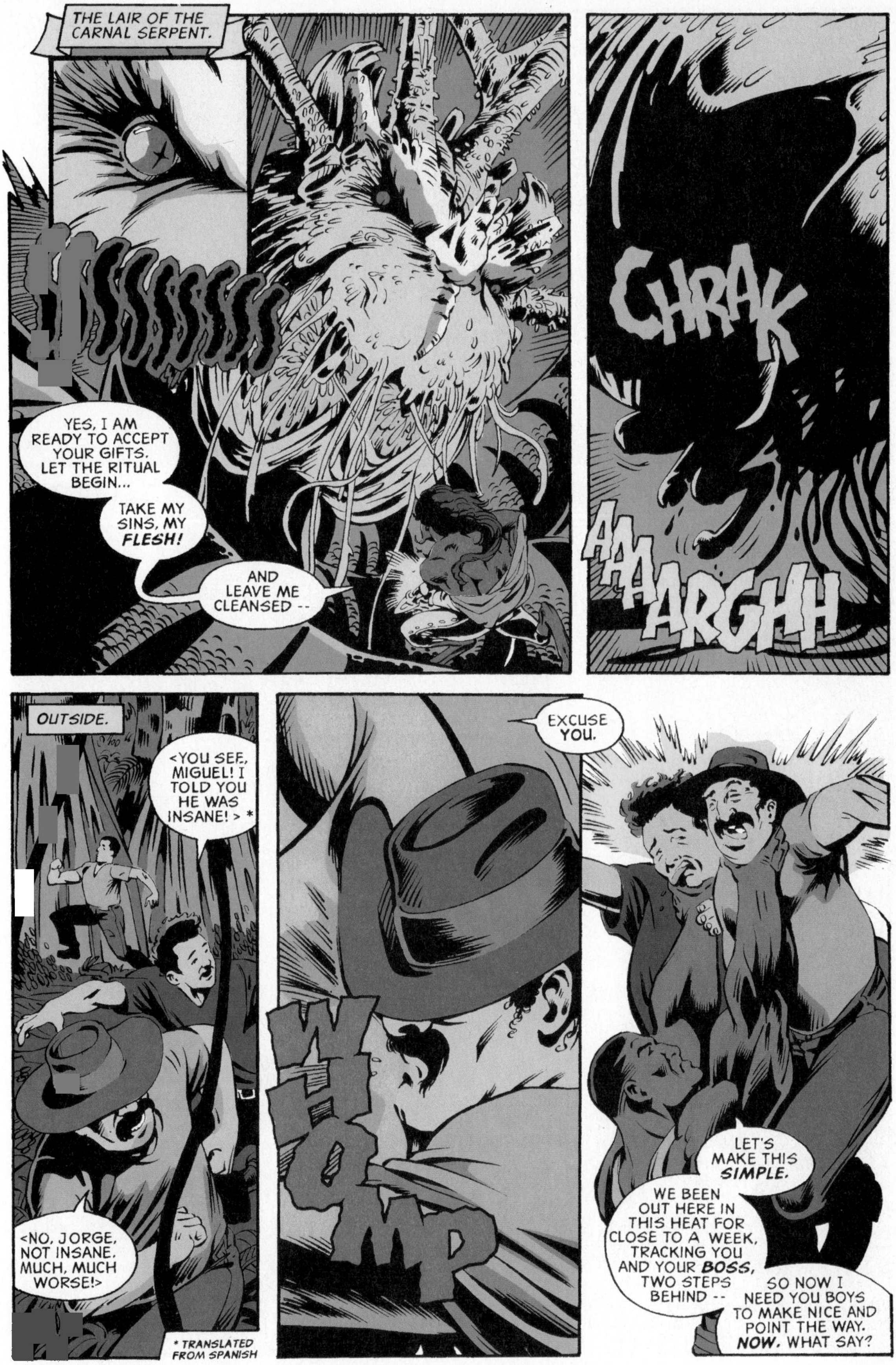
THE LAIR OF THE CARNAL SERPENT.
YES, I AM READY TO ACCEPT YOUR GIFTS. LET THE RITUAL BEGIN...
TAKE MY SINS, MY FLESH!
AND LEAVE ME CLEANSED --
CHRAK
AAAARGHH
OUTSIDE.
<YOU SEE, MIGUEL! I TOLD YOU HE WAS INSANE! > *
<NO, JORGE, NOT INSANE. MUCH, MUCH WORSE!>
* TRANSLATED FROM SPANISH
EXCUSE YOU.
LET'S MAKE THIS SIMPLE.
WE BEEN OUT HERE IN THIS HEAT FOR CLOSE TO A WEEK, TRACKING YOU AND YOUR BOSS, TWO STEPS BEHIND --
SO NOW I NEED YOU BOYS TO MAKE NICE AND POINT THE WAY. NOW. WHAT SAY?

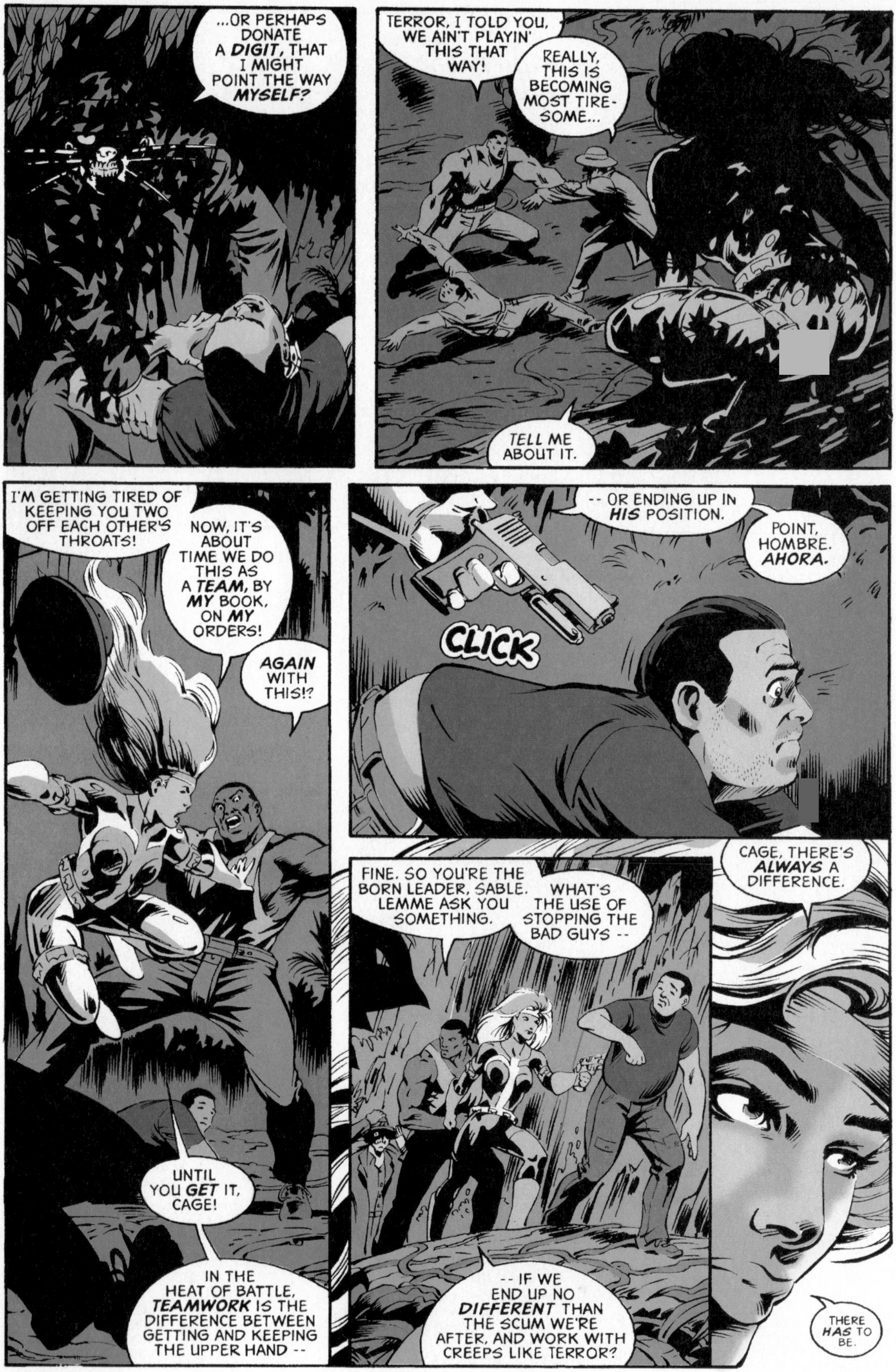
...OR PERHAPS DONATE A DIGIT, THAT I MIGHT POINT THE WAY MYSELF?
TERROR, I TOLD YOU, WE AIN'T PLAYIN' THIS THAT WAY!
REALLY, THIS IS BECOMING MOST TIRE-SOME...
TELL ME ABOUT IT.
I'M GETTING TIRED OF KEEPING YOU TWO OFF EACH OTHER'S THROATS!
NOW, IT'S ABOUT TIME WE DO THIS AS A TEAM, BY MY BOOK, ON MY ORDERS!
AGAIN WITH THIS!?
UNTIL YOU GET IT, CAGE!
IN THE HEAT OF BATTLE, TEAMWORK IS THE DIFFERENCE BETWEEN GETTING AND KEEPING THE UPPER HAND --
-- OR ENDING UP IN HIS POSITION.
POINT, HOMBRE. AHORA.
CLICK
FINE. SO YOU'RE THE BORN LEADER, SABLE. LEMME ASK YOU SOMETHING.
WHAT'S THE USE OF STOPPING THE BAD GUYS --
-- IF WE END UP NO DIFFERENT THAN THE SCUM WE'RE AFTER, AND WORK WITH CREEPS LIKE TERROR?
CAGE, THERE'S ALWAYS A DIFFERENCE.
THERE HAS TO BE.

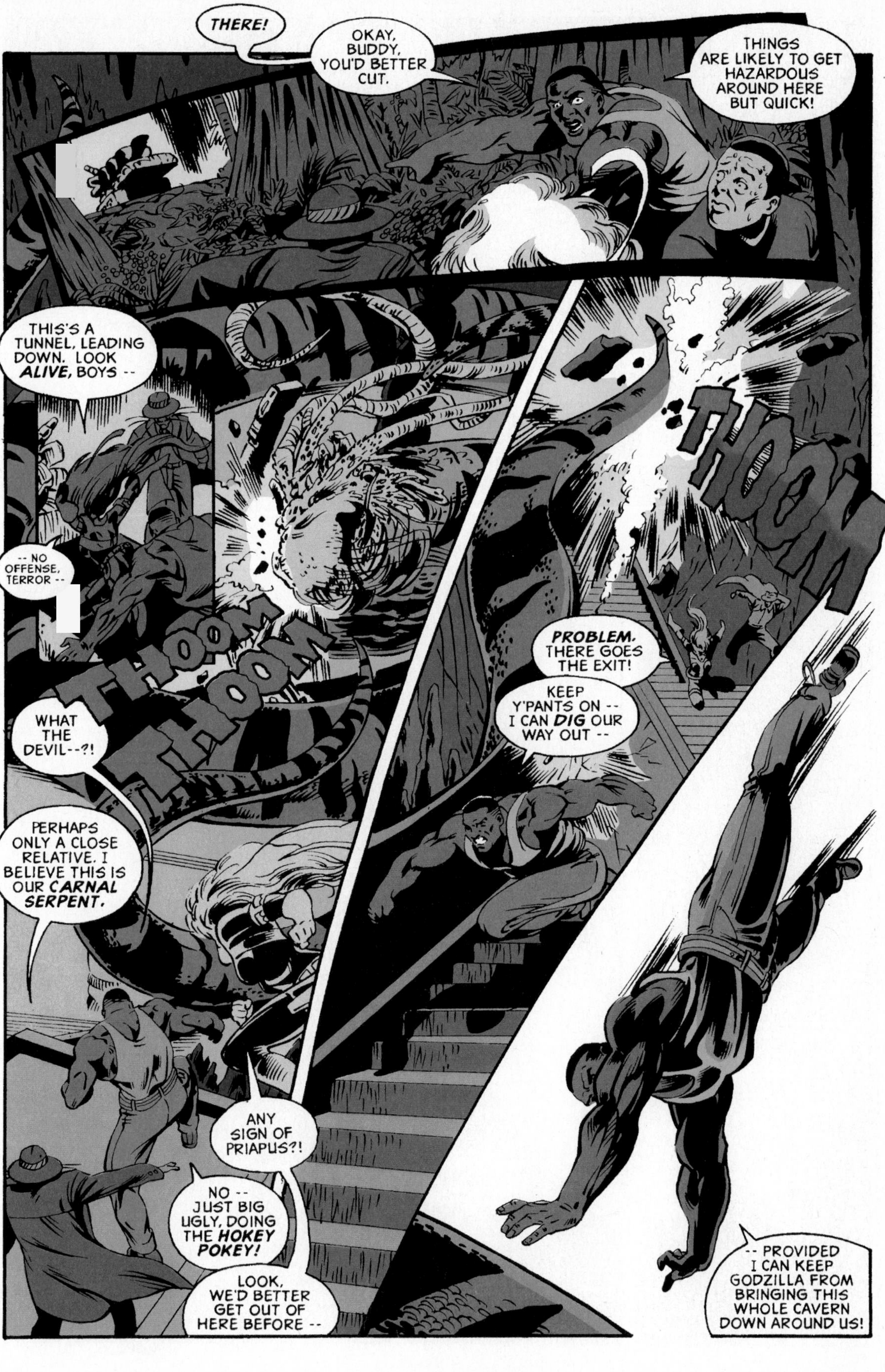

THERE!
OKAY, BUDDY, YOU'D BETTER CUT.
THINGS ARE LIKELY TO GET HAZARDOUS AROUND HERE BUT QUICK!
THIS'S A TUNNEL, LEADING DOWN. LOOK ALIVE, BOYS --
-- NO OFFENSE, TERROR --
THOOM
THOOM
WHAT THE DEVIL--?!
PERHAPS ONLY A CLOSE RELATIVE. I BELIEVE THIS IS OUR CARNAL SERPENT.
ANY SIGN OF PRIAPUS?!
NO -- JUST BIG UGLY, DOING THE HOKEY POKEY!
LOOK, WE'D BETTER GET OUT OF HERE BEFORE --
THOOM
PROBLEM. THERE GOES THE EXIT!
KEEP Y'PANTS ON -- I CAN DIG OUR WAY OUT --
-- PROVIDED I CAN KEEP GODZILLA FROM BRINGING THIS WHOLE CAVERN DOWN AROUND US!

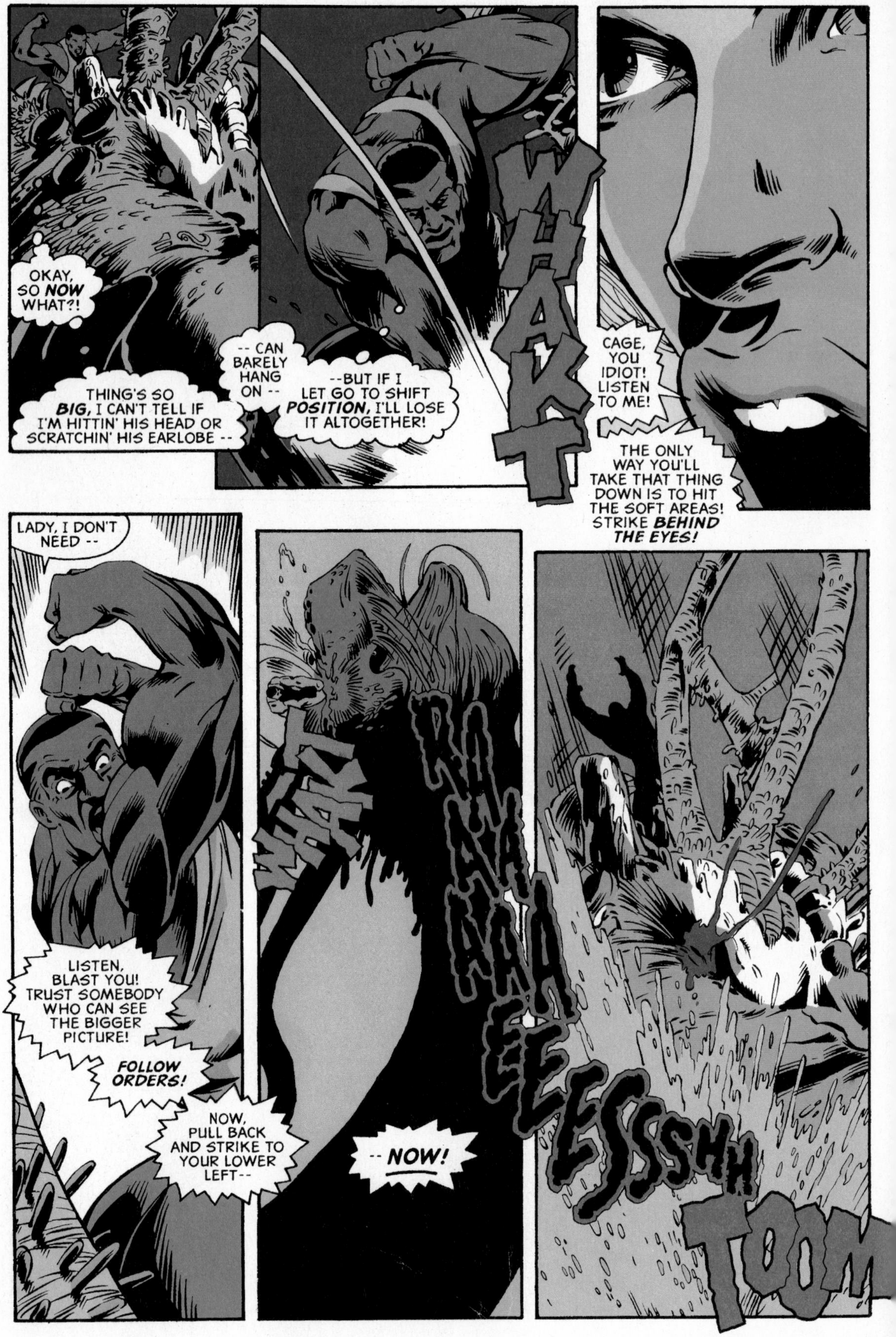
OKAY, SO NOW WHAT?!
THING'S SO BIG, I CAN'T TELL IF I'M HITTIN' HIS HEAD OR SCRATCHIN' HIS EARLOBE --
-- CAN BARELY HANG ON --
--BUT IF I LET GO TO SHIFT POSITION, I'LL LOSE IT ALTOGETHER!
WHAKT
CAGE, YOU IDIOT! LISTEN TO ME!
THE ONLY WAY YOU'LL TAKE THAT THING DOWN IS TO HIT THE SOFT AREAS! STRIKE BEHIND THE EYES!
LADY, I DON'T NEED --
LISTEN, BLAST YOU! TRUST SOMEBODY WHO CAN SEE THE BIGGER PICTURE!
FOLLOW ORDERS!
NOW, PULL BACK AND STRIKE TO YOUR LOWER LEFT--
-- NOW!
WHAK
TOOM

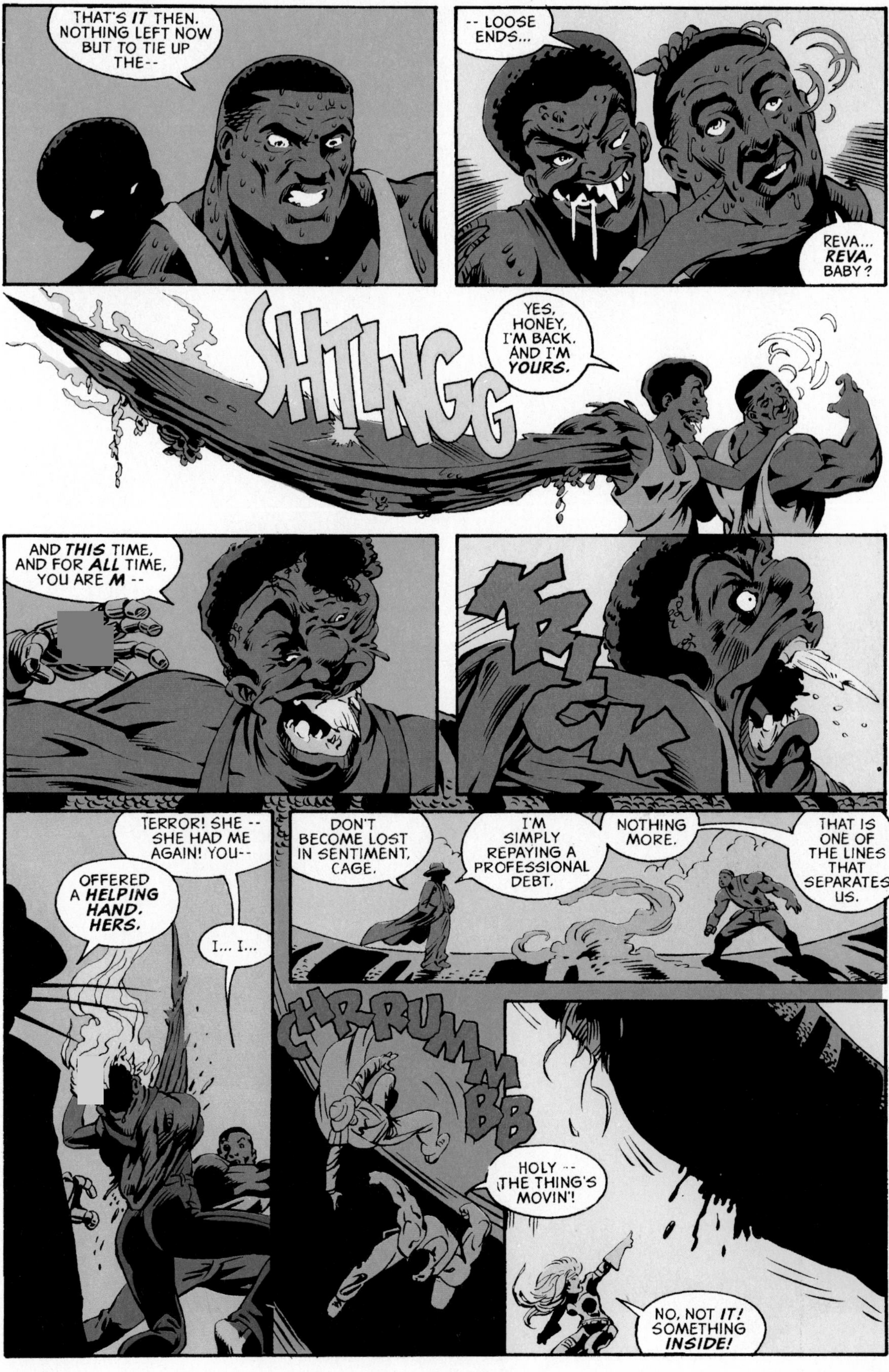
THAT'S IT THEN. NOTHING LEFT NOW BUT TO TIE UP THE--
-- LOOSE ENDS...
REVA... REVA, BABY?
SHTLINGG
YES, HONEY, I'M BACK. AND I'M YOURS.
AND THIS TIME, AND FOR ALL TIME, YOU ARE M --
TERROR! SHE -- SHE HAD ME AGAIN! YOU--
OFFERED A HELPING HAND. HERS.
I... I...
DON'T BECOME LOST IN SENTIMENT, CAGE.
I'M SIMPLY REPAYING A PROFESSIONAL DEBT.
NOTHING MORE.
THAT IS ONE OF THE LINES THAT SEPARATES US.
CHRRUMMMBB
HOLY -- THE THING'S MOVIN'!
NO, NOT IT! SOMETHING INSIDE!

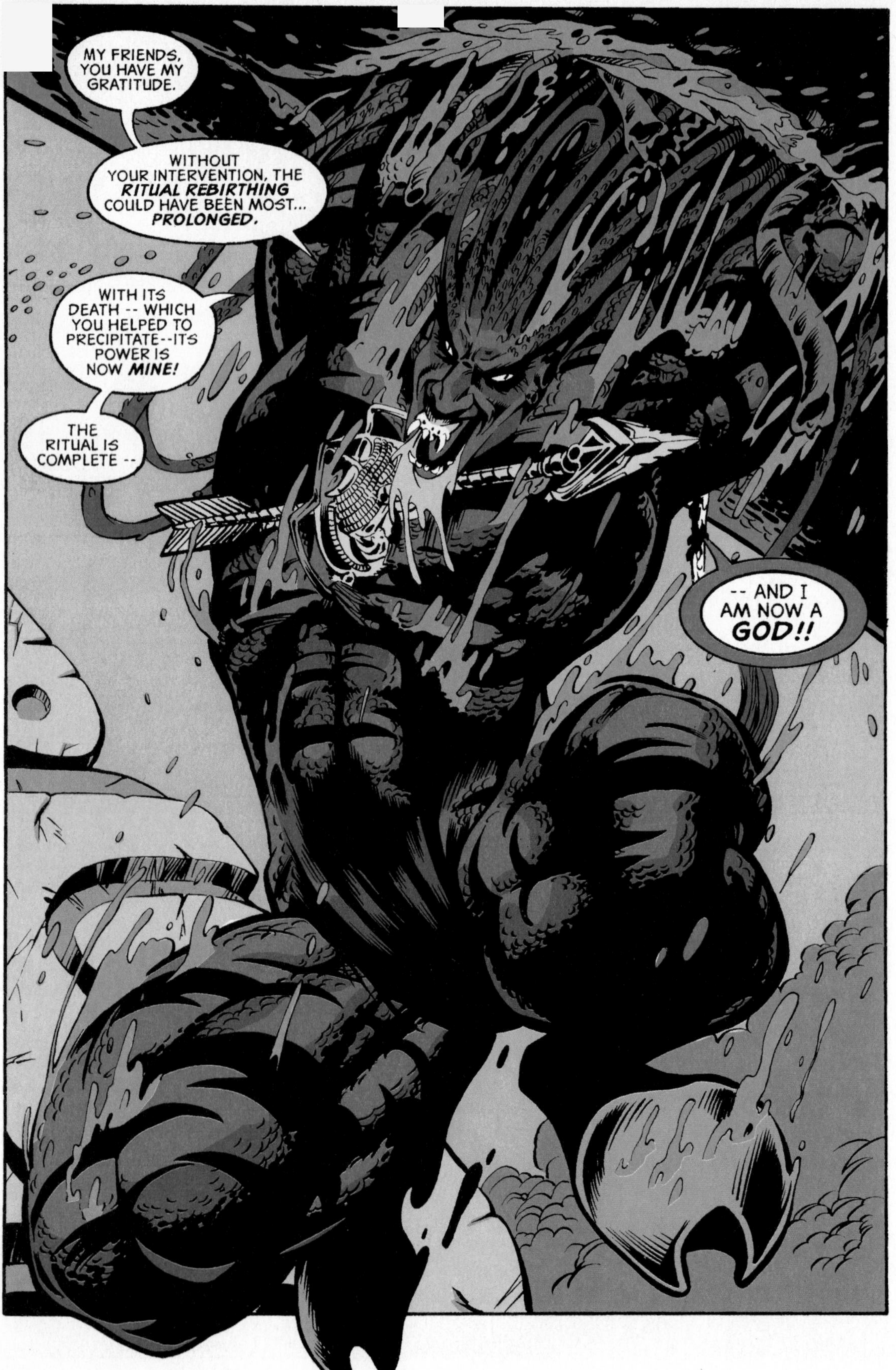
MY FRIENDS, YOU HAVE MY GRATITUDE.
WITHOUT YOUR INTERVENTION, THE ***RITUAL REBIRTHING*** COULD HAVE BEEN MOST... ***PROLONGED.***
WITH ITS DEATH -- WHICH YOU HELPED TO PRECIPITATE--ITS POWER IS NOW ***MINE!***
THE RITUAL IS COMPLETE --
-- AND I AM NOW A ***GOD!!***

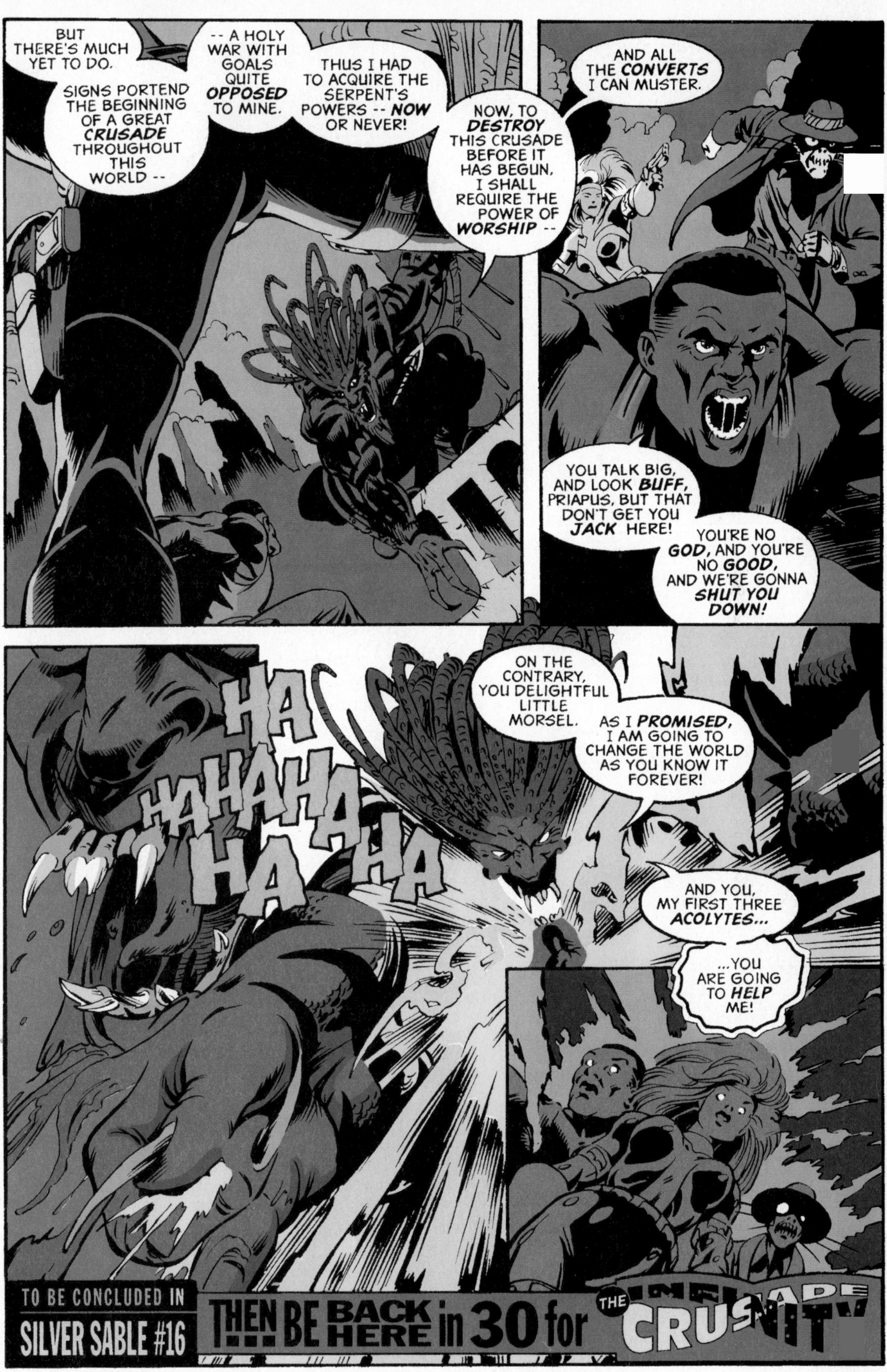

BUT THERE'S MUCH YET TO DO.
SIGNS PORTEND THE BEGINNING OF A GREAT CRUSADE THROUGHOUT THIS WORLD --
-- A HOLY WAR WITH GOALS QUITE OPPOSED TO MINE.
THUS I HAD TO ACQUIRE THE SERPENT'S POWERS -- NOW OR NEVER!
NOW, TO DESTROY THIS CRUSADE BEFORE IT HAS BEGUN, I SHALL REQUIRE THE POWER OF WORSHIP --
AND ALL THE CONVERTS I CAN MUSTER.
YOU TALK BIG, AND LOOK BUFF, PRIAPUS, BUT THAT DON'T GET YOU JACK HERE!
YOU'RE NO GOD, AND YOU'RE NO GOOD, AND WE'RE GONNA SHUT YOU DOWN!
HA HAHAHA HA HA
ON THE CONTRARY, YOU DELIGHTFUL LITTLE MORSEL.
AS I PROMISED, I AM GOING TO CHANGE THE WORLD AS YOU KNOW IT FOREVER!
AND YOU, MY FIRST THREE ACOLYTES...
...YOU ARE GOING TO HELP ME!
TO BE CONCLUDED IN SILVER SABLE #16
THEN BE BACK HERE in 30 for THE

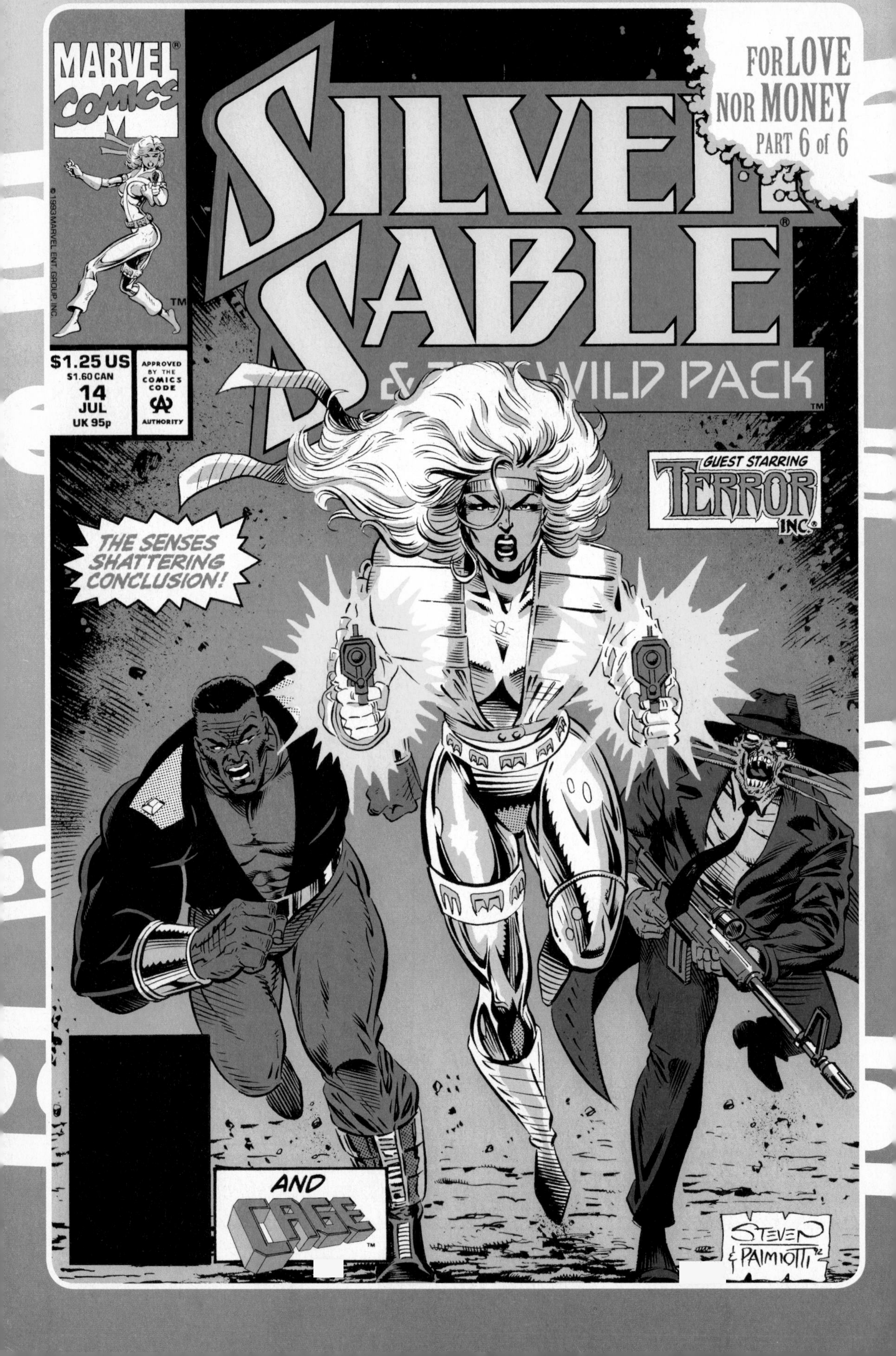
MARVEL COMICS
© 1993 MARVEL ENT. GROUP, INC.
$1.25 US
$1.60 CAN
14
JUL
UK 95p
APPROVED BY THE COMICS CODE AUTHORITY
SILVER SABLE
& WILD PACK
FOR LOVE NOR MONEY
PART 6 of 6
GUEST STARRING
TERROR INC.
THE SENSES SHATTERING CONCLUSION!
AND
CAGE
STEVEN & PALMIOTTI

RELENTLESSLY TRAINED IN MULTIPLE FORMS OF HAND-TO-HAND AND ARMED COMBAT, SILVER SABLE WAS DESTINED TO INHERIT THE COMMAND OF HER FATHER'S PROFESSIONAL SOLDIER UNIT, THE WILD PACK. UNDER THE AUSPICES OF SILVER SABLE INTERNATIONAL, SHE HAS SINCE TRANSFORMED THEM INTO THE ULTIMATE MERCENARY COMBAT FORCE, NOW THE ECONOMIC FOUNDATION OF HER BELOVED HOMELAND, SYMKARIA. STAN LEE PRESENTS. . .SILVER SABLE AND THE WILD PACK

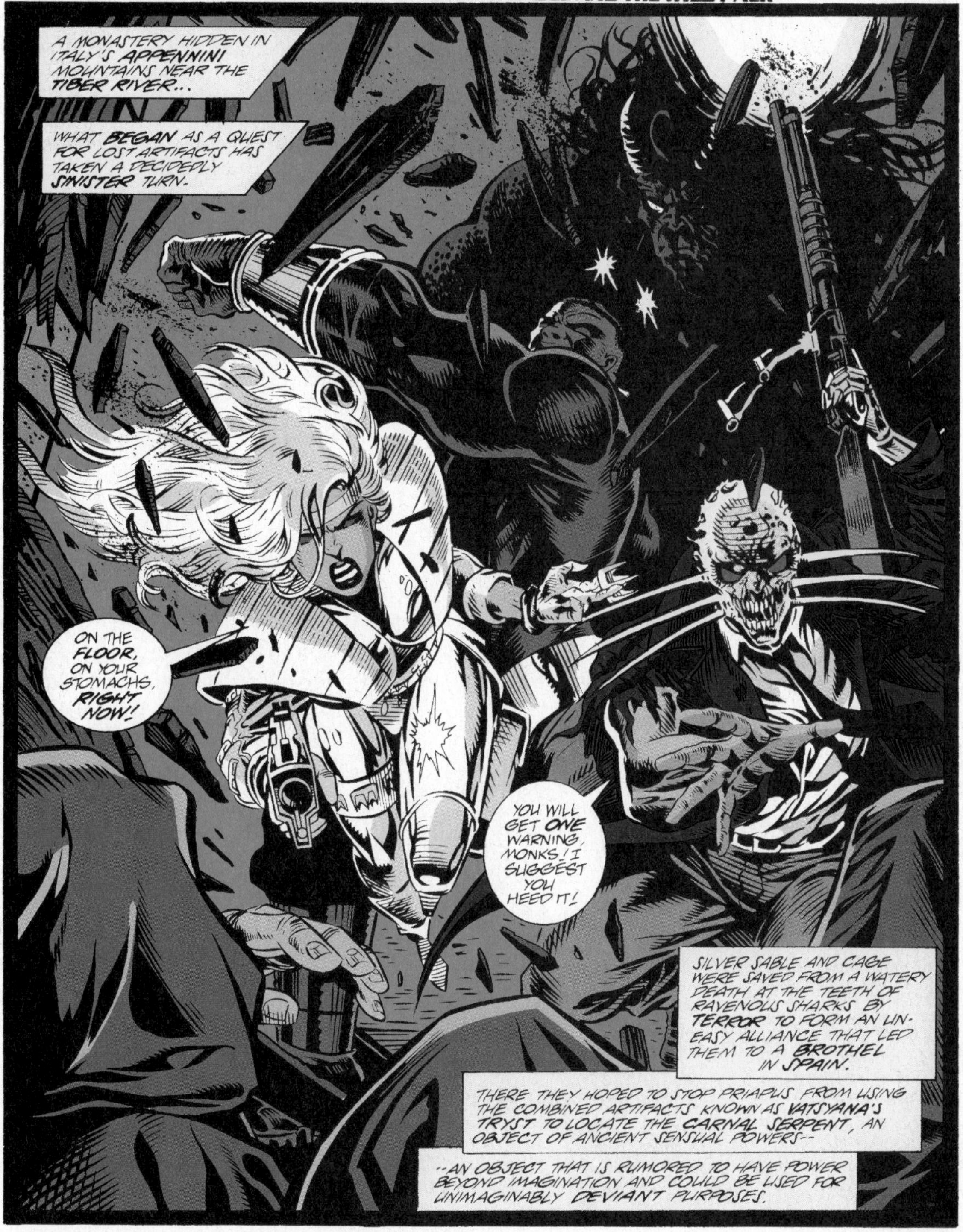

A MONASTERY HIDDEN IN ITALY'S APPENNINI MOUNTAINS NEAR THE TIBER RIVER...
WHAT BEGAN AS A QUEST FOR LOST ARTIFACTS HAS TAKEN A DECIDEDLY SINISTER TURN.
ON THE FLOOR, ON YOUR STOMACHS, RIGHT NOW!
YOU WILL GET ONE WARNING, MONKS! I SUGGEST YOU HEED IT!
SILVER SABLE AND CAGE WERE SAVED FROM A WATERY DEATH AT THE TEETH OF RAVENOUS SHARKS BY TERROR TO FORM AN UNEASY ALLIANCE THAT LED THEM TO A BROTHEL IN SPAIN.
THERE THEY HOPED TO STOP PRIAPUS FROM USING THE COMBINED ARTIFACTS KNOWN AS VATSYANA'S TRYST TO LOCATE THE CARNAL SERPENT, AN OBJECT OF ANCIENT SENSUAL POWERS--
--AN OBJECT THAT IS RUMORED TO HAVE POWER BEYOND IMAGINATION AND COULD BE USED FOR UNIMAGINABLY DEVIANT PURPOSES.

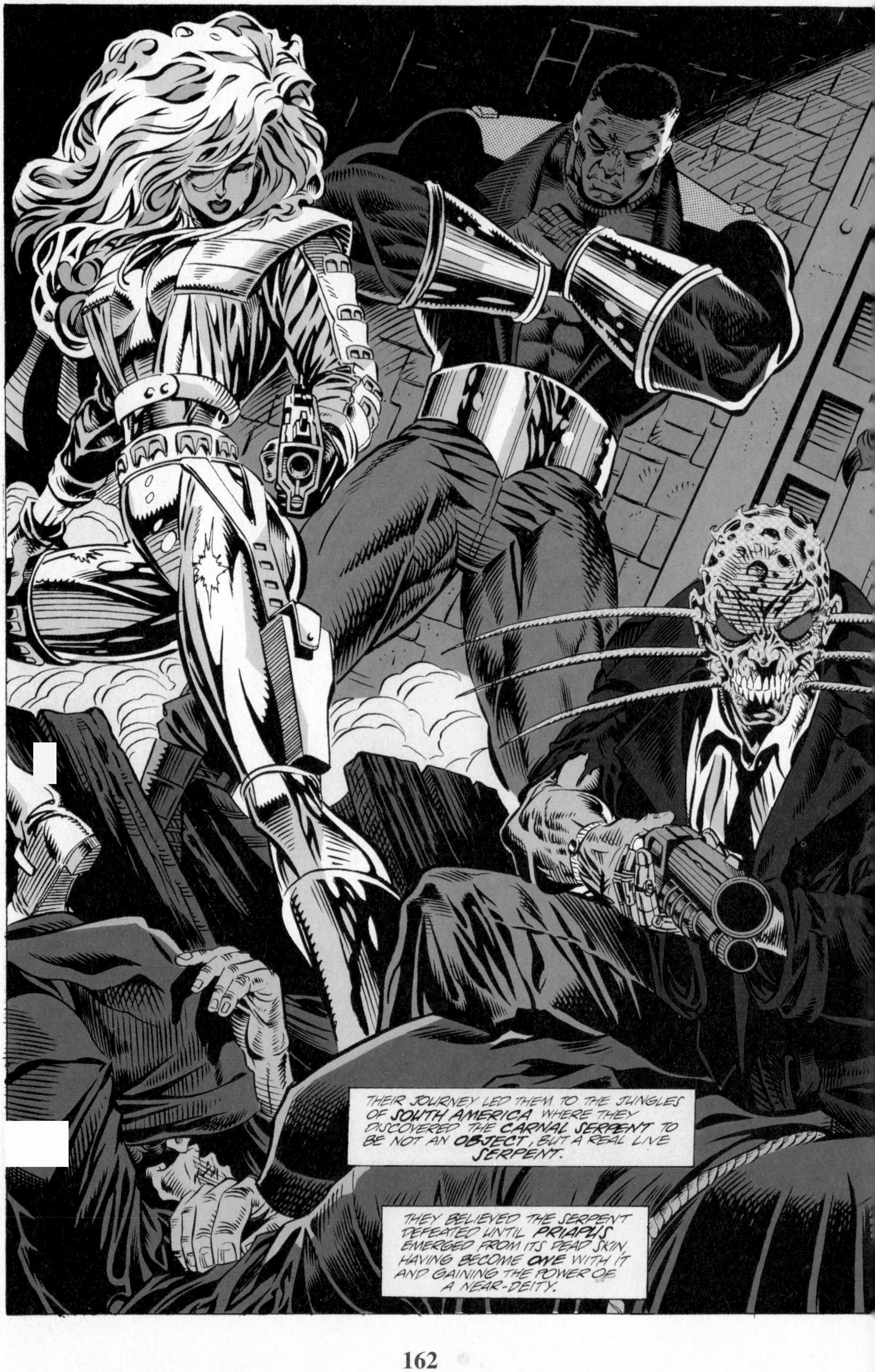
THEIR JOURNEY LED THEM TO THE JUNGLES OF SOUTH AMERICA WHERE THEY DISCOVERED THE CARNAL SERPENT TO BE NOT AN OBJECT, BUT A REAL LIVE SERPENT.
THEY BELIEVED THE SERPENT DEFEATED UNTIL PRIAPUS EMERGED FROM ITS DEAD SKIN, HAVING BECOME ONE WITH IT AND GAINING THE POWER OF A NEAR-DEITY.

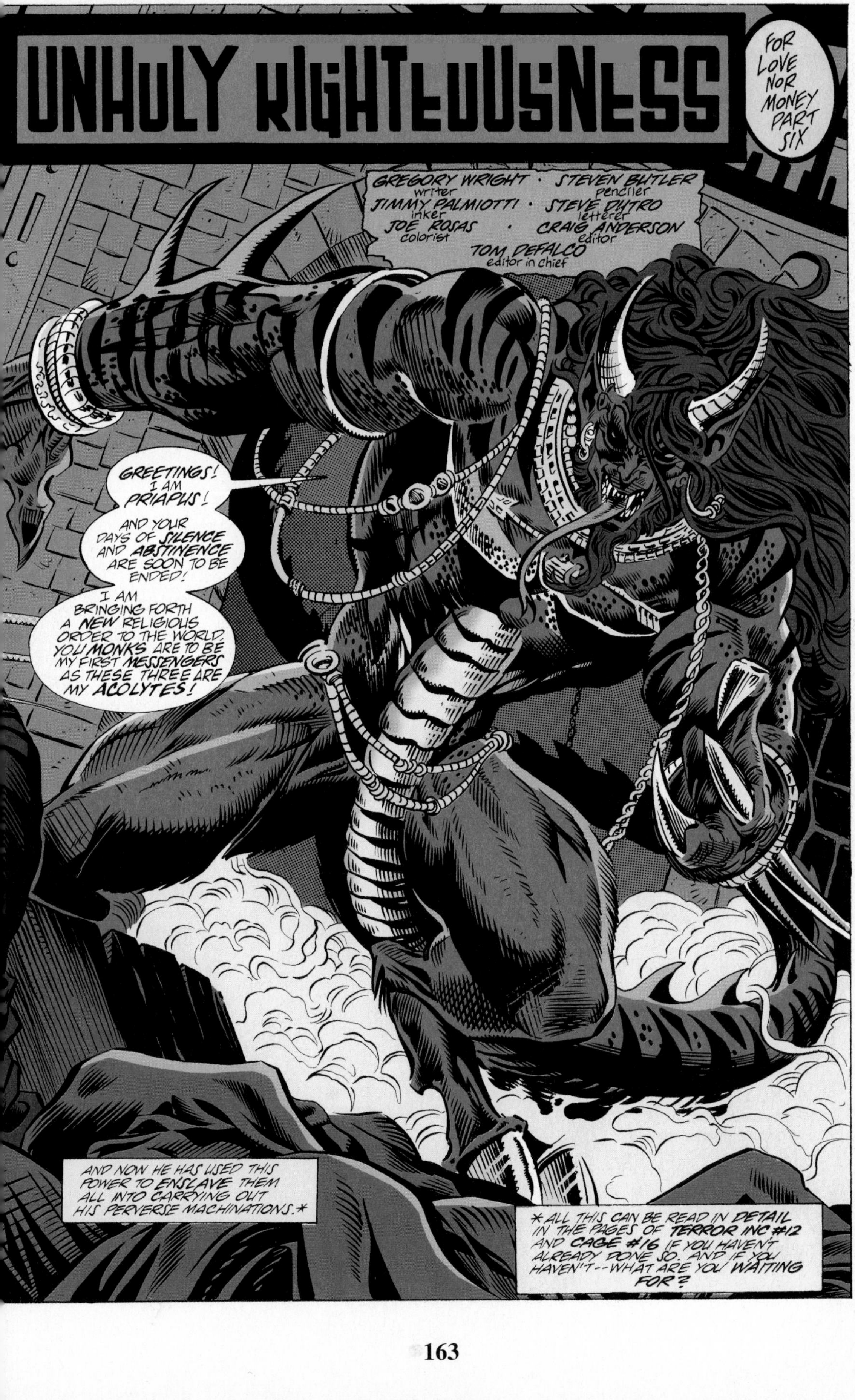
UNHOLY RIGHTEOUSNESS
FOR LOVE NOR MONEY PART SIX
GREGORY WRIGHT · writer
STEVEN BUTLER · penciler
JIMMY PALMIOTTI · inker
STEVE DUTRO · letterer
JOE ROSAS · colorist
CRAIG ANDERSON · editor
TOM DEFALCO editor in chief
GREETINGS! I AM PRIAPUS!
AND YOUR DAYS OF SILENCE AND ABSTINENCE ARE SOON TO BE ENDED!
I AM BRINGING FORTH A NEW RELIGIOUS ORDER TO THE WORLD. YOU MONKS ARE TO BE MY FIRST MESSENGERS AS THESE THREE ARE MY ACOLYTES!
AND NOW HE HAS USED THIS POWER TO ENSLAVE THEM ALL INTO CARRYING OUT HIS PERVERSE MACHINATIONS.*
*ALL THIS CAN BE READ IN DETAIL IN THE PAGES OF TERROR INC #12 AND CAGE #16 IF YOU HAVEN'T ALREADY DONE SO. AND IF YOU HAVEN'T--WHAT ARE YOU WAITING FOR?

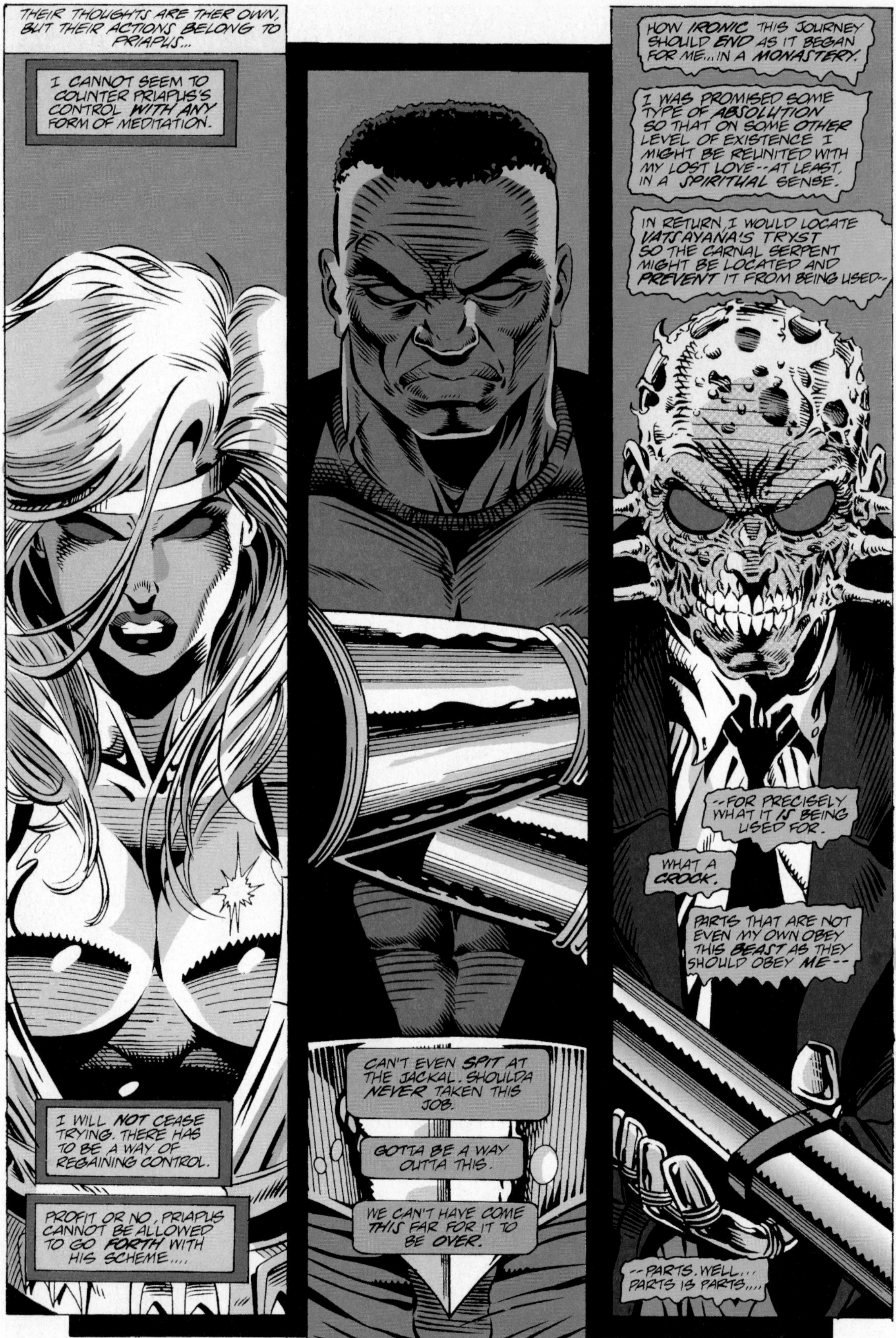
THEIR THOUGHTS ARE THER OWN, BUT THEIR ACTIONS BELONG TO PRIAPUS...
I CANNOT SEEM TO COUNTER PRIAPUS'S CONTROL WITH ANY FORM OF MEDITATION.
I WILL NOT CEASE TRYING. THERE HAS TO BE A WAY OF REGAINING CONTROL.
PROFIT OR NO, PRIAPUS CANNOT BE ALLOWED TO GO FORTH WITH HIS SCHEME....
CAN'T EVEN SPIT AT THE JACKAL. SHOULDA NEVER TAKEN THIS JOB.
GOTTA BE A WAY OUTTA THIS.
WE CAN'T HAVE COME THIS FAR FOR IT TO BE OVER.
HOW IRONIC THIS JOURNEY SHOULD END AS IT BEGAN FOR ME...IN A MONASTERY.
I WAS PROMISED SOME TYPE OF ABSOLUTION SO THAT ON SOME OTHER LEVEL OF EXISTENCE I MIGHT BE REUNITED WITH MY LOST LOVE--AT LEAST, IN A SPIRITUAL SENSE.
IN RETURN, I WOULD LOCATE VATSAYANA'S TRYST SO THE CARNAL SERPENT MIGHT BE LOCATED AND PREVENT IT FROM BEING USED--
--FOR PRECISELY WHAT IT IS BEING USED FOR.
WHAT A CROCK.
PARTS THAT ARE NOT EVEN MY OWN OBEY THIS BEAST AS THEY SHOULD OBEY ME--
--PARTS. WELL... PARTS IS PARTS....

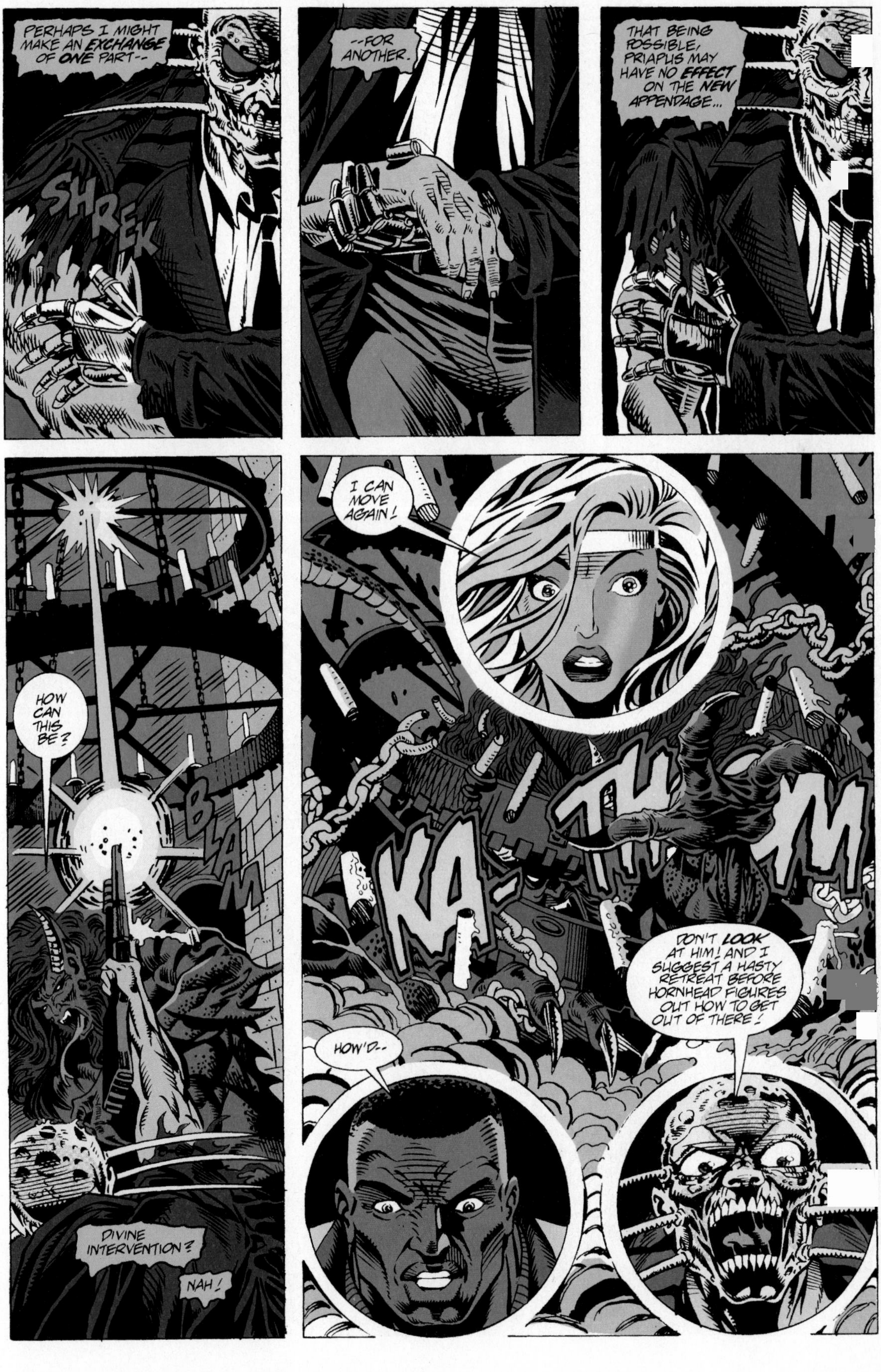
PERHAPS I MIGHT MAKE AN EXCHANGE OF ONE PART--
SHREK
--FOR ANOTHER.
THAT BEING POSSIBLE, PRIAPUS MAY HAVE NO EFFECT ON THE NEW APPENDAGE...
HOW CAN THIS BE?
BLAM
DIVINE INTERVENTION?
NAH!
I CAN MOVE AGAIN!
KA-THOOM
DON'T LOOK AT HIM! AND I SUGGEST A HASTY RETREAT BEFORE HORNHEAD FIGURES OUT HOW TO GET OUT OF THERE!
HOW'D--

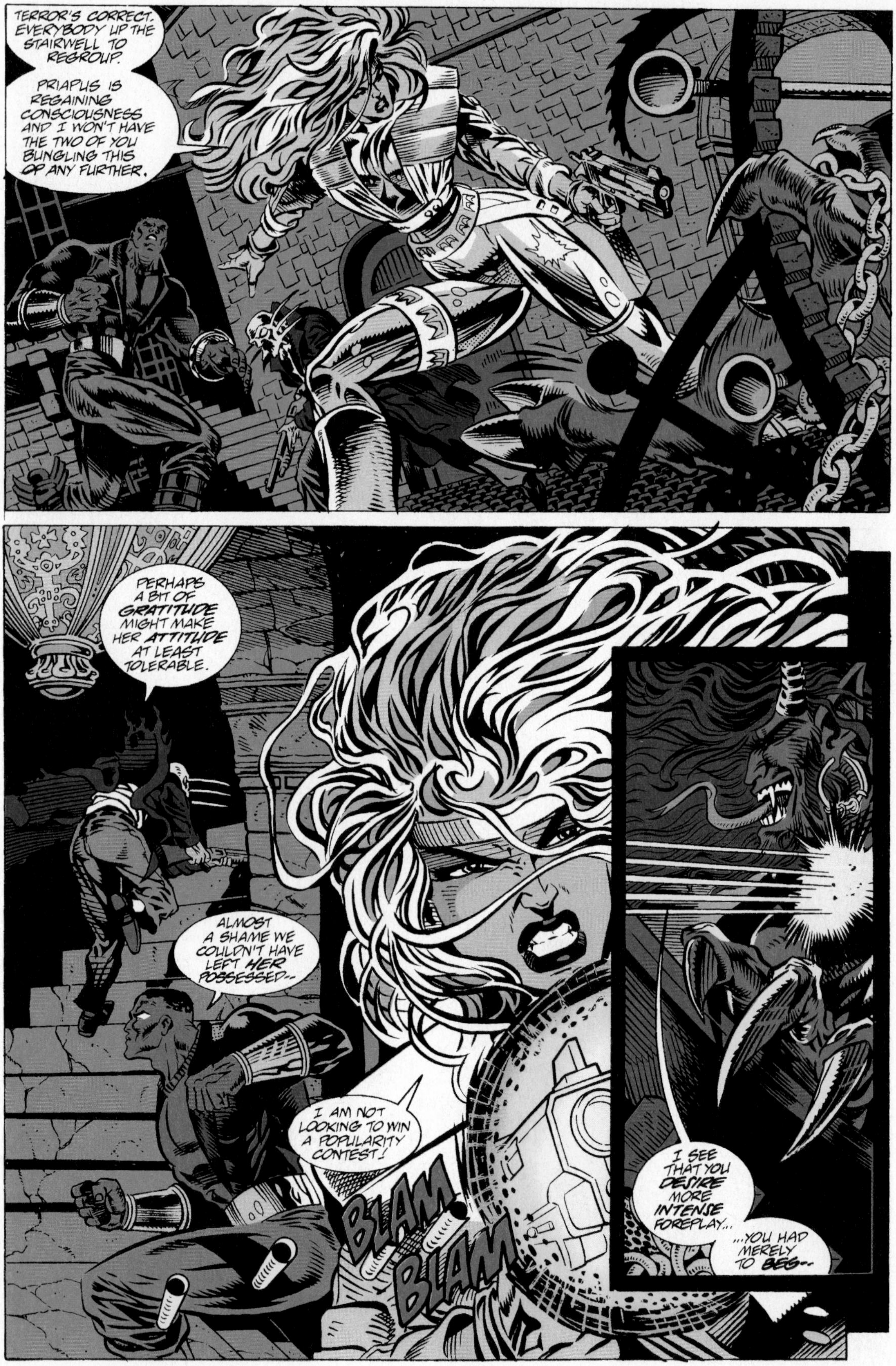
TERROR'S CORRECT. EVERYBODY UP THE STAIRWELL TO REGROUP.
PRIAPUS IS REGAINING CONSCIOUSNESS AND I WON'T HAVE THE TWO OF YOU BUNGLING THIS OP ANY FURTHER.
PERHAPS A BIT OF GRATITUDE MIGHT MAKE HER ATTITUDE AT LEAST TOLERABLE.
ALMOST A SHAME WE COULDN'T HAVE LEFT HER POSSESSED--
I AM NOT LOOKING TO WIN A POPULARITY CONTEST!
BLAM
BLAM
I SEE THAT YOU DESIRE MORE INTENSE FOREPLAY...
...YOU HAD MERELY TO BEG--

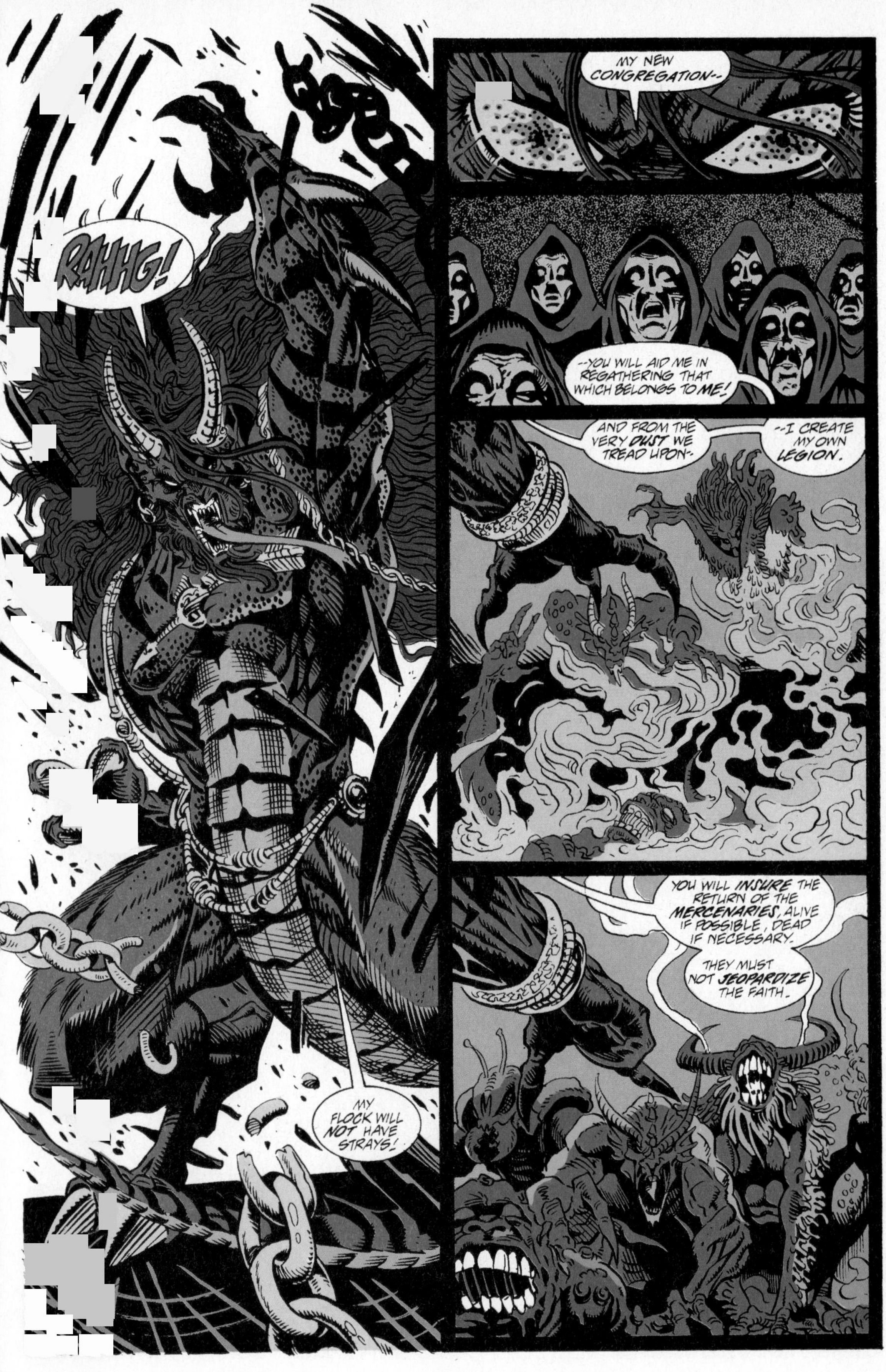
RAHHG!
MY FLOCK WILL NOT HAVE STRAYS!
MY NEW CONGREGATION--
--YOU WILL AID ME IN REGATHERING THAT WHICH BELONGS TO ME!
AND FROM THE VERY DUST WE TREAD UPON--
--I CREATE MY OWN LEGION.
YOU WILL INSURE THE RETURN OF THE MERCENARIES, ALIVE IF POSSIBLE, DEAD IF NECESSARY.
THEY MUST NOT JEOPARDIZE THE FAITH.

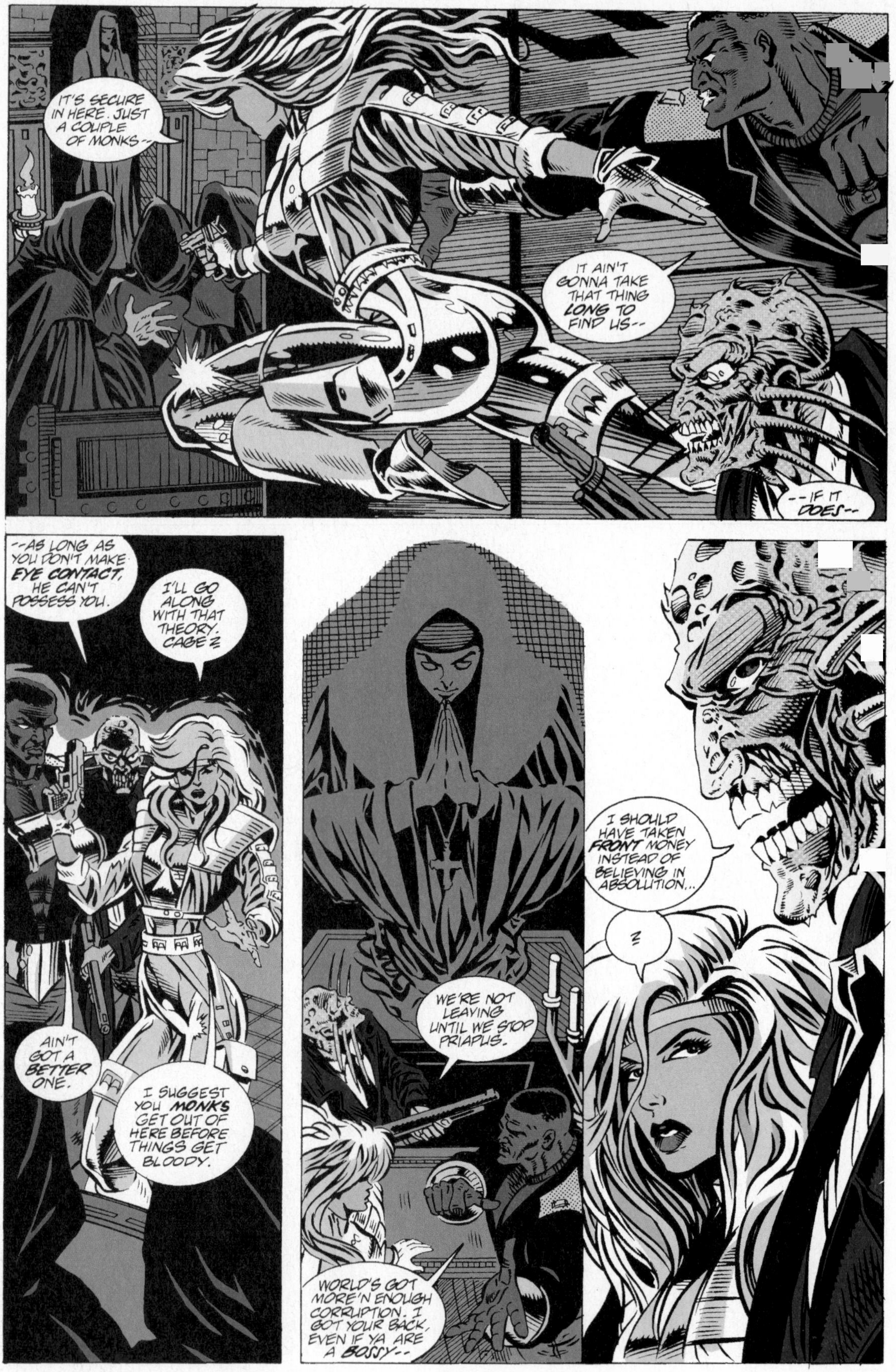

IT'S SECURE IN HERE. JUST A COUPLE OF MONKS--
IT AIN'T GONNA TAKE THAT THING LONG TO FIND US--
--IF IT DOES--
--AS LONG AS YOU DON'T MAKE EYE CONTACT, HE CAN'T POSSESS YOU.
I'LL GO ALONG WITH THAT THEORY. CAGE?
AIN'T GOT A BETTER ONE.
I SUGGEST YOU MONKS GET OUT OF HERE BEFORE THINGS GET BLOODY.
WE'RE NOT LEAVING UNTIL WE STOP PRIAPUS.
WORLD'S GOT MORE'N ENOUGH CORRUPTION. I GOT YOUR BACK, EVEN IF YA ARE A BOSSY--
I SHOULD HAVE TAKEN FRONT MONEY INSTEAD OF BELIEVING IN ABSOLUTION...
?

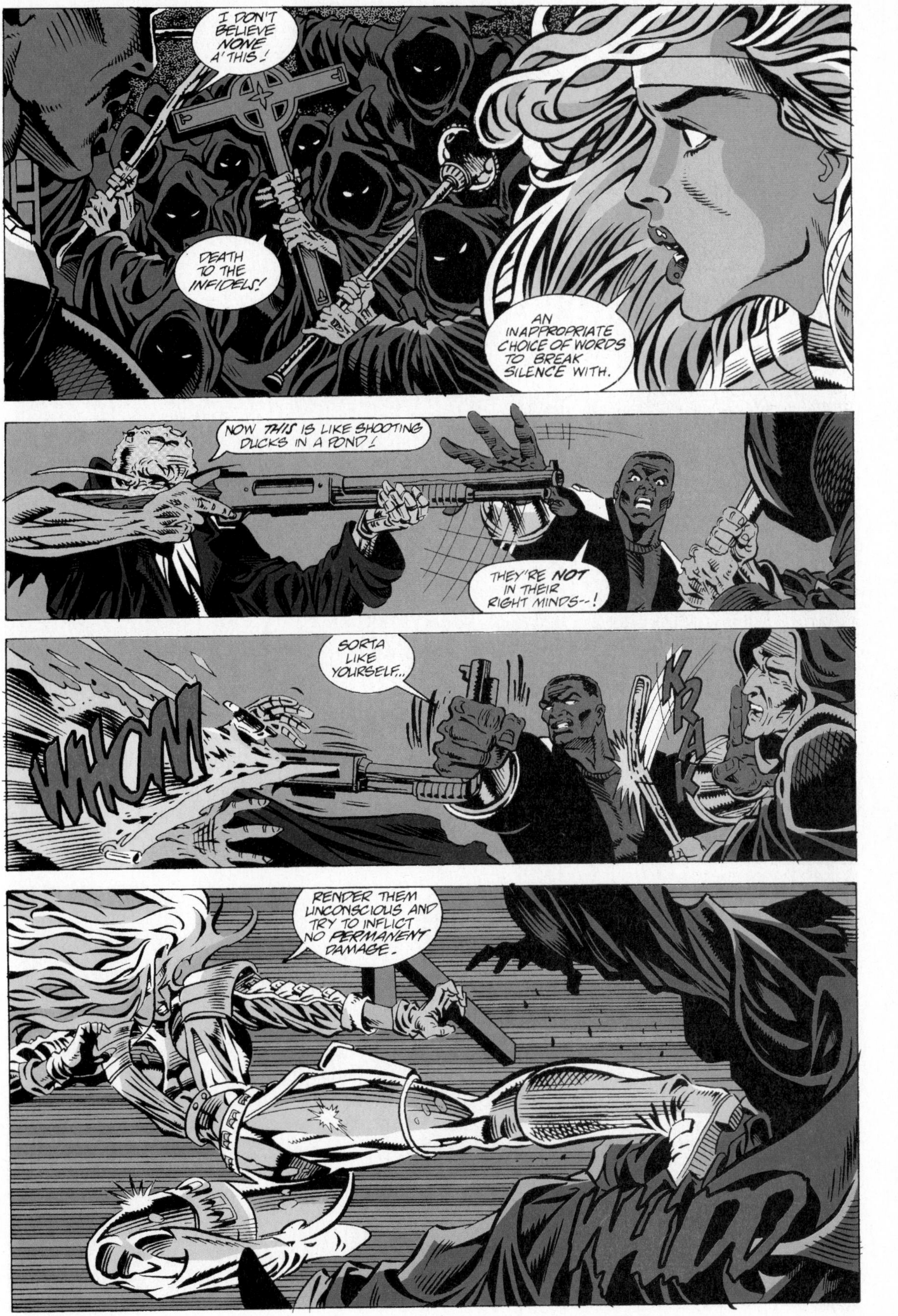
I DON'T BELIEVE NONE A'THIS!
DEATH TO THE INFIDELS!
AN INAPPROPRIATE CHOICE OF WORDS TO BREAK SILENCE WITH.
NOW THIS IS LIKE SHOOTING DUCKS IN A POND!
THEY'RE NOT IN THEIR RIGHT MINDS--!
SORTA LIKE YOURSELF...
KRAK
WHOM
RENDER THEM UNCONSCIOUS AND TRY TO INFLICT NO PERMANENT DAMAGE.

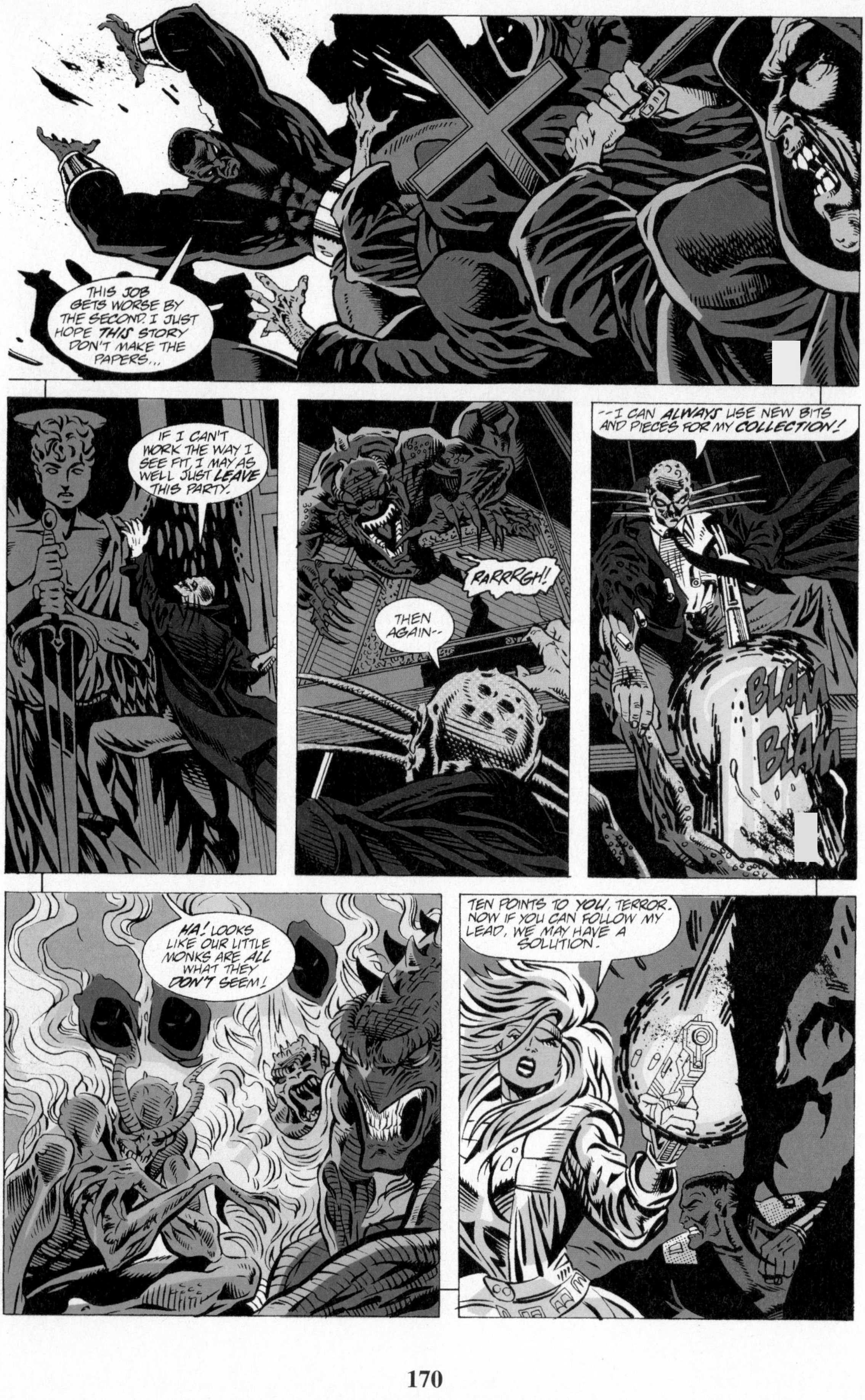
THIS JOB GETS WORSE BY THE SECOND. I JUST HOPE THIS STORY DON'T MAKE THE PAPERS...
IF I CAN'T WORK THE WAY I SEE FIT, I MAY AS WELL JUST LEAVE THIS PARTY.
RARRRGH!
THEN AGAIN--
--I CAN ALWAYS USE NEW BITS AND PIECES FOR MY COLLECTION!
BLAM
BLAM
HA! LOOKS LIKE OUR LITTLE MONKS ARE ALL WHAT THEY DON'T SEEM!
TEN POINTS TO YOU, TERROR. NOW IF YOU CAN FOLLOW MY LEAD, WE MAY HAVE A SOLUTION.

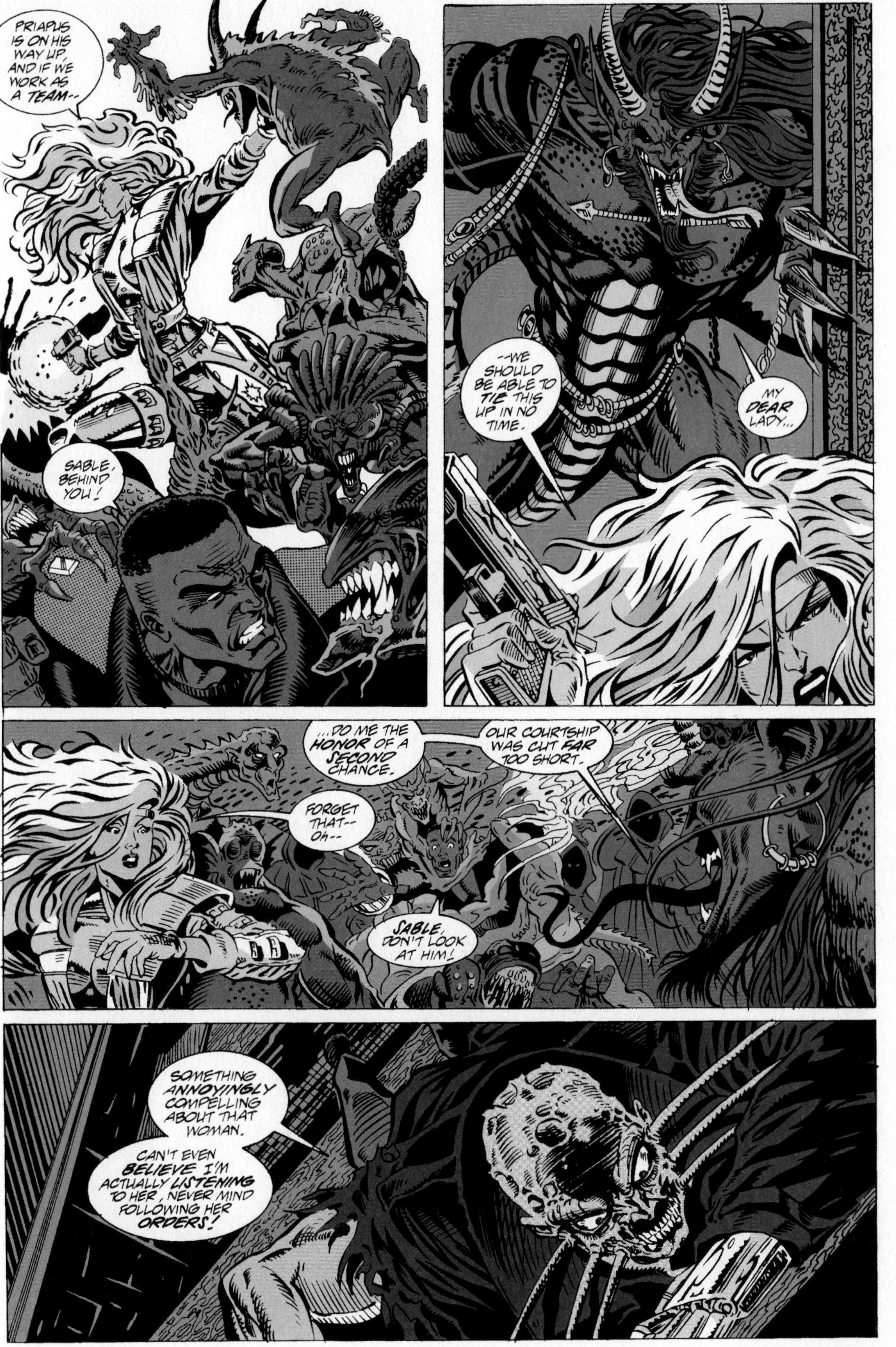

PRIAPUS IS ON HIS WAY UP, AND IF WE WORK AS A TEAM--
--WE SHOULD BE ABLE TO TIE THIS UP IN NO TIME.
SABLE, BEHIND YOU!
MY DEAR LADY...
...DO ME THE HONOR OF A SECOND CHANCE.
OUR COURTSHIP WAS CUT FAR TOO SHORT.
FORGET THAT-- Oh--
SABLE, DON'T LOOK AT HIM!
SOMETHING ANNOYINGLY COMPELLING ABOUT THAT WOMAN.
CAN'T EVEN BELIEVE I'M ACTUALLY LISTENING TO HER, NEVER MIND FOLLOWING HER ORDERS!

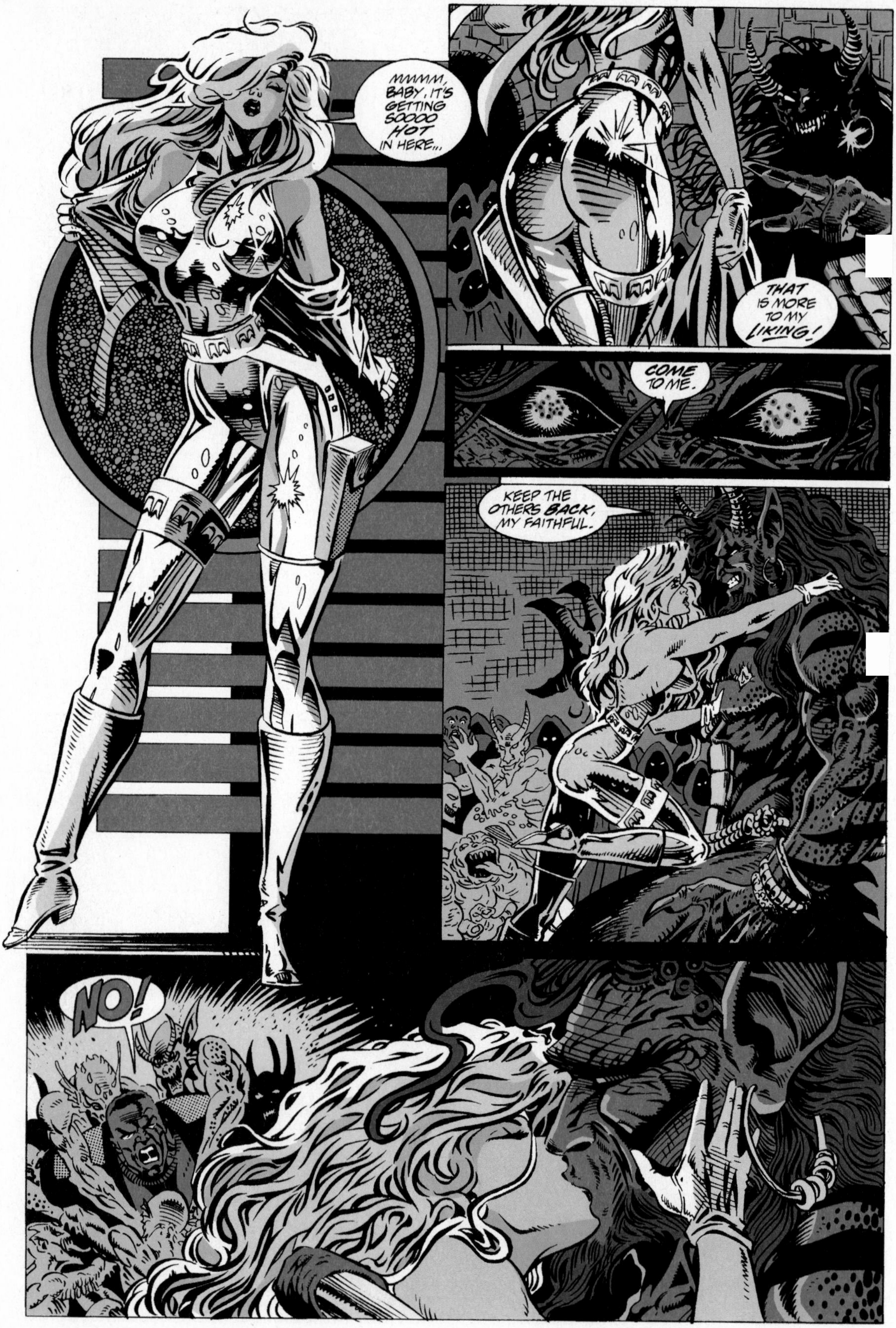
MMMM, BABY, IT'S GETTING SOOOO HOT IN HERE...
THAT IS MORE TO MY LIKING!
COME TO ME.
KEEP THE OTHERS BACK, MY FAITHFUL.
NO!

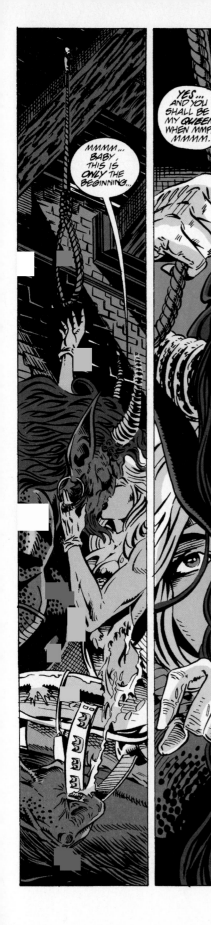

MMMM... BABY, THIS IS ONLY THE BEGINNING...

YES... AND YOU SHALL BE MY *QUEEN* WHEN MMPH! MMMM.

ONLY IN YOUR *DREAMS.*

EH?

GAKK!

CAN'T BREATHE? GOOD. YOUR FOUL BREATH IS NOT APPRECIATED!

NOW, TERROR!

UH! WISH I HAD ONE OF *SCHWARZE-NEGGER'S* ARMS ABOUT NOW!

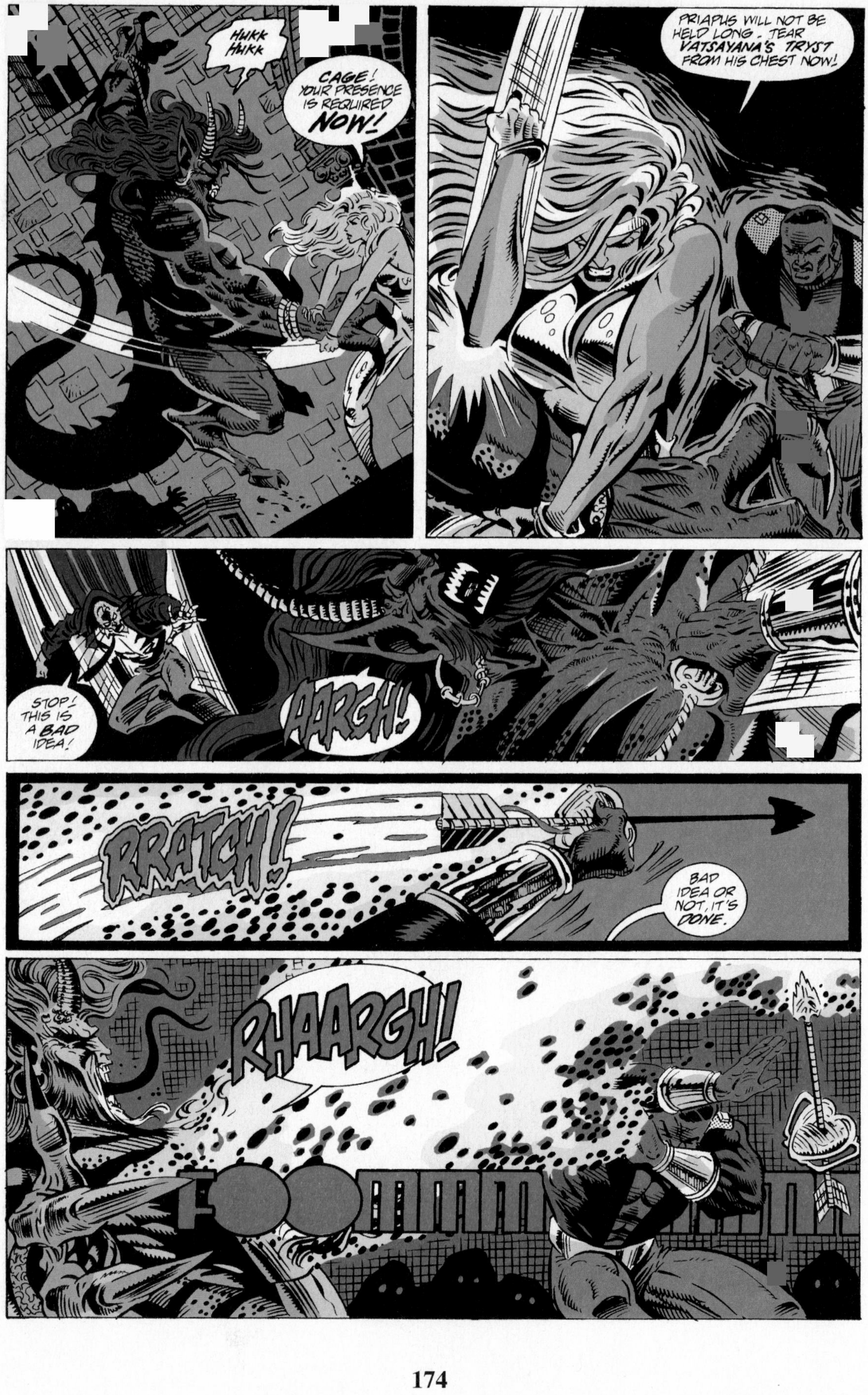
HUKK HUKK
CAGE! YOUR PRESENCE IS REQUIRED NOW!
PRIAPUS WILL NOT BE HELD LONG. TEAR VATSAYANA'S TRYST FROM HIS CHEST NOW!
STOP! THIS IS A BAD IDEA!
AARGH!
RRATCH!
BAD IDEA OR NOT, IT'S DONE.
RHAARGH!

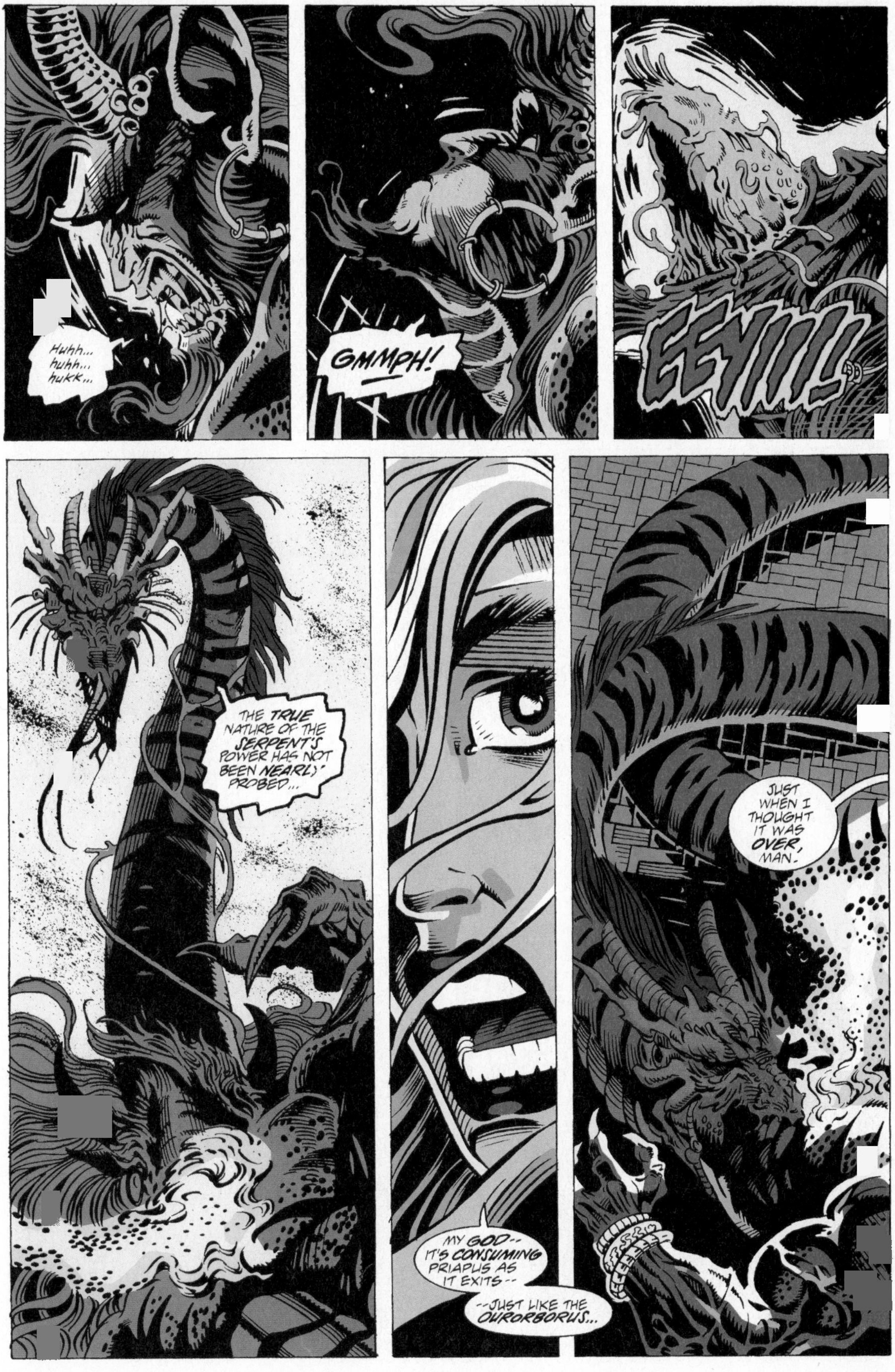

Huhh...
huhh...
hukk...
GMMPH!
EEYIII!
THE TRUE NATURE OF THE SERPENT'S POWER HAS NOT BEEN NEARLY PROBED...
MY GOD-- IT'S CONSUMING PRIAPUS AS IT EXITS--
--JUST LIKE THE OUROBORUS...
JUST WHEN I THOUGHT IT WAS OVER, MAN.

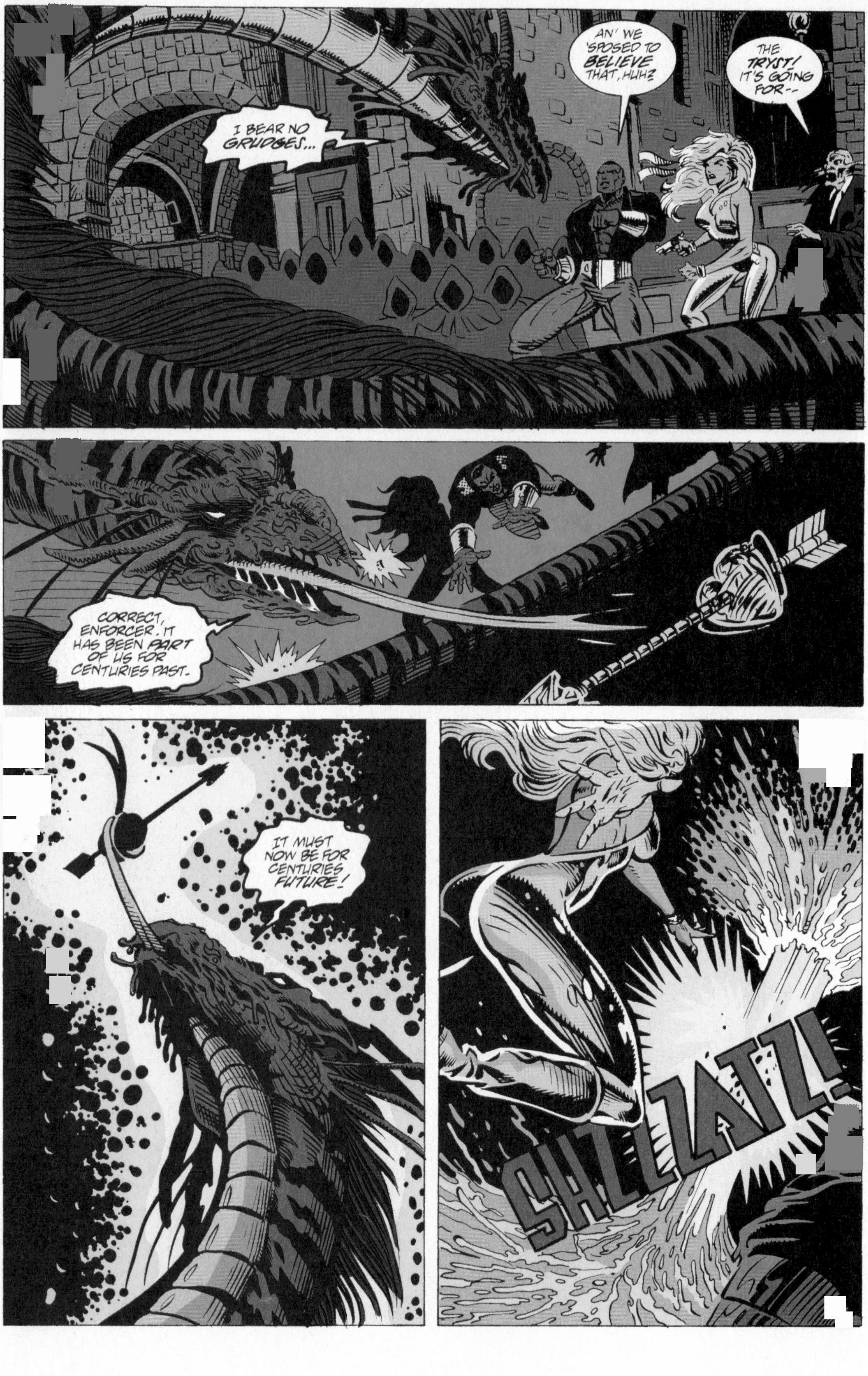
I BEAR NO GRUDGES...
AN' WE 'SPOSED TO BELIEVE THAT, HUH?
THE TRYST! IT'S GOING FOR--
CORRECT, ENFORCER. IT HAS BEEN PART OF US FOR CENTURIES PAST.
IT MUST NOW BE FOR CENTURIES FUTURE!
SHZZATZ!

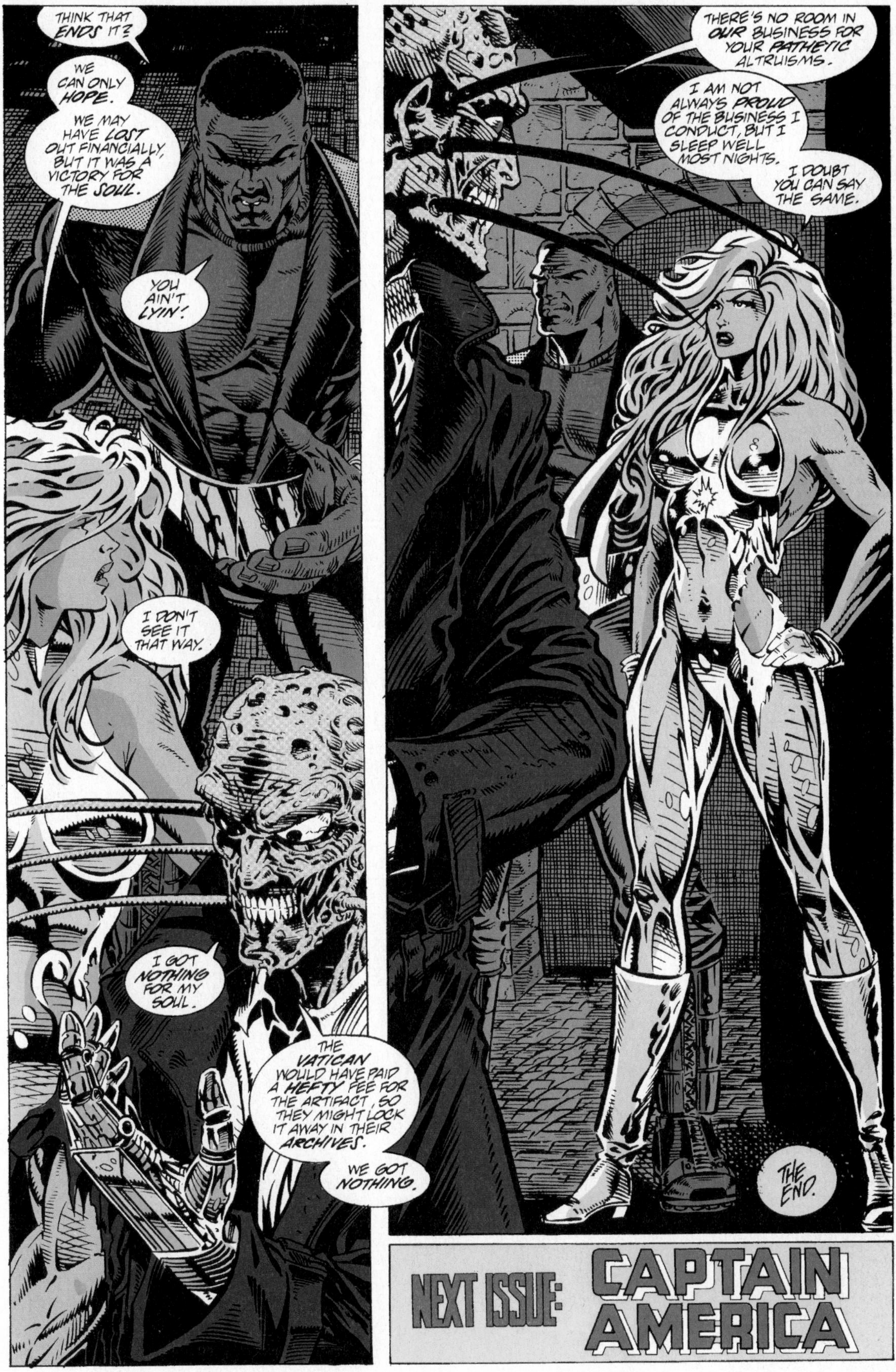
THINK THAT ENDS IT?
WE CAN ONLY HOPE.
WE MAY HAVE LOST OUT FINANCIALLY, BUT IT WAS A VICTORY FOR THE SOUL.
YOU AIN'T LYIN'!
I DON'T SEE IT THAT WAY.
I GOT NOTHING FOR MY SOUL.
THE VATICAN WOULD HAVE PAID A HEFTY FEE FOR THE ARTIFACT, SO THEY MIGHT LOCK IT AWAY IN THEIR ARCHIVES.
WE GOT NOTHING.
THERE'S NO ROOM IN OUR BUSINESS FOR YOUR PATHETIC ALTRUISMS.
I AM NOT ALWAYS PROUD OF THE BUSINESS I CONDUCT, BUT I SLEEP WELL MOST NIGHTS.
I DOUBT YOU CAN SAY THE SAME.
THE END.
NEXT ISSUE: CAPTAIN AMERICA

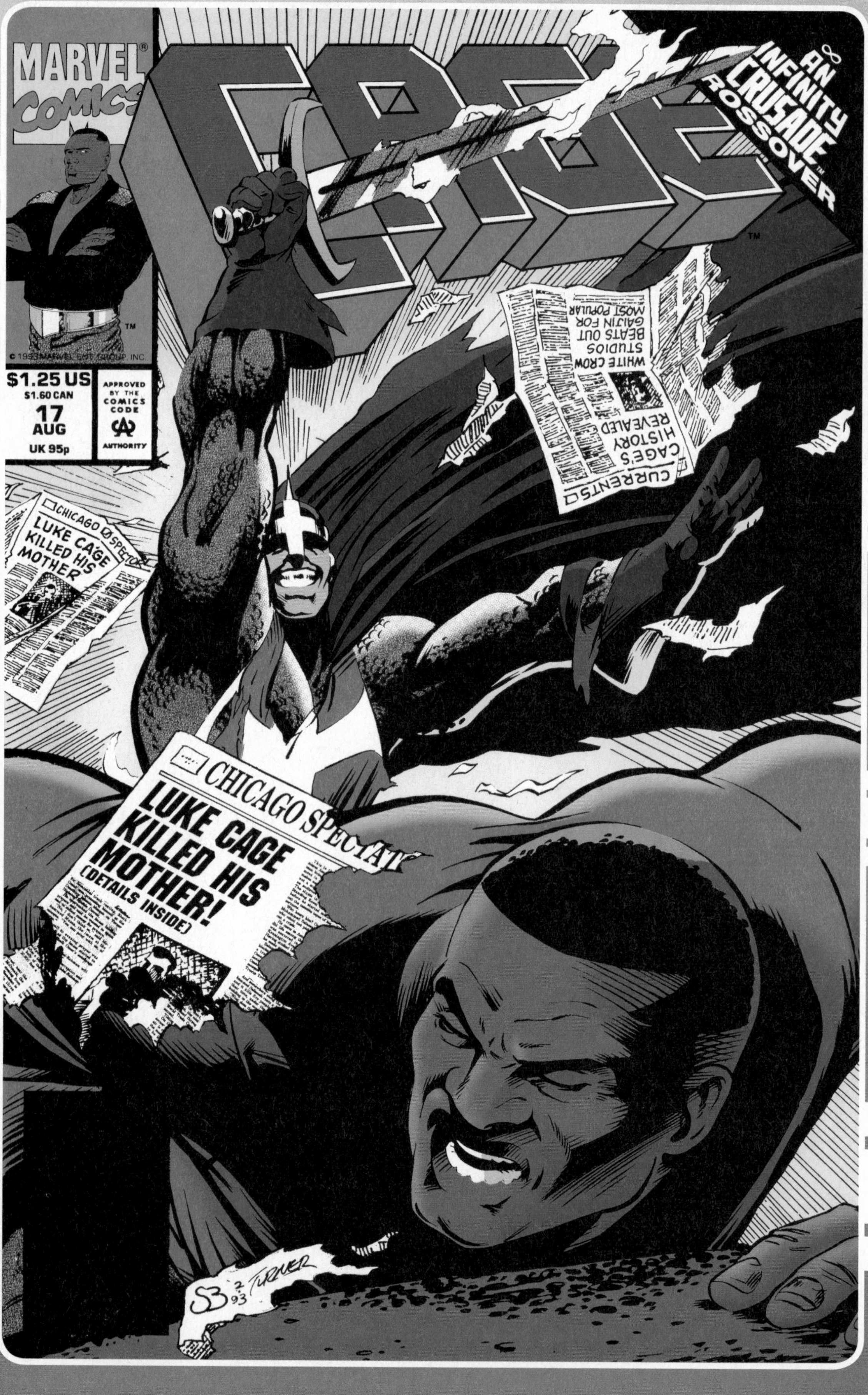
MARVEL COMICS
CAGE
AN INFINITY CRUSADE CROSSOVER
$1.25 US
$1.60 CAN
17
AUG
UK 95p
APPROVED BY THE COMICS CODE AUTHORITY
CURRENTS
CAGE'S HISTORY REVEALED
WHITE CROW STUDIOS BEATS OUT GAIJIN FOR MOST POPULAR
CHICAGO SPECTATOR
LUKE CAGE KILLED HIS MOTHER
CHICAGO SPECTAT
LUKE CAGE KILLED HIS MOTHER!
(DETAILS INSIDE)

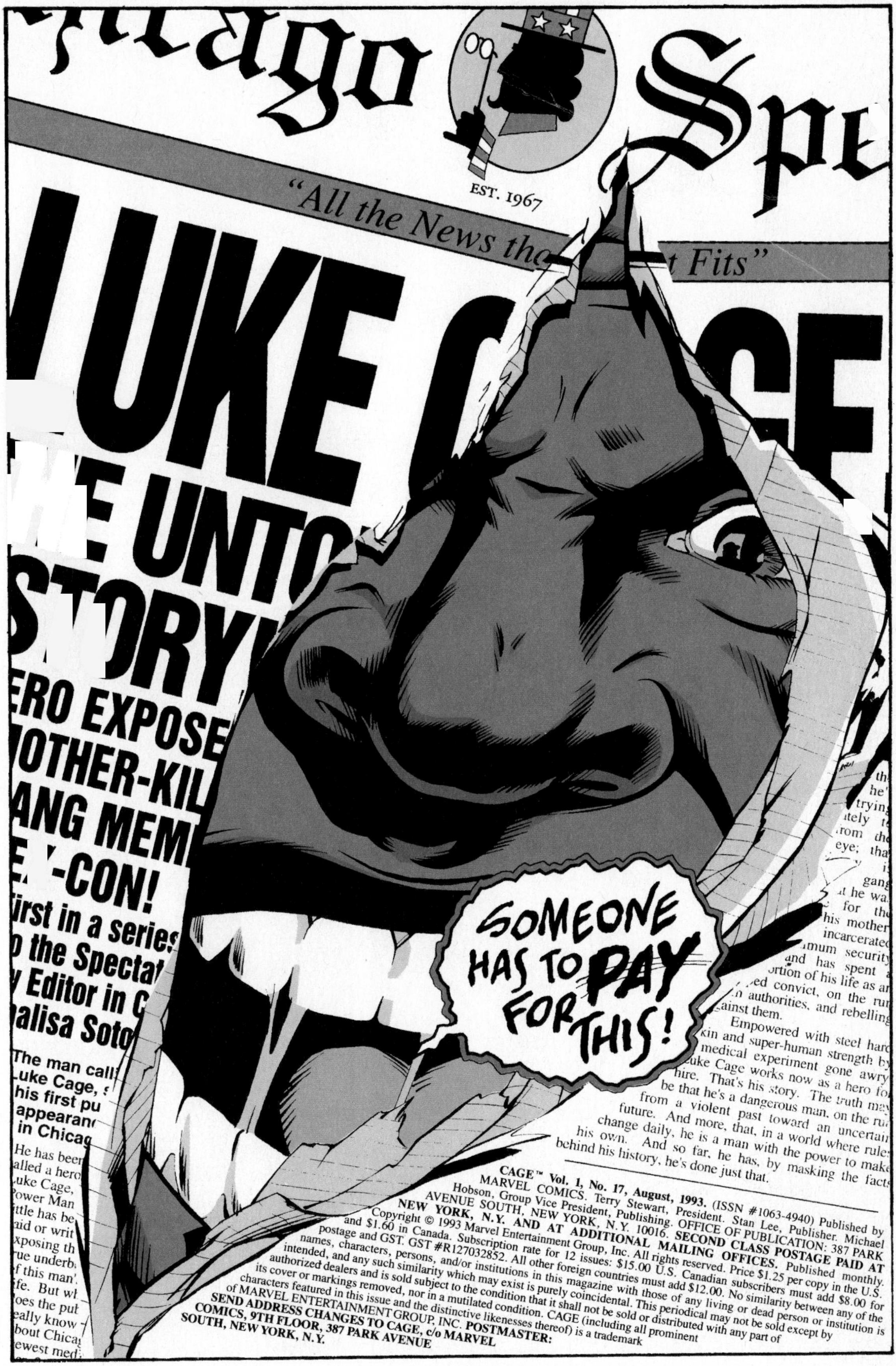
EST. 1967
"All the News tha t Fits"
LUKE C GE
E UNTO
STORY
ERO EXPOSE
OTHER-KIL
ANG MEM
E -CON!
SOMEONE HAS TO PAY FOR THIS!
CAGE™ Vol. 1, No. 17, August, 1993. (ISSN #1063-4940) Published by MARVEL COMICS. Terry Stewart, President. Stan Lee, Publisher. Michael Hobson, Group Vice President, Publishing. OFFICE OF PUBLICATION: 387 PARK AVENUE SOUTH, NEW YORK, N.Y. 10016. SECOND CLASS POSTAGE PAID AT NEW YORK, N.Y. AND AT ADDITIONAL MAILING OFFICES. Published monthly. Copyright © 1993 Marvel Entertainment Group, Inc. All rights reserved. Price $1.25 per copy in the U.S. and $1.60 in Canada. Subscription rate for 12 issues: $15.00 U.S. Canadian subscribers must add $8.00 for postage and GST. GST #R127032852. All other foreign countries must add $12.00. No similarity between any of the names, characters, persons, and/or institutions in this magazine with those of any living or dead person or institution is intended, and any such similarity which may exist is purely coincidental. This periodical may not be sold except by authorized dealers and is sold subject to the condition that it shall not be sold or distributed with any part of its cover or markings removed, nor in a mutilated condition. CAGE (including all prominent characters featured in this issue and the distinctive likenesses thereof) is a trademark of MARVEL ENTERTAINMENT GROUP, INC. POSTMASTER: SEND ADDRESS CHANGES TO CAGE, c/o MARVEL COMICS, 9TH FLOOR, 387 PARK AVENUE SOUTH, NEW YORK, N.Y.

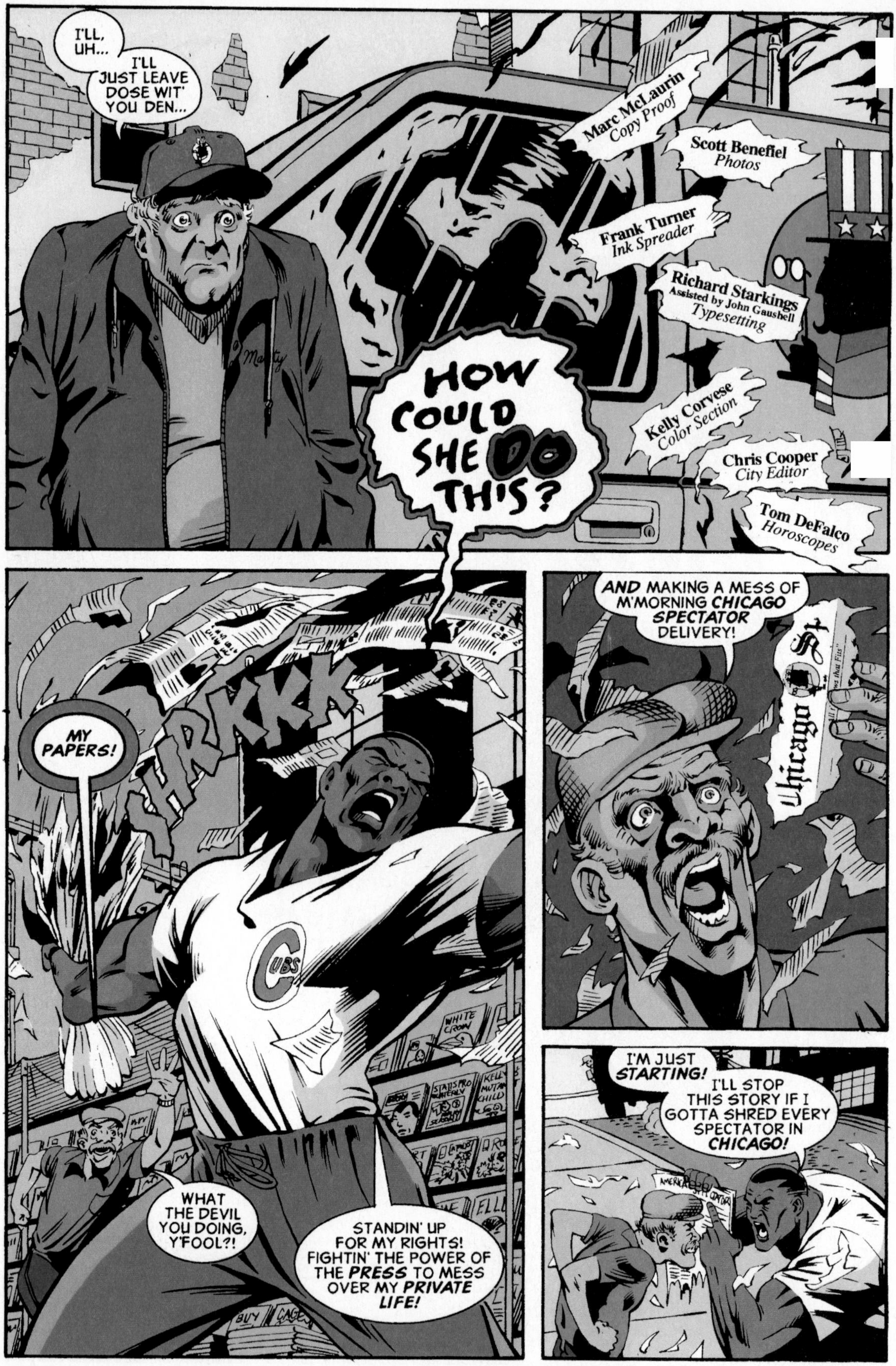
I'LL, UH...
I'LL JUST LEAVE DOSE WIT' YOU DEN...
Marc McLaurin Copy Proof
Scott Benefiel Photos
Frank Turner Ink Spreader
Richard Starkings Assisted by John Gaushell Typesetting
Kelly Corvese Color Section
Chris Cooper City Editor
Tom DeFalco Horoscopes
HOW COULD SHE DO THIS?
SHRKKK
MY PAPERS!
AND MAKING A MESS OF M'MORNING CHICAGO SPECTATOR DELIVERY!
Chicago
WHAT THE DEVIL YOU DOING, Y'FOOL?!
STANDIN' UP FOR MY RIGHTS! FIGHTIN' THE POWER OF THE PRESS TO MESS OVER MY PRIVATE LIFE!
I'M JUST STARTING!
I'LL STOP THIS STORY IF I GOTTA SHRED EVERY SPECTATOR IN CHICAGO!

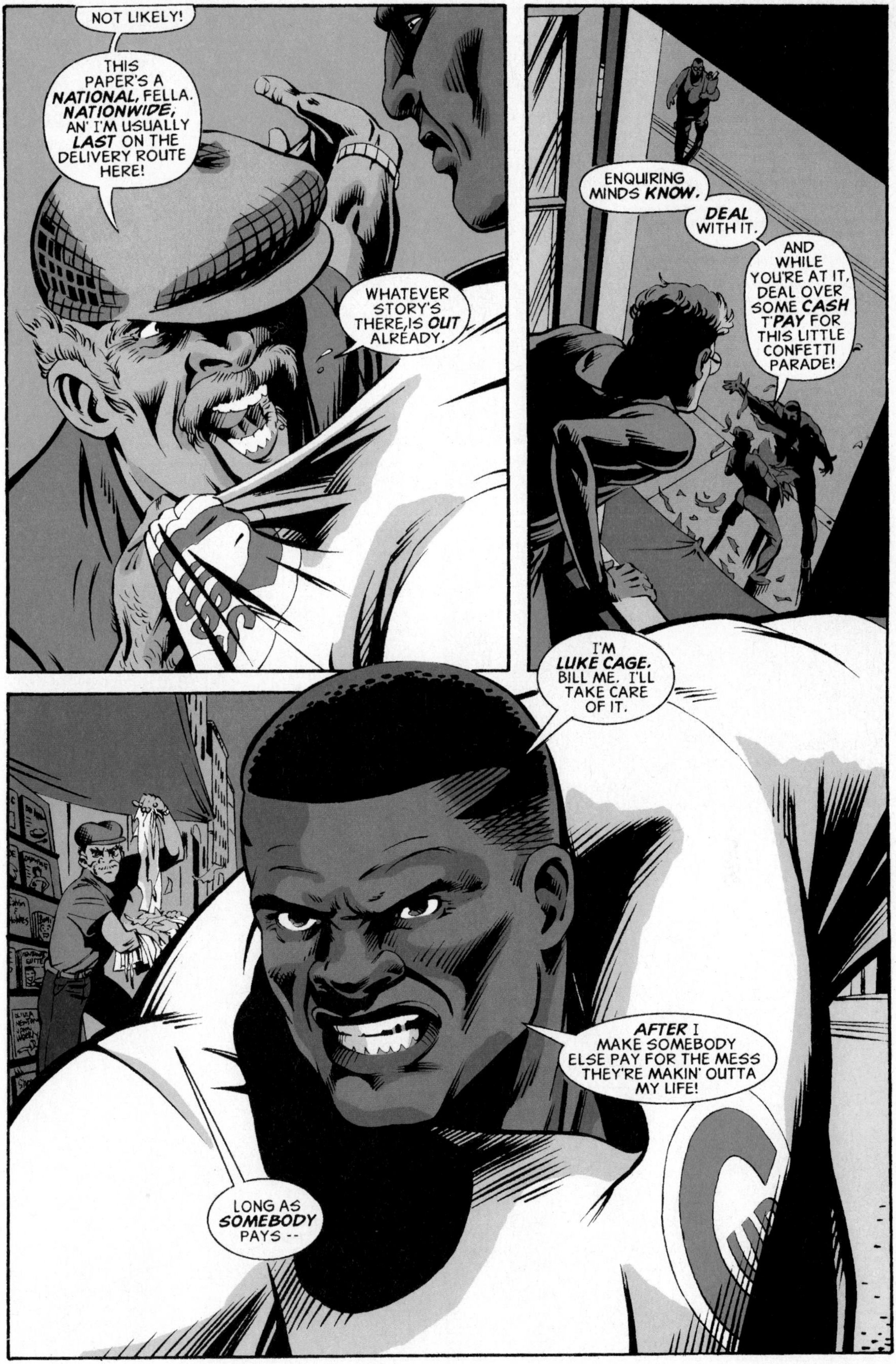

NOT LIKELY!
THIS PAPER'S A NATIONAL, FELLA. NATIONWIDE, AN' I'M USUALLY LAST ON THE DELIVERY ROUTE HERE!
WHATEVER STORY'S THERE, IS OUT ALREADY.
ENQUIRING MINDS KNOW.
DEAL WITH IT.
AND WHILE YOU'RE AT IT, DEAL OVER SOME CASH T'PAY FOR THIS LITTLE CONFETTI PARADE!
I'M LUKE CAGE. BILL ME. I'LL TAKE CARE OF IT.
AFTER I MAKE SOMEBODY ELSE PAY FOR THE MESS THEY'RE MAKIN' OUTTA MY LIFE!
LONG AS SOMEBODY PAYS --

power to make
sking the facts
hat.

There are elements of his past Cage won't reveal even to his closest friends – if any can be considered close to the powerful loner. Born **Carl Earl Lucas,** in East Harlem, New York City, his early life was marred by extremes of gang violence which still plague many major cities today. Cage's involvement in this particularly violent gang's history was abruptly ended following the murder of Cage's mother, **Esther Lucas,** by one of his fellow gang members. Cage himself witnessed the murder, and was later brought up on charges revolving around the incident.

Mrs. Lucas had apparently been actively involved in trying to free her son from the grip of the gang. She apparently only succe sacrifice of her life. Cage's famil learn of Cage's involvement i own mother. Cage's father, retired police officer, was esp the incident, and withdrew Carl, moving in with his elde

As a result of this incident protective of his father, to the young Carl's repeated attempts to But none of this was sufficient to br own new resolve to leave the gang life behind and start his life anew.

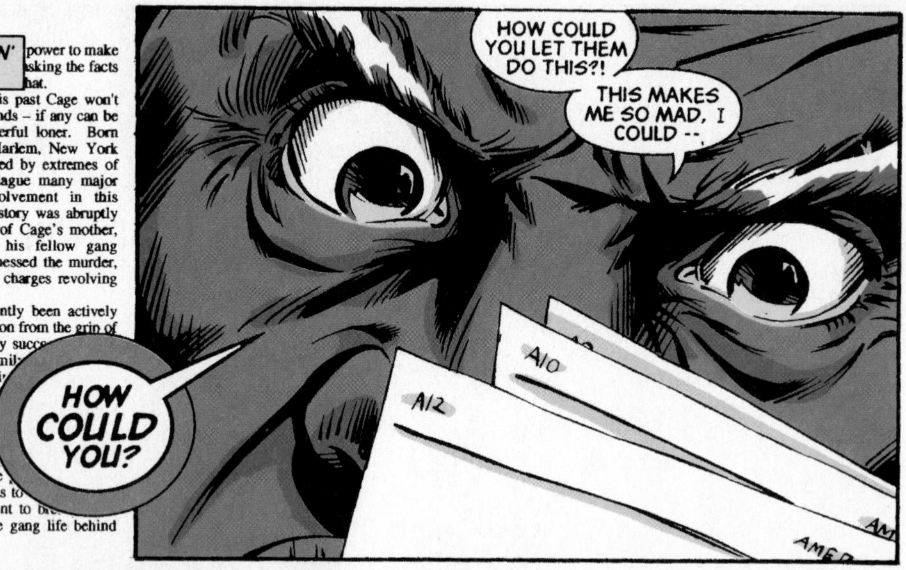
"THOUGH I'M BETTIN' IT'LL BE YOU."
HOW COULD YOU LET THEM DO THIS?!
THIS MAKES ME SO MAD, I COULD --,
HOW COULD YOU?
A10
A12

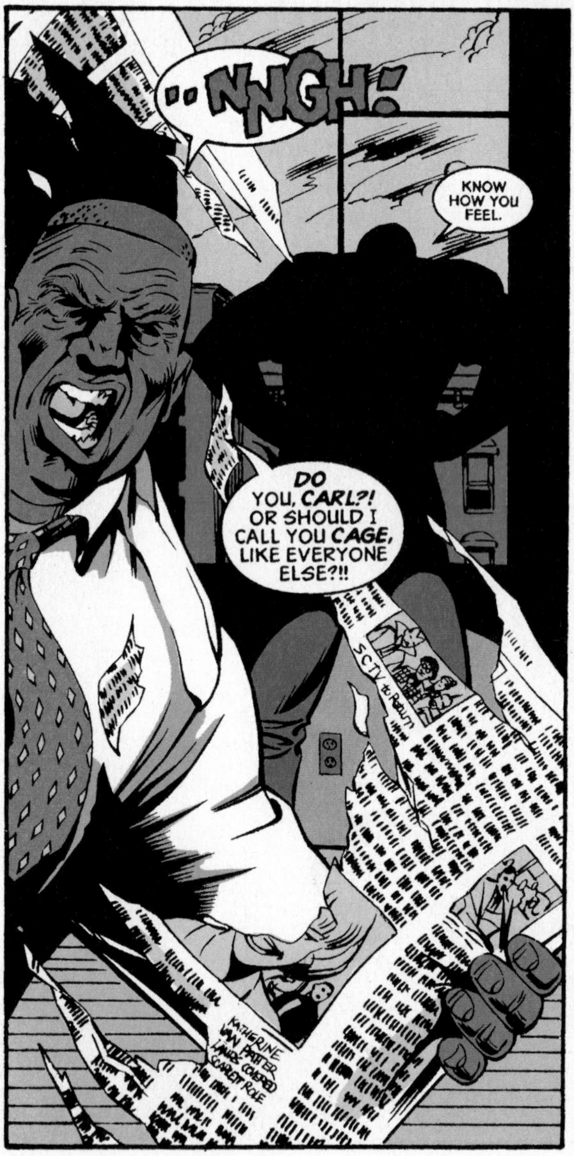
..NNGH!
KNOW HOW YOU FEEL.
DO YOU, CARL?! OR SHOULD I CALL YOU CAGE, LIKE EVERYONE ELSE?!!

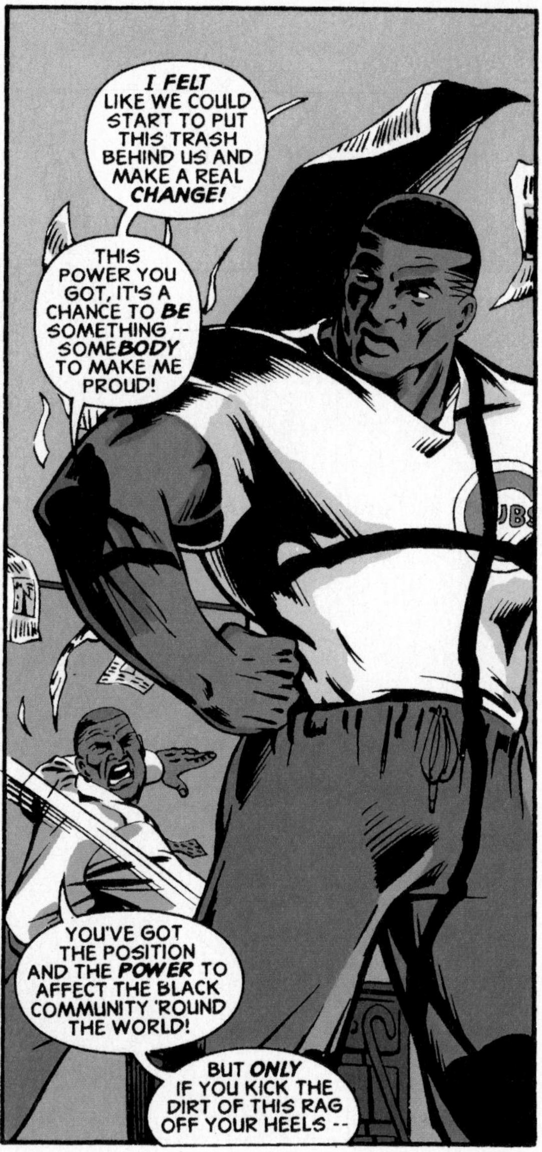
I FELT LIKE WE COULD START TO PUT THIS TRASH BEHIND US AND MAKE A REAL CHANGE!
THIS POWER YOU GOT, IT'S A CHANCE TO BE SOMETHING -- SOMEBODY TO MAKE ME PROUD!
YOU'VE GOT THE POSITION AND THE POWER TO AFFECT THE BLACK COMMUNITY 'ROUND THE WORLD!
BUT ONLY IF YOU KICK THE DIRT OF THIS RAG OFF YOUR HEELS --

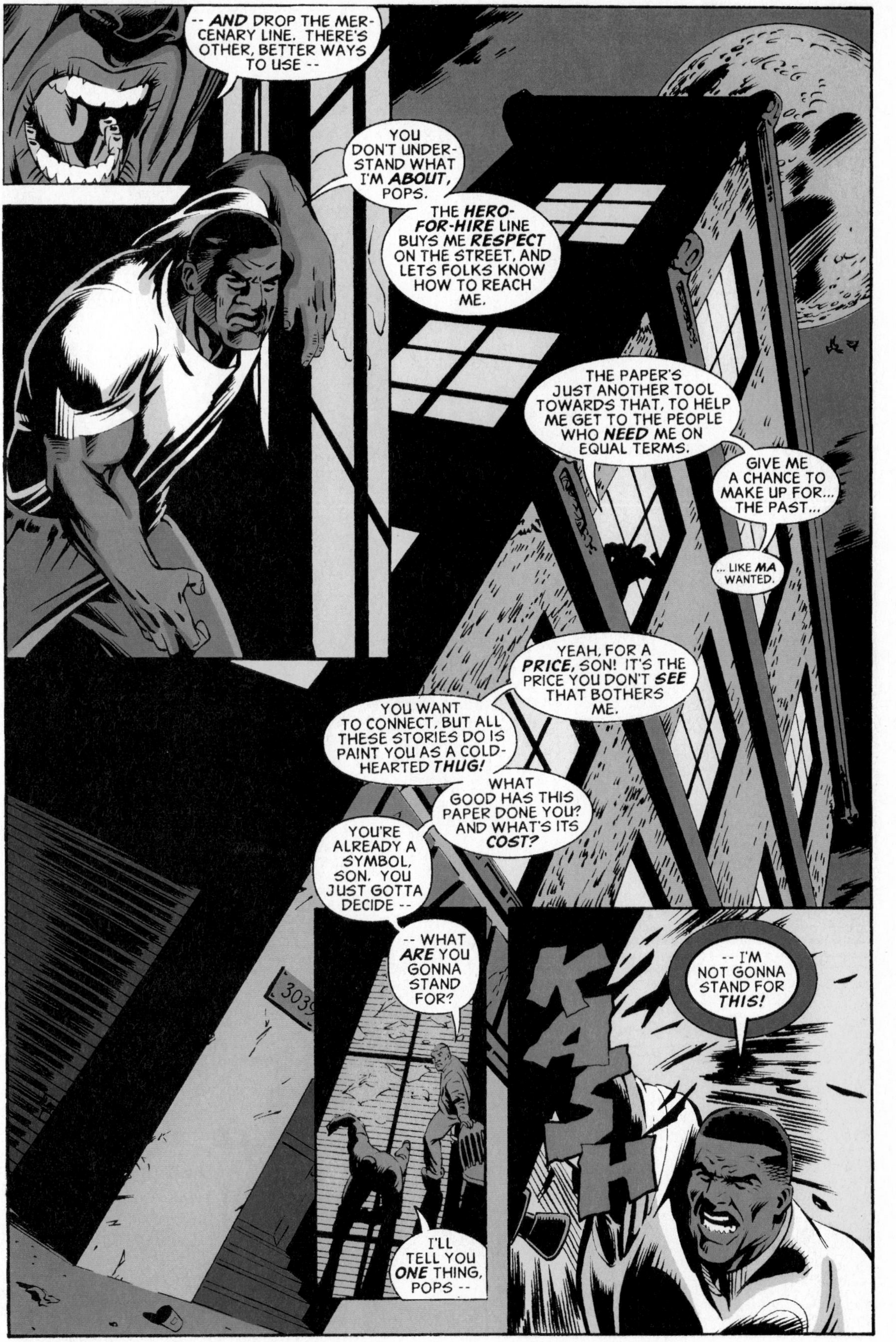
-- AND DROP THE MERCENARY LINE. THERE'S OTHER, BETTER WAYS TO USE --
YOU DON'T UNDERSTAND WHAT I'M ABOUT, POPS.
THE HERO-FOR-HIRE LINE BUYS ME RESPECT ON THE STREET, AND LETS FOLKS KNOW HOW TO REACH ME.
THE PAPER'S JUST ANOTHER TOOL TOWARDS THAT, TO HELP ME GET TO THE PEOPLE WHO NEED ME ON EQUAL TERMS.
GIVE ME A CHANCE TO MAKE UP FOR... THE PAST...
... LIKE MA WANTED.
YEAH, FOR A PRICE, SON! IT'S THE PRICE YOU DON'T SEE THAT BOTHERS ME.
YOU WANT TO CONNECT, BUT ALL THESE STORIES DO IS PAINT YOU AS A COLD-HEARTED THUG!
WHAT GOOD HAS THIS PAPER DONE YOU? AND WHAT'S ITS COST?
YOU'RE ALREADY A SYMBOL, SON. YOU JUST GOTTA DECIDE --
-- WHAT ARE YOU GONNA STAND FOR?
I'LL TELL YOU ONE THING, POPS --
KRASH
-- I'M NOT GONNA STAND FOR THIS!

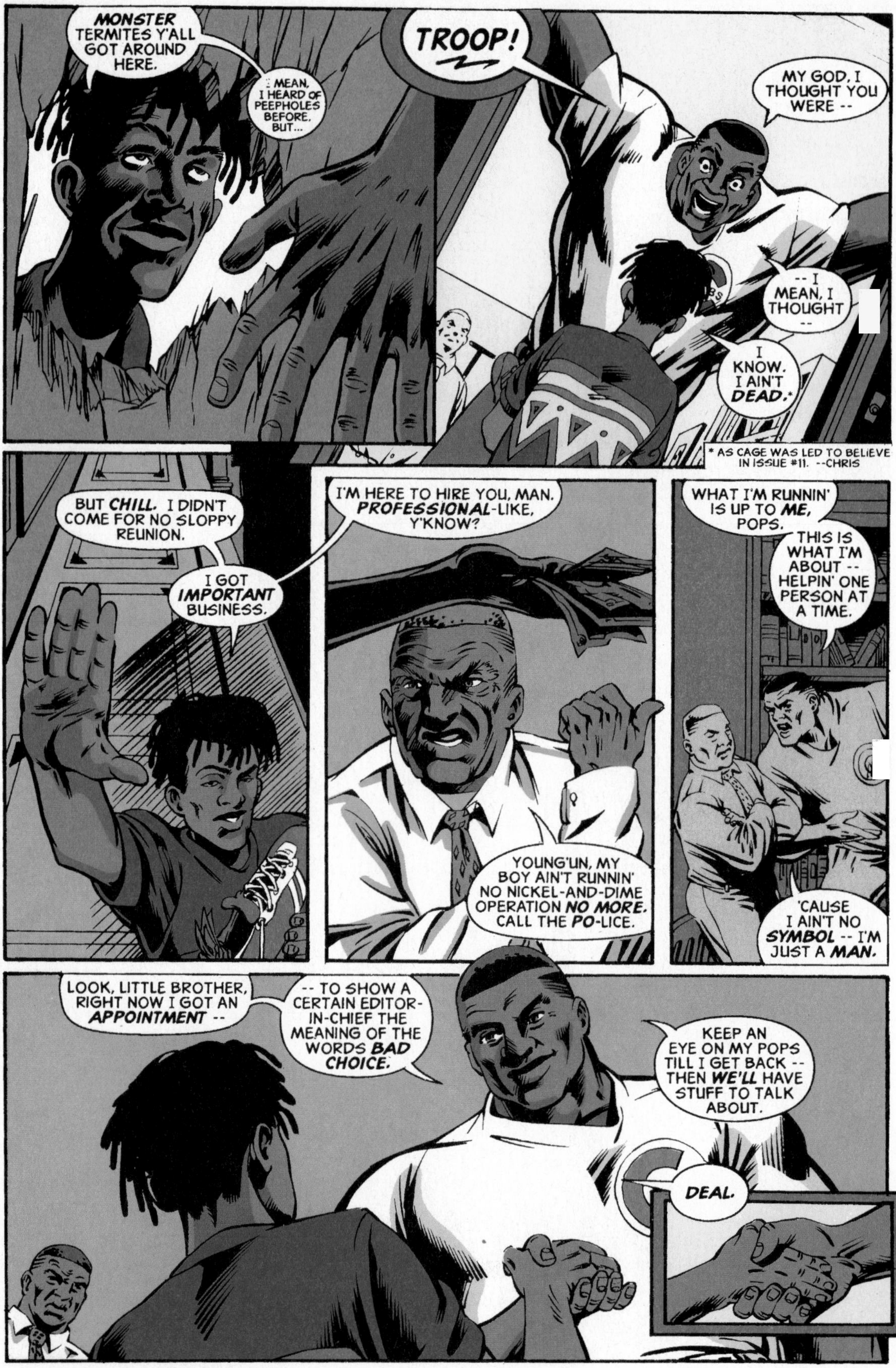
MONSTER TERMITES Y'ALL GOT AROUND HERE.
I MEAN, I HEARD OF PEEPHOLES BEFORE, BUT...
TROOP!
MY GOD, I THOUGHT YOU WERE --
-- I MEAN, I THOUGHT --
I KNOW. I AIN'T DEAD.*
* AS CAGE WAS LED TO BELIEVE IN ISSUE #11. --CHRIS
BUT CHILL. I DIDN'T COME FOR NO SLOPPY REUNION.
I GOT IMPORTANT BUSINESS.
I'M HERE TO HIRE YOU, MAN. PROFESSIONAL-LIKE, Y'KNOW?
YOUNG'UN, MY BOY AIN'T RUNNIN' NO NICKEL-AND-DIME OPERATION NO MORE. CALL THE PO-LICE.
WHAT I'M RUNNIN' IS UP TO ME, POPS.
THIS IS WHAT I'M ABOUT -- HELPIN' ONE PERSON AT A TIME.
'CAUSE I AIN'T NO SYMBOL -- I'M JUST A MAN.
LOOK, LITTLE BROTHER, RIGHT NOW I GOT AN APPOINTMENT --
-- TO SHOW A CERTAIN EDITOR-IN-CHIEF THE MEANING OF THE WORDS BAD CHOICE.
KEEP AN EYE ON MY POPS TILL I GET BACK -- THEN WE'LL HAVE STUFF TO TALK ABOUT.
DEAL.

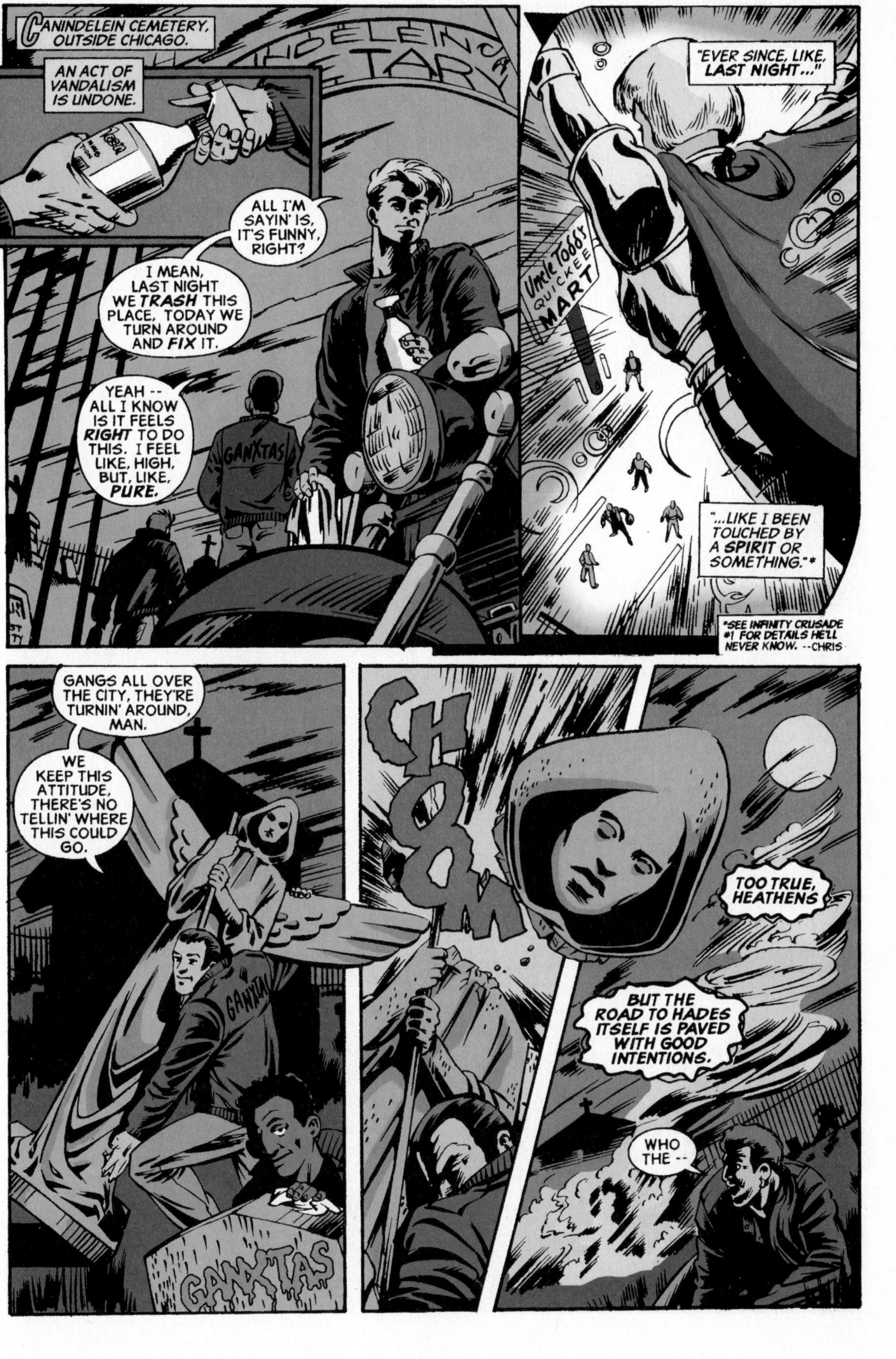
CANINDELEIN CEMETERY, OUTSIDE CHICAGO.
AN ACT OF VANDALISM IS UNDONE.
ALL I'M SAYIN' IS, IT'S FUNNY, RIGHT?
I MEAN, LAST NIGHT WE TRASH THIS PLACE, TODAY WE TURN AROUND AND FIX IT.
YEAH -- ALL I KNOW IS IT FEELS RIGHT TO DO THIS. I FEEL LIKE, HIGH, BUT, LIKE, PURE.
GANXTAS
"EVER SINCE, LIKE, LAST NIGHT..."
Uncle Todd's QUICKEE MART
"...LIKE I BEEN TOUCHED BY A SPIRIT OR SOMETHING."*
*SEE INFINITY CRUSADE #1 FOR DETAILS HE'LL NEVER KNOW. --CHRIS
GANGS ALL OVER THE CITY, THEY'RE TURNIN' AROUND, MAN.
WE KEEP THIS ATTITUDE, THERE'S NO TELLIN' WHERE THIS COULD GO.
GANXTAS
CH
&
M
TOO TRUE, HEATHENS
BUT THE ROAD TO HADES ITSELF IS PAVED WITH GOOD INTENTIONS.
WHO THE --

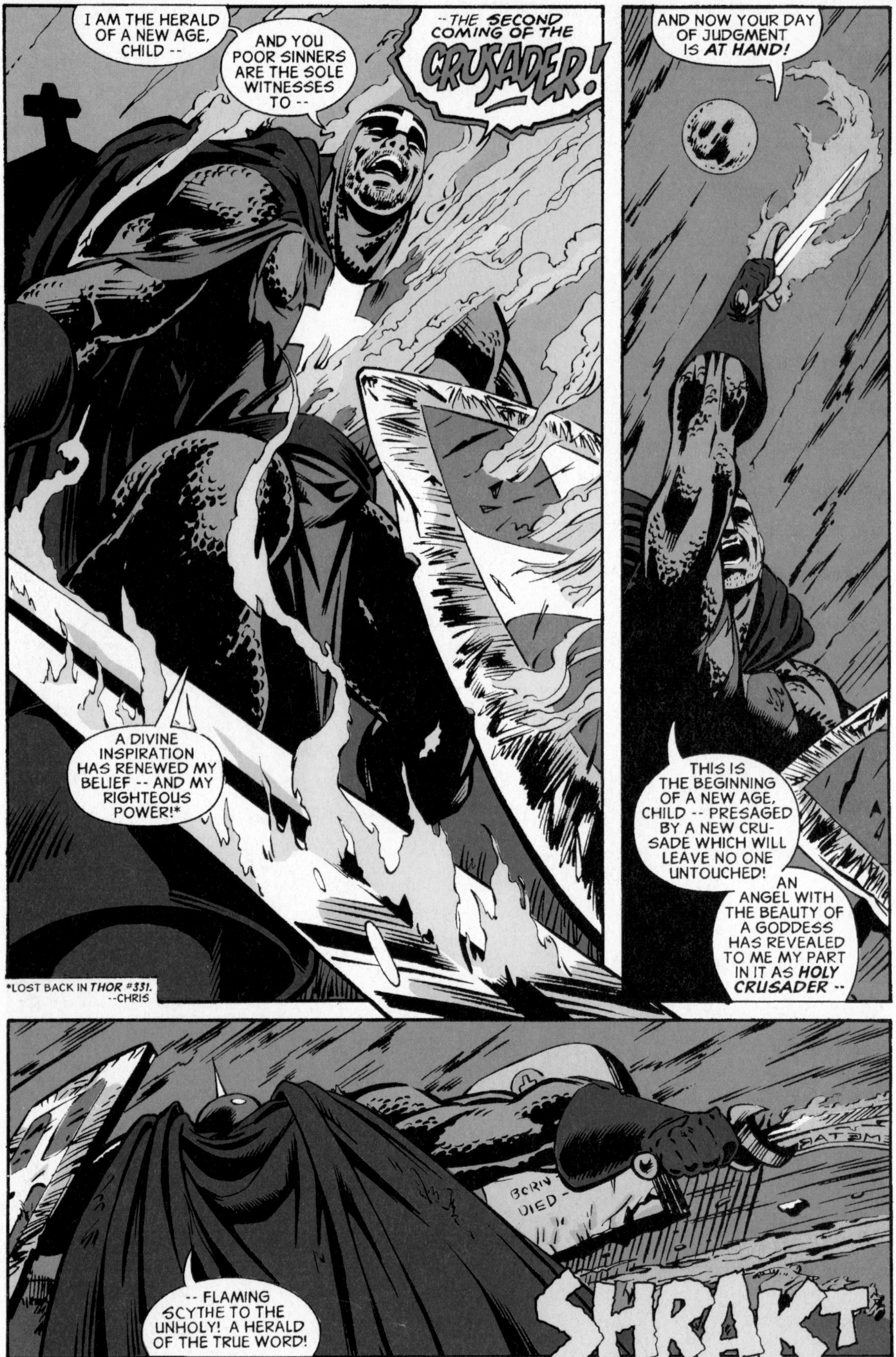
I AM THE HERALD OF A NEW AGE, CHILD --
AND YOU POOR SINNERS ARE THE SOLE WITNESSES TO --
--THE SECOND COMING OF THE CRUSADER!
A DIVINE INSPIRATION HAS RENEWED MY BELIEF -- AND MY RIGHTEOUS POWER!*
*LOST BACK IN THOR #331. --CHRIS
AND NOW YOUR DAY OF JUDGMENT IS AT HAND!
THIS IS THE BEGINNING OF A NEW AGE, CHILD -- PRESAGED BY A NEW CRUSADE WHICH WILL LEAVE NO ONE UNTOUCHED!
AN ANGEL WITH THE BEAUTY OF A GODDESS HAS REVEALED TO ME MY PART IN IT AS HOLY CRUSADER --
BORN
DIED
-- FLAMING SCYTHE TO THE UNHOLY! A HERALD OF THE TRUE WORD!
SHRAKT

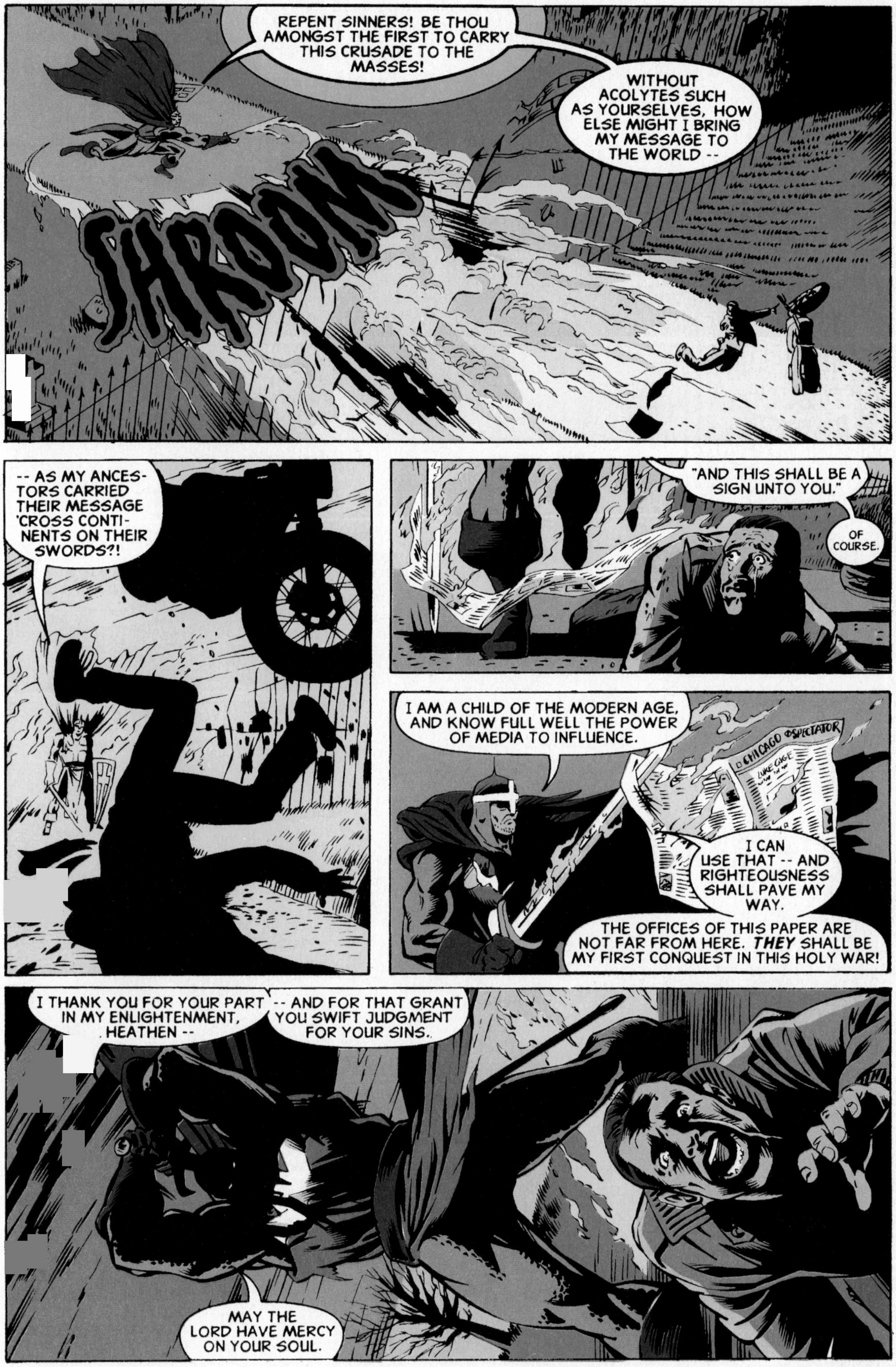
REPENT SINNERS! BE THOU AMONGST THE FIRST TO CARRY THIS CRUSADE TO THE MASSES!
WITHOUT ACOLYTES SUCH AS YOURSELVES, HOW ELSE MIGHT I BRING MY MESSAGE TO THE WORLD --
SHROOM
-- AS MY ANCESTORS CARRIED THEIR MESSAGE 'CROSS CONTINENTS ON THEIR SWORDS?!
"AND THIS SHALL BE A SIGN UNTO YOU."
OF COURSE.
I AM A CHILD OF THE MODERN AGE, AND KNOW FULL WELL THE POWER OF MEDIA TO INFLUENCE.
CHICAGO SPECTATOR
I CAN USE THAT -- AND RIGHTEOUSNESS SHALL PAVE MY WAY.
THE OFFICES OF THIS PAPER ARE NOT FAR FROM HERE. *THEY* SHALL BE MY FIRST CONQUEST IN THIS HOLY WAR!
I THANK YOU FOR YOUR PART IN MY ENLIGHTENMENT, HEATHEN --
-- AND FOR THAT GRANT YOU SWIFT JUDGMENT FOR YOUR SINS.
MAY THE LORD HAVE MERCY ON YOUR SOUL.

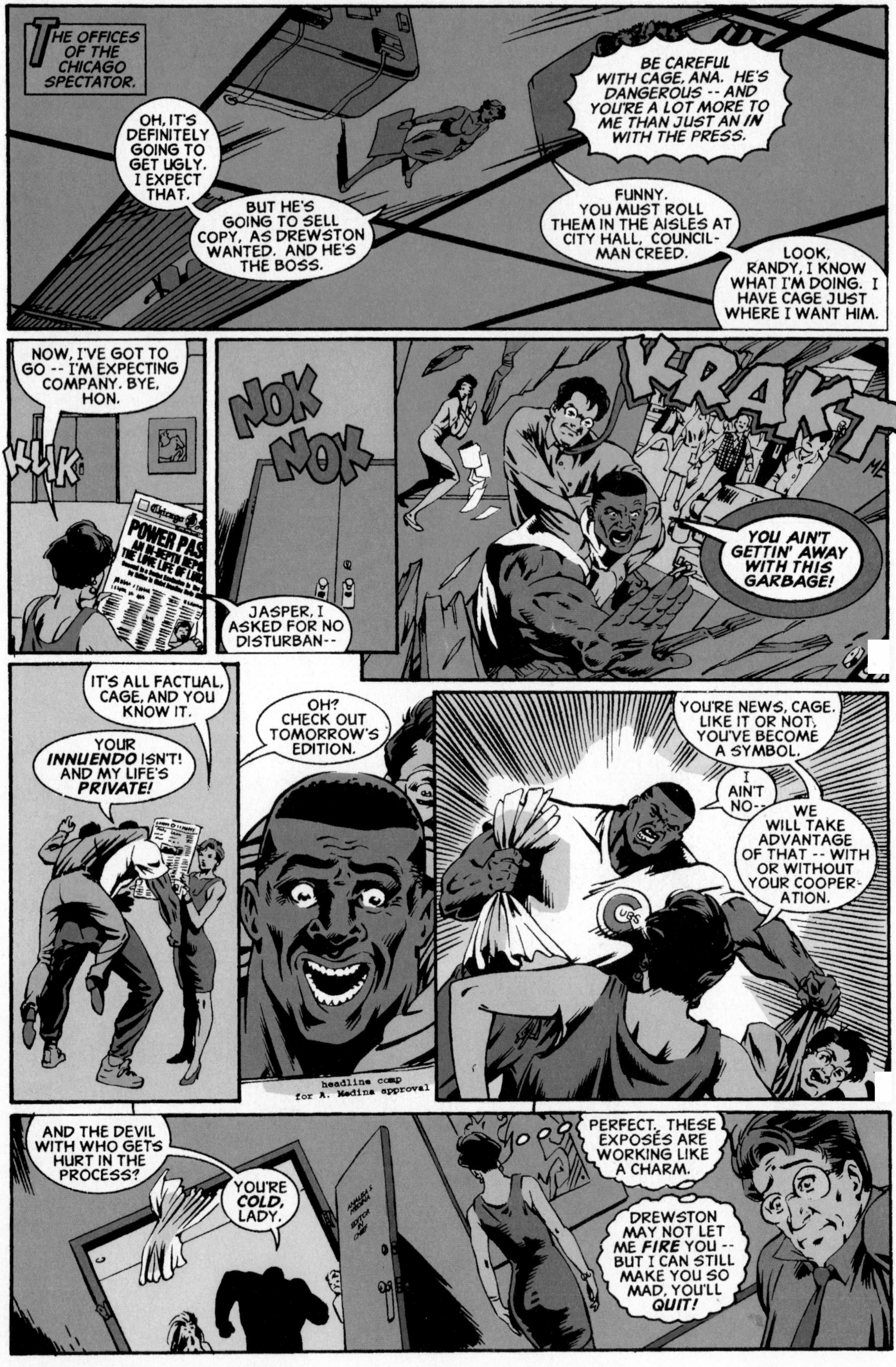
THE OFFICES OF THE CHICAGO SPECTATOR.
OH, IT'S DEFINITELY GOING TO GET UGLY. I EXPECT THAT.
BUT HE'S GOING TO SELL COPY, AS DREWSTON WANTED. AND HE'S THE BOSS.
BE CAREFUL WITH CAGE, ANA. HE'S DANGEROUS -- AND YOU'RE A LOT MORE TO ME THAN JUST AN IN WITH THE PRESS.
FUNNY. YOU MUST ROLL THEM IN THE AISLES AT CITY HALL, COUNCILMAN CREED.
LOOK, RANDY, I KNOW WHAT I'M DOING. I HAVE CAGE JUST WHERE I WANT HIM.
NOW, I'VE GOT TO GO -- I'M EXPECTING COMPANY. BYE, HON.
KLIK
POWER PAS
JASPER, I ASKED FOR NO DISTURBAN--
NOK NOK
KRAKT
YOU AIN'T GETTIN' AWAY WITH THIS GARBAGE!
IT'S ALL FACTUAL, CAGE, AND YOU KNOW IT.
YOUR INNUENDO ISN'T! AND MY LIFE'S PRIVATE!
OH? CHECK OUT TOMORROW'S EDITION.
headline comp for A. Medina approval
YOU'RE NEWS, CAGE. LIKE IT OR NOT, YOU'VE BECOME A SYMBOL.
I AIN'T NO--
WE WILL TAKE ADVANTAGE OF THAT -- WITH OR WITHOUT YOUR COOPERATION.
AND THE DEVIL WITH WHO GETS HURT IN THE PROCESS?
YOU'RE COLD, LADY.
PERFECT. THESE EXPOSÉS ARE WORKING LIKE A CHARM.
DREWSTON MAY NOT LET ME FIRE YOU -- BUT I CAN STILL MAKE YOU SO MAD, YOU'LL QUIT!

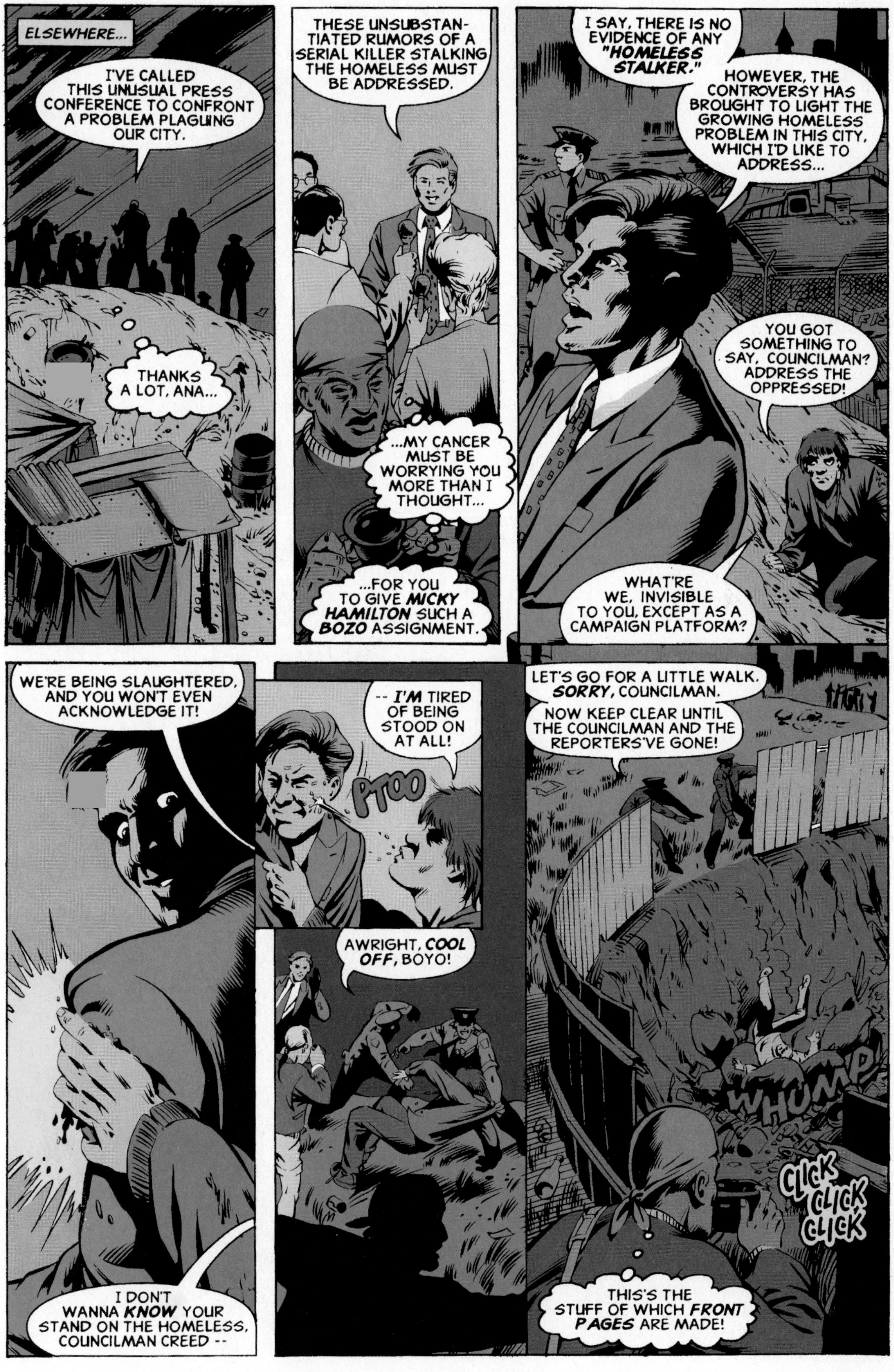
ELSEWHERE...
I'VE CALLED THIS UNUSUAL PRESS CONFERENCE TO CONFRONT A PROBLEM PLAGUING OUR CITY.
THANKS A LOT, ANA...
THESE UNSUBSTANTIATED RUMORS OF A SERIAL KILLER STALKING THE HOMELESS MUST BE ADDRESSED.
...MY CANCER MUST BE WORRYING YOU MORE THAN I THOUGHT...
...FOR YOU TO GIVE MICKY HAMILTON SUCH A BOZO ASSIGNMENT.
I SAY, THERE IS NO EVIDENCE OF ANY "HOMELESS STALKER."
HOWEVER, THE CONTROVERSY HAS BROUGHT TO LIGHT THE GROWING HOMELESS PROBLEM IN THIS CITY, WHICH I'D LIKE TO ADDRESS...
YOU GOT SOMETHING TO SAY, COUNCILMAN? ADDRESS THE OPPRESSED!
WHAT'RE WE, INVISIBLE TO YOU, EXCEPT AS A CAMPAIGN PLATFORM?
WE'RE BEING SLAUGHTERED, AND YOU WON'T EVEN ACKNOWLEDGE IT!
I DON'T WANNA KNOW YOUR STAND ON THE HOMELESS, COUNCILMAN CREED --
-- I'M TIRED OF BEING STOOD ON AT ALL!
PTOO
AWRIGHT, COOL OFF, BOYO!
LET'S GO FOR A LITTLE WALK. SORRY, COUNCILMAN.
NOW KEEP CLEAR UNTIL THE COUNCILMAN AND THE REPORTERS'VE GONE!
WHUMP
CLICK CLICK CLICK
THIS'S THE STUFF OF WHICH FRONT PAGES ARE MADE!

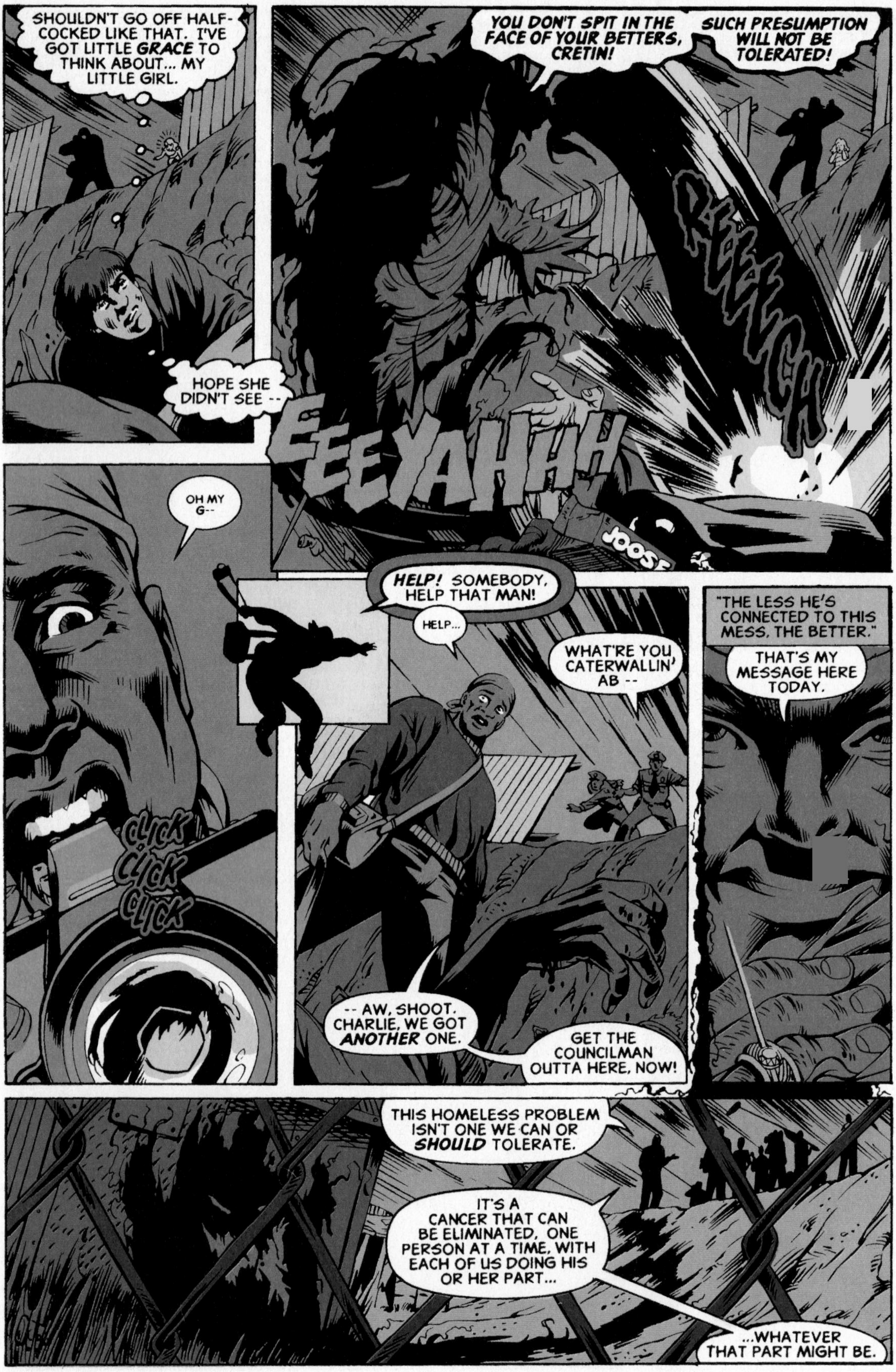
SHOULDN'T GO OFF HALF-COCKED LIKE THAT. I'VE GOT LITTLE GRACE TO THINK ABOUT... MY LITTLE GIRL.
HOPE SHE DIDN'T SEE --
YOU DON'T SPIT IN THE FACE OF YOUR BETTERS, CRETIN!
SUCH PRESUMPTION WILL NOT BE TOLERATED!
EEEYAHHH
OH MY G--
CLICK CLICK CLICK
HELP! SOMEBODY, HELP THAT MAN!
HELP...
WHAT'RE YOU CATERWALLIN' AB --
-- AW, SHOOT. CHARLIE, WE GOT ANOTHER ONE.
GET THE COUNCILMAN OUTTA HERE, NOW!
"THE LESS HE'S CONNECTED TO THIS MESS, THE BETTER."
THAT'S MY MESSAGE HERE TODAY.
THIS HOMELESS PROBLEM ISN'T ONE WE CAN OR SHOULD TOLERATE.
IT'S A CANCER THAT CAN BE ELIMINATED, ONE PERSON AT A TIME, WITH EACH OF US DOING HIS OR HER PART...
...WHATEVER THAT PART MIGHT BE.

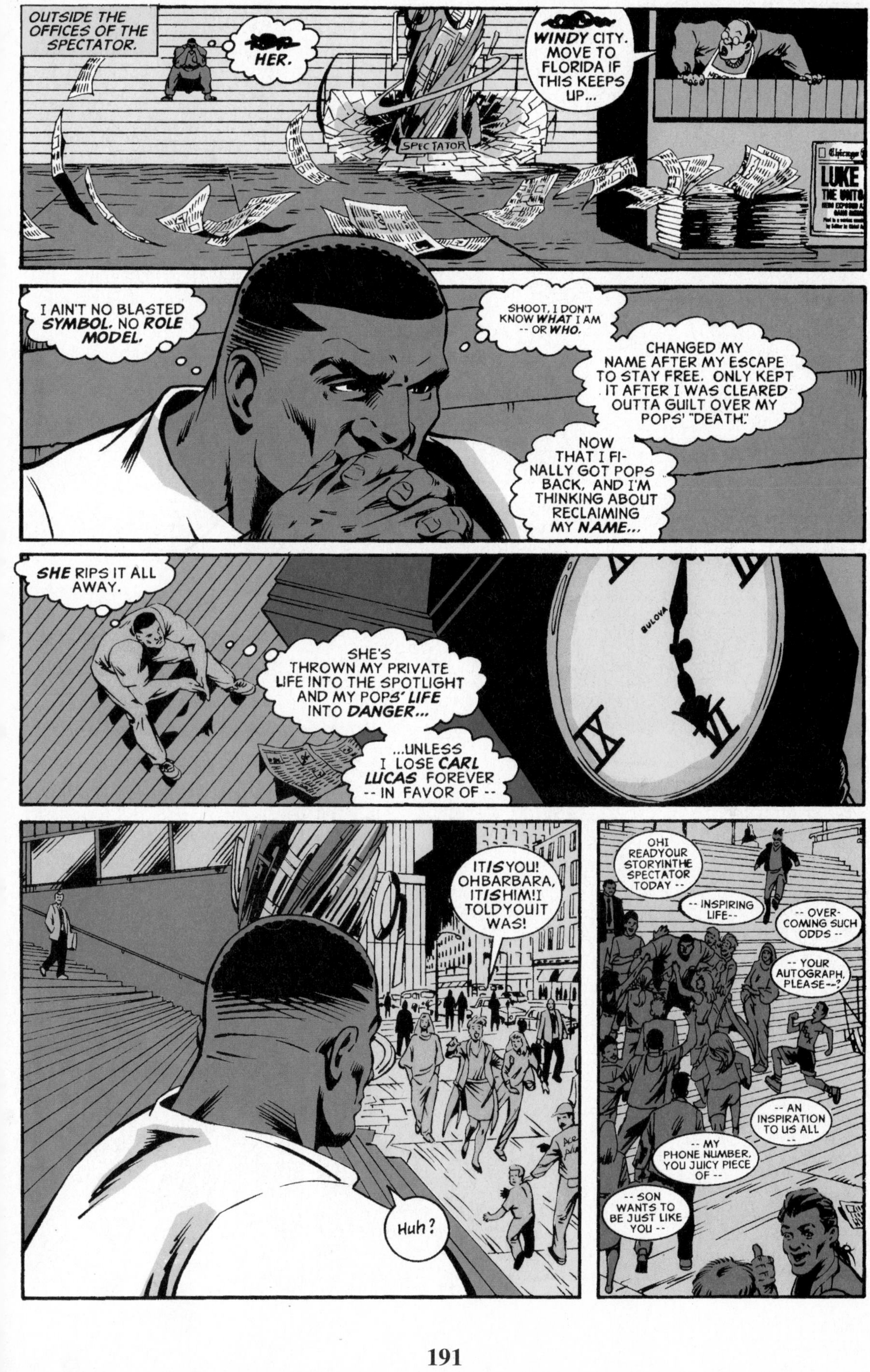
OUTSIDE THE OFFICES OF THE SPECTATOR.
HER.
WINDY CITY. MOVE TO FLORIDA IF THIS KEEPS UP...
SPECTATOR
LUKE
I AIN'T NO BLASTED SYMBOL. NO ROLE MODEL.
SHOOT, I DON'T KNOW WHAT I AM -- OR WHO.
CHANGED MY NAME AFTER MY ESCAPE TO STAY FREE. ONLY KEPT IT AFTER I WAS CLEARED OUTTA GUILT OVER MY POPS' "DEATH."
NOW THAT I FINALLY GOT POPS BACK, AND I'M THINKING ABOUT RECLAIMING MY NAME...
SHE RIPS IT ALL AWAY.
BULOVA
SHE'S THROWN MY PRIVATE LIFE INTO THE SPOTLIGHT AND MY POPS' LIFE INTO DANGER...
...UNLESS I LOSE CARL LUCAS FOREVER -- IN FAVOR OF --
IT IS YOU! OH BARBARA, IT IS HIM! I TOLD YOU IT WAS!
Huh?
OH! I READ YOUR STORY IN THE SPECTATOR TODAY --
-- INSPIRING LIFE --
-- OVERCOMING SUCH ODDS --
-- YOUR AUTOGRAPH, PLEASE --?
-- AN INSPIRATION TO US ALL --
-- MY PHONE NUMBER, YOU JUICY PIECE OF --
-- SON WANTS TO BE JUST LIKE YOU --

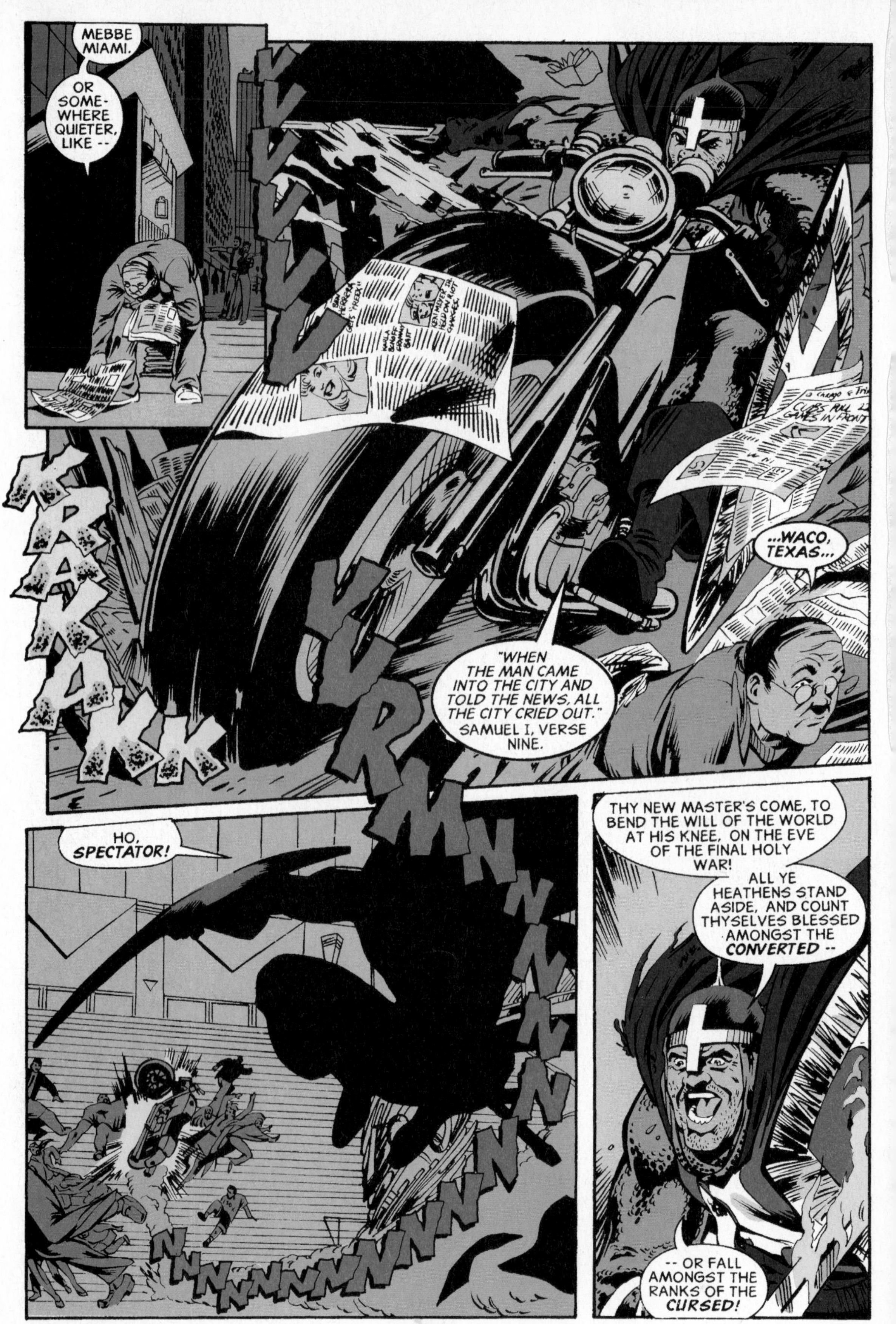

MEBBE MIAMI.
OR SOME-WHERE QUIETER, LIKE --
...WACO, TEXAS...
"WHEN THE MAN CAME INTO THE CITY AND TOLD THE NEWS, ALL THE CITY CRIED OUT." SAMUEL I, VERSE NINE.
KRAKAKAKK
VRMNNNNNNNNNNNNNNNNNNNNNNN
HO, SPECTATOR!
THY NEW MASTER'S COME, TO BEND THE WILL OF THE WORLD AT HIS KNEE, ON THE EVE OF THE FINAL HOLY WAR!
ALL YE HEATHENS STAND ASIDE, AND COUNT THYSELVES BLESSED AMONGST THE CONVERTED --
-- OR FALL AMONGST THE RANKS OF THE CURSED!

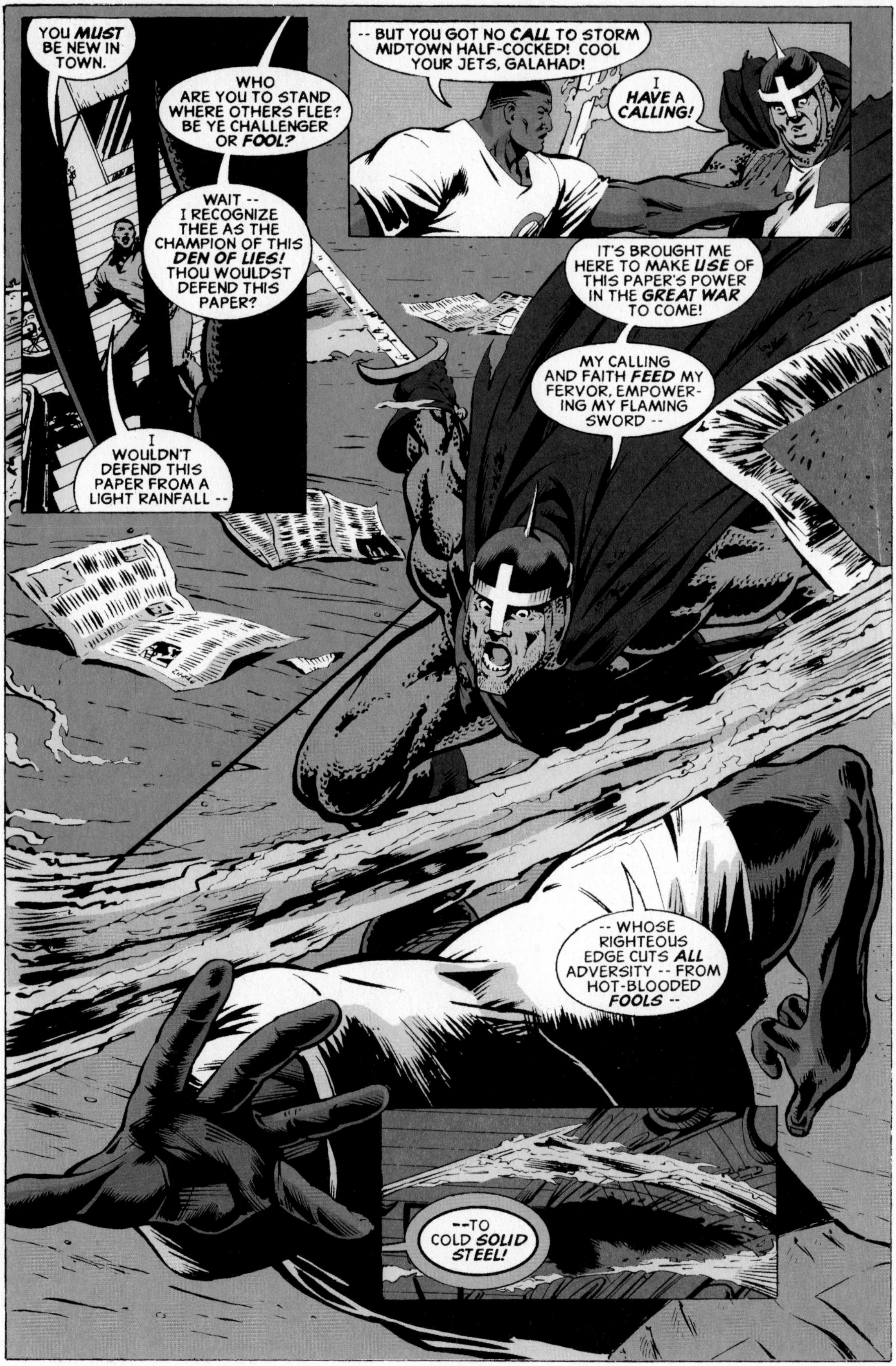
YOU MUST BE NEW IN TOWN.
WHO ARE YOU TO STAND WHERE OTHERS FLEE? BE YE CHALLENGER OR FOOL?
WAIT -- I RECOGNIZE THEE AS THE CHAMPION OF THIS DEN OF LIES! THOU WOULDST DEFEND THIS PAPER?
I WOULDN'T DEFEND THIS PAPER FROM A LIGHT RAINFALL --
-- BUT YOU GOT NO CALL TO STORM MIDTOWN HALF-COCKED! COOL YOUR JETS, GALAHAD!
I HAVE A CALLING!
IT'S BROUGHT ME HERE TO MAKE USE OF THIS PAPER'S POWER IN THE GREAT WAR TO COME!
MY CALLING AND FAITH FEED MY FERVOR, EMPOWERING MY FLAMING SWORD --
-- WHOSE RIGHTEOUS EDGE CUTS ALL ADVERSITY -- FROM HOT-BLOODED FOOLS --
--TO COLD SOLID STEEL!

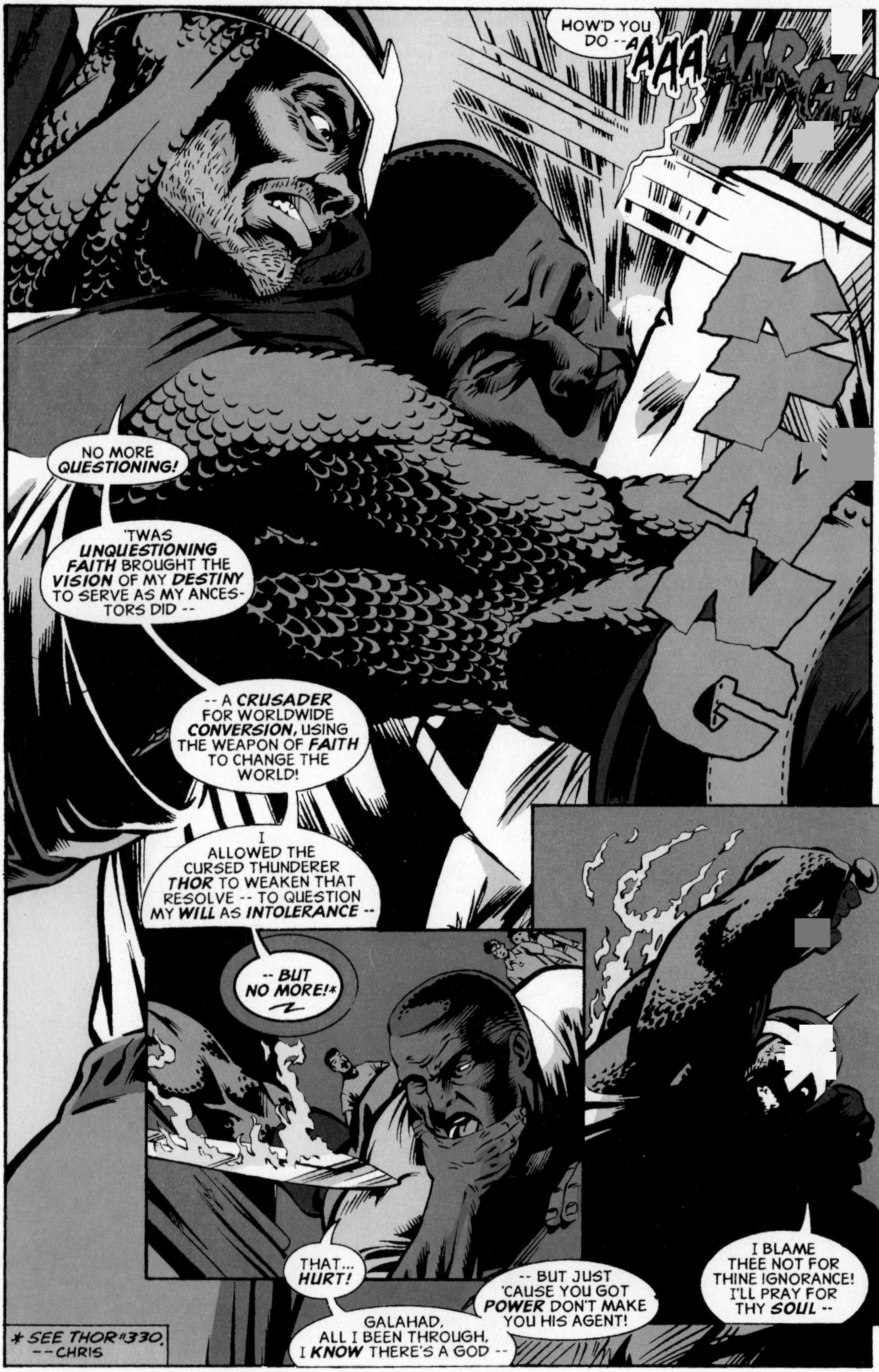

HOW'D YOU DO -- AAAAARGH
KZANG
NO MORE QUESTIONING!
'TWAS UNQUESTIONING FAITH BROUGHT THE VISION OF MY DESTINY TO SERVE AS MY ANCESTORS DID --
-- A CRUSADER FOR WORLDWIDE CONVERSION, USING THE WEAPON OF FAITH TO CHANGE THE WORLD!
I ALLOWED THE CURSED THUNDERER THOR TO WEAKEN THAT RESOLVE -- TO QUESTION MY WILL AS INTOLERANCE --
-- BUT NO MORE!*
THAT... HURT!
GALAHAD, ALL I BEEN THROUGH, I KNOW THERE'S A GOD --
-- BUT JUST 'CAUSE YOU GOT POWER DON'T MAKE YOU HIS AGENT!
I BLAME THEE NOT FOR THINE IGNORANCE! I'LL PRAY FOR THY SOUL --
* SEE THOR #330. --CHRIS

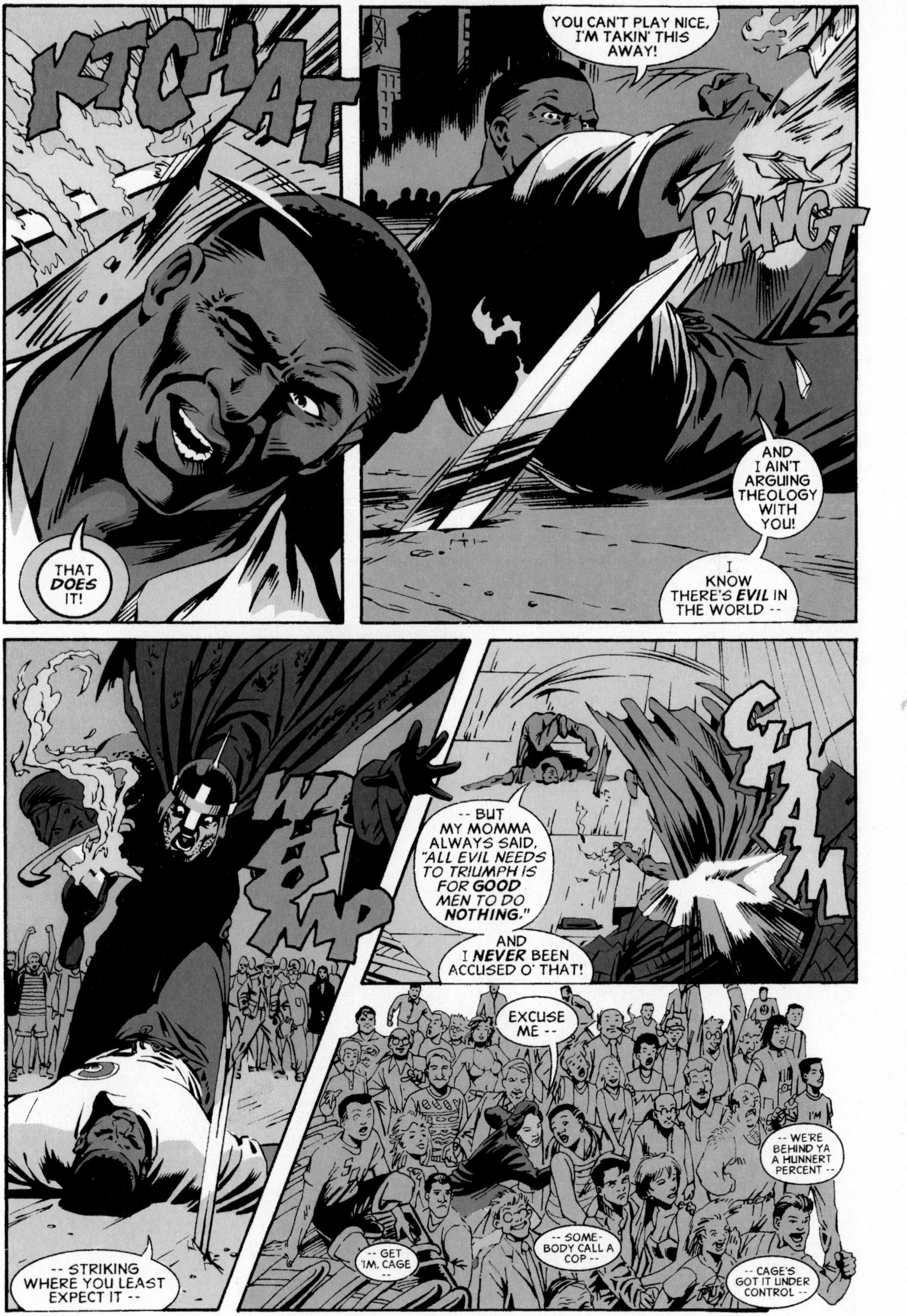
KTCHAT
THAT DOES IT!
YOU CAN'T PLAY NICE, I'M TAKIN' THIS AWAY!
RANGT
AND I AIN'T ARGUING THEOLOGY WITH YOU!
I KNOW THERE'S EVIL IN THE WORLD --
WHOMP
-- BUT MY MOMMA ALWAYS SAID, "ALL EVIL NEEDS TO TRIUMPH IS FOR GOOD MEN TO DO NOTHING."
AND I NEVER BEEN ACCUSED O' THAT!
CHAM
-- STRIKING WHERE YOU LEAST EXPECT IT --
EXCUSE ME --
-- WE'RE BEHIND YA A HUNNERT PERCENT --
-- GET 'IM, CAGE --
-- SOME-BODY CALL A COP --
-- CAGE'S GOT IT UNDER CONTROL --

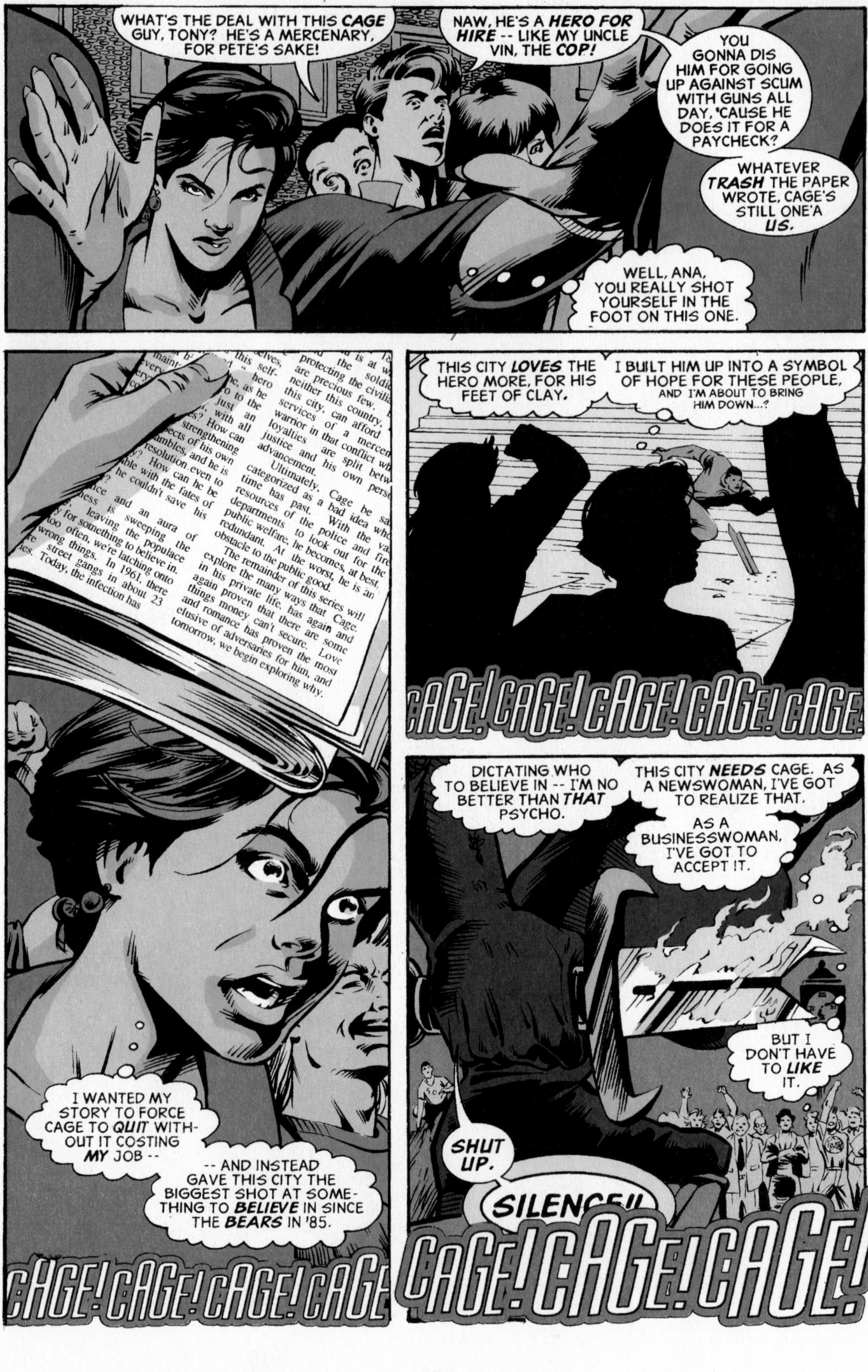

WHAT'S THE DEAL WITH THIS CAGE GUY, TONY? HE'S A MERCENARY, FOR PETE'S SAKE!
NAW, HE'S A HERO FOR HIRE -- LIKE MY UNCLE VIN, THE COP!
YOU GONNA DIS HIM FOR GOING UP AGAINST SCUM WITH GUNS ALL DAY, 'CAUSE HE DOES IT FOR A PAYCHECK?
WHATEVER TRASH THE PAPER WROTE, CAGE'S STILL ONE'A US.
WELL, ANA, YOU REALLY SHOT YOURSELF IN THE FOOT ON THIS ONE.
I WANTED MY STORY TO FORCE CAGE TO QUIT WITHOUT IT COSTING MY JOB --
-- AND INSTEAD GAVE THIS CITY THE BIGGEST SHOT AT SOMETHING TO BELIEVE IN SINCE THE BEARS IN '85.
CAGE! CAGE! CAGE! CAGE
THIS CITY LOVES THE HERO MORE, FOR HIS FEET OF CLAY.
I BUILT HIM UP INTO A SYMBOL OF HOPE FOR THESE PEOPLE, AND I'M ABOUT TO BRING HIM DOWN...?
CAGE! CAGE! CAGE! CAGE! CAGE!
DICTATING WHO TO BELIEVE IN -- I'M NO BETTER THAN THAT PSYCHO.
THIS CITY NEEDS CAGE. AS A NEWSWOMAN, I'VE GOT TO REALIZE THAT.
AS A BUSINESSWOMAN, I'VE GOT TO ACCEPT IT.
BUT I DON'T HAVE TO LIKE IT.
SHUT UP.
SILENCE!!
CAGE! CAGE! CAGE!

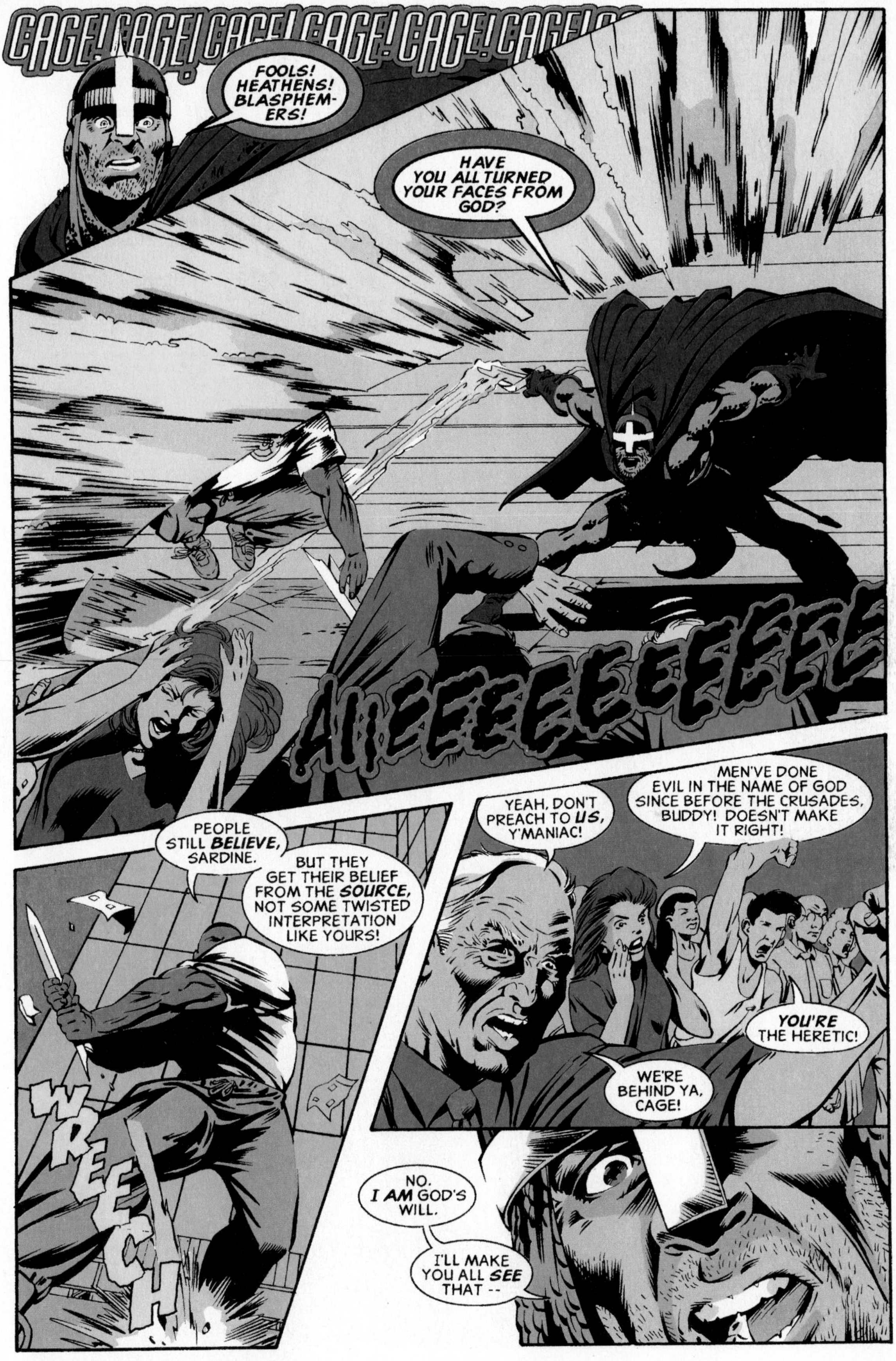
CAGE! CAGE! CAGE! CAGE! CAGE! CAGE!
FOOLS! HEATHENS! BLASPHEM-ERS!
HAVE YOU ALL TURNED YOUR FACES FROM GOD?
AIEEEEEEEEEEE
PEOPLE STILL BELIEVE, SARDINE.
BUT THEY GET THEIR BELIEF FROM THE SOURCE, NOT SOME TWISTED INTERPRETATION LIKE YOURS!
WREECH
YEAH, DON'T PREACH TO US, Y'MANIAC!
MEN'VE DONE EVIL IN THE NAME OF GOD SINCE BEFORE THE CRUSADES, BUDDY! DOESN'T MAKE IT RIGHT!
YOU'RE THE HERETIC!
WE'RE BEHIND YA, CAGE!
NO. I AM GOD'S WILL.
I'LL MAKE YOU ALL SEE THAT --

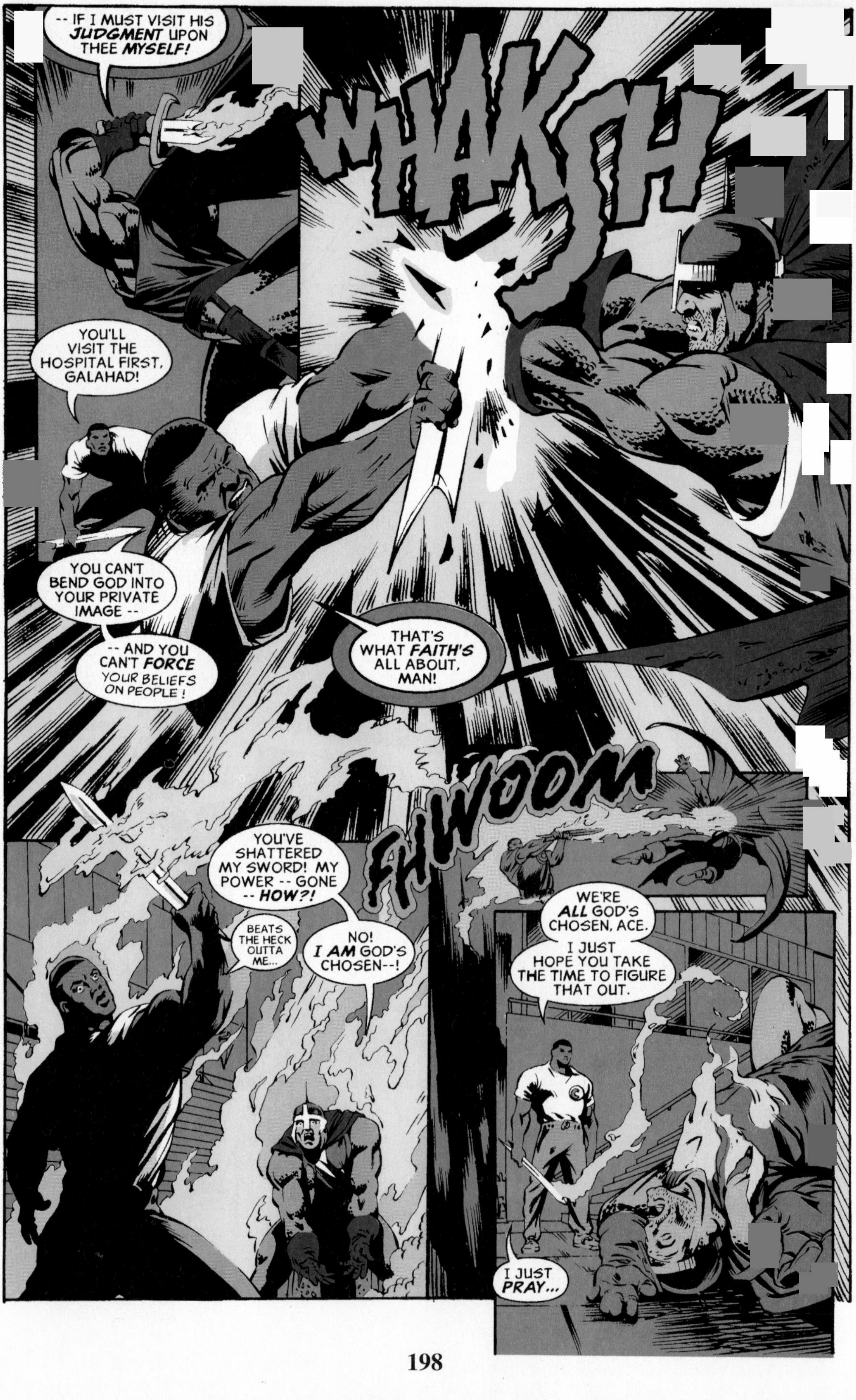
-- IF I MUST VISIT HIS JUDGMENT UPON THEE MYSELF!
WHAKSH
YOU'LL VISIT THE HOSPITAL FIRST, GALAHAD!
YOU CAN'T BEND GOD INTO YOUR PRIVATE IMAGE --
-- AND YOU CAN'T FORCE YOUR BELIEFS ON PEOPLE!
THAT'S WHAT FAITH'S ALL ABOUT, MAN!
FHWOOM
YOU'VE SHATTERED MY SWORD! MY POWER -- GONE -- HOW?!
BEATS THE HECK OUTTA ME...
NO! I AM GOD'S CHOSEN--!
WE'RE ALL GOD'S CHOSEN, ACE.
I JUST HOPE YOU TAKE THE TIME TO FIGURE THAT OUT.
I JUST PRAY...

ROLL IT!

MR. CAGE, WOULD YOU COMMENT, IN RELATION TO TODAY'S *SPECTATOR* ARTICLE --

-- EXPLORING YOUR *FATHER'S* ATTITUDE TOWARD --

-- EXPOSING YOUR *HOME* TO PUBLIC REVIEW --

-- TRUE RELATIONSHIP WITH YOUR *MOTHER* --

-- STAND ON THE *FANTASTIC FOUR*, IN LIGHT OF --

-- *RACISM* WITHIN THE PARA-NORMAL COMMUNITY --

LOOK, I'D LOVE TO TALK, BOYS, BUT I GOT UNFINISHED BUSINESS --

-- REVEAL YOUR *FULL HISTORY* TO THE PUBLIC --

" -- AND AN *EXCLUSIVE* MESSAGE T'DELIVER."

MEDINA, WE GOTTA TALK.

NOTHING LEFT TO SAY, CAGE. YOU'RE OFF THE HOOK.

WHAT --?

SUDDEN ATTACK OF INTEGRITY. DON'T RUB IT IN. YOU'RE *FREE.*

Chicago Spectator
"All... News that F..."

POWER PASS...
AN IN-DEPTH REPORT...
...LOGY OF LUK...

FIRED

YEAH, RIGHT. LOOK, YOUR STORY WASN'T *ALL* TRASH. OPENED MY EYES.

MY POPS SAID IT -- LIKE IT OR NOT, I'M IN THE SPOTLIGHT, IN A POSITION TO AFFECT THINGS.

BUT THE FOLKS OUTSIDE SHOWED ME I NEED SOME KINDA *CONTROL* OVER WHAT'S WRITTEN ABOUT ME.

IF I WANNA HAVE SOME SAY IN PEOPLE KNOWIN' WHAT I *STAND* FOR, I *NEED* THE OUTLET THE SPECTATOR GIVES.

WITH MICKY CUTTING BACK WITH HIS *SICKNESS,* I'LL NEED SOME-ONE TO COVER MY STORIES.

SO IF YOU WANT *ME,* I WANT *YOU.*

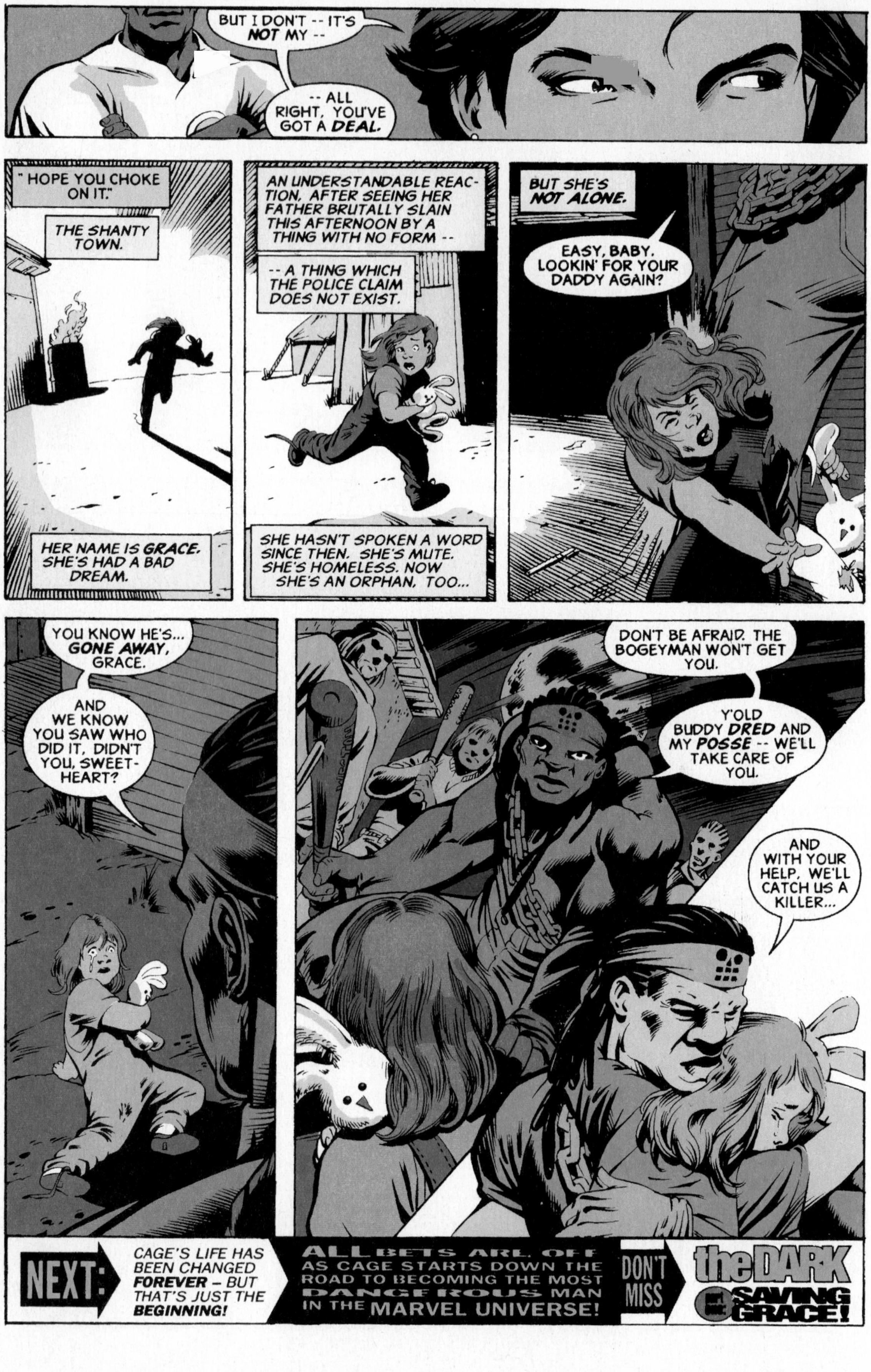
BUT I DON'T -- IT'S NOT MY --
-- ALL RIGHT, YOU'VE GOT A DEAL.
"HOPE YOU CHOKE ON IT."
THE SHANTY TOWN.
HER NAME IS GRACE. SHE'S HAD A BAD DREAM.
AN UNDERSTANDABLE REACTION, AFTER SEEING HER FATHER BRUTALLY SLAIN THIS AFTERNOON BY A THING WITH NO FORM --
-- A THING WHICH THE POLICE CLAIM DOES NOT EXIST.
SHE HASN'T SPOKEN A WORD SINCE THEN. SHE'S MUTE. SHE'S HOMELESS. NOW SHE'S AN ORPHAN, TOO...
BUT SHE'S NOT ALONE.
EASY, BABY. LOOKIN' FOR YOUR DADDY AGAIN?
YOU KNOW HE'S... GONE AWAY, GRACE.
AND WE KNOW YOU SAW WHO DID IT, DIDN'T YOU, SWEETHEART?
DON'T BE AFRAID. THE BOGEYMAN WON'T GET YOU.
Y'OLD BUDDY DRED AND MY POSSE -- WE'LL TAKE CARE OF YOU.
AND WITH YOUR HELP, WE'LL CATCH US A KILLER...
NEXT:
CAGE'S LIFE HAS BEEN CHANGED FOREVER -- BUT THAT'S JUST THE BEGINNING!
ALL BETS ARE OFF AS CAGE STARTS DOWN THE ROAD TO BECOMING THE MOST DANGEROUS MAN IN THE MARVEL UNIVERSE!
DON'T MISS
the DARK
SAVING GRACE!

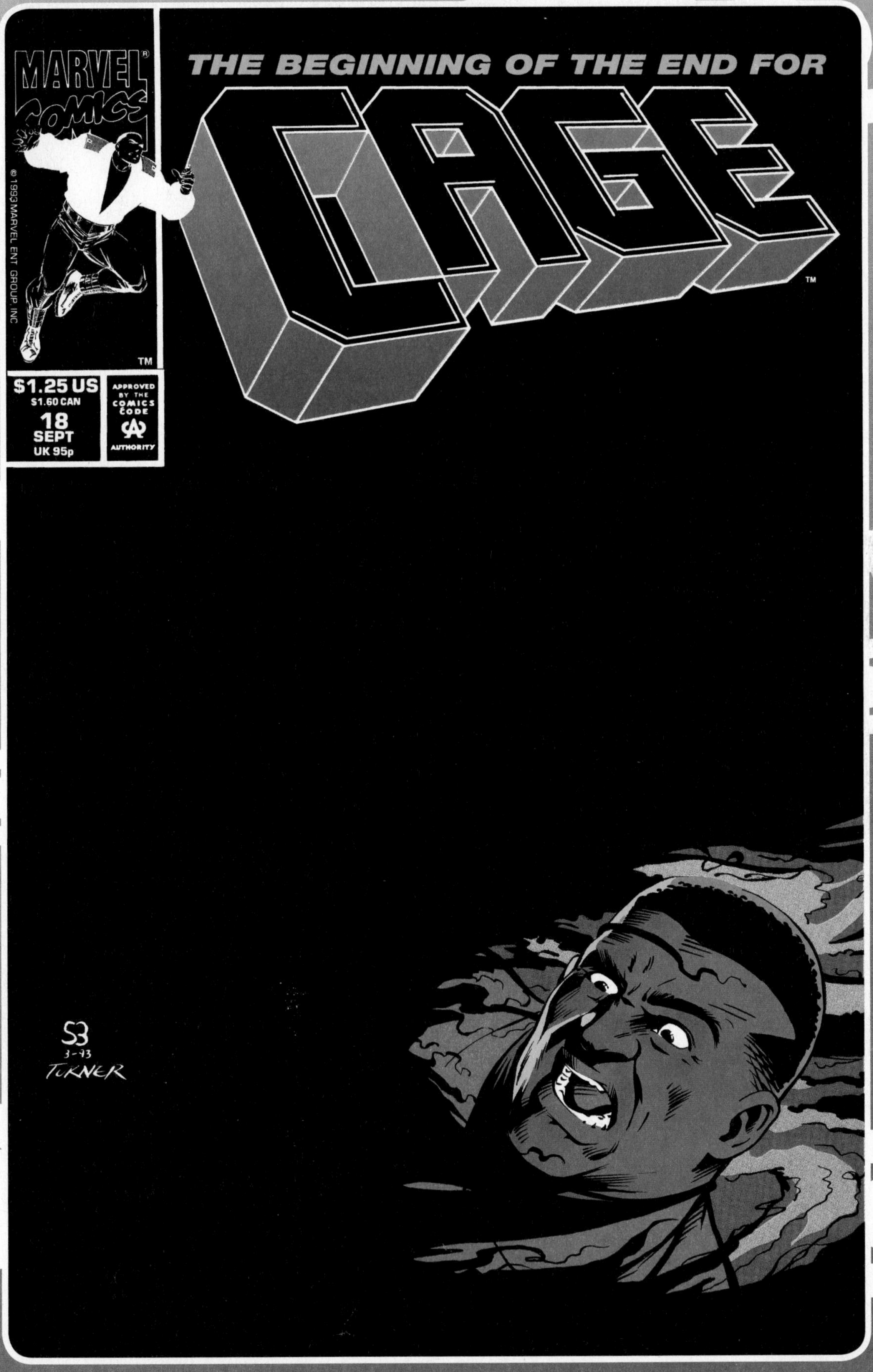

MARVEL COMICS
© 1993 MARVEL ENT GROUP, INC
TM
$1.25 US
$1.60 CAN
18
SEPT
UK 95p
APPROVED BY THE COMICS CODE AUTHORITY
THE BEGINNING OF THE END FOR
CAGE
TM
SB
3-93
TURNER

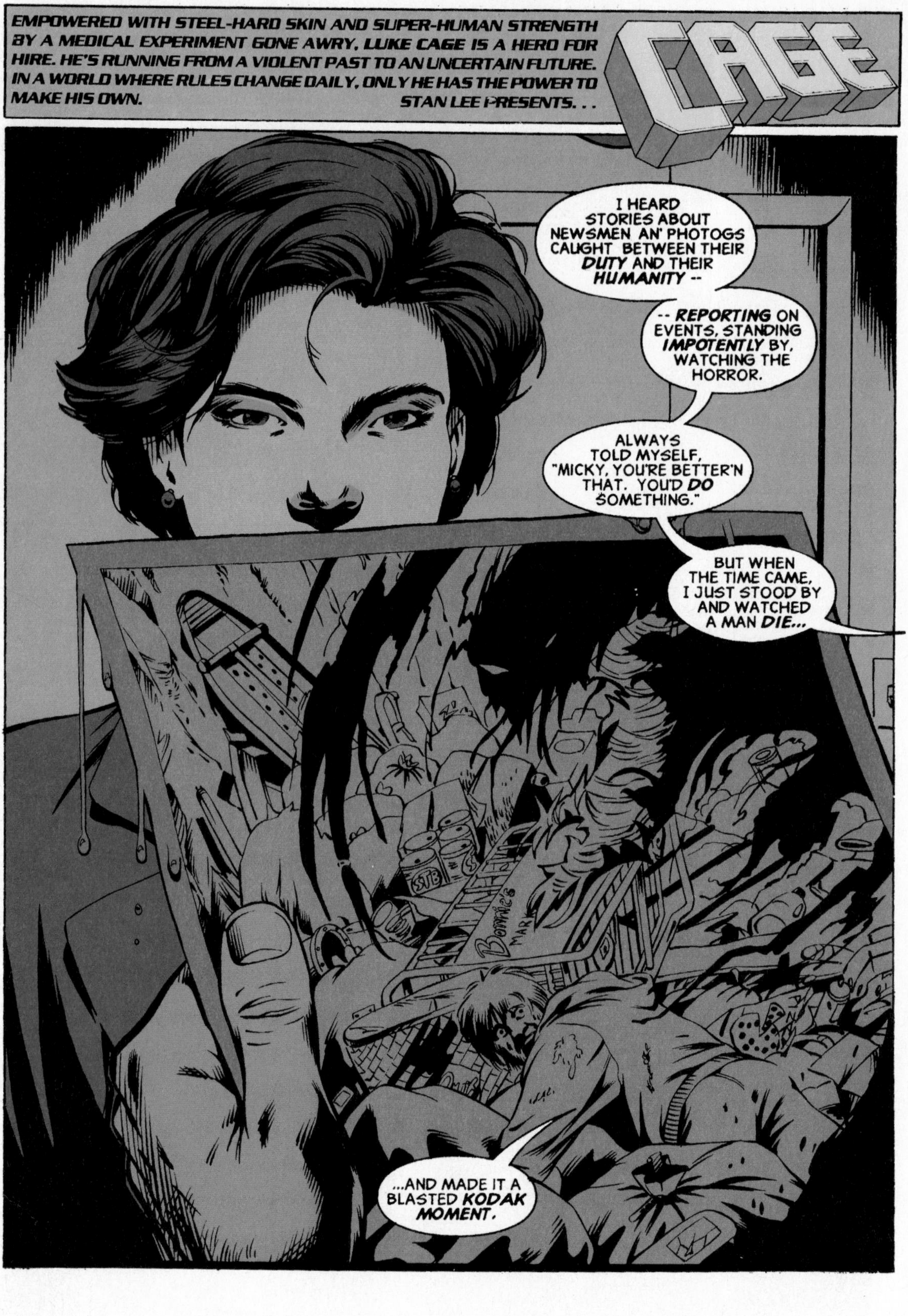
EMPOWERED WITH STEEL-HARD SKIN AND SUPER-HUMAN STRENGTH BY A MEDICAL EXPERIMENT GONE AWRY, LUKE CAGE IS A HERO FOR HIRE. HE'S RUNNING FROM A VIOLENT PAST TO AN UNCERTAIN FUTURE. IN A WORLD WHERE RULES CHANGE DAILY, ONLY HE HAS THE POWER TO MAKE HIS OWN.
STAN LEE PRESENTS. . .
CAGE
I HEARD STORIES ABOUT NEWSMEN AN' PHOTOGS CAUGHT BETWEEN THEIR DUTY AND THEIR HUMANITY --
-- REPORTING ON EVENTS, STANDING IMPOTENTLY BY, WATCHING THE HORROR.
ALWAYS TOLD MYSELF, "MICKY, YOU'RE BETTER'N THAT. YOU'D DO SOMETHING."
BUT WHEN THE TIME CAME, I JUST STOOD BY AND WATCHED A MAN DIE...
...AND MADE IT A BLASTED KODAK MOMENT.

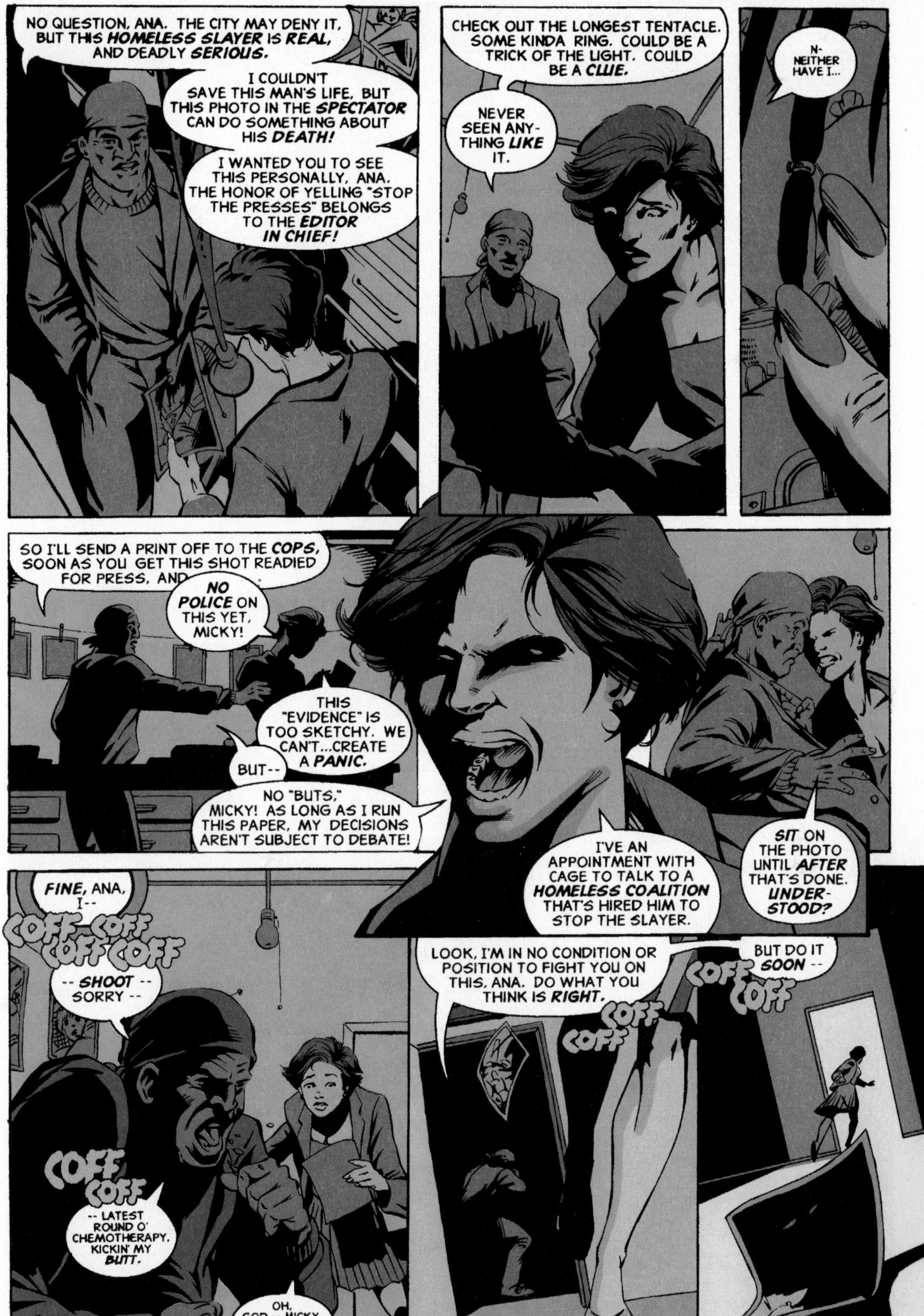
NO QUESTION, ANA. THE CITY MAY DENY IT, BUT THIS HOMELESS SLAYER IS REAL, AND DEADLY SERIOUS.
I COULDN'T SAVE THIS MAN'S LIFE, BUT THIS PHOTO IN THE SPECTATOR CAN DO SOMETHING ABOUT HIS DEATH!
I WANTED YOU TO SEE THIS PERSONALLY, ANA. THE HONOR OF YELLING "STOP THE PRESSES" BELONGS TO THE EDITOR IN CHIEF!
CHECK OUT THE LONGEST TENTACLE. SOME KINDA RING. COULD BE A TRICK OF THE LIGHT. COULD BE A CLUE.
NEVER SEEN ANYTHING LIKE IT.
N-NEITHER HAVE I...
SO I'LL SEND A PRINT OFF TO THE COPS, SOON AS YOU GET THIS SHOT READIED FOR PRESS, AND
NO POLICE ON THIS YET, MICKY!
THIS "EVIDENCE" IS TOO SKETCHY. WE CAN'T...CREATE A PANIC.
BUT--
NO "BUTS," MICKY! AS LONG AS I RUN THIS PAPER, MY DECISIONS AREN'T SUBJECT TO DEBATE!
I'VE AN APPOINTMENT WITH CAGE TO TALK TO A HOMELESS COALITION THAT'S HIRED HIM TO STOP THE SLAYER.
SIT ON THE PHOTO UNTIL AFTER THAT'S DONE. UNDERSTOOD?
FINE, ANA, I--
COFF COFF COFF COFF
-- SHOOT -- SORRY --
COFF COFF
-- LATEST ROUND O' CHEMOTHERAPY, KICKIN' MY BUTT.
OH, GOD -- MICKY, YOUR CANCER. I FORGOT. I--
LOOK, I'M IN NO CONDITION OR POSITION TO FIGHT YOU ON THIS, ANA. DO WHAT YOU THINK IS RIGHT.
COFF COFF
BUT DO IT SOON --
COFF COFF

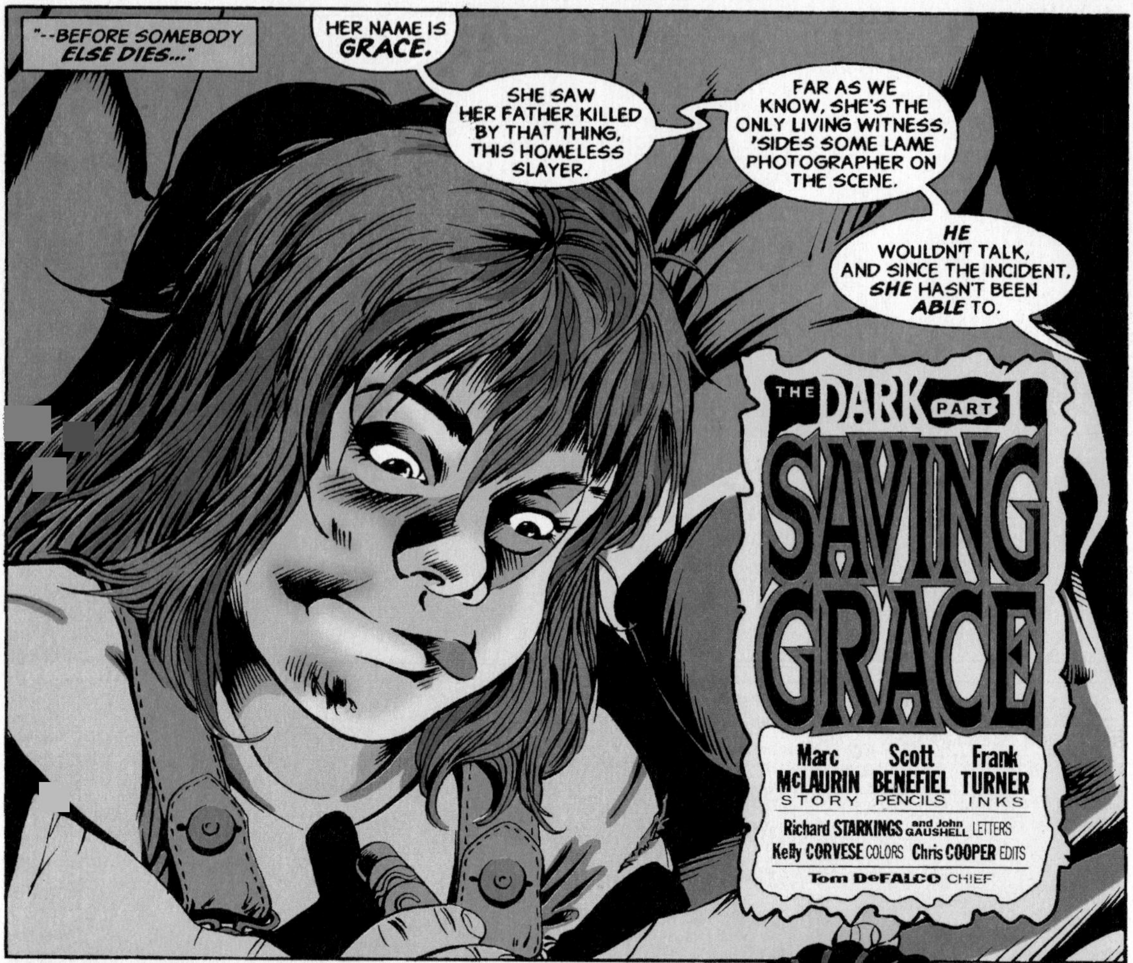
"--BEFORE SOMEBODY ELSE DIES..."
HER NAME IS GRACE.
SHE SAW HER FATHER KILLED BY THAT THING, THIS HOMELESS SLAYER.
FAR AS WE KNOW, SHE'S THE ONLY LIVING WITNESS, 'SIDES SOME LAME PHOTOGRAPHER ON THE SCENE.
HE WOULDN'T TALK, AND SINCE THE INCIDENT, SHE HASN'T BEEN ABLE TO.
THE DARK PART 1
SAVING GRACE
Marc McLAURIN STORY
Scott BENEFIEL PENCILS
Frank TURNER INKS
Richard STARKINGS and John GAUSHELL LETTERS
Kelly CORVESE COLORS Chris COOPER EDITS
Tom DeFALCO CHIEF

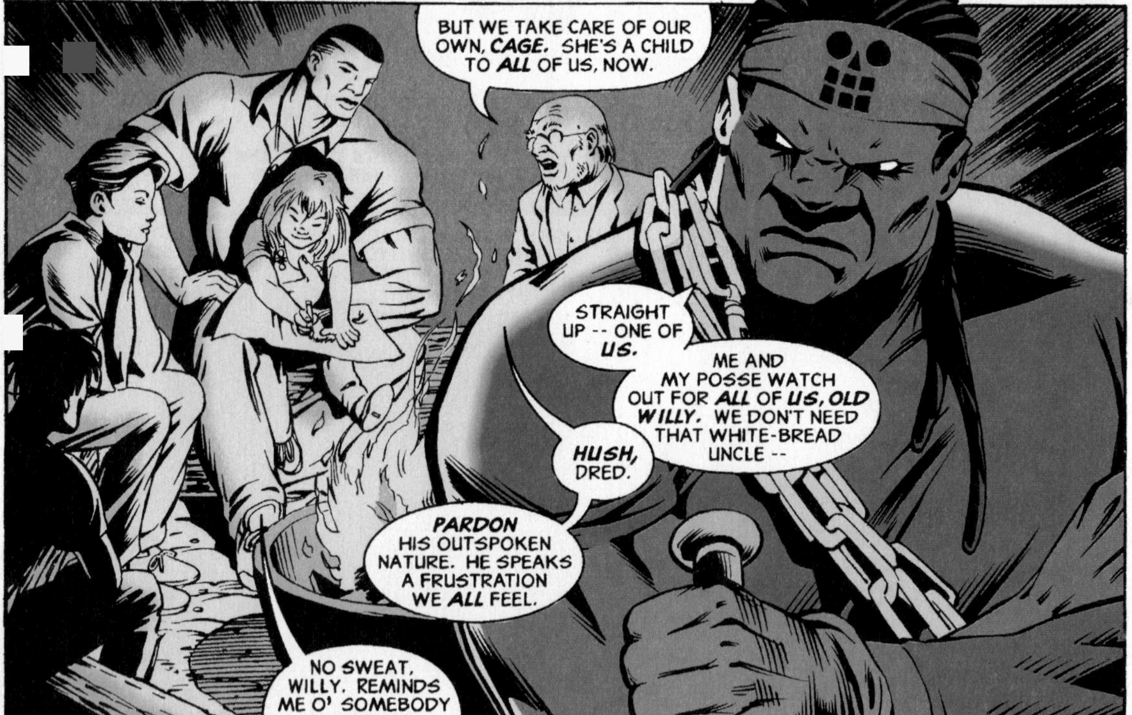
BUT WE TAKE CARE OF OUR OWN, CAGE. SHE'S A CHILD TO ALL OF US, NOW.
STRAIGHT UP -- ONE OF US.
ME AND MY POSSE WATCH OUT FOR ALL OF US, OLD WILLY. WE DON'T NEED THAT WHITE-BREAD UNCLE --
HUSH, DRED.
PARDON HIS OUTSPOKEN NATURE. HE SPEAKS A FRUSTRATION WE ALL FEEL.
NO SWEAT, WILLY. REMINDS ME O' SOMEBODY I USETA BE.

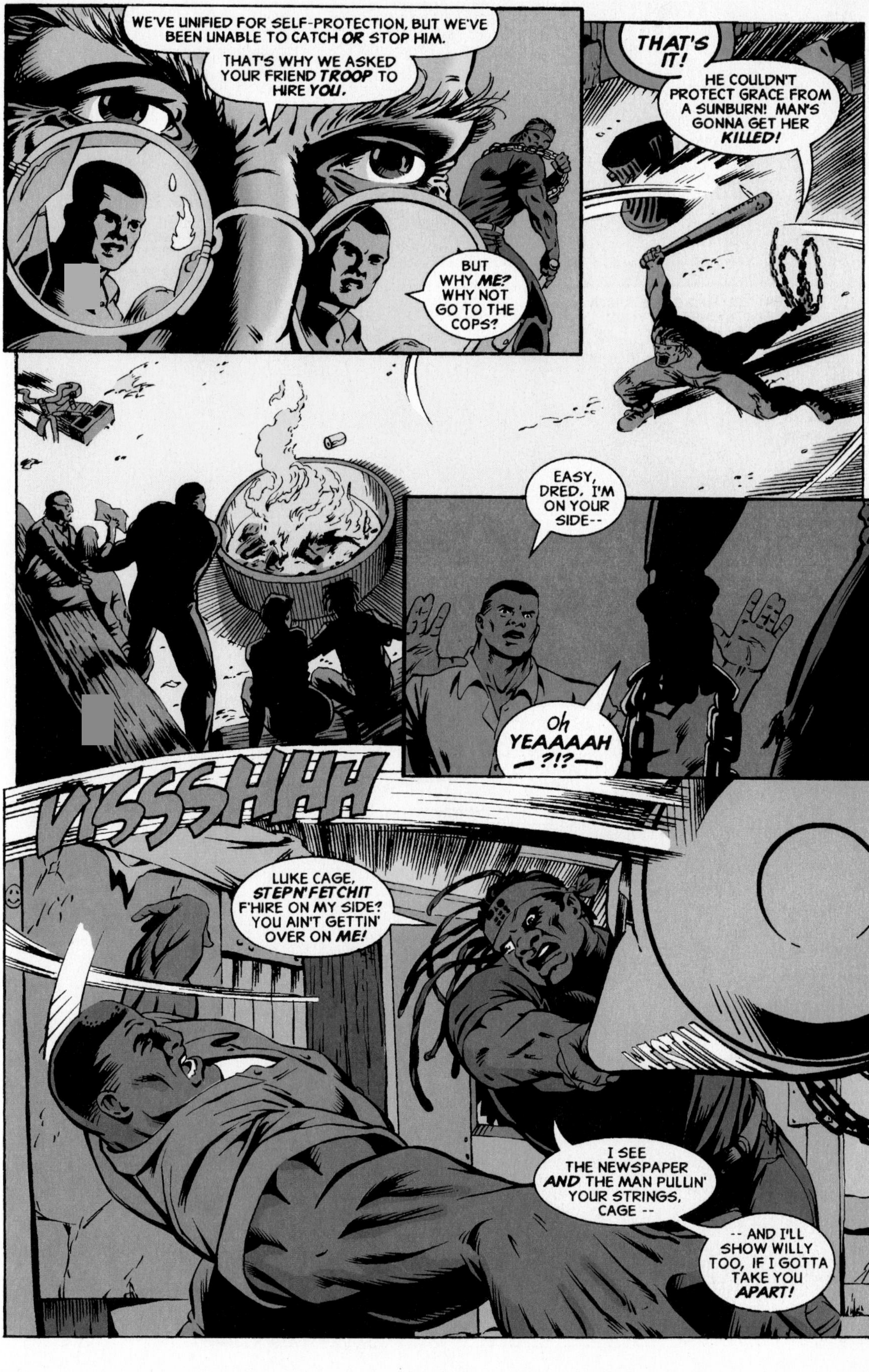
WE'VE UNIFIED FOR SELF-PROTECTION, BUT WE'VE BEEN UNABLE TO CATCH OR STOP HIM.
THAT'S WHY WE ASKED YOUR FRIEND TROOP TO HIRE YOU.
BUT WHY ME? WHY NOT GO TO THE COPS?
THAT'S IT!
HE COULDN'T PROTECT GRACE FROM A SUNBURN! MAN'S GONNA GET HER KILLED!
EASY, DRED. I'M ON YOUR SIDE--
Oh YEAAAAH --?!?--
VISSSHHH
LUKE CAGE, STEPN'FETCHIT F'HIRE ON MY SIDE? YOU AIN'T GETTIN' OVER ON ME!
I SEE THE NEWSPAPER AND THE MAN PULLIN' YOUR STRINGS, CAGE --
-- AND I'LL SHOW WILLY TOO, IF I GOTTA TAKE YOU APART!

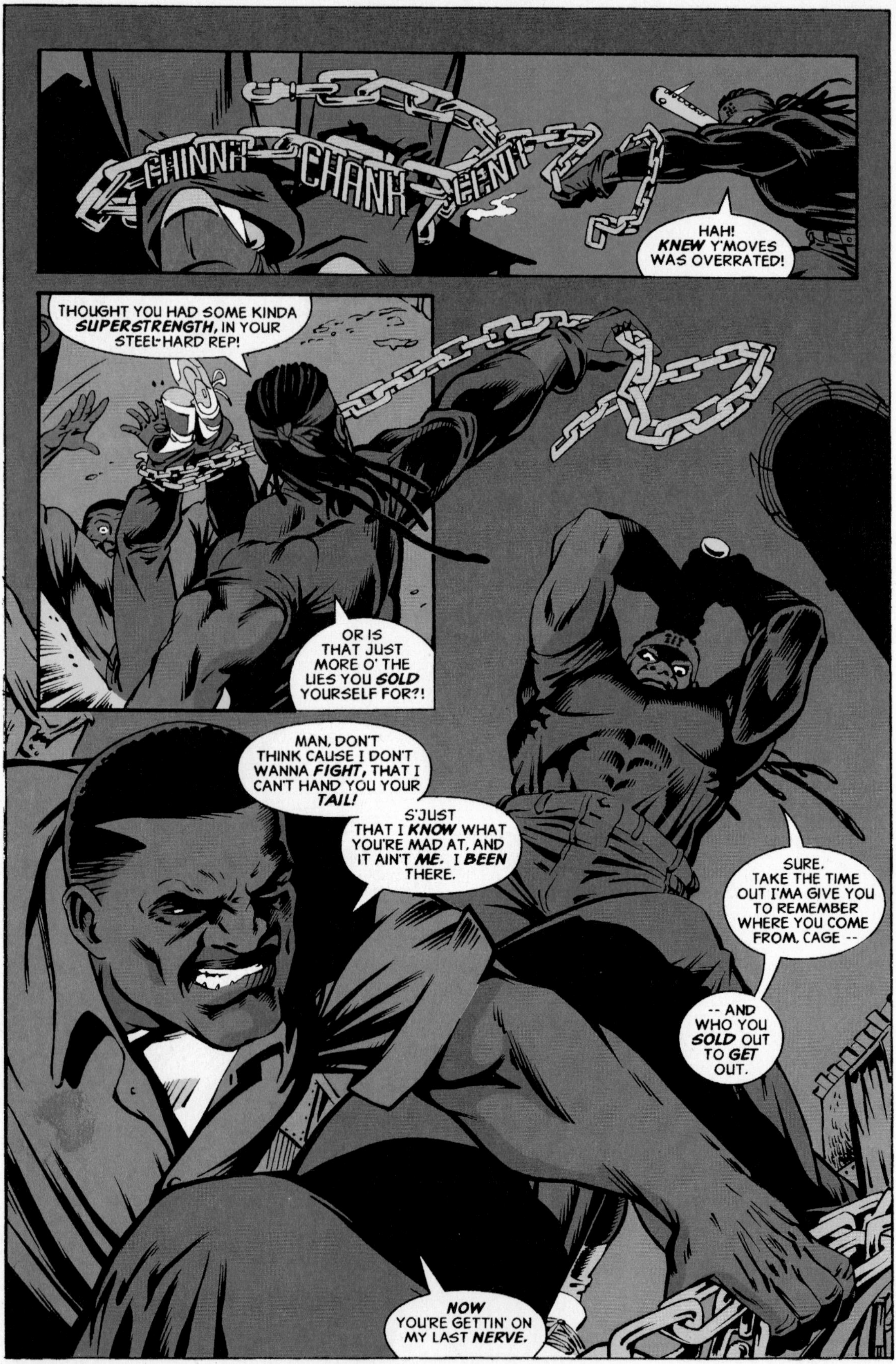
CHINNK
CHANK
CLNK
HAH! KNEW Y'MOVES WAS OVERRATED!
THOUGHT YOU HAD SOME KINDA SUPERSTRENGTH, IN YOUR STEEL-HARD REP!
OR IS THAT JUST MORE O' THE LIES YOU SOLD YOURSELF FOR?!
MAN, DON'T THINK CAUSE I DON'T WANNA FIGHT, THAT I CAN'T HAND YOU YOUR TAIL!
S'JUST THAT I KNOW WHAT YOU'RE MAD AT, AND IT AIN'T ME. I BEEN THERE.
SURE. TAKE THE TIME OUT I'MA GIVE YOU TO REMEMBER WHERE YOU COME FROM, CAGE --
-- AND WHO YOU SOLD OUT TO GET OUT.
NOW YOU'RE GETTIN' ON MY LAST NERVE.

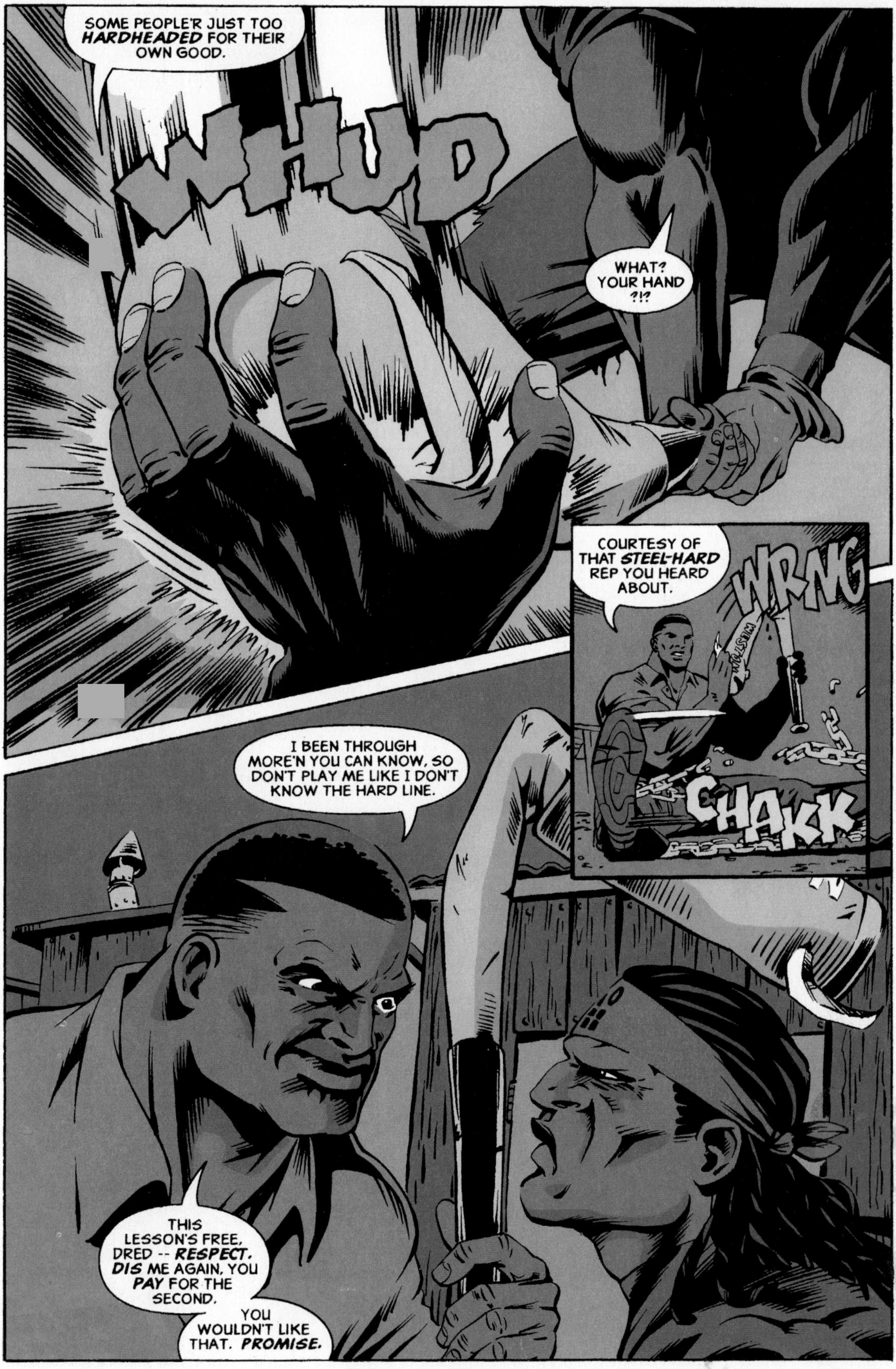
SOME PEOPLE'R JUST TOO HARDHEADED FOR THEIR OWN GOOD.
WHUD
WHAT? YOUR HAND ?!?
COURTESY OF THAT STEEL-HARD REP YOU HEARD ABOUT.
WRNG
CHAKK
I BEEN THROUGH MORE'N YOU CAN KNOW, SO DON'T PLAY ME LIKE I DON'T KNOW THE HARD LINE.
THIS LESSON'S FREE, DRED -- RESPECT. DIS ME AGAIN, YOU PAY FOR THE SECOND.
YOU WOULDN'T LIKE THAT. PROMISE.

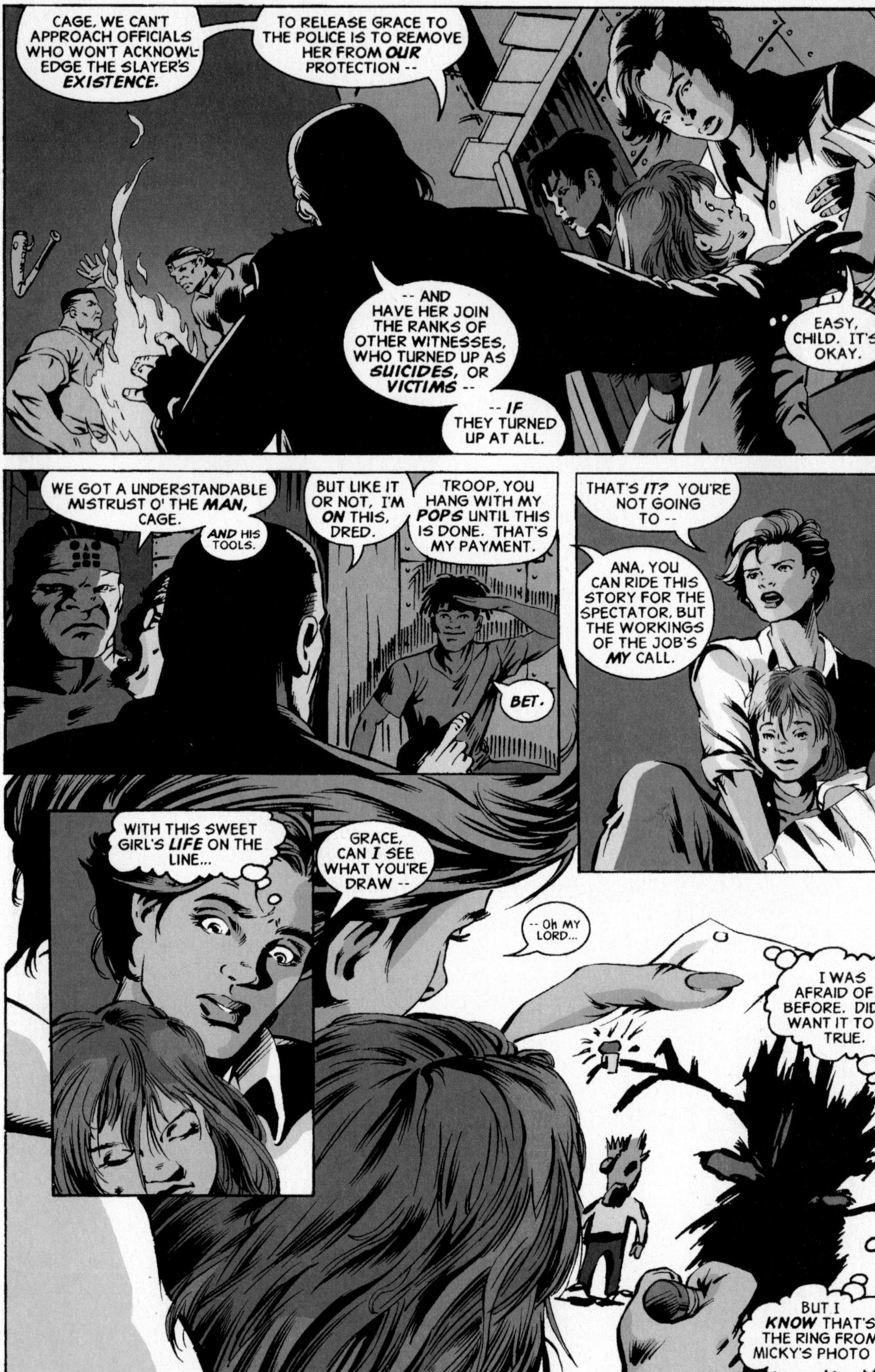

CAGE, WE CAN'T APPROACH OFFICIALS WHO WON'T ACKNOWLEDGE THE SLAYER'S EXISTENCE.
TO RELEASE GRACE TO THE POLICE IS TO REMOVE HER FROM OUR PROTECTION --
-- AND HAVE HER JOIN THE RANKS OF OTHER WITNESSES, WHO TURNED UP AS SUICIDES, OR VICTIMS --
-- IF THEY TURNED UP AT ALL.
EASY, CHILD. IT'S OKAY.
WE GOT A UNDERSTANDABLE MISTRUST O' THE MAN, CAGE.
AND HIS TOOLS.
BUT LIKE IT OR NOT, I'M ON THIS, DRED.
TROOP, YOU HANG WITH MY POPS UNTIL THIS IS DONE. THAT'S MY PAYMENT.
BET.
THAT'S IT? YOU'RE NOT GOING TO --
ANA, YOU CAN RIDE THIS STORY FOR THE SPECTATOR, BUT THE WORKINGS OF THE JOB'S MY CALL.
WITH THIS SWEET GIRL'S LIFE ON THE LINE...
GRACE, CAN I SEE WHAT YOU'RE DRAW --
-- OH MY LORD...
I WAS AFRAID OF IT BEFORE. DIDN'T WANT IT TO BE TRUE.
BUT I KNOW THAT'S THE RING FROM MICKY'S PHOTO --

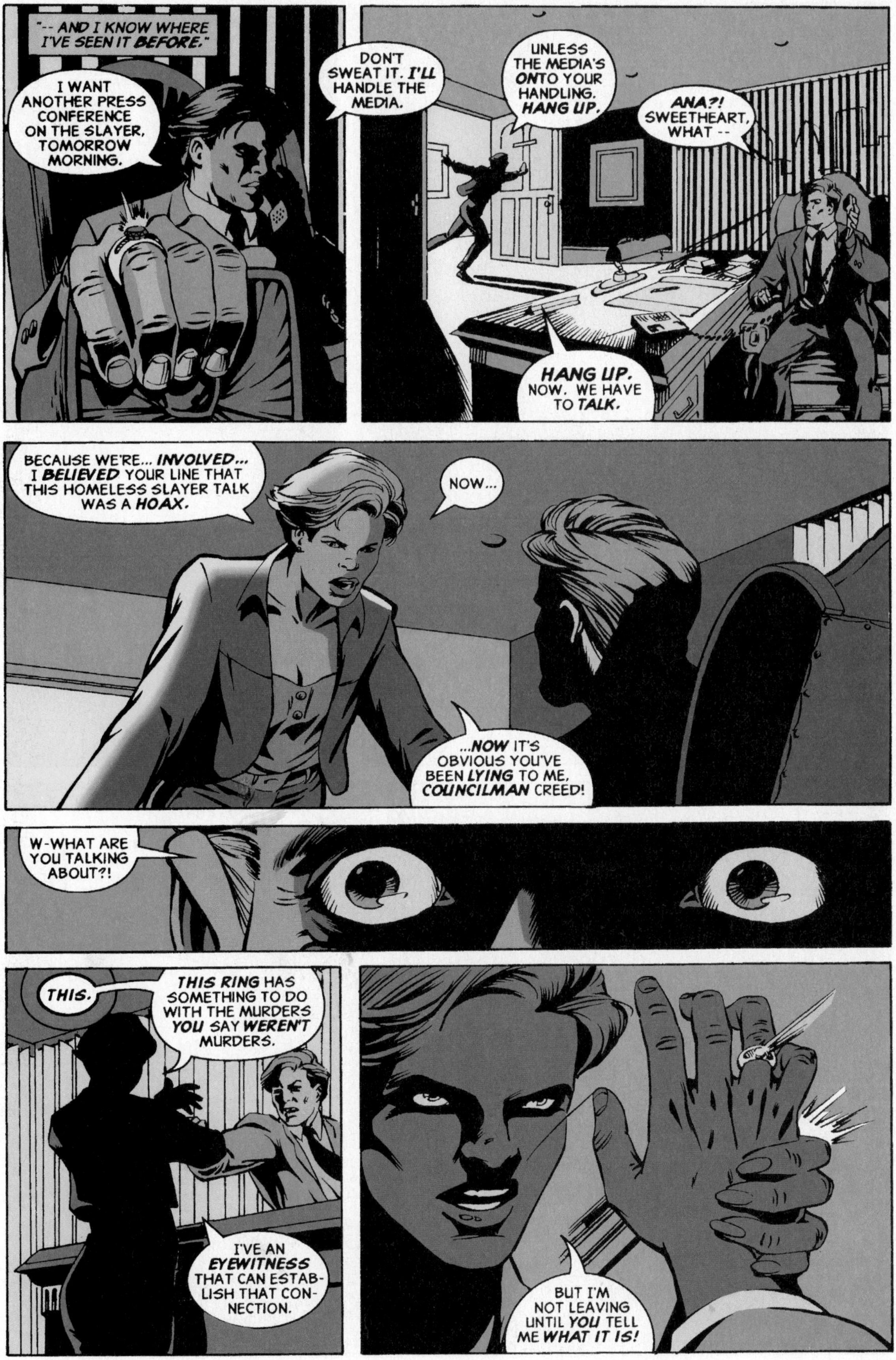
"-- AND I KNOW WHERE I'VE SEEN IT BEFORE."
I WANT ANOTHER PRESS CONFERENCE ON THE SLAYER, TOMORROW MORNING.
DON'T SWEAT IT. I'LL HANDLE THE MEDIA.
UNLESS THE MEDIA'S ONTO YOUR HANDLING. HANG UP.
ANA?! SWEETHEART, WHAT --
HANG UP. NOW. WE HAVE TO TALK.
BECAUSE WE'RE... INVOLVED... I BELIEVED YOUR LINE THAT THIS HOMELESS SLAYER TALK WAS A HOAX.
NOW...
...NOW IT'S OBVIOUS YOU'VE BEEN LYING TO ME, COUNCILMAN CREED!
W-WHAT ARE YOU TALKING ABOUT?!
THIS.
THIS RING HAS SOMETHING TO DO WITH THE MURDERS YOU SAY WEREN'T MURDERS.
I'VE AN EYEWITNESS THAT CAN ESTABLISH THAT CONNECTION.
BUT I'M NOT LEAVING UNTIL YOU TELL ME WHAT IT IS!

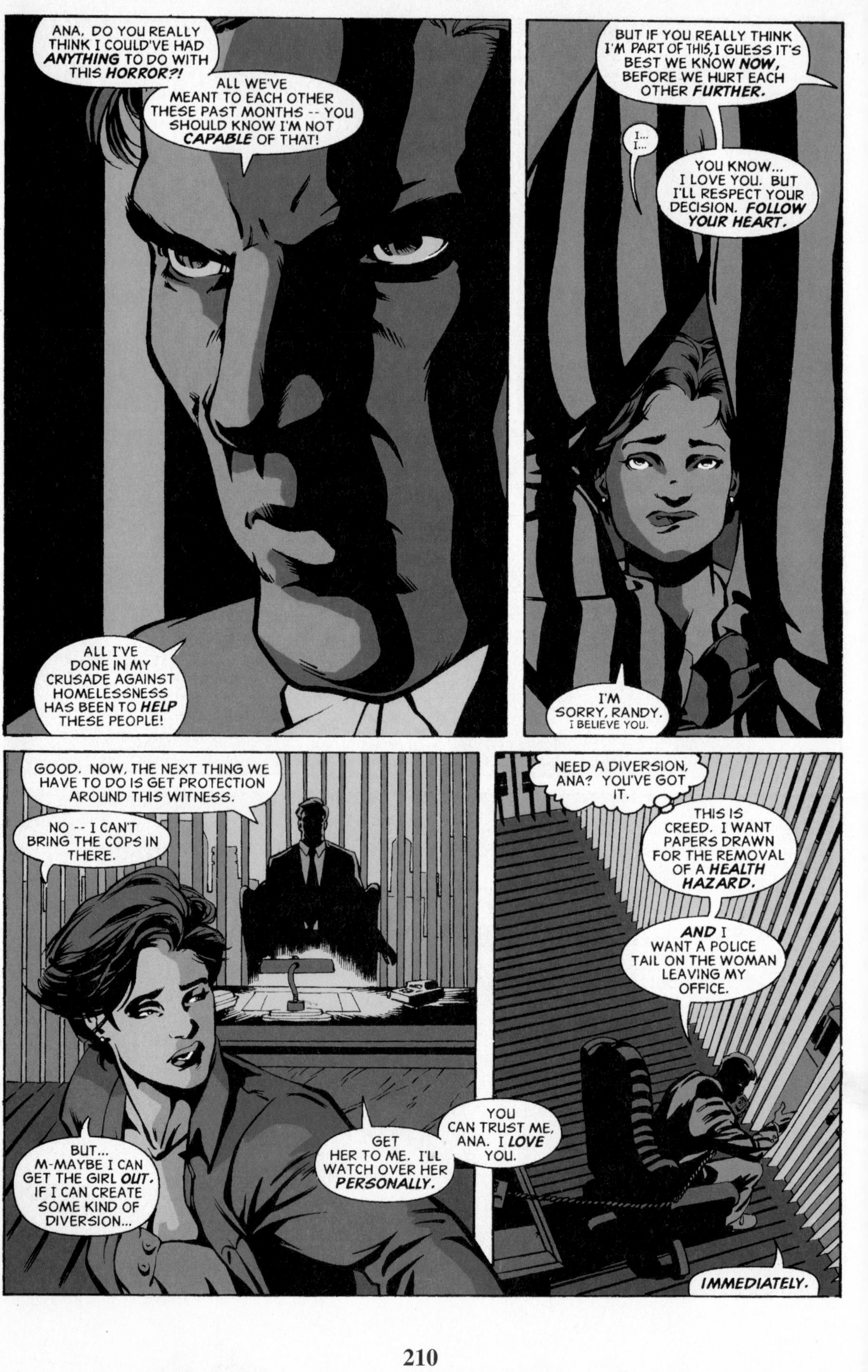
ANA, DO YOU REALLY THINK I COULD'VE HAD ANYTHING TO DO WITH THIS HORROR?!
ALL WE'VE MEANT TO EACH OTHER THESE PAST MONTHS -- YOU SHOULD KNOW I'M NOT CAPABLE OF THAT!
ALL I'VE DONE IN MY CRUSADE AGAINST HOMELESSNESS HAS BEEN TO HELP THESE PEOPLE!
BUT IF YOU REALLY THINK I'M PART OF THIS, I GUESS IT'S BEST WE KNOW NOW, BEFORE WE HURT EACH OTHER FURTHER.
I... I...
YOU KNOW... I LOVE YOU. BUT I'LL RESPECT YOUR DECISION. FOLLOW YOUR HEART.
I'M SORRY, RANDY. I BELIEVE YOU.
GOOD. NOW, THE NEXT THING WE HAVE TO DO IS GET PROTECTION AROUND THIS WITNESS.
NO -- I CAN'T BRING THE COPS IN THERE.
BUT... M-MAYBE I CAN GET THE GIRL OUT. IF I CAN CREATE SOME KIND OF DIVERSION...
GET HER TO ME. I'LL WATCH OVER HER PERSONALLY.
YOU CAN TRUST ME, ANA. I LOVE YOU.
NEED A DIVERSION, ANA? YOU'VE GOT IT.
THIS IS CREED. I WANT PAPERS DRAWN FOR THE REMOVAL OF A HEALTH HAZARD.
AND I WANT A POLICE TAIL ON THE WOMAN LEAVING MY OFFICE.
IMMEDIATELY.

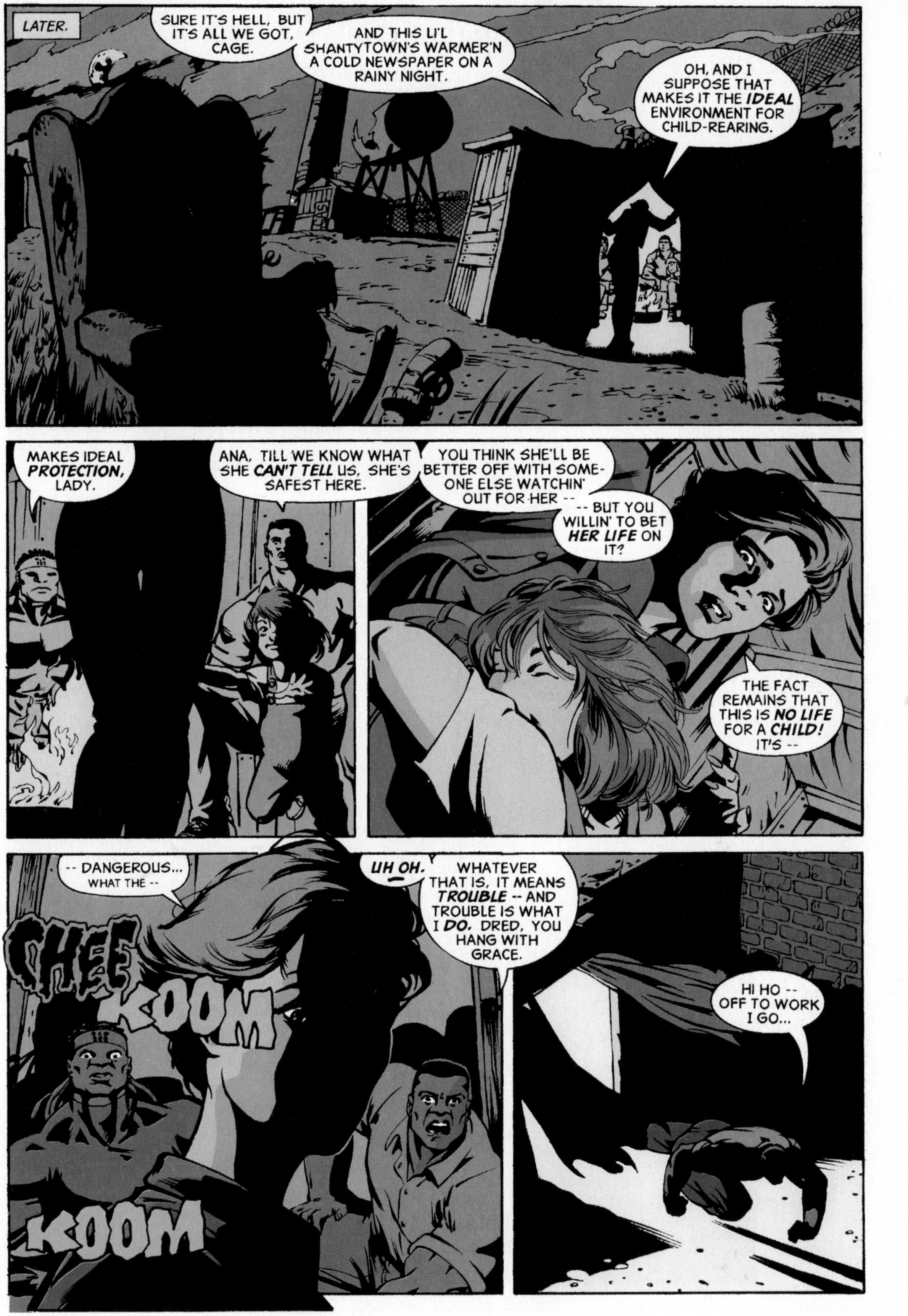
LATER.
SURE IT'S HELL, BUT IT'S ALL WE GOT, CAGE.
AND THIS LI'L SHANTYTOWN'S WARMER'N A COLD NEWSPAPER ON A RAINY NIGHT.
OH, AND I SUPPOSE THAT MAKES IT THE IDEAL ENVIRONMENT FOR CHILD-REARING.
MAKES IDEAL PROTECTION, LADY.
ANA, TILL WE KNOW WHAT SHE CAN'T TELL US, SHE'S SAFEST HERE.
YOU THINK SHE'LL BE BETTER OFF WITH SOME-ONE ELSE WATCHIN' OUT FOR HER --
-- BUT YOU WILLIN' TO BET HER LIFE ON IT?
THE FACT REMAINS THAT THIS IS NO LIFE FOR A CHILD! IT'S --
-- DANGEROUS... WHAT THE --
CHEE KOOM
KOOM
UH OH.
WHATEVER THAT IS, IT MEANS TROUBLE -- AND TROUBLE IS WHAT I DO. DRED, YOU HANG WITH GRACE.
HI HO -- OFF TO WORK I GO...

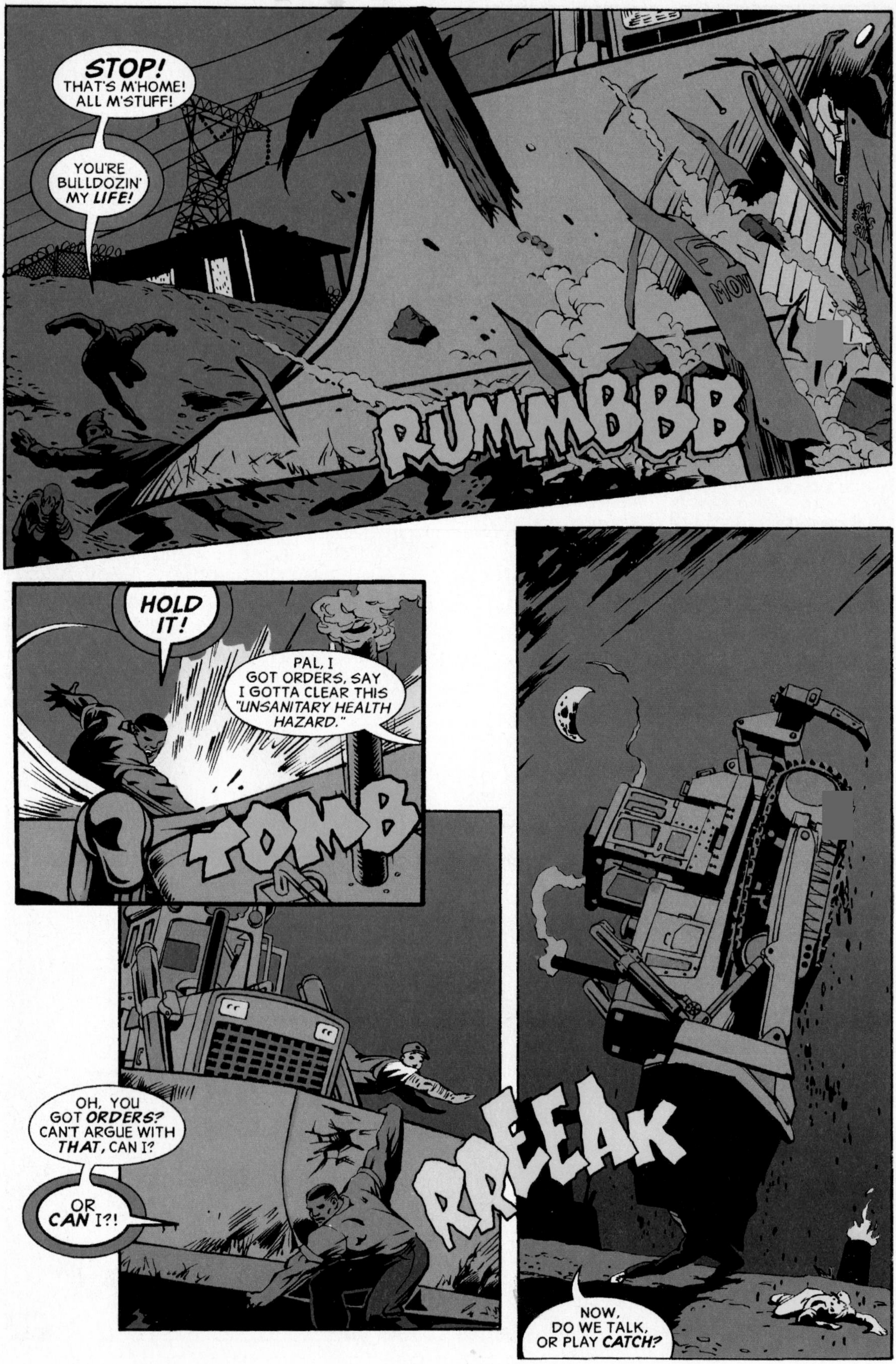
STOP! THAT'S M'HOME! ALL M'STUFF!
YOU'RE BULLDOZIN' MY LIFE!
RUMMBBB
HOLD IT!
PAL, I GOT ORDERS, SAY I GOTTA CLEAR THIS "UNSANITARY HEALTH HAZARD."
TOMB
OH, YOU GOT ORDERS? CAN'T ARGUE WITH THAT, CAN I?
OR CAN I?!
RRREEAK
NOW, DO WE TALK, OR PLAY CATCH?

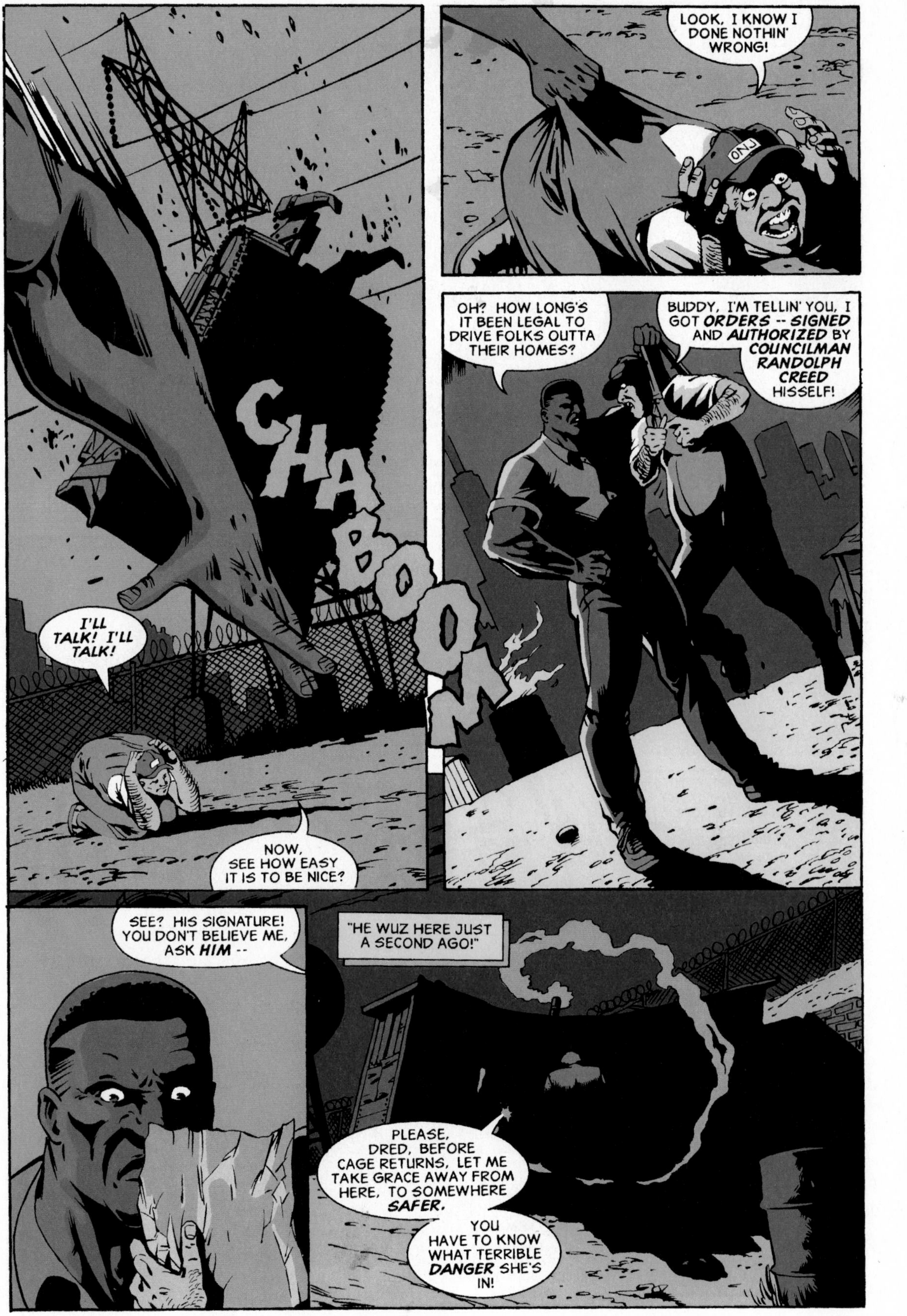
LOOK, I KNOW I DONE NOTHIN' WRONG!
CHABOOOM
I'LL TALK! I'LL TALK!
NOW, SEE HOW EASY IT IS TO BE NICE?
OH? HOW LONG'S IT BEEN LEGAL TO DRIVE FOLKS OUTTA THEIR HOMES?
BUDDY, I'M TELLIN' YOU, I GOT ORDERS -- SIGNED AND AUTHORIZED BY COUNCILMAN RANDOLPH CREED HISSELF!
SEE? HIS SIGNATURE! YOU DON'T BELIEVE ME, ASK HIM --
"HE WUZ HERE JUST A SECOND AGO!"
PLEASE, DRED, BEFORE CAGE RETURNS, LET ME TAKE GRACE AWAY FROM HERE, TO SOMEWHERE SAFER.
YOU HAVE TO KNOW WHAT TERRIBLE DANGER SHE'S IN!

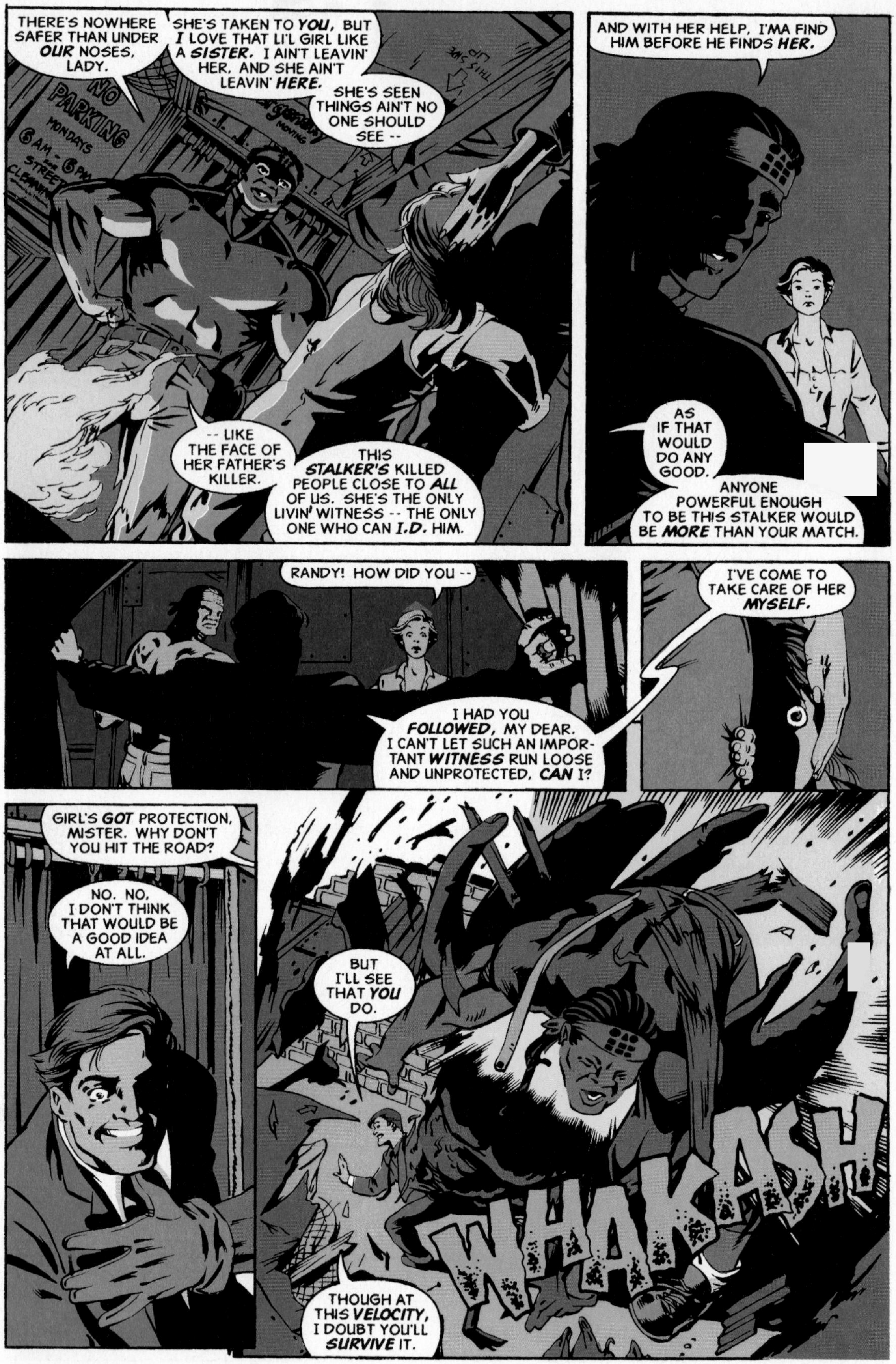

THERE'S NOWHERE SAFER THAN UNDER OUR NOSES, LADY.
SHE'S TAKEN TO YOU, BUT I LOVE THAT LI'L GIRL LIKE A SISTER. I AIN'T LEAVIN' HER, AND SHE AIN'T LEAVIN' HERE.
SHE'S SEEN THINGS AIN'T NO ONE SHOULD SEE --
NO PARKING
MONDAYS
6 AM - 6 PM
-- LIKE THE FACE OF HER FATHER'S KILLER.
THIS STALKER'S KILLED PEOPLE CLOSE TO ALL OF US. SHE'S THE ONLY LIVIN' WITNESS -- THE ONLY ONE WHO CAN I.D. HIM.
AND WITH HER HELP, I'MA FIND HIM BEFORE HE FINDS HER.
AS IF THAT WOULD DO ANY GOOD.
ANYONE POWERFUL ENOUGH TO BE THIS STALKER WOULD BE MORE THAN YOUR MATCH.
RANDY! HOW DID YOU --
I HAD YOU FOLLOWED, MY DEAR. I CAN'T LET SUCH AN IMPORTANT WITNESS RUN LOOSE AND UNPROTECTED, CAN I?
I'VE COME TO TAKE CARE OF HER MYSELF.
GIRL'S GOT PROTECTION, MISTER. WHY DON'T YOU HIT THE ROAD?
NO. NO, I DON'T THINK THAT WOULD BE A GOOD IDEA AT ALL.
BUT I'LL SEE THAT YOU DO.
THOUGH AT THIS VELOCITY, I DOUBT YOU'LL SURVIVE IT.
WHAKASH!

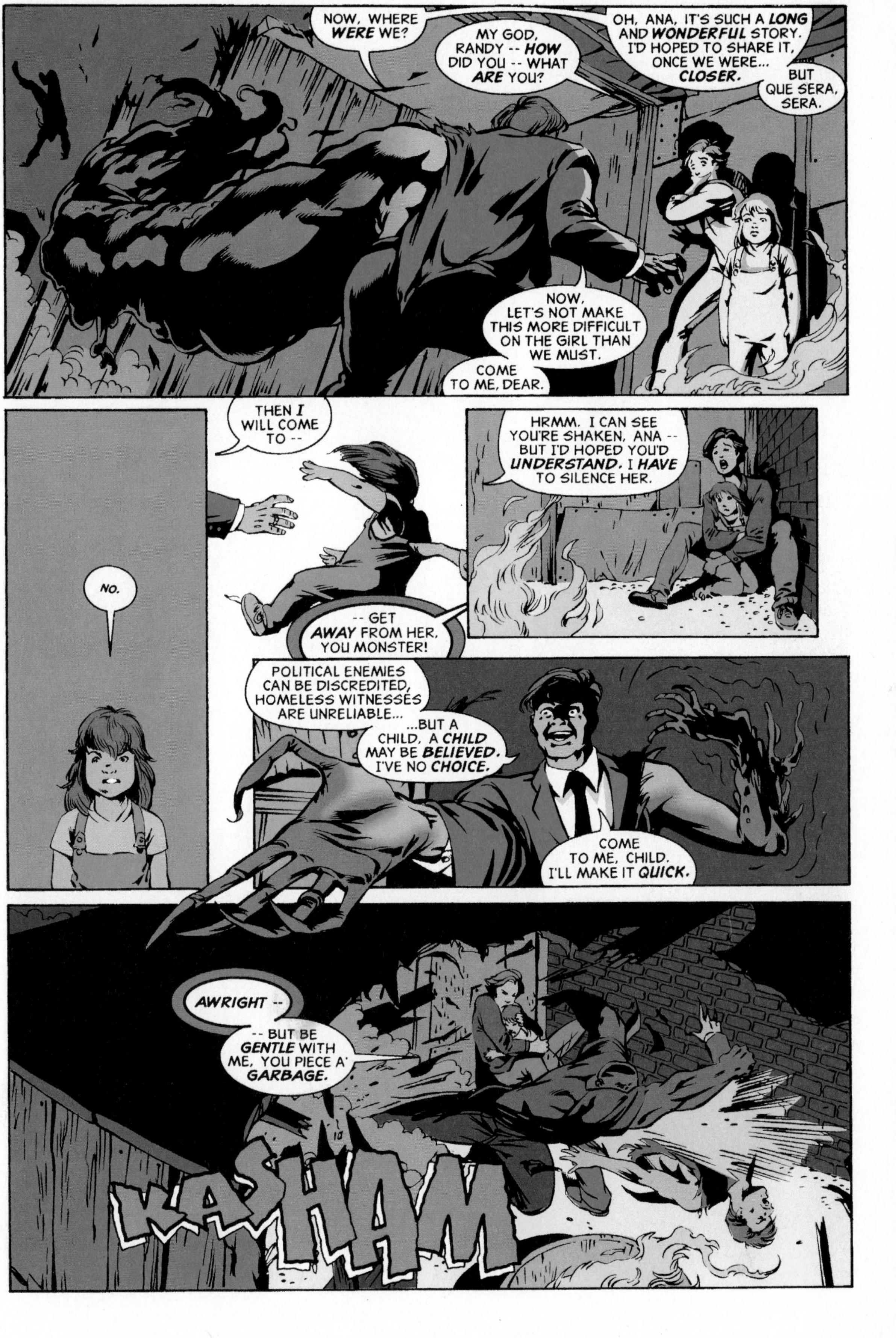
NOW, WHERE WERE WE?
MY GOD, RANDY -- HOW DID YOU -- WHAT ARE YOU?
OH, ANA, IT'S SUCH A LONG AND WONDERFUL STORY. I'D HOPED TO SHARE IT, ONCE WE WERE... CLOSER.
BUT QUE SERA, SERA.
NOW, LET'S NOT MAKE THIS MORE DIFFICULT ON THE GIRL THAN WE MUST.
COME TO ME, DEAR.
NO.
THEN I WILL COME TO --
-- GET AWAY FROM HER, YOU MONSTER!
HRMM. I CAN SEE YOU'RE SHAKEN, ANA -- BUT I'D HOPED YOU'D UNDERSTAND. I HAVE TO SILENCE HER.
POLITICAL ENEMIES CAN BE DISCREDITED, HOMELESS WITNESSES ARE UNRELIABLE...
...BUT A CHILD, A CHILD MAY BE BELIEVED. I'VE NO CHOICE.
COME TO ME, CHILD. I'LL MAKE IT QUICK.
AWRIGHT --
-- BUT BE GENTLE WITH ME, YOU PIECE A' GARBAGE.
KASHAM

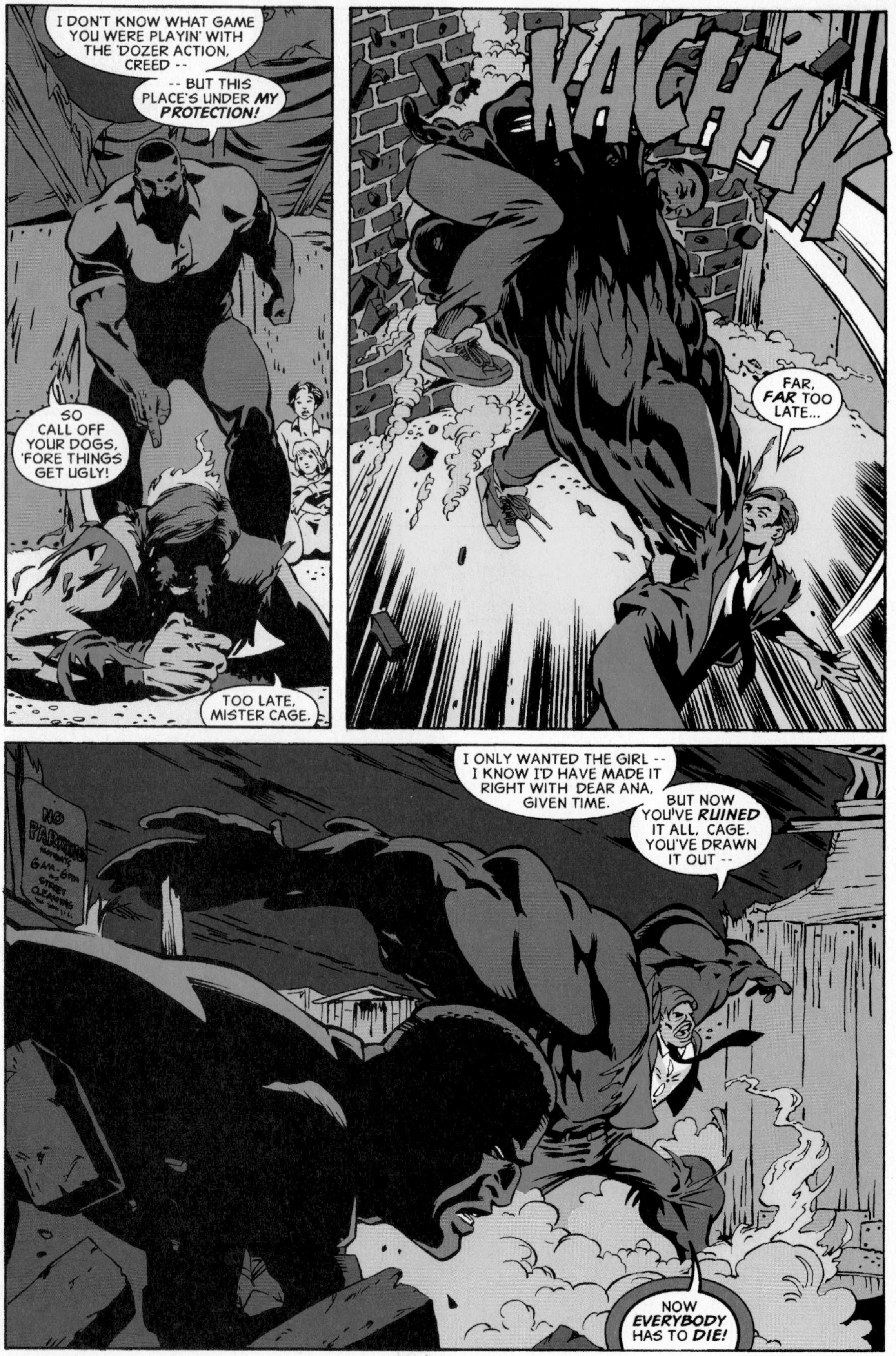
I DON'T KNOW WHAT GAME YOU WERE PLAYIN' WITH THE 'DOZER ACTION, CREED --
-- BUT THIS PLACE'S UNDER MY PROTECTION!
SO CALL OFF YOUR DOGS, 'FORE THINGS GET UGLY!
TOO LATE, MISTER CAGE.
KACHAK
FAR, FAR TOO LATE...
NO PARKING
STREET CLEANING
I ONLY WANTED THE GIRL -- I KNOW I'D HAVE MADE IT RIGHT WITH DEAR ANA, GIVEN TIME.
BUT NOW YOU'VE RUINED IT ALL, CAGE. YOU'VE DRAWN IT OUT --
NOW EVERYBODY HAS TO DIE!

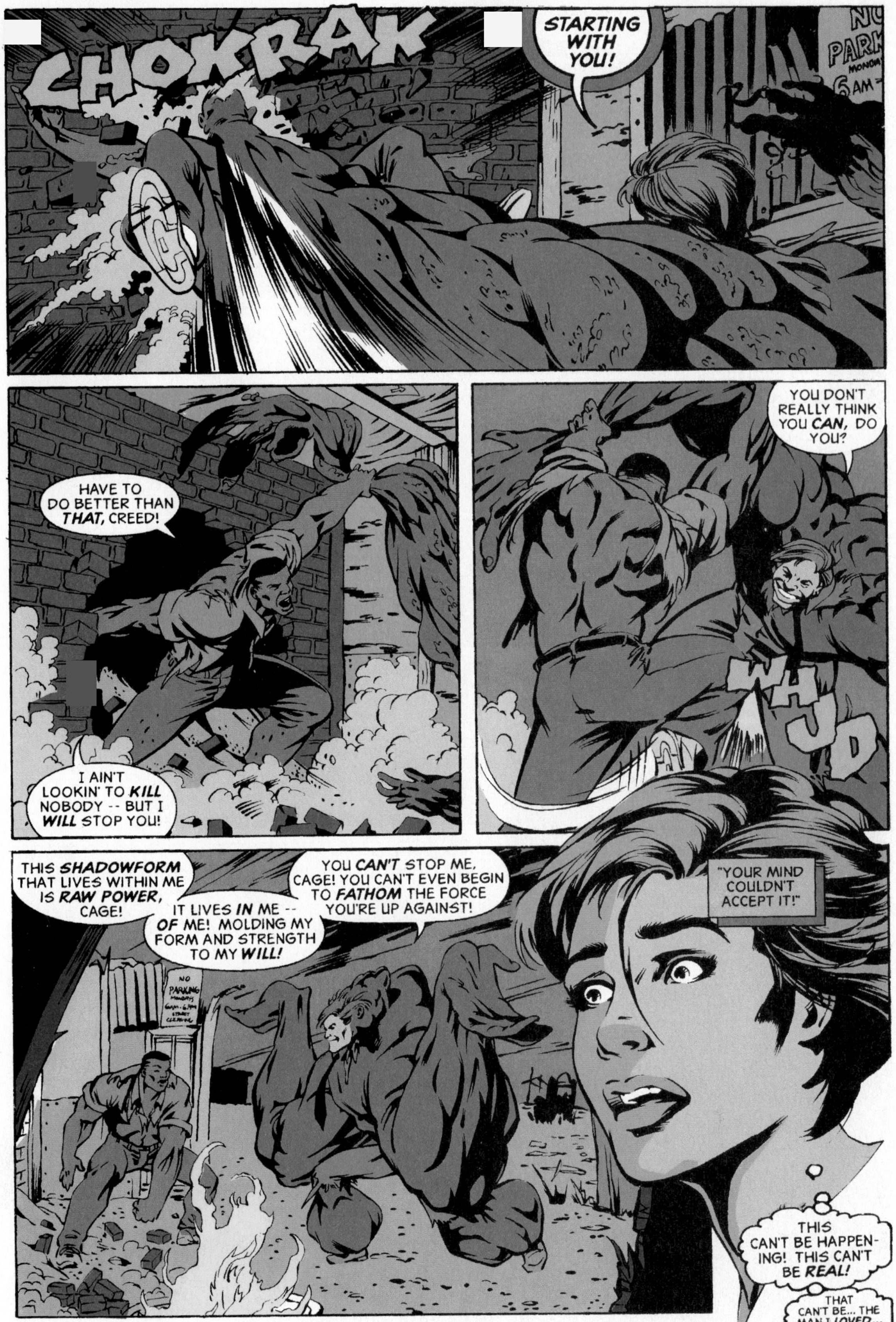
CHOKRAK
STARTING WITH YOU!
NO PARK MONDAY 6AM
HAVE TO DO BETTER THAN THAT, CREED!
I AIN'T LOOKIN' TO KILL NOBODY -- BUT I WILL STOP YOU!
YOU DON'T REALLY THINK YOU CAN, DO YOU?
WHUD
THIS SHADOWFORM THAT LIVES WITHIN ME IS RAW POWER, CAGE!
IT LIVES IN ME -- OF ME! MOLDING MY FORM AND STRENGTH TO MY WILL!
YOU CAN'T STOP ME, CAGE! YOU CAN'T EVEN BEGIN TO FATHOM THE FORCE YOU'RE UP AGAINST!
"YOUR MIND COULDN'T ACCEPT IT!"
NO PARKING
THIS CAN'T BE HAPPENING! THIS CAN'T BE REAL!
THAT CAN'T BE... THE MAN I LOVED...

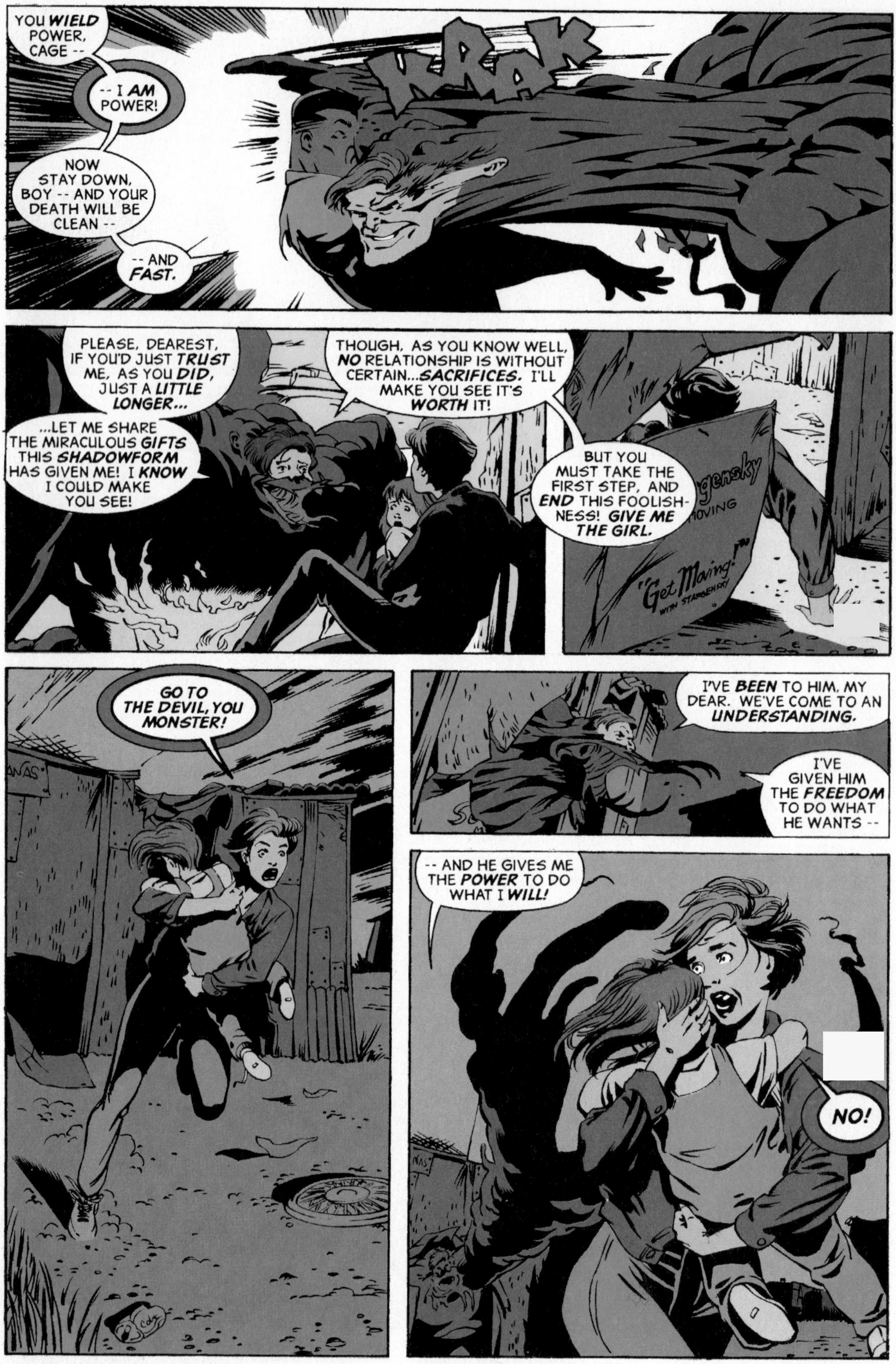
YOU WIELD POWER, CAGE --
-- I AM POWER!
NOW STAY DOWN, BOY -- AND YOUR DEATH WILL BE CLEAN --
-- AND FAST.
KRAK
PLEASE, DEAREST, IF YOU'D JUST TRUST ME, AS YOU DID, JUST A LITTLE LONGER...
...LET ME SHARE THE MIRACULOUS GIFTS THIS SHADOWFORM HAS GIVEN ME! I KNOW I COULD MAKE YOU SEE!
THOUGH, AS YOU KNOW WELL, NO RELATIONSHIP IS WITHOUT CERTAIN...SACRIFICES. I'LL MAKE YOU SEE IT'S WORTH IT!
BUT YOU MUST TAKE THE FIRST STEP, AND END THIS FOOLISHNESS! GIVE ME THE GIRL.
"Get Moving!"
GO TO THE DEVIL, YOU MONSTER!
I'VE BEEN TO HIM, MY DEAR. WE'VE COME TO AN UNDERSTANDING.
I'VE GIVEN HIM THE FREEDOM TO DO WHAT HE WANTS --
-- AND HE GIVES ME THE POWER TO DO WHAT I WILL!
NO!

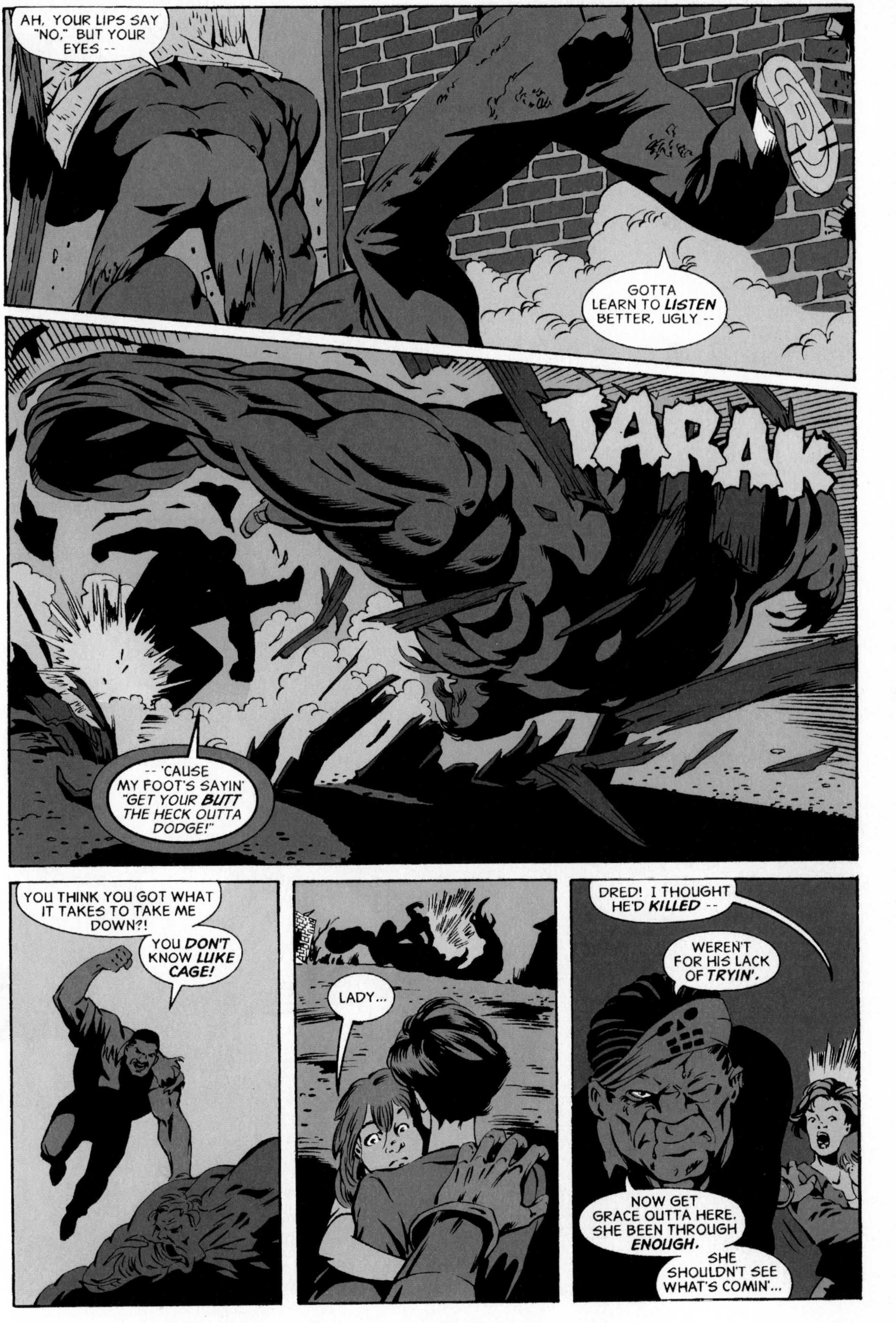
AH, YOUR LIPS SAY "NO," BUT YOUR EYES --
GOTTA LEARN TO LISTEN BETTER, UGLY --
TARAK
-- 'CAUSE MY FOOT'S SAYIN' "GET YOUR BUTT THE HECK OUTTA DODGE!"
YOU THINK YOU GOT WHAT IT TAKES TO TAKE ME DOWN?!
YOU DON'T KNOW LUKE CAGE!
LADY...
DRED! I THOUGHT HE'D KILLED --
WEREN'T FOR HIS LACK OF TRYIN'.
NOW GET GRACE OUTTA HERE. SHE BEEN THROUGH ENOUGH.
SHE SHOULDN'T SEE WHAT'S COMIN'...

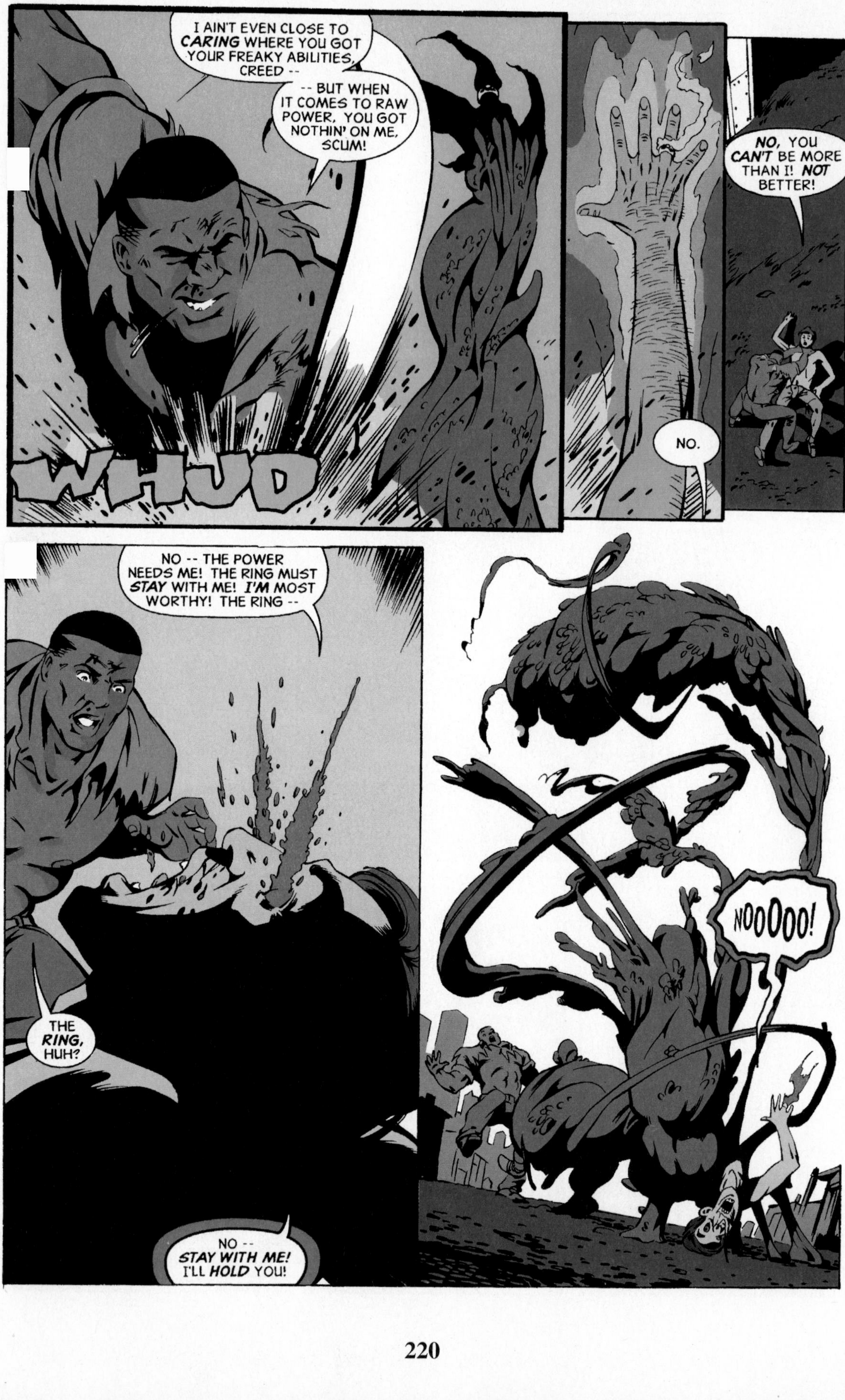
I AIN'T EVEN CLOSE TO CARING WHERE YOU GOT YOUR FREAKY ABILITIES, CREED --
-- BUT WHEN IT COMES TO RAW POWER, YOU GOT NOTHIN' ON ME, SCUM!
WHUD
NO.
NO, YOU CAN'T BE MORE THAN I! NOT BETTER!
NO -- THE POWER NEEDS ME! THE RING MUST STAY WITH ME! I'M MOST WORTHY! THE RING --
THE RING, HUH?
NO -- STAY WITH ME! I'LL HOLD YOU!
NOOOOO!

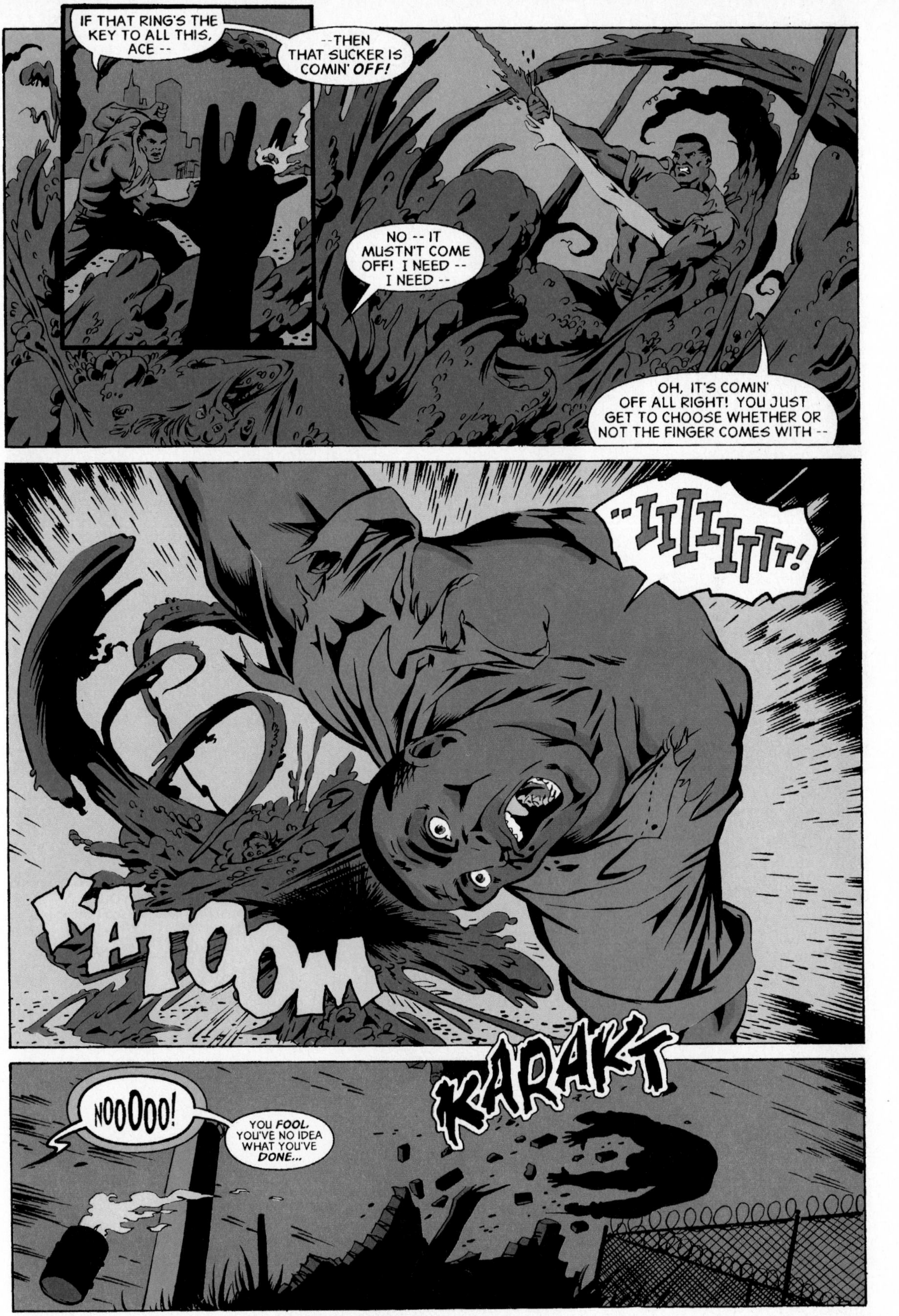
IF THAT RING'S THE KEY TO ALL THIS, ACE --
--THEN THAT SUCKER IS COMIN' OFF!
NO -- IT MUSTN'T COME OFF! I NEED -- I NEED --
OH, IT'S COMIN' OFF ALL RIGHT! YOU JUST GET TO CHOOSE WHETHER OR NOT THE FINGER COMES WITH --
--IIIIITTT!
KATOOM
KARAKT
NOOOOO!
YOU FOOL, YOU'VE NO IDEA WHAT YOU'VE DONE...

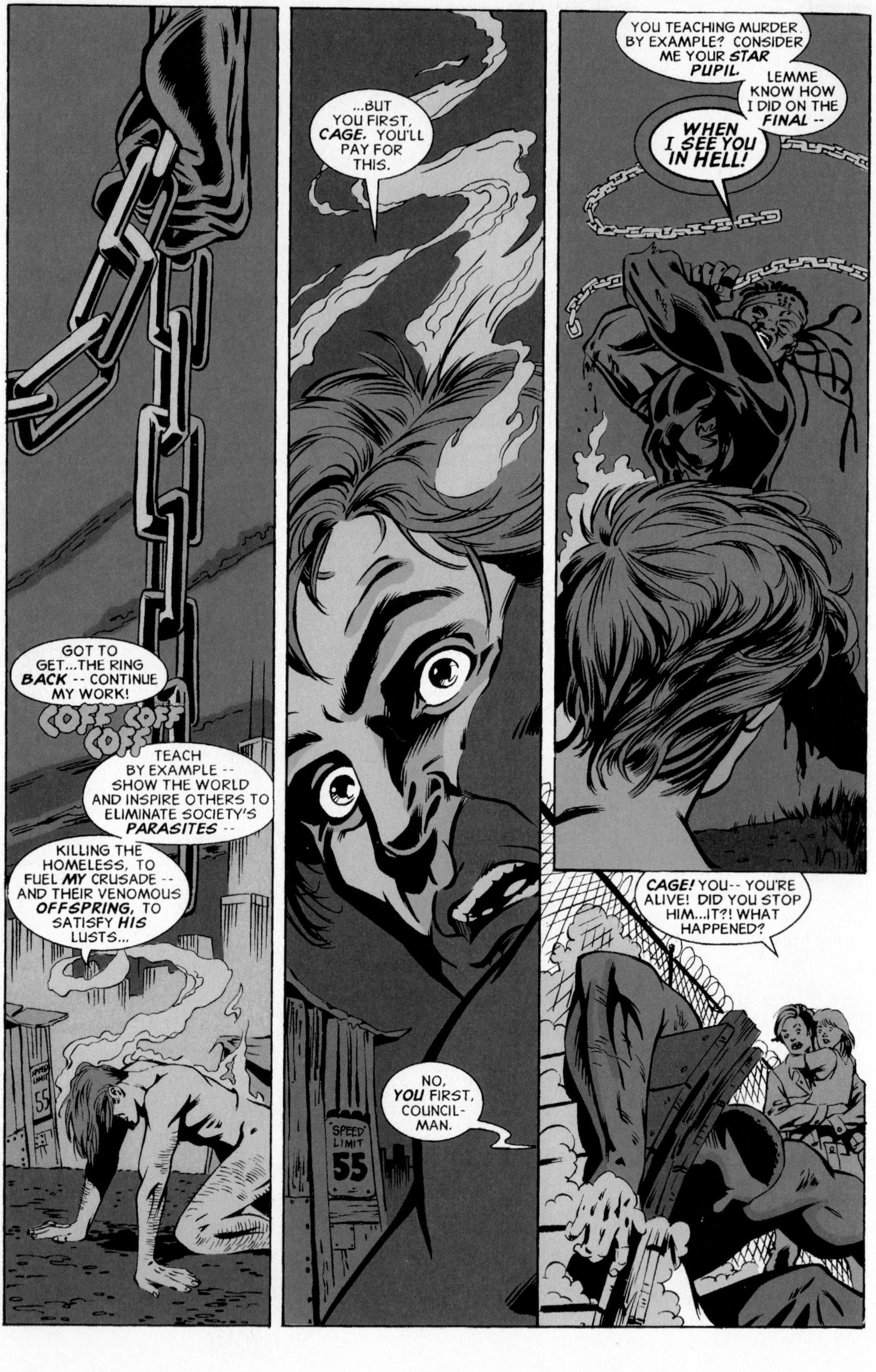
GOT TO GET...THE RING BACK -- CONTINUE MY WORK!
COFF COFF COFF
TEACH BY EXAMPLE -- SHOW THE WORLD AND INSPIRE OTHERS TO ELIMINATE SOCIETY'S PARASITES --
KILLING THE HOMELESS, TO FUEL MY CRUSADE -- AND THEIR VENOMOUS OFFSPRING, TO SATISFY HIS LUSTS...
SPEED LIMIT 55
...BUT YOU FIRST, CAGE. YOU'LL PAY FOR THIS.
NO, YOU FIRST, COUNCIL-MAN.
SPEED LIMIT 55
YOU TEACHING MURDER BY EXAMPLE? CONSIDER ME YOUR STAR PUPIL.
LEMME KNOW HOW I DID ON THE FINAL --
WHEN I SEE YOU IN HELL!
CAGE! YOU-- YOU'RE ALIVE! DID YOU STOP HIM...IT?! WHAT HAPPENED?

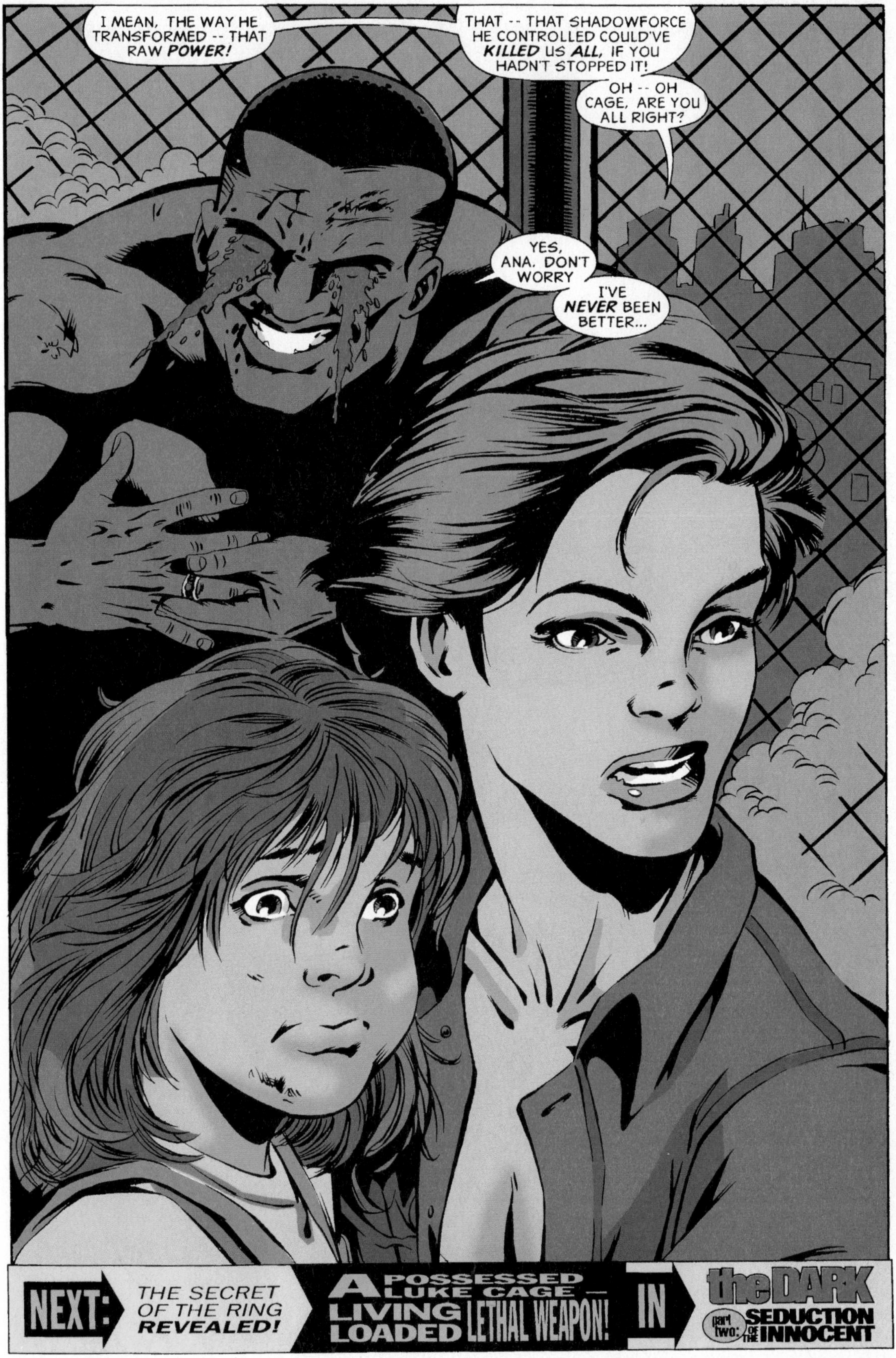
I MEAN, THE WAY HE TRANSFORMED -- THAT RAW POWER!
THAT -- THAT SHADOWFORCE HE CONTROLLED COULD'VE KILLED US ALL, IF YOU HADN'T STOPPED IT!
OH -- OH CAGE, ARE YOU ALL RIGHT?
YES, ANA. DON'T WORRY
I'VE NEVER BEEN BETTER...
NEXT:
THE SECRET OF THE RING REVEALED!
A POSSESSED LUKE CAGE -- LIVING LOADED LETHAL WEAPON!
IN
the DARK
part two: SEDUCTION OF THE INNOCENT

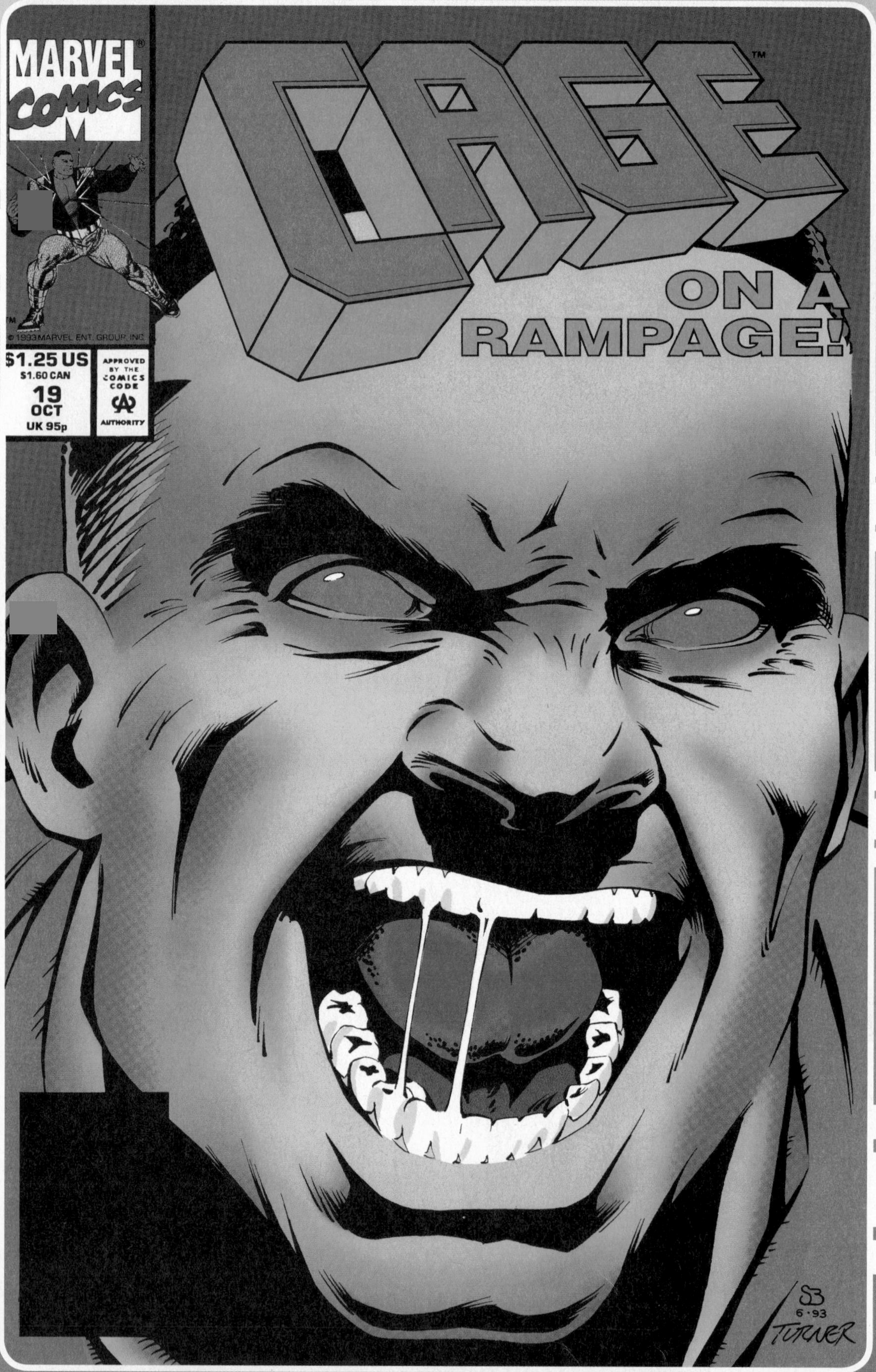
MARVEL COMICS
CAGE
ON A RAMPAGE!
© 1993 MARVEL ENT. GROUP, INC.
$1.25 US
$1.60 CAN
19
OCT
UK 95p
APPROVED BY THE COMICS CODE AUTHORITY
SB 6·93
TURNER

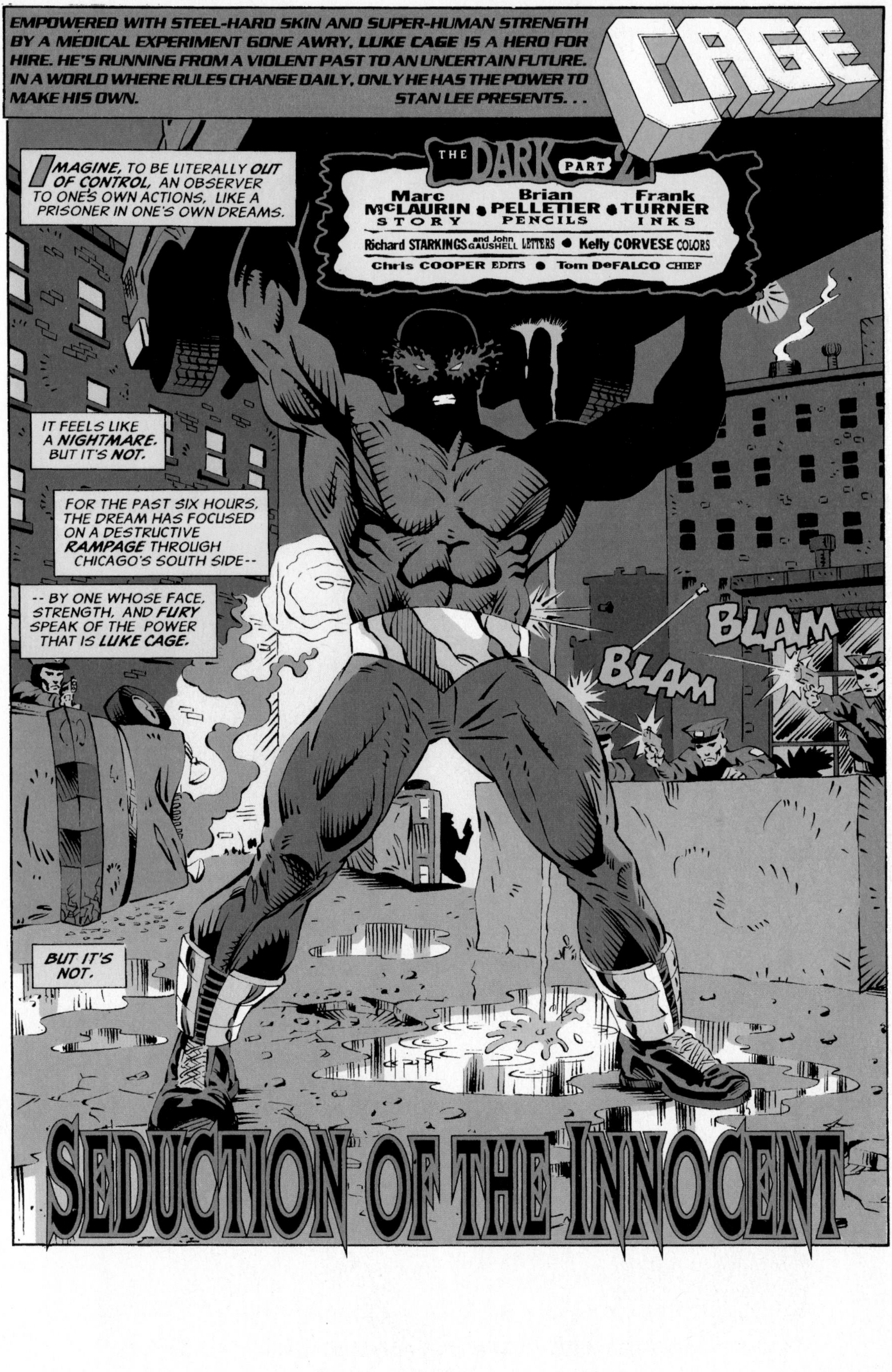

EMPOWERED WITH STEEL-HARD SKIN AND SUPER-HUMAN STRENGTH BY A MEDICAL EXPERIMENT GONE AWRY, LUKE CAGE IS A HERO FOR HIRE. HE'S RUNNING FROM A VIOLENT PAST TO AN UNCERTAIN FUTURE. IN A WORLD WHERE RULES CHANGE DAILY, ONLY HE HAS THE POWER TO MAKE HIS OWN.
STAN LEE PRESENTS. . .
CAGE
THE DARK PART 2
Marc McLAURIN STORY • Brian PELLETIER PENCILS • Frank TURNER INKS
Richard STARKINGS and John GAUSHELL LETTERS • Kelly CORVESE COLORS
Chris COOPER EDITS • Tom DeFALCO CHIEF
IMAGINE, TO BE LITERALLY OUT OF CONTROL, AN OBSERVER TO ONE'S OWN ACTIONS, LIKE A PRISONER IN ONE'S OWN DREAMS.
IT FEELS LIKE A NIGHTMARE. BUT IT'S NOT.
FOR THE PAST SIX HOURS, THE DREAM HAS FOCUSED ON A DESTRUCTIVE RAMPAGE THROUGH CHICAGO'S SOUTH SIDE--
-- BY ONE WHOSE FACE, STRENGTH, AND FURY SPEAK OF THE POWER THAT IS LUKE CAGE.
BLAM
BLAM
BUT IT'S NOT.
SEDUCTION OF THE INNOCENT

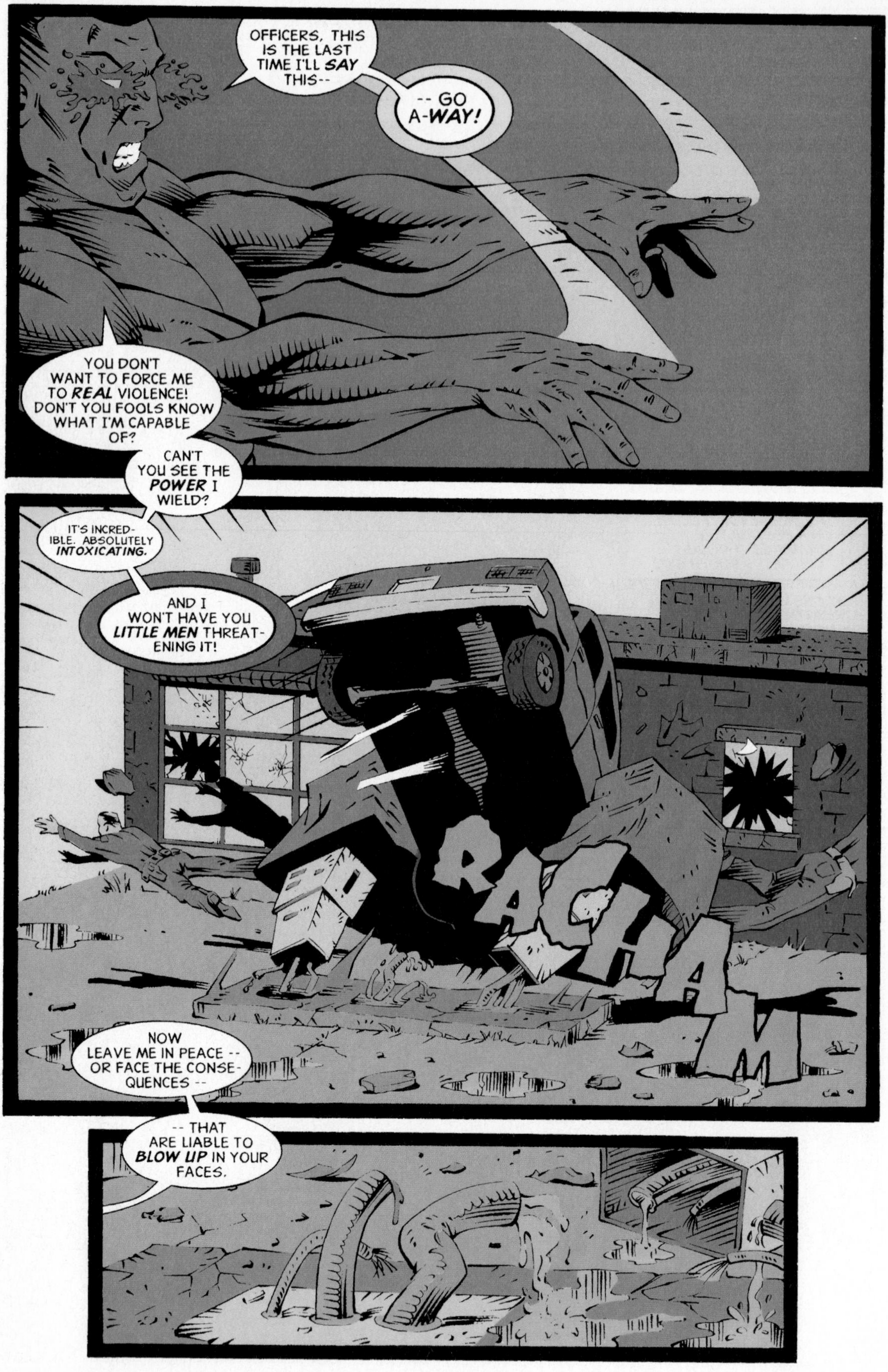

OFFICERS, THIS IS THE LAST TIME I'LL SAY THIS--
-- GO A-WAY!
YOU DON'T WANT TO FORCE ME TO REAL VIOLENCE! DON'T YOU FOOLS KNOW WHAT I'M CAPABLE OF?
CAN'T YOU SEE THE POWER I WIELD?
IT'S INCREDIBLE. ABSOLUTELY INTOXICATING.
AND I WON'T HAVE YOU LITTLE MEN THREATENING IT!
RACHAM
NOW LEAVE ME IN PEACE -- OR FACE THE CONSEQUENCES --
-- THAT ARE LIABLE TO BLOW UP IN YOUR FACES.

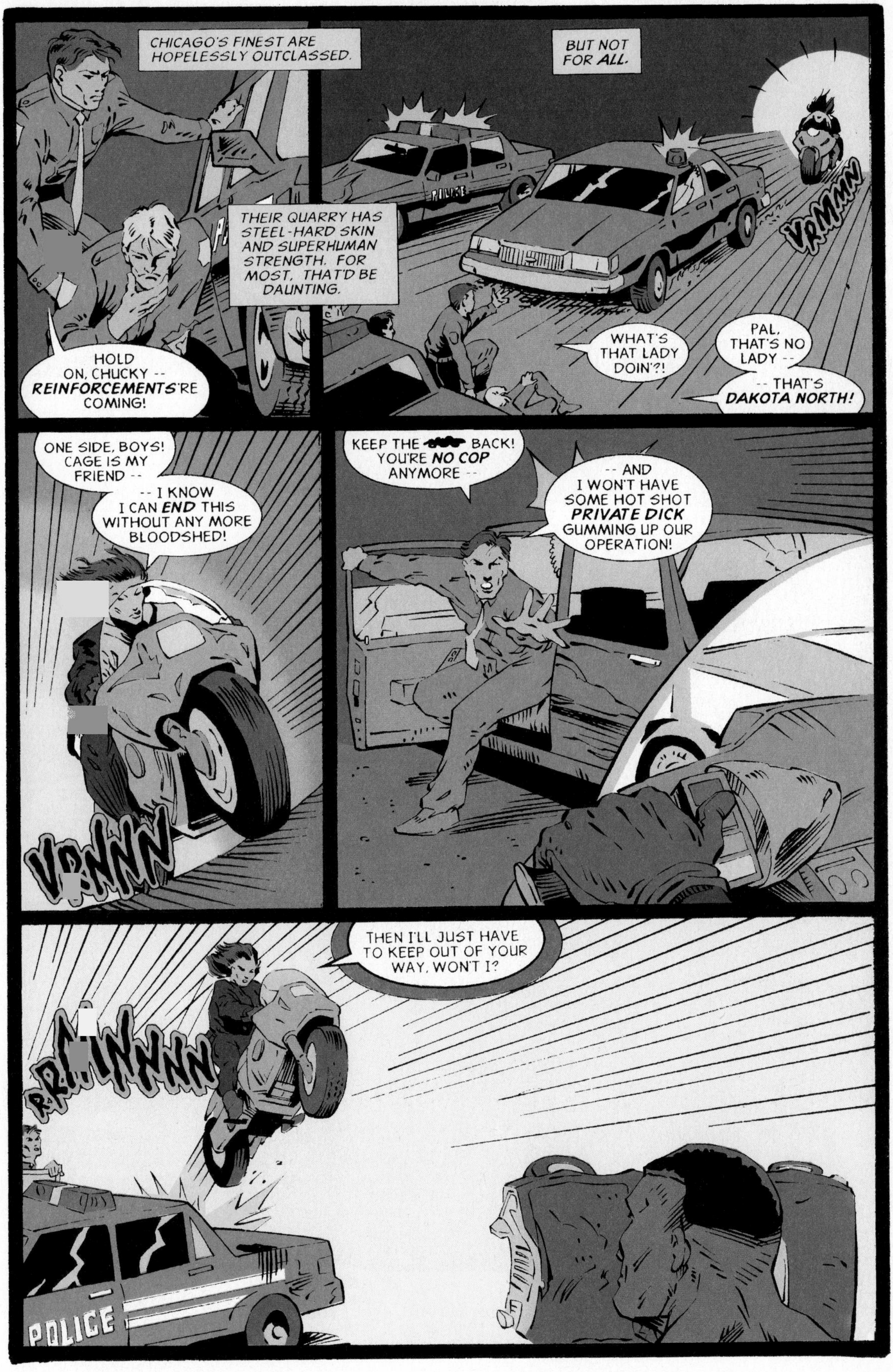
CHICAGO'S FINEST ARE HOPELESSLY OUTCLASSED.
THEIR QUARRY HAS STEEL-HARD SKIN AND SUPERHUMAN STRENGTH. FOR MOST, THAT'D BE DAUNTING.
HOLD ON, CHUCKY -- REINFORCEMENTS'RE COMING!
BUT NOT FOR ALL.
VRMMMN
WHAT'S THAT LADY DOIN'?!
PAL, THAT'S NO LADY --
-- THAT'S DAKOTA NORTH!
ONE SIDE, BOYS! CAGE IS MY FRIEND --
-- I KNOW I CAN END THIS WITHOUT ANY MORE BLOODSHED!
KEEP THE [redacted] BACK! YOU'RE NO COP ANYMORE --
-- AND I WON'T HAVE SOME HOT SHOT PRIVATE DICK GUMMING UP OUR OPERATION!
THEN I'LL JUST HAVE TO KEEP OUT OF YOUR WAY, WON'T I?
POLICE

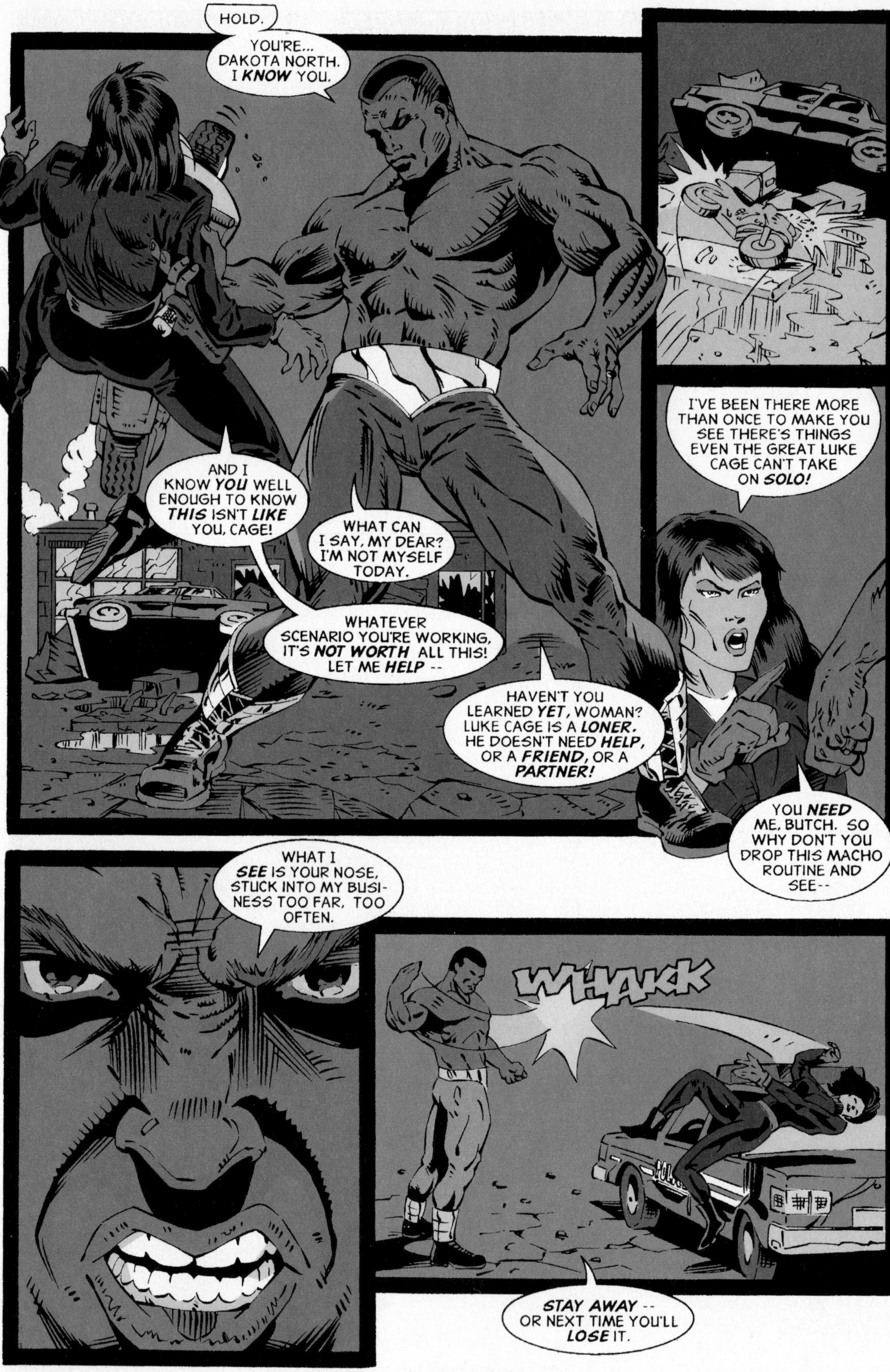
HOLD.
YOU'RE... DAKOTA NORTH. I KNOW YOU.
AND I KNOW YOU WELL ENOUGH TO KNOW THIS ISN'T LIKE YOU, CAGE!
WHAT CAN I SAY, MY DEAR? I'M NOT MYSELF TODAY.
WHATEVER SCENARIO YOU'RE WORKING, IT'S NOT WORTH ALL THIS! LET ME HELP --
HAVEN'T YOU LEARNED YET, WOMAN? LUKE CAGE IS A LONER. HE DOESN'T NEED HELP, OR A FRIEND, OR A PARTNER!
I'VE BEEN THERE MORE THAN ONCE TO MAKE YOU SEE THERE'S THINGS EVEN THE GREAT LUKE CAGE CAN'T TAKE ON SOLO!
YOU NEED ME, BUTCH. SO WHY DON'T YOU DROP THIS MACHO ROUTINE AND SEE--
WHAT I SEE IS YOUR NOSE, STUCK INTO MY BUSINESS TOO FAR, TOO OFTEN.
WHAKK
STAY AWAY -- OR NEXT TIME YOU'LL LOSE IT.

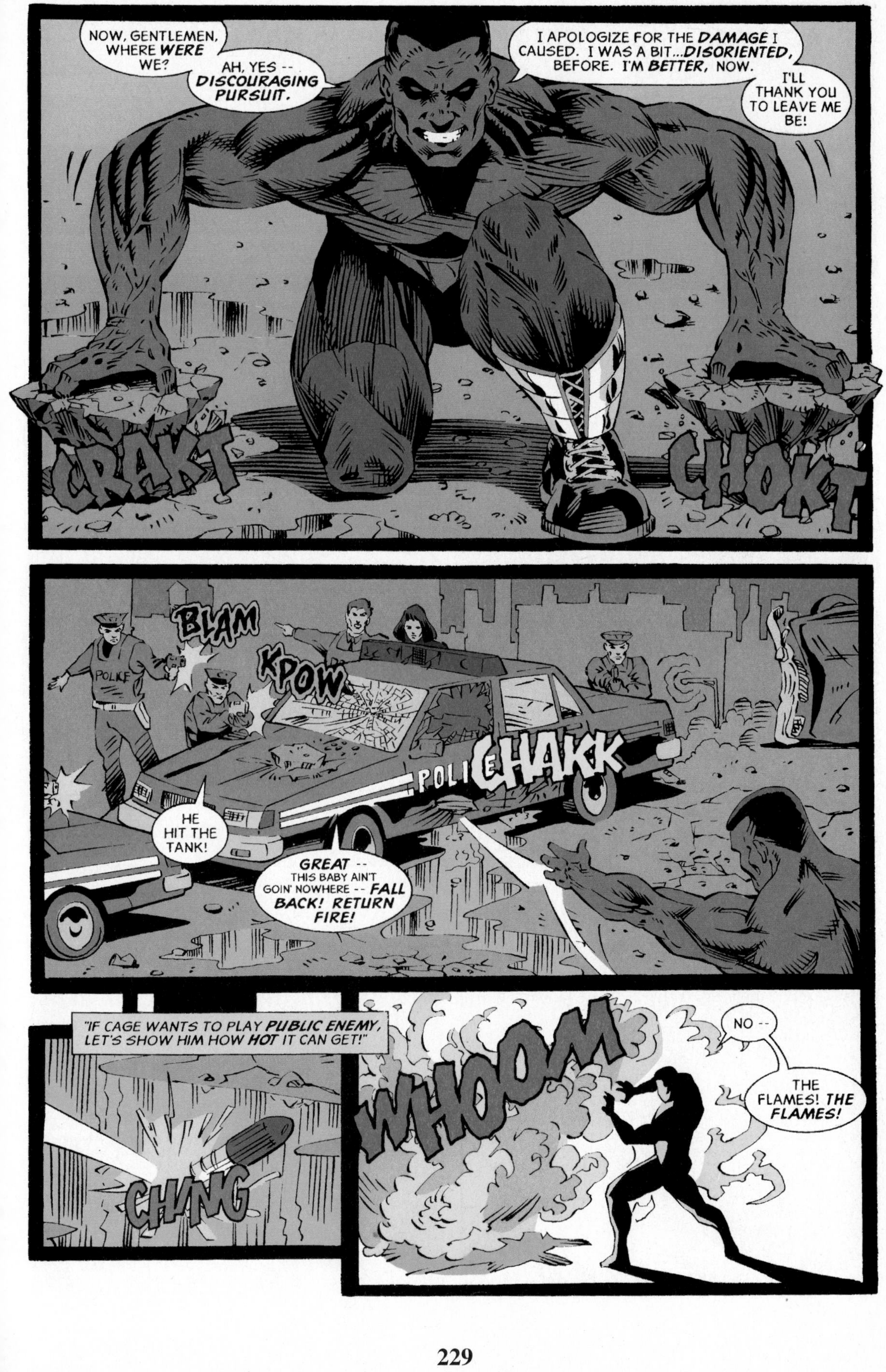
NOW, GENTLEMEN, WHERE WERE WE?
AH, YES -- DISCOURAGING PURSUIT.
I APOLOGIZE FOR THE DAMAGE I CAUSED. I WAS A BIT...DISORIENTED, BEFORE. I'M BETTER, NOW.
I'LL THANK YOU TO LEAVE ME BE!
CRAKT
CHOKT
BLAM
KPOW
CHAKK
HE HIT THE TANK!
GREAT -- THIS BABY AIN'T GOIN' NOWHERE -- FALL BACK! RETURN FIRE!
"IF CAGE WANTS TO PLAY PUBLIC ENEMY, LET'S SHOW HIM HOW HOT IT CAN GET!"
CHING
WHOOM
NO --
THE FLAMES! THE FLAMES!

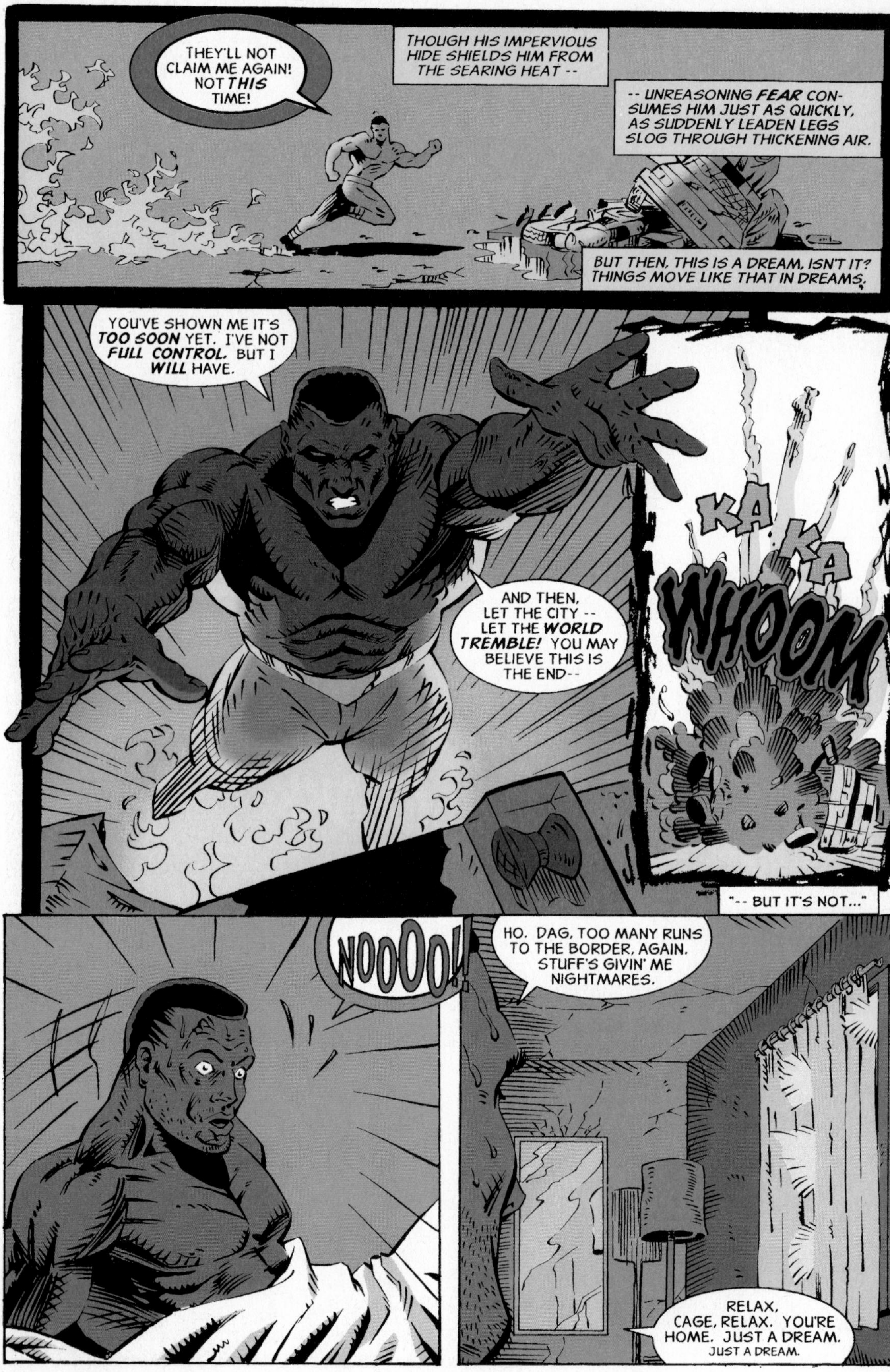
THEY'LL NOT CLAIM ME AGAIN! NOT THIS TIME!
THOUGH HIS IMPERVIOUS HIDE SHIELDS HIM FROM THE SEARING HEAT --
-- UNREASONING FEAR CONSUMES HIM JUST AS QUICKLY, AS SUDDENLY LEADEN LEGS SLOG THROUGH THICKENING AIR.
BUT THEN, THIS IS A DREAM, ISN'T IT? THINGS MOVE LIKE THAT IN DREAMS.
YOU'VE SHOWN ME IT'S TOO SOON YET. I'VE NOT FULL CONTROL. BUT I WILL HAVE.
AND THEN, LET THE CITY -- LET THE WORLD TREMBLE! YOU MAY BELIEVE THIS IS THE END--
KA KA WHOOM
"-- BUT IT'S NOT..."
NOOOO!
HO. DAG, TOO MANY RUNS TO THE BORDER, AGAIN. STUFF'S GIVIN' ME NIGHTMARES.
RELAX, CAGE, RELAX. YOU'RE HOME. JUST A DREAM. JUST A DREAM.

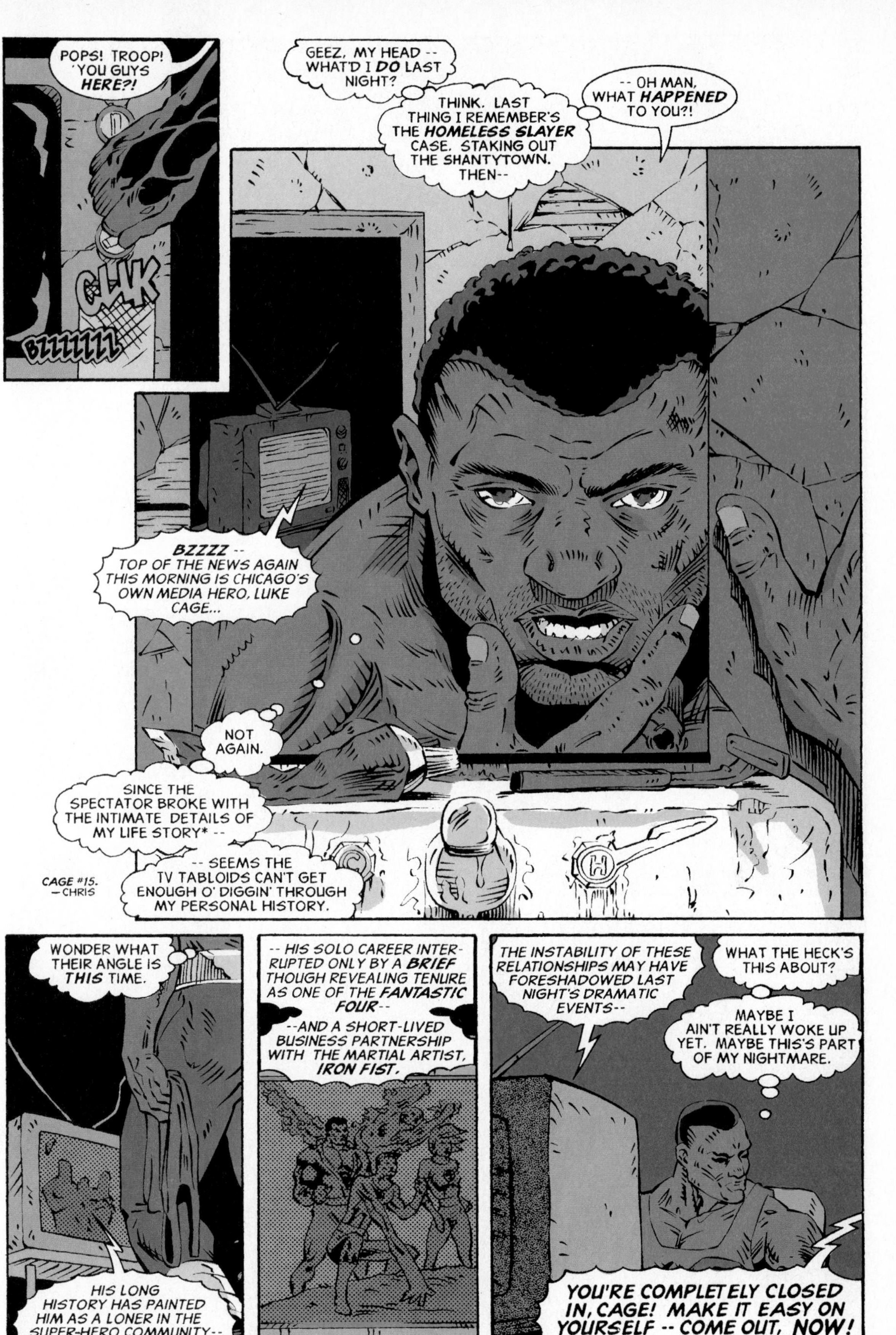
POPS! TROOP! 'YOU GUYS HERE?!
CLIK
BZZZZZZZ
GEEZ, MY HEAD -- WHAT'D I DO LAST NIGHT?
THINK. LAST THING I REMEMBER'S THE HOMELESS SLAYER CASE. STAKING OUT THE SHANTYTOWN. THEN--
-- OH MAN, WHAT HAPPENED TO YOU?!
BZZZZ -- TOP OF THE NEWS AGAIN THIS MORNING IS CHICAGO'S OWN MEDIA HERO, LUKE CAGE...
NOT AGAIN.
SINCE THE SPECTATOR BROKE WITH THE INTIMATE DETAILS OF MY LIFE STORY* --
-- SEEMS THE TV TABLOIDS CAN'T GET ENOUGH O' DIGGIN' THROUGH MY PERSONAL HISTORY.
CAGE #15. —CHRIS
WONDER WHAT THEIR ANGLE IS THIS TIME.
HIS LONG HISTORY HAS PAINTED HIM AS A LONER IN THE SUPER-HERO COMMUNITY--
-- HIS SOLO CAREER INTERRUPTED ONLY BY A BRIEF THOUGH REVEALING TENURE AS ONE OF THE FANTASTIC FOUR--
--AND A SHORT-LIVED BUSINESS PARTNERSHIP WITH THE MARTIAL ARTIST, IRON FIST.
THE INSTABILITY OF THESE RELATIONSHIPS MAY HAVE FORESHADOWED LAST NIGHT'S DRAMATIC EVENTS--
WHAT THE HECK'S THIS ABOUT?
MAYBE I AIN'T REALLY WOKE UP YET. MAYBE THIS'S PART OF MY NIGHTMARE.
YOU'RE COMPLETELY CLOSED IN, CAGE! MAKE IT EASY ON YOURSELF -- COME OUT, NOW!

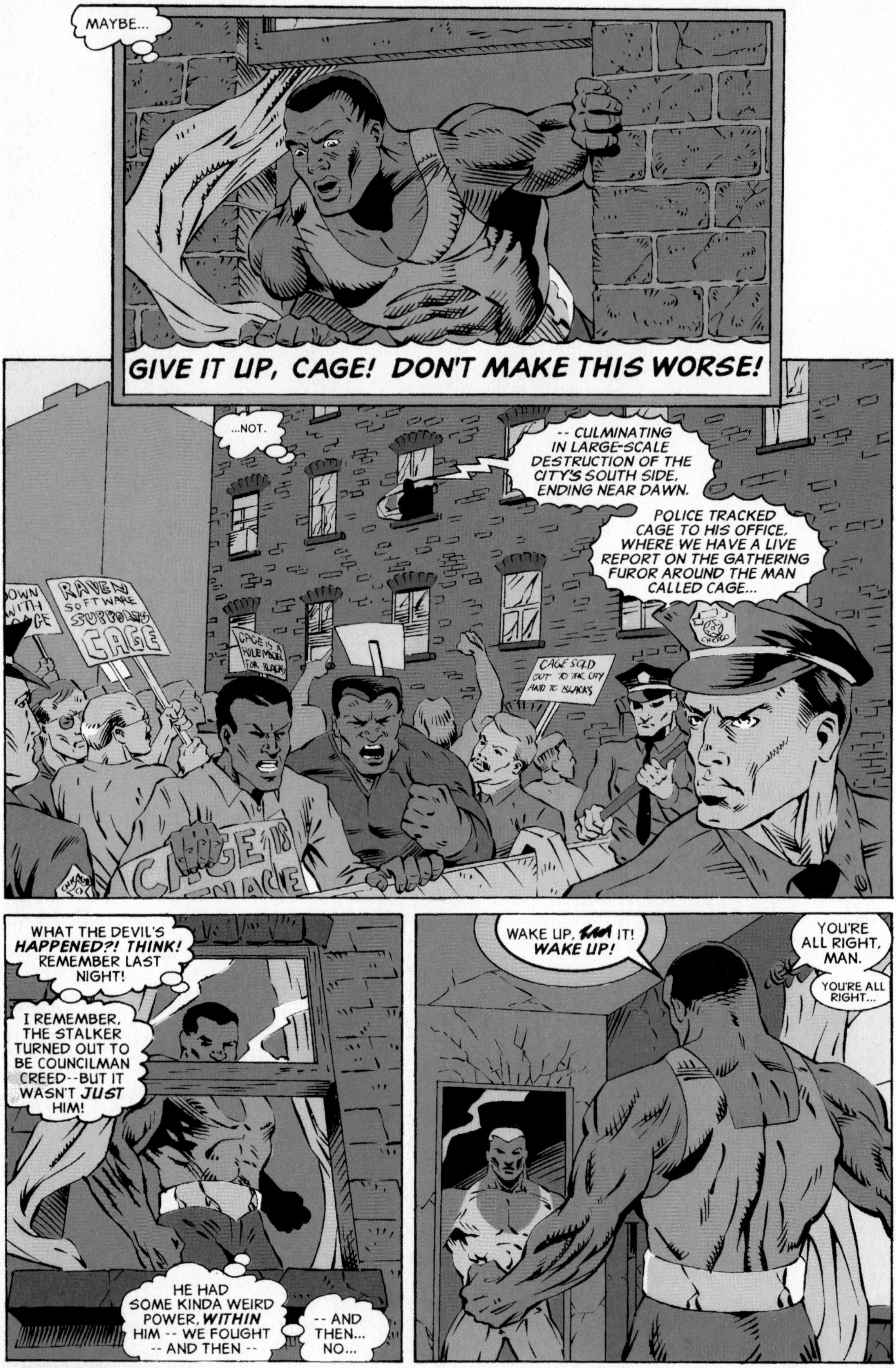
MAYBE...
GIVE IT UP, CAGE! DON'T MAKE THIS WORSE!
...NOT.
-- CULMINATING IN LARGE-SCALE DESTRUCTION OF THE CITY'S SOUTH SIDE, ENDING NEAR DAWN.
POLICE TRACKED CAGE TO HIS OFFICE, WHERE WE HAVE A LIVE REPORT ON THE GATHERING FUROR AROUND THE MAN CALLED CAGE...
RAVEN SOFTWARE SUPPORTS CAGE
CAGE IS A ROLE MODEL FOR BLACKS
CAGE SOLD OUT TO THE CITY AND TO BLACKS
WHAT THE DEVIL'S HAPPENED?! THINK! REMEMBER LAST NIGHT!
I REMEMBER, THE STALKER TURNED OUT TO BE COUNCILMAN CREED--BUT IT WASN'T JUST HIM!
HE HAD SOME KINDA WEIRD POWER, WITHIN HIM -- WE FOUGHT -- AND THEN --
-- AND THEN... NO...
WAKE UP, IT! WAKE UP!
YOU'RE ALL RIGHT, MAN.
YOU'RE ALL RIGHT...

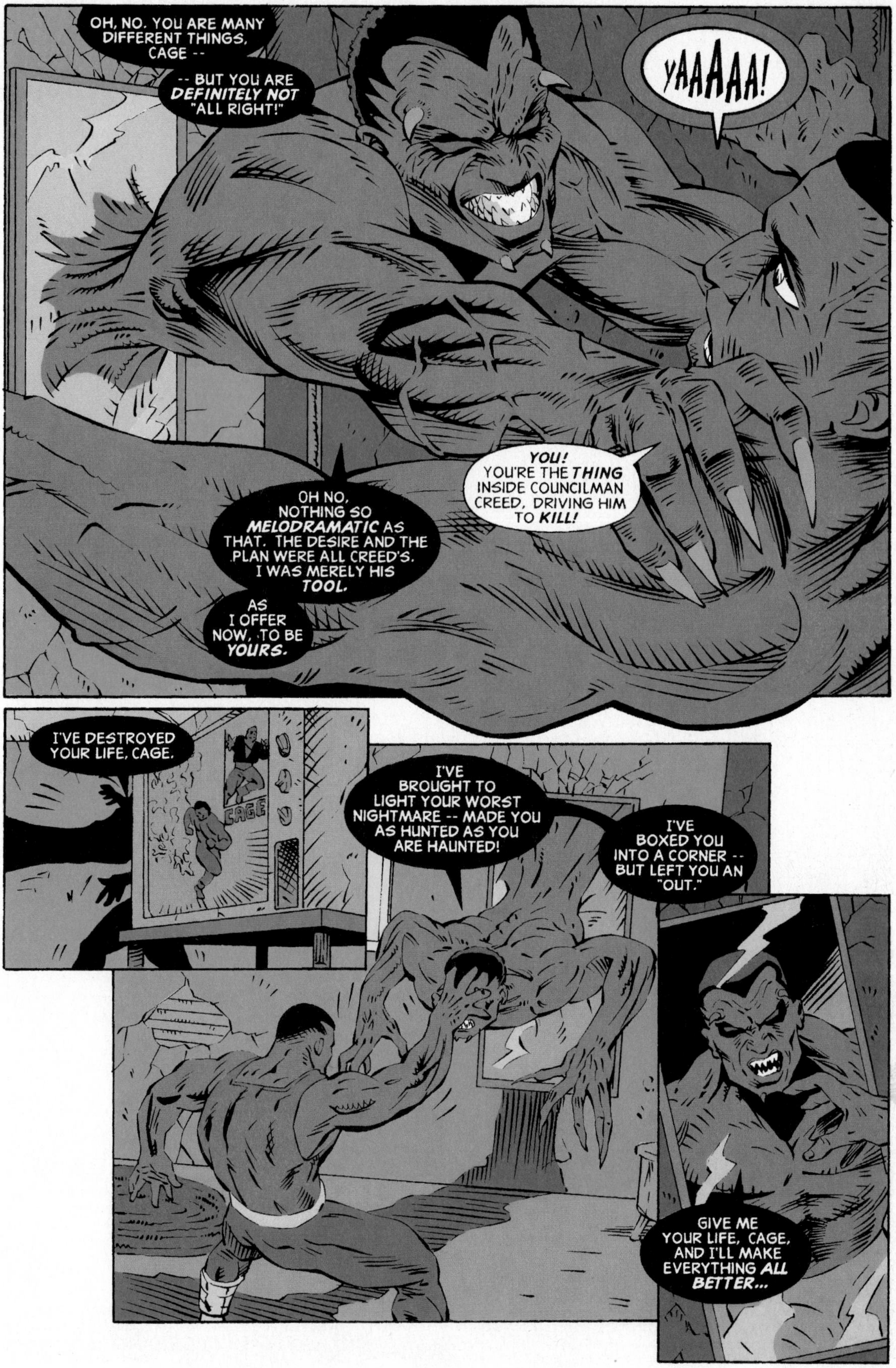
OH, NO. YOU ARE MANY DIFFERENT THINGS, CAGE --
-- BUT YOU ARE DEFINITELY NOT "ALL RIGHT!"
yAAAAA!
YOU! YOU'RE THE THING INSIDE COUNCILMAN CREED, DRIVING HIM TO KILL!
OH NO, NOTHING SO MELODRAMATIC AS THAT. THE DESIRE AND THE PLAN WERE ALL CREED'S. I WAS MERELY HIS TOOL.
AS I OFFER NOW, TO BE YOURS.
I'VE DESTROYED YOUR LIFE, CAGE.
CAGE
I'VE BROUGHT TO LIGHT YOUR WORST NIGHTMARE -- MADE YOU AS HUNTED AS YOU ARE HAUNTED!
I'VE BOXED YOU INTO A CORNER -- BUT LEFT YOU AN "OUT."
GIVE ME YOUR LIFE, CAGE, AND I'LL MAKE EVERYTHING ALL BETTER...

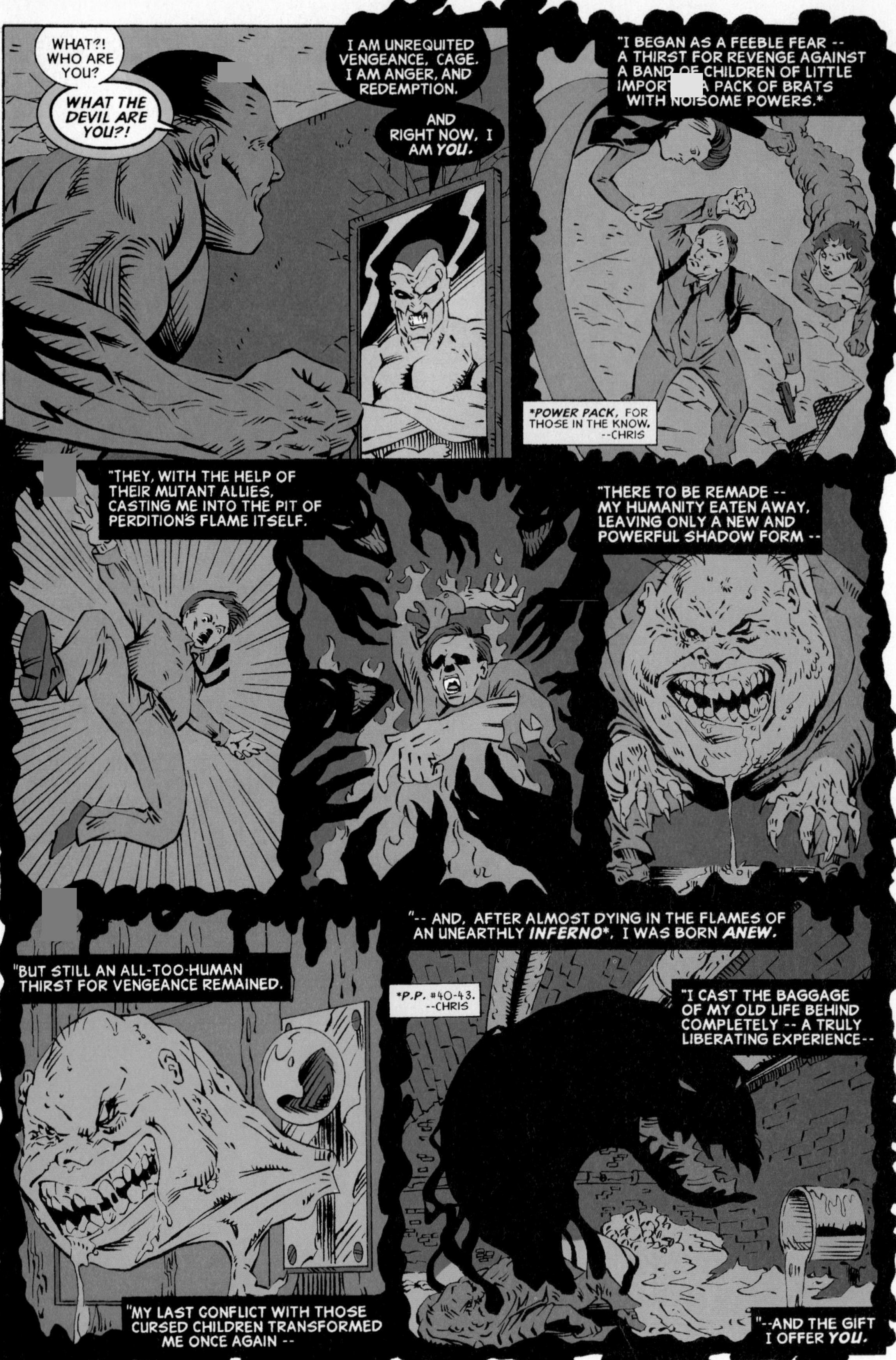
WHAT?! WHO ARE YOU?
WHAT THE DEVIL ARE YOU?!
I AM UNREQUITED VENGEANCE, CAGE. I AM ANGER, AND REDEMPTION.
AND RIGHT NOW, I AM YOU.
"I BEGAN AS A FEEBLE FEAR -- A THIRST FOR REVENGE AGAINST A BAND OF CHILDREN OF LITTLE IMPORT A PACK OF BRATS WITH NOISOME POWERS.*
*POWER PACK, FOR THOSE IN THE KNOW. --CHRIS
"THEY, WITH THE HELP OF THEIR MUTANT ALLIES, CASTING ME INTO THE PIT OF PERDITION'S FLAME ITSELF.
"THERE TO BE REMADE -- MY HUMANITY EATEN AWAY, LEAVING ONLY A NEW AND POWERFUL SHADOW FORM --
"BUT STILL AN ALL-TOO-HUMAN THIRST FOR VENGEANCE REMAINED.
"MY LAST CONFLICT WITH THOSE CURSED CHILDREN TRANSFORMED ME ONCE AGAIN --
"-- AND, AFTER ALMOST DYING IN THE FLAMES OF AN UNEARTHLY INFERNO*, I WAS BORN ANEW.
*P.P. #40-43. --CHRIS
"I CAST THE BAGGAGE OF MY OLD LIFE BEHIND COMPLETELY -- A TRULY LIBERATING EXPERIENCE--
"--AND THE GIFT I OFFER YOU.

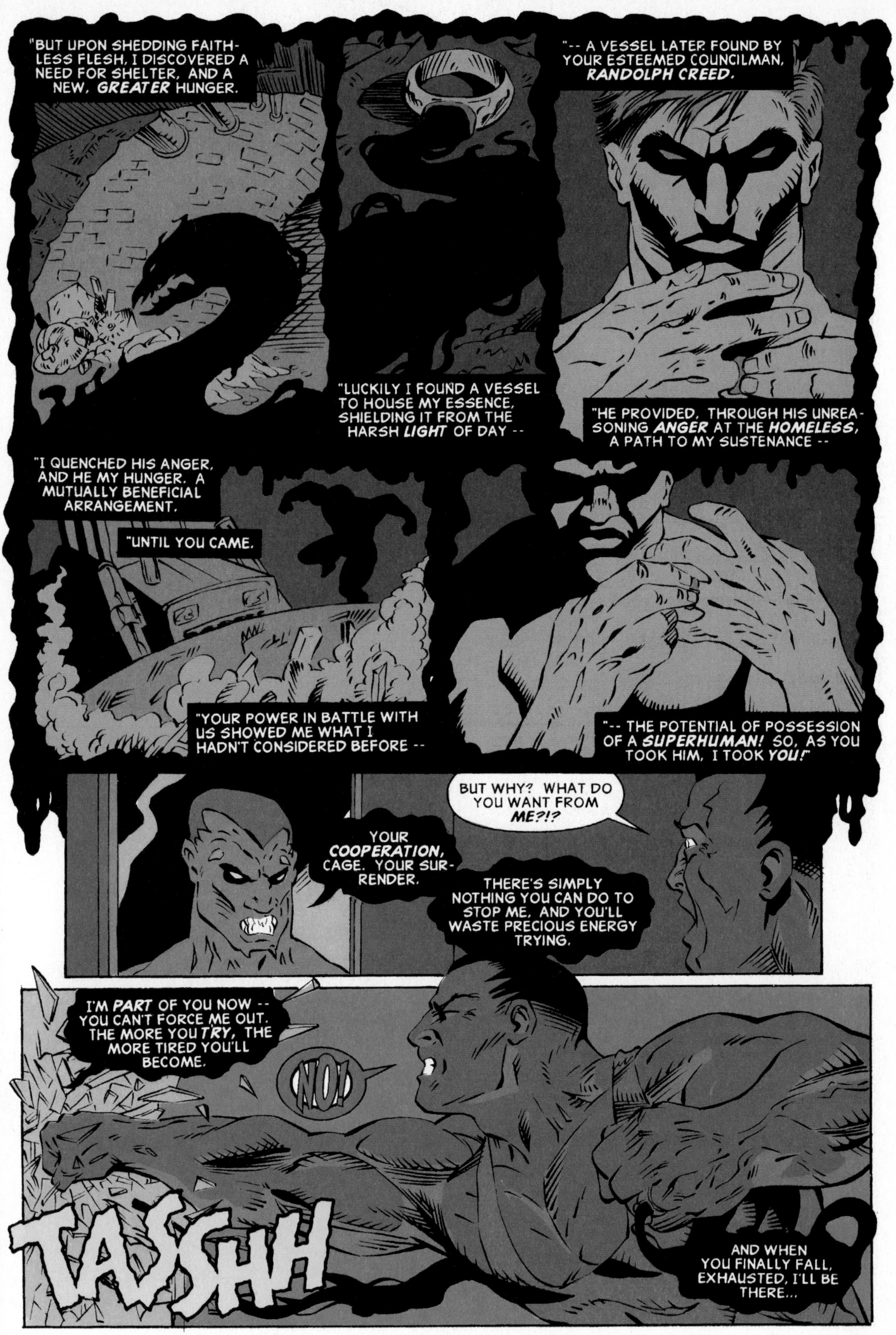
"BUT UPON SHEDDING FAITH-LESS FLESH, I DISCOVERED A NEED FOR SHELTER, AND A NEW, GREATER HUNGER.
"LUCKILY I FOUND A VESSEL TO HOUSE MY ESSENCE, SHIELDING IT FROM THE HARSH LIGHT OF DAY --
"-- A VESSEL LATER FOUND BY YOUR ESTEEMED COUNCILMAN, RANDOLPH CREED.
"HE PROVIDED, THROUGH HIS UNREA-SONING ANGER AT THE HOMELESS, A PATH TO MY SUSTENANCE --
"I QUENCHED HIS ANGER, AND HE MY HUNGER. A MUTUALLY BENEFICIAL ARRANGEMENT.
"UNTIL YOU CAME.
"YOUR POWER IN BATTLE WITH US SHOWED ME WHAT I HADN'T CONSIDERED BEFORE --
"-- THE POTENTIAL OF POSSESSION OF A SUPERHUMAN! SO, AS YOU TOOK HIM, I TOOK YOU!"
BUT WHY? WHAT DO YOU WANT FROM ME?!?
YOUR COOPERATION, CAGE. YOUR SUR-RENDER.
THERE'S SIMPLY NOTHING YOU CAN DO TO STOP ME, AND YOU'LL WASTE PRECIOUS ENERGY TRYING.
I'M PART OF YOU NOW -- YOU CAN'T FORCE ME OUT. THE MORE YOU TRY, THE MORE TIRED YOU'LL BECOME.
NO!
TASHH
AND WHEN YOU FINALLY FALL, EXHAUSTED, I'LL BE THERE...

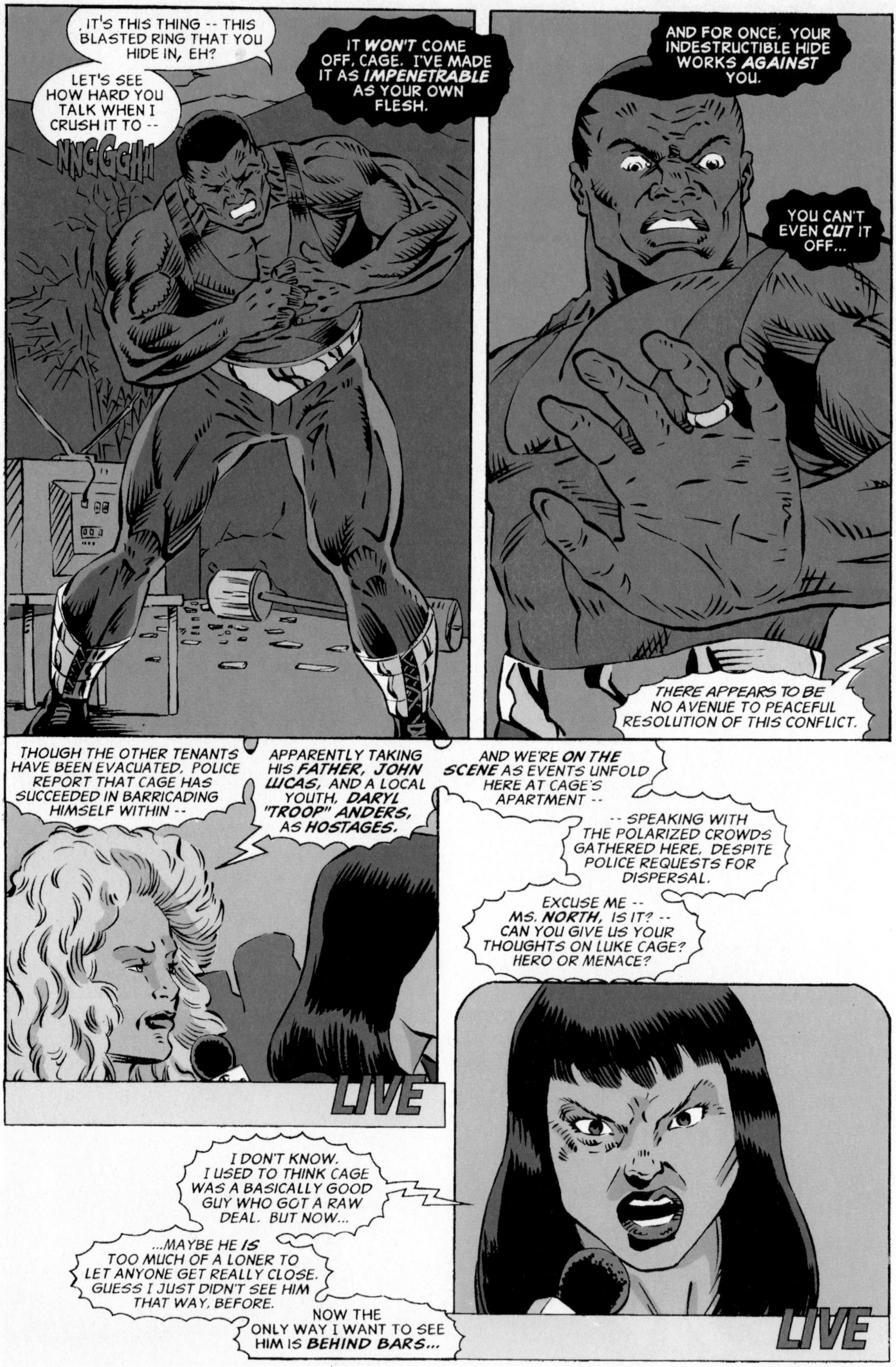
IT'S THIS THING -- THIS BLASTED RING THAT YOU HIDE IN, EH?
LET'S SEE HOW HARD YOU TALK WHEN I CRUSH IT TO --
NNGGGHH
IT WON'T COME OFF, CAGE. I'VE MADE IT AS IMPENETRABLE AS YOUR OWN FLESH.
AND FOR ONCE, YOUR INDESTRUCTIBLE HIDE WORKS AGAINST YOU.
YOU CAN'T EVEN CUT IT OFF...
THERE APPEARS TO BE NO AVENUE TO PEACEFUL RESOLUTION OF THIS CONFLICT.
THOUGH THE OTHER TENANTS HAVE BEEN EVACUATED, POLICE REPORT THAT CAGE HAS SUCCEEDED IN BARRICADING HIMSELF WITHIN --
APPARENTLY TAKING HIS FATHER, JOHN LUCAS, AND A LOCAL YOUTH, DARYL "TROOP" ANDERS, AS HOSTAGES.
AND WE'RE ON THE SCENE AS EVENTS UNFOLD HERE AT CAGE'S APARTMENT --
-- SPEAKING WITH THE POLARIZED CROWDS GATHERED HERE, DESPITE POLICE REQUESTS FOR DISPERSAL.
EXCUSE ME -- MS. NORTH, IS IT? -- CAN YOU GIVE US YOUR THOUGHTS ON LUKE CAGE? HERO OR MENACE?
LIVE
I DON'T KNOW. I USED TO THINK CAGE WAS A BASICALLY GOOD GUY WHO GOT A RAW DEAL. BUT NOW...
...MAYBE HE IS TOO MUCH OF A LONER TO LET ANYONE GET REALLY CLOSE. GUESS I JUST DIDN'T SEE HIM THAT WAY, BEFORE.
NOW THE ONLY WAY I WANT TO SEE HIM IS BEHIND BARS...
LIVE

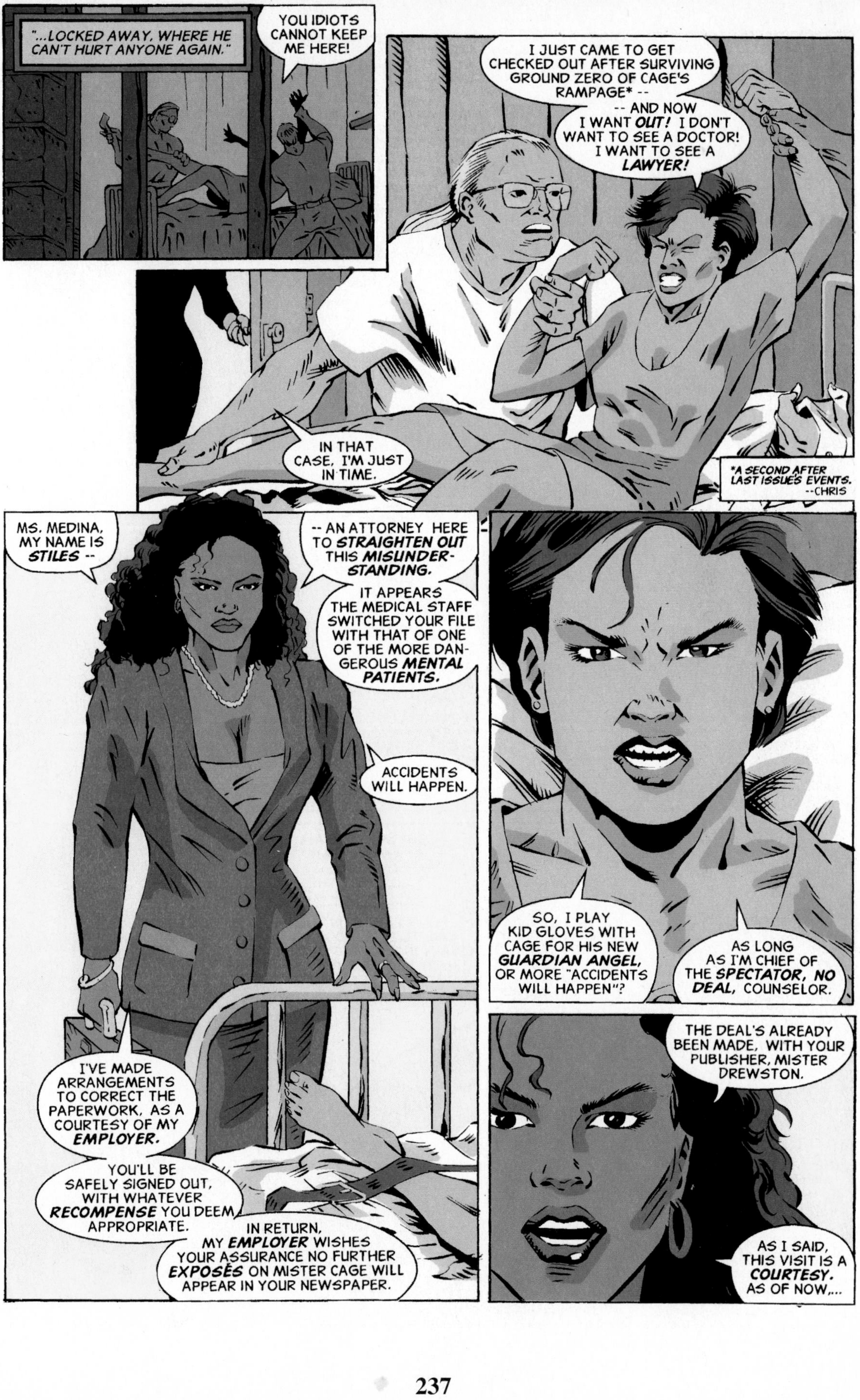
"...LOCKED AWAY, WHERE HE CAN'T HURT ANYONE AGAIN."
YOU IDIOTS CANNOT KEEP ME HERE!
I JUST CAME TO GET CHECKED OUT AFTER SURVIVING GROUND ZERO OF CAGE'S RAMPAGE* --
-- AND NOW I WANT OUT! I DON'T WANT TO SEE A DOCTOR! I WANT TO SEE A LAWYER!
IN THAT CASE, I'M JUST IN TIME.
*A SECOND AFTER LAST ISSUE'S EVENTS. --CHRIS
MS. MEDINA, MY NAME IS STILES --
-- AN ATTORNEY HERE TO STRAIGHTEN OUT THIS MISUNDER-STANDING.
IT APPEARS THE MEDICAL STAFF SWITCHED YOUR FILE WITH THAT OF ONE OF THE MORE DAN-GEROUS MENTAL PATIENTS.
ACCIDENTS WILL HAPPEN.
I'VE MADE ARRANGEMENTS TO CORRECT THE PAPERWORK, AS A COURTESY OF MY EMPLOYER.
YOU'LL BE SAFELY SIGNED OUT, WITH WHATEVER RECOMPENSE YOU DEEM APPROPRIATE.
IN RETURN, MY EMPLOYER WISHES YOUR ASSURANCE NO FURTHER EXPOSÉS ON MISTER CAGE WILL APPEAR IN YOUR NEWSPAPER.
SO, I PLAY KID GLOVES WITH CAGE FOR HIS NEW GUARDIAN ANGEL, OR MORE "ACCIDENTS WILL HAPPEN"?
AS LONG AS I'M CHIEF OF THE SPECTATOR, NO DEAL, COUNSELOR.
THE DEAL'S ALREADY BEEN MADE, WITH YOUR PUBLISHER, MISTER DREWSTON.
AS I SAID, THIS VISIT IS A COURTESY. AS OF NOW,...

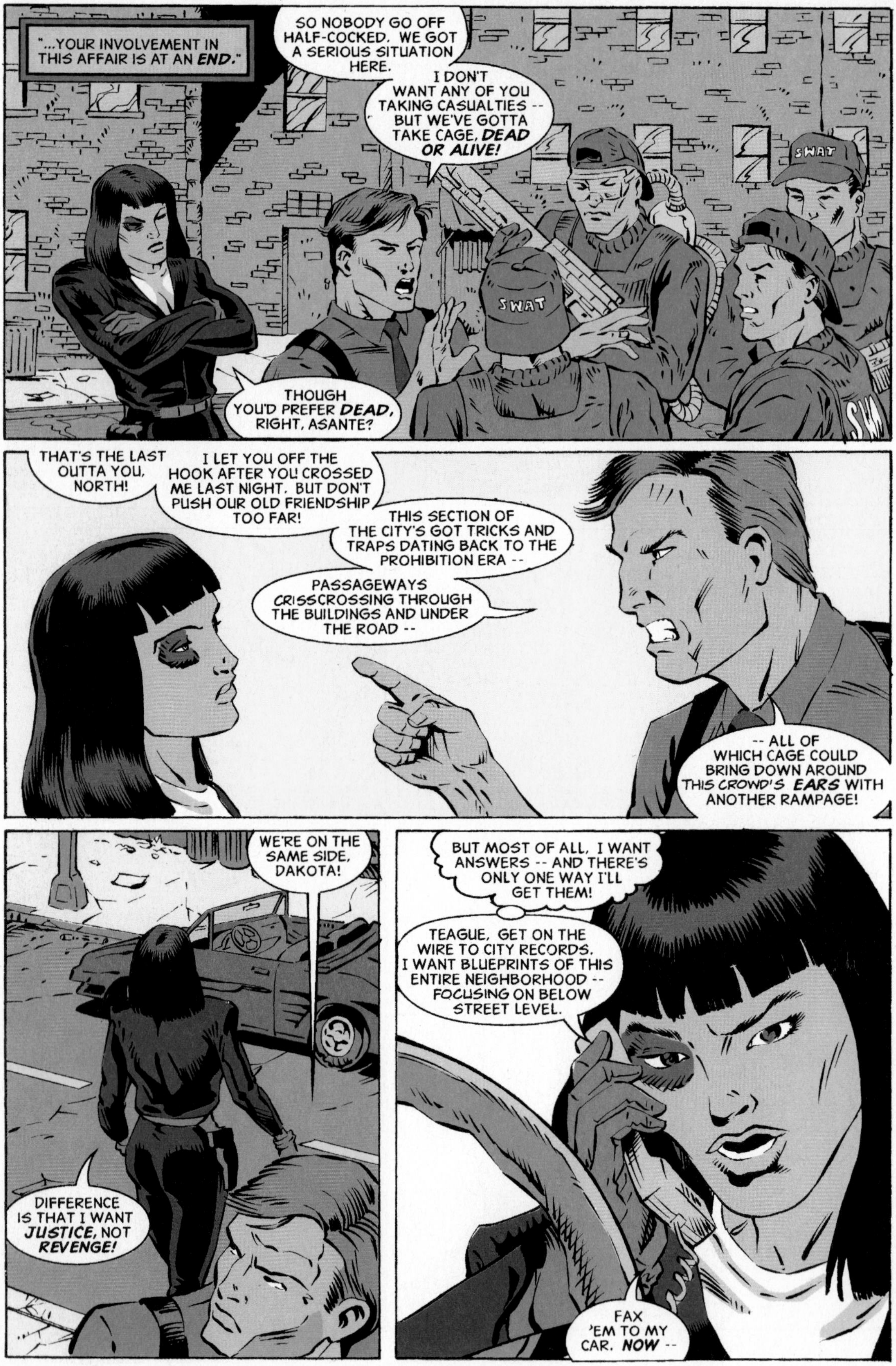
"...YOUR INVOLVEMENT IN THIS AFFAIR IS AT AN *END.*"
SO NOBODY GO OFF HALF-COCKED. WE GOT A SERIOUS SITUATION HERE.
I DON'T WANT ANY OF YOU TAKING CASUALTIES -- BUT WE'VE GOTTA TAKE CAGE, *DEAD OR ALIVE!*
SWAT
SWAT
THOUGH YOU'D PREFER *DEAD,* RIGHT, ASANTE?
THAT'S THE LAST OUTTA YOU, NORTH!
I LET YOU OFF THE HOOK AFTER YOU CROSSED ME LAST NIGHT. BUT DON'T PUSH OUR OLD FRIENDSHIP TOO FAR!
THIS SECTION OF THE CITY'S GOT TRICKS AND TRAPS DATING BACK TO THE PROHIBITION ERA --
PASSAGEWAYS CRISSCROSSING THROUGH THE BUILDINGS AND UNDER THE ROAD --
-- ALL OF WHICH CAGE COULD BRING DOWN AROUND THIS CROWD'S *EARS* WITH ANOTHER RAMPAGE!
WE'RE ON THE SAME SIDE, DAKOTA!
DIFFERENCE IS THAT I WANT *JUSTICE,* NOT *REVENGE!*
BUT MOST OF ALL, I WANT ANSWERS -- AND THERE'S ONLY ONE WAY I'LL GET THEM!
TEAGUE, GET ON THE WIRE TO CITY RECORDS. I WANT BLUEPRINTS OF THIS ENTIRE NEIGHBORHOOD -- FOCUSING ON BELOW STREET LEVEL.
FAX 'EM TO MY CAR. *NOW* --

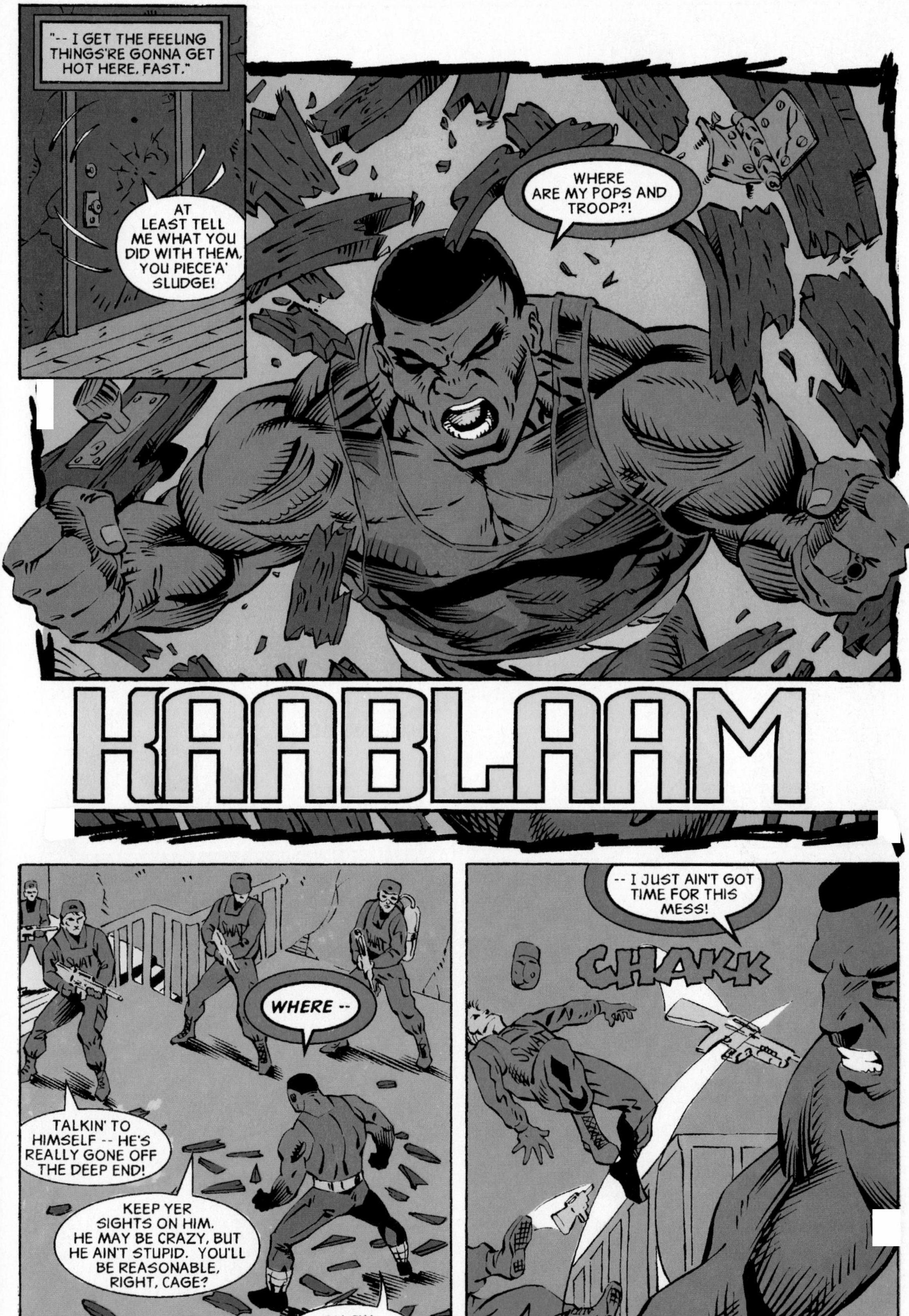
"-- I GET THE FEELING THINGS'RE GONNA GET HOT HERE, FAST."
AT LEAST TELL ME WHAT YOU DID WITH THEM, YOU PIECE'A' SLUDGE!
WHERE ARE MY POPS AND TROOP?!
KAABLAAM
WHERE --
TALKIN' TO HIMSELF -- HE'S REALLY GONE OFF THE DEEP END!
KEEP YER SIGHTS ON HIM. HE MAY BE CRAZY, BUT HE AIN'T STUPID. YOU'LL BE REASONABLE, RIGHT, CAGE?
OH, I'M REASONABLE --
-- I JUST AIN'T GOT TIME FOR THIS MESS!
CHAKK

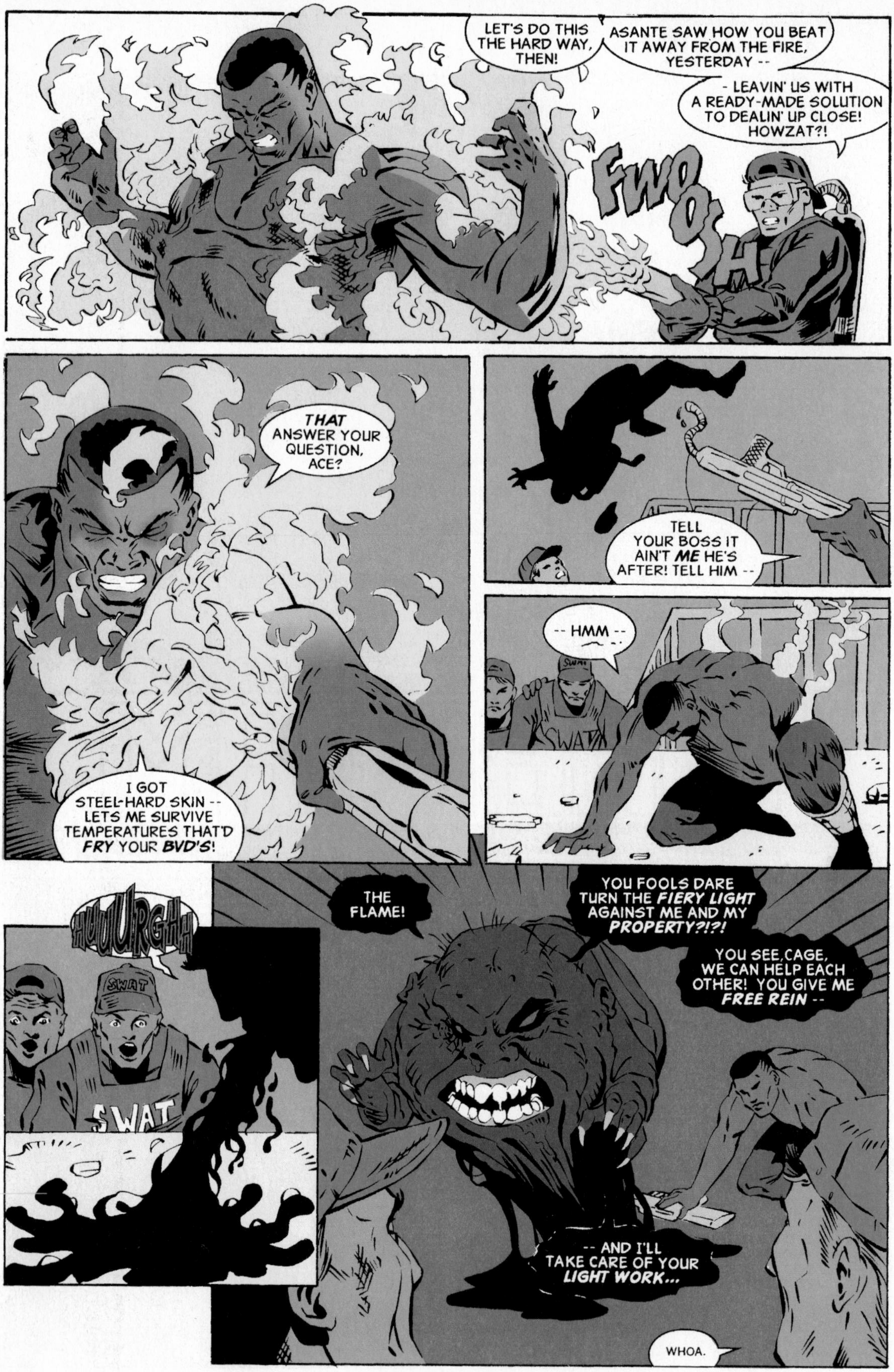
LET'S DO THIS THE HARD WAY, THEN!
ASANTE SAW HOW YOU BEAT IT AWAY FROM THE FIRE, YESTERDAY --
- LEAVIN' US WITH A READY-MADE SOLUTION TO DEALIN' UP CLOSE! HOWZAT?!
FWOOSH
THAT ANSWER YOUR QUESTION, ACE?
I GOT STEEL-HARD SKIN -- LETS ME SURVIVE TEMPERATURES THAT'D FRY YOUR BVD'S!
TELL YOUR BOSS IT AIN'T ME HE'S AFTER! TELL HIM --
-- HMM --
HUUURGHH
THE FLAME!
YOU FOOLS DARE TURN THE FIERY LIGHT AGAINST ME AND MY PROPERTY?!?!
YOU SEE, CAGE, WE CAN HELP EACH OTHER! YOU GIVE ME FREE REIN --
-- AND I'LL TAKE CARE OF YOUR LIGHT WORK...
WHOA.

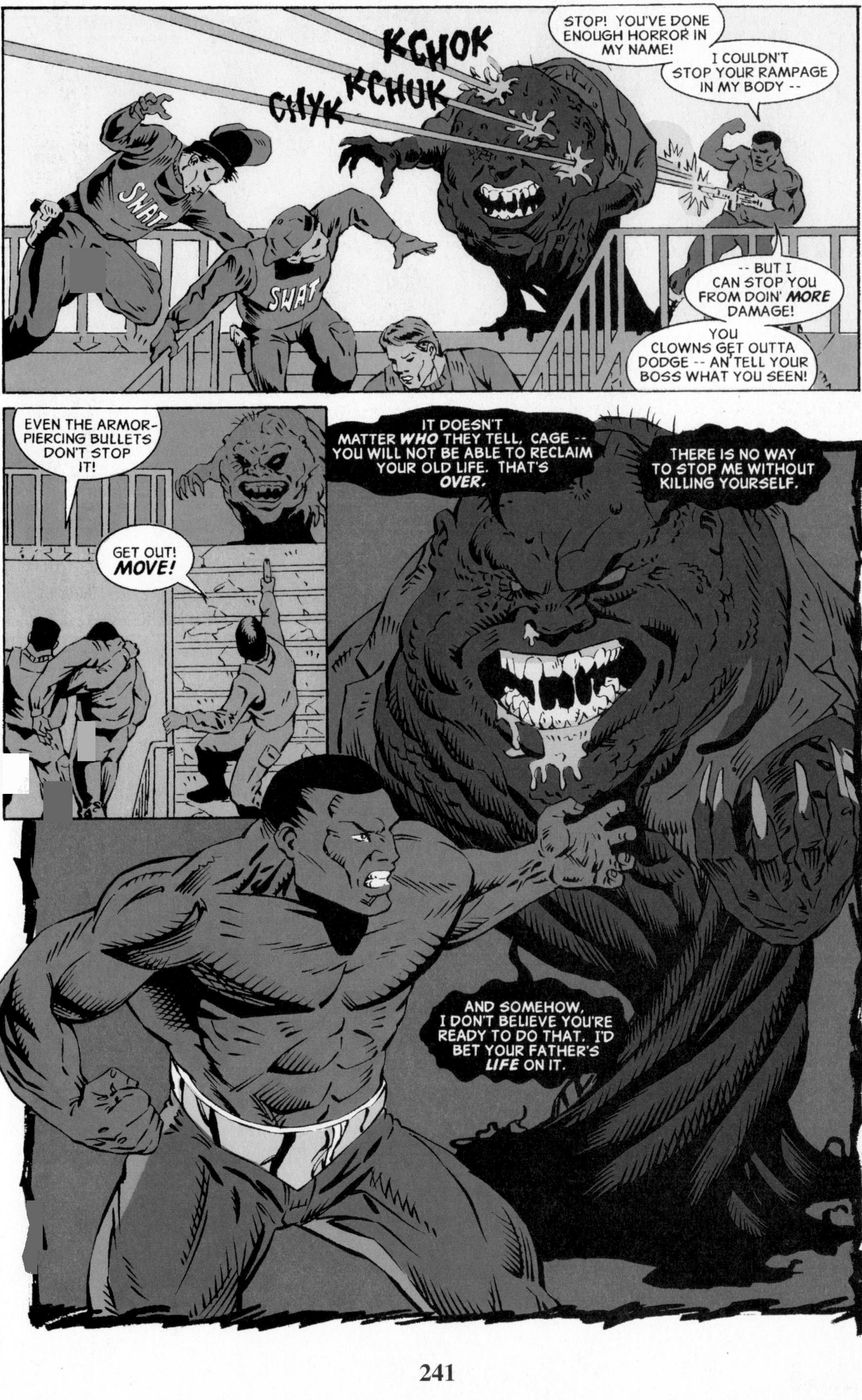
KCHOK
CHYK
KCHUK
STOP! YOU'VE DONE ENOUGH HORROR IN MY NAME!
I COULDN'T STOP YOUR RAMPAGE IN MY BODY --
-- BUT I CAN STOP YOU FROM DOIN' MORE DAMAGE!
YOU CLOWNS GET OUTTA DODGE -- AN' TELL YOUR BOSS WHAT YOU SEEN!
SWAT
SWAT
EVEN THE ARMOR-PIERCING BULLETS DON'T STOP IT!
GET OUT! MOVE!
IT DOESN'T MATTER WHO THEY TELL, CAGE -- YOU WILL NOT BE ABLE TO RECLAIM YOUR OLD LIFE. THAT'S OVER.
THERE IS NO WAY TO STOP ME WITHOUT KILLING YOURSELF.
AND SOMEHOW, I DON'T BELIEVE YOU'RE READY TO DO THAT. I'D BET YOUR FATHER'S LIFE ON IT.

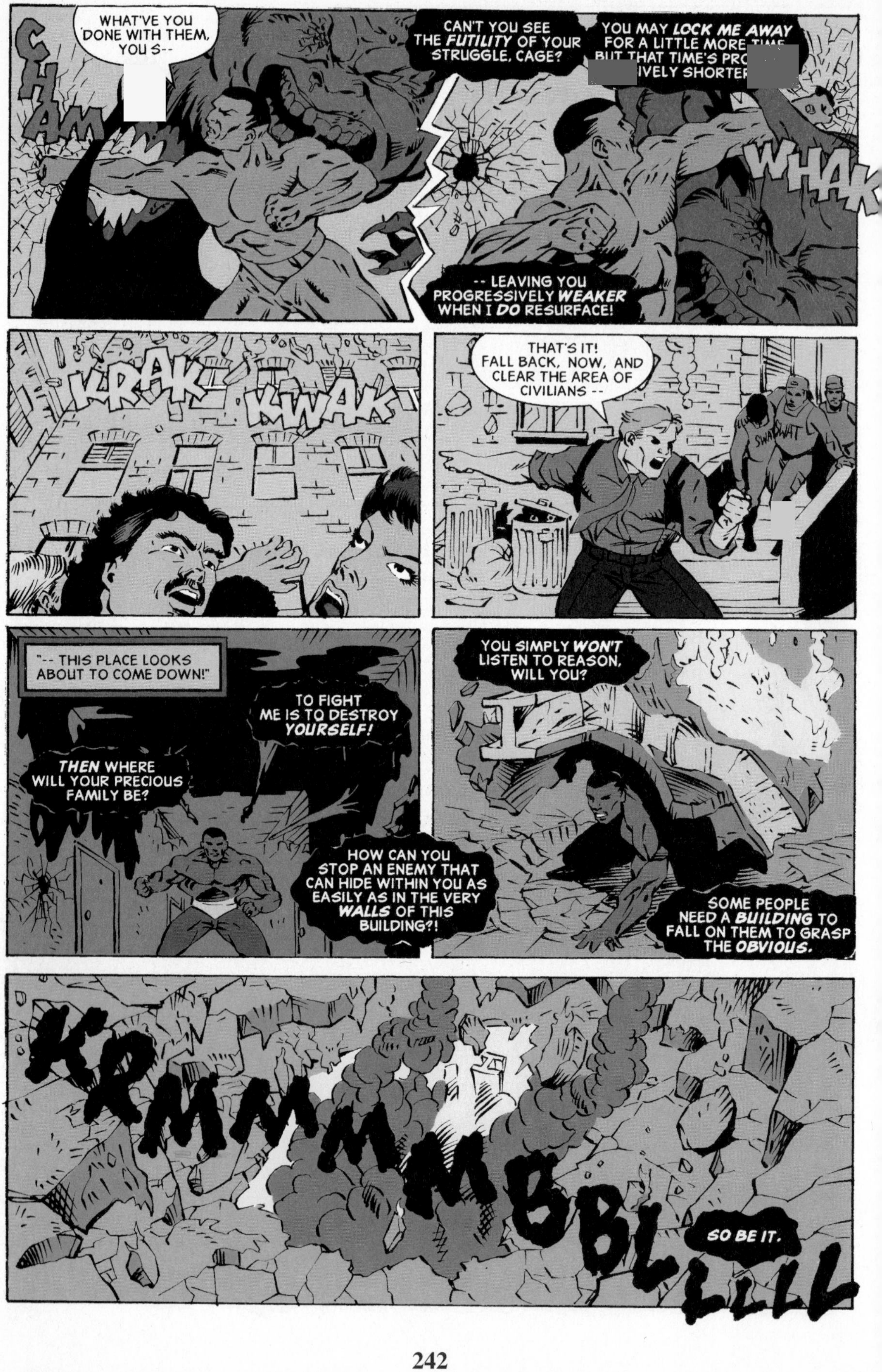
CHAM
WHAT'VE YOU DONE WITH THEM, YOU S--
CAN'T YOU SEE THE FUTILITY OF YOUR STRUGGLE, CAGE?
YOU MAY LOCK ME AWAY FOR A LITTLE MORE TIME
BUT THAT TIME'S PRO
IVELY SHORTER
WHAK
-- LEAVING YOU PROGRESSIVELY WEAKER WHEN I DO RESURFACE!
KRAK
KWAK
THAT'S IT! FALL BACK, NOW, AND CLEAR THE AREA OF CIVILIANS --
"-- THIS PLACE LOOKS ABOUT TO COME DOWN!"
TO FIGHT ME IS TO DESTROY YOURSELF!
THEN WHERE WILL YOUR PRECIOUS FAMILY BE?
HOW CAN YOU STOP AN ENEMY THAT CAN HIDE WITHIN YOU AS EASILY AS IN THE VERY WALLS OF THIS BUILDING?!
YOU SIMPLY WON'T LISTEN TO REASON, WILL YOU?
SOME PEOPLE NEED A BUILDING TO FALL ON THEM TO GRASP THE OBVIOUS.
KRMMMMBBLLLLL
SO BE IT.

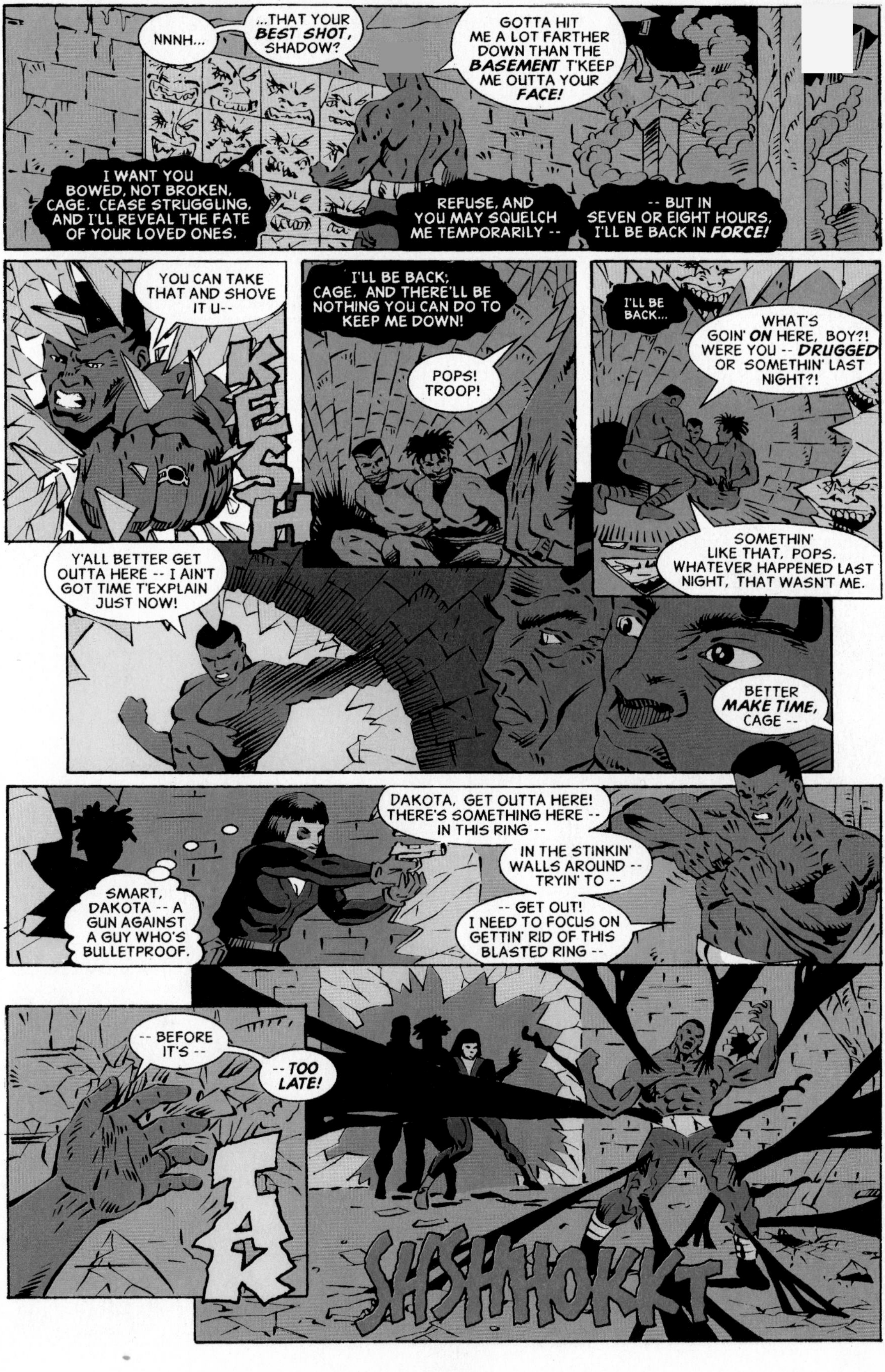
NNNH...
...THAT YOUR BEST SHOT, SHADOW?
GOTTA HIT ME A LOT FARTHER DOWN THAN THE BASEMENT T'KEEP ME OUTTA YOUR FACE!
I WANT YOU BOWED, NOT BROKEN, CAGE. CEASE STRUGGLING, AND I'LL REVEAL THE FATE OF YOUR LOVED ONES.
REFUSE, AND YOU MAY SQUELCH ME TEMPORARILY --
-- BUT IN SEVEN OR EIGHT HOURS, I'LL BE BACK IN FORCE!
YOU CAN TAKE THAT AND SHOVE IT U--
KESH
I'LL BE BACK; CAGE. AND THERE'LL BE NOTHING YOU CAN DO TO KEEP ME DOWN!
POPS! TROOP!
I'LL BE BACK...
WHAT'S GOIN' ON HERE, BOY?! WERE YOU -- DRUGGED OR SOMETHIN' LAST NIGHT?!
SOMETHIN' LIKE THAT, POPS. WHATEVER HAPPENED LAST NIGHT, THAT WASN'T ME.
Y'ALL BETTER GET OUTTA HERE -- I AIN'T GOT TIME T'EXPLAIN JUST NOW!
BETTER MAKE TIME, CAGE --
DAKOTA, GET OUTTA HERE! THERE'S SOMETHING HERE -- IN THIS RING --
IN THE STINKIN' WALLS AROUND -- TRYIN' TO --
SMART, DAKOTA -- A GUN AGAINST A GUY WHO'S BULLETPROOF.
-- GET OUT! I NEED TO FOCUS ON GETTIN' RID OF THIS BLASTED RING --
-- BEFORE IT'S --
-- TOO LATE!
SHSHHOKKT

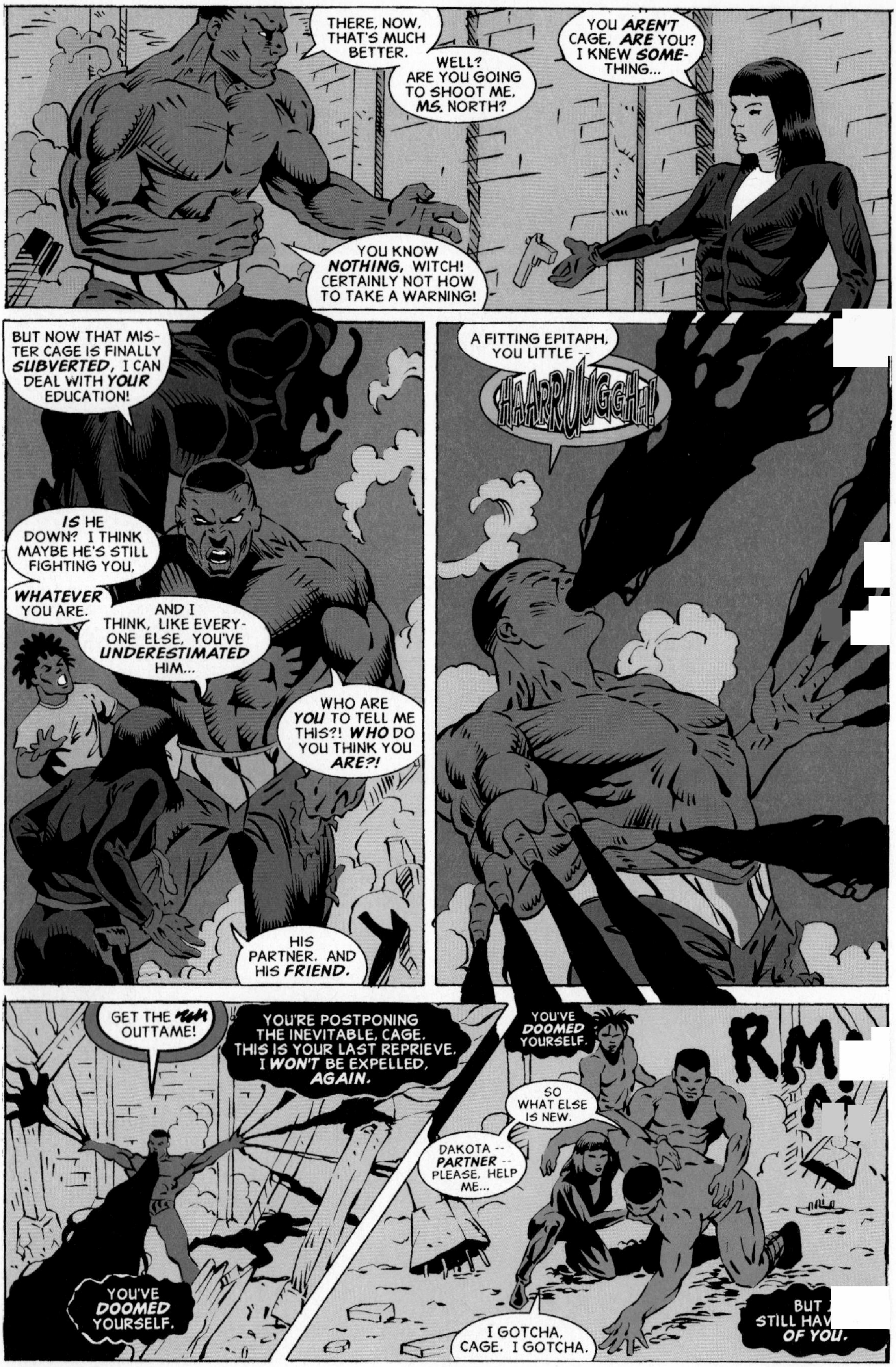
THERE, NOW, THAT'S MUCH BETTER.
WELL? ARE YOU GOING TO SHOOT ME, MS. NORTH?
YOU AREN'T CAGE, ARE YOU? I KNEW SOMETHING...
YOU KNOW NOTHING, WITCH! CERTAINLY NOT HOW TO TAKE A WARNING!
BUT NOW THAT MISTER CAGE IS FINALLY SUBVERTED, I CAN DEAL WITH YOUR EDUCATION!
IS HE DOWN? I THINK MAYBE HE'S STILL FIGHTING YOU,
WHATEVER YOU ARE.
AND I THINK, LIKE EVERYONE ELSE, YOU'VE UNDERESTIMATED HIM...
WHO ARE YOU TO TELL ME THIS?! WHO DO YOU THINK YOU ARE?!
HIS PARTNER. AND HIS FRIEND.
A FITTING EPITAPH, YOU LITTLE --
HAARRUUGGHH!
GET THE OUTTAME!
YOU'RE POSTPONING THE INEVITABLE, CAGE. THIS IS YOUR LAST REPRIEVE. I WON'T BE EXPELLED, AGAIN.
YOU'VE DOOMED YOURSELF.
YOU'VE DOOMED YOURSELF.
SO WHAT ELSE IS NEW.
DAKOTA -- PARTNER -- PLEASE, HELP ME...
I GOTCHA, CAGE. I GOTCHA.
BUT
STILL HAV
OF YOU.

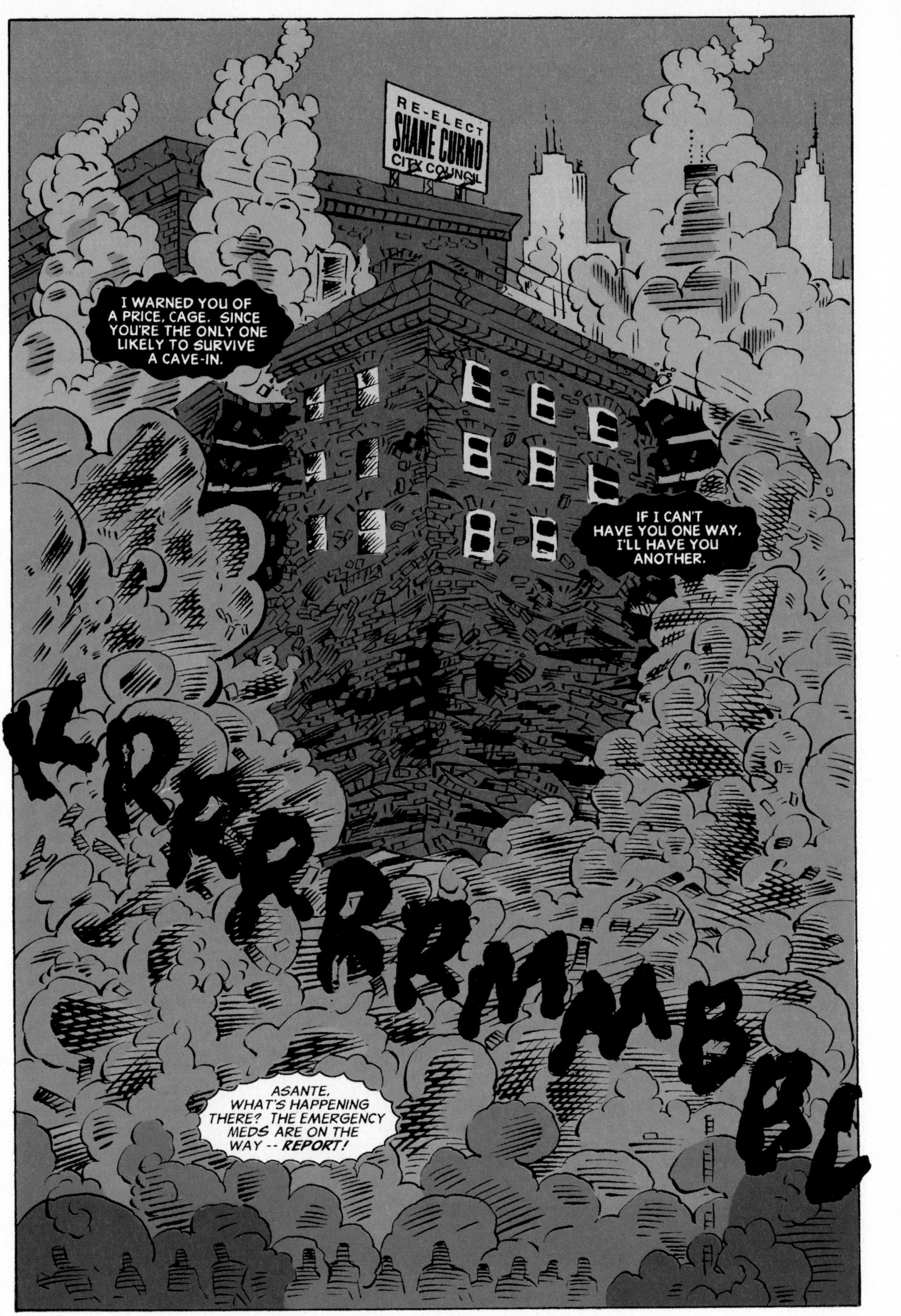
RE-ELECT
SHANE CURNO
CITY COUNCIL
I WARNED YOU OF A PRICE, CAGE. SINCE YOU'RE THE ONLY ONE LIKELY TO SURVIVE A CAVE-IN.
IF I CAN'T HAVE YOU ONE WAY, I'LL HAVE YOU ANOTHER.
KRRRRRRMMBBL
ASANTE, WHAT'S HAPPENING THERE? THE EMERGENCY MEDS ARE ON THE WAY -- REPORT!

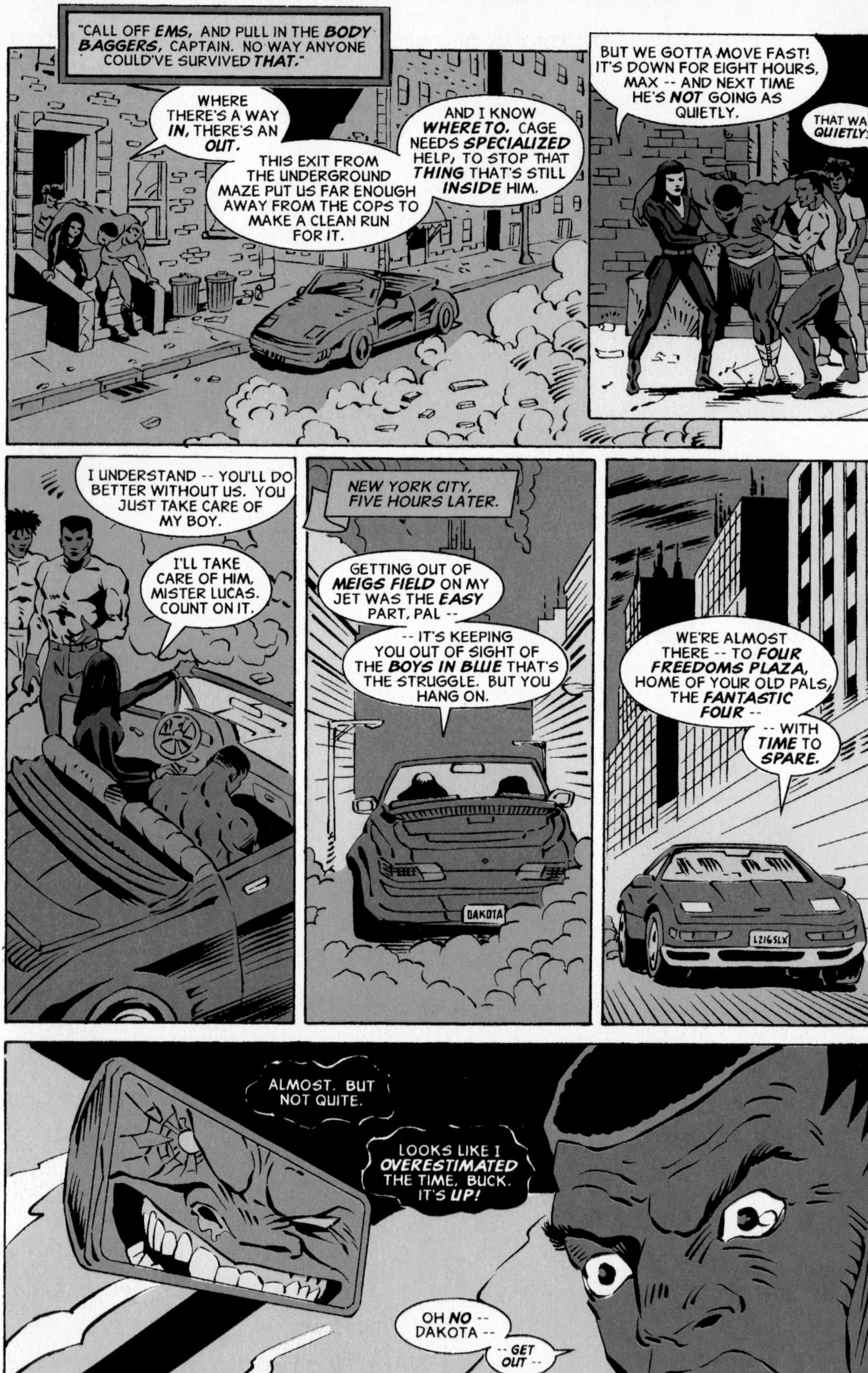
"CALL OFF EMS, AND PULL IN THE BODY BAGGERS, CAPTAIN. NO WAY ANYONE COULD'VE SURVIVED THAT."
WHERE THERE'S A WAY IN, THERE'S AN OUT.
THIS EXIT FROM THE UNDERGROUND MAZE PUT US FAR ENOUGH AWAY FROM THE COPS TO MAKE A CLEAN RUN FOR IT.
AND I KNOW WHERE TO. CAGE NEEDS SPECIALIZED HELP, TO STOP THAT THING THAT'S STILL INSIDE HIM.
BUT WE GOTTA MOVE FAST! IT'S DOWN FOR EIGHT HOURS, MAX -- AND NEXT TIME HE'S NOT GOING AS QUIETLY.
THAT WAS QUIETLY?
I UNDERSTAND -- YOU'LL DO BETTER WITHOUT US. YOU JUST TAKE CARE OF MY BOY.
I'LL TAKE CARE OF HIM, MISTER LUCAS. COUNT ON IT.
NEW YORK CITY, FIVE HOURS LATER.
GETTING OUT OF MEIGS FIELD ON MY JET WAS THE EASY PART, PAL --
-- IT'S KEEPING YOU OUT OF SIGHT OF THE BOYS IN BLUE THAT'S THE STRUGGLE. BUT YOU HANG ON.
DAKOTA
WE'RE ALMOST THERE -- TO FOUR FREEDOMS PLAZA, HOME OF YOUR OLD PALS, THE FANTASTIC FOUR --
-- WITH TIME TO SPARE.
LZ16SLX
ALMOST. BUT NOT QUITE.
LOOKS LIKE I OVERESTIMATED THE TIME, BUCK. IT'S UP!
OH NO -- DAKOTA --
-- GET OUT --

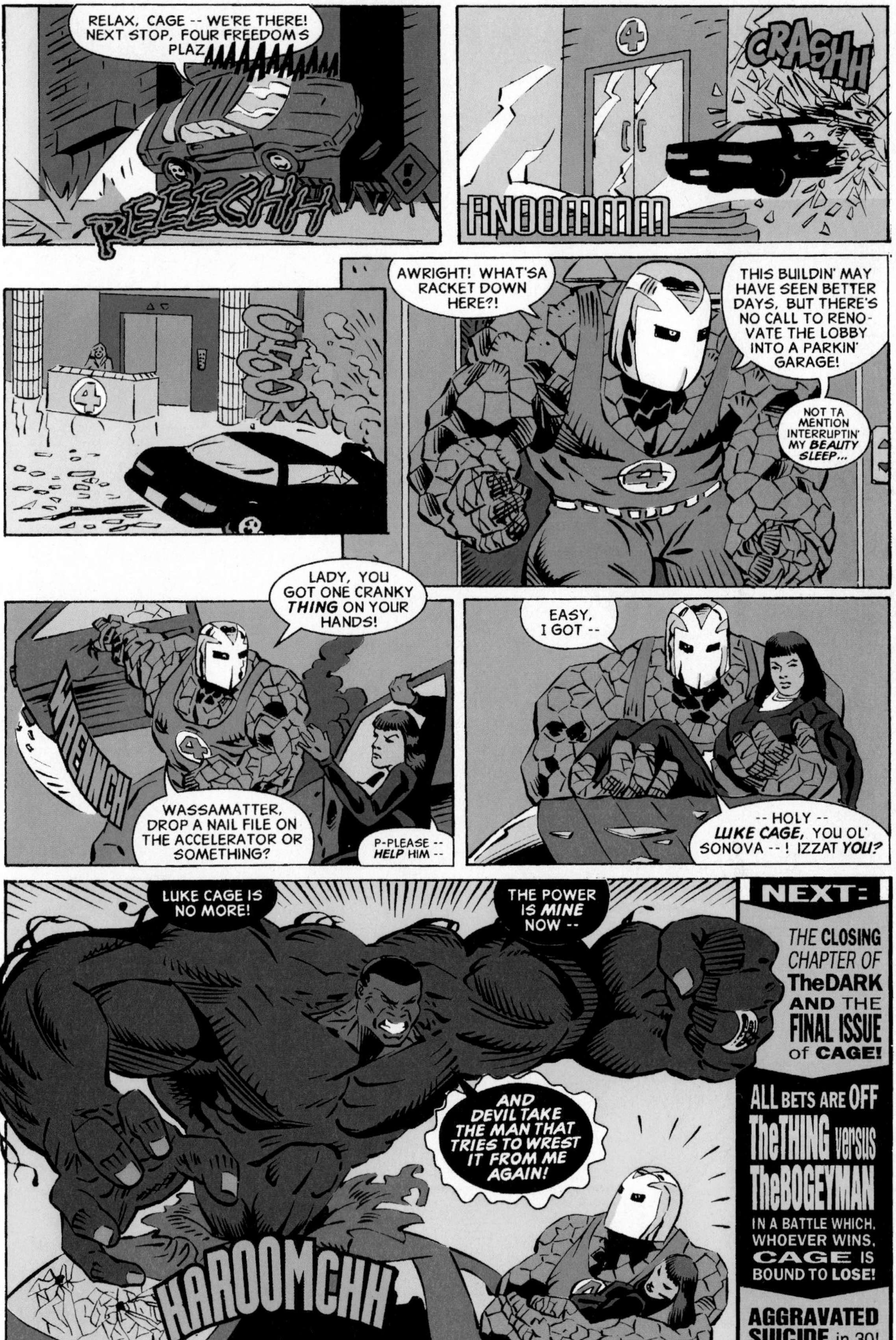
RELAX, CAGE -- WE'RE THERE! NEXT STOP, FOUR FREEDOMS PLAZAAAAAAAAA
REEEECHHH
CRASHH
RNOOMMMM
CHOOM
AWRIGHT! WHAT'SA RACKET DOWN HERE?!
THIS BUILDIN' MAY HAVE SEEN BETTER DAYS, BUT THERE'S NO CALL TO RENOVATE THE LOBBY INTO A PARKIN' GARAGE!
NOT TA MENTION INTERRUPTIN' MY *BEAUTY SLEEP*...
LADY, YOU GOT ONE CRANKY *THING* ON YOUR HANDS!
WRENNCH
WASSAMATTER, DROP A NAIL FILE ON THE ACCELERATOR OR SOMETHING?
P-PLEASE -- *HELP* HIM --
EASY, I GOT --
-- HOLY -- *LUKE CAGE,* YOU OL' SONOVA -- ! IZZAT *YOU?*
LUKE CAGE IS NO MORE!
THE POWER IS *MINE* NOW --
AND DEVIL TAKE THE MAN THAT TRIES TO WREST IT FROM ME AGAIN!
HAROOMCHH
NEXT:
THE CLOSING CHAPTER OF TheDARK AND THE FINAL ISSUE of CAGE!
ALL BETS ARE OFF TheTHING versus TheBOGEYMAN IN A BATTLE WHICH, WHOEVER WINS, CAGE IS BOUND TO LOSE!
AGGRAVATED SUICIDE in 30!

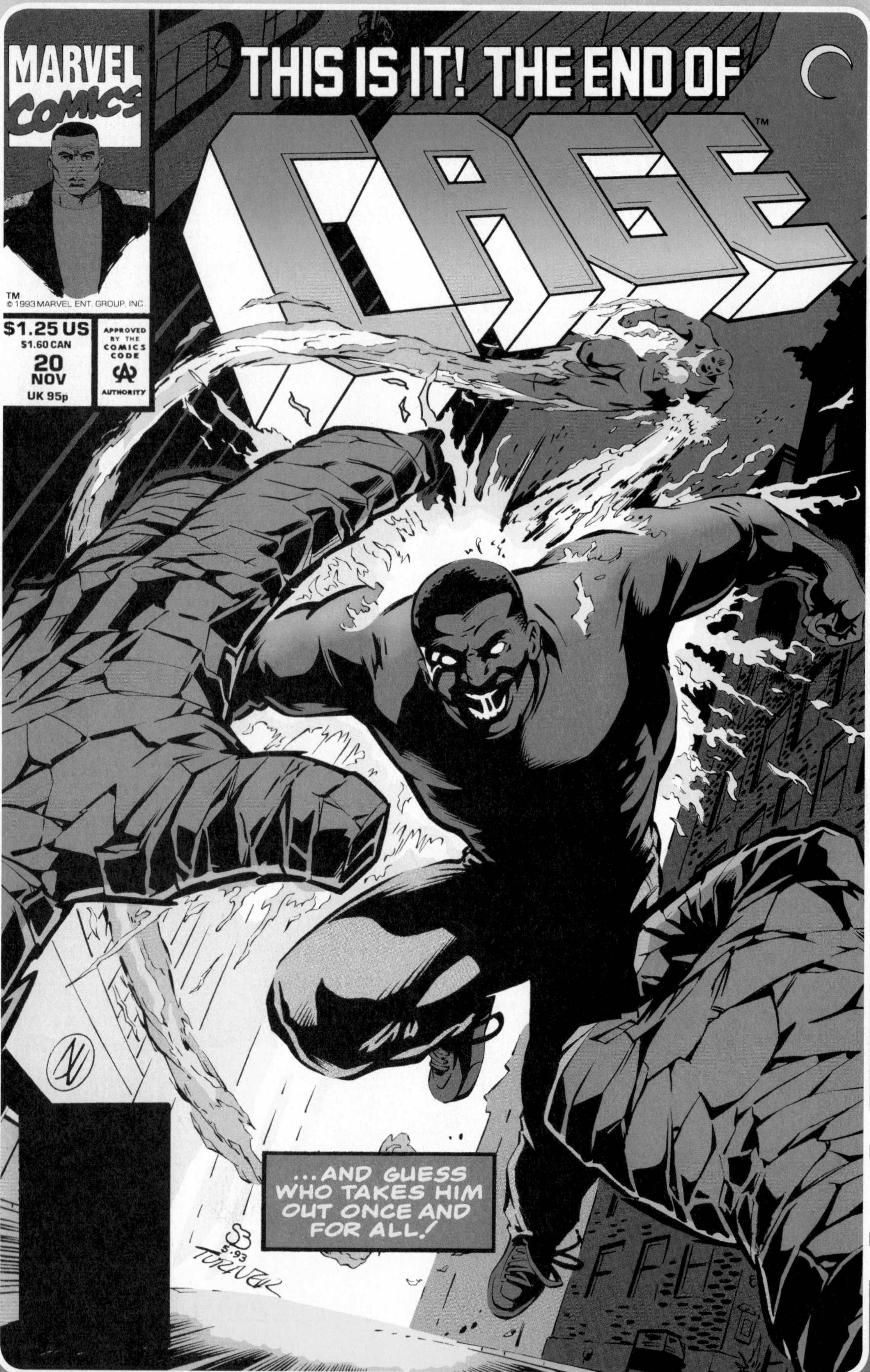
MARVEL COMICS
THIS IS IT! THE END OF
CAGE™
TM
© 1993 MARVEL ENT. GROUP, INC.
$1.25 US
$1.60 CAN
20
NOV
UK 95p
APPROVED BY THE COMICS CODE AUTHORITY
...AND GUESS WHO TAKES HIM OUT ONCE AND FOR ALL!
SB 5·93
TURNER

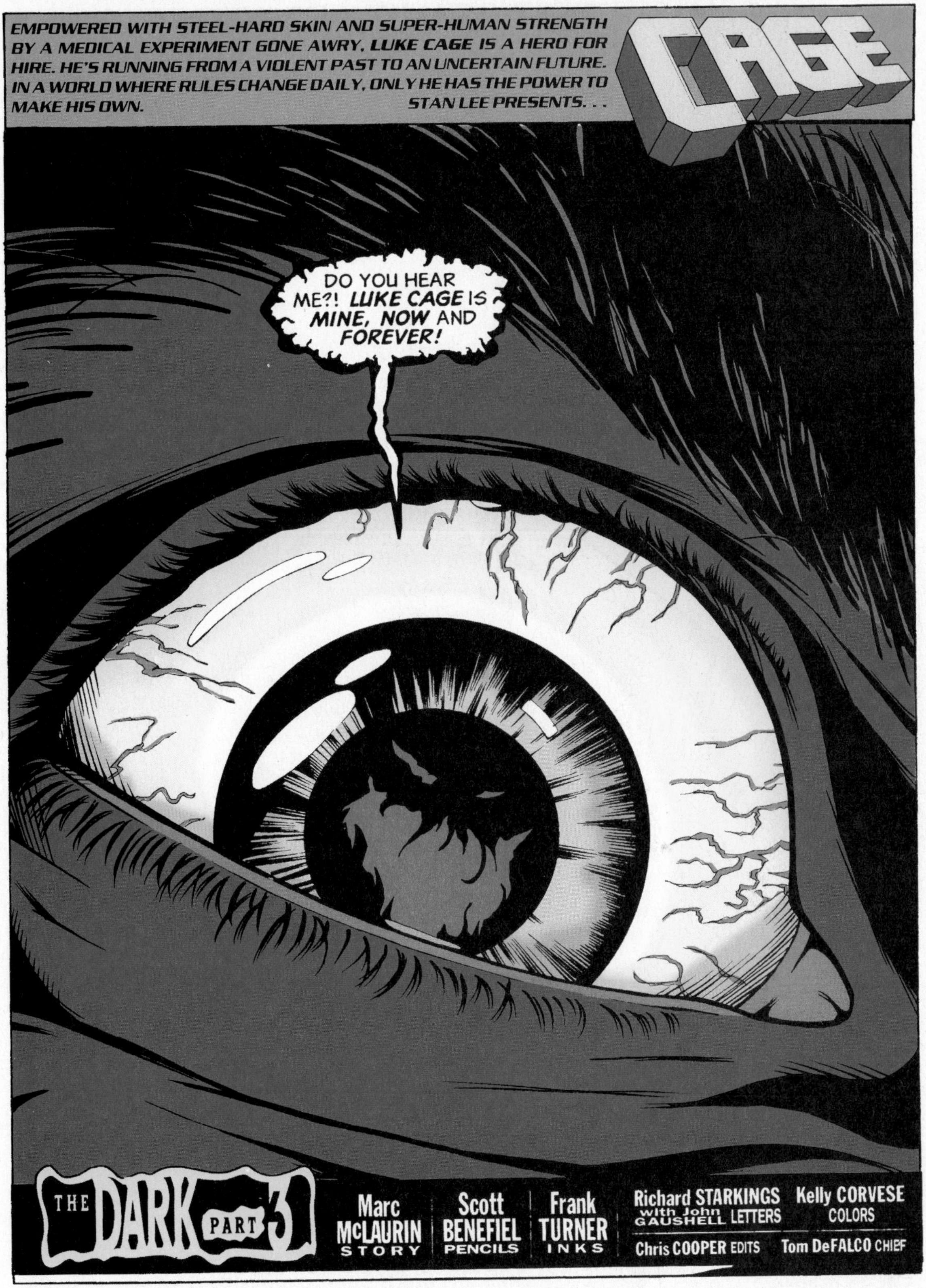
EMPOWERED WITH STEEL-HARD SKIN AND SUPER-HUMAN STRENGTH BY A MEDICAL EXPERIMENT GONE AWRY, LUKE CAGE IS A HERO FOR HIRE. HE'S RUNNING FROM A VIOLENT PAST TO AN UNCERTAIN FUTURE. IN A WORLD WHERE RULES CHANGE DAILY, ONLY HE HAS THE POWER TO MAKE HIS OWN.
STAN LEE PRESENTS. . .
CAGE
DO YOU HEAR ME?! LUKE CAGE IS MINE, NOW AND FOREVER!
THE DARK PART 3
Marc McLAURIN STORY
Scott BENEFIEL PENCILS
Frank TURNER INKS
Richard STARKINGS with John GAUSHELL LETTERS
Kelly CORVESE COLORS
Chris COOPER EDITS
Tom DeFALCO CHIEF

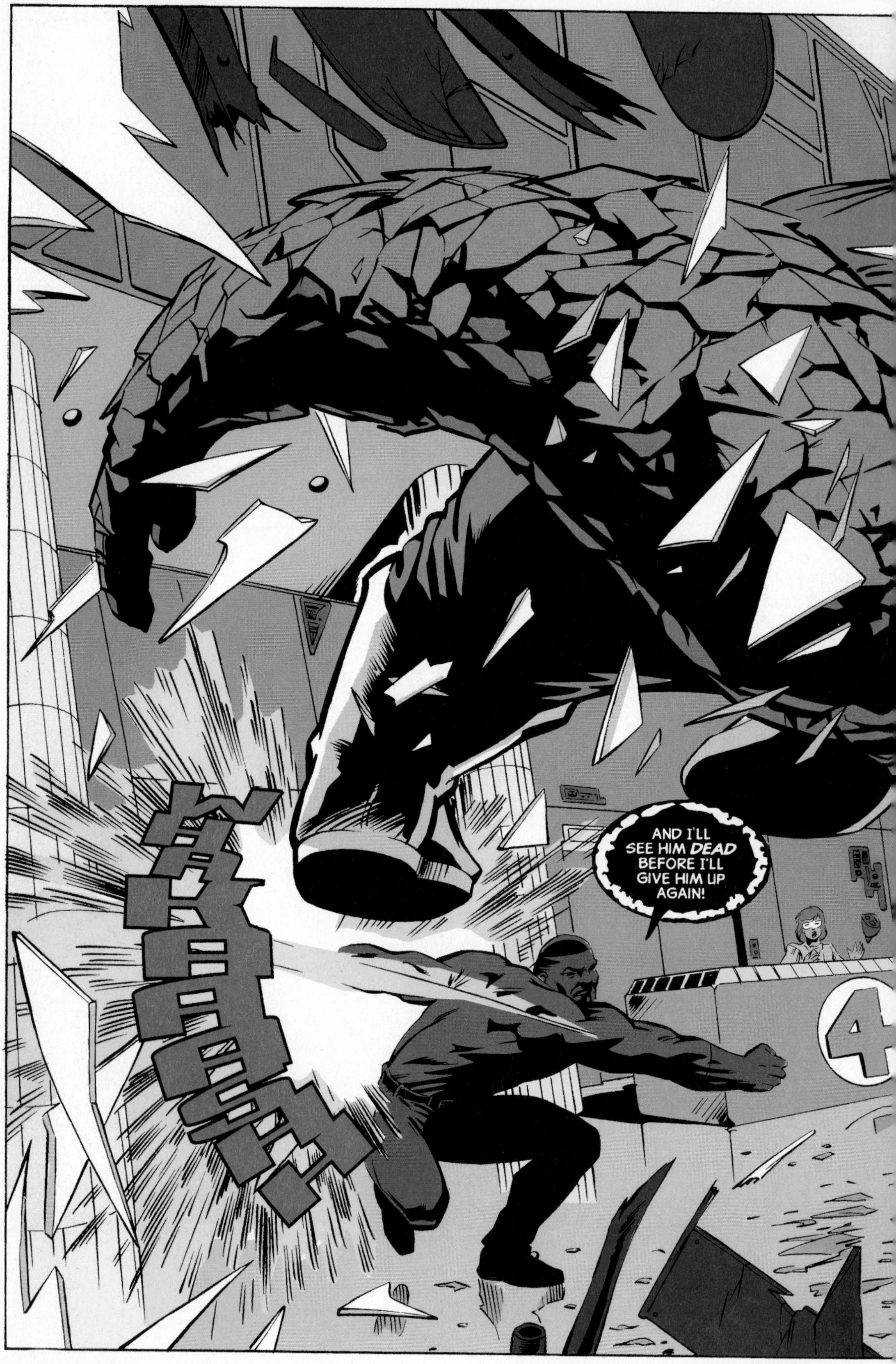
AND I'LL SEE HIM DEAD BEFORE I'LL GIVE HIM UP AGAIN!

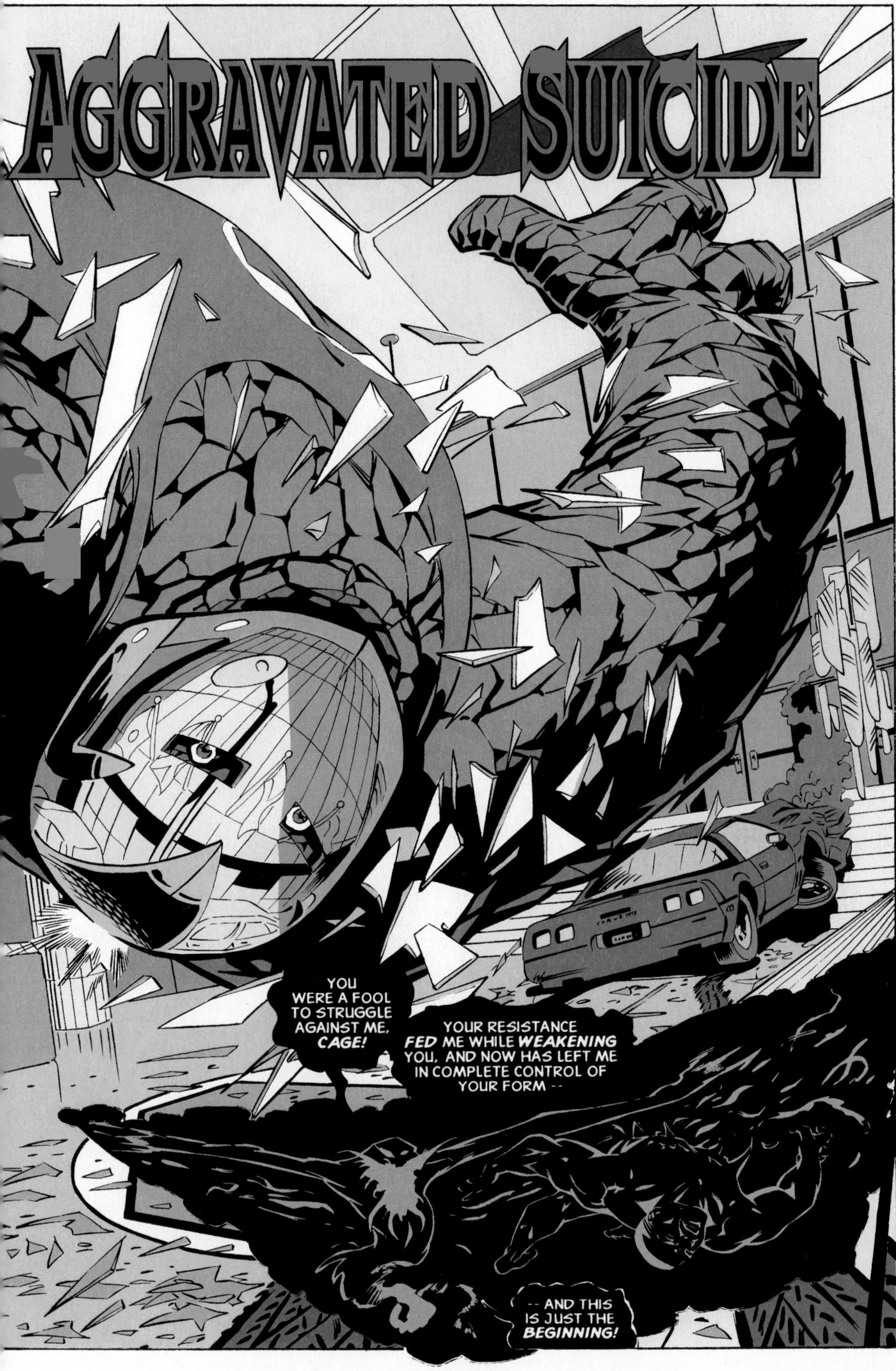
AGGRAVATED SUICIDE
YOU WERE A FOOL TO STRUGGLE AGAINST ME, CAGE!
YOUR RESISTANCE FED ME WHILE WEAKENING YOU, AND NOW HAS LEFT ME IN COMPLETE CONTROL OF YOUR FORM --
-- AND THIS IS JUST THE BEGINNING!

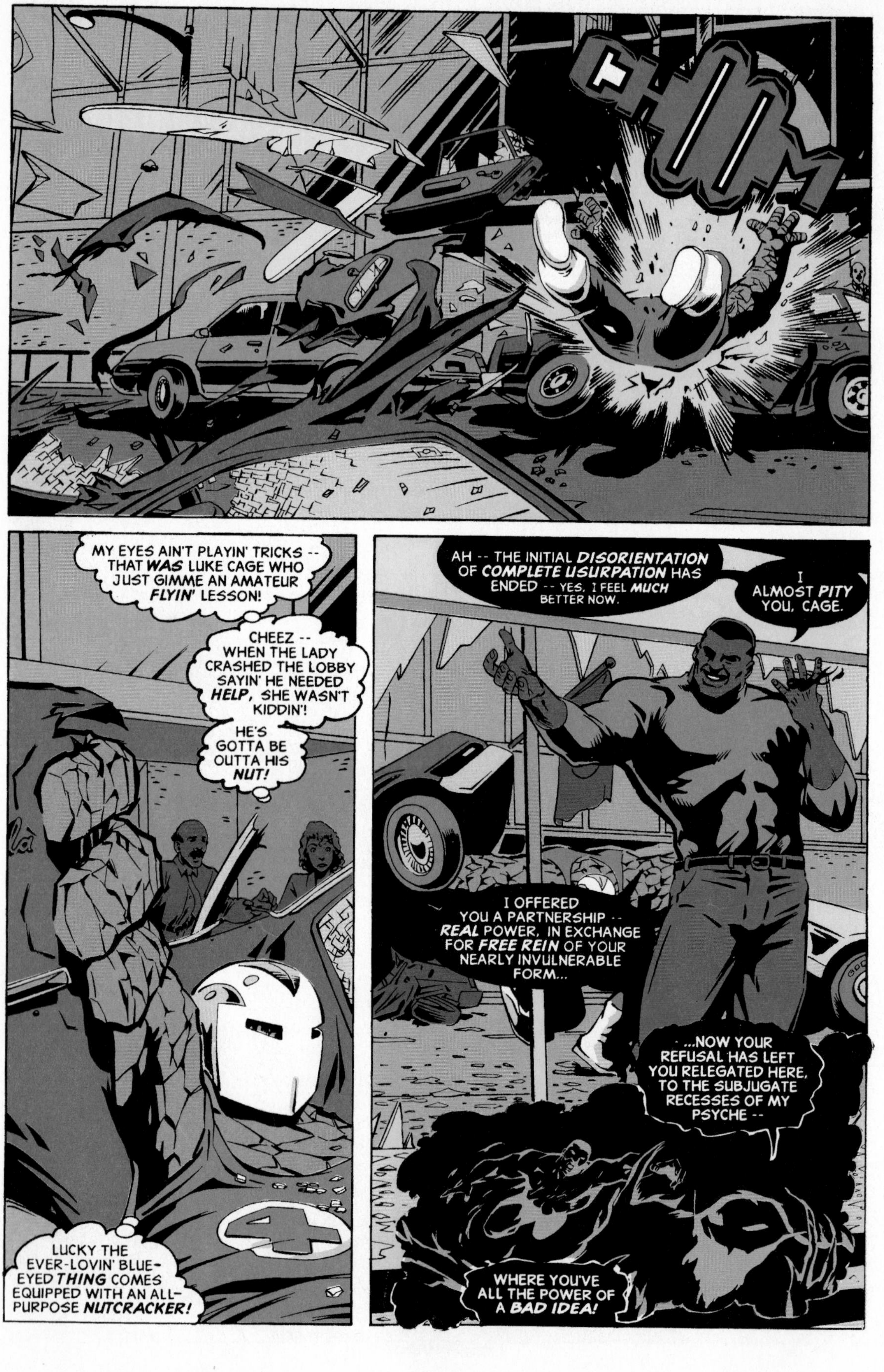
THOOM
MY EYES AIN'T PLAYIN' TRICKS -- THAT WAS LUKE CAGE WHO JUST GIMME AN AMATEUR FLYIN' LESSON!
CHEEZ -- WHEN THE LADY CRASHED THE LOBBY SAYIN' HE NEEDED HELP, SHE WASN'T KIDDIN'!
HE'S GOTTA BE OUTTA HIS NUT!
LUCKY THE EVER-LOVIN' BLUE-EYED THING COMES EQUIPPED WITH AN ALL-PURPOSE NUTCRACKER!
AH -- THE INITIAL DISORIENTATION OF COMPLETE USURPATION HAS ENDED -- YES, I FEEL MUCH BETTER NOW.
I ALMOST PITY YOU, CAGE.
I OFFERED YOU A PARTNERSHIP -- REAL POWER, IN EXCHANGE FOR FREE REIN OF YOUR NEARLY INVULNERABLE FORM...
-- ...NOW YOUR REFUSAL HAS LEFT YOU RELEGATED HERE, TO THE SUBJUGATE RECESSES OF MY PSYCHE --
WHERE YOU'VE ALL THE POWER OF A BAD IDEA!

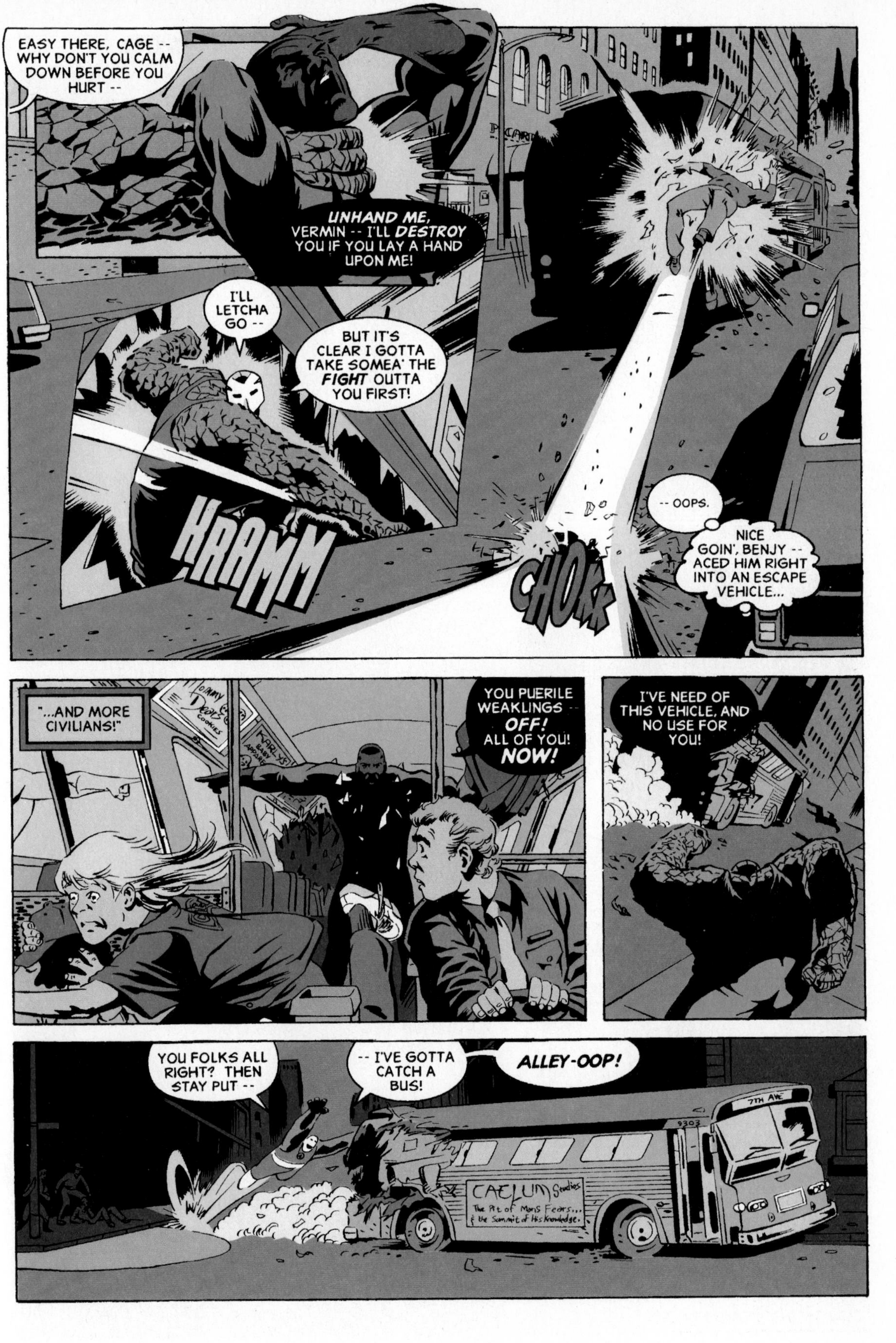
EASY THERE, CAGE -- WHY DON'T YOU CALM DOWN BEFORE YOU HURT --
UNHAND ME, VERMIN -- I'LL DESTROY YOU IF YOU LAY A HAND UPON ME!
I'LL LETCHA GO --
BUT IT'S CLEAR I GOTTA TAKE SOMEA' THE FIGHT OUTTA YOU FIRST!
KRAMM
CHOKK
-- OOPS.
NICE GOIN', BENJY -- ACED HIM RIGHT INTO AN ESCAPE VEHICLE...
"...AND MORE CIVILIANS!"
YOU PUERILE WEAKLINGS -- OFF! ALL OF YOU! NOW!
I'VE NEED OF THIS VEHICLE, AND NO USE FOR YOU!
YOU FOLKS ALL RIGHT? THEN STAY PUT --
-- I'VE GOTTA CATCH A BUS!
ALLEY-OOP!
7TH AVE
CAELUM Studios
The Pit of Mans Fears... & the Summit of His Knowledge.

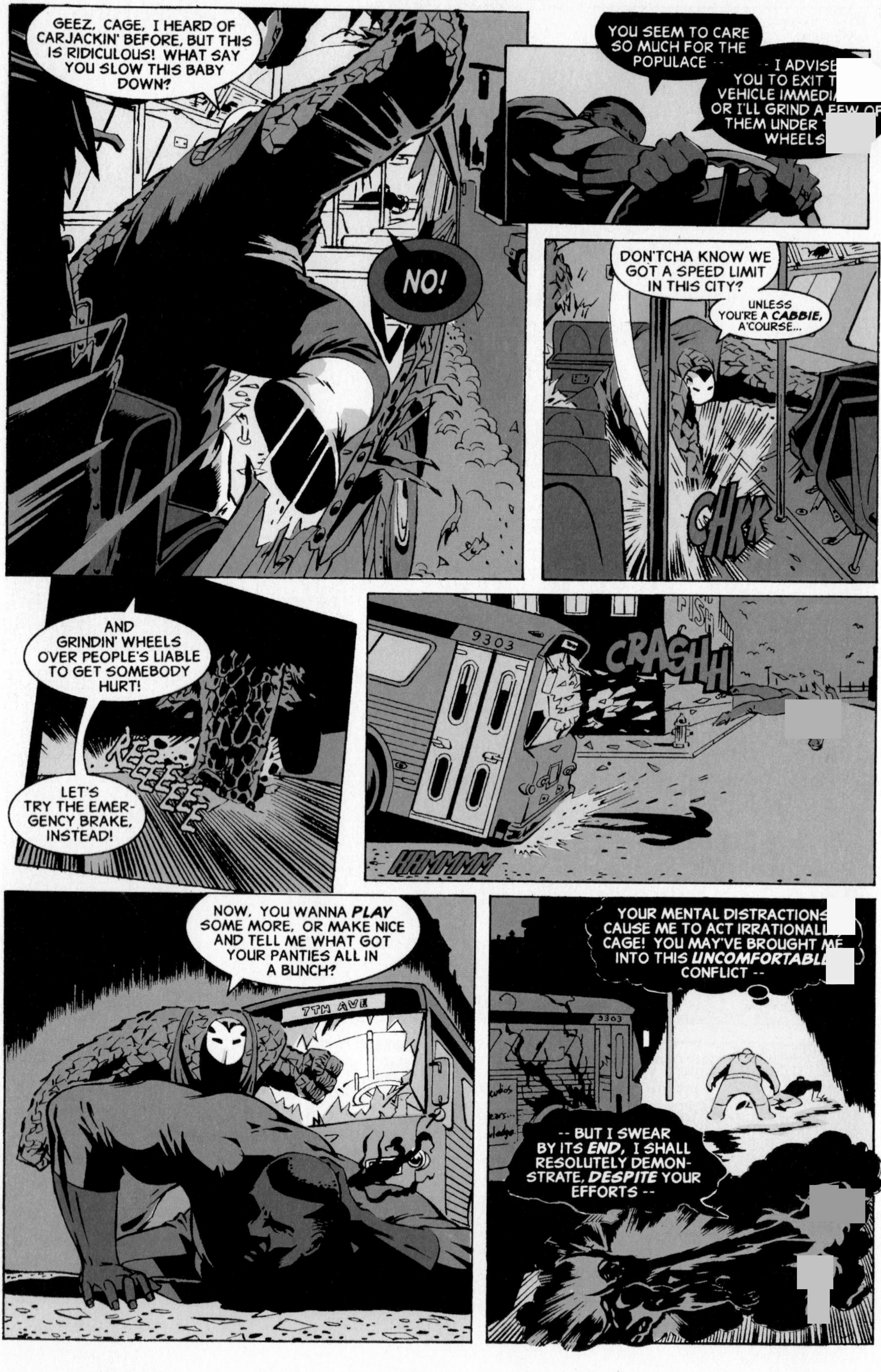
GEEZ, CAGE, I HEARD OF CARJACKIN' BEFORE, BUT THIS IS RIDICULOUS! WHAT SAY YOU SLOW THIS BABY DOWN?
NO!
YOU SEEM TO CARE SO MUCH FOR THE POPULACE --
-- I ADVISE YOU TO EXIT T VEHICLE IMMEDIA OR I'LL GRIND A FEW OF THEM UNDER T WHEELS
DON'TCHA KNOW WE GOT A SPEED LIMIT IN THIS CITY?
UNLESS YOU'RE A CABBIE, A'COURSE...
CHKK
AND GRINDIN' WHEELS OVER PEOPLE'S LIABLE TO GET SOMEBODY HURT!
LET'S TRY THE EMERGENCY BRAKE, INSTEAD!
9303
CRASHH
HRMMMM
NOW, YOU WANNA PLAY SOME MORE, OR MAKE NICE AND TELL ME WHAT GOT YOUR PANTIES ALL IN A BUNCH?
7TH AVE
YOUR MENTAL DISTRACTIONS CAUSE ME TO ACT IRRATIONALL CAGE! YOU MAY'VE BROUGHT ME INTO THIS UNCOMFORTABL CONFLICT --
-- BUT I SWEAR BY ITS END, I SHALL RESOLUTELY DEMONSTRATE, DESPITE YOUR EFFORTS --

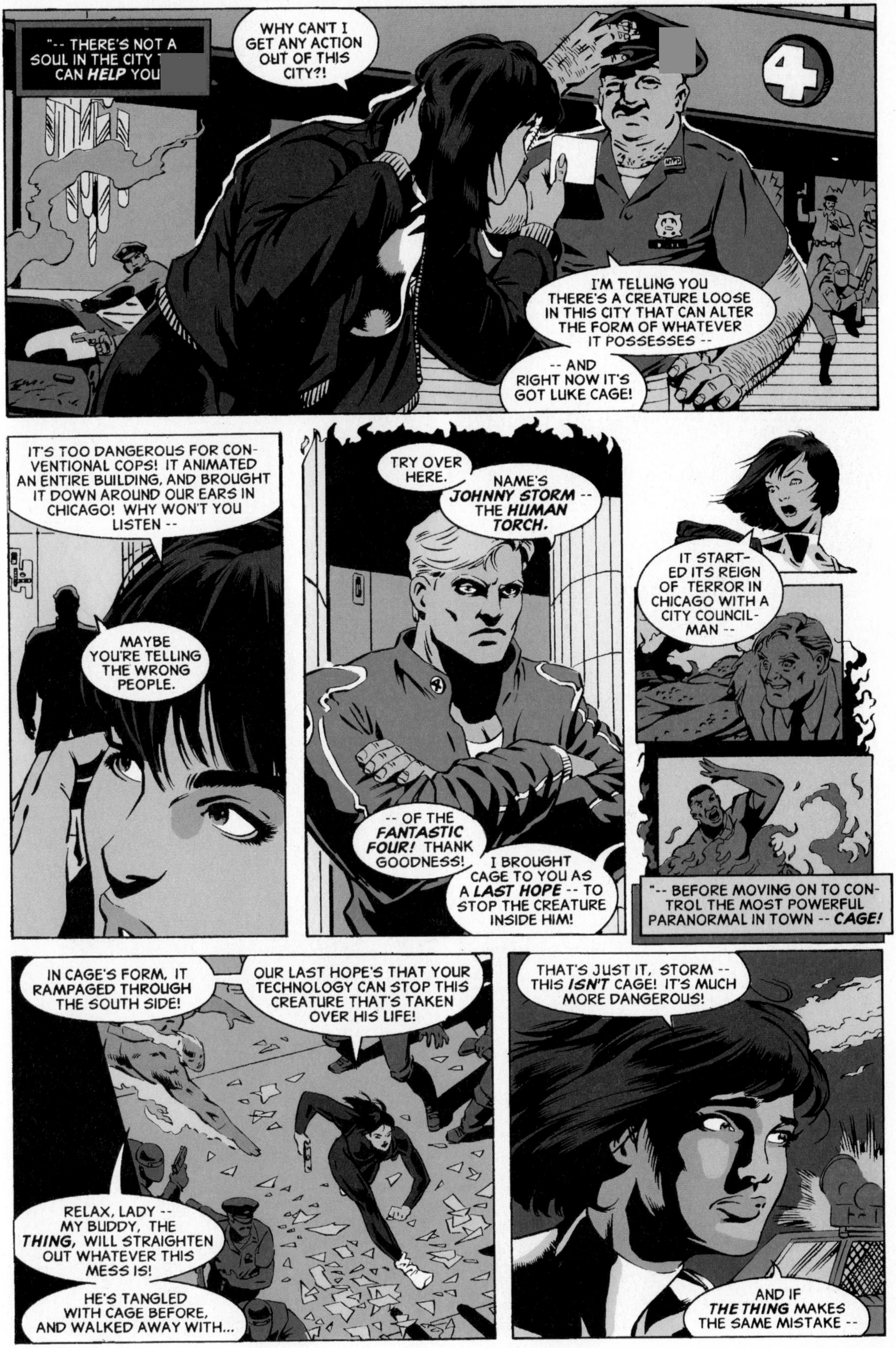
"-- THERE'S NOT A SOUL IN THE CITY T CAN HELP YOU
WHY CAN'T I GET ANY ACTION OUT OF THIS CITY?!
I'M TELLING YOU THERE'S A CREATURE LOOSE IN THIS CITY THAT CAN ALTER THE FORM OF WHATEVER IT POSSESSES --
-- AND RIGHT NOW IT'S GOT LUKE CAGE!
IT'S TOO DANGEROUS FOR CONVENTIONAL COPS! IT ANIMATED AN ENTIRE BUILDING, AND BROUGHT IT DOWN AROUND OUR EARS IN CHICAGO! WHY WON'T YOU LISTEN --
MAYBE YOU'RE TELLING THE WRONG PEOPLE.
TRY OVER HERE.
NAME'S JOHNNY STORM -- THE HUMAN TORCH.
-- OF THE FANTASTIC FOUR! THANK GOODNESS!
I BROUGHT CAGE TO YOU AS A LAST HOPE -- TO STOP THE CREATURE INSIDE HIM!
IT STARTED ITS REIGN OF TERROR IN CHICAGO WITH A CITY COUNCILMAN --
"-- BEFORE MOVING ON TO CONTROL THE MOST POWERFUL PARANORMAL IN TOWN -- CAGE!
IN CAGE'S FORM, IT RAMPAGED THROUGH THE SOUTH SIDE!
OUR LAST HOPE'S THAT YOUR TECHNOLOGY CAN STOP THIS CREATURE THAT'S TAKEN OVER HIS LIFE!
RELAX, LADY -- MY BUDDY, THE THING, WILL STRAIGHTEN OUT WHATEVER THIS MESS IS!
HE'S TANGLED WITH CAGE BEFORE, AND WALKED AWAY WITH...
THAT'S JUST IT, STORM -- THIS ISN'T CAGE! IT'S MUCH MORE DANGEROUS!
AND IF THE THING MAKES THE SAME MISTAKE --

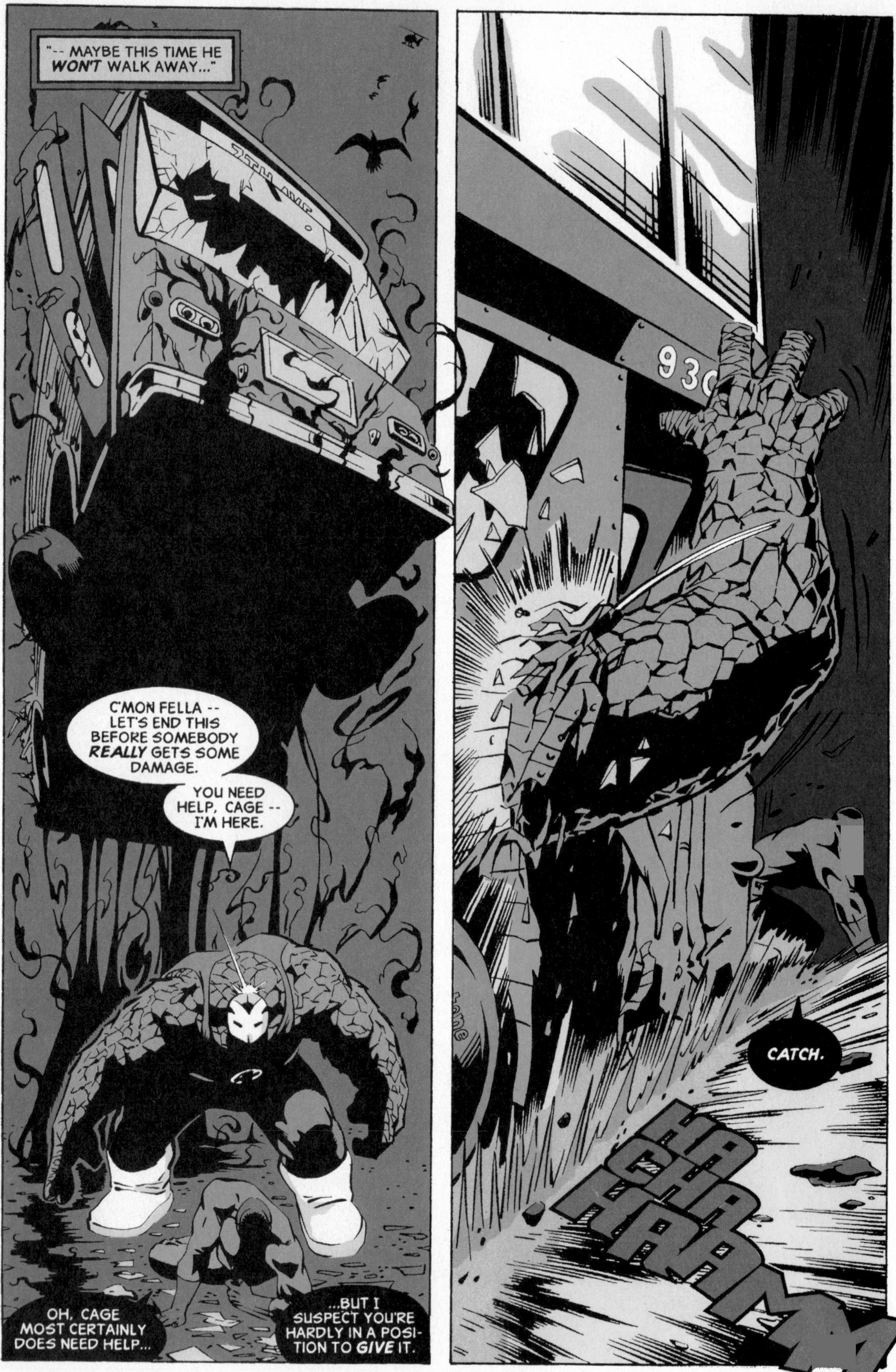
"-- MAYBE THIS TIME HE WON'T WALK AWAY..."
C'MON FELLA -- LET'S END THIS BEFORE SOMEBODY REALLY GETS SOME DAMAGE.
YOU NEED HELP, CAGE -- I'M HERE.
OH, CAGE MOST CERTAINLY DOES NEED HELP...
...BUT I SUSPECT YOU'RE HARDLY IN A POSITION TO GIVE IT.
CATCH.
KA CHA KRAMM

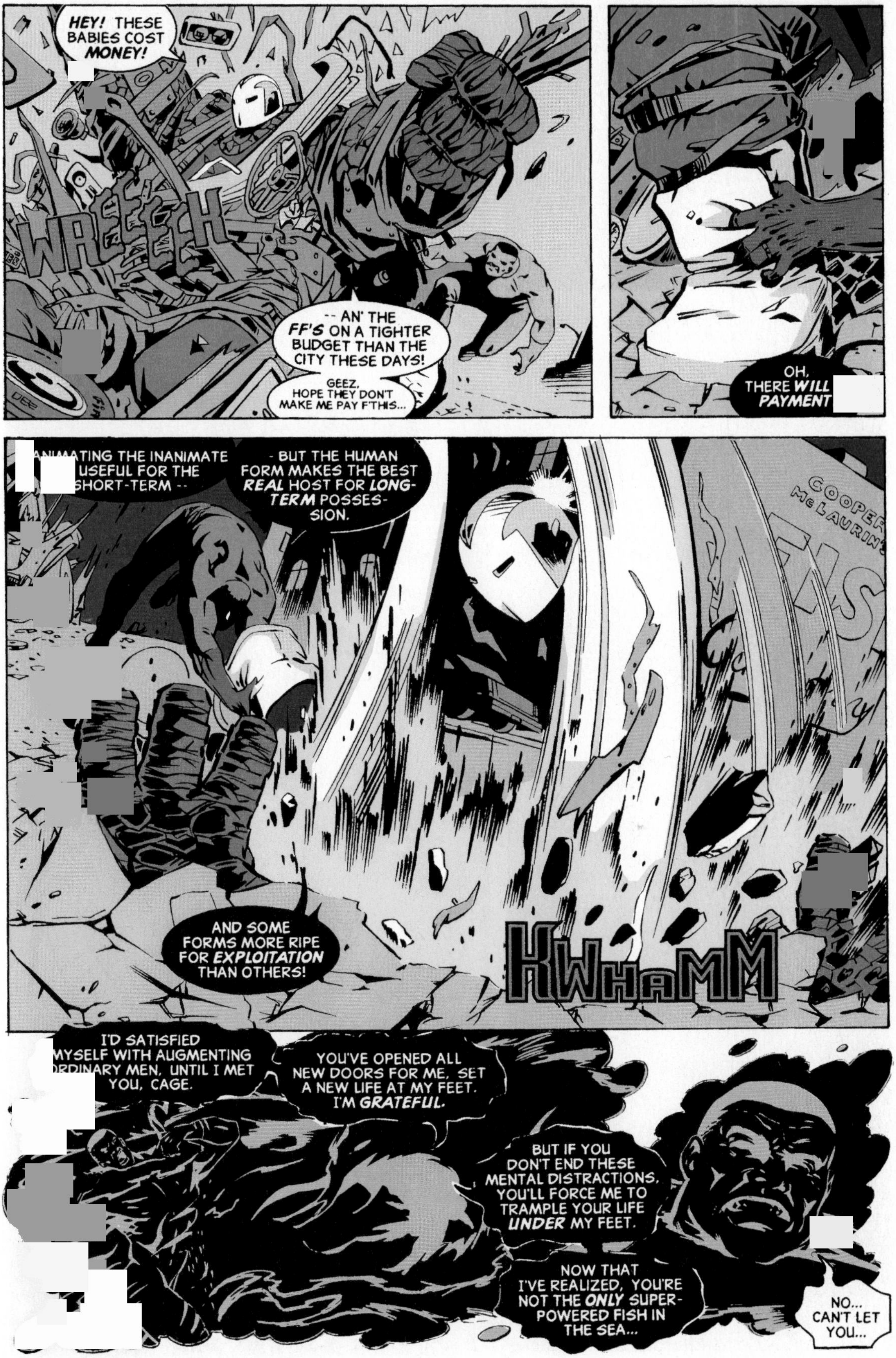

HEY! THESE BABIES COST MONEY!
WREEECH
-- AN' THE FF'S ON A TIGHTER BUDGET THAN THE CITY THESE DAYS!
GEEZ, HOPE THEY DON'T MAKE ME PAY F'THIS...
OH, THERE WILL PAYMENT
ANIMATING THE INANIMATE USEFUL FOR THE SHORT-TERM --
- BUT THE HUMAN FORM MAKES THE BEST REAL HOST FOR LONG-TERM POSSES-SION.
AND SOME FORMS MORE RIPE FOR EXPLOITATION THAN OTHERS!
KWHAMM
I'D SATISFIED MYSELF WITH AUGMENTING ORDINARY MEN, UNTIL I MET YOU, CAGE.
YOU'VE OPENED ALL NEW DOORS FOR ME, SET A NEW LIFE AT MY FEET. I'M GRATEFUL.
BUT IF YOU DON'T END THESE MENTAL DISTRACTIONS, YOU'LL FORCE ME TO TRAMPLE YOUR LIFE UNDER MY FEET.
NOW THAT I'VE REALIZED, YOU'RE NOT THE ONLY SUPER-POWERED FISH IN THE SEA...
NO... CAN'T LET YOU...

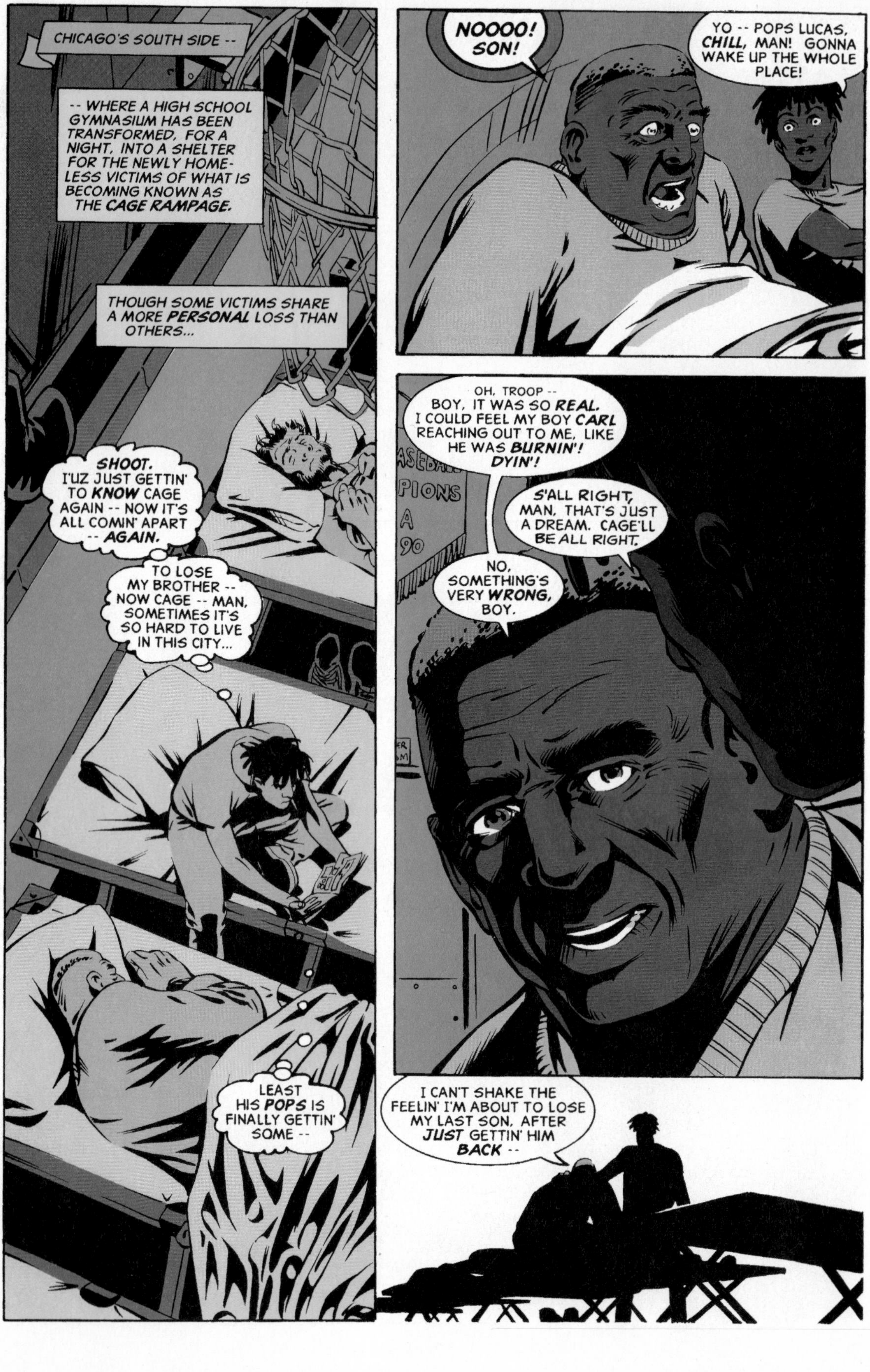
CHICAGO'S SOUTH SIDE --
-- WHERE A HIGH SCHOOL GYMNASIUM HAS BEEN TRANSFORMED, FOR A NIGHT, INTO A SHELTER FOR THE NEWLY HOMELESS VICTIMS OF WHAT IS BECOMING KNOWN AS THE CAGE RAMPAGE.
THOUGH SOME VICTIMS SHARE A MORE PERSONAL LOSS THAN OTHERS...
SHOOT. I'UZ JUST GETTIN' TO KNOW CAGE AGAIN -- NOW IT'S ALL COMIN' APART -- AGAIN.
TO LOSE MY BROTHER -- NOW CAGE -- MAN, SOMETIMES IT'S SO HARD TO LIVE IN THIS CITY...
LEAST HIS POPS IS FINALLY GETTIN' SOME --
NOOOO! SON!
YO -- POPS LUCAS, CHILL, MAN! GONNA WAKE UP THE WHOLE PLACE!
OH, TROOP -- BOY, IT WAS SO REAL. I COULD FEEL MY BOY CARL REACHING OUT TO ME, LIKE HE WAS BURNIN'! DYIN'!
S'ALL RIGHT, MAN. THAT'S JUST A DREAM. CAGE'LL BE ALL RIGHT.
NO, SOMETHING'S VERY WRONG, BOY.
I CAN'T SHAKE THE FEELIN' I'M ABOUT TO LOSE MY LAST SON, AFTER JUST GETTIN' HIM BACK --

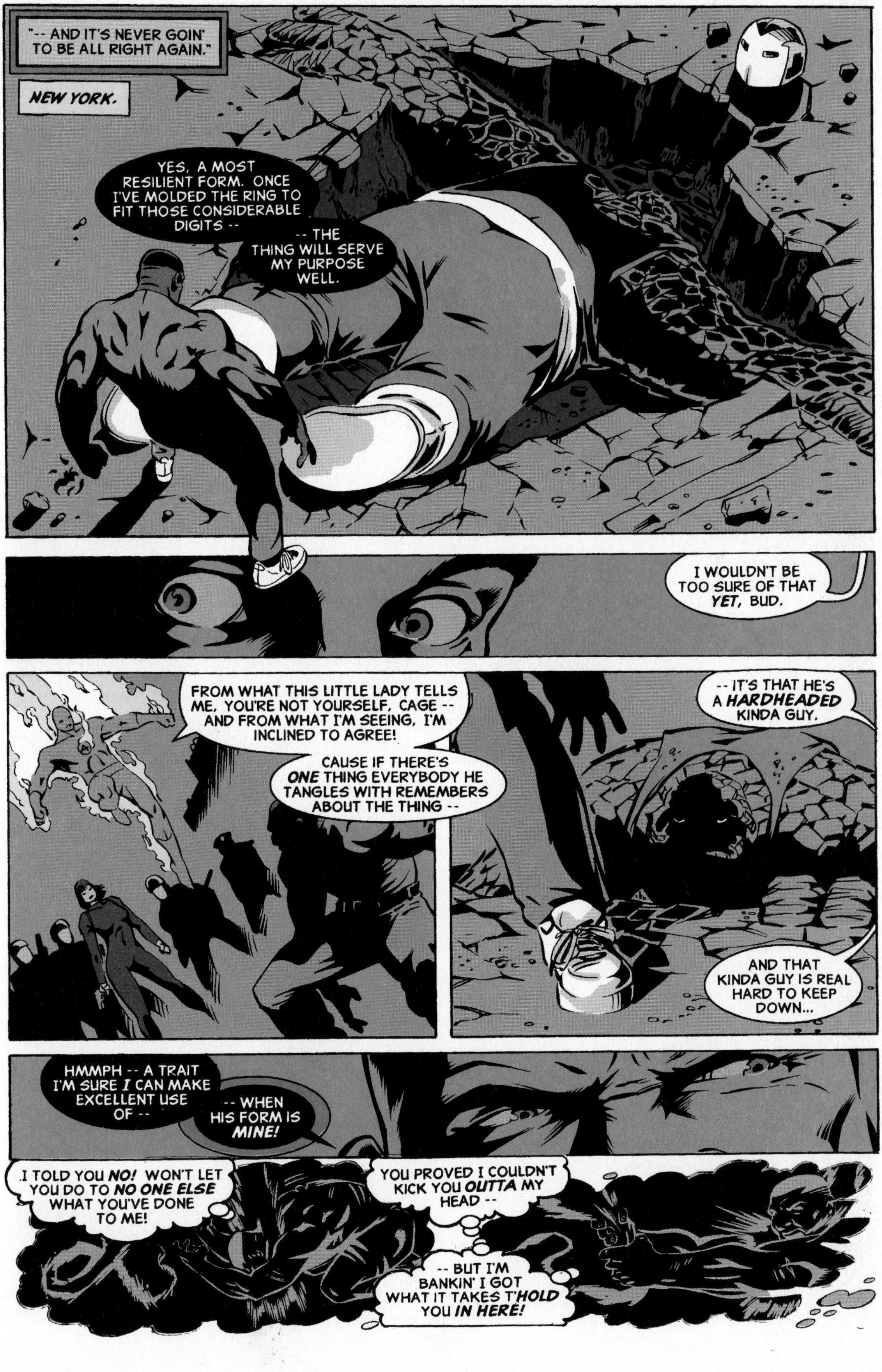
"-- AND IT'S NEVER GOIN' TO BE ALL RIGHT AGAIN."
NEW YORK.
YES, A MOST RESILIENT FORM. ONCE I'VE MOLDED THE RING TO FIT THOSE CONSIDERABLE DIGITS --
-- THE THING WILL SERVE MY PURPOSE WELL.
I WOULDN'T BE TOO SURE OF THAT YET, BUD.
FROM WHAT THIS LITTLE LADY TELLS ME, YOU'RE NOT YOURSELF, CAGE -- AND FROM WHAT I'M SEEING, I'M INCLINED TO AGREE!
CAUSE IF THERE'S ONE THING EVERYBODY HE TANGLES WITH REMEMBERS ABOUT THE THING --
-- IT'S THAT HE'S A HARDHEADED KINDA GUY.
AND THAT KINDA GUY IS REAL HARD TO KEEP DOWN...
HMMPH -- A TRAIT I'M SURE I CAN MAKE EXCELLENT USE OF --
-- WHEN HIS FORM IS MINE!
I TOLD YOU NO! WON'T LET YOU DO TO NO ONE ELSE WHAT YOU'VE DONE TO ME!
YOU PROVED I COULDN'T KICK YOU OUTTA MY HEAD --
-- BUT I'M BANKIN' I GOT WHAT IT TAKES T'HOLD YOU IN HERE!

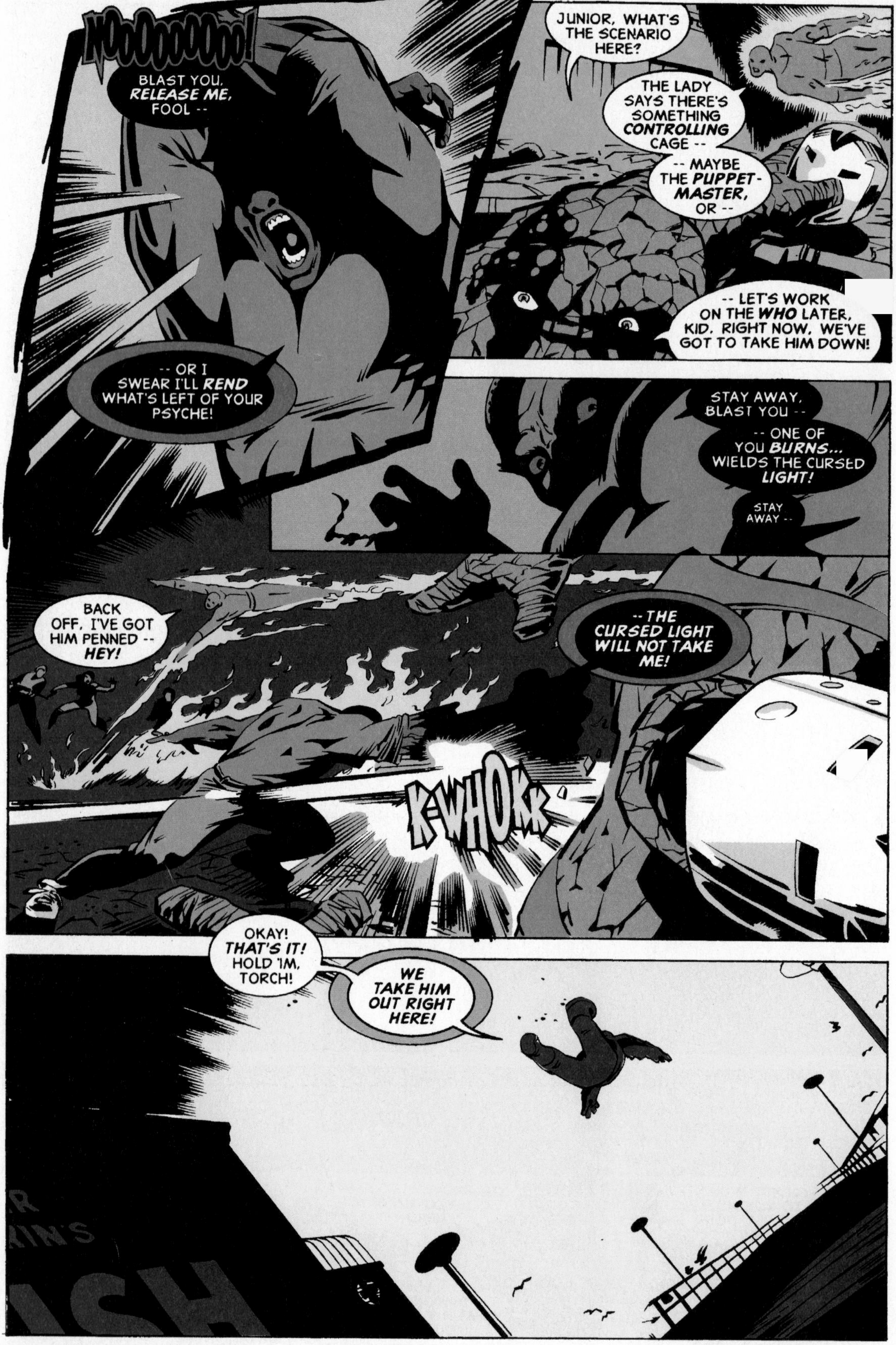
NOOOOOOOOO!
BLAST YOU, RELEASE ME, FOOL --
JUNIOR, WHAT'S THE SCENARIO HERE?
THE LADY SAYS THERE'S SOMETHING CONTROLLING CAGE --
-- MAYBE THE PUPPET-MASTER, OR --
-- LET'S WORK ON THE WHO LATER, KID. RIGHT NOW, WE'VE GOT TO TAKE HIM DOWN!
-- OR I SWEAR I'LL REND WHAT'S LEFT OF YOUR PSYCHE!
STAY AWAY, BLAST YOU --
-- ONE OF YOU BURNS... WIELDS THE CURSED LIGHT!
STAY AWAY --
BACK OFF, I'VE GOT HIM PENNED -- HEY!
-- THE CURSED LIGHT WILL NOT TAKE ME!
K-WHOKK
OKAY! THAT'S IT! HOLD 'IM, TORCH!
WE TAKE HIM OUT RIGHT HERE!

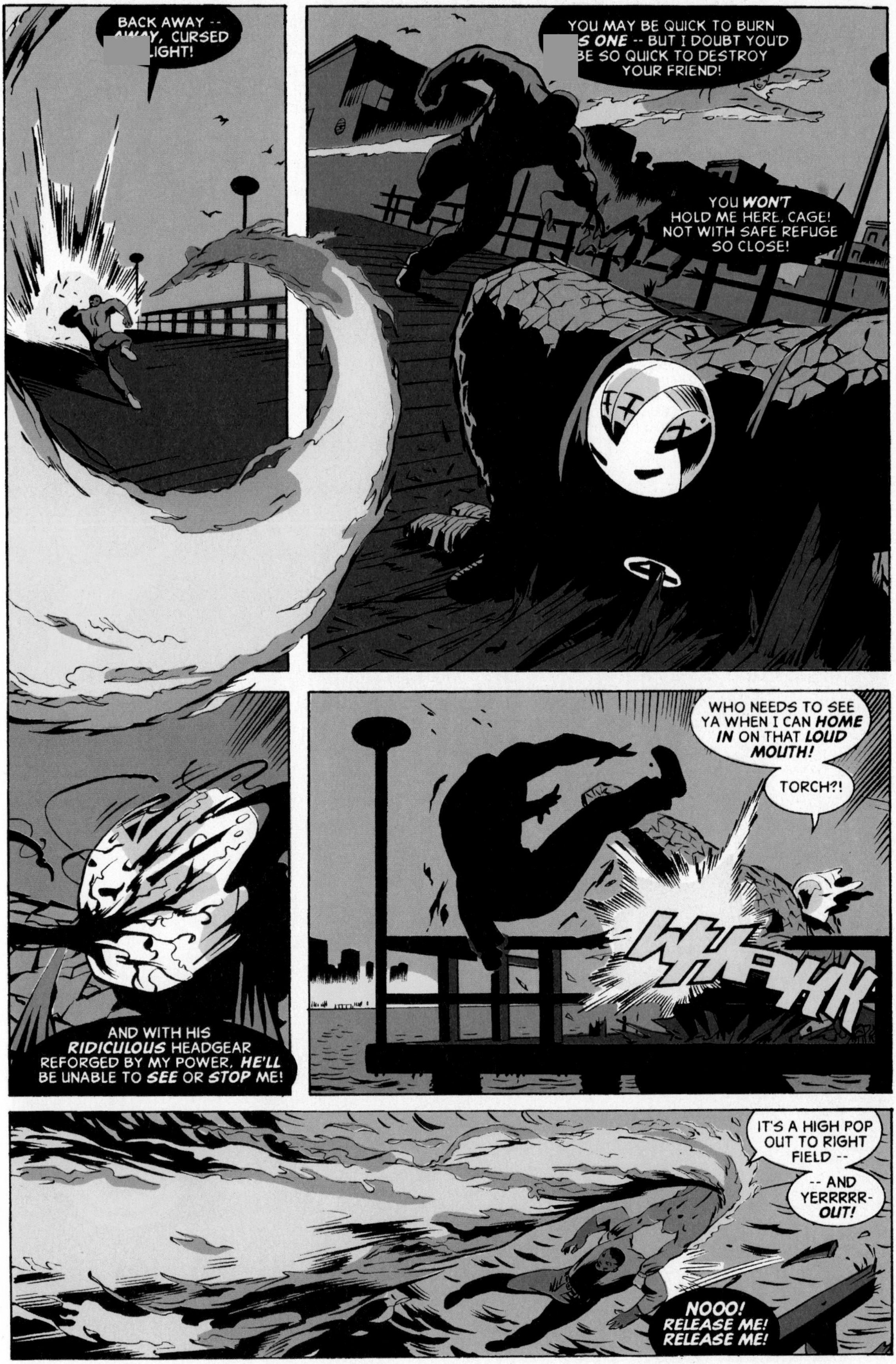
BACK AWAY -- AWAY, CURSED LIGHT!
YOU MAY BE QUICK TO BURN S ONE -- BUT I DOUBT YOU'D BE SO QUICK TO DESTROY YOUR FRIEND!
YOU WON'T HOLD ME HERE, CAGE! NOT WITH SAFE REFUGE SO CLOSE!
AND WITH HIS RIDICULOUS HEADGEAR REFORGED BY MY POWER, HE'LL BE UNABLE TO SEE OR STOP ME!
WHO NEEDS TO SEE YA WHEN I CAN HOME IN ON THAT LOUD MOUTH!
TORCH?!
WHA-KK
IT'S A HIGH POP OUT TO RIGHT FIELD --
-- AND YERRRRR-OUT!
NOOO! RELEASE ME! RELEASE ME!

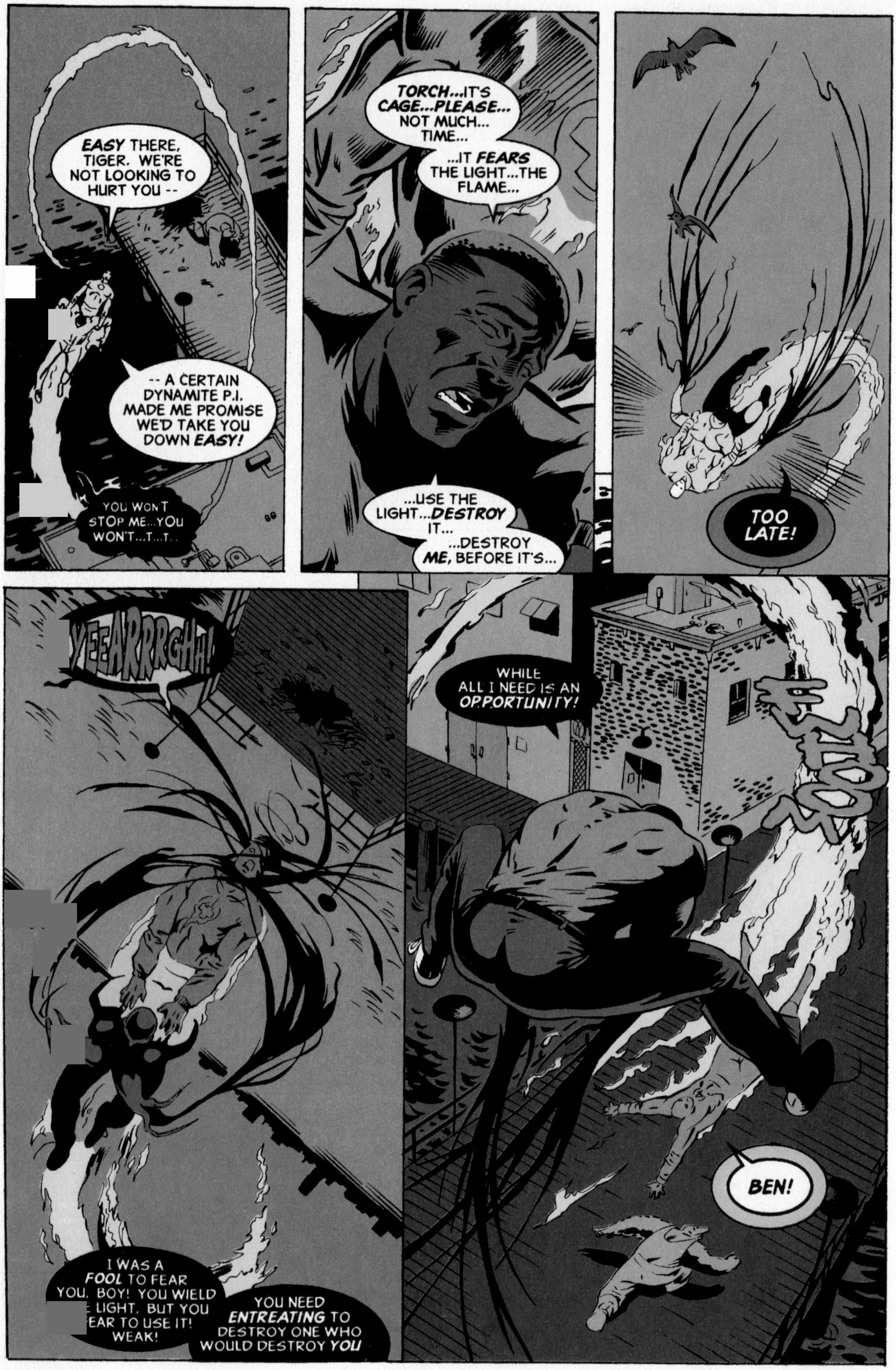
EASY THERE, TIGER. WE'RE NOT LOOKING TO HURT YOU --
-- A CERTAIN DYNAMITE P.I. MADE ME PROMISE WE'D TAKE YOU DOWN EASY!
YOU WON'T STOP ME...YOU WON'T...T...T...
TORCH...IT'S CAGE...PLEASE... NOT MUCH... TIME...
...IT FEARS THE LIGHT...THE FLAME...
...USE THE LIGHT...DESTROY IT...
...DESTROY ME, BEFORE IT'S...
TOO LATE!
YEEARRRGHH!
I WAS A FOOL TO FEAR YOU, BOY! YOU WIELD
E LIGHT. BUT YOU
FEAR TO USE IT! WEAK!
YOU NEED ENTREATING TO DESTROY ONE WHO WOULD DESTROY YOU
WHILE ALL I NEED IS AN OPPORTUNITY!
BEN!

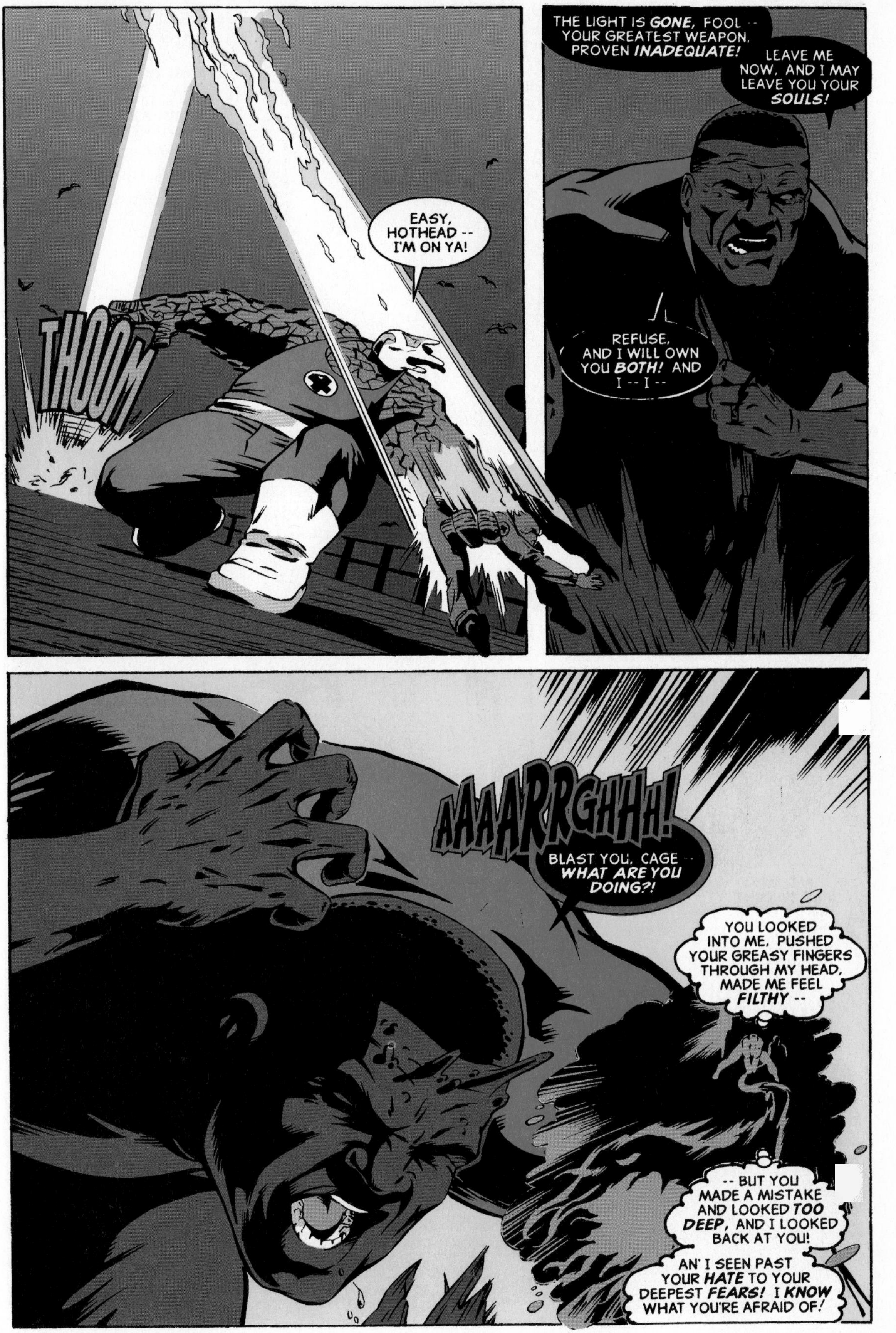
THOOM
EASY, HOTHEAD -- I'M ON YA!
THE LIGHT IS GONE, FOOL -- YOUR GREATEST WEAPON, PROVEN INADEQUATE!
LEAVE ME NOW, AND I MAY LEAVE YOU YOUR SOULS!
REFUSE, AND I WILL OWN YOU BOTH! AND I -- I --
AAAARRGHHH!
BLAST YOU, CAGE -- WHAT ARE YOU DOING?!
YOU LOOKED INTO ME, PUSHED YOUR GREASY FINGERS THROUGH MY HEAD, MADE ME FEEL FILTHY --
-- BUT YOU MADE A MISTAKE AND LOOKED TOO DEEP, AND I LOOKED BACK AT YOU!
AN' I SEEN PAST YOUR HATE TO YOUR DEEPEST FEARS! I KNOW WHAT YOU'RE AFRAID OF!

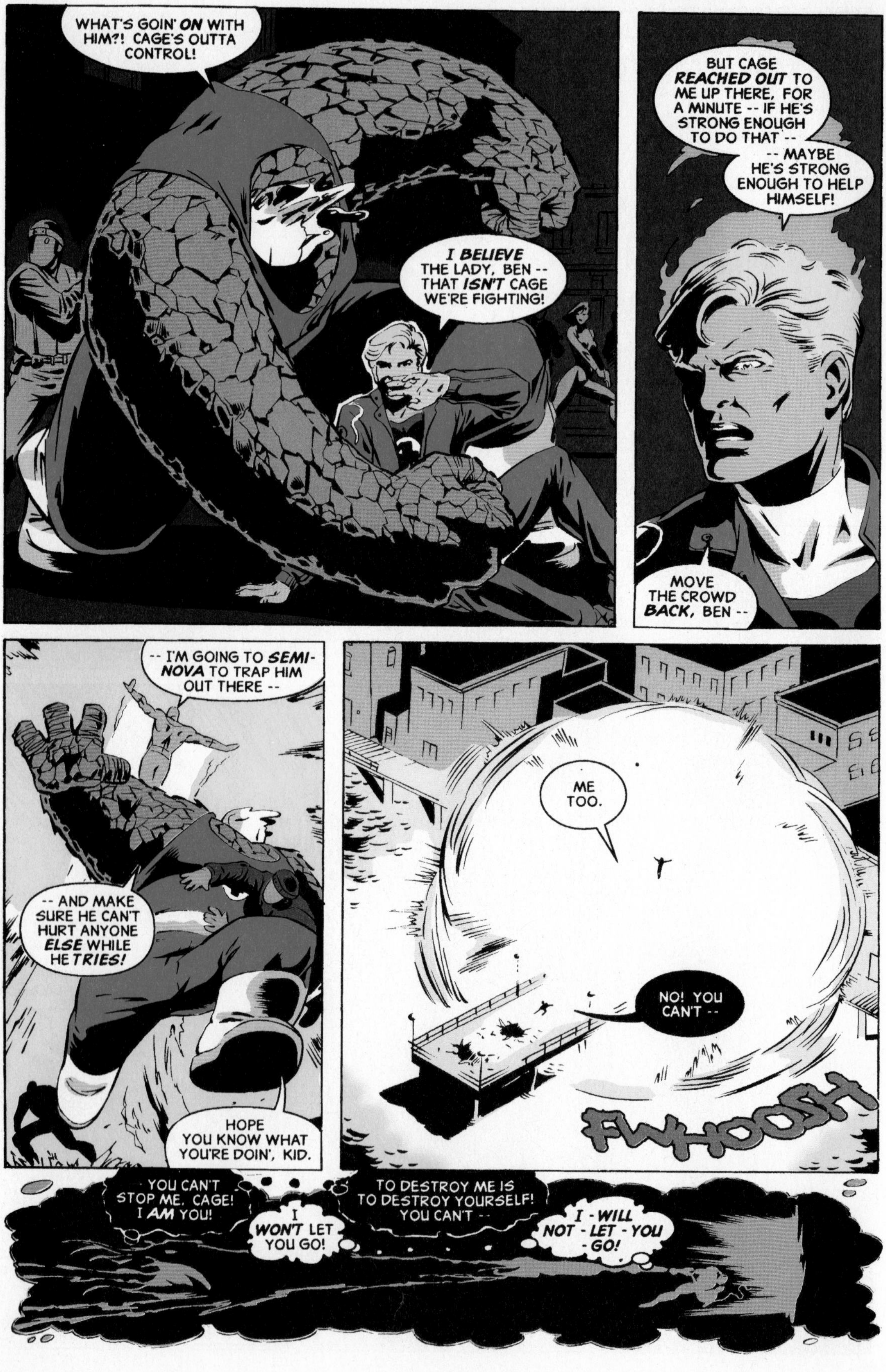

WHAT'S GOIN' ON WITH HIM?! CAGE'S OUTTA CONTROL!
I BELIEVE THE LADY, BEN -- THAT ISN'T CAGE WE'RE FIGHTING!
BUT CAGE REACHED OUT TO ME UP THERE, FOR A MINUTE -- IF HE'S STRONG ENOUGH TO DO THAT --
-- MAYBE HE'S STRONG ENOUGH TO HELP HIMSELF!
MOVE THE CROWD BACK, BEN --
-- I'M GOING TO SEMI-NOVA TO TRAP HIM OUT THERE --
-- AND MAKE SURE HE CAN'T HURT ANYONE ELSE WHILE HE TRIES!
HOPE YOU KNOW WHAT YOU'RE DOIN', KID.
ME TOO.
NO! YOU CAN'T --
FWHOOSH
YOU CAN'T STOP ME, CAGE! I AM YOU!
I WON'T LET YOU GO!
TO DESTROY ME IS TO DESTROY YOURSELF! YOU CAN'T --
I - WILL NOT - LET - YOU - GO!

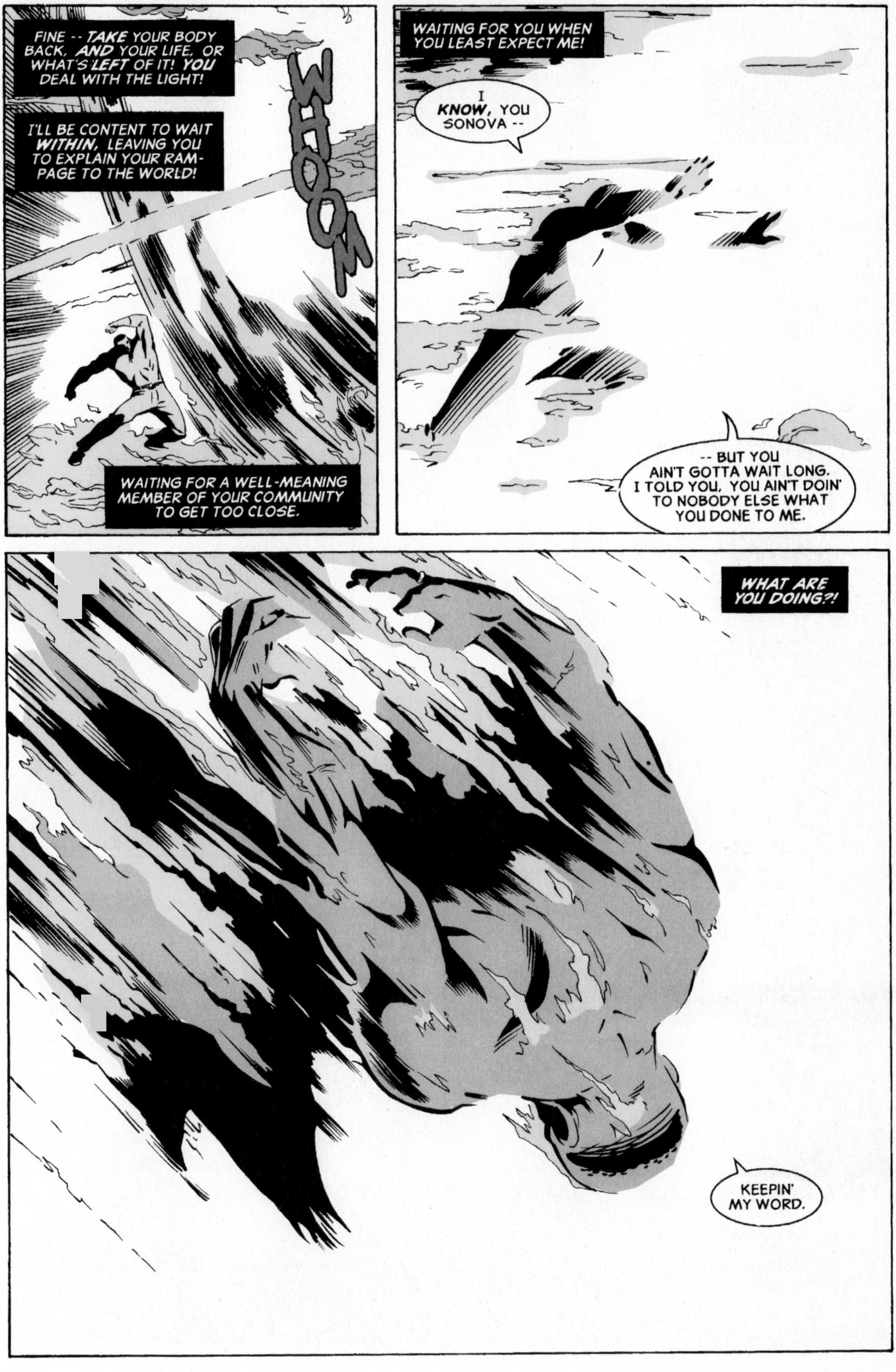
FINE -- TAKE YOUR BODY BACK, AND YOUR LIFE, OR WHAT'S LEFT OF IT! YOU DEAL WITH THE LIGHT!
I'LL BE CONTENT TO WAIT WITHIN, LEAVING YOU TO EXPLAIN YOUR RAMPAGE TO THE WORLD!
WHOOM
WAITING FOR A WELL-MEANING MEMBER OF YOUR COMMUNITY TO GET TOO CLOSE.
WAITING FOR YOU WHEN YOU LEAST EXPECT ME!
I KNOW, YOU SONOVA --
-- BUT YOU AIN'T GOTTA WAIT LONG. I TOLD YOU, YOU AIN'T DOIN' TO NOBODY ELSE WHAT YOU DONE TO ME.
WHAT ARE YOU DOING?!
KEEPIN' MY WORD.

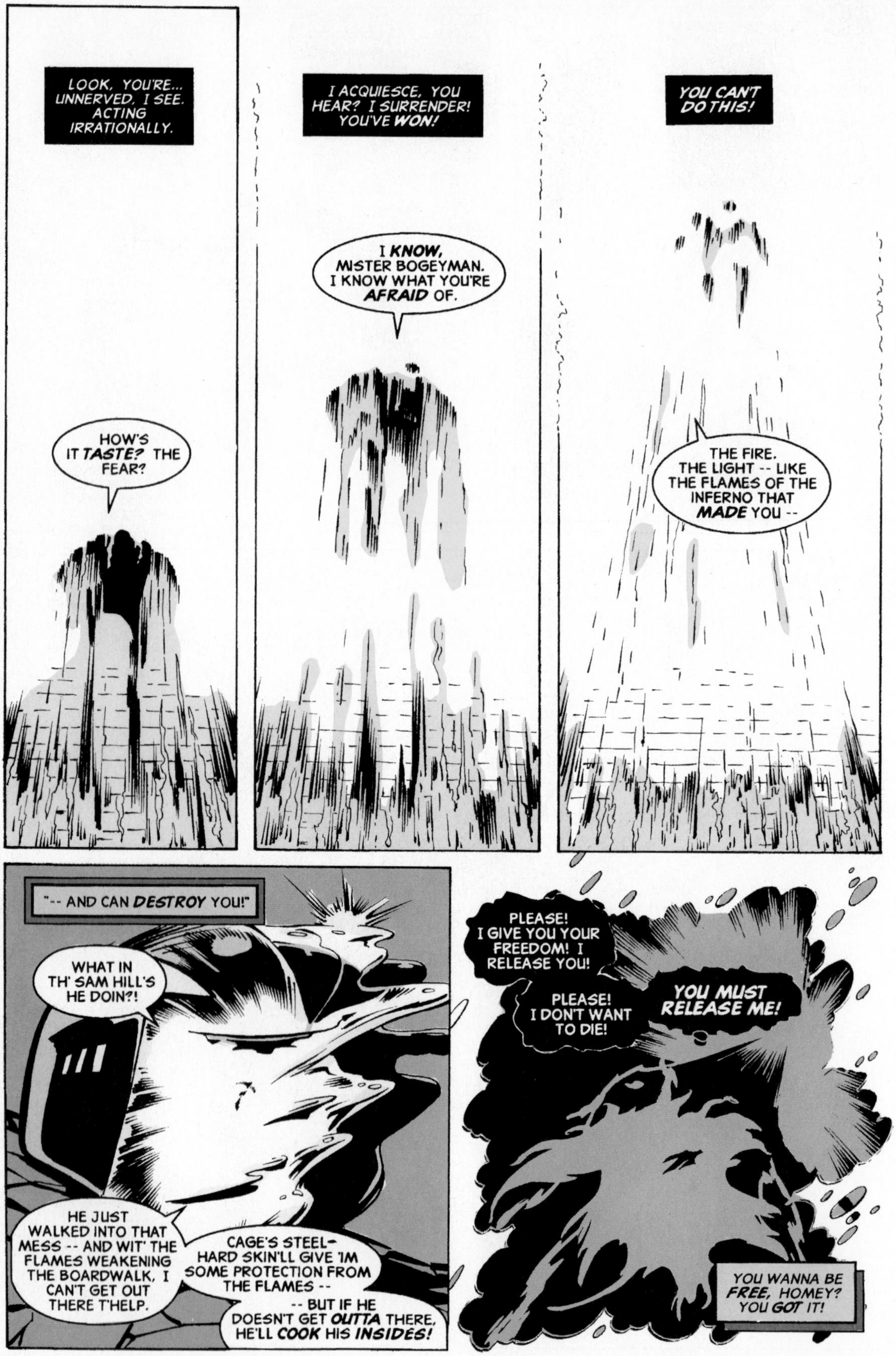

LOOK, YOU'RE... UNNERVED, I SEE. ACTING IRRATIONALLY.
HOW'S IT TASTE? THE FEAR?
I ACQUIESCE, YOU HEAR? I SURRENDER! YOU'VE WON!
I KNOW, MISTER BOGEYMAN. I KNOW WHAT YOU'RE AFRAID OF.
YOU CAN'T DO THIS!
THE FIRE. THE LIGHT -- LIKE THE FLAMES OF THE INFERNO THAT MADE YOU --
"-- AND CAN DESTROY YOU!"
WHAT IN TH' SAM HILL'S HE DOIN?!
HE JUST WALKED INTO THAT MESS -- AND WIT' THE FLAMES WEAKENING THE BOARDWALK, I CAN'T GET OUT THERE T'HELP.
CAGE'S STEEL-HARD SKIN'LL GIVE 'IM SOME PROTECTION FROM THE FLAMES --
-- BUT IF HE DOESN'T GET OUTTA THERE, HE'LL COOK HIS INSIDES!
PLEASE! I GIVE YOU YOUR FREEDOM! I RELEASE YOU!
PLEASE! I DON'T WANT TO DIE!
YOU MUST RELEASE ME!
YOU WANNA BE FREE, HOMEY? YOU GOT IT!

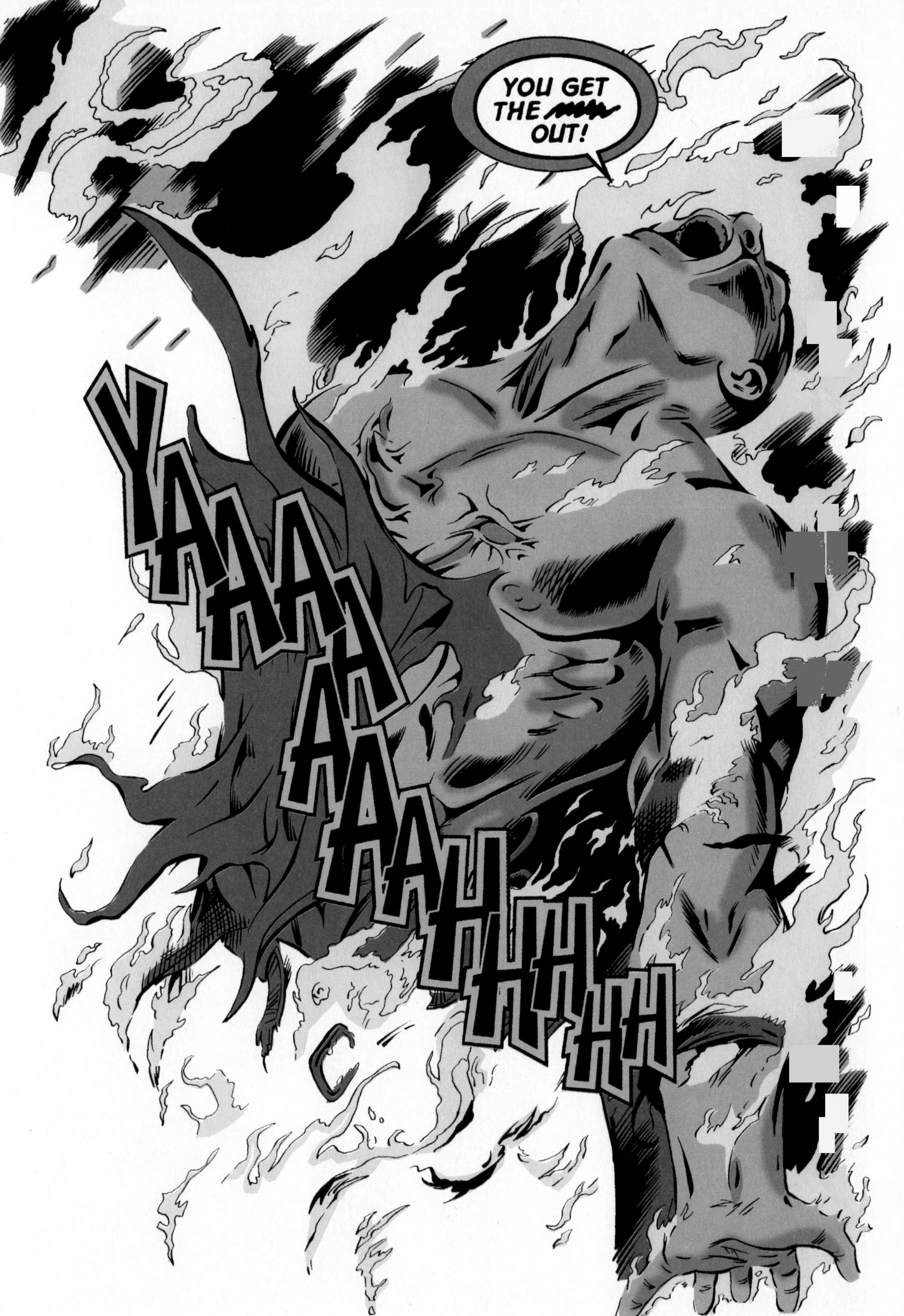
YOU GET THE
OUT!
YAAAAAAAHHHHHH

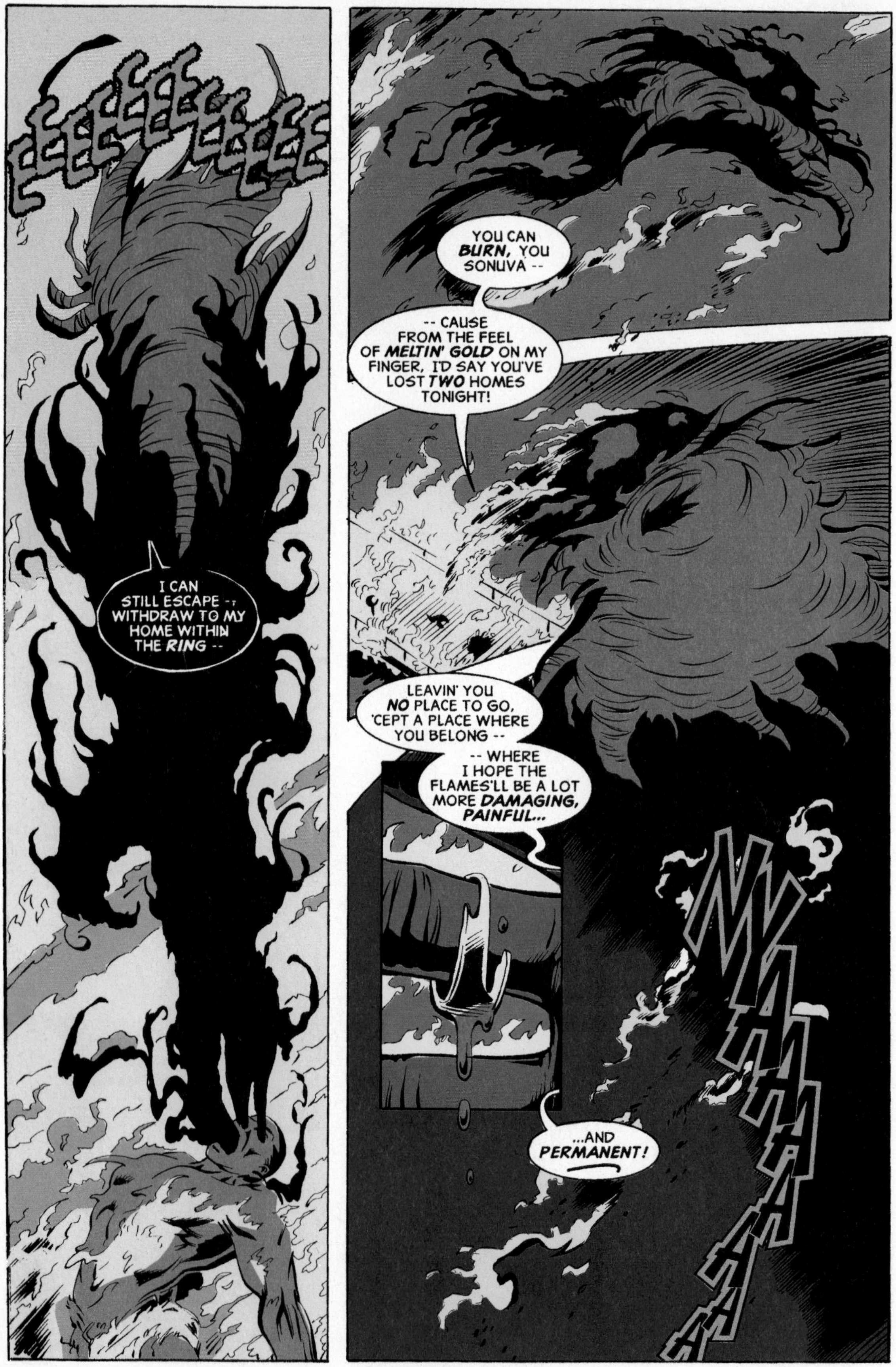
EEEEEEEEEEEEEEEEEEE
I CAN STILL ESCAPE -- WITHDRAW TO MY HOME WITHIN THE RING --
YOU CAN BURN, YOU SONUVA --
-- CAUSE FROM THE FEEL OF MELTIN' GOLD ON MY FINGER, I'D SAY YOU'VE LOST TWO HOMES TONIGHT!
LEAVIN' YOU NO PLACE TO GO, 'CEPT A PLACE WHERE YOU BELONG --
-- WHERE I HOPE THE FLAMES'LL BE A LOT MORE DAMAGING, PAINFUL...
...AND PERMANENT!
NYAAAAAAAAAA

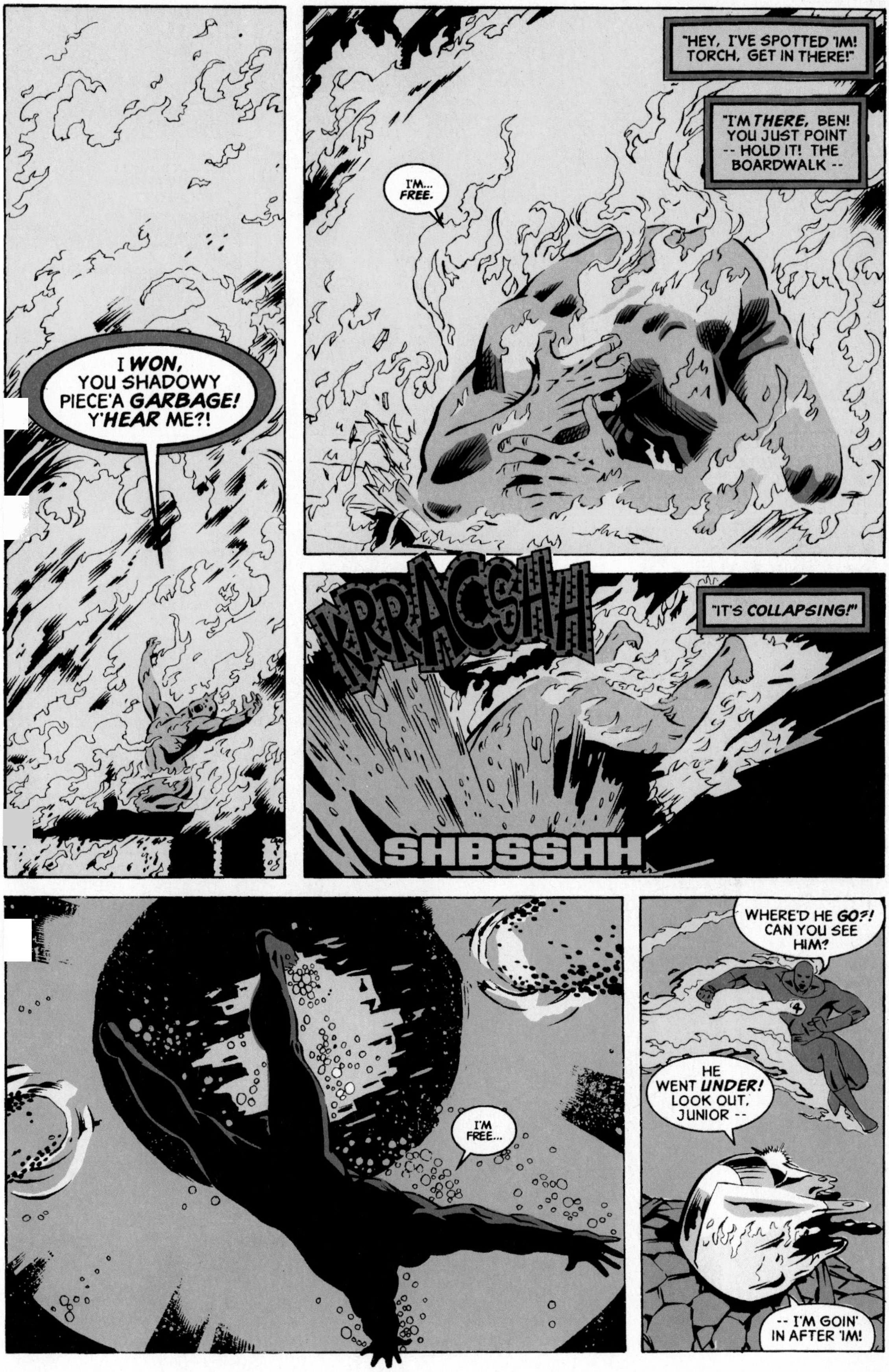
I WON, YOU SHADOWY PIECE'A GARBAGE! Y'HEAR ME?!
"HEY, I'VE SPOTTED 'IM! TORCH, GET IN THERE!"
"I'M THERE, BEN! YOU JUST POINT -- HOLD IT! THE BOARDWALK --
I'M... FREE.
KRRACSHH
"IT'S COLLAPSING!"
SHBSSHH
I'M FREE...
WHERE'D HE GO?! CAN YOU SEE HIM?
HE WENT UNDER! LOOK OUT, JUNIOR --
-- I'M GOIN' IN AFTER 'IM!

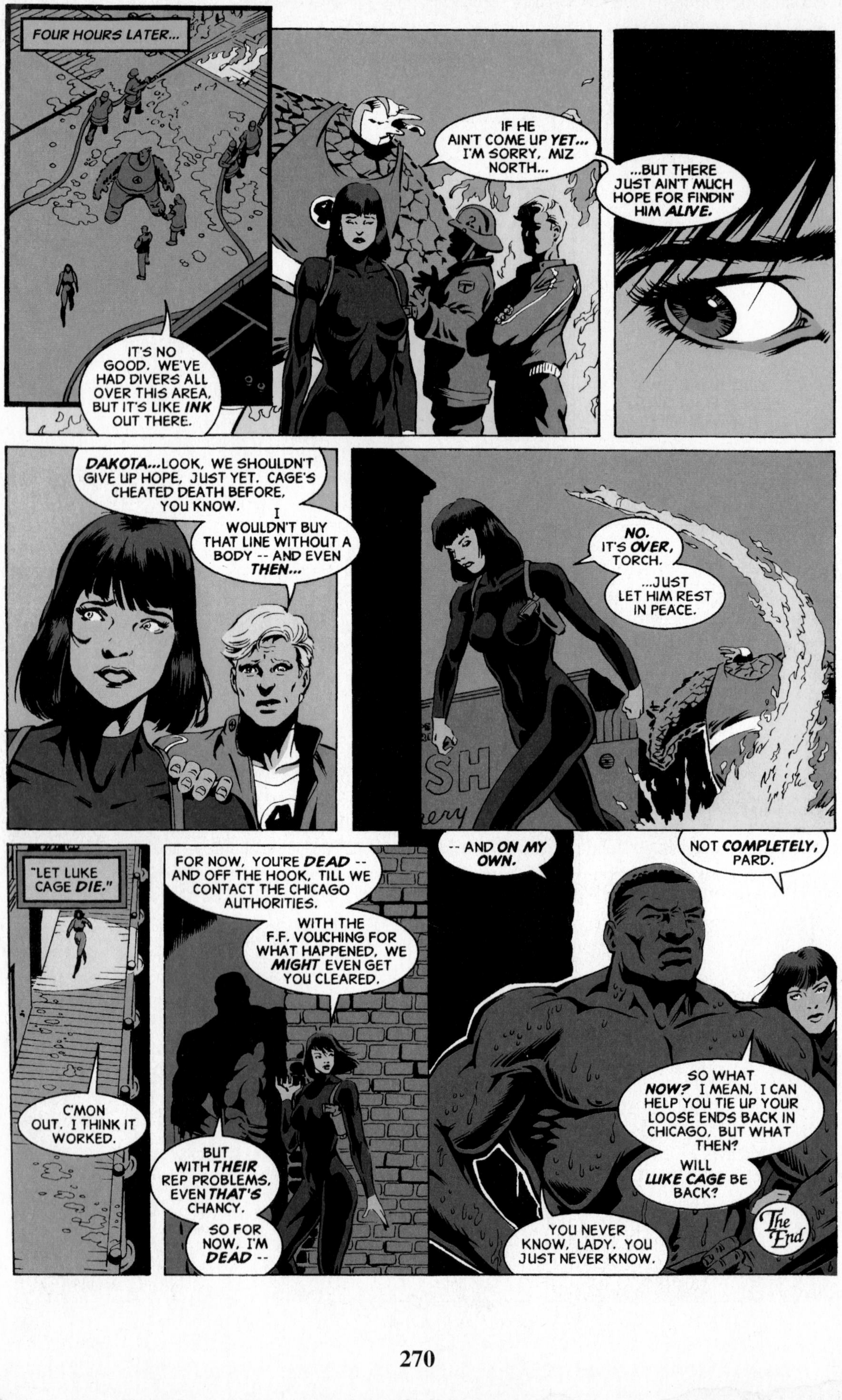
FOUR HOURS LATER...
IT'S NO GOOD. WE'VE HAD DIVERS ALL OVER THIS AREA, BUT IT'S LIKE INK OUT THERE.
IF HE AIN'T COME UP YET... I'M SORRY, MIZ NORTH...
...BUT THERE JUST AIN'T MUCH HOPE FOR FINDIN' HIM ALIVE.
DAKOTA...LOOK, WE SHOULDN'T GIVE UP HOPE, JUST YET. CAGE'S CHEATED DEATH BEFORE, YOU KNOW.
I WOULDN'T BUY THAT LINE WITHOUT A BODY -- AND EVEN THEN...
NO. IT'S OVER, TORCH.
...JUST LET HIM REST IN PEACE.
"LET LUKE CAGE DIE."
C'MON OUT. I THINK IT WORKED.
FOR NOW, YOU'RE DEAD -- AND OFF THE HOOK, TILL WE CONTACT THE CHICAGO AUTHORITIES.
WITH THE F.F. VOUCHING FOR WHAT HAPPENED, WE MIGHT EVEN GET YOU CLEARED.
BUT WITH THEIR REP PROBLEMS, EVEN THAT'S CHANCY.
SO FOR NOW, I'M DEAD --
-- AND ON MY OWN.
NOT COMPLETELY, PARD.
SO WHAT NOW? I MEAN, I CAN HELP YOU TIE UP YOUR LOOSE ENDS BACK IN CHICAGO, BUT WHAT THEN?
WILL LUKE CAGE BE BACK?
YOU NEVER KNOW, LADY. YOU JUST NEVER KNOW.
The End

ITEM! Beginning this month, a new six part adventure weaves its way through TERROR INC., CAGE and SILVER SABLE. Titled, "For Love Nor Money" this Big Guns "Merc War" is the search for a mystical artifact called Vatsyana's Tryst.

Whoever possesses all three pieces of Vatsyana's Tryst will have the power to fulfill their deepest sensual desires. The story begins when an ancient evil named Priapus announces that he'll pay a great deal of money to the mercenary who brings him the pieces. Terror, Cage and Sable are in a race against time, and each other, to recover them.

Parts 1 and 4 in TERROR INC. are written by Dan Chichester (DAREDEVIL, NIGHTSTALKERS) and penciled by new artist Richard Pace. CAGE #15 and 16 are written by Marcus McLaurin and penciled by Scott Benefiel. The third installment and conclusion, both appearing in SILVER SABLE, are written by Greg Wright (DEATHLOK, MORBIUS) and penciled by Steven Butler.

"For Love Nor Money"

Part 1	TERROR INC. #11
Part 2	CAGE #15
Part 3	SILVER SABLE #13
Part 4	TERROR INC. #12
Part 5	CAGE #16
Part 6	SILVER SABLE #14

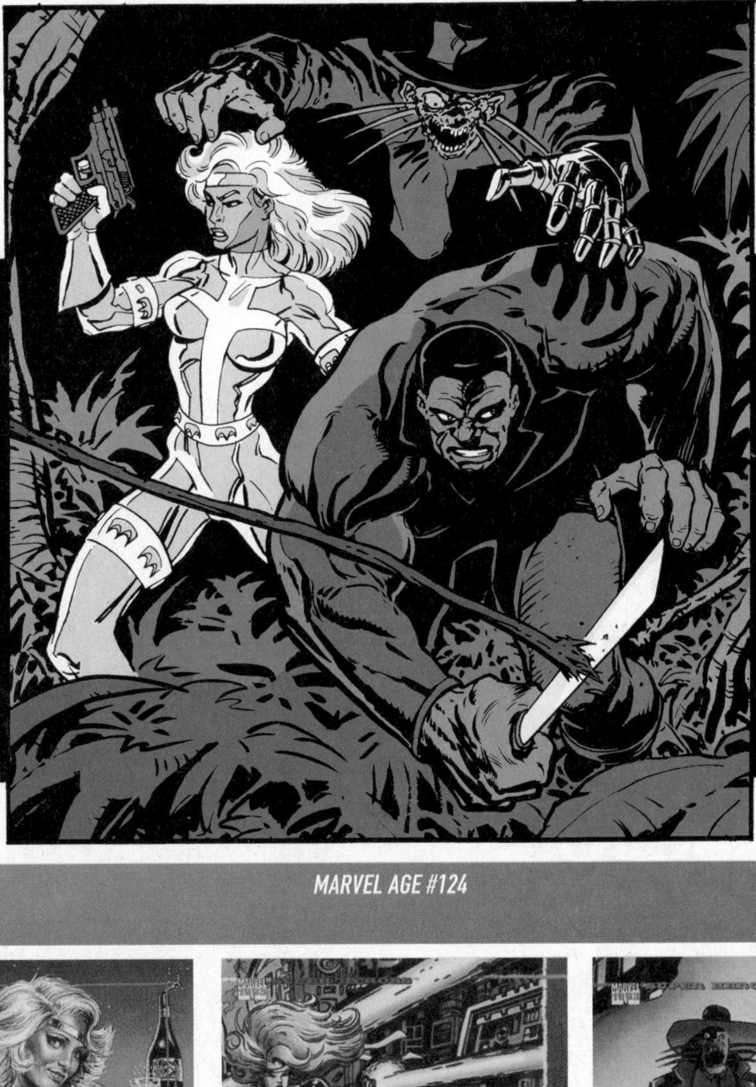

MARVEL AGE #124

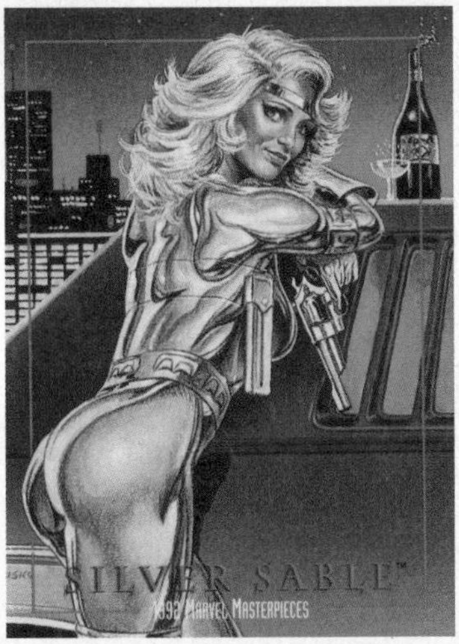
SILVER SABLE™
1992 MARVEL MASTERPIECES

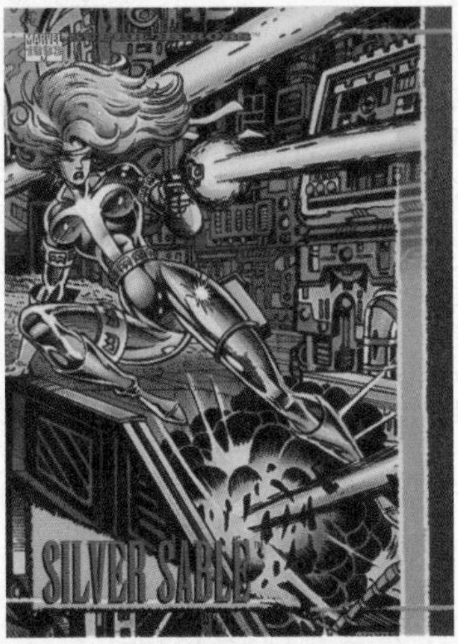
SILVER SABLE™

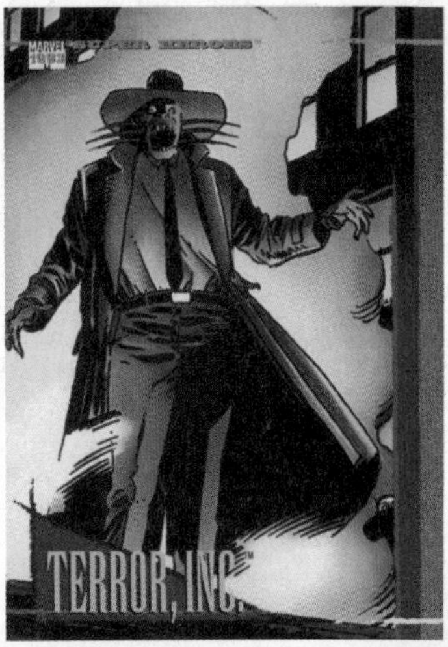
TERROR, INC.™

1992–93 TRADING-CARD ART BY JOE JUSKO, STEVEN BUTLER, LEE WEEKS & PAUL MOUNTS

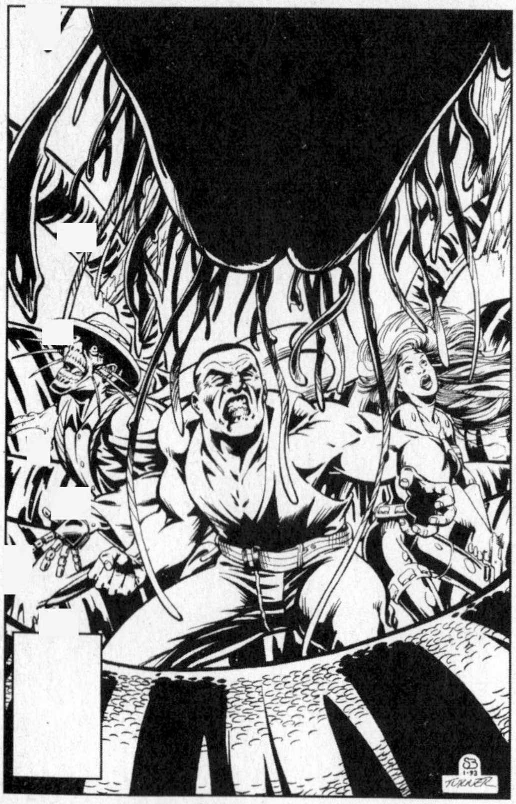
SB 1·93
TURNER

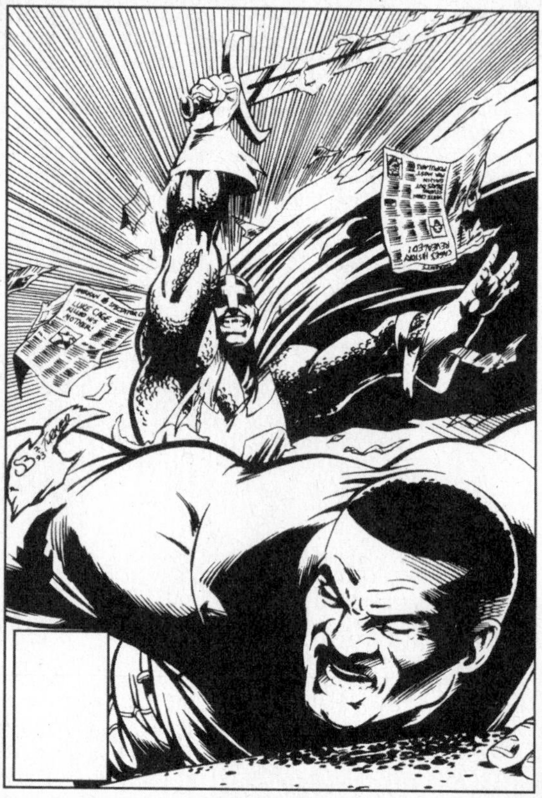

CAGE #16–17 COVER ART BY SCOTT BENEFIEL & FRANK TURNER

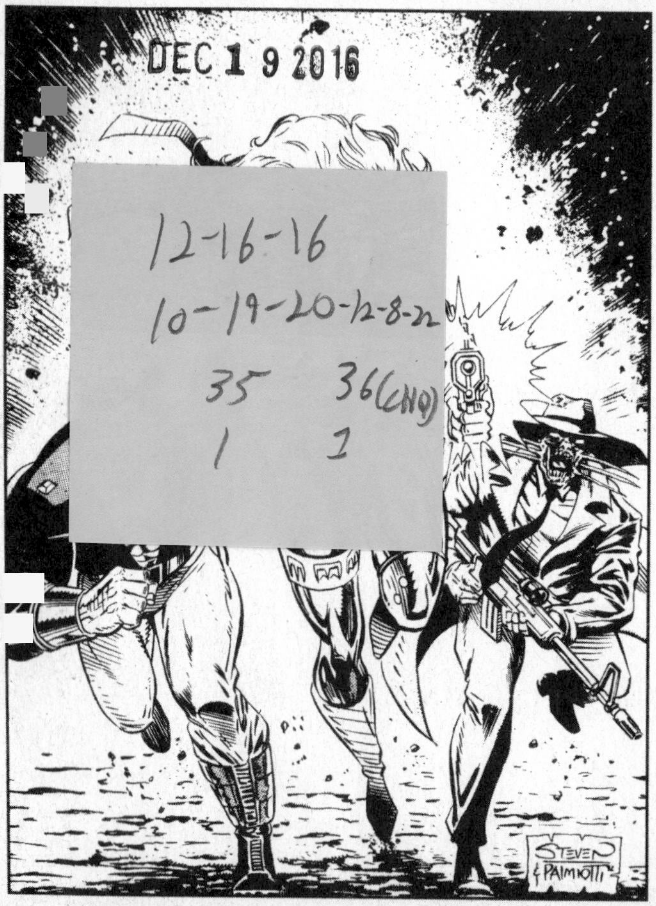
STEVEN
& PALMIOTTI

SILVER SABLE #14 COVER ART BY
STEVEN BUTLER & JIMMY PALMIOTTI